D0295054

ERIC LINKLATER

ERIC LINKLATER

A Critical Biography

Michael Parnell

JOHN MURRAY

LONDON

To Mary, my wife, in love and gratitude

*The publisher acknowledges subsidy
from the Scottish Arts Council
towards the publication of this volume*

© Michael Parnell 1984
Foreword © Andro Linklater 1984

First published 1984
by John Murray (Publishers) Ltd
50 Albemarle Street, London WIX 4BD

All rights reserved
Unauthorised duplication contravenes applicable laws

Typeset by Fakenham Photosetting Ltd, Fakenham
Printed and bound in Great Britain
by Butler & Tanner, Frome

British Library Cataloguing in Publication Data
Parnell, Michael
Eric Linklater.
1. Linklater, Eric—Biography   2. Authors,
Scottish—20th century—Biography
I. Title
823'.912   PR6023.1582Z/
ISBN 0-7195-4109-3

Contents

Foreword by Andro Linklater   ix

Preface   xiii

I   IN SEARCH OF AN IDENTITY

1   Child in Exile   3

2   Orkney Youth   8

3   Schoolboy in Aberdeen   15

4   A Sniper in France   20

5   Student   29

6   Journalist in Bombay   45

7   Poet Manqué   61

8   Commonwealth Fellow   77

9   Professional Writer   95

10   Scottish Nationalist   122

II   THE WANDERING ORCADIAN

11   Family Man in Italy   145

12   Orkney Householder   166

13   Traveller in the Orient   187

14   Uncertain Pacifist   201

15   Soldier to the Wars Returning   216

III   HIGHLAND GENTLEMAN

16   Leaving Orkney   249

17   Lure of the Theatre   258

18   Old Warrior Goes Walkabout   273

Contents

19 Honoured by The Queen   285

20 Eclipse at Noon   297

21 A Man Over Sixty   315

22 An Old Peasant with a Pen   329

EPILOGUE

23 Sentinel Stone   345

    Notes on Sources   351

    Selected Bibliography   361

    Index   369

Illustrations

Eric in 1944, from a drawing by Michael Ayrton   *Frontispiece*

1 Eric, Elspeth and their mother, Orkney, 1907   *f.p.* 96

2 Family picnic at the Dounby Show, 1914   96

3 L/Cpl Linklater, Fife & Forfar Yeomanry, 1917   97

4 Eric, with Isobel Walker, collecting for charity during an Aberdeen University rag, *c.* 1922   97

5 Douglas Walker, Elspeth and Eric drying out after a swim off Orkney, 1922   97

6 Eric, with Billy 'Pin-leg' Robertson, in Orkney   112

7 Merkister, overlooking the Loch of Harray, Orkney   112

8 Eric, with Compton Mackenzie, at the National Mòd, Fort William, 1932   113

9 Aspiring politician: Eric in November 1932   113

10 Marjorie and Eric, Edinburgh, May 1933   192

11 Portrait of Eric, 1933, by Stanley Cursiter, RSA   193

12 Marjorie and Eric being welcomed to Barra by Compton Mackenzie, June 1933   193

13 A drawing by Nancy Kirkham for *The Crusader's Key* (1933)   208

14 A wood-engraving by Joan Hassall for *Sealskin Trousers* (1947)   208

15 Major Linklater bound for the Faroes, May 1941   209

16 Lt-Col Linklater visits the front line in Korea, August 1951   209

17 Eric, John Gielgud and Barry Morse at rehearsal for *Crisis in Heaven*, 1944   288

18 Eric and Peter Ustinov confer during the filming of *Private Angelo* (1949) in Italy   288

19 Pitcalzean House, looking out over Nigg Bay, Easter Ross   289

20 Eric and Marjorie enjoying a crack at Pitcalzean, 1955   289

21 William Hewison's cartoon of Eric in *Punch*, 1958   *f.p.* 304

22 Emilio Coia's caricature of Eric, 1967   304

23 Distant roots: Eric enjoying the sunshine in Uppsala, 1964   305

MAP OF ORKNEY   p. 10

ILLUSTRATION SOURCES

Grateful acknowledgement is given to the following for their permission for illustrations to be reproduced in this book: Frontispiece and 1–7, 12, 19: Marjorie Linklater, Kirkwall; 8, 10: George Outram & Co Ltd, Glasgow; 9, 17, 20: BBC Hulton Picture Library, London; 11: University Court of the University of Aberdeen; 14: Joan Hassall and Rupert Hart-Davis; 15, 16: Imperial War Museum, London; 18: National Film Archive Stills Library, London, and Peter Ustinov; 21: William Hewison and Punch Publications Ltd, London; 22: Emilio Coia, Glasgow; 23: Karl W. Gullers, Stockholm. The map of Orkney on p. 10 was drawn by Denys Baker.

Foreword

by Andro Linklater

When I was a child in the 1950s, my father's reputation as a writer had passed its peak. He was one year older than the century and his great fame had come in the 1930s and 1940s with a succession of best-selling novels beginning with *Juan in America* and ending with *Private Angelo*. Nevertheless his reputation remained sufficiently powerful to breed in me a distinct expectancy of recognition. In the company of strangers voices above my head would say 'This is Eric Linklater's boy' or a face would duck down to my level and assert brightly, 'So you're the great man's son', and I would feel the spread of a wider penumbra than a small boy could throw. To be Eric Linklater's son then seemed no hardship.

With my father on hand, however, the expectancy was shot through by a fearful apprehension that something might go wrong. Like some infant Duke of Norfolk superintending a coronation, I felt it imperative that his importance be acknowledged by those around him. My worries reached a peak when he appeared in public—on a local 'Matter of Opinion' panel where he was bound to be contradicted, or on the radio where the interviewer would surely fail to catch his jokes, or on television where the camera would reveal him, as indeed it did, with his flies undone. To be his son in those circumstances was to feel his dignity threatened at every turn.

To some extent these were the natural misgivings of any child seeing his parent perform in public, but they also had a source in Eric's own apprehensions. One of the many merits of Michael Parnell's biography is his recognition that beneath his subject's exuberant exterior ran a layer of uncertainty. My father disliked his physical appearance and emotional inhibition, and from adolescence had fought to overcome these shortcomings, as he perceived them to be. Anything which reminded him of them was liable to provoke a fury quite disproportionate to its overt cause. There was a manner in which people *should* behave and a way in which things *should* be done, and it was crucial that the people or things around him should measure up to the standards he had set himself. Thus my Norfolk-like concern for appearances echoed in some degree that of the monarch.

From our different standpoints we were both familiar with the ideal. It came when he was in the company of men he admired, for the most part those who added writing to other accomplishments: soldiers, such as Robert Henriques or Bernard Fergusson; a doctor such as O. H. Mavor (James Bridie); and above all Compton Mackenzie whose additional guises defy brief description. With them he became the person he wanted to be, extravagant in affection, hospitality and discourse.

When they came to stay the house swelled in sympathetic grandeur. The dining-room table grew in length, the cellar was harvested of bottles, and dark corners of the hall sprouted sheaves of roses, lupins or gladioli. From a mingled sense of drama and terror the butcher produced his best mutton, my mother her best cooking, and the four children their best behaviour. It was a pleasure to be present on such occasions, and to offer a second helping of carrots was to stand on the edge of glory.

Eric then made a splendid companion. His conversation was served by a Jacobean wit and a prodigious memory crammed with reading and experience, but most importantly admiration unstoppered his feelings so that his friends were bathed in their warmth. Driven by the gale of his personality their talk grew boisterous and its direction unpredictable. Allusion served for explanation, personal experience stood in for definition. A quotation from Racine comprehended France and war was caught in the memory of a battle. Like wizards they leapt from one conversational peak to another, and wherever they landed an entire mountain of knowledge was assumed to stand beneath their feet.

There was something of Cinderella in this gaiety and the departure of the guests represented the chimes of midnight. Then the saddle of mutton turned to rissoles, the claret bottles became a water-jug, and in place of the glittering talkers sat four bespectacled, unattractive children. I surmise that nothing reminded Eric more forcibly of his secret faults than his children, for he strove repeatedly and angrily to mould us to a less irritating form.

In memory these attempts have their focus on the long-polished table in the dining-room from one end of which he sat facing the window so that its westerly light illuminated the pink, imperial dome of his bald head and made his spectacles gleam like mirrors. Meals took place in an atmosphere which I recall as being so charged the squeal of a knife on china or the slurrup of soup on lip could trigger an explosion. 'If you can't eat like a civilised human being,' he bellowed, 'you can finish your meal at the bottom of the garden.' At his most irritable, he had a habit of addressing us through my mother as though she were the NCO of a slovenly platoon he had to inspect. 'Marjorie! Have you seen this boy's tie? Does he have to come to table looking like a slum child?' or, on the occasion I first tried to carve a chicken, 'Marjorie! What's that bloody boy been doing? The bird looks as though it's been attacked with a Mills grenade.'

When he shouted, his voice had a percussive force at which I usually cried, as much for my own failure as his anger. Despite straining every Norfolk nerve, things could not be prevented from going wrong. There were sudden unannounced purges against the smell of peeled oranges or grapes pulled from the stalk, and if these were avoided paralysing interrogations exposed my ignorance about people, places and dates.

The other children, being older, had presumably run this gauntlet before me, and our collective failings must have seemed part of a conspiracy against him. For all his shouting, deficiencies continued to appear on every side. Plates were served cool when they should have been hot, drinking water was tepid instead of cold, and spoons were dull instead of sparkling. There was, in consequence, no mistaking who was at the centre of the conspiracy—the woman responsible for plates, spoons, children and, most infuriatingly of all, for boiled potatoes which either dissolved to flour or split as crisply as apples. 'Good God, woman, look at this!' he bawled in disbelief. 'After twenty-three years of married life you *still* haven't learned to boil a potato.' And despite the years, he would still be goaded into slinging the potato at my mother, though either because she was only a silhouette against the light, or out of good manners, he usually missed.

The emotional drama left no one untouched, and viewed on the distorting screen of memory, meal-times have a decidedly operatic quality. Conversations are shouted arguments, unforgivable accusations are hurled across the table, people break down and cry, exits are made to the sound of slammed doors—my elder sister once exited with a slam which dislodged a full-length portrait of my maternal grandmother from the wall and two painted plates from the sideboard. Acknowledging a force as elemental as himself, my father relapsed briefly into silence.

I do not present this as the whole truth—the sunnier moods are absent, and as we grew older and tougher, and thus more acceptable, they often predominated—but it is accurate as to the intemperate quality of his frustration. For a child it was impossible to understand that the violence of his emotions was inseparable from his writing, and that what enraged him in life could become comedy in fiction. In fact I remember my embarrassment at the age of seven when I first read *The Pirates in the Deep Green Sea*, a book which he wrote for my brother Magnus and me. There for all to see was my father in the person of the ferocious pirate, Dan Scumbril, who terrified half the North Atlantic with his blazing temper and loud voice. 'Split my liver with a brass harpoon,' thundered Dan Scumbril, and I quailed, not with fright but shame that my father's rages should now be known to everyone. When, so far from being thought the worse of, he was congratulated on the creation of an exceptionally comic character, I logged it as one more of those bewildering quirks of existence which had to be accepted even though they made no sense.

As it happens, it is more complex than most childhood matters to understand how fiction transforms reality. In my adolescence and early twenties, I found—as did most of my contemporaries to judge by reviews and comments—a lack of sensitivity in his resort to comedy. It was too obviously the right thing to do, not to take the world very seriously—even his nightmare of service on the Western Front in the First World War was presented in *The Man on My Back* in comic form.

Yet, when I read his books today it seems to me that what underlies his writing is not an absence but an excess of feeling. Michael Parnell illustrates with admirable clarity the violent sentiment which runs through his most extravagant comedy so that it dances on the edge of blackness or slips abruptly into tragedy. The variety of his approaches to fiction which once irritated his critics—the rollicking *Juan in America* followed by the gut-spilling *Men of Ness*, the macaroni jollity of *Private Angelo* and the sombre *Roll of Honour*—now appear much more of a piece. A word which he liked was inenarrable, or untellable, and what strikes me is the persistent attempt to convey the inenarrable exorbitance of his feelings.

Had he been born with a poet's head, with tragic brows and an aquiline nose, he would have had a mask to suit his inner being. As it was, the sergeant-major's jaw was surmounted by a massive skull and a nose which he explained as the outcome of eight hundred years of peasant ancestry exposed to the bulbous gales of Orkney. The physical ideal was subverted before he began, and his spirit met a similar stumbling-block in the weighty Victorian values instilled by his parents. It was little wonder that he raged so furiously, sometimes to be free of the encumbrances, sometimes to make sense of them.

They bred in him a lust for beauty—for the sense of liberation which it conferred and for the model which it offered of the way things should be. No moment exposes him more clearly than when in wartime he found himself alone in the room where Botticelli's *Primavera* had been stored for protection, and stretching up on tiptoe he pressed his lips to those of Spring. He married a beautiful wife, he built and bought houses for their views rather than their suitability as homes, and he purchased pictures even faster than poverty required him to sell them. He kept Highland cattle for their shaggy grandeur, and allowed a succession of elegant, self-possessed Siamese cats to step with impunity across his writing-paper. Even the aggressive pattern of his tweed jackets I suspect of answering some aspiration which he felt to be bold and carefree.

His laugh was always loud and in old age his tears grew copious. He cried at memories of soldiering, at a pipe tune or a reading of *Danny Deever*. Perhaps they sprang in part from an old man's sentimentality, but I also remember the remark made by a neighbour, Donald MacGillivray, a supreme piper and teacher of piping. When he played *The Lament for the Children* Eric was not the only one moved to tears, but it was for him in particular that the piece was performed. 'I always like playing for your father,' Donald said. 'You see, he has the soul for it.'

25 January 1984   ANDRO LINKLATER

Preface

Eric Linklater came into my life one afternoon in 1956 when, on my way to spend a couple of hours supine in a punt on the Cherwell, ostensibly studying Klaeber's *Beowulf*, I stopped at the tray of second-hand books being offered at 6d each outside Dollond's in the High. Among the bargains I carried with me to the river was a fat book called *Juan in America*; and after I had read the first two pages, *Beowulf* had no further attraction.

The Prologue to *Juan in America* seemed to me an almost perfect piece of writing: elegant, comic, controlled. The story of Juan's adventures in fabulous 1920s America was funny, persuasive, provocative and extraordinarily satisfying in texture. Who was this Eric Linklater? Why had I, studying literature at Oxford, never had my attention even drawn to his work?

The question was rhetorical, since I knew that for my teachers real literature had stopped in 1830 or thereabouts. It was surprising, however, to discover that Eric Linklater's work did not apparently merit much attention from those who did perceive that recent and contemporary literature might usefully be studied. There were endless books and articles on James Joyce, Virginia Woolf, D. H. Lawrence, E. M. Forster and Joseph Conrad; and there was some evidence that Evelyn Waugh, Graham Greene and Aldous Huxley were not completely negligible; but nobody had anything to say about Linklater at all.

Over the years, for the sheer pleasure of it, I made myself better acquainted with his work. It was a considerable and impressive *oeuvre*. Twenty-three novels, three collections of short stories, half a dozen plays, a volume of poems, two children's novels, and a long list of biographies, histories, essays and articles constituted a fair claim to be noticed among the notable British writers of the century. I was just, at last, plucking up sufficient courage to write to the man behind the books when I heard that he was ill, and then that he had died; I felt a sense of personal loss. Later I met Marjorie Linklater and other members of his family, and gradually came to the position where I was entrusted with the task of writing his biography.

It had only gradually been borne in upon me that Eric was a Scot, and that his writings were valued more highly in Scotland. His novels do have at times a special Scottish flavour, and about half of them are set, to a greater or lesser extent, in Scotland. But it would be wrong to regard him as a 'regional novelist', with any corollary implication of limited stature. Joyce and Shaw were Irish; Dylan Thomas was Welsh; Robert Louis Stevenson was Scottish; what mattered was that they all wrote well in English and, like Eric Linklater, did honour to the language by their particular use of it. The Scottish Arts Council kindly agreed to support the project, and it is undeniable that in many ways Eric Linklater belongs to Scotland; but I am sure it will offend no Scot when I declare my interest in him as a distinguished though still curiously undervalued contributor to English literature in the largest sense.

I have tried, therefore, to tell the story of a man who will be remembered in the end as a storyteller of rare ability and as a writer whose English is quite wonderfully lucid, individual and pleasurable. But as a man, too, he was endlessly interesting, unpredictable and challenging. He was full of wit, energy and humour, a romantic who loved all life's good things: food, wine and whisky, women, sport and physical achievement, poetry, music, art, and beautiful and exotic places; but he was also saddened by life's ugliness, brutality and unfairness, and by a sense of his own failure. He had the gift of laughter, and used it in the face of a perception that life is a profound and tragic mystery.

The book could not have been written without the full and willing co-operation of the Linklater family, who have given their time to talk and write to me with unflagging courtesy and interest over a period of several years. I am especially grateful to Marjorie Linklater, who, over the past ten years, has come to treat me like a loved friend of the family and has given me her whole-hearted trust and support, allowing me to see all Eric's papers and books, answering all my questions even when the memories so stirred caused her to suffer again the pain of loss, and extending to me and my family her generous hospitality; and to Andro Linklater, whose Foreword so vividly presents a vision of the man who was his father.

I am also indebted to many of Eric's friends and acquaintances who have given me invaluable help; special mention should be made of the great encouragement and assistance given to me by the following: Mrs Lucile Bell (Mrs John Moore); George Bruce; Elspeth Cormack; the Hon. Mrs C. J. Y. Dallmeyer (Ursula Balfour); Ian Grimble; Sir Rupert Hart-Davis; Alison Sheppard; James Sutherland; and Peg Walker.

A great deal of my information has come from public sources, and I should like to record my gratitude for kindly assistance from the following in particular: Mrs M. I. Anderson-Smith and Mary Williamson, the Library, University of Aberdeen; Ellen S. Dunlap, Humanities Research Center, University of Texas, Austin; Dr J. A. Edwards, the Library, University of Reading; Jacqueline Kavanagh and Gwyniver Jones, BBC Written Archives Centre, Caversham Park; David Machin, Jonathan Cape Ltd; Alan Maclean, Macmillan Ltd; Professor Andrew Rutherford, University of Aberdeen; Stanley Simpson, National Library of Scotland; Margaret Stephens and Michael Sissons, A. D. Peters & Co Ltd; and Patrick Walker, BBC Scotland.

I should like also to acknowledge help with information or with permission to quote from letters from: Dr W. R. Aitken; L. A. H. Arndt; Basil Ashmore; A. W. Badenoch; Sir John Betjeman; John L. Broom; George Mackay Brown; C. E. Tatton Brown; Mrs Margaret Clarke; Allan Colquhoun; Jean Cruickshank; Monja Danischewsky; Lt-Cdr H. W. Drake; Lt-Col R. H. Edwards; L. Marsland Gander; Val Gielgud; Karl Ragnar Gierow; Alan J. Grant; Jo Grimond; Karl W. Gullers; H. Forsyth Hardy; Francis Russell Hart; Celia Henderson; Jack House; Margaret Cursiter Hunter; Storm Jameson (Mrs Margaret Chapman); Lt-Col Jack Lambert; Kristin Linklater; Gordon L. McCullough; Finlay J. Macdonald; Colin Mackenzie; John MacRitchie; J. Montgomery MacRoberts; Magnus Magnusson; Ronald Mavor; Bruce Marshall; Naomi Mitchison; Jack Morpurgo; George C. Morrison; Sean O'Faolain; Col A. Paton; J. B. Priestley; Isobel Ramsay; Sir Ralph Richardson; Charles T. Rioch; A. Rodgers; Donald and Ismay Ross; Stewart F. Sanderson; Annabelle Skarda; L. A. Stronach; Ragnar Svanstrom; Anthony Walker; Isobel Walker; Eleanor H. B. Walsh; Molly Weir; Dame Rebecca West.

The following publishers kindly allowed me to quote from books and periodicals: Aberdeen University Press; Allen & Unwin Ltd; W. H. Allen & Co Ltd; William Blackwood & Sons Ltd; Jonathan Cape Ltd; Chatto & Windus Ltd; André Deutsch Ltd; William Heinemann Ltd; Longman Group Ltd; Macmillan Ltd; John Murray Ltd; James Thin and the Mercat Press; and I am indebted to Jonathan Cape Ltd to quote from letters in the Cape archive at the Library, University of Reading.

Thanks are also due to the following agencies who gave permission to quote from books of which they control the copyright: BBC Written Archives Centre; Harry Ransom Humanities Research Center, University of Texas; A. D. Peters & Co Ltd; and Society of Authors.

I owe thanks, too, to colleagues at the Polytechnic of Wales, particularly to Dr Mike Slater, who, as head of my department, arranged for me to have some timetable abatement and financial assistance from the Polytechnic's research funds. Duncan McAra at John Murray has been ceaselessly encouraging and helpful, and I owe him special thanks for his tactful editing and for the enthusiasm and kindness with which he set about finding photographs from sources unknown to me.

There are others who have helped me whose names may inadvertently have been omitted; to all those, my thanks and apologies. Finally, my thanks and love to my wife, Mary, who has been a tower of strength throughout the long period I have been working on this book and without whose patient and generous support I could never have completed it.

M.P.

I

IN SEARCH
OF AN IDENTITY

1   Child in Exile

Until he was over seventy, Eric Linklater never publicly admitted that he had been born in south Wales, that he had passed his childhood there, and that he had begun his education at the Intermediate School that was to become the Cardiff High School.

Instead, he had so successfully fostered the notion that he was, like his father before him, a native of Orkney, that all the newspapers and reference books for more than forty years gave his birthplace as Dounby, Orkney. He finally disclosed the truth in a third volume of autobiography, *Fanfare for a Tin Hat*, in which he devoted three pages to his real birthplace and early years. He explained to an inquirer: 'I have never said that I was born in Orkney, but my close connection with the islands prompted that assumption.'[1] It was an assumption he never corrected, even when confirmed by the blurb on many of his books.

The northern identity which he forged for himself was of enormous importance for him. His first autobiographical book, *The Man on My Back*, written at the end of his greatest decade of success in 1940, began with a marvellous evocation of the Loch of Harray, centre of all his boyhood memories. A few pages later he recorded his first fight with a twelve-year-old bully whom he 'threw down in a deserted bicycle-shed and, taking in both hands his essenced hair, hammered his head upon the concrete floor.'[2] This incident must have taken place in Cardiff, or just conceivably Aberdeen, but the reader is led to assume that it is a memory of Orkney schooldays, where in fact Eric never went to school. The second chapter briefly sketched in his Aberdeen schooldays, but still implied that Orkney was home. The book was dedicated to 'the Land and Seas and the People of Orkney'.

In the decade before *The Man on My Back*, nothing of the many and memorable things he wrote suggested anything other than that he was an Orkneyman born and bred. His first and evidently autobiographical novel, *White-Maa's Saga*, featured a young Orcadian central character, whose most significant adventures happened in Orkney. His fourth novel recounted the story of Orkney Vikings, Kol and Skallagrim, in *The Men of Ness*. His fifth novel, *Magnus Merriman*, again had an Orcadian hero who eventually returned to settle in his native islands after an extensive testing of life in the larger world.

Even where his focus was not Orcadian, there was a profound and pervasive suggestion that matters of Scottish or Norse concern were more interesting and important than others. When he turned his hand to biographies, his subjects, Mary Stewart and Robert the Bruce, were Scots, and in his book about Ben Jonson the liveliest chapter recounted Ben's visit to the Scot, Drummond of Hawthornden.

When he took an interest in politics, it was as a Scottish Nationalist that he went to the poll. His essay, *The Lion and the Unicorn*, commissioned by Lewis Grassic Gibbon, examined the relations between Scotland and England in history, politics and economics.

During the 1930s he became so widely known as a Scot—and in particular an Orkneyman—that he was frequently called upon to contribute essays to books about those northern territories. His short stories more often depended upon Scottish characters and settings, despite his cosmopolitan experience. And in the persona which he created for the newspapers during the days of his most considerable lionisation, it was always as a warlike, braw and canny Scot that he projected himself.

Yet he was born in Penarth, in Glamorganshire, on 8 March 1899. Christened Eric Robert, he was the son of Robert Baikie Linklater, a master mariner who had married a girl whom he had met in Greenock and who would have preferred to live in the north if possible. An Orkneyman himself, Captain Linklater was happy enough to sail from the Clyde, but by the end of the century the steamships had almost completely taken over from the sail he loved. The greatest coal-ports in the world were then in south Wales, and though Robert's employers, the Elder-Dempster Line, did not carry coal as cargo, they found Cardiff a useful base from which to work, and Robert had to adjust to sailing from the Bristol Channel. When he realised that their first child was on the way, he decided to set up a shore home for his family in his new southerly home port of Penarth, at 31 Grove Place.

Within a year a move was made to a respectable brick villa in a terrace in a newly expanding part of Cardiff.

> While I was still an infant—or perhaps a little older—we removed to a new, protruding limb of the city of Cardiff. The limb was a benign and well-gardened series of public parks which modest rows of small houses accompanied. I have never returned to Cardiff since we left it ... but now, when town-planning is so highly regarded, I am inclined to think that, sixty years ago, it must have been in the vanguard of municipal progress.[3]

The new house, 23 Fairoak Road, was indeed in a pleasant position on the edge of the city. Nearby was the newly created Roath Park, with its lawns and flowerbeds and large boating lake; beyond the back garden was open, unspoilt country. At the new house, on 12 July 1900, the family was enlarged by the birth of a daughter, Elspeth, and there they lived for eleven years.

The children were very happy in Cardiff. Eric wrote many years later of his memories of attending the Miss Jennings's dame school and the Cardiff Intermediate School for Boys without any sense that the first twelve years of his life had been in some way deprived or uncomfortable. He recalled some of the teachers at the school which later became much respected under its new name of the Cardiff High School:

> There was a splendid man, who taught classics, called Mr Brace or Mr Bryce. He was an atheist who stood defiantly erect during morning prayers ostentatiously despising their unwarranted appeal ... There was Todger Evans, excessively Welsh, with a strange domestic smell, of whom I was very fond ... There was a delightful man—called, I think, Greig—who took some of us to see Glamorgan play Gloucestershire at cricket and told us to watch, with close attention, everything that Gilbert Jessop did.[4]

Among the pleasures of life in Cardiff Eric remembered 'bicycles, small rowing-boats ... and food':

> The boats were for hire on a large lake in one of the parks, and from an early age I had a season-ticket that let me take useful exercise and enjoy the unfailing pleasure of plank-thin proximity to water.[5]

Elspeth remembered:

> I can see myself bowling a hoop in the park, and, later on, bicycling under a railway bridge with—I think—wagons labelled TAFF VALE RAILWAY ... I was very happy in Cardiff, and never liked Aberdeen—quite the opposite of Eric. Not that, as far as I can remember, he was *un*happy in Cardiff: as time passed on, he simply closed his mind to the facts that he had been born in Penarth and lived in Cardiff.[6]

Elspeth remembered that they were allowed to go rowing on the lake at Roath Park, but only as a special treat. 'There was no swimming that I can remember. But lovely bicycle rides to Caerphilly and round about.'

There were also plenty of other children to make friends with, because several of the new villas were similarly occupied by young couples with new or recent families. Still living in the area, one of those children, Roy Edwards, remembers his elder brother going off hand-in-hand with the five-year-old Eric all dressed up in his sailor suit towards the park to play. He also recalls being taught by Elspeth to ride her bicycle when he was about seven: 'I had to stand on the pedals as the saddle was too high.' Roy was a little bit in love with Elspeth, and once he offered Eric an exchange that seemed quite sacrificial:

> I suggested to Eric that he might be disposed to swap his sister for my model railway engine. He considered the bargain seriously for a while, but then, noticing that one of the wheels on the engine was buckled, rejected it, saying: 'My sister's not broken.'[7]

There were also, according to Eric, 'a series of plump, dark-haired little girls—most of them, I think, called Gwyneth', among the pleasures of life in Cardiff, and Elspeth commented: 'I think it is perhaps better to remember Cardiff as it was and not as it is. Remember, my day was pre-motor-car; we drove to the station to start our long journey to Orkney in a cab, and our good Scotch doctor came to visit us on a bicycle.'

The long journey to Orkney was an annual event for the Linklater children and their mother from about 1906 on, and its importance in Eric's subsequent development cannot be over-estimated. All told, it seems that the life of Cardiff would have been sufficient, had it not been for the special combination of circumstances that gave him a particularly potent inherit-ance of Norse blood and a mother who could not resign herself to living in south Wales.

Mrs Elizabeth Linklater had herself lived an adventurous life at sea before settling down ashore. She was the daughter of a Swedish sailor who had naturalised his name from Ljung to Young and worked his way up to become a captain in the English merchant service. In this capacity he took his English wife and little daughter to sea with him aboard the barque *Parajeiro* in 1872, when Elizabeth was four years old. For eighteen years after that she sailed the seven seas at intervals on his ships. In 1938 she published, with the help of her son, *A Child Under Sail*, her story of those exciting and unsettling years, and in his Preface Eric referred to the pleasure which, in fragments, his mother's story had given his childhood, 'when Rio de Janeiro, the coast of Java and the village down the road were all equidistant in a familiar landscape'.[8]

After such a childhood, Elizabeth Young might have found it difficult to settle anywhere; indeed, Eric frequently referred to her as having been 'neurotic' until his father's untimely death turned her into someone who had to cope on her own. Besides, she thought of herself as being essentially Scottish from having lived in Scotland with her Swedish father; and the fact that her blood was half English by virtue of her mother's having been Sarah Dodd, daughter of a Northamptonshire farmer, counted not at all. She yearned for the Clyde and Greenock of her youth, and for her husband's native Orkney, which she had come to love. Her unrest was communicated to her children, especially Eric, who later wrote: 'Her resentment had a curious effect on my childhood: I was led to believe that we were living in exile.'[9]

At Fairoak Road Elizabeth also provided a home for her mother and retired father, and for her sister; there was also a maid: 'a short, stoutly built Welsh maid—sad of aspect, but possibly contented'.[10] Despite the absence of a father kept away by duties at sea, Eric found his life full of interest, much of it derived from his grandfather's sea-lore and his grandmother's sometimes lurid tales of the poverty and pains of farming life in the English Midlands.

In the rich characters and well-stocked minds of these relations, Eric found much inspiration and pleasure. In his delight in his grandmother's eccentric old-fashioned English pronunciation may be seen the beginning of his own joy in language, and in his appreciation of her fabulous cooking lay the seeds of the celebration of the good things of life which gives a special character to so much of his writing. There can be few more mouth-watering pages than Eric's tribute to Mrs Young's culinary arts:

Her pastry was superlative—feathery flakes that swiftly dissolved in the mouth and enclosed, in a richly flavoured gravy, fragments of tender steak and succulent, taut kidney; or encircled, in little tarts, her home-made strawberry, blackcurrant or gooseberry jam. I remember with gratitude deep sirloins of beef, dripping red under a cornice of fat, and Welsh mutton redolent of hill pasture; dark, sombre Christmas puddings full of impacted opulence, and plump mince-pies bursting their frail encasement. Lemon-hued suet puddings, light and friable under sweet-sour sauces, and ponderous beef-steak puddings in their fast-melting coverlets ...[11]

These pleasant aspects of life in Wales notwithstanding, the young Eric was not content. There was something not quite right, something missing, and if this sense was partly due to his mother's restlessness, it was also because of what he gradually learned about the origins of the father he all too rarely saw.

2 Orkney Youth

Eric Linklater's father was the youngest of five children of Magnus Linklater, a crofter of Mossetter, near the village of Dounby, on the West Mainland of Orkney. Although Magnus had an estate no bigger than sufficient to keep a single cow, he could trace his ancestry in Orkney back several centuries. His son Robert was very proud of his family's long connection with the islands, and though he prospered in south Wales, he listened with ever closer attention to the voice of his wife, constantly yearning for a return to Scotland, and to the promptings of his own heart. In 1909 he made the first positive move towards a return by building a house near the site of his father's home.

For a couple of years before this, since Eric was seven, Elizabeth had been taking the children for summer holidays all the way from Cardiff to Orkney, and it was not long before the son began to recognise in the island of his ancestors his own spiritual home.

When he was about ten, his essentially Orcadian identity was confirmed. Many years later he wrote:

> I had always known that my mother, soon after her marriage, had spent some months in Orkney with my father; and lately I had acquired some deeply exciting information about the human condition and the curious exercises on which humanity depends for its continuance. I had overcome my original estrangement from arithmetic, and a simple calculation proved beyond doubt that I had been conceived in Orkney.[1]

The holidays spent in Orkney continued every year, and though the family never lived there, the times spent in the islands were sufficient to provide Eric with the roots and connections that Cardiff could not offer. The true centre of the boy's world became the house that his father built 'on an acre of land, overlooking a delectable bay, at the north-eastern corner of the Harray Loch'.[2] Given the name Ingleneuk by Eric's mother, the house was much later enlarged by Eric and, re-named Merkister, became the Orkney home for himself, his wife and children that he had always longed for.

Rather than the house, it might be even truer to say that the loch itself was at the heart of his world as a boy, and the little boat which his father gave him and in which he spent many hours exploring the water:

Day after day I spent, solitary as a dog at sea, or fishing with a mind intent only on the dropping flies and the bubble of a rising trout. My chief talent was idleness, and to lie in a drifting boat was a pleasure that did not grow stale.[3]

Throughout his life Eric claimed he was one of nature's idlers, and ranked idling as life's chief pleasure, but so restless was his nature, so great his compulsion to work, and so vital his determination to wrest from life as much experience as possible, that he had little enough time to indulge his love of it.

Besides teaching him the appreciation of leisure and the skills of fishing, the Orkney interludes formed a specially important and personal kind of knowledge for him, and helped him towards a highly specific self-identification. The islands of his origin—mysterious, remote northern islands, some flat and green and treeless, some rising to great heights from which fell mighty cliffs and strange sentinels of rock—had a history 'beyond the perimeters of ancient knowledge'.[4] Cut off from Scotland by the swirling, dangerous waters of the Pentland Firth (or Pictland Firth as Eric declared it should properly be known), Orkney contained strange, cold burial-chambers thousands of years old, and rings of ancient standing stones with which were associated different vintages of magic.

He later described the islands many times in novels, stories, broadcasts, guidebooks, histories and autobiographies. Their magic never faded for him; he celebrated, time and time again, the peculiar beauty of the landscapes they offered, the individuality and character of the people who lived on them, the might and changeable moods of the sea that surrounded them, the power and exhilaration of the great winds that swept over them. Here he isolates a special feature of the way Orkney affects the eye:

Light is the dominating factor in its scenery, and the town-dweller, on his arrival in Orkney, will screw up his eyes and ask where all the light is coming from. Except Hoy, there are no hills high enough to intercept it. There are no trees to diminish it. There is, on the entire circumference, the sea to reflect it. And beneath a changing sky Orkney can change from ugliness and bleakness to a radiant panorama of lakes more brightly blue than the Mediterranean, a dazzling chequer-board of grass and ploughland, the shadow-and-claret of hills that flow in sweet unbroken lines. It can put on beauty like a song or a dance, so light and airy it is, so brisk, and tender, and gay. And then, in less time than it takes to count the colours, the colours will change again, and the land looks grave and peaceful.[5]

What comes through most powerfully in much of Eric's writing, especially those stories arising most directly from Orkney settings, is his sense of the majesty, beauty and irresistible might of the sea. No one who lived in Orkney could fail to be aware of the sea that so incessantly swept the never-far-distant shore, sometimes with great noise and violence. For

those who could get to the islands each year, as the Linklaters did, only by taking the ferry from Aberdeen, there was the additional acquaintance with the sea in its various moods which the journey afforded—'a voyage that was often stormy and never comfortable', as Eric recalled it:

> The ships that ran between Aberdeen and Kirkwall were primarily designed for the carriage of sheep and cattle. They stank of wet wool, ordure, vomit and vile cooking. But the crew and stewards were friendly, and if we were lucky the voyage would last no more than twelve hours. In rough weather we would have time to add to the accumulated sour odour of sickness, and sometimes we lay becalmed in a sinister fog and looked out at an oily sea closely circumscribed by a wet, white invisibility.[6]

The sea was already a vast and exciting concept for him before he ever went to Orkney, for it had been brought into the Cardiff house through the tales told by his grandparents and by his father and mother. But now it began to enter his blood and become a passion. Across the seas were the lands of adventure that he longed to see with his own eyes, and the swans' road by which they might be attained held its own fascination. Going to Orkney, a land of sea-farers and sea-fearers, whose history was deeply affected by the Viking sea-adventurers of the dark ages, concentrated his interest, and one of the most charged expressions to enter his vocabulary was the Norse 'west over sea'. Over those wastes of water that surrounded the islands of Orkney had come Picts and Scots and Irish adventurers, and Norsemen who, after succumbing to Christianity, had built with the aid of Durham masons the great red Cathedral of St Magnus in Kirkwall. Eric learned with passionate delight that it was from such men that he had descended, and he honoured the sea that had brought them. He discovered with satisfaction that there was actually a place on the island of South Ronaldsay called by his name, Linklater. With the help of a friend who dabbled in genealogy he traced his ancestry back 400 years to a Cristi Aelingaklaet: Cristi who lived near a stone (*klaet*) in the heather (*ling*), and who was mentioned in a Norwegian document of the fifteenth century. No wonder the mere fact of having been born in a far southern place dwindled in importance so much that in the end it disappeared.

And in Orkney, besides the ever-present sound of the sea, there was the wind. Rarely less than at least a perceptible breeze, the wind in those islands sometimes becomes a wild, screaming tempest that little can withstand, and Eric was excited, amazed and sometimes terrified by its force. He explained:

> The islands stand at the meeting-place of the winds. They guard the upper gate of the North Sea, and west of them lie the stormiest parts of the Atlantic from Iceland down past Greenland's Cape Farewell to Labrador. Their climate is mild, because the Gulf Stream bends about them, but they are in the latitude of

northern Labrador, and between them and Labrador there is nothing to check a gale or stop the march of Atlantic waves. And from the other side, out of the North Sea, come turbulent southeasters.[7]

In 1952 Orkney weathered a storm such as few who lived there had ever known before, and Eric, with a kind of awed satisfaction at the wind's devastating strength, described the havoc in a broadcast:

In the early hours of 15 January 1952, people in all the twenty-eight inhabited islands of Orkney began to stir uneasily in their sleep, and as the noise grew worse the more nervous wondered if their walls would stand the strain. They were not unaccustomed to the great voices of the Atlantic that roar and bellow from their oceanic lungs, but this was something different from the ordinary chorus of the winter's rage. This was a hard and solid impact on their ears, a continuous deluge of sound that seemed to hurt the mind...

When daylight came, the two little towns of Kirkwall and Stromness looked like targets that had been 'softened-up' by the sky's artillery. Chimney-pots lay shattered in the streets, windows were smashed, slates had been ripped off roofs, and waterfalls ran down the stairs. But out in the country the scene was grimmer still. There the wind had left a scorched earth. Hay-ricks and corn-stacks had been swept away, scattered over the fields, or carried out to sea. Hundreds of chicken-houses, standing in the fields, had been killed. Here a barn stood roofless, and there the top-end of a telegraph-pole hung by the wires, cut in two by a flying sheet of corrugated iron. To the eastward, where the islands slope down over sandy beaches to the North Sea, the channels and bays of the archipelago were carpeted with straw, with splintered wood, and broken doors, and drowned hens.[8]

In addition to his love of the wildness and romance of the islands, grew an affection and respect for the island people whom he came to know, the fishermen and the crofters and their wives and daughters, with their canny ways and subtle humours, their endlessly interesting eccentricities. In *The Man on My Back* he described several of them, giving usually their local name or nickname in accordance with the principle by which in that book almost no one was fully identified and few things were rendered without some artistic modification of the truth. There was, for instance, Billy Pin-leg, the farmer of such surpassing and unOrcadian meanness that he would hurry home 'in anxious haste to obey a call of nature on his own land lest the riches thereof be wasted on another's field'[9]—the biblical tone of the language was appropriate, for Billy Pin-leg was the Bible-thumping neighbour of Eric's mother when she went to live in Ingleneuk. His name was Billy Robertson, and when he died Eric bought his house (The Cottage) for his mother to live in while he and his wife set up their home in Ingleneuk/Merkister. Another was 'Tom of the Mill'; he was Tom Scott, who lived across the road from Ingleneuk at Twagarn, and who taught Eric all he knew about fishing and thus planted in him one of the great sporting obsessions of his life. Tom Scott liked to eat plovers' eggs in season, breaking them into his mouth. 'Occasionally, late in the season, the bird was in the egg, but down it went; "Thoo spoke too late," he said, as the bird disappeared down his throat.'[10]

'Johnny of Tiveth' was one whose temper was always on the shortest possible fuse; he was Johnny Sinclair, a nephew of Storer Clouston's father, Sir Thomas Clouston. Another colourful character may in fact have been called Dan Stephen, as he is in the book; Eric remembered how he used to see visions of the Fairy Court, and how he could use a scythe with extraordinary grace.

Eric delighted in these people, and especially in their talk. As a boy he read the sagas of Iceland and Norway, and noted with satisfaction in the conversation of the Orkney people pleasing echoes of the Norse style of speech. He found:

> There is the same humour, a humour of understatement, of the objective eye and the balancing intelligence. There is a great appreciation of irony. There is—though it may seem extravagant to say so—something of the same aesthetic judgment of conduct. Much is forgiven, as it was in saga times, to anyone who acts in character.[11]

Their humour, especially as it revealed itself in gossip, entranced him, and the books which germinated from these Orcadian observations gained life and colour from the accurate and vivid way in which he was able to reflect it. One of his favourite stories, told many times, was included in a radio programme he wrote about Orkney. Two farmers are discussing their trade after hearing Eric say to someone in the programme that he wouldn't want to be a farmer, because the work would interfere with his fishing:

1ST FARMER Did thoo hear that, min?
2ND FARMER Ay, faith did!
1ST FARMER Did thoo hear him say that he wouldna tak a fairm because it would interfere with his catchin' *troots*?
2ND FARMER I doot that's not the only reason.
1ST FARMER Not hid, faith. But I'll tell thee the true reason, and that is he's no' fit for it.

They indignantly point out that you need brains to be a farmer. And a capacity for hard work, as the women especially knew, for they bore the brunt. Not that the women were *all* successful helpmeets to their men:

2ND FARMER Does thoo mind on the take aboot Mansie Harra's wife? ... Weel, Mansie Harra's wife kept the dirtiest hoose in the parish—this was in the old days, thoo kens—and whan a' the neebour-women were getting fivepence a pund for their butter, or maybe saxpence, Mansie's wife got fowerpence, and never mair nor that. Mansie stood it for as long as a man could, but one day lost all patience, and he said to his wife, 'Wife, afore thoo kirns today, thoo'll go into the back-hoose and strip to thee sark, and thoo'll wesh thee and thoo'll kirn in thee sark. And we'll see if we canna mak clean butter for wance.' So Mansie's wife did as she was telt, and kirned in her sark, and when the butter cam she took it oot o' the kirn and wesht it and set it intil a pan and set the pan on a chair. Then cheust as she was turning away in triumph the cat came in, and ran atween her legs, and trippit her, and doon she sat square in the butter. And 'God,' says Mansie, 'God, wife, thoo've done it again. That's fowerpenny butter still.'[12]

The fruits of those Orkney holidays were the set which they gave to Eric's maturing character and self-concept, and the many writings directly inspired by them when he finally—and it did take a long time—awoke to the power in his pen. When it began to dawn on him that he might be able to write a novel, it was inevitably the Orkney experience that he first quarried. 'Write about what you know' is a good rule, and young people undertaking their first novel usually find that first they must write out of themselves their own story and circumstances. But for Eric the Cardiff experience had been obliterated by more important adventures; it was as if it had never been. So Peter Flett came into being in *White-Maa's Saga*, and his Orkney childhood and background are so vividly recreated that you would swear that they were the author's own.

But even as he learned to think of himself as an Orkneyman, circumstances were conspiring to offer him an identity as more generally a Scot—it sometimes seems doubtful whether the inhabitants of Orkney think of themselves as Scots at all—by taking him to live in Aberdeen. It was a translation he welcomed unreservedly.

3 Schoolboy in Aberdeen

In 1913 Captain Robert Linklater was transferred to a Far Eastern trade route. His home port became London, and his home-comings much less frequent. There was no further need for his wife to endure her Welsh exile, and she began to arrange a return to Scotland. She might have considered going to Greenock, which she knew well from her youth, but, as Eric wrote, 'The advantages of Aberdeen were obvious. It had good schools for a growing family, a university of its own, and between it and Orkney lay only a few miles of rough sea.'[1]

Aberdeen was a fine, compact city, and Eric decided that he liked it. As he described it:

> The greater part of it had a shining and adamantine precision. It was all granite, and it shone with intrinsic brilliance as soon as the bright northern sun came out to illumine the glittering streets that rain had lately washed. I was fascinated by its jewelled domestic walls.
> It lay between two noble rivers, it faced the crashing onset of the North Sea, and its back windows looked out on a hinterland that gradually rose to Lochnagar and the high plateaux of the Cairngorms. It was a splendid city to which we had removed, and with exemplary decision I became an Aberdonian as well as an Orkneyman.[2]

To that hinterland he returned to live the last two or three years of his life, and in two novels he celebrated the city memorably. In *White-Maa's Saga* and *Roll of Honour* it is called not Aberdeen but 'Inverdoon', and may have some touches of Inverness in its fictional ambience, but readers who know the place recognise with pleasure his lively and affectionate projection of it and the people, and not least of its school and university.

Aberdeen Grammar School he found 'a strenuous, ancient and sensible kind of school'.[3] He settled quickly enough as a pupil there, and was relieved to find that although the teachers seemed more impressive and solid men than those he had met in Cardiff, the school's standards were not beyond his reach. Rather, he was ahead of his new class-mates in most subjects, the exception being in writing Latin 'versions', an exercise given much more emphasis in Scottish schools than the mere ability to read the Roman classics.

Idly though he may have spent his time in the Orkney holidays, there is no evidence other than that he was a gifted and hard-working pupil at school. He loved to tell the story against himself of how one of the school reports commented: 'On the whole he is doing fairly well, but is handicapped by a sense of humour.'[4] He left the Cardiff school, however, with a prize for French ('Molière in red calf'), and in Aberdeen was quickly recognised by other boys and teachers as a 'character' with a rare ability with words. The Aberdeen Grammar School prospectus for 1915 records 'E. R. R. Linklater' as a multiple prize-winner, taking 'the Smith Gold Medal for the best Latin version; the Classical VIth Prize for the Third Total in Latin; the First English, First French and Fourth Mathematics Prizes; and the Dr Alexander Walker Prize for his essay in local history'. He had awarded himself an extra name, too, at some step along the way to creating a satisfactory identity, adopting the forename 'Russell' and thus giving a certain pleasing resonance to the roll of his initials. It was a style he retained at least until he was nearly thirty, when the pleasant simplicity of 'Eric Linklater' had become famous across the English-speaking world.

The name Russell, meaning 'red-haired', and chosen by Eric for himself in his unconfident adolescence, could be said to stand for all those soldierly and traditionally red-haired Scots heroes in whose steps the boy ached to follow. Whether he knew it or not, his choice reflected the image of himself he wanted to create. More than one of the more admirable characters in his novels was to flaunt red hair.

Nobody but himself seems to have thought him unattractive. He was highly regarded by his fellow pupils for his waggishness, wit and boisterous good humour, and evidence of his future skill and craftsmanship in language is present in various contributions to the school magazine. But even in his sweetest dreams he can hardly have imagined that the time would come when he would be regarded as the greatest literary pupil to be produced by the school, excepting only one predecessor. The most famous pupil of the Grammar School was Byron, and in celebration of this there was before the school 'a statue of him in robes of flowing bronze'. Eric recalled how reading *Don Juan* and *The Vision of Judgment* at fourteen was a revelation to him:

> My affection for romance was cut in two, and the other half of my mind fell far in love with wit. Dirty fingered, we sat at our desks—rough with deep-cut initials—and gave glum attention to *Samson Agonistes* and *The Causes of the Recent Discontents*; but Byron, through the window, undid the schoolroom teaching that literature must be a solemn thing.[5]

Despite this reflection on the school's teaching of literature, he praised, in a passage reminiscent of one in Churchill's *My Early Life*, the old-fashioned English teaching by which 'we were firmly guided into an exact knowledge of all its tropes and ornaments, such as irony, synecdoche, meiosis and hendiadys ... The practice of writing English was encouraged by compression into a précis of some passage from Addison, Temple or Ruskin.'[6] Eric acknowledged his gratitude for the discipline so learned, for when he turned to journalism he found that 'it had taught me to gut a Blue Book or a White Paper in no time at all'.

At school Eric was notorious, too, for the fire and courage he showed in games, though here commensurate skills were often lacking. Throughout his youth he worked hard to cultivate and compensate for the strengths of a body that seemed to him inadequate. He thought of himself as so unprepossessing that, in retrospect, he deduced that he was 'either truly unattractive or pathologically modest . . . My head was too big for my body . . . I was short-sighted and soon bespectacled.'[7] And later: 'I was rather a narrow-shouldered fifteen.'[8] He was glad he had at least his sense of humour to set against his 'physical unattractiveness', and complained:

> My hair grew with such witless profusion, so thick and harsh and wilfully forward, that no brush could persuade it into decency; with such wanton exuberance that by my twenties it had exhausted my follicles and left me bald.[9]

To compensate for this sense of physical deficiency, he threw himself into physical activity with mental fury, and tried various schemes of exercise to improve himself. It may have seemed an ironic and unfair contrast that his father was a powerful, broad-shouldered man, though tending to run to fat.

As the war against Germany progressed, Eric, partly driven by the jingoistic spirit of the time, and partly by a conviction that life in the army would make a man of him, tried to join up. When his first attempt was frustrated because of his obvious youth, he wrote to his father about the whole problem, and received an illuminating reply:

> My dear Eric,
> Thanks very much for your letter of the 16th inst, and I am very pleased that you and Elspeth are both well and getting along all right, but *you* must have patience and don't do anything rash, keep on at the school until you are seventeen at any rate, after which I promise that I won't interfere with your aspirations. You will then be of military age, and perhaps you will *have* to go into training and I am quite at one with you in regard to physical development etc etc & I know it will do you good but you know yourself that the first thing is to pass the medical inspection & to be able to do this I hardly think that any artificial appliances will help you, so I wouldn't advise you to call on your mother for *cash* indiscriminately, but rather depend on your *own self* and do everything in your power to strengthen your physical developments, which in the course of time will doubtless respond to good natural exercise. And always bear in mind that at any time now you may be called upon to be the one and only support of your mother. These are hazardous times for everyone and especially for sea-farers. And by all accounts you have good talents for education, so take my advice and be prepared to put them to the very best advantage at the

shortest of notice, both for your own sake and that of your mother. Therefore, I
say, give up this idea of enlisting at the present moment.

This was in April 1915, but the doubts about his physical attributes
revealed by the episode are representative of doubts about himself and his
ability and acceptability which in a way he harboured all his life. It helps
account for the discrepancy between the comparatively brash, confident,
sometimes brusque exterior manner often noted in him, and the sensitive,
reserved and self-doubting inner figure perceived by only a few close
friends. It is a tribute to the success of his determination to overcome what
he thought of as his physical inadequacy that later in life people perceived
him as anything but a seven-stone weakling, and his wife, from whom
perhaps he concealed some of the sense of inferiority that had once
bedevilled him, indignantly pointed out that he 'had exceedingly broad
shoulders, was strong, and a great walker'.[10]

As the First World War began to take its toll, the clever Aberdeen
schoolboy became increasingly determined to see some action. His father's
letter may usefully have reminded him of his duty to his mother, but the
sensible advice about patience and natural exercise was less acceptable.

Sixteen months later, the veiled prediction in that letter about the
possibility of the war taking his father's life was fulfilled. Captain Linklater
died, killed not in battle but as a direct consequence of an engagement with
a German submarine in the South Atlantic. Exhausted after the strain of
two years' war service in distant and dangerous waters, he now succumbed
to exposure and contracted pneumonia. Put ashore from his ship in
Colombo, Ceylon, he never recovered.

Eric recalled his last walk with his father, when he had tackled the
difficult paternal task of advising his son about the opposite sex. 'You're at
an age to be taking some interest in girls—and it's not impossible that
some girls are taking an interest in you. Well, what I want to say is this:
make up your mind that you'll never take more from a girl than she's
willing to give you.' Good advice from a good man, even if it was a little
undercut by his muttered continuation: 'And if you take all that she's
willing to give you, you'll have more on your plate than you'll know what to
do with.'[11] Such a man, such a father, had to be avenged, but for a while,
obedient to Robert's wishes, Eric controlled his anger, concentrated on
pleasing his mother, stayed at school and continued his studies.

His extra-curricular studies included a fair amount of exploration of the
field indicated in Robert's last walk with him, but it no longer seems
possible to establish details or names. In *The Man on My Back* he wrote of
the beginnings of his associations with women in a characteristically
generalised and amusing way, again admitting the problems of his self-
doubt.

I was by then of the proper age for falling in love; which I did with a fearful regularity and the assistance of a friend called Bonner. I have always been handicapped by a stupid shyness, a state of being that consists of a thorny and sensitive exterior within which I lurk in dull ineptitude ... I have always needed a catalyst, one who will break down the tiresome barriers of myself, and by his own composure in it familiarise what company I may have wandered into. For such catalysis there was, in Bonner, a natural genius.[12]

Not everything in *The Man on My Back* should be taken, by Eric's own later admission, as gospel, and it may be that he exaggerated his shyness for artistic purposes. But that passage has the ring of truth, and might be borne in mind when he is accused, as sometimes he is, of having been unpredictable and even occasionally boorish in company. He was never one to suffer fools gladly, anyway, but the stress of social occasions is much greater for those afflicted in the way he described. He was young, too, at a time when it was probably more difficult than now for a boy to realise that girls are as deeply attracted by wit and intellect in a man as they are by physical accomplishment. Eric's experience should soon have taught him this, but he did not begin to see things more clearly until after he had passed through a phase (which perhaps in one sense never really ended) when he set himself up as the university misogynist.

There were, in fact, girls and lessons in plenty, and Eric's books, both fictional and non-fictional, are full of references to tall and darkly pretty and pleasantly laughing girls. But his words are revealing, and add a poignancy to one's concept of a man who later created many successful and easy lovers, such as Peter Flett, Magnus Merriman, and especially Juan Motley, with whom he was often and perhaps ironically identified by readers of his books.

After leaving school in 1916 he went, true to his determination to please his mother, straight into Aberdeen University as a medical student. The choice of medicine seems to have been as arbitrary as it was surprising, though it is true that the range of acceptable professions in Scotland in those days was effectively limited to minister, lawyer, doctor, architect or schoolmaster, and he may have selected the least of several evils. Eric gave as his reasons that he wanted to remain in the company of his friend Bonner, that he was tired of Latin and Greek, and that 'the Medicals had a livelier reputation than the Arts students'.[13]

The real concern in his life, however, was to get into the war and prove himself as a soldier. There was little attempt to engage with the studies recommended by his tutors in those first two terms, and then, rather before his eighteenth birthday, with the connivance of a disgruntled officer friend, he joined the Fife & Forfar Yeomanry, and his life as a soldier had begun.

4 A Sniper in France

Joining the Army was in a way like entering into a love affair to which Eric was never really unfaithful for the rest of his life. It was not the Army itself which was the true object of his affections, but the men who made it up. The Army was a monolithic and imperfect institution which often enough was boring and irritating, inefficient in its use of men, cluttered in its operations by red tape of unimaginable proportions, and irrational in its actions. The men were a different matter: they were bound together by causes and circumstances, ready to give everything for their countries, families, wives and sweethearts, and sharing in some measure the most heroic and delightful characteristics of mankind at its best: courage, humour and friendship. That was the way 85831 Private Linklater perceived things in 1917, and his view was little changed half a century later when he accepted what was to be the last commission of his life: a history of his old regiment, The Black Watch, offered him by the man of whose friendship he was most fiercely proud, the soldier Lord Ballantrae, who, as Bernard Fergusson, had become Colonel of the Royal Highland Regiment.

At first the military life was almost wholly fun, more like an extended schoolboy/Territorial Army camp than the horrible mix of blood and mud which thoughts of the First World War usually bring to mind. Passed fit for home service by Captain Jimmy Stewart of the RAMC, he had now to 'cook his own claim for a passage'[1] before he could overcome the twin drawbacks of poor sight and youth, and get across the Channel to exact from the Germans revenge for his father's death. The spring and summer of training soon contributed to a growth of muscle and physical fitness that delighted him, and the poor sight of his naked eyes was sufficiently improved by his spectacles to make his aim unerring; very soon he wore the stripe of a lance-corporal and the crossed-rifles badge of a marksman. When his relative slightness early on opened up a possibility that he might be bullied, a fortunate boxing bout left him with 'the pleasing reputation of being a dangerous person',[2] for his fierceness took him into attack before his opponent expected it, and left the man temporarily astonished and with a good deal of blood on his face. Although after this encounter Eric forswore boxing, 'determined to leave pugilism to the rougher sort for whom it was intended',[3] he did later at university demonstrate on several occasions similar impassioned courage in the ring, coupled with a remarkable inability to perceive when he was beaten.

The summer under canvas in the north of England was almost idyllic. He wrote:

> The camp was situated on a high sloping field with a distant view of the sea, and behind it, running deeply through a wood, was a stream with green and sunshot pools where—though they were out of bounds—one could swim in slow-running water beneath a far high roof of cathedral beeches, or lie warming on white pebbles under a ferny bank. There was rifle-shooting in a desert of sand-dunes, pudding-basin hillocks rough with wiry grass, and beyond them a misty sea crumbling on the shore; and deliberate fire was slow delight, the serious exercise of muscle and eye and tender finger, with the grave reward of a bull, a bull, the tight-lipped annoyance of a magpie, and then—oh, bliss!— another bull; while rapid fire was a sensual ecstasy in which the rifle, well cared for and cosseted with oil, became an almost living thing, its butt-plate firm and faithful, its bolt flying quickly with an eagerness like the soldier's own.[4]

So pleasant were these days, and so remote were the realities of war, that it was some years before Eric had much idea of what happened during that year on the Western Front; detailing the pleasures, he noted the irony:

> These and like simplicities are my memories of the summer when there was mutiny among the French, and the menace of the submarines was at its height; when Russia was making its last weak offensive, and Haig was throwing his doomed armies into the mud at Passchendaele.[5]

The shooting and the marching, the comic adventures and the adjustment to the astonishing and marvellous obscenities of military language, the learning of a little discipline and authority, all contributed to the making of a much more soldierly Linklater who, towards the end of 1917, at last found an opportunity to bring about his translation to France. On duty as orderly corporal one day, and alone for a few minutes in the orderly office, he changed on his documents the year of his birth from 1899 to 1898, so that he became of sufficient age to be sent abroad; and gave himself improved vision in case his spectacles might still be held against him. At last his requests to be included in a fighting regiment prevailed, and he was transferred to The Black Watch. In early December his battalion crossed the Channel, and he was breathing the air of Boulogne.

Eric wrote lightly enough about much of his experience of the war in France, too, from the distances in time from which he recalled them, but the pain and tragedy are not hard to find beneath the surface of his writing. His disposition always was to lighten the dark by seeing the funny side of things, but he knew, too, that the farcical contains and perhaps ultimately conquers the tragic; his humour, sometimes very grim, was a weapon with which to beat back the horror and transmute the pain; he described the occasion of his being wounded as 'pure farce'[6]; but his escape from death was by the narrowest margin. He later remarked that he had written of his 'brief, undistinguished introduction to war with a mannerly reticence which was too mannered to be true',[7] but this too modestly plays down the fearful power his narrative had gained from its comic, understated treatment of material too terrible for tears.

It was not long after his arrival in Boulogne to join the 4th Battalion, The Black Watch, before Eric got his first chance to see what war was really all about. They moved to Passchendaele, relatively quiet now after the brutal offensive of the previous months, but far from the summer picknicking in Yorkshire. The mud, the flooding, the duckboarded trenches, the dead still lying wretchedly in spots where their bodies were as yet irrecoverable, the shortage of food, and the lice all contributed to physical and mental discomforts that became engraved on the young man's memory:

> Our forward positions were holes in the mud. Shell-holes deepened and extended to give cover to a section of ten or a dozen men. They were waterlogged craters in which we were never dry. Our feet and our arses were sodden-wet, and we seldom got enough to eat because ration-parties on their way up the line were usually shot at, and lost not only several men but also what they carried.[8]

But youthful ebullience was not easily stifled, and Eric's memories included much that was bleakly, some that was farcically, funny. So cold and wet was it when they marched towards the Somme that their company commander told them to take off their kilts and wear them as capes about their shoulders. 'So we said goodbye to Passchendaele with a flutter of grey shirt-tails dancing behind our bums.'[9] When a shell fell near them one man caught sufficient of the blast to be knocked aside and receive a bloodied face. When bandaged and comforted with the information that he had lost only a bloody ear, he 'lost self-control as well as his ear. "My ear, my bloody ear!" he shouted, and like a retriever seeking a dead grouse in the heather he went down on his hands and knees to search for it.'[10] There was an Irish sergeant for whom the whole war was nothing but a marvellous opportunity to get practice in battle conditions ready for the coming struggle against England. There was a Commanding Officer who, after watching Eric's attempts to handle a pick and shovel, asked:

> 'What are you doing?'
> I turned and stood rigidly at attention. 'Digging a trench, sir.'
> 'My wife', he said, 'has a small dog, a Pekinese, that gets out every morning to do its business in the garden. And that little Pekinese dog makes a bigger hole than you do!'[11]

When Ludendorff's sixty-two divisions launched their massive offensive against the Fifth Army in March 1918, Eric was in hospital in Rouen, recovering from a severe attack of trench fever, contracted after a fearsome attack by lice; so he missed the worst part of the fighting, but returned to the lines to assist in keeping the retreat as counter-offensive as possible in early April.

On his way back he enjoyed a curious experience reminiscent of an episode in Conrad's *Typhoon*, and his telling of it in *The Man on My Back* merits quotation:

> I became, for a night, a warder of Chinese coolies ...
> There were about fifty coolies in the hut, and all so thickly wadded with clothing, so wrapt about with indescribable garments and old sand-bags, that their apparent bulk was enormous. They had fat round faces that appeared, at one moment, the mirror of immutable calm; but next were twisted and writhen in a maniacal hysteria. When the first bomb fell, a few hundred yards away, they let out a chattering yell, and in a suddenly massing herd ran up the floor of the hut; but stopped a few yards away from us. The next bomb was much closer, and a third, almost simultaneously, roared against the iron walls and set them deeply vibrating. Like madmen the coolies rushed, and my fellow-warder, putting his rifle behind him, dropped three of them with accurate long punches. I, being much smaller than he, retained my rifle and hammered their toes with the butt. We kept them off; but in many of them fear had produced a simple physiological effect, and by the preternatural smell that arose we were nearly stifled. It seemed a long time before All Clear sounded, for though by then the Chinese were sitting happily on the floor, and discussing their private affairs, we were faint and queasy from the extravagance of their inenarrable stink.[12]

There is a good deal of the essential Linklater in the style of that passage: the grotesque humour of the situation, the dispassionate narration of violent action, the interest in the contrast between the wise and phlegmatic countenances of the Chinese and their volatile behaviour, and the vocabulary which enjoys polysyllables and even employs one word that nine out of ten English speakers would simply not know. 'Inenarrable' means 'incapable of being told'; 'indescribable' would do equally well in the context, better in the sense of conveying meaning to the majority, slightly worse in securing the euphony that was part of Eric's stylistic aim. It was a word that he would insist on using again, in the final line of a short story, even after an attempt at disuasion by his publisher,[13] and its use exemplifies a Linklater characteristic that sometimes led to criticism: his extensive and experimental vocabulary.

Although 'the bloodiest and most feverishly distraught days of that magnificent rearguard action'[14] were finished before he rejoined his unit, now much reduced, Eric was now to see action unlike anything he had so far encountered. By the end of the month there were officially only thirty-one survivors of the 4th/5th Black Watch, though Eric always maintained that in fact there were rather more than that. After a brief rest, these few were re-formed into a composite battalion with remnants of other regiments, and marched back into the Salient.

Here Eric's first job was as company runner, but before long his marksman's badge led to his being recruited as a sniper. For three weeks he lived an almost solitary life, remote from his platoon, engaged in what seemed like 'a succession of deliberately invited duels in which I had, admittedly, the initial advantage of choosing my position, and the inherent advantage of being a better shot—as things turned out.'[15] In this way he fought and killed his enemy, as he never forgot. Often he deliberately lightened the memory by the tone in which he referred to it: 'I earned, very honestly, a private's pay by killing several Germans'[16] and again, years after the Second World War: 'In July I think I am going to Frankfurt for the International PEN Congress: the Germans (the Germans, mark you—I used to kill them) have asked me as a Guest of Honour.'[17] It is a profoundly disturbing thing, however, to have visited this ultimate sanction on another human being, and Eric's response was complex. He felt pride in having served his country, in having survived the bitter fighting in the trenches, in having found within himself resources of strength and courage that matched him with his hour; but at the same time his instinct was to mock his own pretensions and himself. In much of his writing later the sardonic tone and macabre imagination would often displace the romantic view of life which was his by nature.

His love for the good soldier notwithstanding, Eric had no doubt that war was 'intellectually intolerable—as well as economically destructive and socially atrocious', and that this was no modern discovery:

> It became insufferable, though sufferance continued, when Napoleon summoned his *levée en masse*, and more evidently when the Germans first used poison-gas. The massive slaughter that modern weapons made possible in 1916 and 1917 destroyed all lingering notions that war retained a romantic appeal which could balance its brutality and multitudinous grief. By 1917 war had become an outrage against common sense as well as against humanity ... but we had decided to fight, *à outrance*, against aggression, and I, a microscopic projection of general insanity, shared to the full its insensate purpose, and with a robust perversion enjoyed the brief remnant of my active service. My few weeks as a sniper gave my life an excitement, an intensity, which I have never known since ... In my nineteenth year I lived at a high pitch of purpose, a continuous physical and mental alertness, that has never again suffused my mind and body.[18]

Such heights of experience must be paid for, and his sense of himself as basically a clown, doomed invariably to lose his trousers at the moment when he was about to win the jackpot, was duly confirmed on 11 April 1918, when his active service was effectively brought to an end. He recalled it as 'a conclusion in pure farce',[19] though some might think that it takes rather a special way of looking at things to see it in such a light. That it was consonant with an outlook he developed in life may be confirmed by a glance at his books; as Marjorie Linklater pointed out: 'Eric, like many of his heroes—or anti-heroes—regarded himself as the chap beset by banana-skins.'[20]

The banana-skin on which he slipped in 1918 took the form of a German bullet that hit him in the back of the head as he fled along a trench, obeying rather late an order to retreat. In an early narration of this event he wrote:

> I heard a wild shout behind me, and looking round saw the trench empty save for one man, who had come back to warn me that we were retreating. He was an old regular soldier, and had also been a nurse in a lunatic asylum. He was a big, good-looking man, but his cheeks had strangely fallen in. He must have lost his false teeth, I thought.
>
> I threw my second bomb, more usefully than the first, and turned to run. I ran so very fast that, although I was the last by a long way to leave the trench, within two hundred yards I had passed several of those who had preceded me; including an officer who was looking back with an expression of reluctance that, in the circumstances, seemed strangely ill-timed.
>
> I continued to run till, in a mingling of righteous indignation and utter dismay, I felt on my head a blow of indescribable force. It was a bullet, and probably a machine-gun bullet, for the rifle-fire of the German infantry was poor.[21]

In a later version of the story, Eric added an element that reinforced the idea that the event was somehow grotesquely comic; a friend had witnessed the moment when Eric was hit, and according to him 'my response to a German bullet was exactly that of a rabbit when it is shot in the head. A rabbit, in that moment of death, leaps high in the air; and so—there was something like admiration in his voice—so, he said, did I.'[22]

In the helmet that he had been wearing there was 'a neat little hole where the bullet had made its entrance; and there was a large and jagged hole where the bullet, flattened and disappointed by the density of my Nordic skull, had forced an exit and gone off in the general direction of Ypres.'[23] He always told the story as if it was funny, though only the fact that he had survived the blow could have rendered it so, and when he was in a good mood he would make jokes about the gutter in his skull and let children make a ceremony of examining it. He kept the helmet 'with the determination of the slightly insane' as a kind of talisman for the rest of his life. When, in his old age, the National Library of Scotland honoured him with an exhibition celebrating his life and work, the battered helmet was a central feature[24]; and it is immortalised in a photograph on the jacket and in the title of his third volume of autobiography, so frequently pillaged in this book, *Fanfare for a Tin Hat*.

It is difficult to see how anyone could ever quite recover from such a shock, and Eric's life was deeply affected by his skirmish with death. Having been so close to oblivion himself, and having seen so many strangers, acquaintances and dear friends succumb to what he had so narrowly escaped, he came to value life more preciously than others, and to feel obliged to celebrate it, to live it more fully, to honour it more completely than people who had not known such a crisis; and in this attitude lay the seeds of the celebrant artist he was to become. At the same time he had seen by what slender threads life is supported, how easily it may be aborted, in what filth and horror it may become embroiled; and in this experience originated the peculiar flavour of much of his art where the farcical may lead to sunny uplands of pure delight or to more grotesque or macabre imaginings where the cruel side of life almost takes precedence.

The rest of Eric's war was spent in hospitals, at first in Boulogne, then in London; and then, when he began to get well, apparently little the worse for his adventure, at convalescent hospitals in Birmingham and Staffordshire. In his chapter 'Soldiers in Bed' in *The Man on My Back*, Eric wrote with humour and style about the various wards in which he spent time; the nurses, some angels, some she-dragons, who helped him back to recovery; the gruesome operations to repair the back of his skull; the dreams and nightmares which for a while dominated his sleeping—and which would provide an element in his writing throughout his life, most notably in his last novel, *A Terrible Freedom*; and his fellow patients, whose humanity and lively idiosyncrasies helped promote in him both the driving interest in individuality and character and the ability to capture its essence in well-chosen words that gave his fiction from the start a special vitality.

After a while, recovering his youthful sprightliness, despite occasional pain from the wound in the back of his head, Eric became less than a model patient, and finally brought contumely upon himself when he and a friend were surprised by the Matron in a bedroom with two VAD nurses. 'McGregor and his crutches were being taught to dance, while I with the other nurse held innocent hands on the bed. A laughing and harmless picture, but the old woman thought otherwise, so McGregor and I were returned forthwith to the depot hospital.'[25]

Despite the still raw and open wound in his head, the military authorities decided that Lance-Corporal Linklater was still needed in the Army and, after a week's leave, he was posted in September to the Reserve Battalion of The Black Watch in Edinburgh Castle. It was not a very pleasant time; the Castle was cold and uncomfortable, and his duties, though 'light', were menial and unfulfilling. He was made more unhappy when a rumour 'poisoned his mind with a wild and hopeless longing'[26]; for it was being said that his bravery in the trenches had earned him a DCM. Alas, it turned out to be without foundation.

But, as Eric recorded in his book about Edinburgh, written forty years later, this first acquaintance with the city began a lifelong delight in it: 'I do, indeed, dote upon the place; and though its faults and frailties can move me to querulous annoyance, I know of much to awaken love, and keep it awake—as well as qualities that are quite unloveable, yet rouse a deep respect.'[27] He celebrated her qualities not only in his guidebook but also in three novels in particular where Edinburgh is the setting, and in one of his most famous short stories, 'Kind Kitty'; and among other debts that he owed the capital was that, more than a decade after his uncomfortable stay in the Castle, Edinburgh would provide him with a beautiful wife.

After a few weeks with The Black Watch in Edinburgh Eric, tired of the inane and unrewarding life of a telephone operator, applied for a Medical Board in the hope of a discharge to civilian life; but this resulted only in his being put into a lower physical category and being dispatched to a labour battalion at Fort George, on the Moray Firth. Here he liked his situation even less, but

> this despairing and dissolute camp was stricken by a wave of that epidemic of influenza which swept the world in 1918, and suddenly I became a medical orderly in a hospital which had to be guarded by two sentries with fixed bayonets, because among the patients were criminals from the guard room ... In this dismal company I celebrated the Armistice; and celebrated it on the parade-ground, doing punishment-drill in full pack. A false rumour of peace, two days before, had provoked a riot, of which a serious view was taken because an obscene and drunken hooligan attacked the sergeant of the guard with a loaded rifle and a bayonet. I entirely agreed with the authorities in deprecating his behaviour, for I was on guard at the time and sorely frightened—the sergeant ordered me to disarm the fellow, but as my nerve was unequal to the task he had to do it himself—yet I and my small coterie of friends were agreed that it was monstrously unfair to punish the innocent with the guilty, and assemble us to welcome peace in full marching order.[28]

The drily comic tone of this little piece of narrative from *The Man on My Back* is typical of the book as a whole. The last sentences of the chapter of reminiscence of the First World War show, however, the romantic side of Eric's character, for there is dramatic impact and genuine pain in them:

> These were my friends when I learned of the death of him who had been my inseparable friend.
> Bonner was dead, with whom I had laughed all through a winter of the war, and whose gay spirit I had breathed like mountain air. He had been killed in France, in the last weeks of the fighting, thrusting forward against a nest of German machine-guns.[29]

At the end of the year Eric was finally discharged from the Army, and it was time for him to resume his interrupted medical studies at Aberdeen

University. Despite the anti-climax and low comedy of his experience in the later part of his service he never forgot the exhilaration and sense of splendour that accompanied the self-sacrifice and comradeship of truly necessary military service, and whenever he wrote of them, in truth or in fiction, his admiration and love for the devoted soldier were manifest. He did not put aside the life of the soldier, or attempt to leave the military life wholly behind, when he went back to Aberdeen, but joined immediately the Officer Training Corps when it was established, kept company particularly with those who had survived wartime service, went regularly to camp and preserved a soldierly bearing.

His experiences in France were of profound significance for his future development. In all three of his volumes of autobiography the period is returned to and described in grim and vivid terms, and it formed the basis for his understanding of and sympathy for the soldier throughout his life. And of course it left its mark on his fiction. In *White-Maa's Saga*, his first novel published in 1929, he was still close enough to those experiences of the First World War for the mood to be powerfully affected by his memories of it and of its aftermath. In 1934 another hero, Magnus Merriman, was endowed with wartime adventures that closely resembled those of his creator, and is similarly affected by the experience in his attempts to make sense of peaceful civilian life. In Eric's gesture towards writing a pacifist novel, *The Impregnable Women*, undertaken in 1938 as he saw Europe rolling forward into another hellish conflict, all the details of the war he described were ineluctable memories of what he had seen in 1918; and they were presented, as he himself admitted, in a less restrained way than in *The Man on My Back*, for in the novel he was 'protected by the good mask of fiction' and achieved, he thought, 'a very respectable approximation to the truth'.[30]

But for a while it was time to put off the uniforms and routines of soldiering and return to the life of study.

5 Student

If his military career was undistinguished and fraught with banana-skins, the next five years offered ample compensation, for Eric became one of the most outstanding and best-remembered students of his day. It was soon evident that he had chosen an inappropriate course: his enthusiasm for his studies in medicine was small and grew less; but university life was wonderful, and in its social and extra-curricular aspects he found a *modus vivendi* most congenial to his vital and expansive spirit.

While the previous eighteen months had nourished his love of the soldier and his arts, the new ambience brought into bud and allowed to blossom two new loves. One was relatively simple: an unequivocal, passionate commitment to the English language. He found himself powerfully gifted, and began increasingly to exploit a linguistic ability that charmed and amazed his contemporaries. The most interesting aspect of his medical studies proved to be the opportunity to acquire new and recondite expressions, and to appreciate with new understanding the value of precise and accurate terminology. A certain medical tang continued to flavour his use of language long after he had abandoned the idea of being a doctor.

The other love was much more shadowy and complicated, much more subject to moods and reviews: it was his love of women, or womankind, and it was far from straightforward, for he was far from single-minded on the subject. His confidence in himself had been increased by the maturing experiences of war and military life, and college life soon confirmed that girls were moved not only by conventional notions of virility, but equally or even more by intelligence, verbal dexterity and a relish of life. But he was a man's man in so many ways, and his view of women included some chauvinistic notions. The result was that Eric fell in love, more or less, with every attractive girl he met; he practised love-making, verbally at any rate, with many willing partners, but succeeded generally in ensuring that things neither went too far nor lasted too long; and, to convince both his fellow students and himself that he was really far from the romantic soul he suspected himself to be, he even developed a public role as the very model of a modern misogynist.

It was all part of the fun because, despite the gradually growing awareness that he was academically on the wrong course, Eric was in his element. In three books in particular he later wrote evocatively and wittily about his student days and, in the chapters numbered V ('Gaudeamus') in *The Man on My Back* and Nine in *Fanfare for a Tin Hat* he reviewed his university days with striking honesty and engrossing art.

The third book indispensable for a full perception of the undergraduate Linklater is his first attempt at an extended fiction, *White-Maa's Saga*, published in 1929. In that novel a young Orcadian by the name of Peter Flett attends the medical school of a university called Inverdoon; the life he leads, the trials he suffers, the joys he delights in are strikingly similar to those of its author. Its lively recreation of the student life of Eric Linklater's time and place is as sound and rewarding an account as we are likely to get.

Further, many of Eric's contemporaries have recalled with great pleasure moments in which he figured, and the University of Aberdeen's records and publications of the time seem to have his name on almost every page. He had many friends, some of them destined to remain friends throughout his life; indeed he had a special gift for friendship which testifies to the solid core of caring and generosity in his character. Once he had formed a friendship it endured, though sometimes keenly tried, and this is as true of friendships formed later in life as it was of those made at school and university. Although he was often short-tempered and difficult, and although he became crustier as time went on, he was basically a faithful and loving man; and this is one of the reasons why now, ten years after his death, his life is still worth writing about.

As an ex-soldier who had seen action in France and sustained a severe wound Eric had, by the time he returned to Aberdeen a little before his twentieth birthday, a solemn maturity in his character which contrasted oddly with his youthful sense of fun and his flashing wit, and many stories are still told about him by those who were at Aberdeen in those days. His handicap of a sense of humour and his perception of himself as one of nature's clowns continued to bring trouble to himself and delight to all who knew him as he made the university his personal property.

For almost two and a half years he continued to wage a losing battle in his medical studies, for though he greatly enjoyed the companionship of his fellow students he could not muster sufficient interest in the items of knowledge he was supposed to commit to memory, and his performance in sessional examinations was less than satisfactory. He wanted not so much to be a doctor as to enter a profession which, he calculated, would more readily than most allow him to travel freely about the world.

That was my real desire: to see the variety of Asia and Africa, and the seas around them. I never regarded the practice of medicine as an end, but only as the means of a vagrant livelihood; and that, of course, was the principal reason why I never came in sight of the necessary degrees.[1]

There was no question of his finding his teachers unsympathetic, for, with the exception of one, he liked them all, considering them the most interesting and jovial of men. The exception was Professor Soddy, later to be a Nobel Prize winner, 'a man of cold and haughty demeanour' who 'did not conceal his dislike of ex-servicemen, and on one occasion was so offensive that his whole class rose and walked out'.[2] But Eric was not personally offended, for he was not there; finding the man's lectures as uninteresting as his personality was unappealing, he seldom attended them. He took pleasure in the skills and ebullient or eccentric characters of the others, and made some attempt to master what they had to teach him, as far as the other demands upon his time permitted.

There were financial difficulties when his failure to pass the examin-ations with sufficient promptitude brought about the loss of his ex-serviceman's grant of about thirty pounds a term, the arrival of which gratuity, he said, 'used to be celebrated with much enthusiasm'. He was driven to the pawnshop to alleviate his distress, depositing against an advance of four pounds the gold medal he had won at school for Latin composition. It was entirely due to the determination and generosity of his mother that he remained at college after this. When he failed, he spoke of finding a job perhaps as a tea-planter in Assam or Ceylon, anything to remove himself from dependence on Elizabeth, who had been left no better than moderately provided for after the early death of her husband. She would not hear of it. In tribute to her, Eric wrote:

> Like Bernard Shaw I can say, 'I never threw myself into the battle of life. I threw my mother into it ...' She would say—she who was so reverent of traditional Scottish education—'You will not leave Aberdeen until you have taken your degree.'[3]

Writing more astringently of the same period in the earlier volume of autobiography he put it this way: 'By mixing hard work and domestic sapience with every shilling, she kept me in flesh and comparative idleness for half a dozen years.'[4]

Eric was everything to his mother; now that his father had died he was and would remain the only man in her life. One of the friends who visited the Linklater ménage frequently was James Sutherland, who commented:

> Mrs Linklater was a remarkable woman. There was clearly a deep relationship between her and her son: the house was run for Eric, and any visitor like me was welcomed as her son's friend. We often sat up late and then stayed in bed until noon: we came and went as we saw fit, or, to do myself justice, as Eric thought fit. Looking back on it in my old age, I am ashamed to think how casually— indeed abominably—I behaved to my hostess.[5]

Supported by this formidable woman, Eric continued for a while in the medical school. The opening chapter of *White-Maa's Saga*, called 'Prelude:

The Pub-Crawl', captures something of what it was like to be at college at that time, when many of the students were veterans of the recent hideous war, hardened in battle, matured by suffering and responsibility, and well used to adult ways. Now they were given a new lease of youth and irresponsibility, and took the best advantage of it they could. They often drank too much; but the conversation that resulted, and the comic belligerence it brought about, and the companionship it encouraged, helped compensate for the darker side of their memories. There were still all-too-frequent reminders of the war as young men, who had somehow survived the trenches, now succumbed to death because of gas in the lungs or some other such insidious legacy; Eric recorded 'a black day in 1922 when I said, "Now I have shot my load of grief, and I'll give death no more attention"'[6]—but it was not so easy.

So, in his first novel, Eric wrote of the bar called the Frigate:

> There was not much light in the Frigate. A pair of dingy incandescent gas-mantles, shaded at the top, threw out descending cones of brightness which overlapped at the level of the tables and gleamed redly in tall beer tumblers, and with pallid radiance in the lesser whisky glasses. Somewhere in the shadows of the roof the dirty model of a frigate hung.... Talk swelled in eager groups and met in a general hubbub, growing afresh as more men came in, and now and then sinking so that a categorical imperative might dominate Babel with a demand for three large whiskies. Tobacco-smoke rose like a drifting mist about the lamps; laughter, now individual and now again a chorus, broke like trumpets through the hubbub of talk; and a warmth of content, a contagious geniality, moved through the crowded tavern.[7]

That well-loved place and such occasions were worked into Eric's early writing because they had been so important to him; the people in the book, too, were very closely modelled on the students he had known. One especially, called Garry Duncan both in the novel and in *The Man on My Back*, was to the life Eric's most admired friend, another who was to die meaninglessly within a year or two. In the autobiography he is described:

> Garry's appearance made him conspicuous, his character added fame. He wore generally a suit of greenish tweed, with tight knickerbockers and a tweed hat of a sporting shape. His cheeks and upturned nose were the colour of a geranium, his eyes were little and bright blue, his hair a golden fire. His energy was unceasing, and he was ever stirring and prodding those about him to some new enterprise. He was generous beyond measure, radiantly kind, but in his cups a sly fantastic rogue. And his weakness, that magnified his fame into legend, was an excessive and recurrent thirst.[8]

Eric was to develop in his life something of a healthy and recurrent thirst himself, and his delight in drinking and the companionship and conversation that goes with it became legendary in time. His use of it as a theme and as a catalyst in several of his novels was noted by Kurt Wittig as a significant component in his art, in which drink is 'not so much a vice, nor an escape or stimulant, but a gateway to a new kind of world that provides distortion, new perspectives and surprising insights'.[9]

In the intervals of drinking and enjoying life with his witty and ribald companions, Eric applied himself hopefully to his studies, and found a degree of pleasure and success in some of the actual practice in doctoring for which he found opportunities. Later in life he loved to surprise people by pointing out that, among his other competencies, he was a qualified midwife, and his account of how Peter Flett in *White-Maa's Saga* spends a Christmas holiday practising midwifery may be taken as an accurate representation of his own experience.[10] He also wrote, much later, about one confinement which he attended as a raw young locum:

> I was summoned to a woman in labour, and dreadful fears assailed me, on my motor-cycle, of a breech presentation, of twins, of haemorrhage, and a twisted cord. But she, thank God, had neither doubt nor fear. She had had healthy children before, and calmly she gave birth to another. I remembered all I had been taught, I was tolerably quick and earnestly careful. I bathed the child, and left both of them tidy, and with my knees still trembling a little went down into the kitchen. Warmly the husband shook my hand, and gave me a tumbler half-filled with rum. The night air was frostily cold, the motor-bike steered itself and swiftly ran of its own impulse, and through dark clouds a wild moon sprang to play absurdly with its reflection in the loch.[11]

That little narrative finely catches the excitement, the sense of achievement and the tenderness which Eric felt in finding his newly acquired skills useful; but his memories were also of more comic moments, as in a story of his brash over-confidence when he found himself called in by a local farmer to establish whether his cow had died of anthrax or of some other less dreadful malady:

> We flayed the skin from the upper half of the body, and with a carpenter's saw I cut out a great section of its ribs. I was somewhat puzzled by what appeared to be a gross confusion of organs lying beneath, but after laborious inspection of what, I suppose, were its lungs, I discovered the heart; and then, triumphantly, was able to show a collection of yellow globules about the valves. 'There's no sign of anthrax here,' I said, firmly.—I had no idea what the signs of anthrax were, but time had not yet invaded the pure confidence of youth.—'It's fatty degeneration of the heart that killed her.' The farmer was grateful to me. For several years I shot over his hill and marsh free of payment, and with a meal waiting for me whenever I cared to stop at his house; and always I congratulated myself on the profits of ignorance—for if I had known more about anthrax I would certainly never have gone near his cow.[12]

These more positive achievements in the practical sphere of medicine notwithstanding, Eric's performance in examinations was repeatedly discouraging. His contemporaries expected him to withdraw from the course after each reversal, and several thought that the time had come indeed when, as one of them wrote:

> A notice appeared on the Union Board in bold legible handwriting that was never going to be that of a doctor. It read:
>
> FOR SALE: Gray's *Anatomy*
>   Halliburton's *Physiology*
>   Schaefer's *Histology*
>
> Condition almost indistinguishable from new.
> Apply E. R. R. Linklater.[13]

Eric had in fact not yet given up the idea of completing his course in medicine; the notice was 'a poet's gesture', for, having fallen in love with a girl 'who provoked a similar wildness of emotion in a good many other young men; for she was uncommonly lovely and not always aloof though always virtuous',[14] he needed money to take her out. The girl, Mabel Cowie, was one of many who caused Eric's heart to miss a beat or two. His love led him in high romanticism, 'with the narrow logic and nonsensical heroism of youth', to sell his books, the tools of his trade, just before making his second attempt at the Second Professional Examination. He consoled himself with the thought that he would have failed the examination anyway.

He simply could not make himself remember all the multitude of details that had to be mastered. 'The growing burden of uncongenial work and examinations that could not be passed grew at last unbearable'[15] and, anticipating by a narrow margin the decision of Faculty, he decided to abandon medicine. According to one story:

> Linklater's difficulty in Anatomy was his utter repugnance to a partially dissected cadaver. It made him ill. After several questions, all indifferently answered, the examiner produced a visiting card and suggested that Linklater might write all he knew of Anatomy upon the back of it. The examinee, fortified by the knowledge that he would not be continuing in medicine, tore the card in two and gave one half back, with the words: 'Half may be enough for both of us', and hurried out.[16]

But Alan Grant, who told me the story, didn't think it could be true; the Eric he had known would never have been so rude. But perhaps he would. If he was, it was certainly not for the last time.

The decision at last made, Eric moved from Marischal College to King's College to read English literature under Professor A. A. Jack. He was undoubtedly humiliated by his failure in medicine, as he would have been, as he always was, by any failure. He wrote: 'I should like to pretend that I suffered failure without a bruise; but the truth is otherwise.' But after the transfer to Arts had been made, he realised the sense of it: 'I entered then upon a new curriculum, and found content.' Everything he needed for his new studies came naturally to him, and he was now able to take an even more prominent part in the life of the university, if that was possible, without detriment to his examination prospects.

He had applied himself from the beginning of his university life to a fine variety of extra-curricular activities, and is remembered by his contemporaries as having fearful, almost maniacal, energy. Part of his determination was still to strengthen his bodily faculties, already much improved by his life as a soldier, and he took the field in various gladiatorial disguises. Rugby he seems to have regarded as too beautiful a game to be sullied by his own participation; that he would celebrate for its aesthetic and companionable delights in his writing. But he played hockey—'not very well', according to one witness, but frequently and usefully for the Former Pupils of the Grammar School according to another—and tried to get a rowing club going. One of the recruits for this enterprise recalls:

> The first outing upon the dangerous waters of the Dee was my last. With Linklater supervising despairingly from a skiff, I found myself floundering and flustered in a coxless four with three men of double my muscle-power. There was never any subsequent allusion to this hazardous farce, which we all survived, and I have no idea what happened to the rowing club.[17]

Despite his resolution as a soldier to renounce pugilism, Eric returned not infrequently to the ring at Aberdeen, where he boxed 'with more enthusiasm than science'. His need for spectacles to render his sight at all useful must have been something of a handicap. An article in *Alma Mater* referred to him as being 'generally carried out of the ring looking like an early Christian martyr'. In 1923 he got to the final of a middleweight competition for a place in the university's team to meet Edinburgh University's team, by winning on points in a lively contest against one J. A. Spark:

> In the initial session, Linklater was knocked down and took a count of nine, rising quite fresh ... Matters livened up in the second meeting, Linklater putting in some telling two-handed work to the face and body ... Linklater again took the aggressive in the third round, but Spark's long left kept him out ... In the final session, Linklater landed some fine crisp blows to both head and body, Spark spoiling his display by clinching too freely. Linklater was awarded the decision.[18]

Alas, in the final Eric met a formidable opponent in W. B. Macdonald, with the result suggested by a cartoon in the *Aberdeen Evening Express* portraying a much-battered and bewildered Linklater.

His attitude towards boxing may perhaps best be gauged from passages in *White-Maa's Saga*. In one Peter Flett's lack of training tells and he is defeated, but the excitement and atmosphere are well caught, and the justification for it all is suggested by:

There is a beauty in boxing when men stand upright and step lightly. There is a design in their movements, a significance as charged as that of ballet. Counter-poise follows on poise, defence on attack, reaction on action with a balance, a trim symmetry that quickens as the blood heats and grows and swells into a pounding orchestration of thudding fists and shifting, sidling feet; eyes and heart and every muscle are attuned to it; for an instant there is repose, the sculptured austerity of two figures, motionless, poised like statues on the verge of life; and then their static energy is again released to mingle dynamically in a crescendo of action.[19]

His interest in the sport took Eric a couple of years later to a boxing tournament in Bombay, an occasion so curious, beautiful and hilarious that he devoted five pages to it in his autobiography.[20] To read his account of the evening's business is to come close to the spirit of the essential man.

Eric's greatest sporting joy, however, lay then, as throughout his life, in more natural surroundings, and it was in fishing, sailing, shooting and mountain-walking that he most excelled. It is impossible to read many of his books, especially the non-fiction, without appreciating very quickly how greatly these activities mattered to him. His friend James Sutherland described some of their walking and fishing together:

> I spent several long vacations with Link at his mother's house in Orkney, on the northern shore of Loch Harray. We fished most days, unless the water was too rough, and caught plenty of small trout: ¼lb was acceptable, ½lb would be a good fish, a ¾lb would call for a celebration ...
>
> We varied the fishing with occasional excursions to places like Scapa Flow, where the bulk of the German fleet was still lying where it had been scuttled. I remember particularly a visit we made to the island of Hoy. We set off in Link's boat on a fairly boisterous sunny morning, and when we were about a third of the way down the loch a gale blew up. Something went wrong with one of the rowlocks (probably mine), and for some time we were drifting dangerously until we were able to make some temporary repairs with a piece of rope. We managed to reach the southern end of Loch Harray, beached the boat, and set off to walk however many miles it took to reach the coast. Link had brought his red setter with him: it had been violently sick in the boat, but now it went coursing about the heather as if nothing had happened.
>
> In due course we arrived at Stromness, where a little steamer was waiting to cross over from the Orkney Mainland to Hoy ... On Hoy Link knew a place where he could buy lobsters, and he got two enormous ones for a few shillings. They were so big that they had to be put in a sack, and as we sat in the steamer on the way back to Mainland we could hear the clattering of those creatures inside the sack. We took turns to carry them back to where we had beached our boat, and reached home late that night. I don't know how Mrs Linklater coped with them—probably in her jam kettle—but we feasted on them next day.

Eric's pleasure in the outdoor sporting life is most potently conveyed in *A Year of Space* in the chapter 'A Memory of Hills', where he wrote nostalgically of various occasions of shooting and fishing in the Highlands. At the end of one summer vacation, short of money as usual, he and two other medical students with whom he was friendly went off to Ballater to act as beaters on the Glorious Twelfth and subsequently. On the grouse-moors he, Stewart and Cheyne worked hard, sometimes having to walk twenty-five miles in the course of a day, and learned to do a little poaching on their own account; they 'borrowed a big iron pot from the shepherd's wife and lived on stewed grouse'. They tried boldly to get into the line of beaters for the King, George V, who was said to be the best shot in Britain, but the head keeper explained that he had to give the local lads their chance. Their disappointment was well and truly dispersed when the King and the Duke of York came over and briefly spoke with them.

> He was sorry we had been disappointed. We stood, a little breathless, and muttered, 'Yes, Sir.' The King, in his voice that was rough about the edges and genial in essence, asked who we were and what we did. Shyly, in overlapping words, we told him, and with a flicker of amusement in his beard—looking at our posture—he asked, 'Have you been in the Army?' We told him the names of our regiments, and he talked to us a little longer; and at his right shoulder the Duke of York looked at us with steady and percipient eyes. He was of our generation, he knew us better than the King. The old King was quite simply the Chief of the Clan, the Captain of the Ship; but the Duke had trodden the years that we had trodden, and he did not smile when the King smiled.[21]

The King invited the three young men to stay and watch him shoot, if they would like to, and they were glad of the opportunity to watch 'the very summit of marksmanship, the nonpareil of shooting' in a performance that could be described only as 'supernacular'.

Although in the student politics in which he played yet another role in the University Eric set himself up as a Liberal, he was already essentially a Tory, even by his own admission. The reverence and respect shown for the King that was and the King that would be in the passage just quoted is partly traceable to its having been written in 1953, directly stimulated by thoughts of the recent and widely lamented death of King George VI, but in another sense it might have been written at any time in the previous thirty years. Eric's admiration for the traditional, for the Royal Family, for the British Empire, for all comparable institutions grew more evident as the years advanced, but it was natural to him from the beginning. It was part of his romanticism, allied to that element in his nature that tended to hero-worship in a more general way; he was far from blind to the inadequacies of the average human being, and of the larger part of human institutions, but he was also in no doubt that there were some men whose stature was simply heroic, and these men he loved to celebrate.

In the University Eric was himself quite a hero, though he did not think of himself as such, regarding himself basically as a comic figure. His extraordinary energy took him into most of the social and cultural areas of the life of the place, usually with some kind of distinction. Early in 1920 he contributed to the University magazine, *Alma Mater*, some verses entitled 'Don Juan—Lamb', signed 'Silenus'; it was the beginning of his flirtation with the idea that he might be a poet and the first step towards his taking over the paper as its Editor the following year. It was here that his friendship with James Sutherland began, for 'Suddy' was Editor of *Alma Mater* in 1919–20. Eric's breezy style and superb confidence in this early stage of his career as a journalist show the ease with which he could already move in the medium of words. Having a great variety of activities requiring his attention, Eric would always be in a great hurry, as his contemporary, Alan Grant, remembered:

> He would rush in on a Tuesday afternoon (publication Wednesday morning), sit down and literally dash off his editorial in minutes. He might throw the paper across to one of us—'Do me a favour and proof-read it for me'—and he would disappear again as fast as he had come.

Isobel Walker also commented on the excitement and pace which Eric generated in his passage from one activity to another:

> My real friendship for him began in my teens when he encouraged me to draw in black and white and later illustrate his nonsense verses in *Alma Mater*. We were both on the committee, and went to desperate lengths to get anything ready in time for publication. He would seize any old drawing of mine and write like mad—and so our efforts were not exactly masterpieces![22]

Masterpieces or not, they were very entertaining, and Eric's leading articles, though often executed in the minimum of time, were witty and provocative. He would hold forth on all sorts of topics, for instance 'Afternoon', 'Gaudeamus' (a Christmas editorial celebrating the virtues of good food and drink), 'Jazz' (of which he did not in the least approve) and 'The Noble Art' (boxing). They were not a bad sort of introductory practice for the career in journalism which he later decided to follow—or at any rate to try for a year or two.

Egged on by 'Garry Duncan', he also played a considerable part in reviving the University's defunct Debating Society and acted as its Secretary in 1920–1 and as its President in the following year. At the first meeting of the regenerated society he proposed the motion 'That women are a wet blanket in any society'—James Sutherland said that he had chosen the topic himself as part of his comic campaign to be seen as a misogynist. In this he seems to have been partly successful, for several of his contemporaries remembered him as having such a reputation. They were men, though. None of the women who have offered testimony suggested that he did not like them: quite the opposite.

At first the debating took a great personal toll, for despite his apparent extroversion he was very shy and the thought of speaking in public filled him with terror:

> Indeed, I found the whole business of the Debating Society a torture as well as a delight. I would wait my turn to speak in a livid distress—often I lost the latter half of a sentence, and even of a word, in the black void of aphasia.[23]

In such beginnings a considerable talent struggled to develop, but was not long in learning to make light of the psychological barriers that sought to restrain it. His debating ability became legendary for its wit and verbal legerdemain. He spoke frequently and sufficiently forcefully to win more debates than he lost, including—an easy and appropriate topic for him to move—'That alcohol makes the world go round' in the year of his Presidency.

Besides debating for its own sake, he took his newly acquired skills into the political arena as President of the Liberal Society. One student of the time remembers well his making in this capacity during a Rectorial Election 'a quite long speech in which he cleverly disguised the fact that he had almost nothing concrete to put across'.[24] Tribute was paid to his astonishing verve and fluency in an article recording the occasion of his leaving the University:

> The face of Link was an illumination, in more ways than one. It was an outward and visible symbol of the brains behind the face. It was a memorable rather than a handsome face, but it was the sort of face that one could live with and be pleased to exist. That is more than could be said of many handsome faces. They are so often frontispieces for books that do not materialise. Link's face, like Link himself, spoke volumes ...
>
> Never has the face of Link been more illuminate, never did it speak so well and so voluminously as at the farewell dinner at which he was entertained on the eve of his departure for a warmer climate ...
>
> Link's speech, which lasted for three-quarters of an hour, was peculiarly and particularly intimate and inclusive. There were certain passages in it which, both for the matter and the manner, will not soon be forgotten. And when Link had finished his detailed 'ticking off' of the company, he suddenly realised that he had come to the end of his last speech at a varsity function for some time to come. There was a second's flash of something which we who knew him knew existed in him though he seldom or never showed it. It came and it was gone, and with a peculiarly Linklaterian chuckle, the speech was finished.
>
> Yes, Link has gone out, as he should, in a blaze of oratory, leaving with those of us who remain the echo of a voice that has that peculiar huskiness which has distinguished the voices of so many fine artists.[25]

Eric was remembered as much for his sterling work in the Gala Charity Week activities as for almost anything else. Having inaugurated the Gala Week idea, to win money for charities, he then combined his skills as organiser, poet and actor to bring about, each year for three or four years, the staging of a musical play to crown the festivities of the week.

He had first tried his hand at acting when Professor Harrower, Professor of Greek, who was greatly interested in amateur theatre, produced with some professional help Greek plays in his own translation. In Eric's account:

> Well-designed costumes encouraged some charmingly pretty girls to enlist in his choruses, and in my vain pursuit of one or more of them I suffered deeply. I joined the cast of an ambitious *Oedipus Tyrannus*, and wore a violet-bordered grey himation. There were two girls who, in peplos and chiton, acquired a beauty, an unfamiliar attraction, that far exceeded their everyday appearance; and I may have let my mind stray beyond the Sophoclean dialogue.
>
> I played the dullish part of Creon, and advancing to the foremost edge of a promontory intruding into the audience exclaimed, 'Hear me, men of Thebes!'—and in that loneliness, a loneliness beyond help, forgot the message I had to deliver. I stood there, mute and miserable, for three, five, seven seconds before my memory returned. Later in the evening I was congratulated on the unexpected emotion I had given to my speech. In my agony my forehead was bedewed with sweat that glistened very prettily. Or so I was told.[26]

The would-be misogynist is singularly absent from this recollection, but he is present in one of the plays which Eric wrote for the climax of Gala Week, 1922. Called *Stella the Bajanella*, it was about a first-year girl at the University and her adventures among a motley crew of recognisable college types. (In the argot of Aberdeen University a 'bajan' was a first-year Arts student, and the female of the species was a 'bajanella'. A first-year medical student was a 'lamb', as in the title of Eric's Byronesque poem mentioned earlier.) Eric's friend A. I. Cheyne, who was with him when they watched the King shooting, played the hero, Theodore Dollop, and Eric himself played 'Jonathan Gane, a Misogynist'. He gave himself lines such as:

> GANE: Probably half the fascination about Marcelle is that you can see her only at certain hours. That would be rather a good idea to apply to all women—let them out on a lead from 12 till 2, and from 6 to 9.30 only, and then—[27]

It was clearly nothing but a provocative pose—and yet ...

In the two subsequent years, so great had been the success of *Stella*, he wrote two more such comedies, *Rosemount Nights* (1923) and *The Prince Appears* (1924); these two were in fact immortalised in print, issued in a paper binding by an Aberdeen printer, and thus constitute the first published works in the Linklater *oeuvre*. Many years later, in answer to a question about them, Eric described them as 'very juvenile musical comedies', neither of which, he imagined, had survived. 'Their disappearance cannot be counted a loss,' he wrote.[28] As a matter of fact he had done what he could soon after they were published to make sure they would not survive, buying up from the printer all the remaining copies and destroying them. But almost fifty years later copies of both plays eventually found their way back, and now reside in the library of Eric's widow. They were much appreciated at the time, by the audience for which they were written, and much fun was had by all concerned in putting them on.

Among these were two members of a family which Eric had practically adopted in Aberdeen. One was Douglas Walker, who had been at the Grammar School with Eric; he later became a Writer to the Signet (a member of an historic society of solicitors in Scotland) and Eric's personal lawyer. Douglas's youngest sister was Isobel Walker; for years she was in thrall to Eric, and he always treated her, half-mockingly, half-seriously, as if he was in love with her, or would be one day. She adored his funny ways, romantic and comic language, and his many talents; and he encouraged her in her drawing, and to act little parts in his musical plays, and generally to develop her own skills. Isobel in the end married another of Eric's friends, a medical student confusingly also called Walker, though no relation to the family. Charles Walker, whose greatest interest was in ornithology, used to undertake the direction of the plays; Douglas wrote some of the tunes and acted various roles. Most of the music was written by another student whom they all thought of as a genius, Dr John Stevenson ('Johnny') Taylor.

Eric's friendship with this group of people, especially with the Walker family, was a source of great delight to him, as was the friendship and respect of a great number of people throughout the University. Among these were those who, despite having 'suffered the pains of military service, felt no dislike of uniform'.[29] By 1921 they had re-formed the old University Company of the 4th Gordon Highlanders, and Eric became a leading light in this circle, too, attending camps, enjoying the drills, and flourishing in the male environment. He became a sergeant, and later Company Sergeant Major, 'under the redoubtable command of John Boyd Orr', before being commissioned when the Officer Training Corps was established.

All these enterprises, from amateur militarism to journalism to theatricals to poetastering to debating to the multifarious sportive undertakings, even his ultimate and inevitable Presidency of the Union, were not sufficient to interfere with his new line of study, and in reading English literature he again distinguished himself notably. He was very happy under the tutelage of Professor Jack, comic figure though Eric certainly found him at times, and later he paid generous tribute to him in the autobiographies and in an appreciation published in the Aberdeen University *Review* in 1946. He also derived much pleasure from the teaching and companionship of Claud Colleer Abbott, a young lecturer in the

English department, who was aware of some of the new forces in literature and who tried to interest Eric in the poetry of T. S. Eliot and the moderns. Though unconvinced by what he read of the new poetry, Eric rounded off his academic career by taking First Class Honours in his Finals. At the same time he picked up several university prizes: the Seafield Gold Medal, the Minto Memorial Prize, the Senatus Prize in English literature and the Calder Verse Prize for his long poem, 'The Queen of Scots'.

It is typical of his essential modesty and amused sense of proportion, if not of a genuine and consistent self-undervaluation, that in his last review of his life he reported his university success in this way:

> In an undistinguished year I had taken my degree and decorated it with several prizes. That gratified my mother, but when I met Professor McKerron [the Professor of Midwifery and Eric's former tutor] in Broad Street he beckoned me from the pavement, and as I crossed the road he shouted: 'Clever fellow, aren't you, Linklater? You stay here till there's no competition left—all the good ones have gone—so you walk in and scoop the pool. Well, well, good luck to you. There's a lot of art in good timing.'[30]

Less well documented than other aspects of his time at the university, there remains the question of just how well, in reality, he got on with the girls. If his misogyny was, as I have suggested, not more than an affectation, what facts can now be recovered from the past about his friendships and affairs of the heart? Was there any resemblance between the love life of his characters, such as Peter Flett, Juan Motley and Magnus Merriman, who enjoyed fully consummated love-affairs in the novels he wrote about them, and his own? Even if they were more imaginative projections of what might have been than fictional reconstructions of what was, they are very suggestive of what he would have liked.

According to his own statements he was not infrequently in love with or in pursuit of some girl or other, despite his public avowal of an impatience with and distrust of womankind. He claimed to have been in love with the five daughters of the Principal and Vice-Chancellor, Sir George Adam Smith, each in turn, but their recollections admit rather of warm friendship and mutual regard than of passionate embroilments. There was Isobel Walker, but that was closer to a form of loving brother-and-sister bond rather than anything else. There was Mabel Cowie, the beautiful girl for whose sake he sold his medical books; she later became quite famous as a playwright, under the pseudonym of Lesley Storm, and Eric retained a close friendship with her for many years afterwards. When she married Dr James Clark he remained in touch, acted as a friendly uncle to her children; their shared interest in the theatre held them together, too, and when in the 1940s they both had plays running in London at the same time they met again with old affection.

Clearly there was a powerful attraction and enduring relationship there, though whether it was anything other than sexually innocent would be hard now to establish and seems unlikely. Eric wrote in retrospect of those days: 'Of the girls who came up to the University the majority were chaste, and chastity was still regarded as a normal temper and condition for the young.' I do not think he would have had it any different, though he comically contrasted that relatively innocent state of affairs with a problem mentioned to him twenty years later by the Supervisor of Women Students at the University of which he had by then been elected Rector: '"I'm finding it difficult", she said, "to keep the girls from bringing their carry-cots into the Union." *Autres temps, autres moeurs.*'[31] Which is not, however, to suggest that the facts of life were unknown in the University of the early twenties, especially to the medical students who qualified in midwifery—only that there was a different attitude to what use could be made of knowledge of those facts. That Eric was not embarrassed by them is suggested by a recollection of Alan Grant's:

> The SRC were faced with difficulties when the Manager of the University Union complained of the activities by students of both sexes in the gallery of the theatre-hall, after the weekly Saturday hops. Moreover, the Manager said, he had concrete proof. The difficulties arose because the Chairman of the SRC that year was Dr Mary Esslemont. The delicacy of the matter was left to Eric to handle at the next meeting, and I heard from Alex Badenoch that the Chairman had been advised by Mr Linklater of 'tangible tokens of illicit love being left lying about in the students' gallery', but with the Chairman's permission he would convene a subcommittee to deal with the complaint and the matter in the meantime need not be discussed further.

The presence of Mary Esslemont in the Chair, the first woman to hold the office of President of the Students' Representative Council, was due partly to Eric's efforts as 'one of a clique—or coterie or faction—that engineered her election'.[32] Their campaign roused bitter feeling and angry opposition, and after its success no woman was elected again. Eric's bringing his influence to bear in such a unique campaign and his pride in its outcome—for Mary Esslemont was by this elevation started on a road to a lifetime of service to the University—would seem curious behaviour in a dedicated misogynist.

Eric's friend Douglas Walker announced in 1924 his engagement to a girl called Margaret Murray, who, after leaving Aberdeen in 1922 to live in South Africa, had now returned to Scotland. In a delighted letter of congratulation to Douglas Eric made fun of his own position and lavished praise on the intended bride—to whom, indeed, he had written poems in years gone by:

> My dear man,
> The truly appalling rapidity with which I am answering your letter is directly referable to an EVENT, the nature of which you may possibly surmise.

In the normal course of things such an event would be unlikely to stir me to a paean (add 'e's and 'a's where necessary) of congratulation. At most a pang of genuine pain and loss—at least a cynical snort—that, I think, would be my normal reflex. As it is I passed the news to Johnny Taylor with a wild laugh of despair and in a tone of hollow anguish. Johnny—but it was hypocrisy on his part—pressed the bell again and said: 'Another good man gone. God bless bachelors and keep 'em safe.' Hypocrisy, my dear fellow, damned affectation. The thought of Mabel was in his mind all the time, and his flung-out regret was but a barren gesture. *My* Mabels, bless their little hearts, are all married or lost, and I drink my drink alone, without the sugared interpolation of any woman's finger ...

I do congratulate you and, curiously enough, Peggy ... In addition to her more obvious attractions—and it is not everyone who is comely, wise and witty, and only one woman in ten can laugh properly and Glory-to-God-good-jokesily—in addition to these there is one that you should cherish in your heart. She reads Kipling ...

In a man, that is little more than a certificate of character. Every good man does, and knows every thumb-mark on the page. But women, poor creatures, are denied so much. They see that the Cardinal's Hat is red, and doubtless judge that it is a very pretty red, though it doesn't match his nose, but they don't see that the Hat stands for Holy Rome and poisoned gloves and ambition and ecstasy and the herd-complex of swarming peasants and a key to locks more wonderful than anything devised by Mr Yale. Women chatter incessantly from the desire to make a noise, or from curiosity, or to provide a decent interval between kisses. But they don't see that syllabic vocalised noises are all that distinguish us from the higher apes.

But a girl who knows her Kipling stands apart and has a soul to save.

The words of an unusually romantic misogynist, one might think. Peggy had a younger sister, Marris, and several years later she and Eric had a stormy and passionate affair, until she fled to London. The answer seems to be simply that he wanted the best of both worlds, to be loved and cherished by a woman, but also to be a free agent to travel the world and find himself. To an enviable extent he achieved this high ambition, both before and after the marriage he eventually made.

The word which most accurately sums up his life as a student would seem to be 'exuberant'—life, after the black miseries of the war, was essentially to be enjoyed with every scrap of energy at one's command. Eric's exuberance at times bordered on the frenetic: he was a great lover of life. Here is a final snapshot of him as a student by Alan Grant:

> In the annual bonfire of torches that closed the student procession at the end of charity week, Linklater, dressed as Silenus, would lead some extroverted hardened souls in leaping across the bonfire, screaming wildly.

It is a picture that helps capture the pagan vitality of an extraordinary young man.

6 Journalist in Bombay

Somewhere in the back of Eric's mind as he stuck with reasonable dogged-
ness at his medical studies was the notion that the profession of doctor
would give him more chances than most to travel and see the world; similar
reasoning, as he drew towards the close of his more rewarding career as a
literary student, led him to look for a job in journalism. As Editor of and
frequent contributor to *Alma Mater* he had gained some experience of
working under pressure and had proved an ability to spin words onto
paper. During his last year as a student he made himself better known to
the editorial staff of the local newspaper, the Aberdeen *Press and Journal*,
and as soon as his Finals were over and he had returned from Summer
OTC camp in Rhyl he attached himself to the paper while waiting for
something more exciting to turn up.

Something of the flavour of this experience may be learned from a letter
he wrote to his friend Douglas Walker, who was at the time on holiday in
Paris:

I am writing this in the elaborate offices of the *Press and Journal*. Hence the
paper, which is not, as you wickedly surmised, the lost property of some public
lavatory. I come down about 8 p.m. and wander away about 1, having filled in
the time by reading a selection of papers from the *Morning Post* to the *Daily
Herald*; by occasionally playing at sub-editing the strange case of Major Sheppard, the Balkan bigamy of a Hampshire clergyman, the infidelity of an MP,
the Sheffield Gang Trial, and occasionally the less important messages of
M—and then—Reuter. I have also done the obituary of a woman missionary,
whom I just found spread over two columns of the *North China Observer*, or
some such thing, and tactfully boiled down to five unobtrusive lines; and three
or four of those ridiculous little 2nd or 3rd leaders, two of which have actually
appeared ...

At that point the Editor came in, made some polite noises, and said that
my ideas on dress the previous evening had frightened him. My God. A chaste
soul. He said, 'I must give you duller things to write about. Do you know
anything about China?' A deprecating silence implied that the name was
familiar to me ...

PS: I am now commissioned to write a critical appraisal of the Unemployment Insurance Bill, which has just passed its third reading. And nobody
knows, nobody cares. O swift hurricanes of death and the bubbling coil of
bursting gum factories. Coma and death. I hear 10,000 little silver bells tinkling

in the blankness of night, and Burton is washed to sea on his own bright flood.
A long farewell.

When he wrote this letter, however, Eric knew that more exciting times
were not far away, for he had secured an appointment as Assistant Editor
of *The Times of India*, and was due to go out to Bombay in October 1925. He
gave three reasons why this came about:

> I had been educated in Aberdeen, and two members of the editorial staff were
> Aberdonians, whose common virtue is local patriotism; I had had a couple of
> poems published in the *London Mercury*, which may have revealed incipient
> ability to write about Hindu-Moslem politics; and being summoned to an
> interview in London, the editor took me out to lunch, and, yawning, protested
> that he could not be bothered with the deciphering of so large and ill-written a
> menu, and would I order lunch for both of us? I did, and got the job.[1]

This is typical of his attitude towards himself throughout *The Man on
My Back*. His qualifications, which included a first-class degree, a sharp
and inquiring mind, a marked way with words, a measure of valid and
useful experience, and a hardy and energetic character, must have been
more evident both to himself and to his prospective employers than he
represented in this episode, and in this he was true to an image of himself
that he cultivated through most of his life. According to his own self-
estimate he was incurably idle, sometimes undeservedly fortunate and
more often deservedly unfortunate, earning the inevitable reward of the
inveterate buffoon. Or so he projected himself all too often, knowing well
enough that, despite some superficial truth in the image, behind it there
was a very different person indeed, sadly confused at times.

His eighteen-month period of life in India was enormously enriching,
although there were times when he was unhappy and homesick or bored
with his work. He wrote at length about the period in *The Man on My Back*
and gave a further ten pages to it in *Fanfare for a Tin Hat*. Some additional
information and colour has been drawn from his surviving letters to
members of the Walker family, but it is hard to forgive him for the act of
vandalism by which he destroyed, after his mother's death, all the great
pile of long and fascinating letters which he had dutifully and lovingly
written to her whenever he was away from home. His confession of this
barbarous act may be found on pages 72 and 92 of *Fanfare for a Tin Hat*.

Eric sailed out to India on the TSS *California* in October 1925. In a
letter to Douglas Walker's mother he waxed lyrical about the food:

> One lunches, simply enough, on, shall we say, lobster—we cut out the soup and
> the flummeries—some curry, perhaps cold turkey, or a pigeon or two. Then
> something fruitish, and a plain ice, and some coffee. But perhaps at dinner one
> spreads oneself a little.... But I do two half-hours a day very strenuous work in
> the gym, walk at least seven miles round the deck, and cut out entirely the

eleven o'clock soup, tea, supper, wine and women—and there are swarms of these.

In Bombay he was welcomed onto a staff which suffered such periodic decimation because of the endemic illnesses and dangers of the country that there was on the one hand continual pressure of work and on the other opportunity for quick promotion. He soon found that the £540 per annum salary which had sounded so generous in Scotland was barely adequate in India, where living conditions for Europeans were unexpectedly expensive, and for a while he was engaged in a continual battle to persuade his employers to improve his pay. This once achieved, he settled down to learn his trade, soak up perceptions of the astonishing Indian milieu, and enjoy life as he might in the not unpleasant companionship of colleagues who were amusingly eccentric or youthfully high-spirited. At first he lived in a meagre flat above the office with the chief sub-editor, a man named Peacock but called 'Ostrich' in *The Man on My Back*; later he moved into a more palatial bachelor establishment shared with two other men and looked after by 'seven or eight servants who attended, promptly and efficiently, to our domestic needs'.[2]

One of his colleagues was a very serious young man named Leonard Marsland Gander. Appointed Chief Reporter of *The Times of India* when he was barely twenty-one, he had already been in Bombay for more than a year when Eric arrived, and it fell to him to meet the new recruit at Ballard Pier and introduce him to his responsibilities. He was impressed with Eric's mature appearance, 'a strongly built man of medium height, prematurely bald, with a finely domed forehead and rimless pince-nez glasses', and soon discovered that he was not a man who could be patronised just because he was in a new and unfamiliar situation. The younger Gander found the new Assistant Editor moderate, quiet and studious, toughened and tempered by his war experiences, but showing little of the verbal dexterity and flair which would later make him 'one of the most amusing, inventive and original of contemporary writers'. He was 'markedly self-confident and, if dour, exceptionally good-natured'.[3] Gander, who in 1926 became one of the casualties, having to go into hospital suffering from a liver abscess, was greatly touched by the solicitude with which Eric looked after him and wrote kindly and reassuringly to the invalid's anxious mother, far away in London.

A frequent visitor to the offices of *The Times of India* was L. A. Stronach, an executive connected with advertising and business aspects of the paper. He, too, recalled Eric as somewhat long-faced and dour in what he thought a typically Scottish way, but noted also a very positive and occasionally volatile side to his personality. Stronach told a story which in a way justifies Eric's belief in himself as a natural victim of farcical catastrophe. He joined

Eric and Peacock late one evening after they had been dining in Green's Hotel, 'celebrating some Scottish event', and were both 'well oiled'. Seated at a neighbouring table was a rather notorious lady who had acquired a title by marriage to a pleasant young Italian count, but who had been a barmaid in Rangoon before he got inextricably involved with her. Stronach urged Peacock to keep his voice down and speak with less impropriety because there was a countess at the next table. Peacock, seeing a woman somewhat the worse for wear, said incredulously: 'What, that a bloody countess?' The woman rose unsteadily to her feet, crossed to their table, gave Peacock a terrific smack across the face and said: 'That's right, this is a bloody countess.' At which Eric began to laugh so immoderately that she turned towards him and slapped him even harder, saying: 'You may as well have one for yourself.' Stronach managed to beat a strategic withdrawal before coming in for any attention; it was an incident he would never forget.[4]

Actually Eric worked much harder than he played and had less time than he had expected for social pleasures. This was partly because he was unprepared for and unenamoured of the kind of society he found there; he had never learned to ride, and had always been rather contemptuous of the kind of skills required for golf, tennis and bridge. As these four were the basic pastimes of the European community in Bombay, he considered himself rather unqualified for joining it. Besides, he felt guilty about the British attitude towards the Indians, and for some time tried to hold out, be his own man and make friends among the indigenous people. It did not work, and he felt he had failed to find the real India. He wrote: 'One had to acquire a protective insensibility, a sort of social blindness, that let one ignore the fearful evidence of a poverty beyond help.'[5] When he tried to talk with his servant, Laloo Bhika, the problem of his knowing no Hindi and Laloo's knowing little English soon became sufficient reason for making no further effort. 'Presently,' Eric recollected, 'I became afflicted with the *morbus Indicus* that reveals itself in shortness of temper and an irritated withdrawal into the society of one's own kind and colour.'[6] In the end he found himself oddly and eternally troubled by thoughts of India. Half a century later he admitted: 'Even today I read news of India with an emotion that no other part of the world—outside our own bewildered islands—can elicit.'[7]

It was not that he felt the British were wrong to be in India—quite the reverse. His ardour for Kipling and his admiration for the British Empire never dimmed.

If the balance-sheet could be struck, the account would show that we had given India more than we took from her. But having seen something of the way we behaved in India—of the insensate pretence of superiority that white people, of no intrinsic distinction, exhibited in their dealings with the Indians—I left

Bombay with a feeling of uneasiness, related to guilt, of which I had been innocent when I landed there.[8]

It may have been partly such reflections that at times made him deeply depressed and dissatisfied, as when he wrote to Douglas Walker in early 1926:

> To stay at home, when your home is in England or Scotland, is the best thing in the world. Foreign countries—and how utterly, essentially, almost devastatingly foreign such a country as India is you have no idea—are a delusion and a snare. I'm not saying this in a spirit of bitterness or regret, but merely stating a truth which I have found out, which probably I shall forget in a few months, when familiarity has robbed the newness out of it. I wouldn't have been satisfied staying at home, but the mistake I made was in thinking that I'd be satisfied here. But I'm not—not a bit.

His depression at the time admittedly may have been partly due to something of a shock his system had sustained after 'too much exercise, tennis in the morning, rowing at night, and so on, and my heart went queer'. Warning Douglas not to say anything about this to anyone, in case worrying news should reach his mother by some circuitous route, Eric assured him that he was now quite recovered; and indeed, although he was to suffer various illnesses over the years, there was no further trouble from his heart for almost half a century. Eric put it down to a combination of overwork, physical over-extension and reduced morale by reason of being too far from home in a not wholly congenial place:

> There's no intellectual life out here, not a scrap. Money-making's the guiding light, the moon of the universe, and tennis and whisky are the supporting constellations. Games in the early morning, money all day, and drink and women at night. Brothels do a big trade here. They're not awfully interesting. I've been in several, but even the very bad whisky they give you didn't prevent me from seeing everything quite dispassionately and declining to yield to the temptations of the flesh; after all, rabbits do that most readily. Not that conventional immorality offends me, but commercialised lust is degrading—I always think of a dog's expression during street-corner coitus. Some of the girls dance well. The most disgustingly amusing place is the Street of the Cages, where the women, black, brown and yellow, sit behind bars and shout at you as you pass, 'Come inside, Sahib, come inside!'
> Bombay, of course, isn't India. It's a seaport town, with an amazing conglomeration of races ... But it's a hopeless country, and its politics are the most exasperatingly fatuous tissue of cant, hypocrisy, double-dealing and damn stupidity that ever happened. Graft is everywhere.

Nevertheless, he was deeply impressed by the extraordinary variety, social complexity and picturesque multifariousness of the people, customs, religions, languages and places that surrounded him. More than a

decade later his first attempt at autobiography contained forty pages
devoted to lively and amusing recollections of the period. They are full of
colourful, poetic description and powerful evocation of locale and atmosphere that testify to the extent of the mark made upon him by his stay in
India. Of all the peoples he saw, the Pathans were the most unforgettable.
He described them to Douglas:

> Talking of beards, you ought to see the Pathans. They're beautiful, and the
> terror of all the fat Hindus and Parsis in the place. They're better than Captain
> Hook in *Peter Pan*; they're always murdering somebody.

In one of the earliest newspaper articles to carry the by-line E. R. R.
Linklater, the death of a vagrant Pathan led him to some reflections on
what he had learned about them from 'my friend Holly', a stereotyper in
the machine-room. Eric had come to like Holly particularly for his vocabulary 'built on the whimsical knowledge of the day, and magnificently
buttressed by a peculiar intimacy with Shakespeare'. According to Holly
the Pathans were 'Ugly beggars. They're not meant to court an amorous
looking glass. Not 'alf. Nor strut before a wanton ambling nymph—she
wouldn't 'alf amble, too, if she met one of them on a dark night.'⁹ It took
tact to handle them, and occasionally a sort of benign credulity to understand their motives. The only item in the estate of the unknown Pathan was
one cane stick: 'a *lathi*, a five-foot staff, iron-shod, that may in its time have
birled about the ears of upstanding opponents, or merely given comfort to
its owner when out walking'.¹⁰ One of Eric's earliest short stories,
'Pathans', derived from his observations of these curious and violently
disposed people.

But all sorts of people and impressions enliven the chapters on the year
and a half in Bombay: intelligent young men from the Indian universities,
elderly Rajputs, a Parsi high priest, a Yoga acolyte from Bikanir, the
oriental strangeness of Indian singing, the problems of child-marriage and
barter, and the intense humid heat of the summer and the eventual blessed
relief when the monsoons arrived. In a letter to Isobel Walker he described
a visit to an Indian lady's household:

> I had tea with [the Begum Saheba of Jaujira] one day not long ago, and she was
> stiff with gold; she had a necklace of gold coins about three yards long
> consisting of about three hundred things the size of half-sovereigns, and her
> finger-nails were painted red and her eyes touched most marvellously with
> kohl; they're about the size of hen's eggs, and her nose is a most beautiful
> hooked beak. She's great. The tea was awful—all sorts of little things with nasty
> vegetable smells and funny names, and sherbet. And there were some dreadful
> touts there—a Parsi degenerate who read ninety-nine poems like Oscar Wilde
> at school ... The Begum sang Indian songs, funny wailing rather nasal things;
> temple songs and love songs, they were, and rather nice ... There was a

professional musician there, too, a temple-singer with, they say, an enormous reputation in Bombay. He accompanied himself on a thing like a harmonium, one hand playing and the other pumping wind into it, and threw back his head and howled like a dog. Then he cleared his throat—very thoroughly—and howled some more. Then he grumbled a bit, low down, and beamed at us, and suddenly hit the roof with a terrific falsetto shriek; off into a minor wail again with his lips drawn back from his teeth, and then a bull-like roaring till the tears came to his eyes. 'Struth!

Whether it was in a kind of unconscious revenge for what he had suffered, or in an involuntary demonstration of that buffoon side of his character that he used to complain of, one cannot know, but before he left the Begum's house Eric tripped over the temple-singer's 'monkey organ' and rendered it unusable for some time.

There were also all around him the appalling poverty, the casual deaths and the leprous beggars of the Bombay street, *lacrimae rerum* indeed, and he was both moved and horrified by what he saw.

Occasionally real life was invaded by the sort of grotesque events that sometimes disturb and deepen the tenor of his comic novels, such as when a dog belonging to a friend went mad. Lacking a gun, and rejecting the only weapons handy in the form of a niblick or a brassie from a bag of golf clubs, Eric managed to capture the animal by throwing his dressing-gown over it and wrapping it securely. There then seemed to be nothing to do but drown it horribly in the bath. There was later evidence that their hideous task had been necessary when an examination at a nearby Pasteur institute showed the dog to have been rabid. Consequently they had 'on fourteen successive days to submit to inoculation with anti-rabies serum and the tiresome humour of our friends, who barked when they saw us'.[11]

There was much that was agreeable, too, as he described to Isobel:

I had a rattling good Easter weekend at a small pseudo hill-station called Mahableshwar. It is situated on a thing known as a ghat, which is an irrational species of hill ... All the roads are at an angle of 45° and abound in hairpin bends. A meagre parapet stands between you and a valley 3000 feet below—except where, every hundred yards or so, it has been broken down by a car going over.

Mahableshwar was beautiful, cool in the mornings and cool in the evenings, and we drank gallons of beer and played golf on a comic course cut out of the jungle. At three or four holes you played from a plateau, seeing the green far beneath. At one you lash out over a patch of jungle and an old Muslim cemetery.

There were friendships with girls, two of whom he wrote about in *Fanfare for a Tin Hat*; he described them in a letter to Douglas's mother at Christmas:

Last night I dined with an American millionaire ... The night before that two very nifty young things dined with us in our flat. One is a Canadian and teaches gym and can protrude her diaphragm three inches. We don't get much money but we do see life. She is very, very beautiful, but she sings out of tune so much that even I can hear it. Life is like that. How I love her. The other has red hair and a lisp; I am going surfing with her tomorrow.

More details of the high life were conveyed to Douglas after Christmas and further junketings:

I have done some sailing and a lot of bathing parties and such, with occasional moonlight picnics (O silver beaches and phallic palms, O whispering sea and fringe of silent jungle that night transmutes to a black and silver Arcady!) and surfing. Surfing on the seven-mile face of the harbour, the fifteen-mile fore-head of the bay, with a boatload of men and maidens, slim-built, round of breast and leg and comely of haunch; laughing bravely (if unintelligently) and looking each like Atalanta on her surf-board riding superbly the leaping sea as the fast motor-boat tows her away from the dying West. Which reminds me that the fairest brace of all come to dinner tonight ...

[Later] It was a good dinner last night. We danced latterly. I did a most gorgeous Apache dance with Lucille, and an even better Tangoish one with Jo—very contorted-like and writhy. Charming girls, you would love them even as I do ... If only Lucille were as intelligent as your Peggy I should fall most hideously in love with her. 'Intelligent' is an arid kind of qualification, but I can't think of the proper word. A kind of mental charm which affects you like a subtler physical charm is what I'm trying to get at. There's probably a French word for it.

He still felt uncomfortable at times and consequently joked about his relationship with women, as in an incident he mentioned to Isobel:

At this moment probably you are wandering through a leafy lane in Hertford-shire talking to Charles about Scarlet Fever and Diphtheria and so on. [Isobel's fiancé was a doctor.] Ah, love's young dream! *Et in Arcadia vixi*, but I always spoil it. The other night, for example, a cold wind swept through a taxi speeding homewards ... and all because in a moment of tender confidence I confessed and said that deep in my heart I preferred beer to women really. Oh, truth never pays, for her eyes grew hard and I could scarcely borrow enough from her to pay the driver.

What he meant was that he didn't care for women *en masse*, for he often flirted enthusiastically with individual women. As often as not it was married women that he most liked, as in another situation he described to Isobel:

The man I live with has been grievous sick but is now almost better, which is such a shame, for he sits and stares sourly at his Beautiful Wife and Me as we dance languorously and not ungracefully along the veranda after dinner;

previously he would shut his bedroom door and we would be Alone. Now, alas! we are in a crowd. I shall take her to the pictures tonight, instead. He is not a bad fellow, but such a fool, and they have a thoroughly unpleasant child of about two or so, with deficient kidneys, and it comes into my room of a morning when I have only a towel on, because 'Uncle is such a funny man!' But the Missus is Marvellous.

No doubt there was a kind of safety in such a relationship, as long as the husband tolerated it; there was no danger of a marriage trap suddenly closing. The following May, writing to Isobel from Vienna, he referred to a new friendship of a similar kind:

What fun we travellers have. The ship from Constantinople to Venice took twelve days, ambling slowly round the Greek coast. There was a most beautiful girl aboard, with great dark eyes; Lord, how I loved her! And after she had gone to bed I used to sit up on deck and drink beer with her husband. An ideal arrangement.

All this of course was in fun; he even claimed that although he had been invited by this girl to stay with her and her husband, he couldn't remember her name, Cyril, was it, or Cecil? But there is much truth in fun. His letter to Isobel in April 1926 contained another passage which, while showing both his homesickness at the time and something of his attitude to Isobel, also demonstrates his remarkable skill and facility in developing the comic possibilities of an idea:

I never felt really homesick till you told me you were cast as a child with lots of legs and so forth, and then I remembered your brief ragged appearance in *Rosemount Nights* and shook the startled office with my sobs. Editors, sub-editors, sepoys, machine-men, stereotypers, peons, clerks and readers and the bearded havildar from the outer gate came rushing in, and a fire-engine stopped outside. 'What is it?' they said anxiously. 'Time,' I answered. 'Time, the strong thief who steals from us our April and our May. Shall we not weep if in the arid heat of my August I remember the cool delights and new green ways of my dead April? God', I said, 'has set my foot in the Gateway of India, which is indeed full of rubies and precious stones, and do not the match-girls at my right hand wear anklets of purest gold, and are not the swords of the jugglers on my left hand hilted with emerald and chrysophrase, very precious and carved about the seventh incarnation of Vishnu? And is not Buddha sitting benign upon his lotus, and the thousand and three gods of Hind upon elephants, and the Prophet of God, very terrible and green, upon the lap of the fairest of ten thousand houris? And yet I', I said, sadly and a little bitterly, 'think nothing of these, remembering a small and apparently somewhat dirty child with holes in her stockings.' Whereat they all went away, very quietly, first taking all pins, paperclips and typewriters lest I should do myself an injury.

In the round of newsworthy happenings, one other event of late 1926 caught Eric's imagination particularly. In a letter to Douglas, he described how he went as accredited press correspondent to observe one of the earliest of combined naval and military exercises when a thousand troops were put ashore in a selected area south of Bombay:

> The week has passed in a storm of blue seas and green jungle and Indian infantry and flat-footed matelots and night-landings and sweat and emergency rations ...
>
> It was a good show, that started very merrily by one getting semi-bottled in the ward-room of the *Emerald*, one of our new cruisers, and proceeded by way of being sun-smitten on high and blazing hot plateaus, and lost in impenetrable jungle-covered mullahs, to embarkation at night from a crowded beach—troops and sailors and mules and coolie transport—and copious beer aboard again.

Reading Bernard Fergusson's account of the development of Combined Operations in *The Watery Maze* many years later, and noting a brief reference to the Kasid exercise, Eric felt a definite pleasure in having been present at what was, in a way, a historic occasion. He wrote:

> I had the good luck to share in an intelligently conducted but almost unique anticipation of a mode of warfare that became obligatory fourteen or fifteen years later.[12]

Though he liked writing, however, and was increasingly sure that there was a living to be made from his pen somehow, he did not care for the life of a journalist very much. There were too many restrictions, too little freedom of action. Regular office hours were a bore. The people he worked with were pleasant enough but frequently petty-minded or concerned only with their own authority. The topics on which he had to write were not what he wanted to write about. He admired and worked well with Francis Low when he took over the reins during the illness of the Editor, and had no qualms about establishing his point of view when people who were in his opinion less competent sought to obstruct him. He told Douglas:

> There was an acting editor (he has just gone up to Delhi today and we shan't see him again) who made himself tiresome, till I went in and thumped his desk and told him that I had stood enough senseless interference from him and didn't propose to stand any more; a squalid brawl, but he apologised eventually and we lived fairly happily ever after.

And he amused himself by making his leaders considerably more radical in tone than the conservative owners of the newspaper expected as editorial policy. But his attitude to his job as reflected in several of his letters to Douglas was not devoted:

> There's a pile of work waiting for me which I have no mind to tackle, and news to look for to hang my pitiful shreds of leaders onto, like dirty washing strung across the public street, which is a foul habit ... By God, I'm fed up! It's utterly

ridiculous that Man who has legs to walk, eyes to see, and hands to feel, should only use his bottom for sitting on and his eyes to read foul news from foreign cities, most of which is lies anyway. I don't know how people stand it—I am in a state of impotent rebellion.

He was already itching to be on the move, although he had been working at *The Times of India* for only four or five months, and the desire to travel was greater by far than the impulsion to become a first-rate journalist. There were moods when he found the job more interesting and exciting, especially when greater responsibilities descended upon him. He naturally made a joke of it when he outlined his position to Isobel in July 1926:

[This is] a city of heat and steam and exotic stinks. Now it is raining like as though the sump of heaven had fallen out and it washing day, and indeed the sky looks very like half-washed blankets. But it is much cooler, and that is good, for everyone is dead or dying, except me and my pal Low who comes from Finzean and hiccups after drinking as a man should.

At the moment of writing I am Acting Editor of the Greatest Paper in Asia, the Editor Sahib being sick of a quinsy or so, and the next fellow having gout, or some such thing . . . so I hold the fort, though with only one hand, having been inoculated against something or other but yesterday.

A week later he was writing again, rather more forcefully:

Two hours ago I was stabbed deeply for the second time with a horrid great lance dipt in the inspissated venom of typhoid . . . The Editor Sahib totters frailly to his grave, the Assistant Editor [Senior] is brought to bed of an undiagnosable ailment, the Chief Sub is down with malaria . . . and I, like a croaking raven, flap agueishly about their fevered bones pondering mine own decease but jesting obscenely the while on life. Which is indeed an obscene jest out here.

As his own physical condition improved, so did his pleasure in the new degree of freedom which seemed his for the taking; by September he was quite enjoying himself, as he told Isobel:

All our heid yins have died of awful diseases and gone home to recuperate, and for the last two months nearly I have been writing leaders on whatever I pleased and saying whatever I pleased about it all. It has been good fun, though it has meant pretty hard work; I average about a column and a half a day and say the most dreadful things and make lewd jokes about respectable people. Our Big Noise in London is getting all hot and bothered. He will be worse by next mail as I have written a column of Vulgar Abuse of that Mr Evan Williams (the mine-owners' Secretary) whom he likes very much . . .

I am also Bombay Correspondent of the *Daily Mail*, now, which is a Jest, for they want Blood. I sent 'em a message the other day quoting leader *Times of India* gravely warning Government serious situation Afghanistan watch Russia military circles profoundly alarmed encroachment Soviet influence Gawd help us all stop Linklater, hoping to get us embroiled in hellish fight with the Bolshies. The leader from which I quoted was my own: as was the alarm in military circles. But they didn't know that, bless them. I do hope they used it. I'll get a guinea if they did.

More of the time, however, he was frustrated, working in an inappropriate element. Despite the evidence that in the end he would always do what he had to as well as he could, according to his own account the work suffered because it did not sufficiently matter, either to him or to anyone else:

Well, I have dawdled through the day with a minimum of work. I prepared a column of 'Points from Letters', giving facetious titles to serious epistles and cutting large chunks out so as to make them read even more ridiculously than they did at first—for your Indian is an inveterate babbler whether with pen or tongue. I wrote a paragraph about something or other, and I have just finished a middle on the situation in China; I shall send it to you, I think, as China is one of the few subjects I still get some amusement out of. I am, on occasion, Our Chinese Correspondent.[13]

If he had had an opportunity, he would have gone to China without hesitation. As it was, a pressure to go and see the Far East for himself continued to motivate him for almost a decade, until at last the chance he had been waiting for presented itself and was not resisted. Meanwhile, the writing required of him professionally in India proved to be something he could do quite facilely and without real involvement, and he set himself from time to time to write something more demanding, more true to his personal concept of where his verbal skills ought to lead. His poems continued to take first place in his efforts, but he began to try his hand at short stories, too. As well as 'Pathans', which he sold in England after his return home, several other short stories grew out of his experiences: 'Country-born' and 'The Prison of Cooch Parwanee' are the most obvious.

The ramifications of the Indian experience were long, and India was to recur several times in Eric's fiction. If he began writing fiction in the form of short stories while in India, however, there was not much of it. Perhaps encouraged by memories of his success as librettist for the Gala Week musical plays, Eric was tending to think of himself as a potential dramatist, and indeed remained unshaken in that view of himself for the next thirty years, despite considerable setbacks and only minor successes. In his leisure time in Bombay the project to which he devoted most energy was a play. He explained to Douglas:

I'm working on a slight verse-play thing that I want Isobel to illustrate, but this is the most damnable place in the world for trying to do a spot of writing in, and it moves slowly. If I polish it off at all satisfactorily, I want you to help with trying to market it.

By September the playscript was indeed finished and Douglas dutifully sent it off to various publishers and to Nigel Playfair at the Lyric Theatre, Hammersmith. It was called *Harlequin's Hour, or The Devil's an Old Man*, and had as a central character Polly Peachum from *The Beggar's Opera*. Even with Isobel's comical line drawings to illustrate it, the play raised no enthusiasm among publishers or producers, and when he returned to Scotland Eric put it in a drawer and forgot about it—for a few years, anyway.

Before the end of 1926 Eric knew that he would never be able to keep going for the full three years of his contract with *The Times of India*. He was very restless. In his debates with himself about the wisdom or otherwise of leaving before his time was up the strongest argument for going was 'a feeling that if I was ever to find satisfaction in work, it must be work more certainly creative than leader-writing'.[14] But it would be hard to leave; he had made friends, his income was reasonably comfortable, and the voice of common sense urged him to stay where he was. The catalyst proved to be a plan hatched by a friend, called 'Radcliffe' in *The Man on My Back*, but in reality Walter Lucas. Marsland Gander described him as 'black-haired Walter Lucas, who spoke with the slightest impediment and had a reputation for mordant wit ... He was not a journalist, but had some job with the BB & CI [Bombay, Baroda and Central India] Railway. He was an old Wellingtonian and a fine cricketer, making many centuries for the Bombay Gymkhana.'[15]

According to Eric, Lucas was chronically footloose and, having been promised a few months' leave, had conceived a plan for 'going home through Afghanistan, the Uzbek and Turkestan republics, the northern provinces of Persia, the port of Krasnovodsk, the Caspian Sea, the bleating pastures of Astrakhan, the river Volga, and so to Moscow.'[16] When offered the opportunity—or when challenged—to join Lucas on this adventurous undertaking, Eric could not resist.

Fortunately a job turned up, possibly with Lucas's help, which provided funds for the journey. Eric recalled:

> I made some money by writing a series of pamphlets for one of the Indian railway companies: brochures that described in brilliant phrasing, and with a wealth of picturesque detail, the charms of Delhi, Lucknow, and other places that I had never seen.[17]

He never, in fact, saw the pamphlets, as he left Bombay before they were printed and did not even correct the proofs. He was paid 'the handsome sum of 500 rupees', he told an inquirer many years later, but claimed that someone at the railway company had adulterated his texts:

> *Jaipur* is mainly, if not entirely, by me. The beginning, with its quotation from Kipling, is typical of me-in-1927 ... There's a reference to Pierre Loti, and I

used to read him. Towards the end there have been, I think, some additions, but I accept *Jaipur . . . Mount Abu* is the real puzzle. I think quite a lot of it is by me. There's a good deal of show-off—the use of Indian words, for instance, typical of a young man pretending that he knows more than he does. But see p. 12: 'A nice restful way . . . potter about . . . worn to a *frazel* (?) . . . as we glimpse it we thank our stars' and so on—that's Indian writing, babu English, beyond a doubt.[18]

Even with the money from this enterprise the young men's joint finances were not sufficient for them to go quite as far round as they had intended, and they settled instead for what still proved to be a 'hazardous and hilarious' route by sea to the Persian Gulf, and thence by land and sea to Constantinople. In April 1927 they sailed from Bombay, and anyone who wants the full flavour of the journey should read Chapters IX to XII of *The Man on My Back*, where Eric described it with a wealth of humour, poetic description and romantic enthusiasm. At Karachi they were joined on board their ship by a friend of Lucas, called 'Mrs Rodney' in Eric's account, and her splendidly English characteristics enlivened the journey:

Wherever we went, she demanded the rigorous maintenance of impossible amenities, but accepted without dismay discomfort of many sorts; while her shooting-stick seemed always capable of growing into a flagstaff from which at any moment the Union Jack might be broken with bugles blowing underneath.[19]

They disembarked at Bushire and, going to catch the train to Baghdad, were much impressed by a notice in the station which read: CHANGE AT HILLA FOR BABYLON AND KISH. Baghdad itself, with its bazaars and magic carpets and its intriguing mixture of the ages-old with the brash-new, did not disappoint. From there they travelled overland in a hired car, driven by a world-wandering Englishman to whom Eric gave the name 'Poins' for his fancied resemblance in behaviour to an admired character from *Henry IV*. A couple of near disasters on the edges of precipices in the Paitak Pass kept their senses suitably excited, and for a while there was a threat of long delay and perhaps even of jail sentences after their car unavoidably knocked over an old man who was not accustomed to such modern vehicles.

In Tehran they had to wait several days trying to secure Russian visas for the next stage of their journey; then they drove back to Kasvin and turned northwards, over the Elburz mountains and down to the Caspian Sea. Eric noted the astonishing contrast in the terrain:

For behind us the houses, few enough, were flat-roofed, and the country was bare and brown: a country clothed in lion-skins and camel-hide. But ahead of us the houses—not many indeed—had sloping high-pitched roofs, a fantastic difference to behold so suddenly, and the country was luxuriant and green: a country clothed in great forests, and laced with the white falling of turbulent rivers.[20]

From the port of Pahlevi they sailed, aboard a Russian ship called the *Udarob*, northwards over the Caspian towards the port of Baku on the western coast of the 'Sturgeon Sea'. They found themselves unable to accept the cabin accommodation which they had booked when they discovered it was to be shared with 'two Circassian girls, one plump and painted, the other like a dishevelled and dissipated Madonna', and spent the mild night not uncomfortably on deck instead. Baku proved to be a dingy grey town where the winds seemed colder in a distinctly Russian sort of way. Unable at first to get seats on the train they were forced to see more of the unexciting night-life of the town, and Eric received something of a frisson from observing a Russian policeman fondly cleaning and re-loading his revolver. After a while they caught a train to Tiflis, which was at least on the way to Batum; it started three hours late, and rolled slowly over the plain, stopping frequently at small villages and once to remove a dead buffalo from amongst its wheels. They would have been stuck at Tiflis, too, had not a beautiful dramatic performance of longing for home and present impecuniousness been improvised by Lucas. Moved by his pleas, a council of workers decided that room could, after all, be found for the trio on the next train for Batum, and a couple of hours later they were rumbling into Georgia. Eric's delight in every moment of the journey is manifest in the pictures he later sketched in his autobiography, such as his memory of the train labouring through the last hours of darkness and coming at length 'to a bare plain, white in the morning and stretching to the distant snowy wall of the Caucasus'; or the unexpected and idyllic view they got on the descent to the Black Sea:

> Another night in the train took us into a great open valley, into vineyards and rich meadows rolling down to a river from huge wooded heights, while in the distance snowy peaks scarred with their dazzling spears the blue expanse of a cloudless sky. This was Georgia, a gracious country nobly inhabited, for at the little stations enormous broadbuilt men, like giants in their hairy boorkas and astrakhan caps, strode magnificently or stood and laughed in open mirth with handsome, rosy-faced girls.[21]

They rather liked Batum, but were forced to stay much longer than they had intended, for getting passages on a ship for Constantinople proved to be quite a problem. It was ten days, during which they had many comic encounters and witnessed the local May Day celebrations, before the regular passenger ship arrived and the strangest part of their homeward journey was over. The rest of the journey was mild and ordinary in comparison. Eric stayed in Vienna until he had no money left, and finally arrived back in England just as summer was beginning to make itself felt.

He did not know what he was going to do, but was sure now that full-time journalism was not for him.

He began to cast about for some kind of job teaching in a university, for now he had the glimmerings of another possibility of travel in mind. He lived meanwhile on the hundred pounds he had managed to save in India, and earned small cheques from *Blackwood's Magazine* and the *Daily Mail* for articles about his experiences in Russia and Persia. It was not that he scorned the journalist's trade, or was contemptuous of the money it could bring him; throughout his life he returned at intervals to various kinds of involvement with magazines and newspapers, partly for the opportunity or platform they afforded him, and partly because there were, and continued to be, periods when he particularly needed some extra money. In the summer of 1927, home again after his first taste of the great world, he still thought of himself as wanting primarily to be a poet. True, he would need some sort of job, perhaps somewhere in the academic world if journalism were not the answer, by which to support himself. Anything might do, provided it gave him further opportunities to travel, to gather further experience out of which one day, with more confidence, he might write novels. But in his heart there still lay the thought—despite some of the evidence to the contrary which his intelligence could not help perceiving—that it was in poetry that he would one day make his name.

7 Poet Manqué

It was by no means uncharacteristic that Eric, when seeking a more creative outlet for his growing verbal talent in India, should have devoted his spare time not to prose but to the verse-play that he persuaded Douglas Walker to try to market for him. Aspects of the theme and style, and the idea that his intended medium was poetry, had been occupying him fairly obsessively since his return to Aberdeen University in 1919, and were to continue to engage him deeply for many years. He had a dream of being a poet, and in his free time in India the dream drove him to work in various verse forms, some rather more successfully than others. The parallel notion, that he might write for the theatre, was also powerful; he had, after all, been successful in the musical plays written for his friends for the Gala Week festivities, and was not unacquainted with the excitement of the theatrical experience. His discovery of *The Beggar's Opera*, his delight in the themes of magic, disguise and transformation, and the theatrical traditions of *commedia dell'arte* and pantomime which flourished on such matters, all helped to bring together in his mind the twin ambitions in theatre and poetry. Though he then and later shrugged off the experiment as mere pottering about, he worked on it seriously. When it failed to raise interest in 1927, he put it by, only to resurrect it later and try again, reshaping it from new experiences, until it was eventually both staged and published as *The Devil's in the News* in 1934. When it then failed after all that time and effort, Eric finally let it go, but theatrical ambitions continued to plague him at intervals for at least another quarter of a century, and his attempts to write poetry continued to the end of his life.

He had begun by writing verse at school, and enjoyed the facility in rhyming and the metrical talent which he discovered in himself. His verses were often mere doggerel, scribbled rapidly in fun, but there was also in him, more often than not consciously suppressed, a deeply romantic, serious turn of mind which suggested real poetic possibilities. His appreciation of the craftsmanship of language led him to extensive study, imitation and parody of the English verse forms of tradition, and essentially to see them as impeccable models on which any genuine new poetry would have to be based.

Soon after his return from the Army to the Medical School at Aberdeen he began submitting poems to *Alma Mater*, the undergraduates' magazine. The Editor that year was James Sutherland, who had been a year behind

Eric at the Grammar School and hadn't known him well. But 'Suddy' had missed the war, gone to the university, and was now a year ahead. As Editor he accepted from Eric, as his first contribution to *Alma Mater*, the verses mentioned earlier, called 'Don Juan—Lamb'.

This, Eric's first printed poem—indeed, his first published work—demonstrates several of his interests and characteristics. It is a clever and effective imitation of the Byronic style and stanza form, evincing verbal dexterity and capturing the tone with felicity. The 'Lamb' of the title referred to the university term for a first-year medical student and the poem, being about the adventures of a young man with the girls, has some biographical interest. The hero, called 'Don Juan' to protect his 'real' name, is

> a Lamb,
> An intellectual nonentity . . .
> Of course, he fought in France for four odd years—
> But Profs have such bad memories, poor dears!
>
> His joy in life, I fear, is not to pore
> Long hours in lamplit solitude monastic
> O'er bulky tomes of anatomical lore—
> His attitude to work's iconoclastic.
> His own pet muse sways on some polished floor
> In movements syncopatedly euplastic;
> In homely words, confusion nowise chancing,
> I mean to say he's very fond of dancing.

The humorous tone of the stanza, with its mock-apology for the hero's preference for dancing rather than his medical studies, and the lexical jokes—'movements syncopatedly euplastic' for 'dancing' with the ingenious and unexpected rhymes such words lead to—are persuasively like those of the original; so is Don Juan's response when he fails to persuade the lovely Phyllis to accompany him to a great festive occasion—a Cinder—'a spoonatorium, in point of fact'. For a while his life is blighted, but then:

> Don Juan mused. He knew that suicide
>   Though orthodox, was just a shade old-fashioned.
> He knew 'twas quite plebeian to deride
>   And sneer at love with bitterness impassioned;
> And after all, what use is foolish pride?
>   For girls, thank God! as yet are quite unrationed.
> So Juan, wise, too, in his generation,
> Asked Gwladys, who accepted with elation.[1]

During the next five years, Eric contributed about thirty further poems to *Alma Mater*, ranging in style over a wide variety of traditional forms and showing the influence, sometimes to the point of being more pastiche than poem, of several writers that Eric admired; James Sutherland thought his verse

> owed something to Kipling, Masefield, Belloc and (I add reluctantly) Robert W. Service. Some of it was bacchanalian, some in the sea-shanty vein ... His Norse-Orkney strain comes out in 'Spilt Wine' ... 'Rubáiyát of Omar K. Lamb' is a skit on the FitzGerald poem. 'Carousal' is a pastiche of Meredith's 'Love in the Valley', which I imagined he had just discovered ... All this merely adds up to saying that at the age of circa 24 he was, like other young poets, still experimenting, and very much influenced by what he had been reading last. I have a distinct recollection of rejecting one of his early poems, and marvel now at my editorial courage.[2]

Sutherland also had poetic ambitions, and for some years he and Eric talked constantly of producing a book of poems together, perhaps thinking of themselves as a new Wordsworth and Coleridge. Nothing ever came of it, as each in the end went his own way, but they met for walking holidays in the vacations and talked endlessly about poetry. Eric recalled the frustration he felt even while enjoying a reputation as a poet at college:

> And yet I was dissatisfied. I could string verses, but I wanted to be a poet. I had a light hand for triviality, but broke my knees whenever I essayed a nobler leap. To express and find rhymes for a whimsy became easy enough, but never could I set forth in clear, compulsive, inevitable and comely lines the emotions that made their transitory abode in me.
>
> As often as I was invaded by fragments of the eternal doubt, despair and bliss of youth, I tortured myself in futile efforts to give them articulate expression. I barked my knuckles and bruised my heart against the fine hard themes of rebellion, friendship, the slope of a hill drawn clear against the empty sky, the metastasis of drinking, and total love. It was intolerable to be in love yet powerless to immortalise its cause.[3]

Dissatisfied or not, he certainly versified with great facility, and evidently much enjoyed doing so. He wrote nonsense verses for Isobel in the manner of Edward Lear, such as 'The Christmas Mumps: a Fairy Story for Bad Children', when she had suffered an attack of that ailment; or the Harry Grahamish 'Mr Benn':

> That careless man, Elijah Benn,
> Got badly into trouble when
> His wife in 1923
> Presented him with twins, and he
> Gave one of them to Mr Parkin,
> A bachelor friend of his, remarkin':
> 'It's quite all right; don't hesitate,
> For this one's just a duplicate.'[4]

Many of his published verses were equally playful, as, in a way, his public persona demanded, and as the irrepressible humour of his outlook rendered inevitable. But there was, too, in more poems than one might at first expect, evidence of the deeper vein of seriousness which secretly drove Eric on to try to be a real poet. When tackling potentially more emotional subjects, such as 'friendship', to draw a topic from the list he provided, he deliberately kept mawkishness at bay by verbal fun. 'De Amicitia', inspired by his great affection and admiration for Douglas Walker, begins, after its pretentious title, with a fine mock-heroic flourish followed immediately by a bathetic descent into a confession of inadequacy for the purpose:

> Life's keenest joys are in contrasted shades:
>   Night's sombre purple gains full half its glamour
> In sick remembrance as the dawn-rose fades;
>   The shrilly sweetness of the blackbirds' clamour
> Is sweet but in the quiet of tree-girt glades;
>   The anvil's bass is tuned to tenor hammer,
>   And so on. These sentiments, though somewhat trite,
>   To sequent darkness lend a little light.

The poem then grandly refers to other themes the author has at various times attempted ('faint love-lyrics', 'an ale-song', 'satires, crost and crusty') before coming to its point: 'I have a friend to notice'. The rest of the poem offers a sketch of Douglas in four snapshots of remembered shared moments. The glimpses that follow, of Douglas at a dance, or camping—

>   see him bend
> Pyjama-clad, to tend a steaming stew,
>   And probe with questing fork its bubbling deeps,
>   And curse it as the scalding gravy leaps—[5]

or walking in the rugged Highlands, or talking in a bar about 'the purport of God's great World-Making Jest', are vivid, amusing and tender, suggesting, behind the distance-preserving rhetoric, real feeling.

In few of his poems did he give much away about himself, but occasion-ally personal comments were allowed a place, and the range of topics and modes of treatment are in themselves indicative. In a poem addressed 'To My Beloved Master, Eric Linklater', Sutherland, who had gone on to Oxford to read for his doctorate, called his friend 'Thou great colossus striding King's and Marischal' and summed up his stature as:

> Thou Triton in the minnowy pool of King's,
>   Son to Silenus, kin to Rabelais,
>   Thou rib of Belloc, limb of Chesterton[6]

Eric's reply, a week later, cursed James for disturbing him from his attempts to work by reminding him of the orgies of drinking and talking till the small hours which they had so much enjoyed, and to which Eric could so easily be seduced again:

> And—plague upon it!—here am I among
> Threescore of books, most noble books, that fill
> Their shelves with portly grace, and I have sung
> My love to each, and wooed all with a will,
> Have walked with work as Beaumont walked with Fletcher,
> Have played, in fact, the literary lecher.
>
> The Devil take thee, James! Or stay—instead
> The Devil take my sixty mistresses,
> Buckram and paste and all. Their charm is fled
> As quick as nimbler buckram rogues than these
> Once fled before an old fat man . . . I read
> One day, and thanked the writer on my knees,
> 'Small have continual plodders ever won
> Save small authority . . .' I envy none
>
> This poor reward.[7]

In such moments the reader can see many elements in the complex of attitudes that made Eric such a notable and memorable individual: the love of companionship and talk, and of the drink that helps promote them; the literary basis of so much of his knowledge; the ambition behind the careless, life-enjoying façade of the inveterate toper and idler. His interest in 'the old fat man' was more than passing. The character of Falstaff appealed enormously to him. He saw something of Falstaff's amoral rumbustiousness in himself, and loved the Elizabethan richness and wholeness of the concept. The verses published in *Alma Mater* show or suggest several of the varied interests that coloured his life, and in many cases adumbrate themes that would later be returned to and developed much more fully, mostly in fiction.

In May 1923 he published a poem called 'Rosemount Nights: In Memoriam', a light-hearted confessional about his relationships with women met socially at the Rosemount Hall. He praises the character of Macheath, from the pages of *The Beggar's Opera*:

> a certain strutting knave,
> A cloak and pistol amorous rascal; he
> Who loving still his Polly, yet could save
> For Lucy half a sigh, and easily
> A score of kisses—

For Eric the essence of Macheath ('all Honour to him') was:

> He lived with Love with only love to pay;
> Then, leaving Love, for quittance dropped a tear,
> And sought at other inns the same good cheer.

Such, claimed Eric, was his own problem, for

> Fortune, with distressing carelessness,
>> Has given me two most discerning eyes
> Appreciating Beauty no whit less
>> Than did Macheath's, but—here the trouble lies—
> Without the silver tongue that might caress
>> (As did Macheath's) with flattery and sighs
> The stubborn head of Beauty.

Consequently:

> So Stella, when she sings, enraptures me
>> And Daphne has my heart at her sweet will—
> Diana, looking oh! so guilelessly
>> Can twist me round her little finger still—[8]

and so on, with Madeline, Mary, Jane and Peggy. While the poem may be no more than a *jeu d'esprit* springing from the idea of being like Macheath, it is happy, persuasive and amusingly ironical, and throws more doubt on the misogynistic pose he adopted. No wonder if about that time an article about him in *Alma Mater* contained the following paragraph:

> In the Ladies' Room he is tenderly thought of as the Misogynist who changed his mind. Indeed he has become a Lion in the Ball-Room, though his individualistic style with its inevitable 'Sorry, Partner!' tends to create the illusion of a mixed double at King's.[9]

Eric seems to have discovered *The Beggar's Opera* at about the same time as Brecht did, but his use of Gay's world was more eclectic and referential in the play which eventually found shape as *The Devil's in the News* than in the more full and central place it had in *The Threepenny Opera*.

The poem 'Spilt Wine', later reprinted in an anthology of Scottish student verse,[10] was one of a group of more straightforwardly narrative poems which Eric wrote in these years. In high heroic verse it told of Sweyn, the Viking, and his adventures in fighting, carousing and love-making. It ends:

> On Gairsay shore the ruins of Sweyn's hall
> Still stand; and starlings chatter where of old
> The Norsemen drank. But still, beneath the pall
> Of sea-loud nights, the crofters say a cold
> Thin light appears, like ivory and wan gold,
> Wherein, wind-moulded in her saffron gown,
> A maiden walks, keening all unconsoled
> Her stolen joy.
>> But Sweyn, hounding Death down,
> Sweyn rotted long ago to flowers by Dublin town.[11]

It is a poem of some power, in which Eric's sense of his own Viking heritage and his joy in Norse literature are plain.

Some of the poems about university life similarly foreshadow parts of his novel *White-Maa's Saga*. An early poem describes the goodly company to be found at the Frigate and the whole matter of drinking and companionship. In another poem, 'New Lamps for Old', the rhythm and romantic flavour of which seems to owe something to Flecker, Eric tells another story of the ruination of his attempts to work. Side-tracked by the astonishing beauty of a girl, he

> lost the love of printed page and sought the love of Life
> From a maiden, fair and wise with the sooth of summer skies,
> Her eyes the fountainhead of Peace, her lips sweet source of strife.

The same problems beset Peter Flett, and Peter's response, which is to take the girl off in a boat and sail away into the mysterious but promising night, is anticipated in the poem:

> Then I left their chaptered wisdom, for Wisdom of the Night,
> And saw the moon transmute to gold the elfin green of sea,
> And across her shining track stood the shadow, ebon-black,
> Of a schooner with her sails all set and drawing easily.

In the poem, it's all for the best:

> So I've lost (and laughed to lose it) what learned fools esteem,
> Instead I've seen the Night-time and the wonder of the Sea,
> Found the sooth of Vivien and the fellowship of men—
> I ask the gods of all the World, Who would not trade with me? [12]

As the body of poems that he had written grew, Eric sought various ways of achieving further publication. In May of his last year at Aberdeen the newly established Porpoise Press in Edinburgh brought out a pleasantly printed pamphlet entitled *Poobie* containing just four of his poems, with decorations by Isobel Walker; it attracted no attention, but it was pleasing to have a third booklet published. In it he reprinted from *Alma Mater* 'Miss Poobie' and 'Sophonisba', two comic poems more or less satirical in tone and recognisably in the manner of Hilaire Belloc; 'Pan', a strangely impressive exercise in the pastoral idiom; and 'Death from Croup', a comic imitation of modernistic irregular rhymed verse. As it is one of Eric's very few ventures in any but traditional and established forms, this last piece is worth looking at:

> Ten large jam-jars in a hen-run.
> Ten!
> And a hen
> On the edge of each agen,

Unconscious of depravity
Lays an egg in each concavity,
Double-yolks
For a joke,
With an indiarubber shell,
And they bounced about like hell
In the obfuscated gloom of ten jam-jars.
The first egg burst
Unrehearsed;
It was nursed
By a woman recommended in *The Farm Gazette*,
Who was cursed, poor body,
With a thirst for toddy—
Equal parts of strong and wet—
So the egg was neglected,
And the other hens pecked it,
And it grew up ricketty,
The other hennish nuclei, infinitely dismayed by this gloomy
    example of extra-mural activities, one and all declined to
    emerge from their gutta-percha circumvallations, and
    perished miserably within their primitive integuments. So that
    the eggs, deprived, as it were, of their *primum mobile*, no longer
    bounce about like hell
In the obfuscated gloom of ten jam-jars.[13]

As an exercise in nonsense this is witty and works with some of the peculiar logic of the genre. There is something of an attack on the notion of irregular verse with the wildly exaggerated prosaic length and syntactical structure of the penultimate line, but the double and triple rhymes, though irregular, are not a characteristic of free verse. The extremely non-poetic lexis—'obfuscated gloom', 'gutta-percha circumvallations' and 'primitive integuments'—seems also to reflect disapprovingly on aspects of the new poetry. The poem as a whole encapsulates and rejects certain modern developments in poetry; but curiously it rather anticipates the surrealistic verse of people such as David Gascoyne and Philip O'Connor in the mid-thirties.

Eric never attempted a more direct pastiche of the kind of poetry T. S. Eliot had introduced with Prufrock and *The Waste Land*, though he did not like it. He recalled:

In the south, about this time, a new sort of poetry was stirring, a serious and disintegrated kind that reflected, but failed to synthesise, the spirit of the time: the broken thread, the frosty perception of wasted soil, the grim colloquialism, the bright skin of a scar new-healed but aching. The fashion, however, did not reach Aberdeen. We were remote from the contagion of intellect, and remained unserious, old-fashioned and conventional.[14]

There was among Eric's tutors a lecturer, himself a poet, who was very excited by Eliot. Claud Colleer Abbott, however, was clearly unable to convey his enthusiasm even to the brightest member of his class, who, radical though he tried to show himself, was already conservative to his backbone. From the standpoint of 1970 Eric recalled how Abbott

> used to read the brand-new verses of T. S. Eliot. At first hearing they meant little to me and less to Adolphus Jack. Some years after Eliot published *The Sacred Wood*, Jack asked me, 'Have you read it?'—'Yes,' I replied.—'It's very nicely *said*, of course, but is there anything in it we didn't know already?'— 'Very little,' I discreetly answered.—'Nothing at all!' he declared.[15]

To Eric, Eliot's poems were undisciplined and ill-mannered because lacking in clarity. He allowed some reflections on the subject of contemporary poetry to figure in two or three of his earlier novels, where the protagonists were themselves poets.

In *Poet's Pub*, for instance, Saturday Keith, who has walked away from the drudgery of ordinary work in order to devote himself to poetry, has received blistering reviews of his first book of verse. He has been slated for writing 'without a theory ... It is no longer enough to sing, no longer permissible to soar with beautiful and ineffectual wings into a luminous void ...' Keith, whose poems, to judge from what we are allowed to see of them in the book, are not unlike those of his creator, wonders what he should do:

> Through the window he saw a red and white cow and the corner of a haystack. Were those significant? he thought. Here, perhaps, if he could express it with personal emotion, was a microcosm that reflected the macrocosm; individual, raw poetry of the twentieth century; with his ego as the nucleus here was the necessary yolk of experience. Could he state it, a-rhythmically, tonelessly, flatly but significantly, so that it would be recognised as poetry?[16]

These ironic comments are matched by a discussion between Magnus Merriman, eponymous would-be poet of a later novel, and Hugh Skene, a famous modern poet (based upon Hugh MacDiarmid). The dialogue is introduced by authorial reflections on the state of language and literature in the twenties:

> Among the disruptive phenomena that followed the Great War, not the least remarkable was the disruption, or threatened disruption, of language. In most of the so-called civilised countries of the world a group of writers had appeared who stated their belief that existing literary forms were no longer of significance or value, and that to express themselves fully serious writers must rediscover some prime vitality in the roots of language. This belief had shown itself in various degrees. Many authors contented themselves with writing ungrammatically, some acquiring the art and others possessing it by nature ... The poets of the postwar world were fairly united in their belief that poetry, to be poetical,

must be unrhythmical, unrhymed and unintelligible; and by these standards, their output was of a high order. Their leader was the American, Eliot, who, by incorporating in his verse, with frolic wilfulness, tags from half the literatures of the world, had become popular in more than strictly intellectual circles for the likeness of his work to a superior parlour game called 'Spot the allusion'.[17]

There follows an introduction to Hugh Skene, the chief exponent in Scotland of literal revolution, whose work is chiefly notable for its attempts to revive the ancient Scottish forms of speech. But he has found the Scots of Dunbar and Henryson insufficient to contain both his emotion and his meaning, 'and he began to draw occasional buckets from the fountains of other tongues'; Eric provides an example of his work:

> The fleggaring fleichours morgeown on our manheid,
> And jaiput fenyeours wap our bandaged eyes:
> *Progress*! they skirl with sempiternë gluderie—
> The sowkand myten papingyes!
> But Lenin's corp ligs i' the Kremlin still,
> Though Wallace's was quartered like the mune
> By the brankand English for their coclinkis' gain—
> 'Kennst du das Land wo die Zitronen blühn?'

The author of this poem is unequivocal when Magnus declares himself a traditionalist:

> Skene interrupted him.
> As if it were a pistol he aimed his slender and rather dirty forefinger at Magnus and said, with cold and deliberate ferocity, 'You're feeding on corpse-meat. In all its traditional forms English literature is dead, and to depend on the past for inspiration is a necrophagous perversion ...'[18]

Eric Linklater devoted his life to giving the lie to the notion here propounded by one of his characters. His energy as a would-be poet was certainly applied to maintaining the traditional forms. In this he was encouraged by Sir John Squire, the Editor of the *London Mercury*, who accepted several of Eric's poems, and later selected some of them for inclusion in his retrospective anthologies.

Squire liked Eric's exercises in the pastoral. One such that he accepted was 'The Faithless Shepherd', in which Corin, wearying of playing the role of patient lover according to the pastoral rules, turns his attentions to a timely jug of wine, and is inspired by his consequently changed vision to take a more active approach to his Phoebe:

> And now no more on pilgrim knees
> He pleads a docile love and meek,
> But boldly clips her in his arms
> And quiets her modest faint alarms
> With kiss on eager kiss that sips
> The rose-red nectar of her lips.[19]

It is a charming piece, typically for Eric's celebrating love in a context of wine and laughter; it is in a sense a serious poem, in that Eric genuinely felt that the values that it embodied and the kind of poetry it represented were more important and desirable than the new emblems of disintegration and gloom; yet it is odd to find it being written and published at the end of the first quarter of the twentieth century. It might almost have been written at any time in the preceding four centuries; and if it had been signed by Drayton or Prior, no one would have been very surprised.

'Silenus', similarly accepted by Squire, is a more contemporary-sounding, realistic treatment of the pastoral ethos. The figure of the ancient Silenus had a fascination for Eric, who used the god's name as a pseudonym throughout his university career as a poet. Forerunner of all the fat Falstaff figures of later literature including Eric's Flanders in *Juan in China*, Silenus was gross and ugly, but possessed a special kind of wisdom from his deep and endless drinking of wine, and was reputed to be a fabulous storyteller. Hedonist par excellence, ultimate exemplar of the comic drunkard, surrounded ever by acolytes devoted to exploitation of all the bodily appetites, especially drink and sex, Silenus was quite an image for the young Linklater to adopt as his model and alter ego, and to emulate, at least in theory. In an earlier poem Eric had celebrated the wine-bibbing, laughter-making, sensual life of Silenus and his bacchanals in the eternal woods:

> Golden in the light, Silenus and his satyrs
> Strong brown limbs a-sprawling, sun-scarred on the grass,
> Heat their throats with laughter, cool them from the wineskins,
> Laughter speeding hotfoot where the winebags pass.

Silenus pursues a beautiful passing nymph, but is not unduly frustrated when she easily slips 'his sere embraces'; he contents himself with the companionship of his cronies:

> Loud his satyrs hail him: brave his hiccup answers:
> 'Still am I Silenus, still the wine is red!'[20]

Now Eric reworked the material, abandoning the swinging trochaic hexameter in favour of a modified iambic tetrameter, rhyming now in couplets, now alternately, now in more widespread patterns. This, coupled with a somewhat less romantic vocabulary (Silenus awakes 'crapulous', for instance) gave the poem a more dramatic and earthy feeling. The god's discontent is now more central, and is caused by the failure of his arts of seduction with a mortal girl who passes through the scene:

> The girl still mocked him, heartlessly.
> She only saw a fat old man
> Whose most ungodlike belly shook
> With windy sighs.

Silenus tries to console himself with the thought that she is mortal:

> And beauty dies; her breasts would sink
> To heavy shapelessness, her brow
> Grow wrinkled and her laughter shrill.

He returns to the solace of wine:

> and all the roaring crew
> Bring wine and laughter, hailing him
> With shouts and tumbled wreaths of flowers
> And drink and drown the day's last hours.

But there is a poignant ending, for Silenus, for all his powers and consolations, has lost something more wonderful, the loving attention of a real woman:

> But when the moon rode clear and high
> She saw, not very far from there,
> A girl who slept. She was as fair
> As silver or white ivory
> And in her sleep she mocked mortality.[21]

When, several years later, Jonathan Cape admitted that Eric was showing some signs of promise as a novelist, Eric persuaded him to produce a proper volume of his poems. *A Dragon Laughed* appeared in October 1930, only six months before *Juan in America* was to make the name of Eric Linklater very famous indeed. His volume of verses, however, went practically unnoticed, though it did, in a slow but steady sort of way, sell well enough to justify a reprint in 1943. The opening section comprised 'The Faithless Shepherd' and 'Silenus' together with several other poems using the romantic, mythical, fairy-tale or medieval sort of setting which Eric so much enjoyed, including the title poem. They were mostly narrative verses, in which his penchant for storytelling was allowed disciplined rein; a group of poems based on Genesis suggests some Yeatsian influence, with a whispered chorus in 'A Province for Adam' and a sonnet called 'The Adversary' which resembles and which has some of the potency of 'Leda and the Swan'. Of such poems it seems one can only say, either you like them or you don't. A reviewer in *The Times Literary Supplement* wrote that 'the poems reveal a remarkable vitality and versatility'. Technically skilled, humorous in tone and witty in execution, they appeal greatly to those readers who prefer to maintain some contact with the root traditions of English literature: pastoral romance, medieval chivalry, classical and biblical heart-narratives, and associated conventions (sometimes neatly reversed or stood upon their heads); but to those who see only the immediate social and political ills of the twentieth century as the proper study of the poet, to be explored through linguistic experiment and novelty, the poems will seem irrelevant.

Eric did not write exclusively in this vein, though. Increasingly through the later 1920s and afterwards he turned to the immediate scenes of his travels and to emotional experiences in his life for inspiration, and the second and third sections of *A Dragon Laughed* contain a number of poems of this kind. There are personal poems about the loves left behind on his way to India, exploring different farewell moods. Several poems capture neatly and vividly exotic places such as 'The Persian Gulf', 'Iraq Railway' or 'Baghdad'. 'Behind the Sea' is a very personal poem with a moving sense of the urgency of the need to create which Eric was experiencing. Eric, fled to India, as the poem will have it, finds himself assailed by a demon:

> 'Make, make!' it clamoured,
> 'Make!' all through my blood. It hammered
> On my dumb mind, 'Make, make!' It stammered,
> This puny red life, to my sullen brain,
> 'Make, make! Though all creation's vain,
> Creation is the end of all. Oh, make, make, make!'
> And I
> Took sticks of such and such, gaunt spars of my
> Most primal thought, naked imagining,
> And stuck them in the mud for scaffolding;
> Tied planks of rash invention all across
> And built, slow brick by brick, mortared with dross
> Of other men's old theory, and reared
> Ungainly palaces and towers that seared
> The sensitive soft sky. And then
> I pulled them down—easy enough, being so built—
> And scarcely thinking why, started again . . .
> Still, making was the thing,
> Not what was made . . .[22]

This is a nearly naked Linklater that one rarely encounters, and although the formal nature of the poem, with its insistence especially on rhyme, renders it old-fashioned, it has power to move, convince and involve the reader. The comedian, the teller of tales of dragons and satyrs in some bygone day, is revealed as a man of passion, flesh and blood; and one might wish he had written more of such things.

Later, in *A Dragon Laughed*, Eric returned to more familiar ground with the jolly (but also sensuous and provocative) nautical tale of 'Rumbelow', and the comic but frightening 'The Naughty Broomstick', but there is still variety. There is a sardonic poem called 'Wedding Morning'; a simple, tragic haunting song of the betrayal of love in 'The Narrow Bed'; and a brief, cynical love-lyric, 'Song for an Able Bastard'.

The final section of *A Dragon Laughed* is devoted to the long dramatic poem 'The Queen of Scots', for which he was awarded the Calder Verse Prize at Aberdeen University in 1925. It is an impressive poem, following Mary's thoughts through the last night of her life with tremendous sympathy and considerable skill. Using memories, dreams and cameos in an irregular rhymed verse form, Eric recalls the events of Mary's life as she contemplates her approaching execution in alternating moods of calm acceptance and panic fear. At one moment, remembering the murder of Darnley, she thinks:

> I hated him . . .
> But I am guiltless, God, guiltless of blood!
> I did not kill him, God, I did not know
> That they would kill him. I did not know
> What things they meant,
> And I am innocent!
> O God, it was so long ago!

At another period of the night she is reconciled to her fate:

> Death is the only lover who
> Will let you sleep. His coffin-terms
> Are easy, and easily his hands undo
> The weariness, the wedding-dress
> To soothe you into sleepiness
> Where slumber will not cease.
> Death is the only lover who
> Will let you die in peace.

But as this insidious slide into sleep and death begins, the ghost of Bothwell startles her back into awareness, and she flees in nightmare:

> O frantic foolish feet
> And leaden limbs stuck in the mire of sleep!
> O threatening mouths and hands that hungrily
> Reach out for her! O topless hill!
> Teeth bare and streaming eyes
> And heart of agonies
> She fled them still—
> And the top of the hill was a cliff,
> And she fell,
> Fell, fell like a stone
> And alone,
> Over the edge of her dream.[23]

The poem is a fine achievement in itself, but is also interesting as the first evidence of Eric's lifelong absorption in the life of Mary Stewart, and in history more generally.

For all that has been said to suggest that there is much in Eric's poetry that is enjoyable and worthy of rediscovery, he himself was not convinced. In 1940 he was dismissive—or pretended to be—of the desire which had animated him earlier to speak the emotions and thoughts inside him in immortal poetry. He wrote now as a man who had attained to wisdom and put away childish things where no profit lay:

> Self-knowledge was still obscured by self-indulgence—I mean the indulgence of writing verse. With passion in my heart and seven topics in my head, I was going to be a poet. Not yet a novelist, but something with more fire in his heart than prose. Tomorrow or the next day would bring the annealing flame to fuse desire and notion and the beating wings of lovely but invisible words.[24]

He now saw that it was never going to happen as he had hoped. His old-fashioned idea that poetry was about beauty had taken a beating in the light of what was happening in the new poetry, and anyway it was clear—unpleasant though the realisation may have been—that he was never going to write poetry to rival Keats. His reference to this recognition had little of his usual rumbustiousness of tone:

> Failure, recurrent and ever more loudly reiterated, to write anything better than competent versicles, persuaded me at last that I had over-estimated my ability. I could hardly believe the evidence, but there it lay, in wooden lines and the shipwreck of a putty-fashioned epic. Bitter was the knowledge, and when I tried to tramp it down by writing yet another poem, the pain was like walking with a broken leg in a foreign land. My function, I then admitted, was not poetising but only mythopoetising. I might spin a yarn, but I could weave no garment of light, nor rug against the inner cold.[25]

The publication of *A Dragon Laughed* in 1930, however, did give him much pleasure, and it was not wholly a sense of failure which prevented him thereafter from continuing to write poetry with any degree of seriousness. Life became too busy; there were too many deadlines of other kinds; new and varied opportunities presented themselves in astonishing profusion, and poetry had to take a lowlier place. He made no further attempt to join the ranks of the established poets, but his love of poetry and his private practice in the arts of versification continued. He may have derived some vicarious satisfaction from making some of his heroes poets: Saturday Keith, Magnus Merriman, Stephen Sorley (*Ripeness is All*), Albyn (*A Spell for Old Bones*) and Hector MacRae (*The Merry Muse*).

He did publish a further clutch of poems, in the *Scots Review* after the Second World War,[26] and his letters to certain friends were full of snatches of verse. To John Moore, the creator of Brensham Village and Elmbury, he wrote limericks; to Rupert Hart-Davis he sent a sestina and various ballades; to Marjorie, his wife, he wrote a long and intimate poem of love; and to Bernard Fergusson, who also dabbled in light verse and was frequently published in *Punch*, he sent comic stanzas about the goings-on of the soldiery.

One final publication came when, in 1963, he translated Dunbar's satire, 'The Two Married Women and the Widow', and four other poems into modern English. They appeared in *New Saltire*, together with an interesting essay on the background of the original poems and on the problems of bringing such work into modern English with a contemporary setting. His ingenious and highly readable version of poems which otherwise few would be able to read have many felicities; the unrhymed alliterative metre makes for a subtle individual sound, which is successfully retained, and the updated references are comically effective. Though he decided that the scatological strain of the original could be removed without loss, the bawdiness which was essential to the 'savage and double-edged' satire was unobjectionable, he said, because it was robust, boisterous and free from sniggering tones. The result was a poem, long and entertaining, on a theme dear to Eric's heart as it was to Dunbar's: the nature of women and the problems and rewards of the relations between the sexes. Something of the flavour of it may be gathered from a brief extract from the words of the widow who, after the young women have complained about their husbands, explains how she manages herself since her widowhood:

> On Sunday at church, a slim figure in sable attire,
> Feeling like a female wolf in a silly sheep's clothing,
> I kneel down devoutly, hide my head in my hands,
> And open my prayer-book, and read the responses;
> And when next knelt in prayer I peep through my fingers
> To see which of my neighbours are worthy of notice,
> And who looks most likely, if I take him home to luncheon,
> To comfort my loneliness on a cold afternoon:
> As the new moon, in the pallor and perplexity of youth,
> Shows just for a moment serene through serried clouds,
> So between black gloves there's a glimpse, now and then,
> Of my poor pale face taking tally of young men.[27]

This service rendered to Dunbar when Eric was in his sixties shows his interest in poetry to have been still as vital as ever it was, as well as his repaying Dunbar for the germ of a short story, 'Kind Kitty', with which Eric had had a great success thirty years before. When he so humbly confessed his failure as a poet in 1940 he, perhaps provocatively, underestimated his accomplishment. At least part of the reason why, after 1930, he turned to other things was simply that the other things were there, demanding his attention. Very rarely did Eric Linklater say no to a challenge.

8   Commonwealth Fellow

The most urgent challenge which faced Eric on his arrival home from India was to find some sort of job. He had saved about £100 and thought of going off into the wilderness and living off his capital for a year or so while devoting all his energies to developing himself as a poet. More realistically, he was beginning to see himself as a writer of prose: his accounts of his travels in the East had been accepted by *Blackwood's Magazine* and would be published in October 1927, and the storyteller in him was beginning to look for wider canvas than poetry could afford. Besides, his abandonment of India had partly been inspired by

> a scrap of news I discovered in our weekly bundle of English newspapers. Some rich and generous American had founded the Commonwealth Fund, and twenty Commonwealth Fellowships were offered to graduates of British universities who were willing not only to study but to travel in the United States for a period of two years.[1]

His greed for travel now motivated him to look for some kind of academic post from which he could respectably apply for something so grandly titled as a Fellowship. A post at Birmingham University seemed a possibility and he sent in an application for it, but then he fell in with some old cronies and ended up going to walk with one of them for a few days in the Cairngorms. The brief break was blissfully rewarding:

> The smell of the pines at Inverey; the water, solid and dark as peat, then a golden curve, then whiteness filling with thunder the Linn of Quoich; curtain closing upon curtain of mist on Ben Macdhui; the two of us sitting bare to the waist in a hot blue stillness, legs dangling over the precipice, on the rock-and-mossy top of Braeriach.[2]

But when he arrived back in Aberdeen it was to discover that he had missed the date for an interview for the Birmingham job, and his chance had gone. Many years later Eric was told by Walter Allen, the novelist and critic, that he might have been his tutor but for this accident, and thereafter Eric regarded Allen as being 'in some sense *in statu pupillari* to him'.[3] By a fortunate coincidence, a post fell unexpectedly vacant at Aberdeen, and his old professor, Adolphus Jack, invited him to take it on.

The greater part of his duties entailed 'the marking of innumerable essays and countless examination papers written by members of the Graduation Class, who numbered two hundred and fifteen that year'.[4] In later years Eric used to say that he was really employed as 'a sort of superior bottle-washer'[5] in the English Department and, although the £300 a year salary was not to be sneezed at, he was not tempted to try to be anything other than a temporary pedagogue.

The students for the most part greatly enjoyed his effervescent and unconventional approach to teaching, and many thought him highly effective. A first-year student of the time, George Morrison, recalled that Eric was 'the most brilliant and amusing lecturer I ever heard'.[6] Another, Charles Rioch, wrote:

> When lecturing to Honours English classes he used to introduce rather ribald comments into his address to the students, and would preface them by the request to 'lay down your pencils and stop taking notes'. He had been discussing the poet Southey and had mentioned his scheme to set up a Utopian community in South America. Eric's interpolation at this point was the interesting fact that Buenos Aires had the highest percentage of prostitutes of any capital city in the world. At this juncture several young ladies who had been embarrassed by some of Eric's previous comments decided to demonstrate their disapproval and proceeded to leave the lecture room by way of the door at the back. Eric waited patiently until they were approaching the door and then said loudly, 'There's no need to hurry, ladies, the next ship doesn't sail till Tuesday.'[7]

Any arena into which Eric entered would instantly become livelier than before—unless he was in one of his rare but occasional wet-blanket moods. Some students didn't know what to make of him; equally, he could hardly credit the extent of their ignorance about and lack of delight in literature. He found that

> About ten per cent were quite illiterate, and perhaps fifty per cent insensible to the art of writing; incredulous that among the functions of literature is the exact, alarming or ennobled focusing of life; incapable of drawing from their minds more than a stillborn opinion about anything at all.[8]

However, there were some who were very competent and a few very good indeed, and he did his best to interest the whole class. Sometimes he was rewarded with such a roar of approval for some stimulating observation or comical remark that from the next classroom Professor Terry '—gown billowing, face incarnadined—' would come storming in to demand silence.

But the endless marking was more of a burden than he needed, as he confessed to Douglas Walker:

> I have just finished marking the essays of the Grad. Class: about 230 of them. Half of them tripe and paper frills. Two-thirds are under 50%. There will be weeping and wailing, I suppose. Will they remember that the Lord loveth those whom he chastiseth?

The prettiest girl in the bunch (there are about 140 in the bunch) gets 44, which is 10 more than she deserves. Will she realise that and glance shyly at me the next time I pass her, as she did t'other day?
Will she hell!
Heigh-ho!
Duty is a stern path. Would I were 19 again. I would write her the wickedest little notes. Now all I can say—in the margin—is: 'You can do better than this.' She could, too.—Perhaps not on paper, though.
Heigh-ho! Most loving is feigning, but work is pure folly.

A duty which he executed entirely in his own style was to lecture on English poetry once a week to a class of young women in the nearby Teachers' Training College. He began by announcing that

> of the several purposes of poetry the first was entertainment—on a different level from basketball and the moving pictures, but entertainment none the less—and as it appeared anomalous to make entertainment utilitarian or compulsory, I did not propose to call a roll, and I could not promise to teach them anything.[9]

These remarks, he said, were well received, and he wished in retrospect that he had thought of serving tea and small pastries, for his lectures were the merest gossip, and the tinkle of spoon upon china would have been a proper accompaniment. Gossip was a theme to which he would often return, always with approval, when talking of literature and its criticism. The girls, he thought, were probably done little good by his lectures, but at least he avoided fortifying their school-got notions that literature was a grim matter of essays and rote memory. In the end he told them, a week or two before their examinations, what questions he was going to ask; and they all conducted themselves with great credit.

Between the lecturing and marking for which he was paid by the university in his pedagogic year, Eric was busy with his pen, exploring the skills he felt he had been vouchsafed as a writer. He was disappointed when, after a show of interest from Grant Richards and Martin Secker in his Polly Peachum play, it was once again found wanting and sent back to its author. He wrote to Douglas:

> That trollop Polly—poor wench, she has lain in many a bosom, and is none the better for it, nor richer, neither ... I'm sorry, for your sake as well as my own, that nobody saw fit to make an honest woman of her.

Still, 'the inkpot', he reported, was 'teeming with unborn texts' and, undismayed by the rejection of his verse-play, he turned in a new direction. It had long been in his mind that he might write a novel. Looking back in 1940 he described how the notion had gradually crept up on him while he had been in India:

That particular sort of egotism which is a preliminary condition of authorship was beginning to look for a field of its own. I was already on the fringe of the dreadful obsession which, for the last dozen years or so, has sat upon my shoulders, governed my life, falsified my hopes, ruined my digestion, and given me more pain and pleasure than anything else on earth; the need of making from homiletic imagination a series of visible and articulated things called novels: that was the boot that kicked me, yard by yard, from *being*'s blissful state.[10]

Now, with his thoughts bent professionally and academically on literature, the opportunity was ripe, and suddenly he was provoked into a real attempt by the discovery that Mabel Cowie, the girlfriend from college days for whom he had sold his medical books—'and she the despair of her teachers, living on her looks, who had never read anything but a dance programme'[11]—had written a novel. 'Her publishers, moreover, praised it highly and promised a large success . . .' The novel, *Lady, What of Life?*, was published under the pseudonym of Lesley Storm, a name which was later to be much better known in the theatre. It galvanised Eric into action:

Well, really, I said to myself, if that flighty, flipperty, lovely but light-minded four-fifths of a fathom of whimsical femineity can write a novel, I'm damned sure I can too! So I sat down on the instant, and after composing five or six versions of my first chapter, I found one that seemed a little less clumsy than the others, and the rest of my story fell into line with relatively little trouble. But without provocation I might have continued searching for the formula, the magic incantation till this very day; and never finding it, for there is none.[12]

Once started on his novel he worked hard on it through the winter, and by March 1928 *White-Maa's Saga* was almost finished. The material, inevitably, was the stuff of his own life during its most interesting, exciting and fulfilling phase up to that time, the years at the university. Consciously in mind were some observations by Flaubert on imagery and sentence rhythms, and, more important than any other precept, a remembered dictum of the admired Professor Jack: 'A writer should remember his manners, and for a writer the best of good manners is clarity. Clarity is also the debt he owes his readers.'[13] All his life Eric preached the virtue of seeking clarity of expression, and practised it to the best of his ability. He was quite aware of a tendency to over-richness in his early writing, the result of his enthusiastic response to the books he had taken as his mistresses, and he confessed:

I have sometimes been led astray in the matter of illumination by a liking for a fine phrase. I drank deeply of the Elizabethan writers, and the fumes of their prodigious eloquence hung in my brain for years.[14]

But the fumes were so agreeable he had not the heart to blow them away.

He sent off the manuscript of the novel on what proved to be a lengthy round of visits to publishers and turned his mind back to the matter of the

Commonwealth Fund. A whisper from someone at the Harkness Foundation confirmed that his application for a Fellowship had passed the first stage of the selection process. Soon afterwards he was invited to meet the Committee of Award in London, and was faced with a new difficulty:

> I had to propose a particular subject for study and research ... I was not academically inclined, and I doubted the capacity of my scholarship to withstand cross-examination. I concocted, after serious thought, the recipe for a thesis—it had something to do with Ben Jonson and the growth of middle-class comedy—[15]

The selection committee was ponderously impressive, including

> Sir Walter Buchanan-Ridell, Chairman of the University Grants Committee; Sir James Irvine, the wily and formidable Principal of St Andrews; Lord Chelmsford, sometime Viceroy of India; the Vice-Chancellor of the University of Liverpool; and a clutch of dons of scarcely less distinction.[16]

Eric was aware that the interview was not going very well after the small-talk and friendly gestures designed to put the candidate at ease. He was unable to affirm that Jacobean comedy might be better studied in the United States than in Britain; the questioner persisted:

> 'Perhaps you know of certain material, not available to you here, but accessible in some American university?'
> The candidate's reply was inaudible.
> Another of the Committee asked: 'Is there anyone in particular under whom you would like to study?'
> 'Not really. I think I could do the work without much assistance.'
> 'You know the recent investigations of Professor So-and-so and Mr Such-and-such? Wouldn't their research be helpful to you?'
> The candidate was apologetic. He had never heard of the gentlemen in question.
> The sound of a pencil tapping on the table was unhappily reminiscent of coffin-nailing, and the candidate began to perspire a little. Then in a smooth soft voice a white-haired inquisitor said: 'Tell me, Mr Linklater, about your primary motive in applying for a Fellowship. Which is more important, the desire to do this particular piece of work, or the desire to see America?'[17]

Eric never forgot the moment's hesitation before he answered this question, upon which so much depended. He was tempted to give the obvious answer, but had been taught that honesty was the best policy. Hoarsely he spoke the truth: 'The desire to see America.' It was the answer the white-haired gentleman wanted, and Eric, having plumped for honesty, was rewarded with 'two years of liberty in the vast morning of America'[18]—or, as he later put it, 'a couple of years' handsomely subsidised freedom in the United States'.[19]

It was the making of him. From the moment he arrived in New York in October 1928 he was overwhelmed by the strangeness, the greatness, the familiarity and the comicality of the United States. In *The Man on My Back* he devoted nearly forty pages to the adventure; in *Fanfare for a Tin Hat* a further thirty-five, but in the fictional form of the novel, *Juan in America*, he spread his recollections and reconstructions lavishly across four hundred pages. India had moved and intrigued him, but the United States bowled him over; the place and the people provided a cornucopia of impressions on which his creative faculties were richly nourished.

He did not begin immediately to write about the United States, but allowed his mind to soak up the life that surrounded him for several months before looking for a way to record or exploit it. Having rejected the obvious possibilities of Harvard and Yale, he had decided, after poring over maps of the various States, that he would like to go to Cornell. He thought it would be more natively American than the great old institutions that had based themselves on English models, and he liked the look of the lake-divided countryside. After a short period in New York he travelled down to Ithaca, where the university was situated, and found that his choice had been sound. The university

> was built about a large and handsome campus, and surrounding it lay a vast, generous landscape that, as autumn advanced, exposed the bold red hues of ripening maple and sumach, and between its low hills were the long and narrow waters of Lake Cayuga.[20]

To compound his good fortune he found his supervisor, Professor Quincy Adams, agreeable to an unexpected proposal from his new student:

> I made a very good arrangement with my professor who was a sensible man who didn't want to work too hard. When I said to him, 'Sir, if you'll permit me to say so, I don't require any supervision', he said, 'That suits me down to the ground', so I was left entirely on my own resources.[21]

Quickly he settled down to a pleasant but quiet routine. During the day he read in what seemed to him luxurious freedom in the university library, which turned out to be excellent. Notes on the life and times of Ben Jonson and his contemporaries accumulated steadily until, by the end of his Fellowship, he had a suitcase full. He found the air, he said, conducive to work, and besides, it took him a long time to find friends and social engagements; extroverted and confident though he may have seemed on his home ground, there was in him a rooted shyness which prevented him from too eager a visitation of himself upon his hosts. In the 'solitude created by his bashful diffidence in an alien world'[22] he spent his evenings writing a second novel, spurred on by the good news, received soon after arriving in Cornell, that Jonathan Cape had agreed to take *White-Maa's Saga* and would be bringing it out in the spring of the following year. A letter to Douglas Walker described some of his first impressions of America:

> Let Doug put up his feet and Peggy sit on hers (as she is wont) and remark together: 'Say, lissun; I got a letter here from that ol' bum, Link.' Then, looking appropriately surprised, recite in unison, 'For the Lawd's sake!'
> After which, 'Yeah, a letter from Noo Yawk. Pipe the stamp!'
> Peggy: 'Can you read his writing?'
> Doug: 'Sure. That's a pushover for me.'
> Peggy: 'Well, ankle into the buttery, bring out the rye and giggle-water, and let's make whoopee!'
> I can't think of anything more. But perhaps this is enough to provide a Transatlantic atmosphere and suggest a suitable background of Woolworth Buildings, chocolate nut sundaes, and the Eighteenth Amendment ...
> A quiet place this, except for the university, and that is inclined to be noisy. The young American runs naturally to noise. Two of them make a riot ...
> I work on my own—no lectures or nonsense of that kind: I told them, ingenuous-like, that I didn't care for lectures, and I didn't see anything on their programmes (from Aesthetics to Domestic Economy via Bee-Keeping to Hotel Management) that I wanted to listen to. So they said all right ...
> *News Items:*
> Rev. J. Frank Norris, Baptist Minister, recently acquitted on a charge of murder, is widely advertised as God's Gunman.
> Herbert Hoover has never danced with a negress. (This is a political announcement of supreme importance.)

Eric was both surprised and delighted with the wondrous details of the American scene, the vivid eccentricities of their version of spoken English, the dirtiness and naïvety of the Presidential election campaign then in progress, the idiocies of Prohibition, the vigour, charm and oddity of the people he met. Yet what he wrote about in the evenings was far from noticing this novelty; there is an American or two in *Poet's Pub*, but its setting and theme are English to the core, with Scottish undertones. He felt he was doing journeyman work, and looked upon it as a deliberate exercise in craftsmanship, plotting skills, dialogue presentation and so on.

> It was pure fiction, the sheer product of invention, and I wrote it as an exercise from which I hoped to learn something of the strategy and tactics necessary, as I believed, for the construction of a novel.[23]

There is nonetheless something touching about the way in which, set free in a modern foreign world which he had always longed to visit, he spent the many hours necessary for the writing of a novel alone in a room in New York State thinking about England and English ways, English pubs and English poems and stock English characters. There were times, as in

India, when he was lonely and *déraciné*, and writing about that familiar world on the home side of the Atlantic may have been a kind of indulgence, or therapy. Just after the first Christmas in the United States he wrote to Douglas Walker's mother:

> I would like to come in and have supper with you and talk to you until I had driven Mr Walker to bed, and made you look at the clock (very discreetly, of course) three or four times ... In spirit I am sitting in the left-hand corner of the luxurious ottoman in your drawing-room, filling my pipe out of Mr Walker's pouch and quietly purloining Alec's matches (he having gone for the beer, which presently I shall go for, too), and generally preparing to give you my views upon the World (of which I know nothing), the Flesh (I am practically a vegetarian) and the Devil.

But though his mood was nostalgic he soon went on to high-spirited consideration of the alien world he was in:

> This is a quaint little place, just now buried under 18 feet of snow. The wolves are howling in the surrounding hills and every day a child or two goes missing from the village. But we have enough provisions to last the winter without them. Of course there are a lot of deaths from wood-alcohol now that our ordinary supplies of embalming fluid are cut off. But the weak must go to the wall— I almost said 'to the well', but we haven't come to that yet.

By the end of February 1929, however, things were looking up on every point. The months of concentrated work in his comfortless lodging-house in Cornell had brought his new novel to the point where he was sure that it would 'proceed to a live birth' and he had made an important decision. In a couple of months *White-Maa's Saga* would be published; *Poet's Pub* was more than half completed; Eric Linklater the novelist was about to emerge from the chrysalis.

> I had arrived in America with the intention of writing about the development of urban realistic comedy in the late Elizabethan and early Jacobean theatre: the sort of study that might recommend me for employment in a provincial or a Canadian university. But I had already turned my back on a journalistic career in India, and now I dismissed all thought of a scholarly future. I determined to be a novelist; and the material for my third novel lay broadly spread before me in forty-eight united states.[24]

He did not abandon his Jonson studies, though admittedly they were no longer his primary interest, but continued conscientiously to read related materials and add to his notes in a way that was partly inspired by a sense of duty to the Foundation that had given him his Fellowship and partly by an instinct never to waste anything: all would be grist to the writer's mill. So it proved, for before two more years had passed the study had been turned into a very respectable book. At the end of February he was still, as he told

Douglas, suffering from 'a certain sense of ennui' caused by his being buried in Jonsoniana:

> In a word, Work. Which I have never liked. So far I have only nibbled round the edges, being otherwise busy on a second novel. But now the novel is nearly done and off to look for a cardboard house among the publishers, and I go to bed with the demireps of Jacobean times and walk abroad with Ben Jonson. It's not bad fun, but if you think I came to America for a holiday, you're mistaken.

But within a few days of writing this letter, with his hard-won perception of himself and his future career as a novelist the secret that gave him renewed energy and confidence, Eric began much more deliberately to cultivate and enjoy the United States. He accepted more invitations from new friends and travelled about, went to parties and great public occasions, drank in the scene and its people, and began to have a wonderful time. The holiday that really began the 'see America' part of his bargain with the mentors of the Commonwealth Fund was initiated by an invitation from two student acquaintances at Cornell. One had acquired a car and proposed to drive down to Washington to attend the inauguration of President Hoover. It was altogether an eye-opening experience.

They drove the 360 miles of still-wintry roads between Ithaca and the capital in one afternoon and evening in early March, arriving very late at their destination but not too late to join a party which, in the event, continued for several days. By a miscalculation they missed the Inaugural Ball itself but enjoyed such a round of festive occasions that it hardly seemed to matter. Eric was particularly delighted with a trio of young women he met at a party,

> one of whom had lost her fiancé in a motor accident; another her religion in the Smithsonian Institution; and the third a husband in the divorce court. They were quite frank about their misfortunes, which in the aggregate produced an extraordinary effect of carelessness.[25]

Of the inaugural ceremonies themselves one moment more than any other stood out in his mind: in the procession there was:

> a naked Indian, riding a grey pony in the rain, who struck a fearful discord in Mr Hoover's triumph; an impenitent redskin, light glistening on his wet shoulders, and a feather in his hair as brash and all as untimely as the cock who gave the lie to poor St Peter ... Few other countries would have let him ride so publicly, but America will suffer much for freedom ... and therefore admitted the lonely feathered horseman to Mr Hoover's procession, where he commemorated the older cultures on whose destruction were built the new heaven and the new earth that Mr Coolidge was hurrying home to write about.[26]

The ironic symbolism of the lone Indian made a deep impression on Eric, and he used the incident to create a critical moment in *Juan in*

America, when Juan is present at the Inaugural procession for Mr Boomer. In the novel Eric underscored the meaning:

> The rain glistened on his brown skin, his naked thighs gripped the flanks of his rough-clipt pony, and three feathers drooped from his wet black hair. He, in so great a procession, yet seemed alone. He looked neither to the left nor to the right, unaware of the crowd, not come to do honour but to show himself and say, 'I am America. I am he who first saw the caravels of Columbus, who first talked with the English in Virginia, who fought Spaniards and Dutchmen, French and English. It is my blood that paints the maples red and glorifies the crimson sumach. All else that comes here changes, but I have not changed. Yet am I America!'
> ... Mrs Dekker had not been thinking about the Indian—she had seen Indians before and rated them much lower than negroes.[27]

The experience of following the American Presidential campaign from close quarters may have been one of the reasons why Eric became at this time rather more politically aware than formerly. Like any intelligent man he knew that politics cannot be divorced from life, and he had opinions which he supposed to be radical but which were in reality more closely related to a kind of tolerant and humane conservatism. He looked with some incredulity on the American scene, on the mixture of romantic patriotism and practical corruption, on the hopeful element which believed that despite everything man could, and in America would, create a perfect way of life, and was moved to think about the British political situation of the time. He even suggested to Douglas:

> I hope you're going to vote Labour at the coming election. I don't like Socialists or Labourists, but they can't very well be worse or more stupid than Baldwin's tea-party ... In five years the Conservatives have done nothing to deal with unemployment ... that alone is sufficient reason to kick them out ...
> Backing Labour is a bit of a gamble, perhaps, but backing Baldwin is certain loss. America's going to challenge the last remnants of our prosperity with Hoover at the helm, and we need all the brains in the country to meet the challenge.

He did not remain of this opinion for long, and indeed was always his own man no matter with whom he aligned himself, as his short involvement in Scottish politics later showed. His close attention to American politics while he was resident there shows a sharply critical but more gently satirical mind at work, for he was grateful and affectionately disposed towards his hosts and could not by nature help but see the funny side of things. It amused him and sometimes annoyed him to hear Americans criticise the behaviour of the British in India and fail completely to see any fault in their treatment of their own Indians, and he noted too their extraordinarily one-sided view of other aspects of their social and cultural history. The greatest and most ridiculous element in their attempt to create an earthly paradise was the romantic nonsense, as he saw it, of the Eighteenth Amendment. Prohibition was somehow an expression of the essential and touching innocence of a people in a pre-realist age:

> Their initial advocacy of the League of Nations and the reckless experiment of Prohibition both sprang from a romantic belief in their power to cure, by a sudden decision and before morning, the ancient sin in the minds of men. Their abandoning of the League, their return to whisky, were confession of their failure to count the cost of reformation: a romantic weakness.[28]

Eric was intrigued by the curious contrast between the American people and their government; the state was 'clumsy, intractable and covetous' whereas the people were 'congenial, broad-minded (except on the topic of India), and generous beyond measure'.

> Like all other governments, Washington made its own rules and concealed policy under a heavy disguise of righteousness; but the people of America—or those with whom one became friendly—were honourable men, blissfully indiscreet, and lenient to error with the leniency of native magnanimity.[29]

It was a strange and potent mixture, and in its production through the circumstances engendered by Prohibition of a new mythology of 'money, bootleg whisky and blood' to replace the older mythology of the Frontier and the vanishing West, it provided Eric with material for the novel that was to make his name; for which he was duly grateful.

> Though I disliked the government of the United States—its history and continuing practice—I should not reprehend it; for it was my great and permanent benefactor. Writers, it may be, have always owed more to bad governments than to good ones.[30]

After a summer of decent toil at Cornell, he began travelling in earnest, by train and coach but mostly by train. Trains helped a visitor feel, by tactile sensation and the lapse of time, something of the almost unimaginable vastness and variety of the continent of North America. Some of his journeying was done in the company of a young Englishman, Bill Smith—'pink of cheek and Cambridge in his warbling voice'[31]—who, with enormous enthusiasm for all he saw, enlivened the times they spent together.

Crossing the Atlantic the previous October, Eric had struck up a friendship with a fellow passenger called Hamilton Gilkyson. A group of passengers young enough for horseplay had been playing leap-frog rather wildly; Eric had fallen from a jump, knocked his head on the deck, and briefly been rendered unconscious. Hamilton Gilkyson, coming to help the prostrate Eric, discovered the gutter in the back of his head and momentarily feared the worst. Gilkyson and his wife Phoebe lived comfortably with their children in a large old house near Valley Forge, thirty miles from Philadelphia and perhaps eighty from New York. Eric became their frequent visitor, and they remained friends for the rest of their lives. Being at the centre of a large concourse of cultured and talented friends and acquaintances, the Gilkysons were able to give Eric many interesting introductions. He met at their house the then famous novelist Joseph Hergesheimer, and was taken by them to Richmond to call on James Branch Cabell, who seemed to have withdrawn into a world of his own creation: the Poictesme inhabited by his most celebrated character, Jurgen.

With his friend Bill, and furnished by the Gilkysons with an introduction to a young poet called Josephine Pinckney, Eric made an early trip in the summer of 1929 to Charleston. Going for a weekend, they fell in love with the place and remained for almost a month; they became thoroughly southernised in the process, learning to speak with an authentic drawl and live in irresistibly leisurely indolence. The atmosphere and beauty of the place are pleasingly rendered in *The Man on My Back*. Eric was much taken with the Ashley River Gardens:

> The coral and snow of the azaleas was reflected in a windless pool. The water, like thick green glass, mirrored the flaming pyramids and showed again the dead tree like a column of still smoke. It reflected long aisles of colour, burning bushes that burned with a cool flame. There was deep velvety-red blossom against dark-green leaves, and cold starry dogwood. And in the shallow water of the pool were tiny turtles with an archaic Chinese expression, fixed and unwinking under the stony hood of their carapace.[32]

He fell under the spell of the silent Carolina swamps, through which they thrust a canoe beneath 'the grey-curtained roof of over-arching branches', waking 'white egrets that splashed the dark water with their luminous reflexion'. How greatly he was charmed by the whole ethos and scene of South Carolina may be judged from the episodes in *Juan in America* where Juan is rescued from the jungle-like swamps by the mistress of Egret Island, and later spends some time with his great-aunt Rachel Legaré in Charleston. Perhaps, too, Eric's Lalage Gehenna has something in her of the qualities of Josephine Pinckney, 'a poet, young and tremulous amidst the constant perils, the sensational, unexpected rewards of life'; Eric had a brief but delighted acquaintance with her, and was impressed by the way in which she was loved by those whose grandparents had been her grandparents' slaves:

> They came rushing towards her in a radiance of delight that was like the brightness of the egrets in the swamp. They shouted and laughed, they cried and kissed her skirts, they surrounded her with doting affection.[33]

Later Josephine had a great success with a novel, *Hilton Head* (1941), but Eric remembered her best for a moment of tragedy when, on the way to a party, she let fall and broke a precious bottle of whisky that she had been keeping for a special occasion; overcome, she burst into tears, and sobbed on his shoulder.

Later in the summer Bill and Eric together, emulating Robert Louis Stevenson's trans-American journey of 1879, undertook a tremendous tour which began in Boston in June and led them southwards all the way to New Orleans, with a pause for 'a hellish grand society wedding in North Carolina'.[34] From New Orleans ('frogs' legs and damp sticky heat; but nice'[35]) they proceeded westwards into Texas. ('And there was in Texas a handsome young man, 35 years old, attending a Firemen's Convention, who had been travelling for 36 hours continuously without ever getting outside Texas; and thought it a privilege.'[36])

Their next stop was Santa Fé in New Mexico, where Eric responded with emotion to the plight of the indigenous people:

> Some good Indian country. But this humane and commercial country turns its aborigines into a circus—Indians, bears and buffaloes—strictly preserved against aggression, and charging a suitable sum for admission. Exterminate 90%, then sentimentalise over the rest—and make a profit out of them—and complete the story by criticising *our* administration of *our* Indians.[37]

He was less outspokenly ironical in print, but was sufficiently impressed to write one of his most evocative serious poems about what he saw:

Navajo Sand Painting: Santa Fé, New Mexico

Dark and deliberate fingers, heavy with Indian rings,
    Sifting the coloured dust on the levelled sand;
Slender and elegant patterns, like shadows following
    The slow, unerring, turquoise-braceleted hand.

Square and impassive faces, rag-bound coarse black hair—
    The artist hides in the stoic like fire in the old fuel;
Crimson and purple, and necklets of silver, the craftsmen wear—
    The desert yearning for splendour, the lean for a jewel.

Slowly the polychrome pattern is finished and caught in a girth,
    (The Navajo rainbow, angular, narrow and bright);
Now is the pollen scattered that marries the heaven to earth,
    And sanctifies art that is brief as a barncock's night.

Intricate, formal, austere—but the picture is drawn in the sand:
    Though art and the artist die, the sand will remain;
While the sun still illumines the pattern, one comes with a
                       ritual hand
To rake and destroy—and the sand is the desert again.[38]

A couple of days later Eric and Bill were in Colorado, sampling the pleasures of sitting most of the scorching day in a pool of the stream called Bright Angel at the bottom of the Grand Canyon. They tried spending a night at Phantom Ranch, some 4,000 or 5,000 feet below the ordinary surface of the earth, but found the heat insupportable and began to climb up to more comfortable regions in the small hours:

> The moon was shining when we started, and before we began to climb the wall of the main canyon, the sun appeared and lighted mile upon mile of rose-red cliff. While the river was still dark and running loudly in the shadow, the gigantic sides of the canyon were flaming with the dawn, and lordly buttresses returned the glowing salutation of the day.[39]

The next port of call was Los Angeles, which Eric found a terrible disappointment: 'a huge, vulgar, sprawling, noisy village. A million and a quarter people with nothing but movies in their heads. Very, very uninteresting,' he wrote to Douglas Walker. In *Fanfare for a Tin Hat*, forty years later, he unrepentantly called Los Angeles 'an urban calamity that offends the perceptive mind even more than it offends the physical senses'. But the coastline of California was magnificent, San Francisco splendid, Seattle intricate and decorative; a thought that had been in Eric's mind crystallised. He would arrange to spend his second winter on this favoured Pacific sea-board; no more shivering amidst the icicles and snow of another eastern winter; he would transfer to Berkeley.

Eric and Bill now went up to tramp for a week in the Sierra Nevada, the mountain range down the length of eastern California which contains Mount Whitney and several other peaks over 14,000 feet high, and the great National Park of Yosemite. Here his spirit was contented with a vision of true grandeur:

> The biggest day was climbing a mountain called Lyell, 13,090 feet. We set out from the base-camp—ten miles distant—at 4.00 a.m. and reached the summit at 1.30. Rocks and snow, hands and feet, almost perpendicular in parts, and a slidy passage across the corner of a glacier. We should have had ice-axes and ropes, but we hadn't. A superb and rather awful view from the top—range after range of naked, granite mountains, snow-streaked, the glimpse of a lake, a belt of pinewood far below. The descent was difficult at first, like going over the edge of a precipice; and I nearly had an uncomfortable finish to the day, when my foothold broke on the glacier and I slid down a couple of hundred feet at about 30 mph, frantically grabbing at a steep ice-slope that wouldn't be grabbed. Finally, of course, I landed on softer stuff, but my finger-tips are still numb. I was rather anxious to stop, you see, as there was said to be a fault in the glacier unpleasantly deep.[40]

From the heights of the Sierra Nevada they went down to San Francisco, and from there northwards into Oregon and to Portland, where

Bill's fiancée, Dorothy, was anxiously awaiting their arrival. While the young lovers went off for a tour of the Rockies, Eric made his way to Vancouver and dallied there awhile, 'in happy solitude', as he wrote to Phoebe Gilkyson, adding: 'Nature note—the southern part of Vancouver Island is too lovely.' He met Bill again later at the Homestead Hotel in the Banff National Park in Alberta, after Dorothy had left; and while Bill drank beer to drown his sorrows, Eric drank it for pleasure. They swam daily in the sulphur springs, enjoying the curious effect it seemed to have on their ratiocinative processes; it was the health cure that made them tipsy, they insisted, not the beer.

Though they must have been flagging a little after the relentless travelling they had already done, they then went south again to see Salt Lake City, and then took the train to St Paul. This was Dorothy's home, and there they paused again for a while, before moving on once more to Chicago and finally Rhode Island. Eric had for a while almost satiated his desire for travel, and perhaps it had taken more out of him than he realised; but he had with a vengeance seen something of the United States, and his mind was teeming with details that would enliven and colour the novel he was planning. It had been a wonderful summer.

After a visit to the Gilkysons he packed his bags at Ithaca, caught the train all the way back across America to San Francisco, and presented himself at Berkeley for the beginning of the autumn semester. His self-image was subtly different now from what it had been on his arrival in the United States a year before. His confidence in himself had been reinforced by the publication in March 1929 of *White-Maa's Saga*, and now he was the promising author of two novels, for Jonathan Cape brought out *Poet's Pub* in October 1929, just after Eric arrived in California, and promised to have an American edition out soon. Further, he was widely travelled in the States, had good friends to support him, and was now in the regular company of several other Commonwealth Fellows who had congregated in the Californian sunshine. Among these were Sean O'Faolain, whose name was to become famous enough, and Dick White, who would also make a mark in the world, although his name would be less familiar; many years later Eric was thrilled to find that his former friend, with whom he had lost touch, had become the Head of MI5.

Settling in to enjoy life on the Berkeley campus, he made little pretence of working very seriously on a thesis; his study now was of American student life, contemporary social manners, political attitudes and favoured institutions, and the purpose of his clear-eyed gaze at the American way of life was to inform his new fictional undertaking.

There was a problem, however; not for the last time in his life he began to note what he called 'a griping in the guts', and by the end of October he was in a San Francisco nursing home being treated for a duodenal ulcer.

He ascribed it himself to the unfortunate intake of poor-quality illegal liquor at the extended party in Washington six months earlier, but it probably had something to do as well with the pace at which he had been living and travelling ever since, and the emotional tensions connected with being an author. From the Dante Sanatorium he wrote ruefully to Phoebe:

> Do not be alarmed, I beg you, at this sinister address, nor at the mausoleum tinge of the paper.
>
> It is true that I am an inmate, a patient, a sufferer, a prisoner, the hollow-eyed occupant of a mechanical bed that goes up and down at a nurse's will—to keep me from getting comfortable, you see. But mine is not a serious case. Oh no. Not a bit serious. So they all say.

What seemed to be distressing him more than anything was the starvation diet on which he had been put, and visions of glorious food kept interrupting his train of thought:

> All at Mont Clare, Pa., are well, I hope—and getting plenty to eat. Do you get a-plenty ham these days? And does Hamilton get a second helping of grits in the morning? Do you let Paddy eat her chicken off the bone? Is not the chassis of a well-fed hen a pretty ornament for any table? Do you like your eggs sunny side up?
>
> All these gastronomic details have the most poignant interest for me.

He was in the sanatorium for three weeks, and convalescent for many further weeks until he felt properly well again. The episode was something of a shock; it turned out to be the first in a series of such setbacks in his health that were to plague him at intervals for the rest of his life. The illnesses of his digestive tract sometimes extended later to irritating skin troubles as well; there was fairly obviously a link between his health and his nervous disposition, and he learned to live with it as part of the price he had to pay for living life dangerously (in an emotional sense—at some time during the writing of every book he would have a period of feeling sick and ill) and for enjoying the good things of life so fully when he was well. Mostly he made fun of it, especially when recounting his stays in health hydros or sanatoria in letters to distant friends, but he did not like it one bit, and it didn't make him any easier to live with at close quarters.

Early in December he was at the Highlands Inn at Carmel, feeling much better and enjoying the charming gentleness of California's winter. Phoebe Gilkyson was writing short stories to enter for a prize competition, and she suggested to Eric that he should try his hand at a couple, but he replied:

> What do you need a paltry sum like two and a half grand for? Has Hamilton been shooting craps again? Or is it pinochle this time?
>
> No, I can't write short stories. I'm all busy with a simply colossal novel about America. *Very* libellous and improper. A sort of ribald Baedeker with bits of the Bible and Vera Delman. Isn't that fun?

He had in fact sketched out the idea for one short story with an American theme. Inspired by an incident while he was waiting for Bill in New Orleans, it did not appear for several years, but was eventually one of the short stories in Eric's first collection in 1935, by which time the art of the short story had become much more interesting to him. In late 1929 he was more concerned with his work on *Juan in America*, which even as he wrote it he realised was very promising, and on promoting *Poet's Pub*, which was to appear in the USA on 20 January 1930. Phoebe had promised to recruit support among her circle, among them Ellen Glasgow, Josephine Pinckney and Hamilton Owen, and Eric arranged with Harrison Smith, Cape's American partner, for copies to be sent to them, hoping they wouldn't act 'as an immediate emetic to them'.

Though not overwhelmed, he had not been displeased with the British reviews of *Poet's Pub*. He thought it ridiculous that some of them were

> bawling me out for being flippant—just because I did a bit of belly-aching in my first, they expect me to go on belly-aching all my life.[41]

But he would never please the critics by being consistent or even immediately recognisable. Variety was for him the true sign of professional artistry, and appropriateness to context; every book should be its own thing, and different from others in such ways as its theme, setting and characters dictated.

He had not been satisfied with *White-Maa's Saga*, though he was delighted with the high praise it had received from his friend Douglas Walker:

> You were superbly generous in your criticism; and I rejoice—for I believe you to be honest—that *White-Maa* pleased you and Peggy, for there are few people in whose pleasure I take more interest.
>
> It isn't so good a book as I hoped it would be. Here and there it definitely fails. But I had to write it before I could do anything else.

He told Douglas that his second novel was 'altogether lighter in tone: not better, but better done'. It might be supposed that he would have cherished a special feeling for his first novel, but when he was asked forty years later whether he had any particular affection for the book, he answered:

> Affection for that thing? Nothing but embarrassment. It's typical of first novels, the sort of first novel that everybody used to write. Oh no, I think of it with horror now.[42]

Such an attitude was part of his pose; he may to some extent have believed what he was saying, but he would never allow the public fully to know him, and he surely did not speak the whole truth at that moment. On the other hand, his self-criticism was often brutal and his self-regard sometimes far from high; he was possibly more aware of the youthful faults in *White-Maa's Saga* than he was of the marvellously good things in it.

In the spring of 1930 the only thing that really mattered was his progress with *Juan in America*. After a slight hiatus he felt it was moving on satisfactorily again, as he explained to Phoebe:

> We're getting through a week's heatwave here. Up to nearly 80° nearly every day. Quite awful. Very bad for work. Most weather is, I find.
>
> As you discovered, I was in a very bad temper when I last wrote to you, because my quite objectionable hero was in a most unpleasant situation in a dog-wagon at Buffalo, and I couldn't get the damned fellow out. But he's gone a long way since then, and is, indeed, about to succumb to the charms of a female acrobat in a soda-fountain in Michigan: and really, what happens to him after that is his own affair, because I refuse to be responsible for people who associate with female acrobats.

He continued to work hard for what remained of his period in the States, living, as he told Douglas's mother, 'a hermit-like life', trying to get as much work as possible cleared up before he left California at the end of April—'and once a man starts working, well, he's done for. It's the most demoralising influence in the world.' He did get to the movies two or three times a week and was quite an expert on 'the Shouting Screen', but hermit was the only really valid word for him:

> I've not had a drink of ought but the crystal spring (I don't count milk shakes, and chocolate sodas, and banana fizzes, and pineapple juleps, and strawberry oolahs, and other pigmented washes common and indigenous to this uncivilised country; when I say drink I mean Drink)—not a drink, I say, since last Guy Fawkes' day, and that one, I must say, tasted very like a Roman Candle ... Not that there isn't plenty to be got, but my weakened tummy (alas, it's a judgment; just a judgment) shrinks like a Salvation Army band from the smell of gin.[43]

It must have been the longest period of abstinence Eric ever knew, and nothing quite like it ever happened again. There were short periods when his stomach proved similarly recalcitrant, but for the most part he was able to compensate for such intervals very adequately.

On 26 April 1930 he said his last goodbyes to his Californian friends and embarked on the ship *Pennsylvania*, in the company of Dick White. They sailed south via Panama, and docked in New York on 12 May. Ten days with the Gilkysons at Mont Clare provided a most pleasing coda to his period as a Commonwealth Fellow; then, joining Dick White once more, he boarded the *American Farmer* in New York on 22 May and stepped ashore in England on 1 June. Much had happened in his long absence, and he was eager to taste his new future.

9 Professional Writer

The Eric Linklater who returned to England in June 1930 was much clearer about who he was and what his career was going to be than the eager but undirected young man who had sailed westwards two years earlier. With two newly published and not badly received novels behind him, another more than half completed, and a mind full of ideas for further books, he was on the threshold of the writing profession; he had come home in more ways than one.

He made no more than a passing stay in London, calling at 30 Bedford Square to make some arrangements with Cape, and then went north to stay with the Walkers in Aberdeen for a few days.

He spent the summer at home in Orkney, continuing work on the new novel at intervals but mostly idling, fishing, sailing, receiving guests, enjoying the Orcadian peace. He did not feel as well as he normally did, his stomach still troubling him a little. Considerable pleasure, however, resided in preparing for the press the volume of poems which he had first submitted to Cape almost two years previously. Now, anticipating that *Juan in America* was going to be something of a blockbuster in 1931, Cape had agreed to publish the poems 'to keep his name before the public'. *A Dragon Laughed* came out in October, and was given a quite friendly review in *The Times Literary Supplement*, but it was hardly the publishing event of the year. The real excitement lay in the potential of the Juan book; Cape himself cabled to Harrison Smith after reading the draft in October: 'HAVE READ LINKLATER'S NEW NOVEL. IT'S A WOW!'

At the end of the summer Eric went south again to Edinburgh, to work further on the novel in response to criticisms from Edward Garnett. He agreed that 'the first part needs tightening up—the trouble was that I rather enjoyed doing that bit, and was inclined to wander on' and wanted to know what else ought to be pruned. Garnett's reply was helpful, and was gratefully acknowledged by Eric:

Cape has sent me proofs of the first 10,000 words or so, and I've cut 1,600 in various bits and pieces, and also re-fashioned the Duke's death, as briefly as possible, so that he looks less like an Aunt Sally. I'm glad you mentioned that. It's so easy to be undergraduatish, and such a temptation...

The didactic spot you found, which I shall hurriedly and shamefacedly delete—I bottle-washed for a professor for a year...

The meeting in the swamp. That second coincidence was too much—even in

America—but my silly brain had reached its limit of invention just then, and I couldn't see how to avoid it. But an intermediary is, of course, the proper way out of the difficulty.

Eric was greatly taken with Garnett, as he later recorded:

Never have I known anyone more whole-heartedly convinced of the almost-sacred importance of well-chosen, well-appointed words, and his long association with, his great friendship with, Joseph Conrad endued him, for me, with an apostolic magic which neither Rome nor Canterbury could better; for Conrad, by that time, had ousted Kipling from the primacy of my regard.[1]

Jonathan Cape, too, advised Eric on aspects of the new novel:

My own feeling is that it would certainly be improved if the prologue is speeded up and it would be a further improvement if the last chapters were rounded off. I had just a little sense of dissatisfaction at the end ... The whole thing is a sheer delight ... Last summer I read the first half of Robert Graves' *Goodbye to All That* in m/s and was disappointed to come to the end of the material and cried out for more—I felt the same about *Juan in America*.

A day or so after writing this Cape went up to Edinburgh to spend a day with his promising new author and persuaded him to agree to a contract which offered no better terms than had formerly been agreed for the first novels, regardless of the much greater potential of the new one. It was something of a triumph for Cape in one sense, but did less good for the firm in the longer run, for Eric came increasingly to feel that he had been cheated and for some time looked for ways of escaping from Cape to some other publisher. After Rupert Hart-Davis joined Cape in 1933 and took over Eric's portfolio, some of the resentment faded. A great friendship grew between him and Hart-Davis, and although Eric, when he could, took his non-fiction and his children's books to other publishers, he stayed with Cape for the publication of his full-length novels until 1959.

Cape, perhaps aware that Eric's pleasure in the contract might be eroded if anyone more professional were to know its terms, even persuaded Eric not to employ an agent:

Our long and friendly talk on Friday encourages me to feel that the relation between ourselves is one which is not likely to be easily broken by you if competing offers are made to you, providing always that you are satisfied that we are doing fairly by you.

And Eric happily replied:

My Scots blood doesn't take kindly to the thought of parting with 10% of every pound of flesh that I succeed in detaching from you, and if we can manage without an intermediary it will, I think, be all to the good.

1 Eric, Elspeth and their mother, Elizabeth, being carried to Dounby, Orkney, by Robert Linklater's cousin, Alec Flett of Northbigging, 1907

2 Family picnic at the Dounby Show, August 1914. *Back row* (*l–r*): Mary Ritchie, Eric aged 15, Mrs Ritchie, Ellen Merriman, Nell Sinclair, Mimie Flett; *front row* (*l–r*): Deborah Flett, Robert Linklater, Elspeth, Augusta Sinclair, Elizabeth, Jimmie Flett

3 85831 L/Cpl Linklater, Fife & Forfar
Yeomanry, 1917

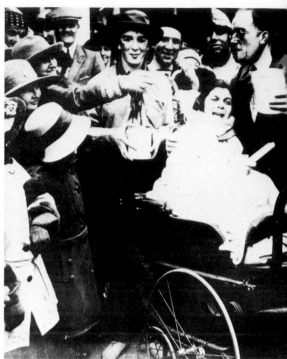

4 Eric, with Isobel Walker in pram, collecting for
charity during an Aberdeen University rag, *c.* 192

5 Douglas Walker, Elspeth and Eric drying out after
a swim off Orkney, 1922

Thinking it over towards the end of his life, Eric wrote with humour of the sharpness with which Jonathan Cape had handled him:

> He scarcely gave me time to finish my first drink before he presented me with a newly drawn contract, pledging my next three novels to him, and—as he commanded a waiter to bring me more whisky—required me to sign it. I, in the innocence that still surrounded me—sometimes a benignant light, but sometimes a blinding fog—gladly obeyed him; and not till some time later did I realise the mistake I had made. Jonathan was a horse-dealer, a cattle-trader, of whom I became oddly fond, even after my realisation that he had taken advantage of my unforgivable innocence.[2]

The essential generosity of Eric's nature, which allowed him to be the victim of such businesslike practice, never changed very much. He did later take himself to the literary agency of A. D. Peters, with whose efforts on his behalf he was very satisfied; they, too, became life-long friends. But, even after handing over his financial affairs to his friend Douglas Walker, he was liable to get into terrible tangles and to make unsound deals, not infrequently running into the kind of bad luck that tends to visit people who naturally trust the people with whom they are dealing. His income tax problems, moreover, occasionally became acute, and he spent many hours writing indignantly, furiously or mollifyingly to the Commissioners trying to explain the peculiar financial difficulties of the professional writer's life, often without much satisfaction.

Even while assuring Eric that success awaited *Juan in America*, Jonathan Cape was anxiously exhorting him to further work. By then Eric had proposed making a biography of Ben Jonson out of the materials he had got together in the United States with a thesis in mind. Now Cape heard that G. M. Thomson would soon be bringing out a book on James VI and his times, and he urged Eric to get down to serious work on his Ben Jonson book, to see if they could beat Thomson into the market place. He further thought that Eric should start putting together ideas for a further Juan book, as Garnett had suggested,[3] taking Juan to Spain, Italy or Germany. Sensible though he was of the shrewdness of this suggestion, Eric had had enough for the time being of Juan, and anyway, the book had yet to appear and earn the success predicted for it. Meanwhile, Eric was not well, and was additionally in a somewhat embarrassed financial state.

Early in 1931, however, came the happy news that *Juan in America* was to be the Book Society's choice for March. Wren Howard at Cape's pointed out that it would mean a nice little cheque for Eric which 'wouldn't do him any harm', even though Book Society trade prices were comparatively low. And, of course, the additional publicity and the prestige of being so selected by J. B. Priestley, Hugh Walpole, Clemence Dane and Sylvia Lynd for the Book Society would not harm the normal sales pattern for the book either. Eric would need to make one or two changes to please the Book Society people; the first part would have to be isolated and called a 'Prologue' ('Priestley will say so in his review, so take the Bull by the Horns and do it yourself'), and Sylvia Lynd wanted a certain passage toned down a little.

Eric replied that he certainly didn't want to upset 'the delicate mind of the General Reader', but that he couldn't understand the complaint: 'Was it a word, or a thought? ... It's difficult to decide which can be more shocking.' He was astonished when the offending passage was precisely indicated, but went about bowdlerising it in his own inimitable fashion. The passage described how Juan and his new acquaintance, Isadore Cohen, observe a pair of amorous yaks at the zoo in Central Park. Eric wrote:

> I was a little bit surprised to see what it was that had been considered as a possible source of offence, but then I read the paragraph carefully and decided there were three words in it capable of upsetting a really refined intelligence: 'leapt', 'embrace' and 'ecstasy', especially as these three were in such close conjunction. And I admit that 'leapt' particularly has a very vulgar Shakespearean sound. So:
>
> '... concluded his addresses. His mate was unshaken by the mountainous occursion.'
>
> 'Occursion' is a very good, obscure sort of word, don't you think? Like putting oatmeal in your bathwater to hide your legs.

Cheered by the continuing optimism at Cape's about the probable reception of *Juan in America*, Eric decided he would not, as he had feared he would have to, look for some kind of job to repair his ailing finances, but opened instead the suitcase full of notes on seventeenth-century theatre and turned his mind back to Ben Jonson. Typically, he rapidly became deeply immersed in the project, and the more he saw it as a biography of Jonson, the more work he realised he still had to do on the background. He returned to Aberdeen to be near the library, explaining to Mrs Walker:

> I shall humble my love of luxury and seek the proper atmosphere for Literary Endeavour—attics, rats and so forth—in some suitably lousy digs.
>
> The new book takes shape very slowly, and I'll have to do some more spadework at King's.

References to the painful progress of the biography continued regularly in his letters till the summer, when at last things fell into place; he worked intently at it in Aberdeen during the spring, but there were constant interruptions from Cape to do with advance publicity for *Juan in America*, and naturally it was the novel that mattered more to him than anything else. Waiting for it to appear was a kind of agony.

There was no need for anxiety. When the papers arrived, the reactions of the reviewers were more or less as Garnett had predicted. Hugh Walpole said: 'I think Eric Linklater's book is brilliant',[4] and J. B. Priestley's review commended the writer's zest and gusto, the 'genuine high spirits of a clever man', the vivid images, the 'gay and crazy kaleidoscope of life', and judged it to be not only more informative about the American scene than anything he had read for years, but 'a carnival of fantastic adventure and satirical humour ... a magnificent frolic'.[5] Eric himself was most pleased with Harold Nicolson's thoughtful review, finding it 'far and away the best—I speak in vanity, perhaps, but unrepentantly', as he confided to Jonathan Cape. It was Nicolson's perception that the book was more than just a frolic that gave Eric pleasure; he had written:

> Mr Eric Linklater is a writer of great intelligence and exuberant fantasy ... *Juan in America* is a supremely amusing book. But it is more than that. It is a serious and sympathetic criticism of American conditions. It is a work of outstanding literary skill.[6]

The moment the novel was launched and under way, Eric decided to go back to Orkney to try and finish the Jonson book. He explained to Cape:

> I'm useless for anything else until he's off my chest. Then there's plenty of other stuff I want to get on with. The trouble is that the conceiving part of my brain works quickly, and the executive part damned slowly.

First he sent a copy of *Juan in America* to the Gilkysons, hoping that they would like it.

> If you don't, I shall be grieved beyond expression. But I think you will. It's the best thing I've done so far.
> I hope America won't misunderstand it. It pulls the American leg, I admit, but there's more in it than that—a lot more, I think—and after all, it's only really big legs that there's any fun in pulling.

Unfortunately, the Americans proved less generous in their response to Eric's mockery than he had hoped. He should have expected something less than an enthusiastic response to ridicule from an outsider; he had noted often enough in the States that while it was perfectly acceptable and indeed desirable that satirical or critical fingers should be pointed at American excesses and peculiarities, it was not for the guest or the stranger to comment. Some months after publication, Wren Howard admitted:

> It continues to sell quietly in the United States, but it has been less than a bang-over success over there. I suppose it was bound to be more appreciated in England than in America, where in spite of their pretensions and professions they still remain very self-conscious and uncomfortable under witty criticism.

In Britain it was one of the biggest publishing successes of the season: 49,000 copies had passed through the shops when Howard reported on the situation in October. By the end of the year a ninth impression was being ordered. For a while, at any rate, Eric's financial problems had disappeared, and he went home to Dounby in late April happy and with his energy sufficiently restored to get down to work on the final stages of *Ben Jonson and King James*.

With the publication, to such pleasing reviews, of his third novel, it might have been expected that Eric would be looked upon as a significant new talent. As Priestley pointed out, in Eric's books 'the writing is uncommonly good'. Years later there would be many to acknowledge that he was one of the most stylishly accomplished writers of his generation. Style alone was insufficient, evidently, for the critical establishment never noticed him. In the fifty years since Eric Linklater appeared on the literary scene there has never been a significant critical study of his work. In many reviews of the century's work in literature his name does not appear at all; in others there is a reference to his flair as a storyteller and the astonishing variety of his output, but there has been no serious attempt to examine his opus, or to suggest that it is particularly valuable. Occasionally there have been more sympathetic glances at his work, especially in the Scottish context, and recently there have been signs of a growing conviction that he has been most grossly neglected.

Eric, who ultimately became resigned to the widespread view that his work was entertaining but not art, thought that perhaps he had signed his own death warrant by the very variety in which he had taken such delight. The critical decision was to write, as his fourth novel, *The Men of Ness*:

> That, I now realise, was the moment when I forfeited all claim to be recognised as a serious novelist. I am, of course, a serious writer: that is to say, I have always shown a proper respect for the language which I write, a respect which is no longer general, or even applauded. But a true novelist is one who imposes his own character, his own way of thought and fashions of writing, on every page that leaves his table ... My own practice has been more humble and realistic. To a very large extent I have allowed my subjects to determine the style and temper in which I have written of them.[7]

He saw himself as a sculptor, much as in a previous consideration of the matter he had called himself a carpenter, a craftsman, a tradesman even, for whom there was not even a rear entrance to the halls of the critically acclaimed.

It is a view which has been echoed by other observers unable to account for the lack of serious consideration of Eric's work. Ernest Marwick, for instance, wrote: 'A man so various is difficult to classify, and dull individuals love to place people in categories. That may be why Eric Linklater has escaped, in very great measure, the attentions of the literary historian.'[8]

But this will not do. Eric's varied novels may have defied easy classification but they do not repel analysis: they have simply not, on the whole, been deemed worthy of it. Another possible explanation has been that they are so entertaining and pleasurable that they cannot be taken seriously. As Lionel Trilling has pointed out: 'The traditional assumptions of pre-Modernist writers, that to give pleasure and comfort to their readers is an important part of their tasks, is too often discounted by Modernist assumptions and criteria.'[9] It could be that Eric's books were thought to be too firmly rooted in the tradition, that they were insufficiently novel. Written in the wake of novelists such as Joyce, Virginia Woolf and D. H. Lawrence, they did too much honour to the values and methods of earlier writers—Peacock, Trollope, Dickens—and their twentieth-century successors: Bennett, Galsworthy and Wells. Eric's cardinal virtue, that of clarity, was almost directly opposed to the cult of opaqueness and difficulty favoured in the twentieth century. His assumption that the central function of a novel was to tell a story was not calculated to endear him to critics for whom the idea of 'story' was false and dead.

The first three novels already indicate the variety which would characterise the Linklater oeuvre. In *White-Maa's Saga* he obeyed a simple but sensible imperative, to write about what he knew. He found material of continuing appeal, and discovered that he had potent resources of language through which to present it. The first responses to the novel were very encouraging. Gerald Gould in the *Observer* found Eric to be 'a new writer of force and promise', and commented: 'There is good fighting as well as good writing in this angry, original novel.' J. B. Priestley in the London *Evening News* said that the scenes and people, from the sophisticated students to the primitive folk of Orkney, were very well presented; later he recalled: 'I remember thinking . . . that here was a new novelist of unusually bright promise'[10] but pointed out at the same time that first novels were not very difficult to write, especially if the author drew on autobiographical material.

This, of course, Eric had done, and he was very clear-eyed about and unimpressed with his own achievement. The novel was, he said, 'a romantic and unsuccessful treatment of matters with which I was very well acquainted'[11]; in his later review of his life he said the book 'had some of the virtues of green things and a naïve enthusiasm, and most of the faults of inexperience'.[12]

There was more to it than such comments allow. *White-Maa's Saga* is a most haunting and memorable novel. It bears comparison with *Portrait of the Artist as a Young Man*, not in terms of linguistic experiment but in terms of the depth and intensity of its examination of a young man's search for meaning and identity among the confusions of life. Eric's protagonist, Peter Flett, is from Orkney. Towards the end of the book he makes a sudden confession to the Orkney girl, Norna, to whom he has been moving closer and closer in the course of the action:

> 'I'm in love,' said Peter, abruptly. 'With you and all these people and your mother and the bride and the Bride's Cog and the fiddlers and the wind; the taste of everything and the smell of everything. With Orkney. By God, I am.'[13]

It is this love of Orkney that imbues the novel with so much of its colour, but also projected with vivid feeling and energy are the university and city of Aberdeen—called here 'Inverdoon', as in other of Eric's books that feature the granite city. Orkney and Aberdeen are the two poles of Peter Flett's axis, as they were for the young Eric Linklater. Peter is a reluctant medical student, just after the First World War; he has a strong-minded sister in Orkney; his sailor father was killed in 1916; he is a boxer and something of a man's man, but is also trying to make sense of his relationship with women; he loves to talk, and fight, and sail, and make love. So far, so like his creator. But he is better-looking and more romantically/conventionally admirable than his creator. Whereas Eric was short and bespectacled, wiry rather than broad until later in life, Peter is tall and powerful,

> a big man with square shoulders. He had a clear, weather-tanned skin and grey, brooding eyes. His mouth was big but the lips were curiously delicate. When he laughed he flushed, his eyes puckered, he showed his white, even teeth; his head went back and he laughed full-heartedly.[14]

Perhaps it was this sort of 'untruth' that made Eric disparage his first novel, feeling that if it was going to be about himself, then it should have eschewed such temptations to project himself as bigger and better than he thought himself to be. But in *Magnus Merriman* Eric made no bones about giving experience very like his own to an imaginary figure, and prefaced the novel with a warning that it was not to be taken as autobiographical. It may have been a matter of other faults in *White-Maa's Saga* which later embarrassed him.

The title indicates something of the nature of the novel. The word 'saga' was appropriate for Eric's purpose and central to some of his most vital interests, but its use necessitated the provision and extension of saga elements which may have led to distortions. It was always Eric's contention that the backbone of a novel was its story; in this early work the demands of story got a little out of hand, and possibly this is what he was uncomfortably aware of. 'Saga' meant an emphasis on action, on violence, on fighting and on love-making which may have led him further than he had intended to go.

What matters, however, is not what Eric thought of his book but what a reader might make of it today. His own Orkney contemporaries found it to be a joy, though as Ernest Marwick recalled, their criticism was not wholly literary:

> The chapter entitled 'Orkney', with its wonderful account of the County Show and 'running in the night', had been read again and again; there were stains on it from the dinner-table and from the evening paraffin lamp ... We tried to decide who were the prototypes of the Fletts and the Sabistons, and whether the story about 'auld John Carrigal wha bade in the upper hoose o' Dykeside' was really taken from life. There was no doubt that it was, for some of the old men could cap it with stories quite as fantastic and many times more Rabelaisian. They shook their heads appreciatively over this new writer, 'a son of Cap'n Linklater frae Dounby', and, savouring some of his phrases, decided he could 'fairly write'.[15]

It is still a powerful evocation of a time and place that has lost none of its vitality, picturesqueness and truth. The conversation of the university students, their perception of the world, their attempts, some more successful than others, to do the academic work required, their thoughts, dreams, anxieties about and responses to women, their male conviviality in the drinking-places and their high spirits which led occasionally to various violent outlets, are presented with enthusiasm and style, and the physical world in which they lived is recreated with pictorial and atmospheric persuasiveness. Their world, though highly coloured at times, is real. It has a sense of being historically true and interesting in a documentary way at the same time as it captures the flavour of being young and at college at any time, combining a kind of universality with the uneasiness and frenetic behaviour of that particular postwar era. Out of this complex scene Eric distilled a narrative about Peter Flett and his friends which dramatically and faithfully rendered the reality.

But the novel is not of interest only to those who want to read about Orkney and Aberdeen and to guess at the extent to which it is a book that reveals hidden things about its author, any more than *Ulysses* is only for those who want to read about Dublin or *The Rainbow* for those who want to read about the Nottinghamshire coal-field. In its charting of the progress of a human soul through many of life's puzzlements and pleasures it, despite the romantic conventions which its story-line follows, convincingly and realistically examines a universal theme. Peter Flett is Jimmy Porter a quarter of a century before he appeared on the stage. At the same time as being the romantic hero who kills his enemy and sails off into the sunrise with his girl, he looks forward to a line of anti-heroes who will in the post-1950 novel challenge and reverse the tradition within which Eric was happy to work. Magnus Merriman is Peter Flett with an added clownishness, and the line from Magnus to Sebastian Dangerfield and Jim Dixon is direct.

A first novel which persuasively examines the psychological and philosophical development of a young man in a way which recalls the achievement of James Joyce and which adumbrates the directions taken much later by Amis, John Wain, and the young Iris Murdoch, and American novelists such as Roth and Updike, is far from negligible. When it does so in such style, one might expect it to command greater respect. The language is fluent and individual, allusive and evocative. There is an aphoristic flavour at times: 'Character is naked in the country and destiny goes steadily through childhood and work to the grave', or: 'Youth is wise in his generation; and it is a clownish jest that he should so often die when his house is built.' There is a resonance in the sentence structures which arises from a keen ear for a satisfying cadence and a sound sense of the need for variety. Literary allusions, sometimes very subtle, give the writing a contextual richness: when Peter Flett walks meditatively along the beach between Inverdoon's two rivers, one remembers Stephen Dedalus walking over the strand at Howth, though for Peter there is no moment of epiphany, only a sense of longing for something he cannot yet identify; when Peter and Mackay discuss the banana with Joyce Macrae, there is an echo of Rupert Birkin on the fig in *Women in Love*. Such echoes and allusions need not be spotted and annotated for the meaning to be clear, but add a richness to the text and set it in the literary tradition to which they refer.

Similarly the presentation of Orkney life, with its appreciation of the farming methods and rhythms, its anecdotes and snapshots, its sense of the islands' uniqueness, its attention to their winds and weather, and its loving exploitation of the customs and attitudes of the people gives the story of Peter's soul a fully realised ambience as potent as Hardy's Wessex or Lawrence's Nottinghamshire. Memorably vivid set-pieces in the book, such as the depiction of the county show at Kirkwall or Jean Sabiston's wedding at Redland, are convincingly accurate and full of life, as well as carrying the story forward.

The narrative becomes a little melodramatic towards the end—as Hardy's stories sometimes do—as the young writer manipulates events to achieve the sense of an ending. The theme of violence stated early by the students' tendency to end their evenings with a fight is expanded in Orkney with the introduction of the villainous Isaac Skea who, like Iago, seems to suffer from a more or less motiveless malignity. But there is a kind of immanent violence in the air, associated perhaps with the islanders' Viking ancestry, and with the atmosphere of superstition which survives alongside their superficial Christianity. What began as a novel rooted, despite its romantic flavour, in realism, moves perhaps too far towards the Gothic for a resolution. The imagination allowed fantastic rein becomes a Linklater characteristic in some later novels, and it is interesting to see him not wholly bound by a realistic imperative right from the beginning.

Eric's second novel was an utterly different kind of undertaking. Though he was more pleased with its technical achievement, and though it became quite well known, it is a less vital book. In it he set out to practise what he conceived of as the art of story-construction; the world of the book was totally invented, he was not personally involved in the tale he had to tell, and he was seeking what he may be said to have found: a mastery of techniques of comic characterisation, dialogue and farcical incident. The reviewers took pleasure in the warmth of his tone and the enthusiasm of his language. 'Mr Linklater is really the greatest fun,' wrote Ralph Strauss in the *Sunday Times*:

> Even at his absurdest moments he is genuinely witty—so witty indeed, that one can forgive him anything, even the disastrous barman. The story is one long series of improbabilities, but that does not matter in the least. The book is first-rate entertainment.[16]

Poet's Pub weaves a complicated and unlikely story out of conventional elements; it is a breathless and absurd business, and very, very funny. The complexity of the comic narrative owes something to the kind of plot devised by P. G. Wodehouse, and the dialogue bears resemblance to that of Wodehouse, with touches of Firbank, Huxley and the young Evelyn Waugh—though as *Decline and Fall* had appeared only a few months earlier, and Eric had probably had no time to see it, let alone be influenced by it, the resemblance is coincidental. Influences are anyway hard to trace. When Waugh condemned Tony Last to the fate of being forced to read interminably from the novels of Charles Dickens, had he any recollection in his mind of the 'boy in Arizona once who tamed a whole camp by reading "Peter Bell" to them', described by Professor van Buren in *Poet's Pub* fifteen years earlier? Eric had probably read some of the young Aldous Huxley, and shared with him his delight in the Peacockian conversation-piece; the literate and philosophical exchanges of the characters in *Poet's Pub* are often of a similar kind.

The book is not memorable for its story, despite the concern of its author, so much as for its pleasant flavour of wit and enjoyment of life. Eric's comments were sometimes mildly satirical, but his observation was usually far too genial and delighted to impress readers with any sense of an attack on human abuses; rather he wrote about human weakness with a sort of joyous and sympathetic recognition, as if laughter alone were the true medicine for the ills of mankind. If one word sums him up at this point of his career, it must be 'celebratory'. In *Poet's Pub* the diversity of human characters and appetites is celebrated in no uncertain terms. The violent and macabre are allowed but a small place, just a reminder in the background that the world can be grotesque and terrifying.

Poet's Pub is a novel that celebrates, even if at times a little ruefully, the poetic instinct, and much of its authorial reflection, as well as that of its characters, is about poetry and the difficulties for the poet who disapproves of the modern tendency towards doom, gloom and obscurity. It celebrates the literary heritage and the delights of food and drink, combining both interests in a chapter describing a gargantuan Elizabethan meal at Saturday Keith's pub, the Pelican.

> Set with the ordered profusion of England's Golden Age, the table already gleamed with fruit, strawberries and cherries and plums and peaches, and sugar-plums and ginger; and jumbals and marchpane and suckets of one kind or another added variety to their happy display. These were not considered or noticed in the menu, which read simply:
>
>
>
> *Salad*
> *Kickshawses*
> *Stewed Pike*
> *Roast Sucking-Pig*
> *Olive Pie*
> *Roast Capons*
> *Marrowbone Pie*
>
>
>
> ... It was notable that although many had exclaimed at the solid substance of the menu, few failed to go steadily through it ... The young man who had spoken in favour of wife-beating was apparently bent on growing big enough to achieve his ambition.[17]

Throughout the book Eric shows a constant pleasure in English manners, English character, English institutions imperfect though they are, and in English literature. Above all, *Poet's Pub* celebrates the pleasures of language both in narration and talk. Eric's extremely wide-ranging vocabulary, with its occasional unexpected rarity or technicality ('The policeman wiped his moustache with the back of his hand. It was a proleptic gesture') or medically learned flavour ('He kissed the upper border of her left trapezius muscle'), varies from the precise and simple to the romantic and orotund, always with well-calculated effect. The snatches of conversation, the amorous exchanges, the literary and philosophical debates are all full of wit and surprises, and at their fullest recall Peacock in *Headlong Hall*; it was a mode to which Eric would occasionally return, most notably in *Laxdale Hall* after the war.

Though *Poet's Pub* was to some extent a deliberate exercise in farce, it is not without its moments of genuine and moving humanity. The love-relationships between its poet-hero and Joan Benbow, and between Quentin Cotton and Nelly Bly, are observed with some gentleness. Nelly's vivid imagination and ability to cobble immediate stories to explain her actions make her something of a forerunner of Henry Tippus in *The Sailor's Holiday*. Her wonderfully comic parody of a Russian political tragedy in tone and setting is related to a trio of short stories Eric wrote a year or two later called 'The Revolution'. She reappears in *Magnus Merriman*, but without the vitality and individuality that makes her the most provocative woman in *Poet's Pub*, where, despite the absurdity of the action, she is sufficiently real and vulnerable at times to move the reader to care. In this sense she is typical of a feature of the whole novel, which is that it does not wholly conform to a type, but has in its texture enough of Eric's individual outlook and control to make it interesting on different levels. It is a very entertaining book, and it is not surprising that Allen Lane should have found it an acceptable offering from Cape for his first ever group of Penguin paperbacks in 1935. But it would be wrong to dismiss it as *mere* entertainment. Like the early novels of Huxley and Waugh, it plays in the world, it jokes and sports a polished and sophisticated surface; a commentator suggested that: 'Mr Linklater in *Poet's Pub* reminds one of a good swimmer playing in the surf with tremendous glee'[18]; but there is in the novel also a too beautifully defined and serious love of life for it to be seen as just a funny book.

Eric felt in tackling his third novel that he had in some way come into his own. Andrew Rutherford, pointing out that all three of his volumes of autobiography are to a significant extent travel books, says:

> By temperament he was more akin to Tennyson's Ulysses ('I cannot rest from travel: I will drink/ Life to the lees') than to the dull but dutiful Telemachus ... Descended from seafarers and farmers on both his father's and his mother's side, he shied away from the life-style of the bourgeoisie. Indeed in several of his early novels we find him toying imaginatively with alternatives—the life of a perpetual student, a poet-publican, a Bohemian author, an Orkney farmer, or in a former age a Viking. But the perfect vehicle for his restlessness, his anarchic aspirations, his delight in life's variety, was provided by the picaresque novel, a traditional form which he realises in *Juan in America*.[19]

Even as he wrote Eric felt that what he was now doing was more important than his earlier attempts. Certainly *Juan in America* made a tremendous splash, and its success transformed his life. Its extraordinary vitality can still be felt, and although the America about which he was writing has disappeared, the book's feeling for and presentation of a whole way of life still seems miraculously vivid. Looking back on it, Eric wrote:

> *Juan in America* is a historical novel, and describes a country and a society which were vanishing even as I left them ... I wrote it open-eyed, with delight, and with total acceptance of what I saw, with little animadversion on the scenes I described except, perhaps, after I had watched, in Detroit, the helpless agent of

an insensate government destroying good whisky on the quays. About that I felt very deeply, as was right and proper ... [The book] presents an accurate picture of North America in its brief heyday of remedial crime and sentimental well-being: 'We have seen the American people create a new heaven and a new earth,' wrote Calvin Coolidge, and the bootleggers did their best to substantiate his words ... *Juan* reflects the country in which Coolidge lived and believed, and deserves a place, now, on a library shelf beside Mark Twain's *Life on the Mississippi*. In the acceleration of time it is almost as far behind us, and quite as true.[20]

The inspiration which gave a shape to what Eric wanted to write about America came from Byron, whose statue outside the school had long been a symbol to him of where literary enterprise might take him. In *Don Juan* Byron had sent his hero through many trials and tribulations half-way across the world, affording himself a perfect opportunity for satirical comment on the world. Eric had already imitated his style in university poems; it now occurred to him to take a descendant of Don Juan to the wondrous New World he had been observing. He actually thought at first of doing it in Byronic stanzas, or so he said, but

having begun to take a pleasure in the looser and more variable rhythms of prose, and flinching when it came to the point of finding thirty thousand rhymes, I unhorsed the infant poem in its first canto and bade it walk.[21]

He may have had other models in mind. His tone and attitude sometimes recall that of Montesquieu in the *Lettres Persanes*, or of Goldsmith in *The Citizen of the World*; in moments of rather more pointed irony or of more grotesque perceptions, the reader might be reminded of Swift in at least the earlier chapters of *Gulliver's Travels*. And while the Byronic inspiration is undeniable, it might be felt that Eric's attitude is less severe and more accepting, more prepared to enjoy what he sees than his predecessor, and that Lewis Carroll's approach in *Alice in Wonderland* was quite possibly just as influential. There is a tendency for action and description in *Juan in America* to become fantastic, and the writing is certainly imbued with a sense of wonder.

There are further flavours which might be mentioned. Commentators were reminded of the celebratory style and jovial humour of Rabelais, with the specially joyous touch of his Scottish translator, of whom Eric wrote with great approval years later when living in Easter Ross:

To the south, through a little wood carefully cleared, we saw the lights of Cromarty, the native place of the fantastical Sir Thomas Urquhart, who had been born in that quiet corner to write so noisily: to translate Rabelais, and die of laughter.[22]

Others thought that Eric's vision of the United States had affinities with that of James Thurber, or saw elements in his handling of language that reminded them of Beckett. There is a Dickensian relish and virtuosity in the conception and projection of many of the characters. But the reader is likely, above all, to think of Candide and his adventures. Eric had a considerable admiration for Voltaire, bringing him into one of the philosophical radio pieces written later in the early years of the Second World War as well as making him an important character in his play, *Crisis in Heaven*. Candide passes from crisis to crisis and disaster to disaster, more or less unaffected by what he sees, losing acquaintances and later meeting them again quite accidentally, his gaze perpetually wide and astonished, his innocence more or less unsullied. Juan's setbacks are somewhat less horrendous, his laughter more frequently moved, but his passage through the New World does not change him much, and what we see by following his adventures never ceases to amaze.

Juan in America, then, is a modern picaresque, following in a notable tradition. It is given shape by its particular relationship with Byron's *Don Juan*. The 'Prologue' gives Juan's genealogical history, complete with family tree, tracing his descent from the original Don Juan through five generations. Far from being the weakest part of the novel, the Prologue is a delightful introduction to the book. Paralleling the similar though less extended opening of Byron's poem, it is a concentrated family saga full of witty historical perceptions and urbane comment, so beautifully written that it is worth an essay to itself; John MacRitchie called it 'English social history as it should be writ'.[23] It performs valuable functions within *Juan in America*. Both in content and in style it establishes a tone of mellow enjoyment and subtle comment, an attitude towards the material, which accounts for much of the effect of the novel. It establishes a character for the wandering hero, compact of Andalusian fire and English reticence; Juan's traditional Englishness provides an important contrast to his American experiences, with each seen more ironically because of its jux-taposition with the other. And in the style—assured, humorous, tolerant, linguistically individual—there is a preparation for the richness and variety of the rest of the novel.

Juan Motley, unlike his illustrious predecessor though not unlike his creator, is less grandly successful in his amours, and more prone to ludicrous accident. Juan has the eyes through which the reader sees North America, but the perceptions are mediated through an attitude more ready to celebrate than to censure. There are moments where serious points are made tellingly with a dry economy or with a kind of romantic grandeur, but there is no personal animus. Authorial comment is lacking; it would be superfluous when the characters are allowed so skilfully to say and do the things by which their folly is manifest.

Eric was surprised by the hostility shown towards his book by some Americans who accused him of betraying his hosts. It is a book which offers an attractive vision of America, gloriously daft though parts of it are made to seem. Criticism of it because it was once offensive to some Americans seems over-sensitive and unjustified. A new generation of Americans would read the novel with enormous delight.

Although accepting basically the episodic nature of the picaresque novel, Eric looked for an element of conventional narrative structure, giving the story rather more of a plot than Byron had troubled himself with. The story mechanism requires several coincidences to occur, and allows characters to disappear from the action only to turn up again later, as in a type of story at least as old as *The Faerie Queene.* The book ends inconclusively as Juan moves on again, this time to catch up with a Chinese girl who has caught his eye. While appearing to adopt a structured plot-line, the novel actually shrugs off any such straitjacket and remains true to the picaresque type. The conclusion takes place when the writer has not so much told the story he set out to tell as said all he has to say about the country and the society under his microscope.

At the end the reader is not sure whether Juan's new pursuit of the Chinese woman is just a reinforcement of the author's sense of something lacking, something plastic and mass-produced, about the average American woman, or whether it portends another story in which China is similarly examined. Cape and Garnett both thought this might be an excellent idea:

> The merit of *Juan* is that you wrote about America, not about seduction, and if you take him to Spain and Italy and Germany, you will write about them, and not about the commonplace—very much the same wherever you go—of tackling a girl on a Spanish, Italian or German pillow. You've made a good start with a well-written, well-contrived set of adventures for a *picaro* of a sort who can go wherever he chooses, and I think you should give him his head.

At the time Eric intended no such thing and, though he was later to have some regrets about his decision on financial grounds, he rejected their advice that he should capitalise on his formula. He wanted to do something different; the idea of attempting to repeat a success with another book in the same manner was anathema to his restless spirit. But the opportunity was there; perhaps subconsciously he had built into the end of *Juan in America* an excuse for a future excursion half-way round the world.

There is, of course, as acknowledged in Eric's description of *Juan in America* as 'a historical novel', a documentary element in the book. This was partly why it was so popular. It appealed immediately to a public that had a huge and comparatively unexploited interest in America, whetted by newspaper reports and the ceaseless flow of films across the Atlantic. Eric's book supplied the need in most gratifying form, presenting a vivid picture of an almost lunatic but highly attractive republic. Prohibition and its associated crimes, the excesses of American university courses and the dominating place in the university culture of brutal and incomprehensible sports, American entertainment including the music-hall and the magical world of Hollywood, American practices in the arts of love and marriage, politics and the inauguration of Presidents, death and the organisation of funerals, society and the treatment of minorities, the vastness and the variety, the beauty and romance of the American continent and its peoples, a thousand new revelations of the American way of life, all teemed invitingly in more than four hundred pages.

It might very possibly have been a bestseller even had it been far less well written; but the sensational details were filtered through the consciousness of an unusually imaginative observer, and the book merits consideration as a major literary achievement because of the qualities in its writing. To reject *Juan in America* because it is documentary would be as wide of the mark as to reject *Ulysses* because it is no more than a guidebook to Dublin. Eric admired *Ulysses* greatly; he wrote of it: 'Joyce, the Irish demi-urge, compounded of Dublin gossip the heroic and comic nonesuch of our age'.[24] But he chose not to write his own nonesuch in the Modernist way. Not for him the modern experimentation with streams of consciousness, invented languages, alternative punctuation, Freudian psychology or any of the associated phenomena. He remained devoted to the principles with which he had begun, where what mattered was craftsmanship and where the highest criterion was clarity. The very considerable pleasure to be gained from reading Linklater derives in great measure from his mastery of language. Though it flows on the page with the appearance of absolute ease and appropriateness, his control of language was painfully and deliberately cultivated. In his own account:

> I am a laborious worker, and must worry myself into a state of pernicious excitement before I can write with an appearance of ease. I have an active imagination, and in a modest way am capable of invention. I have also an interest in words which is like an honest carpenter's interest in wood. Bring together these two conditions, and you have a novelist condemned to work. Rapture, I said. The finding, development and first rough shaping of an idea are among the most compulsive and overwhelming pleasures under the sun. But then comes work. Then comes the finer shaping, the forcing into a pattern, the bending of thought, the discarding of words, the comparing of two good words to find the better. This is labour, and the brain will take heat like a blacksmith's iron in a blown fire, and the heat may sometimes, about midnight, engender a paragraph that gives a little pleasure to the novelist before he stumbles in to bed. But in the morning he must blot and banish and scribble anew. Hard labour.[25]

Though *Juan in America* is a work of considerable sociological interest, as so many novels are, it is not a sociological treatise. There is a heady mixture of comic tones (some of a decidedly darker shade), romantic visions and earthy philosophy; the language is an inexhaustible treasury of felicities in precision, unexpectedness and variety of vocabulary, in tone control and rhythmic subtlety, and in a wonderful profusion of images.

If the epithet 'Linklaterian' has no currency in common parlance, one might well wonder why not. Despite the great number of other writers invoked at various times to account for elements in Eric's style, one thing is clear: that he was his own man. *Juan in America* established him, as *White-Maa's Saga* and *Poet's Pub* had promised, as a writer distinguishable by the way he wrote from any predecessor or contemporary. Fauré wrote that 'Art has every right to be voluptuous and to have as its central aim the giving of pleasure'; with this the author of *Juan in America* would certainly have agreed. But the pleasure Eric gives is peculiar to him.

There is, for instance, the observation and recording within the comic mode of the dark side of life. One of the first things witnessed by Juan in New York is a suicide.

> At this moment Juan saw, no more than ten yards in front of him, a body tumbling through the air. It went into many shapes in its rapid descent, and fell on the outer edge of the pavement with a loud horrible noise like the bursting of a very large paper bag. Immediately a crowd collected with cries of terror and interest.[26]

This happens just as Juan has been considering how the modern art of photography, by showing pictures of everything, has robbed us of the capacity for surprise: 'I can't feel astonishment,' he thinks, 'for I have seen it all before at the cinema and in the illustrated papers.' His thought is rapidly shown to be wrong, though; when the girl throws herself from a high window to his feet he can scarcely believe it. A little man, Isadore Cohen, bobs out of the crowd and explains how it probably happened; it happens all the time. By the time the explanation is complete they have arrived in Central Park, where they witness the 'Himalayan consummation' of the love of the two yaks; Izzy is as unsurprised by this as he was by the suicide and Juan, looking on in Candide-like wonder, considers him a companion to be cultivated.

This touch of dispassion, if not cruelty, in Eric's narration, is not untypical. In a similar cool, dispassionate way Eric tells, in the Prologue, of the effects of an outbreak of smallpox in the family in 1800:

> The lubberly little Earl of Spoon was left with a face like a colander, and his mother, poor lady, was no better. All his brothers and sisters were hideously scarred and the infant William Edward survived with no eyebrows and very little nose.

Details are presented with curious medical accuracy:

6 Eric with Billy 'Pin-leg' Robertson, the Bible-thumping neighbour of the Linklaters at Ingleneuk (later enlarged as Merkister) in Orkney

7 Merkister, overlooking the Loch of Harray, Orkney—the Linklaters' home from 1934 to 1946. To the right is The Cottage, where Eric's mother and, later, his sister Elspeth lived

8 Eric (*r*) with Compton Mackenzie (the first Scottish Nationalist Rector of Glasgow University) at the National Mòd in Fort William, 1932

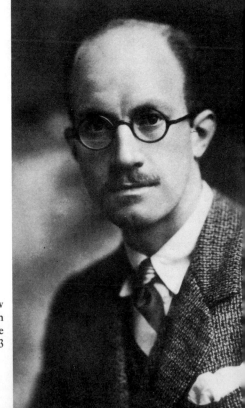

9 Aspiring politician: Eric in November 1932, a few months before he contested, unsuccessfully, as Scottish Nationalist candidate in the East Fife by-election, February 1933

Mr Motley lost an eye and round the vacant orbit clustered a number of lesser foramina.

As if this were not enough he extends and concentrates the horrors, until, perhaps, the very weight of descriptions counters any possible response of pity on the reader's part:

> Pitted and perforated like honeycomb was the row of faces that gathered at last in the vicarage pew to give thanks for their delivery. As tunelessly they sang their hymns it seemed that the pious sound escaped from a score of orifices in each pockmarked visage.[27]

Eric looks hard and with interest at what he sees, the frequent use of precise medical terms adding a sense of scientific detachment. An account of a gunfight in a speakeasy shows how his apparently objective stance sometimes leads to macabre flights of fancy as an idea is developed. A stray bullet smashes an aquarium tank above the head of the intended victim, a gangster known as Wonny the Weeper:

> It hit, indeed, the globular gaping fish that had so long and stupidly stared into the smoky room. Wonny disappeared under the deluge of water and broken glass and the unexpected draught of fishes, and the bullet-struck fish, its silver skin laced with its golden blood, lay on the floor unseen. Its shining plump companions flopped and wriggled beside it, drowning in the hot air of the speakeasy, trampled on by the panic-feet of the men they had seen so often and so uncomprehendingly. Their fishy eyes stiffened into dead jelly, and their silver mail was broken on the floor where customers had thrown the butts of their cigarettes. So, killed astonishingly by a gangster, one by one the silver fishes died, far from the cold native silence of their sea and the jungle softness of waving weed, and the white labyrinthine shelter of coral reefs. And by-and-by a policeman spoke their epitaph in blasphemy as he trod on one, and slipped, and fell bluntly to the wet floor.[28]

This extraordinary passage, with the literary echoes of 'draught of fishes' and 'silver skin laced with its golden blood', the bizarre image of a fish killed by a gangster, the sympathetic extension to the plight of the fish far removed by man from their native haunts, and the uncompromising earthy realism of the conclusion, is Linklaterian. And while it might seem odd to talk of tragedy in reference to the death of a fish (whose demise is dealt with much more fully than that of the man who also perished in the affray), nevertheless it points to an element in Eric's writing which grew more notable as his career developed. He was, where discussed at all, usually described as a light or comic novelist. David Daiches referred to him as:

> a novelist of enormous talent who has remained content to be one of the best comic novelists of the day, but whose wit, imagination and sense of life have always seemed to promise more than that.[29]

Eric's answer to that kind of comment was:

> I have always thought—well, as long as I can remember—that the comic
> attitude to life is just as valid as the tragic attitude. In fact it's probably more
> valid, because tragedy ends in death and with comedy you've got to go on living
> ... In ancient Greece, which set the standard for all things, comedy and tragedy
> were regarded on the same plane, of equal validity as criticism, as comment on
> life.[30]

His all-embracing idea of comedy included the tragic or potentially tragic,
just as Shakespeare's did. Comedy after all is an attitude towards things,
not the thing itself. Comedy depends, as tragedy does, upon disaster. In
the comic view, you either avert the disaster or recover from it or live to
understand that it didn't matter so much after all. Great minds before the
twentieth century have mixed the genres in one way or another; but for
Thomas Mann one of the most striking features of *modern* art was that:

> It has ceased to recognise the categories of tragic and comic, or the dramatic
> classifications, tragedy and comedy. It sees life as tragi-comedy, with the result
> that the grotesque is its most genuine style.[31]

Thomas Mann might have been writing about the work of Eric Linklater
when he said that, and in this sense, if in no other, Eric can be seen as in his
way a Modernist, despite his own preference for seeing himself as a
traditional *makar*.

There are solemnities in *Juan in America* which are neither grotesque
nor tragic, but rather moments of philosophical insight, pauses for reflection. Of such a nature is the sympathetic consideration of the life of the
poor black inhabitants of South Carolina who rescue Juan from the floods:

> Indeed somebody was singing nearly all the time; not always a full-length song,
> but perhaps half a dozen words to which a few casual notes were given ... Their
> laughter too was a pleasant thing to hear. It had much in common with their
> songs, being rich and mellow in sound uncontrollable as hunger, natural as
> thirst ... This, it might be argued, was the result of forcibly transplanting a
> people from one continent to another, using them in slavery for several genera-
> tions, and then bestowing on them a nominal freedom and a position beyond
> the pale of society. They had neither past nor future, no memories of greatness
> and no excuse for ambition.[32]

The overall impression left by the book, however, is of the sunniest high
spirits and of life being relished in all its oddness and richness by a gifted
and infectiously enthusiastic celebrant. Eric's joy in life's possibilities is
perhaps most markedly evident in an incident at the beginning of Book V.
Juan is flying to California with a friend when, above New Mexico, their
light plane is caught in an electrical storm and destroyed by lightning.
They have to take to their parachutes. Initially Juan is terrified, but the

experience turns into something so marvellous that he finds himself shouting with excited laughter:

> Then he sailed down comfortably, blown by the wind, swinging like a pendulum, but scarcely conscious of downward movement except through his eyes, for he saw the clouds go up past him and lightning dance under his feet that did not stay for him to tread upon it...
>
> He plunged into a giant bed of cumulus that swallowed him alive, and as he laughed, deep belly-laughs, he sucked in cloud and blew out great gusts of smoke. Under the cloud was a greenish ocean with a purple floor and billowing canvas walls. Lightning darted across and across it ... He laughed again, shaking in his harness, to think that he, an atom vulnerable at all points, a thing of fragile bones, a coil of guts and two quarts of blood packed in a tenuous envelope of skin, should ride the air and—if he cared to—break wind against thunder in its native place. He did. O potent humanity! O brave and splendid man, that could take Leviathan upon a hook, and fill the empyrean with his songs, and leap the Equator like a skipping-rope, and dance above Aurora Borealis![33]

Neither Juan nor the general tone is always so confident, or so full of Rabelaisian delight, but the final effect of the book is to make the reader as grateful to the writer as Juan felt towards his maker for inventing the parachute.

Despite the warm reception given to *Juan in America* by its first reviewers, and the long period of fame and popularity which it enjoyed (for it remained in print for more than thirty years), it was never to join the select company of novels warranting critical discussion in academic circles. Francis Russell Hart thought *Juan in America* one of the highest points in Eric's career, and he quoted the approval of Eric's Rabelaisian talent expressed by Sydney Goodsir Smith in his Kirkcaldy Lectures of 1947 where he

> placed *Juan in America* in the tradition of the goliardic folk tales, associated its satire with Dunbar and its wit with Byron, and found it almost the equivalent in prose—albeit English prose—of MacDiarmid's *A Drunk Man Looks at the Thistle.*[34]

In a recent essay Andrew Rutherford referred to *Juan in America* as a comic masterpiece which

> engages very directly with 'the realities of life' in its affectionate, amused, at times almost anthropological scrutiny of the American way of life ... The novel is a *tour de force* of comedy, combining the potentially conflicting elements of the anarchic, the satiric and the celebratory.[35]

That these remarks represent virtually all the serious criticism of the novel that exists suggests a curious blindness in the halls where decisions are made about literary greatness.

After the excitement of the publication of *Juan in America*, Eric turned back to his book on Ben Jonson with renewed energy. The summer was coming on, and he had finished his reading in the library at Aberdeen University, so he went home to his mother's house in Orkney to complete the work and the endless associated tasks which he had not anticipated: the provision of suitable illustrations, a bibliography and, worst of all, an index. As it was too early to fish very seriously he was able to concentrate; as he wrote to Mrs Walker:

> As my interest in duck-pens and incubation is rather painfully limited (but do not mention this to the ancient Elizabeth*) I have few distractions. And work is a grand thing when there's nothing else to do.

All went well, and by the middle of May he was able to tell Cape:

> Ben is wearing towards his last chapters, and unless I get aphasia he ought to be jabbed in the solar plexus with a last full stop about the end of the month.

He had by this time developed a tremendous empathy with the subject of his biography, and was so soaked in the Elizabethan and Jacobean matters and manners that he hardly knew which century he was living in. He later called the book he wrote 'opulent, empurpled', an inevitable consequence, he felt, of the bathing in the heady waters of Elizabethan English for so long. His enthusiasm for the project is plain in a letter he wrote to Miss Atkinson at Cape's to help write a blurb for the book:

> Ben was not at all the sort of person people think. The popular view—if there is one, which I doubt—is that he was a dull, pedantic, bad-tempered, scholastic person. Nothing could be farther from the truth. He was a tremendous fellow, with a genius for good-fellowship, and made taverns famous for his patronage of them. He knew everybody, and those who were worthy of his friendship thought the world of him. People who were jealous or frightened of him—he was rather a swashbuckler—hated him like blazes and slandered him. But the best people of the time were his friends—Shakespeare, Donne, Beaumont, Raleigh, Cotton, the Countess of Bedford, Lady Rutland, King James (a *really* learned, humorous old cove whose ill-repute is mainly due to his having been a peace-maker, which is always unpopular in England) . . .
>
> And then his plays: people who have never read them suppose they're dull and difficult. Some of them are. But the best of them are surprisingly modern in tone—much more suited to modern reading than most plays of the time— and *The Alchemist* is probably the best pure comedy in the language. *Bartholomew Fair* is roaring comedy—and there's lovely poetry in the masques, which are almost entirely neglected and absolutely unknown except to a few academical fellows—and me, who once tried to be academical, and failed.

---

* i.e. his mother.

The work on Jonson and his era was to have significant consequences for Eric. The tie with King James redirected his interest to Scottish history and affairs, and helped him on his way towards the deep involvement in Scotland that was to characterise his next few years and ultimately the work of his old age. The focus on the Jacobean theatre required by the book reinvigorated his own theatrical ambitions, and set him at intervals to writing plays as if no medium of communication could be more important; twenty years later he would actually write an updated version of *The Alchemist* to be produced at the Edinburgh International Festival. The scholarly image which the book helped give him (for the next decade or so almost all his journalistic pieces would carry the by-line 'by the brilliant young Scottish author') would be exploited in various ways, in writing and in broadcasting. And the professional writer in him would see the sense and practicality of alternating novels with biographies or, later, other kinds of non-fiction writing, until books of one kind or another would appear annually or more frequently from his pen. The year 1931 really saw the birth of the Eric Linklater who knew that he could earn a satisfactory living from his writing, and the next months were full of flurry as he turned in various directions to put his talent to work.

He was driven almost mad by the detailed work necessary in the compilation of the bibliographical apparatus and index for his book. Playfully he asked Wren Howard: 'God help us all, do you mind if I invent a few authorities?' and later, on delivering the index, said: 'I'd rather pick oakum than do another.' Apart from these irritations he enjoyed the Orkney summer greatly. Isobel Walker and her ornithologist husband Charlie visited in July, and Eric wrote to her mother describing the arrangements he had made to entertain them:

> I don't know anything about birds, of course, but I've discovered where some unlikely ones live and tentatively arranged a hairy expedition to go and look at them. This involves spending the hours of darkness on a hijus barren rock set in the midst of a fierce tideway ... The stormy petrel—which lives a lonely life—carries with it a distinctive odour of decay. So some dark night this coming week Charles and I will spend the dusky hours, girt in with horrid cliffs and the fearsome noises of the sea, crawling about on our hands and knees snuffling up rabbit holes to see if any stormy petrels have lately lodged there.

A week or two later he sailed on the MV *Stella Polaris* to Norway for a short spell, to have a look round the land of his spiritual ancestors. Whether he was already turning over in his mind the idea of writing a Viking story, or whether it was inspired during his holiday in Scandinavia, cannot now be established, but there was another unexpected outcome from the visit. On the boat he had met Frank du Pont, a wealthy American businessman who was as enthusiastic as Eric about the delights of travel and talk, and they concocted a plan to sail around the world together. Eric

returned to Orkney to complete his Jonson index thinking that the projected circumnavigation was just one of those lovely ideas that never come
to anything, but du Pont, he learned a few weeks later, had meant what he
said.

Meanwhile, the date set for the publication of *Ben Jonson and King James*
arrived, and the handsome new book was in the shops. Eric excitedly sent a
copy to Isobel, describing it as 'that laughter-rousing and irresistibly
hilarious masterpiece of biography entitled *Ben Jonson and Queen Boadicea*,
by Annie S. Swan and G. Bernard Shaw'. Another copy went to Miss
Marris Murray, younger sister of his friend Douglas Walker's wife, in
Aberdeen; he did not yet know her very well, but he had seen her emerging
from girlhood into womanhood with some admiration.

Except for a snooty response in *The Times Literary Supplement*, the
reviews of his biography were quite pleasing; unfortunately Eric had to
read them in hospital, for his visceral illness had laid him low once more in
early October. From the Knowles Health Hydro and Dietetic Establishment in Hastings he explained to Douglas:

> A few weeks ago the symptoms of my year-old protein (or proteid—I never
> remember which is which) poisoning began to reappear, and I had heard that
> this place did a more drastic sort of cure, so *tout d'un coup*, I shot down here . . .
> These quack places are much more impressive, more dramatic, than a bottle of
> medicine. For instance, I've just come off a 48-hour fast, and now I'm eating
> stale bread, and nothing but stale bread.

The cure produced the desired effect, perhaps aided by a note from du
Pont asking him to sail with him to New York in mid-November, ready to
embark on their voyage round the world. Frank—or Frank's business
expenses account—would be taking care of the price of the ticket. Eric told
Wren Howard:

> I'm on the verge of a rather comical and altogether improbable adventure,
> which begins by sailing to New York on the 11th, so I shall have to provide
> myself with some moneys . . .

Howard arranged for there to be $300 waiting for Eric in the bank in
New York. The biography, however, had barely sold 1,000 copies yet;
fortunately *Juan in America* continued to do well, so there would be more
money in due course. Eric set off eagerly for the States again, enjoying a
rough crossing aboard the German ship *Europa* which

> like a shapely ness divided the storm, and through four days of frenzied seas
> showed no more unsteadiness than the solemn titubation of a well-trained
> butler with most of the decanter in his wame.[36]

Unfortunately for their plans, Frank du Pont was now involved in
unexpected extra work when his business partner suddenly died. Eric

visited his old friends the Gilkysons again and, now fêted as a successful author, had a good time. He met Owen Wister, and was taken by Emily Balch to call upon Sinclair Lewis, but, the Nobel prize-winner being in bed, Eric spent instead a pleasant evening with Lewis's wife, Dorothy Thompson.[37] Eric had taken very much to du Pont and was disappointed when he found that his intended travelling companion would not be able to travel after all. He wrote:

> Frank was not merely rich but a millionaire and probably more ... He showed none of the alleged deformities of wealth, save abstinence, perhaps, and a small unnecessary collection of watches ... I was sorry indeed to say goodbye, and regarded with much diminished pleasure the ticket that he gave me—a ticket from Sandy Hook to the Grand Central by way of the Pyramids and Angkor Wat.[38]

But life aboard the S S *Empress of Britain* without Frank proved not to be supportable. Eric explained to Wren Howard:

> I've got among agèd wealth and dull respectability—so I'm quitting before contagious senile inertia descends upon me. Middle-aged whoopee? No, Sir!

and in his autobiography:

> Having gone shopping meekly with the throng, in Madeira, Gibraltar and Algiers, I was so weak as to regard with foreboding the prospect of similar excursions in Cairo and Colombo, in Bali and Borneo—in Luxor and Lucknow, Hong-Kong and Hawaii, and all round the world—so in a great hurry I deserted the circumnavigators in Monte Carlo, and momentarily was in worse straits than before.
>
> I had eleven dollars and a letter of credit, but for some reason my letter of credit was unacceptable in Monaco, and eleven dollars insufficient to take me home. There was, however, the Casino, and after some debate I played, with the utmost modesty, a little roulette, and was so happy as to make on Numéro Treize enough to pay my hotel bill and buy a second-class ticket to London.[39]

There followed a busy but largely unproductive two or three months in London, where Eric succumbed to the blandishments of those who assured him that he would benefit from keeping his newly famous face before the public. He took a flat in New Cavendish Street and began a hectic round of making friends and contacts, seeing society, and making some money from occasional journalistic forays into the pages of the daily papers. For several weeks he maintained a salaried post as a columnist for the *Daily Express*, writing as a young innocent or Juan-figure exploring London for the first time. Though he had been offered the freedom of its columns, he soon became annoyed by the extent to which his words were being edited and modified by the management. He also undertook to review new novels for the *Listener*, starting in February 1932. This was a happier though arduous task in which he continued punctiliously for a year, and the reader who would know more about the attitudes and opinions of Eric Linklater on the subject of literature could hardly do better than to start by reading his reviews of almost one hundred novels during that period.

It was quite a good year for novels. He did not of course refer to his own *The Men of Ness*, but among those of which he did write were Huxley's *Brave New World* ('a satire fierce enough for Swift'); J. B. Priestley's *Faraway*; Walpole's *The Fortress*; Lewis Grassic Gibbon's *Sunset Song* ('He has contrived a style that conveys a Scottish rhythm and flavour with singular fidelity, and a style, moreover, that is capable of accommodating beauty, bluntness and humour'); *Cold Comfort Farm* ('a scandalous burlesque, wickedly funny and extraordinarily clever'); Anthony Powell's *Venusberg*; Julia Strachey's *Cheerful Weather for the Wedding*; Graham Greene's *Stamboul Train*; Harold Nicolson's *Public Faces* ('brilliant comedy'); Edwin Muir's *Poor Tom*; and Waugh's *Black Mischief* ('Mr Waugh has wit, and that is a species of gallantry that may defeat the foulest circumstance . . . His narrative is swift and picturesque, and his cutting—if one may borrow a Hollywood term—is masterly'). Eric was an almost uniformly kindly and enthusiastic reviewer, who found good qualities somewhere in most of the books he read; very seldom did he wax waspish, and he must have forsworn altogether the use of the hatchet. There was no shortage of witty generalisations and perceptive particularities in his essays, but the pervasive sense of warmth and good humour which characterised his responses would no doubt suggest to some literary commentators a lack of intellectual penetration and the true critical spirit. Eric, as he grew older, may have been sometimes more than a little moody and irascible, but there was never a more essentially kind-hearted man, and his reviews showed it.

He eventually handed his reviewer's baton on to Edwin Muir with the excuse that he needed more time for his new involvement in politics. He had enjoyed his stint, and had been glad of the occasional chance to do his publishers a good turn by approving the work of some of the Cape authors—for Wren Howard did not hesitate to send him new Cape titles from time to time. One of them, *Touch and Go* by Barbara Starke, led to Eric's meeting the attractive young American author, and for a few months they found themselves affectionately disposed to each other—though mostly separated by three thousand miles of ocean.

Eric's flurry of journalistic activities in the spring of 1932 led to his forming a wide circle of acquaintances in London's literary world. Some of them were Scots, such as Moray McLaren at the BBC, with whom he was to form a lifelong friendship. His description in *Fanfare for a Tin Hat* of how he dined with Beaverbrook, discussed politics with the young Randolph

Churchill, and went with Edward Garnett to visit Mr and Mrs Sean O'Faolain in Richmond, gives an indication of the kind of life he led for a while, as does a sentence from one of his letters to Isobel Walker:

> I would fain write more, but I am weary, for two men—a very respectable critic who writes only for the *most* highbrow papers; and a worthy American publisher—returned with me from a party last night and sat here, varnishing their gastric membranes and talking of this and that, till nearly five o'clock this morning.

Such late-night (or virtually all-night) sittings over glasses and rattling larynxes were to become one of his greatest pleasures, especially after, towards the end of the year, he met Compton Mackenzie and recognised a profound affinity for him.

There were also endless problems to be settled in his business life as he wooed publishers in the United States, trying to decide between Alfred Knopf and Houghton Mifflin, with confusing advice from Cape descending on him every now and again. In Sweden Norstedts were also anxious to finalise contracts with him to publish translations of *Poet's Pub* and *Juan in America* and the proprietors of various Continental cheap edition houses, Tauchnitz and Albatross, were urging him to release titles to them. Howard warned him to have nothing to do with them, but he was sorely tempted to make some money from such sources if he could.

He was also beginning to get confused about his income tax situation, as well as bewildered by the question of just how much he had been paid and was still owed by Cape. There was nothing for it but to call in an expert adviser, and with great relief he informed Wren Howard in April 1932 that in future his financial affairs would be handled by the Edinburgh solicitor, D. S. Walker. His best friend had agreed to look after his interests for him. Thereafter, though often more than a little out of his depth, he at least felt that someone who cared for him and who knew what he was doing was keeping a watch on things.

For all the activity in which he was engaged, Eric felt he was achieving nothing, and never could in the hustle and bustle of the great city. By being a professional writer he had not intended this mad whirl of ephemeral journalism and social interchanges. He wanted to do great things. Besides, his discussions with McLaren had alerted him to exciting developments on the Scottish scene; the term 'Scottish Renaissance' had been uttered; Eric increasingly felt he might have a role to play in such a revival. Suddenly, in March, he gave up his flat in New Cavendish Street, packed his bags, and caught a train to the north.

10 Scottish Nationalist

Eric's motives for going back to Scotland in the late spring of 1932 were complex. Among them was a desire to escape the superficial rounds of London life, though he recognised the possible consequences; as he later wrote:

> Odd jobs came my way with the frequency invited by physical presence: if you live in New Cavendish Street you get more offers of employment than if you live in one of the remoter parts of Scotland. I could have settled down in London, and made a living there; but I was pinched and prodded by irrational desires.[1]

He had even, comically enough, been a little frightened of the fame that had suddenly descended on him; he claimed to have been somewhat shocked in some puritanical recesses of his soul by the blatant advertising of *Juan in America* on London buses, and to have prayed heartily to be saved from the vulgarity of success. But

> Prayer may be answered, and in my case it was. God showed me favour, and spared me the vulgarity I feared. But in my old age, and even in my late middle age, I have deeply regretted his benignity. For several reasons, some of which were good, I have wanted the money that comes with success, and never got it. I seldom pray nowadays, because I am aware of the attendant perils.[2]

More positive reasons, however, were more important. His mind had been constantly occupied with political matters since his travels in India and the United States. Ever since the General Strike of 1926 he had watched the growth of the Labour Party with interest, and had tried so hard to see their point of view that he had convinced himself that they ought to be given a chance. By now, however, he had become disillusioned, though he clung to the belief that some individual socialists had vision and integrity.

From politics on the grander scale, in which he saw little hope for the betterment of the people, he turned more and more to the plight of Scotland. Talking in London with Moray McLaren and others he was reminded of his own Scottishness, and in his personal subconscious quest for identity a lever moved, a cog turned. The Scottish Nationalists were reported to be gaining strength at a time when there was also something of an embryo literary renaissance in the north, associated with the names of Christopher Grieve (Hugh MacDiarmid), James Leslie Mitchell (Lewis

Grassic Gibbon), Neil M. Gunn, Compton Mackenzie, Naomi Mitchison, Edwin and Willa Muir, Dr O. H. Mavor (James Bridie) and George Blake. Perhaps Eric Linklater of Orkney ought to be among such people, helping to establish a newly potent Scotland.

He had, moreover, in considering the passion for vast uniformity in the States and the growth of huge power blocks in the world generally, been inspired with a personal belief in the exact opposite of what was being preached as salvation for the world. Just as Stanley Baldwin was arguing that large units would be more likely to establish world prosperity and that the creation or re-creation of small units would be a retrogressive step, Eric, anticipating Eugene Schumacher by some thirty years, perceived that 'small was beautiful', and resolved to argue as much publicly with a free Scotland as his particular example. He wrote:

> These general ideas being already in my mind, I heard with excitement the muttering noise in the North that Scottish Nationalists were making and the nurseling cry of what was hopefully described as a literary renaissance.[3]

He arrived back in Edinburgh therefore with some sense of a mission. His general determinations were imprecise, comprising some rather idealistic enthusiasms shared with Moray McLaren and later exemplified with irony in an account of one of their conversations given in *The Man on My Back*.[4] Well fortified with Pernod and champagne, McLaren (here called Meiklejohn) and Eric devised a policy for Scotland based upon a model combining the Court of King James IV with Edinburgh in the eighteenth century, incorporating certain Norse and Celtic values, and ignoring 'the cultural blight of Presbyterianism and the industrial revolution'. They would look to the Continent for trade and cultural exchanges, especially France and Vienna, and would persuade Scotland to be 'national in order to be international'. Eric recognised that there might be inadequacies in these proposals, but considered that at least 'our nationalism had not been born of a narrow provincial spirit. Its only defect, indeed, was a total disregard for the prevailing temper and governing conditions of life in Scotland.'

In Edinburgh, where he lived for a while in the Caledonian Hotel before moving to rooms at 11 Murray Park, St Andrews, his broader notions of what he might do for Scotland were sunk into a more specific undertaking. During his discussions of nationalism, Scottishness, Celticness and so on with McLaren and O'Faolain he had found himself more than once quoting a dictum of the German critic and poet Herder: 'Study the superstitions and the sagas of the forefathers.' That was what Yeats and Synge had done, and by so doing had made a significant contribution to the Irish renaissance at the turn of the century. Eric had from his youth read and loved the sagas of the Norsemen. He had bought, soon after their publication by the Cambridge University Press in 1913, the Craigie and Mawer books, *The Icelandic Sagas* and *The Vikings*; he later acknowledged that they were 'the foundation of my real interest in the North'.[5] Why should he not now, as Herder advised and as Yeats had done, draw on the rich and almost untapped heritage that so excited him, and perhaps, in doing so, unleash a new torrent of energy in the Scottish revival?

His knowledge of Orkney, where the Vikings had raided and ruled, and his sense that he was himself descended from those energetic and vital people, perhaps even from Thorfinn the Mighty himself (a possibility suggested by Storer Clouston), added to his conviction that the idea was a good one. He perceived that

> though life in Orkney had changed from a violent to a most peaceful fashion, my neighbours there retained their fathers' trick of hardy understatement, their taste for irony, for a turn of phrase and a sort of fatalistic humour that often reproduced the very note of saga dialogue.[6]

His reading of the sagas of Burnt Njal, of Laxdale, of Grettir the Strong, of Egil, of the Kings of Norway and of the Earls of Orkney had stocked his mind with stories and linguistic rhythms that he was sure he could successfully use; he reflected:

> No one—at the time of which I am writing—had thought of pillaging the Icelandic sagas for such a tale; but I, who knew several of them, and knew also the temper of Orkney speech which in its habitual understatement often preserved the very tone of the sagas, felt myself entitled to confect a story which could borrow what it needed and declare its originality by enclosing between its beginning and its end an account, in some detail, of a sea-voyage. None of the saga-writers had condescended to such a task. Sea-faring, to the Vikings, was what office-life and office-work are to suburbia in our time, and did not call for description.[7]

With this original and galvanising idea in mind he retired to St Andrews, hired a typewriter, and set to work. As the summer advanced his new novel developed most satisfactorily. By early July he was promising Wren Howard that he should have a glimpse of the first draft within a week or two, and was being asked to supply a proposed blurb for the book. At this stage he had given it the provisional title of *Skallagrim's Ship*. He explained that it was because of his having to type it himself that progress was slower than intended, because 'the intricate nature of my handwriting is still too much for the typist-race to unravel'.

Howard complained that the title wasn't simple enough; he feared that potential readers might be deterred by the outlandish sound of the name 'Skallagrim', and he recalled the difficulties they had faced years before when trying to promote *The Worm Ouroboros*. Eric didn't mind, and suggested *The Men of Westness*—'a good plain blunt name'— or *The*

Unafraid—'which is a bit more dramatic'. He reported, 'As a reviewer of current fiction I'm glad to say that it's quite short—I estimate 75,000 words'. Howard was still not quite satisfied until suddenly he thought of a solution: ' "Westness" is too difficult to say ... Simply *The Men of Ness*; that I think is a title which would remain in the memory—not at all difficult to remember—has a good bold ring about it. What say you?'

Eric was delighted with the suggestion, as he was with Howard's reaction to the typescript a few days later. Howard wrote: 'Congratulations. It is very different from anything else you have done, and yet it seems to me that you have brought it off with complete success.'

Good though he acknowledged the book to be, Howard had his doubts about how it would sell. He didn't think it would go as well as *Juan in America*—'the public may be a little coy at first'. He even suggested that Eric might be advised to accept a reduced advance. With great indignation Eric replied:

> The story gathers strength as it goes on. The manner of it compelled a diffusion of interest at the beginning: the interest is concentrated at the end. And to allow for a steady mounting of drama—which I think you will find—I was obviously compelled to begin in a somewhat flat and cool manner. While I was writing it I was definitely conscious of a growing compulsion, and that, I believe, will in some degree be passed on to the reader ... Its earning power may not be wholly despicable. But in any case—taking the long view—I think I am entitled to the advance stated in the contract.
>
> I take a serious and quite immodest view of my writings. I have plans for years ahead. Those plans include another Juan book (the scheme is almost complete in my head) and a large-scale comedy which may well be popular. But I also want to write several things in a different key, and if you are willing to believe in my 'development' as a writer you will agree the necessity of doing these things. But is it desirable that my immediate source of income be cut while I am in the process of establishing myself as what an American publisher would call 'a real property'?

Howard replied very reasonably and sensibly that a reduced advance would not in fact be a reduction in his income, and that there would be income tax advantages in spreading his earnings from the book over more years than one. And what if the book were to fail? It would be a pity to have to work off a dead book for which he had been overpaid. When one first hears of Howard cannily suggesting a reduced advance in this way one is tempted to recall Rupert Hart-Davis's comment to George Lyttelton:

> Jonathan [Cape] was, in fact, despite my obituary notice, one of the tightest-fisted old bastards I've ever encountered, though his partner Wren Howard is even tighter.[8]

But in this case Howard's motive and instinct appear to have been good, and Eric took his point.

The summer was as usual spent in Ingleneuk in Orkney with his mother, and was peaceful enough, except for some worries about his American publishing, since Cape's venture with Harrison Smith had collapsed. Houghton Mifflin were still dragging their feet after initial interest, and when an offer came from the new firm of Farrar & Rinehart Eric sent Cape a telegram asking for his opinion. Cape advised against:

> They are a young firm, and are very active, and I understand have good capital resources. I scarcely think, however, that they can be making much money.

Farrar & Rinehart were keen enough to keep pressing Eric, and a·week or so later Cape changed his mind and told him he thought he should accept—and ask for a 15 per cent royalty—though he was prepared to have another word with Houghton Mifflin. Eric replied:

> It is very good of you to offer to negotiate American rights for me without commission, and if you can fix anything with H. Mifflin I shall be more than glad for you to do so. But if the agreement falls to Farrar, I think it only fair to M. Joseph to let him negotiate it. He had easy pickings from *Juan* but he has done some comparatively hard work in this new matter, and after all it was from him that I heard of the Farrar offer . . . Curtis Brown have been useful to me in selling some short stories, and quite recently M. Joseph came along with an offer from Peter Davies for a short biography (*c.* 30,000 words) of Mary Queen of Scots for their series. I should like to do this very much. It wouldn't take me long. Have you any objections?

In the event Eric closed with the energetic young John Farrar, and Farrar & Rinehart published all his novels in the United States from then until the Second World War.

During the research he had been doing for *The Men of Ness* Eric had also been working on some lecture material on the sagas, in response to a request from university friends with whom he discussed his progress on his Viking story. He told Cape:

> Among my immediate tasks is the writing of a couple of papers on the sagas which I have to deliver in Aberdeen, Glasgow and St Andrews—so one may start a fashion in northern topics!

This undertaking grew larger, as he described to Howard some weeks later:

> I am continuing to make Scotland Viking-conscious. I told Cape that I was booked to give lectures on the sagas, and now I have been asked to broadcast— early in December—on Norse influences. So we'll all be heaving and hacking with coal-choppers and butchers' cleavers very soon.

He naturally hoped that such activities would result in additional pub- licity for *The Men of Ness* when it appeared in November, but his intrinsic interest in the material attracted the scholar in him, and the personal identification with the Viking forefathers was a tremendous spur. At the same time he perceived the significance of this kind of recovery of the past for the emergent Scottish Nationalist movement, and his reflections on the Norse influences in Scotland were amplified by talks on various other Scottish topics. After a while his friend, the journalist George Malcolm Thomson, who, as one of the founders of the Porpoise Press in Edinburgh, had published *Poobie* for Eric in 1925, suggested that the talks might well be gathered together and issued as a contribution to the Nationalist debate which was beginning to attract more attention. When Eric communicated this proposal to Howard, however, he found that Cape's would not wish *anything* of his to be published under some other imprint if this could be avoided; they would rather do it themselves, working with the Porpoise Press if necessary. Eric replied:

> I was surprised but at the same time gratified to discover that you regard me more proprietorially than I imagined. I have six addresses on very Scottish subjects: A Case for Nationalism (given at Edinburgh University); The Prodigal Country (Aberdeen); Limitations of Dialect (Glasgow, Perth, Inverness); The Story of Kari Solmundsson (Glasgow); The Unafraid—a general paper on the Sagas (Aberdeen, St Andrews); and The Norse Influence in Scotland (broadcast).
>
> I don't know to what extent London has become conscious of Scottish Nationalism, but it's news here and the interest grows almost hourly. The opposition particularly is becoming aware of it. The two papers I've already given got quite a lot of publicity in Scottish newspapers.

He suggested putting them out under the general title of *Bait for the Unicorn*. When Wren Howard said he thought the lectures would be publishable, however, Eric had second thoughts and decided: 'There's hardly enough stuff—regular stuff—in the papers to make a proper book.' Though the project came to nothing at this stage, Eric's continuing interest and work on the Nationalist scene in late 1932 eventually led three years later to a little book of essays deriving from this material: *The Lion and the Unicorn, or, What England Has Meant to Scotland*.

At the end of his summer in Orkney he went to live in Edinburgh for a while, sharing a flat with his friend David Cleghorn Thomson, then the first ever Director of Broadcasting for Scotland, at 11 York Place. There he frequently met Moray McLaren and others working with the BBC, and was inclined to make considerable fun of the extent to which their every thought seemed to turn on what Sir John Reith in London might be thinking of their efforts. He lived a hard-working but full and stimulating life for several months. Little did he know it, but the tide of his enjoyable bachelorhood was on the turn, and for the next half-year there was a period of a kind of *Sturm und Drang* as the ebb was subconsciously resisted.

Beside his work on the proofs of *The Men of Ness* and on the various papers and engagements arising from his Scottish Nationalist interests, he was trying his hand at some short stories again, and, as he told Howard, he was encouraged when Michael Joseph, then a literary agent with Curtis Brown, began to find purchasers in the States. It gave him particular pleasure when *Harper's Bazaar* took 'The Abominable Imprecation of Shepherd Alken' in November, and he turned to the chivalric code again for his comic exploration of the problems of ensuring a wife's good behaviour while one was away at a crusade in *The Crusader's Key*. This did not find a publisher until April 1933, when the White Owl Press brought it out as a gift book, nicely printed by Edward Kricorissian and Denis Fairbairns and with drawings by Nancy Kirkham, and then its faint bawdiness got him into trouble with a lady whom he'd rather not have offended.

The *Listener*, while regularly publishing his reviews of novels, accepted occasional other pieces from him. In June he contributed 'The Eleventh Hour of Christopher Marlowe'. Much later this article caught the eye of Basil Ashmore, then a young theatrical producer, with whom Eric as a consequence was to form a friendship, and with whose encouragement he would, in the 1940s, look again towards the theatre as an outlet for his talent.

Another article in the *Listener* in September was on Sir Walter Scott. Already his writing had much authority in its unobtrusive scholarship and polished cadences: there is an adumbration here of the Eric Linklater who, in the 1950s and 1960s, would be constantly in demand for talks and comments on Scott, Stevenson, Burns, Fergusson and other notable Scottish writers.

He must have seemed a distinctive figure to the young people he met in that industrious year of 1932, a man of many parts. His cultivated image was that of the somewhat owlish, solemn-faced, earnest and avuncular middle-aged young man, balding and bespectacled and ready to pontificate on almost any subject with unexpected wit and wisdom. On first acquaintance he seemed a far-from-solemn, rather madcap, socially daring, laughter-loving man; closer knowledge betrayed a more sensitive kind of person who was not very sure of himself. He was trying to go his own way but was perceptibly looking for love. One girl in whom he seemed to find it in the late spring of the year was Marris Murray.

She was the younger sister of Peg Murray, the wife of Eric's greatest friend Douglas Walker. Eric still haunted their home whenever he had a chance, finding there a pleasurable peace and domesticity which he loved, though resolutely up to now refusing to fall into anything so cosy and restricting himself. Douglas and Peg had a baby son, Kenneth, whom Eric called George; he was especially attached to the family just then because his friends' marriage had recently been tested in rocky waters, and his staunch support of them both had 'helped them sail into harbour'.[9] In their house he met from time to time Marris, who was also working on the staff of David Cleghorn Thomson at the BBC. She was impressed with Eric, with his achievements in the world, and with the love and respect he was given in her sister's home, and for a while they grew very close. There was talk of marriage, but it came to nothing, and Marris went away and got a new job in London. No record of their relationship survives, except for the acknowledgement that it did happen. Peg was relieved when they parted, for the affair had been tempestuous; she felt that Eric would have been, indeed was, more than most women could deal with, and she did not want to see either Marris or Eric hurt.

Meanwhile he was as ever fond of Isobel, and in October he was devastated to hear that she had miscarried and lost her first baby. He wrote:

> My sweet and lovely Ylsabyl, I'm so sorry—horribly sorry. Please be very well again soon; and comforted. Though in the next few years you have as many as seventeen children, not one of them will be a quarter so lovely and delectable as you.

He tried to comfort her with a funny fairy story about the Chinese Princess Pin-hi, the point of which was that beautiful princesses are probably better off without children anyway. Charles was going to take Isobel to Cornwall to recuperate, and Eric asked if they would report on their accommodation, because

> I incline to the idea of going thither or thereabouts immediately after the New Year to surround myself with a new and strange environment, in ascetic solitude, to meditate and work upon certain tasks whose airy substance presently burbles in the cauldron of my silly cerebrum. So you would help me considerably if you took a look at this place of your choosing from the point of view of an aged littery gent ... I want a place where I can settle for a couple of months at any rate.

Other things, however, unanticipated at this stage, were to deprive that idea of fruition.

Amid the flurry of work in the autumn, the most important matter was the completion of *The Men of Ness*, and seeing it through the press. In September he returned the proofs with some ironic comment which shows the way in which he was increasingly concerned with the processes of book-making as well as with the words he had supplied:

> Your printer man has taken some pains to improve my punctuation here and there. Doubtless he is fortified by the books that instruct us in that difficult art, but as my scheme of punctuation has been deliberately worked out, I hope he will permit the original commas to be restored.

He also wanted the Skua and the Skarf, the names of the ships, to be in ordinary print, not italic, saying that he did not care himself for the spidery look of italics.

Despite his early optimism, Eric's confidence in *The Men of Ness* was shaken a little by the time of its publication. Howard's tentative anticipation of a less than enthusiastic response from the public was not wholly compensated by Garnett's approval of the book, though Eric was grateful for his comments:

> How very good of you to take the trouble of writing over *The Men of Ness*. But I'm glad you did. I was, in fact, somewhat anxiously waiting to see if you would, because I hoped that you at any rate would like the story. I'm afraid your voice may be a lonely one. I've tried the book out on one or two non-bookish friends, who liked it, but I doubt you will be alone among the learned. Your retention—in the midst of books—of a non-bookish eye is a rare virtue.
>
> I think well of the thing myself. It took care of itself almost from the beginning, and I only did the donkey-work. Then I went over the details of the wreck with a man expert in these matters (we nearly drowned together once) and I think that technically speaking it's all right.
>
> The weaknesses you mention—diffusion and anecdotalism in the early chapters—I'm ready to admit. It's due, I think, to the difficulty of finding a mean between a small and a larger canvas ... On the other hand, it may not be this difficulty that makes it clumsy, but my sin in being led astray by the facts of real history—Harald coming to Orkney, Sigurd getting killed in Caithness—and thrusting these bits in wanton-like. I don't know. At the time of writing it seemed to me that I was just giving young Kol and Skallagrim a chance to grow up before sending them off to be killed.

Wren Howard promised to have a pint when *The Men of Ness* was published, for 'such a book should be launched with a copious libation—if I am up to it, I shall have a second pint!' Things did not go quite as badly as he had feared; by the end of the year he was reporting 9,000 copies sold, and some of the reviews were kind. He pointed out to Eric 'a good bang for *The Men* in today's *Daily Mail*' on 10 November. Eric was very disappointed, however. Looking back he commented:

> *The Men of Ness* was a good story, but so far as I am aware only five people in the Old World really liked it: Edward Garnett; a professor of English literature; a mountainous Warrant Officer from the Royal Navy; an Icelandic reviewer; and a schoolboy.[10]

In fact it later sold well in translation in Scandinavia, and would as late as 1959 see life as a paperback in Britain. Circumstances conspired against the Farrar & Rinehart edition in the United States; in Eric's words:

> In America it was received with such extravagant eulogy that I grew feverish with delight. But unhappily it was published on the very same day that America went off gold, and nobody bought it. So my conceit was inflated but unfed.[11]

Reflecting many years later on his practice in writing, he was clearly still puzzled and a little hurt about what had happened to his career at the time of *The Men of Ness*. His notion was that he had revived a fashion of writing characteristic of the great Scots *makars* of the early sixteenth century, people like Dunbar and Henryson, who 'let their subject call the tune, and found words and style suitable for the music',[12] or that he had been like 'a sculptor who sensibly recognises the formative importance of his material'.[13] Thus:

> I wrote *Juan in America* with the exuberance—an exuberance salted with genial and quizzical satire—that I thought appropriate to my enormous scene ... *Ben Jonson and King James* was hotly coloured by my recollection of the verbal splendours that, in Elizabethan and early Jacobean times, gave to quotidian existence a baroque magnificence of speech. But when I wrote *The Men of Ness* I subdued and restricted my pleasure in words, I composed my story in a stark simplicity that banished all Latinisms from its sentences and relied almost wholly on a vocabulary that could, with some latitude, be called Anglo-Saxon.
>
> I confected a good story. A good, dramatic story with a beginning, a middle and an end. A story peopled by strong and recognisable characters. But did I further, thereby, any claim that I might have to be recognised as a novelist? Most certainly not.[14]

Storm Jameson in Cape's house magazine, *Now and Then*, gave the novel its most perceptive and supportive discussion in England, praising the plain, exciting narrative and the imaginative energy of its conception and execution:

> For Mr Linklater, Time is a narrow strip of water which he crosses and is in the ninth century. He is there with his whole mind—there is none of that uncertainty, that groping after an imperfectly realised vision, which would have betrayed an inferior writer ... *The Men of Ness* is a rounded and perfectly controlled work of art (or imagination, which is the same thing ...) The account of (Kol's and Skallagrim's) voyage ... is a magnificent piece of writing, and to be added to the great sea-pieces in our language. And the fight is flesh and blood on the dry bones of English verse. It would be worth giving students to read alongside their *Beowulf.*[15]

Subsequent criticism has taken little note of the novel. Kurt Wittig, comparing it with Neil M. Gunn's *Sun Circle*, which appeared the following year, commented on the stride forward which the two books represented in contemporary Scottish self-perception:

> Neither is really a historical novel; rather they are both groping towards a mythology of the events which made the forefathers of the race ... This harking back to the primordial beginnings of the race strikes a keynote for modern Scottish fiction, in which the dim ages of history often throw their shadow across the life of modern man.[16]

Except that they were both about the age of the Vikings, there were no similarities between the two books. Eric had met Neil Gunn earlier in the year at a discussion on Nationalist politics, and when he heard in July that Gunn was also working on a Viking novel he wrote to urge him not to withdraw or fear a clash of interests. Though he liked his own story, he didn't think the critics would; 'they will complain about the gore, never having had the advantage of seeing hockey played in Orkney'. The critics didn't complain about the gore; they simply ignored the book.

Francis Russell Hart has pointed out the relationship between *The Men of Ness* and *The Ultimate Viking* in which Eric, twenty-three years later, worked out the historical thesis implicit in the early novel: that the Vikings were 'artists in conduct':

> They were unabashed by social obligation, undeterred by moral prohibition, and they could be quite contemptuous of economic advantage and the safety of their skins. But they saw clearly a difference between right and wrong, and the difference was aesthetic. If what they did became a story that would please the ear, then it was right and beautiful.[17]

It is a theme most movingly and convincingly explored in *The Men of Ness*. Eric was over-modest in his acceptance of Garnett's observations that the story was too diffuse and anecdotal at the beginning. The control of the shape of the book and the control of its linguistic expression are two of its particular triumphs.

Its structure turns on the resolution of a family feud. At the beginning there is a series of incidents which establish the scene and the manners and customs of the time in general terms, gradually focusing on one family, that of Thorlief Ragnarsson of Orkney, and his sons. Although many names occur and many stories are briefly sketched in the first half of the book, relating the fictional story to real historical occasions, the central action is set up very early on as the woman Signy is made a widow by Ivar Ragnarsson, known as Ivar the Boneless, who kills Signy's husband, Bui. It is the persistent determination of the strong-minded Signy to get her revenge for this act that colours the action and eventually decides the tragic outcome. Her disposition and the effect of her implacable will are given a convincing and vivid context by all the other occurrences both fictional and historical. There is no diffusion of interest but, just as Eric claimed in his reply to Garnett, a powerful and inexorable building up towards inevitable catastrophe, a sweep of forward movement that gives the whole a notable sense of unity and intensity.

In language and tone the achievement is even more remarkable. Seeking as far as possible to emulate the style of the saga-makers, bare, laconic, economical, Eric was marvellously successful, blending into the uncompromising action both sufficient descriptive language to evoke places and people with vividness, and a humorous, poetic element that helped counterbalance and humanise the mundane violence and supernatural horrors of the story. It is a man's world that he depicts:

> The names of their sons were Grim, Kol and Einar, and Thorgerd and Hallgerda were their sisters. But little is to be told about the latter.[18]

The narrative catches superbly the stoicism, rugged philosophy and the particular code of honour of these Orkney Vikings with a kind of downbeat humour to complement their fatalistic drift towards destruction, and a lapidary, aphoristic turn of phrase for their speech:

> There was a man called Thord the Swart, a Halogalander. He said, 'It seems to me, Ragnar, that there are farmers enough as it is, and kings enough ... I think that if you want to live ashore, Ragnar, it must be that your strength is going and age is coming on you.'
>
> That put Ragnar in such a wrath that he struck at Thord and cut off his right arm at the shoulder.
>
> Thord looked at his arm, where it lay on the ground, and said, 'You dealt some good blows, and yet I do not think that you had come to your full strength.' Then he fell beside his arm and died.[19]

There is a kind of sweet reasonableness about the men, despite their tendency for sudden violence and their contempt for life. At the siege of Paris a prisoner suggests to Ragnar that to improve his position he should abandon the worship of Thor and Odin and make his men be converted to Christianity:

> 'Let them worship Christ, and pray to him, and they will be healed of their sickness.'
>
> Ragnar thought there might be something in that.[20]

The humorous and philosophical disposition of these men gives the narrative a tone of unexpected tenderness, and makes them admirable; without realising how it has happened, the reader finds himself sharing their outlook and their concerns. The real heroes, Skallagrim and Kol, come into their own during their epic voyage and final confrontation with their renegade uncle in the second half of the book. Eric has built them up skilfully for their dominance of the narrative of their great adventure; they are terrible, but also beautiful and loveable because of the essential humanity Eric has given their characters. Kol is the doomed, tragic figure. From early on his bravery has been particularly challenged, for, in a superstitious time, he has fallen under the influence of the moon, and knows fear in the half-light. His struggle to overcome his fear is poignant, as is his friends' tolerance and understanding when he is almost mastered by it. Yet he is a model of honour and kindliness, and it is Kol's relationship with the ordinary, the little, the cowardly man, Gauk, which figures as the most touching and delightful thing in the whole novel.

The narration is supremely effective during the description of the sons' abortive Viking venture which brings the book to its crisis. The sea forces them to run the gauntlet of all its diverse armoury; lost and unsure after surviving a great wave that all but does for them, they turn northwards by mistake and sail into ice and bitter cold, and then begin a long attempt to row southwards, only to be engulfed in impenetrable mist when the wind at last dies and leaves them directionless. Once they are within hearing of a landfall, but then the wind and tide move them on again through further privations until at last they are wrecked on the shores of Northumbria.

Like the journey of the Ancient Mariner, which in some ways it echoes, this magnificently described voyage has a symbolic power out of all proportion to the thirty or forty pages which it occupies in the book. Much of the reader's pleasure derives from the depiction not so much of the sea's awesome behaviour as of the men and their conduct, their grim humour and indomitable courage, their relapses into quarrelsome argument and their recovery to sensible and hopeful co-operation.

Of the men, Kol and Gauk stay longest in the mind, though there are vivid sketches of many others in their periphery. Gauk is the little man, the sole survivor of the expedition which willy-nilly goes to deal in the end with Ivar the Boneless. For Francis Russell Hart Gauk is the most interesting character in the novel, both because he does survive (and Hart summarises Eric as a 'Novelist of Survival'), and because he

> supplies something of a final comment on the heroic aesthetic of *The Men of Ness*—a comment that will later be embodied in Linklater's most memorable hero, not a Viking bent on the art of adventure but an Italian peasant committed to the art of survival.[21]

While there are elements in his character which make it possible to see him as an antecedent of Private Angelo, Gauk is really only a satellite of Kol. He is largely and comically ineffective as a warrior, despite his pride in his sword, Leg-biter; he prefers to keep in the background, and to hide when it is sensible to do so. In marriage he was hen-pecked, in widowerhood he continues so. Gauk's comments and adventures are often funny, indeed there is something of Falstaff in him, but his loyalty to Kol is greater than his natural cowardice, and his voice often speaks the most sensibly of all; and Kol's savagery is tempered by his disposition to love, by his dutiful and caring leadership, and by the reader's awareness of the inner struggles he undergoes in maintaining the outward fatalistic face of Viking strength.

The story is set almost a thousand years in the past, yet it speaks loudly for our times and for all times. Its values are love, friendship, companionship and courage. In capturing so surely the ethic of manhood, brotherhood and honour in a manner so convincing, Eric produced a novel to be ranked among the finest of his achievements.

Although disappointed by the initial reception of his new book, however, he had no time to brood. On 9 November he told Miss Atkinson at Cape's that he had so far received no reviews—'perhaps, judging from the ones I have seen, this is no great loss. But still I feel a mild morbid curiosity.' The same day he commented to Cape about the tepid reviews he had seen, adding: 'A few people I know who are amateurs of Norse literature say it's hot stuff. My old Prof at Aberdeen has been uncommonly enthusiastic—says definitely it's the best thing I've done, and is very polite about the authenticity of the manner.' Thereafter he was so busy with other things that he put the book behind him and thought about it no more. He was full of plans for his writing future, detailing to Cape on 15 December undertakings already tabled: the Mary Stewart biography; half a dozen short stories 'meant to be amusing, and in some cases, I blush to admit, faintly improper'; a couple of plays; and 'a novel—modern, a comedy, pretty large scale and carried in scenes'.

If the novel he projected was, as seems likely, his first sketch for *Magnus Merriman*, it was about to undergo some modifications as a result of his political experiences of the recent past and immediate future. During the previous few months, working in the ambience of Nationalism he had met, besides Neil Gunn, various other luminaries who had thrown themselves into the same cause, among them Christopher Grieve, Leslie Mitchell and Compton Mackenzie. While he admired Gunn, Grieve and Mitchell, and maintained a somewhat stiff and formal friendliness with them, between him and Mackenzie there was an instant liking, which began when they met at a National Mòd. Mackenzie recalled:

> Looking back on the Fort William Mòd, I think I enjoyed it more than any Mòd at which I have been. One reason for this has nothing to do with Gaelic; it was at this Mòd that I met for the first time Eric Linklater, and from the moment we shook hands we were intimate friends. I remember on that first night the rain gave a downpour notable even for Lochaber. Eric and I were staying at the Highland Hotel where the venerable fathers of the Mòd were staying. We sat up together in the smoke-room. It must have been about midnight when above the swish of the rain without I heard the deep and solemn tones of Eric Linklater.
>
> 'You can always charm the Celt with a song.'
>
> 'Oh that's very interesting, Mr Linklater,' observed one of the venerable fathers turning to another. 'Did you hear what Mr Linklater said, Mr Macleod? "You can always charm the Celt with a song."'
>
> 'Yes,' Eric went on, 'I remember in the war when I was with the Black Watch, my section was getting rattled by heavy shelling. "Who do you think you are?" I said. "The Black Watch or the f——ing windy Sussex?"—You can always charm the Celt with a song.'

The expression on the faces of the venerable fathers is still in my mind's eye.[22]

Mackenzie's friendly support and gift of platform eloquence were soon to be a feature of an unexpected development in Eric's life. One of the most pragmatic and sensible of the political leaders of the National Party of Scotland at the time was John MacCormick. Never one to miss an opportunity, he noted with interest the emergence of the energetic and talented young writer on the scene, and after a while he approached him with a proposition:

> There was going to be a by-election in East Fife, he said. Would I contest it in the Nationalist cause?
> 'But to sit in Parliament', I said, 'is the very last thing I want to do. I should hate it.'
> 'There's not much chance of your winning,' he said.
> 'Oh,' I replied.
> 'We want you to show the flag. If you put up a good show and do some propaganda, you'll help the cause in a general way. It's missionary work really.'
> 'You're quite sure I can't win?'
> 'It's most unlikely.'[23]

Though Eric was aware of a great deal of confusion about the meaning of nationalism among those with whom he discussed political issues, and aware that his own views were hardly those of the official voice of the party, in as far as he could detect one, he allowed himself to be put forward to contest the by-election which was to be held in East Fife on 3 February 1933. Part of his reason for accepting the challenge may have been, as he later noted, professional:

> As a writer, moreover, I have been subject to a weakness which has betrayed many of my fellow countrymen. I have not always been able to find, in writing, a total satisfaction for my natural appetites. From time to time I have felt a craving for more overt action, and ... that craving was about to lead me into a calamitous experiment in a sort of action for which I had no natural gifts, but from which I emerged with the unscrupulous recompense reserved for writers. They can always write a novel—preferably a comic novel—about the misfortunes they suffer.[24]

Whether he embarked on the enterprise quite so cynically may be doubted. In two volumes of autobiography he devoted sufficient space to the adventure and to discussion of the important issues at stake to make one wonder whether he would in fact have been so distressed had he won the seat. Of this, however, there was indeed little likelihood, for the Nationalists at the time were ill organised and wanting in clear and agreed policy, and Eric came bottom in a field of five when the poll was taken. He found himself using terms like 'disgrace' and 'humiliation' when writing about the election later, and although he said that an hour in the company of a pretty and vivacious woman was sufficient to make him forget all about it, his terminology does not appear altogether ironic. There was some sense of the farcical in his involvement in such an adventure; he explained to Phoebe Gilkyson that he had failed to win many votes

> partly because all the time I wore a violently hued tweed suit, which offended people used to a more parliamentary black coat and striped trouserings.

It was part of his view of himself that he was a clown who could expect only to fall on his face, but there was, though unacknowledged, a good deal of quite serious intention in his behaviour. Still surviving from that era there is at least one copy of the manifesto which he addressed to the people of East Fife. When asked about this in 1966, Eric replied that 'no copy survives; thank goodness!'[25] but his interlocutor found one a short time later. It is a remarkable document, combining a certain innocent earnestness with a degree of ironic grandiloquence, suggesting mixed motives in its composition. It is presented in an elegant and rhetorical literary English which may have sounded somewhat foreign and incomprehensible to a fair proportion of the electorate to which it was addressed but which might have seemed not inappropriate from the pen of a coeval of, say, Edmund Burke.

After a declaration that a wholly independent Scotland would be in the world's interest rather than narrowly a cause of concern for Scotsmen at home, he wrote:

> It is a cause for shame and regret that neither interest in Scotland nor pride nor faith in it are apparent except in a minority of the people. But there is cause for hope that that minority is steadily growing, and the first task and purpose of the Nationalist Party are the conversion of the minority into a majority that can demand for Scotland the right to govern itself and with that right acquire the reasonable expectation not only of arresting our national decline, but also, by developing natural resources that have long been neglected, of winning a fair prosperity and commensurate happiness.[26]

East Fife could give Scotland the lead it needed, he argued, but proceeded:

> I am unwilling to bargain for your support with an easy promise of attention to local amenities and zeal in the service of local industries. Should you elect me your member it will indeed be my care and study to foster those amenities and watch the fortune of your industries, but I know too well the difficulties of breaking Westminster's stark wall of indifference to Scottish interests to hope for any large success in procuring special privileges.

Such honesty was not perhaps best calculated to secure a sufficient body of support to elect him. He concluded with a splendid oratorical flourish, appealing to the electors' emotions and sense of history:

In 1320 the nobility and people of Scotland made from Arbroath a declaration of independence in these terms: 'For as long as there are a hundred of us left alive, we will never submit to the domination of the English, for we fight not for glory nor riches nor honour, but for Freedom alone, which no good man giveth up save with life itself.'

The time has come for another such declaration of Scotland's spirit, and no part of Scotland has more right to make it than East Fife. Here are farmers discouraged in their labour; here are miners robbed of their earnings; here is industry decayed and authority stripped of power; here are fishermen who, being helped neither against the elements nor against the malignity of the times, may not even claim protection against foreign piracy. And here is the oldest University in the Kingdom; here stands a Palace of the Kings of Scotland; here is a village that still remembers to honour the men whom it sent to serve the Bruce. Has Fife the courage to declare its faith?

Well, Fife had not, and Eric offered various reasons why his candidacy had been unsuccessful. On the personal level he recognised himself to be 'solemn and ineffective',[27] but forty-five years later Jo Grimond remembered that the first political meeting he ever attended had been eloquently addressed by Eric Linklater[28], and Eric found himself impatient of the requirement that he should make the same speech over and over again with perhaps minor rearrangements at different venues. Rapidly becoming bored with a speech once he had made it, he attempted something new and different at every meeting, wasting thereby his energy and gaining a reputation as a vacillator.

Whereas, however, this inability to repeat himself was a considerable disadvantage for a parliamentary candidate, it accounts for the great variety of his literary output, for which his readers may be grateful. His instinct that the experience would be invaluable to him as a writer soon proved sound, for the campaign had a number of extraordinary and ridiculous aspects upon which he duly capitalised in *Magnus Merriman*, which he began later in the year. The campaign was also briefly described in *The Man on My Back*, where one occasion especially was recalled:

> For a few days there was an excited and uncomfortable feeling that anyone might win. At one point, in a fevered gloom, I even saw the possibility of a Nationalist victory. Compton Mackenzie had come to speak for me, and we had a series of meetings in the little fishing towns on the pleasant coast of Fife. Our audiences here consisted only of men. Men in dark-blue jerseys, newly come from the sea. Their sleeves were swollen with their strength, and there was valiance in their eyes. I was ill-at-ease, wishing only that in Scotland there were ten times as many such, and their prosperity ten times as great. But Mackenzie met the challenge of their hardihood, and with his oratory whipt them to enthusiasm. Their applause was like the breaking of the sea on a stony beach, and for an hour I feared that such a storm might carry me farther than I wanted to go.[29]

In *Fanfare for a Tin Hat* Eric felt himself free after so great a lapse of time to go into fuller detail, and his account is almost as funny as the story of Magnus Merriman's election campaign in 'Kinluce', which itself bears comparison with Dickens's description of the goings-on at Eatanswill in *The Pickwick Papers*. The campaign in East Fife was much enlivened when Lord Beaverbrook took a hand and descended with his entourage upon St Andrews to support his own Empire Free Trade candidate. Lunching one day with Lord Castlerosse at the Royal and Ancient, Eric met Beaverbrook, who greeted his former employee and current political opponent with expansive delight, saying: 'Linklater! I was pretty sure we'd meet again. You've found your way into politics, have you? Well, you're on the wrong side, but you've discovered the greatest game of all. Yes, it's the greatest game there is!'[30]

Eric made friends with David Keir, the Liberal candidate, one of his four opponents and the one destined to come second from bottom of the poll, and was delighted to meet Keir's agent, Basil Murray. He was the son of the classical scholar, Gilbert Murray. It was later widely believed that Basil Murray was at least half the model for Evelyn Waugh's 'deplorable character—so blackly sympathetic, so engagingly destructive',[31] Basil Seal, and Eric found him a most amusing fellow. It was Murray's wife with whom Eric travelled back on the train from St Andrews to Edinburgh after losing the election, and in whose lively company he rapidly forgot the smart of defeat.

Wren Howard and Jonathan Cape were rather alarmed when they first heard of Eric's political adventures, but he reassured them:

> Please tell [Jonathan] that it is only a temporary turning I have taken. I have no political ambitions, and am simply acting as bugleman, trumpeter and herald for the Nationalist Party—which I believe to be a good thing. Fortunately my prospects of being elected are extremely remote—but this is in the *strictest* confidence.

Although Eric blamed himself partly for the electoral failure, the prospect of any Nationalist candidate's being elected, no matter how great his parliamentary ambitions, was pretty remote at the time. At a time when 28 per cent of the labour force of the country was unemployed, the real issues were seen to be in resolving the traditional Tory–Socialist opposition. Eric was, moreover, an unashamed Imperialist who believed in 'the vast importance, to us and the world, of the British Empire to whose creation Scotland had so lavishly contributed',[32] and such convictions sat uneasily in his mind alongside the nationalistic idea that separation from England was the necessary first step to renewed Scottish prosperity.

He returned to work soon after the by-election though suffering for a while, as he told Mackenzie, from a complete loss of mental energy. But the 30,000 words on Mary Stewart had to be written for Peter Davies's series of short biographies, and he had been snatching at various opportunities to renew his acquaintance with her story since completing *The Men of Ness*. He approached his task with a lively interest in the Queen's psychology and based his book on an original and challenging perception about her character. This was that, far from being the 'Swinburnian great and tragic lover' of popular belief and mischievous representation, the only evidence for which was the fact of her three marriages and the report of the Casket letters, she was actually 'not merely chaste, but by constitution averse from love's embraces'.[33]

The book, besides contradicting the accepted picture of Mary, had the merits of brevity and elegance of style, and was quite well received on publication in May 1932. Although Eric was delighted to be assured by John Buchan that this was 'the best and truest thing that had ever been written about Mary',[34] and although he joined with some vigour in an exchange of correspondence on the subject in the columns of *The Times*,[35] he was not greatly surprised to find that his thesis was not generally approved. He wrote: 'I do not suppose that my interpretation of the poor queen will ever be widely accepted.'[36] Subsequent books, films and plays about Mary suggest that he was right in his expectation.

Mary Queen of Scots was reprinted several times during the 1930s. Compton Mackenzie's friendly recommendation of it may have helped; according to him:

> Mr Eric Linklater's biography of Mary Queen of Scots is on another plane (i.e. from that of Clennel Wilkinson's *Richard Coeur de Lion*) ... Those who may be inclined to think that too much has been written about that tragic lady will be astonished by the imagination at work on an aspect of her character to which no justice has been done.
>
> With brevity and with humour, with lucidity, eloquence and beauty, the heartrending story is told again, and on the last two pages the reader may learn why Mr Linklater was able to tell the old tale as if it had all happened but yesterday.[37]

Mackenzie was impressed by the concluding paragraphs where Eric launched into an emotive appeal to the reader which aligns the purpose of the book with that of the manifesto for East Fife; it is evident that Eric felt that through the rediscovery of such a story, the vision of a romantic, vital Scotland of huge potential might be newly kindled:

> There indeed is a proper Queen for the high hills, snow-covered, with the sunlight of a blinding gleam in the corries, and the shadows on the dappled snow; for Scotland, in the gypsy colours of autumn, of silver birch and discoloured leaf and the solid, black-hearted green of the pines; Scotland of swift amber streams and silver firths that take the knees of the mountains in

their arms; of the islands that float in the western sea under sails of indigo and the vapour of gold; Scotland of pibrochs and the silenced music of the harp, of *Christ's Kirk on the Green*, of Urquhart, and rough bothy-singers; of the makars and the ballads, of the chivalry that rode to Flodden, of broken clans and banished men, of battlefields from Lucknow to the Somme; of beauty that brings no profit but to the heart, and of disaster that wrings the heart...

True, there is another Scotland, somewhat provincial in spirit and circumscribed in the imagination; a lion couchant, with the unaspiring steeple of a depressing church and a factory chimney for its supporters; a country whose native violence and traditionally dogged temper have violently asserted and now most doggedly maintain a standard of unflinching mediocrity. The sentiments and the smoke of this other Scotland somewhat obscure the old romantic kingdom, but what of it?

Tecum Scotia nostra comparetur?

O saeclum insapiens et infacetum![38]

Although Eric continued to be concerned about Scotland and its future, he did not, until the idiosyncratic book of essays published in Lewis Grassic Gibbon's series on Scottish matters in 1935, write at length on the topic again. He contributed occasionally to newspapers and magazines; late in the year there was an article 'Scottish Nationalism' in *Everyman* (10 November 1933) and another on 'Why Scots Succeed' in the London *Evening News* (30 December 1933); before that there was a rather ironical piece on 'The Cash Value of a Scottish Accent' in the *Daily Mail* (22 May 1933). Soon after the by-election he castigated Scotland as 'The Prodigal Country' in an address to the Glasgow Literary Society spoken—or preached—from the pulpit of Trinity Church.[39] But there was no question of his being politically active again, and in the end he left the Party in the summer of 1933, irritated beyond measure by their inability to elaborate and declare a constructive agreed policy. He told them in frustration, 'You'll make nothing of this till you bring the English in to run it for you!'[40] After which, he reported, they had very little in the way of friendly association.

The end of Eric's tasting of life as a Nationalist activist coincided with the beginning of quite a different role for him. In the society of Edinburgh in the winter of 1932–3 it would have been difficult to avoid coming face to face sooner or later with the young literary lion-cum-Nationalist politician, and one day in late October Eric's fate was sealed when Marjorie MacIntyre came home from London and did so.

II

THE WANDERING ORCADIAN

Family Man in Italy

Marjorie MacIntyre was a vivacious and attractive young woman who had flirted a little with the idea of being an actress and had been a student at the Royal Academy of Dramatic Art. She had played a minor role on the London stage in Ian Hay's *Sing a Song of Sixpence* under the direction of Jack Lambert, but considered her acting career unpromising. When her brother Duncan died, aged only twenty-seven, she returned to Edinburgh to console her parents. Afterwards she quite happily stayed there, seeing herself in a way as part of a drift of young Scots back from London towards their own world where maybe things were beginning to happen.

Before that she had seen something of the world, especially East Africa where she had been caught up in her sister's divorce—a case which caused a minor scandal in Kenya at the time. Six months of stimulating life together in Kenya when she was only twenty had made Marjorie very close to her elder sister despite the twelve-year age gap, and she found it natural to emulate her independent and lively style. On her return to Edinburgh, she began to devote some of her abundant energy to working with Michael MacOwan in a campaign to establish a Scottish National Theatre, and this fierce enthusiasm for a Scottish revival in arts and politics took her into the midst of circles where Eric, too, had been taken up. They met in late October 1932 'at one of Moray McLaren's incomparable parties' and in Marjorie's words, 'at that very first meeting we "clicked"'. During the weeks that followed she found herself increasingly drawn to the young author; their romance developed steadily and came within a couple of months to a point at which decisions seemed to make themselves.

Looking back, Marjorie could see herself at the time only as 'a far from brilliant, immature twenty-two-year-old', who could hardly believe the miraculous good fortune by which Eric preferred her to the many others who were competing for his attention. Pictures of her, however, testify that she was vibrantly pretty, and men who remember her, such as Jack Lambert and Rupert Hart-Davis (who met her when he was a tyro actor at the Old Vic and she was a drama student) remember her as a pleasure to the eye and a challenge to their manliness. That she was ten years younger than Eric added to her eligibility. They had in common the desire to promote a new age for Scottish achievement which had brought many others home just at that time—Moray McLaren, indeed, had just published an invigorating and hopeful book called *Return to Scotland.* Further,

Marjorie, having recently spent a summer holiday in Orkney, shared Eric's feeling for the islands, and that gave them much to talk about. There were other shared interests; Marjorie recalled:

> I was the first girl he'd met who could share and enjoy a bottle of claret. I also shared his taste for music-hall. We went to the old Theatre Royal in Edinburgh regularly together throughout that winter.[1]

She realised that she was hardly the first love of his life; he was thirty-two and had been around. In time he told her about several earlier affairs, including the not-so-distant one with Marris, and the one with a 'fabulously rich American girl' whom he had courted during his Commonwealth Fellowship days and whom the Gilkysons had hoped he would marry—'but', said Marjorie, 'if he told me her name I have forgotten it—perhaps I didn't want to know too much'. But all those past loves fell into insignificance for him in the spring of 1933.

Eric in a way fell in love not only with Marjorie but with her whole family. He used to flirt enthusiastically with her clever sister Alison, as well as with other of Marjorie's friends, who enjoyed his attentions while recognising them as part of the atmosphere of fun and badinage which, on his good days, he spread all about him. One young lady, Ursula Balfour, daughter of Lord Kinross, responded so much as to say to him one day—as a joke, naturally—that it was she rather than Marjorie whom he ought to marry. He loved the happy and affluent background against which Marjorie moved, and was attracted by her parents too:

> Her father, Ian, sometime player of Rugby Football capped for Scotland ... challenged me to fight for her. Later I became one of his closest friends, and dearly loved my mother-in-law who, when I first met her, told me she so disliked my latest book that she had buried it in her rose-garden.[2]

The story of the fight proposed by Ian MacIntyre, as told in some detail in *The Man on My Back*, reveals through the dialogue something of the magnetism of Marjorie's father, who was a Writer to the Signet with a prosperous practice and had been a Conservative MP for Edinburgh West. The book buried in the rose-garden by Mrs MacIntyre was the engagingly printed *The Crusader's Key*. As the key was that which opened a chastity belt, it is perhaps not altogether a mystery why Eric's future mother-in-law should disapprove of it.

The romance between her daughter and the writer of immodest stories nevertheless flourished, and more or less came to a head on 19 March 1933. It was Marjorie's birthday, and the occasion of a great celebration for Scotland, who had that afternoon recorded a 3–0 rugby win over England at Murrayfield. Later that evening Moray McLaren turned up with Marjorie and Eric at the flat of Colin Mackenzie, 'another urbane and civilised personality in Edinburgh at that time'.[3] Owing to a misunderstanding, their host, thinking they had already dined, gave them no food but sent in plenty of wine until he could join them with his dinner-party guests. By the time Eric left to take Marjorie home they were both convinced that they had found 'the time, the place and the loved one all together'. In Marjorie's recollection it was at the party that she and Eric became engaged:

> Colin's flat was in the middle of Edinburgh. We took a taxi out to Murrayfield where I lived with my parents, and Eric was amazed to discover that I was a virgin. But what he also remembered was that I was so afraid that this seduction might be discovered that at first light (7.00 a.m.) I drove him out of the house and he had to walk two miles to his lodgings—too embarrassed to take a tram because he was wearing a dinner-jacket!

While his relationship with Marjorie was gradually growing towards this gratifying culmination, Eric had also been cementing his friendship with Compton Mackenzie. Their immediate liking for each other was bolstered by their considerable admiration for each other's work. Not long after meeting Marjorie, Eric had already formed some ideas about the possibility of marrying her when in January 1933 he went to spend a couple of days with Mackenzie at Eilean Aigas on the Beauly River. Mackenzie assured him that he recognised a genuine creativeness in him and that he had no doubt whatever that he would be justified in backing his future as a writer; Eric need have no doubts about whether he would be able to support a wife by his pen.[4] This confident declaration from his experienced senior gave Eric great pleasure. He was also very grateful for Mackenzie's promise of support during the East Fife by-election campaign which began the next day. Moved by the older man's interest and confidence in him, and by his knowledge that Mackenzie was going through one of his rougher financial periods, Eric suddenly astonished him by offering a loan of £200. After a gesture of protest Mackenzie accepted the generous offer—on condition, he said, that if Eric succeeded in marrying Marjorie by June, when he would be able to repay the loan, he should bring his bride to Barra for their honeymoon. To this Eric agreed, a good while indeed before Marjorie had been consulted about whether marriage was in prospect. Meanwhile Eric was to visit Barra quite soon to find the lie of the land.

In a letter to Mackenzie three weeks after the by-election in East Fife Eric, complaining that he was rather behind with his work on the biography of Mary Stewart because of the loss of mental energy he had suffered during the campaign, told of another undertaking he had in mind:

> I'm about to lay the foundations of a Scottish navy: I'm on the point of buying a converted fishing-boat, 36 feet long, auxiliary engine, spare jib, three anchors,

w.c. and all modern conveniences. If she's ready for sea by the end of the month I'll sail up to Inverness and we'll go to Barra under our own power. Do you know the way?

Eric's desire to have his own boat was in no way reduced when his engagement to Marjorie intervened; he explained to Mackenzie:

My once-simple life has grown more complicated—but I'm still very anxious to go to Barra, and I hope you haven't abandoned the idea. Having got myself a boat I thought I might as well go the whole hog, so I went and got me a girl as well. The plans are more or less made, and zero is June 1st.

The boat would not be ready till about 21 April, as she was pretty dirty and needed re-rigging, so Eric proposed joining Mackenzie in Barra early in April; he would then return to Leith to pick up *Joy* and 'sail her round'. Mackenzie being ill with one of his bouts of sciatica, Eric in fact went to Barra alone in the second week of April, and was made very welcome by the McNeils of Ardweenish at North Bay, Mackenzie's great friends on Barra. He set Roderick McNeil (known as 'the Crookle') on the trail of a cottage where he and Marjorie might spend their honeymoon; engaged one of the Crookle's sons to crew *Joy* for him when she was ready; and wrote to Phoebe Gilkyson summarising what had been happening to him. He explained that he had bought a boat—'this is very exciting'—for which he had as crew 'a very large, very handsome, very shy and black-haired Highlander' called John McNeil, who was more at home in Gaelic than in English; and that he had got himself engaged to be married:

The poor young woman is called Marjorie MacIntyre, and she's rather nice. I met her last October, and I've taken her to dinner so often that I've pretty well built her up—so I thought it a pity to waste her. She's about 5′ 6″; slim (of course); very dark (blondes get soiled so quickly, don't you think?); good at golf and things like that where I'm a complete dud; no literary pretensions, but believes me when I tell her I'm a swell writer; rather lovely in profile and a bit comic in front; has a really charming voice ... and strictly between ourselves I've gone off the deep end about her and periodically sink into a state of fatuous coma.

That Eric was truly smitten is beyond doubt. His tone was often frivolous and he loved to make jokes, but having once made up his mind about Marjorie he never wavered in his devotion to her. Even his love-letters were as funny as they were romantic. A couple of weeks after their engagement he was writing:

Dearest, I finished up with my surgeon yesterday—charming fellow, he refused to let me pay him, and gave me a drink instead—and then, feeling not *very* well, went to bed and lay down for a long while looking at your photograph (now in a rather chaste and alluring frame) and thought, not as you may expect about your various excellences, but about some fifty or sixty of your faults and frailties. And do you know the conclusion I came to? That we're going to have rather a good time together: that we're going to aid and abet each other pretty satisfactorily: and today I want to marry you even more than I did yesterday—which was quite a lot.

I admit that the faults and frailties I considered were all mild and engaging ones—but then, you haven't let me see any others. Do you harbour any really serious vices? Do you do exercises in the morning, eat hashish, sleep with your head under the blankets, read Emerson, or anything really foul like that? Don't be afraid. Put my love to the test, right now.

I'm being abysmally faithful. A charming French girl came to see me the other night—she's doing a thesis on me (ho! ho!) for the University of Lille— and for an hour and a half I sat right at the other side of the room, and talked severely, and simply kept the idea that she was a girl even from entering my head. Darling, what you've done to me is simply nobody's business...

The good Elizabeth—the widow Linklater, c'est-à-dire—went quite gaga and whoops-sister-with-a-sob-in-the-throat when she got my telegram. I got a high-pitched letter from her written on half a dozen minute scraps of paper apparently salved from a w.p.b. Here it is now—quite unstrung, you see.

However, she seems healthier now and bombards me with questions. I'm going to tell her that you used to be an acrobatic dancer in Mombasa, and your father is a retired lion-hunter who did a bit of slave-trafficking in Tanganyika on the side. Nothing like stimulating interest in our Romance.

Elspeth (my sister) took the news with calm and rudeness—rudeness to *me* my love, not you. She says she never expected me to marry till I was forty, and then to someone not respectable. Darling, she thinks you're respectable!

Marjorie did not learn till some time later how Eric had announced his engagement to his mother. He sent a telegram:

SORRY NOT WRITING HAVE BEEN BUSY GETTING ENGAGED AND BUY-ING A BOAT ONE IS CALLED MARJORIE THE OTHER JOY I CANNOT REMEMBER WHICH IS WHICH.

He found Barra, when he went there on his preliminary visit, a delight-ful place, telling his old friend Mrs Walker:

The air is charmingly sleepy, and the people are uncommonly friendly ... Whenever I go outside I fall into a long and hearty conversation with someone or other; and if I stay inside, someone comes in to see if I'm lonely. They really are delightful people: only poor—Orkney is highly civilised compared with Barra—but happy, of a genuinely literary turn of mind, well-mannered and merry. I had a grand night last night listening to stories of fairies and seals and swimmers and ghosts.

It was a better night than he suspected, for his mind began working on some of the themes that had been aired, and stories germinated. Some were written quite soon; some took longer, and eventually formed the basis of a postwar collection, *Sealskin Trousers* (1947). But his immediate task was to find suitable accommodation to which to take his wife on honeymoon, and this threw up some problems; he joked to Mrs Walker: 'In one way Marjorie will be very safe when she comes here: there won't be a repetition of the brides-in-the-bath case: 'cause there ain't no bath.'

A little while later he had better luck and found what he described to Mrs Walker as 'a marvellous house ... beside a graveyard (so *balancing* for a honeymoon) and actually has a bath and modern plumbing: at least, I'm assured it will have, though at present there's only a hole in the wall.'

The time came to go back to Leith and take over the boat where it was lying in Granton harbour. All did not go well. Marjorie remembered:

> The plan was to take *Joy* through the Forth–Clyde Canal and up the west coast to Barra, and we should, after the wedding, spend happy carefree months and years cruising wherever we fancied. It was a converted fishing-boat. I only saw her once, and she seemed all one could want in the way of basic sea-going amenity. She was victualled, and manned by the Barra men, and off she set from Granton in good high form. Alas, the engine went on fire half-way up the canal and she was ignominiously towed back to Leith.

Eric felt he had slipped on another banana-skin. Thanking Isobel (whom he addressed as 'Dearest and most lovely spectre of my vanished youth') for her wedding present, he told her of his disappointment in *Joy*:

> Come and stay with us some time—but bring your tent, for we have no house of our own; my boat has failed me, and, like Lot to Sodom, I have turned my back on the furry-bottomed and deceptive bitch.

If this was the last of *Joy*, it was far from the end of Eric's desire to own and run a boat. For the time being there was nothing to do but forget the loss and concentrate on the gains accruing to his life. A thank-you letter to the Walkers shows the elevation of his spirits as his wedding day approached:

> Really, the Walker family is turning up a whole pack of trumps—do you know that poor Douglas, in addition to ruining his lifetime's savings with a most opulent gift, and devoting *all* his business time to re-doing-up my mismanaged affairs, is now going to be my Best Man?—and my gratitude is reduced to a state of mere speechless bewilderment.
>
> Always inarticulate when faced with emotional situations, I can now merely say ga-ga-ga—or sometimes, with a great effort, goo-goo-goo—and beam in childish happiness ...
>
> I've been working *fearfully* hard the last couple of weeks, so I start matrimony with a magnificent feeling of Virtue. Don't you think that *goodness*, sheer goodness, is the greatest quality for anyone to possess? Yes, we are one in believing that.

Eric and Marjorie were married at Old St Paul's, Edinburgh, on 1 June 1933. It was a match that was to endure, through minor ups and downs, for the rest of his life. Looking back at the age of sixty-nine he wrote:

> Of my marriage I do not propose to say much. It has lasted, at this writing, about thirty-six years, which is thirty-four more than I envisaged at the hour and the day of our nuptials. How to explain its endurance I do not know, for we have quarrelled loudly and often, and today we still quarrel, though perhaps with less reverberation than the shouting that used to echo from our walls.[5]

It is typical of Eric that he should thus, with a joking dismissal, avoid dwelling on something so private as his love for his wife, for the autobiographical writings, whatever their other merits, rarely come close to exposing much of the inner man. It may seem ungenerous in him that he did not at that point in his final autobiographical statement pay some tribute to the qualities in his wife which had made it possible for the marriage to endure: her patience, devotion, humour, her tolerance, her domestic and social skills, her vitality and strength. It simply was not his way; he preferred a slyer, more ironic kind of statement.

His new state did not in some ways make a great deal of difference to his way of life; Marjorie commented:

> I did not transform Eric's life. He remained a roaming bachelor even after we were married. He adored travelling—by ship, preferably—and unencumbered by domestic ties. He was masterful ... I incline that way myself, but being younger I learned to be docile (more or less).

Reflecting in the *Sunday Express* on the news of Eric's engagement, Lord Castlerosse wondered if he would have a happy married life:

> Linklater is a jolly companion. His wit is highly and drily flavoured ... If his wife gives him a bad time—and purely from a selfish point of view I hope she will—it will make him write like a devil refreshed with molten lead, which will be enjoyable for us who love pyrotechnics. I wonder will he view those days in East Fife as the acme of happiness—when he could think as he wished and speak as he thought? It is funny how men like clatter. It is, I suppose, one of the reasons for marriage. Personally, I am content with a radio that has the advantage of being turn-off-able.[6]

Fifty years later, when this passage was reprinted in the *Orcadian*, Marjorie confirmed that 'Eric always wrote furiously, and better, after we'd had a row—which was frequently', but added:

> To the end of his life he thought as he wished and spoke as he thought. Absurd to suppose that I gave him a bad time! The rows were always caused by him, and he never, never apologised. Apart from that he *was* a jolly companion.[7]

Whatever Eric's adventures in the world may have been, the adventure of creating a family and learning to live with it was as great as any, and whatever his apparent thoughts about women as pungently expressed in some of his writings, he was greatly devoted to the woman he met in Edinburgh in 1932.

Their life together began very well. At the end of June, giving a progress report on the honeymoon to his best man, he wrote:

> I will say a word for marriage. It appears to be a good thing. Marjorie behaves most amiably: she has only once regretted the lost comforts of her maiden home, and once threatened to leave me. This is a striking tribute considering that our landlady couldn't cook for a cat's home ... We keep life in our frail bodies by means of three packing cases of canned goods that I brought here, and by habitually supping with Compton Mackenzie who lives some three and a half miles away—or four when the tide is in.

Mackenzie recalled their arrival on Barra: 'Eric Linklater picked up his bride and carried her down the gangway to the pier. There was a cheer of greeting—and relief perhaps that he had not dropped her in the water.'[8]

They swam frequently, which was just as well, as the much-vaunted new bath wouldn't work, and played ball on the sand, and occasionally sailed to the neighbouring islands of Eriskay and South Uist. One day, for five minutes, they flew over the island in the little aeroplane that had brought George Blake on a visit. On another memorable day they went sailing on a chartered fishing-boat—'a big one, fifty feet long'—with Mackenzie, Chrissie MacSween and their entourage, and put in to Mingulay when the weather turned rough and the sea 'lumpy'.

Early in August they went to Orkney where, lacking a home of their own, they stayed for some months with friends Robert and Hester Scarth at Binscarth. Eric seemed to be in no hurry to saddle himself yet with the responsibility of owning a house; indeed, after the disappointment of losing *Joy* he was already looking for another boat. He and Mackenzie contemplated jointly commissioning the building of a new boat, Eric confessing, 'I'm more than a bit shy of second-hand boats nowadays.' That idea soon perished when they looked more closely into the costs that would be involved. Instead Eric sailed when he could with local friends, needing the relief when he could get it from his work on *Magnus Merriman*, which he described to Mackenzie as 'this damned novel that sits on my back like an old man of the sea'. He sailed on the whole with more enthusiasm than expertise, as he was the first to admit:

> I escaped a day or two ago, sailing as crew on a sixteen-foot boat in the Kirkwall regatta. A grand day, with a nice sailing breeze, though on the bright side, and we came third in our own class (which was better than anyone expected, and largely due to the fact that I only dropped the end of the spinnaker boom

overboard once) and not *quite* so well-placed in the other events. A grand day, I repeat—though I blotted the copy-book at night by getting tight to celebrate it. Despite that the connubial situation is still excellent, and all happiness prevails.[9]

When his spirits were high he was quite irrepressible; his eyes would gleam with wickedness behind his spectacles, and nobody could predict what he might do next. One of his great friends in Orkney was J. Storer Clouston, the local historian well known to the previous generation as the writer of very successful comedy-thrillers such as *The Lunatic at Large*. In August 1934 Clouston's daughter Marjorie was married in St Magnus' Cathedral, and after the convivial reception Eric disappeared, together with Ida Hume, his sister-in-law. His wife, abandoned, returned to Binscarth along with her brother-in-law Julian Hume and other members of her family, who were in Orkney on holiday, and there they waited.

> But no sign of Eric and Ida. By the time they turned up Julian was in a great rage and drove off finally with a somewhat subdued Ida. He left his top-hat behind and Eric solemnly placed it on a gate-post and, egged on by other inebriate wedding guests, peppered it with shots from a .22 rifle.[10]

Julian Hume never really forgave Eric for the incident; it just didn't seem funny to him that a chap could kidnap a chap's wife and murder his top-hat on such an occasion. According to Eric, his reason for kidnapping his sister-in-law was to teach Marjorie a lesson for showing too much favour to their friend Douglas Walker during his stay with them earlier in the summer:

> I tell you, I was beginning to get rather tired of her reiterated remark—in moments of alleged unsympathy on my part—with a sigh, a histrionic upheaval of her eyes—'Ah! *Douglas* would have understood!' ... However, the other day, after Marjorie Clouston's wedding, I revenged myself by kidnapping her sister Ida and taking her to Stromness, while Julian, in the Humber and a Black Rage, furiously pursued us.

Nobody could have lived with Eric without a considerable sense of humour and a generous reserve of tolerance, and fortunately for their marriage Marjorie Linklater had both. Another of Eric's mannerisms, half genuine, half jesting pose, was to treat his wife at times as if she were but an unimportant chattel, a witless slave to be summoned and dismissed without ceremony. Until they got used to it—and to Marjorie's generally unperturbed and amusing responses to such treatment—witnesses were sometimes embarrassed or even angered by it. Marjorie's sister Alison wrote, in retrospect:

> Eric was quite Victorian in outlook, despite his books. He hated Marjorie's going on the County Council. He expected her to wait on him hand and foot.

He deliberately used to humiliate her (or try to) in front of guests, calling her 'wet knickers' or 'my idiot wife'. She would hit back; they used to have great rows. Sally [their eldest child] is said to have got under the table when things got too fierce ... What a domestic tyrant he was! He would come in late for breakfast, long after everyone had finished, and expect his egg to be immediately produced, cooked exactly as he liked it. He was never in his life known to have washed up a single spoon.[11]

Marjorie seemed to learn quite early—or to have by nature—the attitude taken by J. M. Barrie's mother in the episode delightfully recalled by George Lyttelton in a letter to Rupert Hart-Davis:

I love the old mother's reply to J.M.B., after she had said how proud Jane [Carlyle] was to look through the door at her man and think how famous he was. J.M.B. said 'Yes, but what when he roared at her to shut the door?'—'Pooh, a man's roar is neither here nor there.'[12]

Eric roared often enough and loud enough, but Marjorie knew how to handle it. Her unwavering admiration for his talent as a writer led her to make allowances for his bad temper, which she attributed, perhaps rightly, to the emotional stresses to which the creative life is subject. She understood intuitively, moreover, from a very early stage that Eric was prone to quite unreasonable jealousy, and that his disparagement of her was proportionate to his awareness of his dependence upon her. Perhaps his jealousy was not wholly without foundation. She was pretty and vivacious, and attracted men wherever she went, and enjoyed the attentions she got. Eric, although he had won the affections of many women, and had finally drawn a considerable prize in marriage, never quite believed in himself and his ability to hold Marjorie. While it was acceptable, or even *de rigueur*, for him to exercise his charms on new acquaintances, constantly testing what he thought of as his unattractiveness against the actual responses of women he met, Marjorie should have glowed for him alone.

Though there were times when their married life was difficult, however, they were successful in establishing a solid and affectionate relationship, sometimes playful, sometimes exciting, that allowed each of them to work well in his/her own way. If others criticised Eric's behaviour, Marjorie always defended him. It might be a cliché, but one had to learn to take the rough with the smooth; that was her position. Without the rough the smooth would have far less savour.

They were both romantics at heart, and when the idea suggested itself that the young couple might as well winter abroad, they decided it was just what they wanted. After a summer of conscientious writing in which he was able to complete *Magnus Merriman*, Eric took Marjorie for a tour of the south of England—'we looked at a few cathedrals, and spent a good week in London'[13]—and then they prepared for their indefinite visit to Italy. By mid-September they knew that Marjorie was pregnant, but that only made the prospect of a milder southern winter all the more attractive. They accepted the loan of a house in Lerici and Eric, not the most realistic of men, invited numerous friends to come and stay with them in their villino, among them Compton Mackenzie:

> Now look here: we didn't invite you to Italy for a holiday. We thought you might come and stay for a couple of months and do your ordinary work and give us the pleasure of your company in between times ... You can stay in bed all morning and sit up all night, as is your disgusting habit, and no one will force you or cajole you or otherwise prevail upon you to do anything you don't want to do. Whether the villa is big enough to provide you with an exclusive sitting-room I doubt, but surely some arrangement can be arrived at that will be offensive to no one.

Mackenzie, who was working hard at the time to pay off the considerable debts he had accumulated, was unable to accept the invitation. It was just as well, for Eric and Marjorie soon found that the Villino San Carlo was barely big enough for the two of them. He described it to Phoebe Gilkyson as 'this very diminutive and somewhat chilly villa'. They travelled out to Lerici at the end of November and there lived 'a quiet and simple life: we see no one: we walk a little, when the winds do not blow too sheer and bitter off the hills'. He told Douglas Walker:

> We're on a steep, a precipitous slope, with olive trees all round and the sea just below us, coming in to a tiny and almost private bay ... We live on spaghetti, minestrone, pinocchi, ravioli, iron-hard rolls, and floods of Chianti—1s/4d or so for a flask that holds nearly two bottles. So that's all right.

Shortly after Christmas he wrote to Lesley Storm:

> You are thinking, of course, that our invitation to you to come and stay with us in Lerici was one of those things that are meant to be forgotten—and you're right ... [Our villino is] about half the size we expected, and God knows what would have happened if the several people we invited had actually arrived.[14]

He complained that he had nowhere to work except the small sitting-room; hence 'Marjorie is being trained to sit in silence and without movement, poor girl.'

In these circumstances Eric settled down to work again; he had been invited to write a biography of Robert the Bruce for Peter Davies's series, and bent his efforts to the congenial task while awaiting with some anxiety the publication of *Magnus Merriman* in January 1934.

He had also taken some time during 1933 to have another look at the Polly Peachum play, and had submitted a revised version of it to Cape describing it as 'a small but fanciful thing—need I say I think it's rather good?' Cape, perhaps without overwhelming enthusiasm, had agreed to publish it at some time during the following year, encouraged by a possibility that the Cambridge Amateur Dramatic Society would attempt a production of it to coincide with publication. In December Eric heard that this would not now be happening, and he wrote to Cape urging earlier publication:

> Since then their theatre has been burned down—I believe they set it on fire on purpose to provide a gentlemanly excuse for not producing *The Devil's in the News*—so that's off. Hence it might be published earlier, April, don't you think, fairly close in the wake of *Magnus*? Also—this very tentatively—what about getting it illustrated? And work up the price to five bob? It gives plenty of opportunity for pictures—and have a dedication to 'The Unknown Producer'?

Eric's desire to see as many new books in print as possible was partly the result of financial worries which were never very far away. He confessed to Douglas Walker:

> I spent half a day doing furious financial calculations a few days ago—it was *very* interesting—but as the chief expenditure (the matter of my wife's lying-in at Firenze) was assessed on the basis of 'Oh, it can't be more than so-and-so! Well, I mean to say, it really can't!'—perhaps it wasn't very accurate.

Just then, however, he received news that the London *Evening Standard* was going to run 'a kind of Book-of-the-Month stunt', and that it wanted *Magnus Merriman* for its first selection. Eric thought the whole idea comical, and was nervous of it: 'I have a lurking dread of newspaper stunts, and they may ruin it. I hope not. It's rather a good novel, I think.'[15] But the *Evening Standard* people promised that their publicity would increase the sales of the book, and Eric, anxious to make money for projects in mind as well as current maintenance, agreed to the experiment. They would need to buy property before long, since they could not live indefinitely in a rented cottage in Tuscany. Influenced a little by Mackenzie's love of islands and by the pleasure they had found during their Barra honeymoon, Eric had half-persuaded Marjorie that they should seek an island address of their own; he confided to Mackenzie: 'We should be in Orkney again next summer and we have hopes of acquiring a permanent residence there—and on *two* islands, Monty!—each about the size of a small field.' And if they lived in such a situation, then naturally he would have to have the boat he craved as well. A lot depended therefore on the success of the new novel; if a little extra could be made from the play, so much the better.

Meanwhile the Bruce book was beginning to take shape, and should be ready on schedule for Peter Davies in May; and the White Owl Press was going to publish his trio of short stories under the collective title of *The Revolution* at about the same time. Under the pressure to earn money his mind was bursting with ideas, as he told Mackenzie: 'I've got any amount of work in prospect—the *doing* of it is the only difficulty, but the responsibilities of marriage are a good incentive!' Among the ideas was the basis of another novel, 'a roaring lowbrow comedy'[16] which he had already promised Cape, and on which he wanted to get started.

The launch of *Magnus Merriman*, on 4 January 1934, was a great success. Very quickly it became the biggest-selling novel of the season, toppling Hervey Allen's *Anthony Adverse* from the number one position. Reviewers such as Howard Spring, Hugh Walpole, James Agate, Harold Nicolson, all testified to having revelled in the book. Comparisons were made with *Juan in America*, some finding it a little better, some finding it not quite so uproarious. Compton Mackenzie announced that those who had enjoyed *Juan in America* would find in *Magnus Merriman* an added flavour. All found it full of zest and gusto, and brilliantly written. Only J. B. Priestley wasn't sure it should really be called a novel, though he enjoyed its Rabelaisian comic-romantic manner.

In the United States, too, it enjoyed excellent reviews, though there was some sense of misgiving at what was prudishly called its 'naughtiness'. While Walpole in England compared Eric with E. M. Forster, Aldous Huxley and William Plomer as artists *sui generis*, deriving from nobody, in the States Lewis Gannett declared him to be like Sir Walter Scott, Rabelais, P. G. Wodehouse and Voltaire all rolled into one, and William McFee thought Hemingway and Sinclair Lewis might both learn something to their advantage from a study of his technique.

It was off, then, to a good start, and has remained among the most highly regarded of Eric's novels, though like the others it has attracted little or no critical attention. Francis Russell Hart has written approvingly of it as 'Linklater's first large-scale novel of modern Scotland', pointing to certain characteristic qualities such as its 'great setpieces of grotesque hilarity, erupting catastrophically in the midst of elegant manners milieux' and the way in which 'satiric realism fuses with various kinds of fantasy—farcical, erotic and even gothic'.[17] Kurt Wittig analysed the sense of a very special way of looking at things which derives from Eric's disturbingly distorted images and his use of a sort of stereoscopic distortion brought about when characters view things while under the influence of drink.[18]

Whatever readers might make of it, Eric was anxious to establish that it was not a *roman à clef*. In a prefatory 'Admonition' he insisted that his use of autobiographical elements was simply a matter of taking 'an occasional backcloth from reality'; he had, he said, written a novel: 'I have not filled a photograph-album or published confessions of a mis-spent life'. And he concluded: '*Magnus Merriman*, then, is neither photography nor history, but a novel. And the material of a novel is fiction.' This might have been no more than an attempt to vary the sort of declaration that in those days at any rate frequently introduced a novel, to the effect that no person or incident in it had any connection with real life: an attempt to forestall the possibility of libel proceedings against the book. If that was its intention, however, it fell short of the mark. Before the year was half-way through Eric was embroiled in a libel suit. One of the characters in the book, Beaty Bracken, was said to have been so perfervid in her Scottishness that at one stage she flushed a Union Jack down a lavatory. Gwendoline Cuthbert, known in the Scottish political life of the time as 'Wendy Wood', felt that she recognised in this incident a damaging reference to something she was said to have done, and she claimed £1,800 from Eric and Cape.

The case was eventually settled out of court, after causing Eric much worry at intervals during the year, and the offending sentence was excised from subsequent editions of the novel. The business showed him the delicacy of the ground he sometimes trod as a novelist reporting on the world he saw, but the real point of the 'Admonition' was to remind readers that though the book may have started from real life its essential centre lay in the imaginative use and extension of those events into a fiction.

At first sight many of Magnus's experiences and characteristics are so close to those of his creator as to make the reader suppose that the thrust is autobiographical. Proportionally, however, the use of Eric's own past as a basis for Magnus's past is much smaller than it seems; all the details are established in a matter of eight pages only. The Scottish political adventure dominates the middle section of the book. It is preceded by a build-up which draws rather more subtly on Eric's experience in London and Edinburgh in 1932–3 and, showing the real purposelessness of the young man through his flirtations with different women and with literary and political ambitions, begins to set up the tension between the city life and the purer rural rhythms of country life in Orkney. In a sense Magnus is Everyman, and his attempt to come to terms with himself, with women, with notions of responsibility (to oneself, to one's talent, to other individuals, to society), with the nature and purpose of life, give the development of Magnus's story a profound significance. Such a tale, if told with conviction, has the same impact whether it be set in Scotland, England, the United States, China, the Soviet Union or anywhere else.

The underlying seriousness in the novel is not undercut but thrown into high relief by the context of uproarious comedy. Eric views the eccentricities of human action with a kind of baffled sympathy which enjoys the ludicrous aspects of individual behaviour and social organisation but which is essentially concerned with the failed aspirations behind them. But these potentially destructive discoveries are unfolded in no mood of tragic gloom, but rather with a glorious mock-heroic energy which renders the various experiences in love, society and politics as hilarious as they are ultimately disturbing.

That there is no easy solution, however, is a measure of the book's fundamental seriousness. Magnus does not return to a vague promise of satisfying life represented by a sunrise journey into the west with his love in his arms, as Peter Flett does. Orkney is a real place, hard work is the order of the day, and bad weather a feature of the climate; Rose is no ethereal maiden but a practically minded, hard-working woman with some tendency to the shrewish until she gets her way. She is quite incapable of sharing Magnus's imaginative world of books and ideas and poetry. Orkney is no idyllic land beyond the rainbow; it is everywhere, mundane and actual. One of the triumphs of the novel is the way Eric presents and controls this downbeat conclusion. Magnus is defeated; but he finds in his hopes for his son a sufficient reason to continue to enjoy life, and the reader closes the book with a smile.

Not, however, without having first been made to laugh out loud at many points of the narrative, especially the first two-thirds of the novel where the literary world of London and the political world of Scotland are subjected to Eric's genially satirical attentions. Though it is almost fifty years since Eric used his contemporaries in such a way, and although a lot has changed in the Scottish National Party since 1934, there is no loss of impact in the narrative. It has both the quality of history, revitalising a specific period from the past, and a contemporary relevance—for these characters and these problems are recurrent if not eternal.

Apart from the satisfaction of its overall shape, there is an immense amount of pleasure to be gained from the texture of the writing. The debates between Magnus and Meiklejohn are full of Rabelaisian, Falstaffian exchanges. Eric's feeling for place and atmosphere produces vividly realised settings pleasingly differentiated. Magnus's return to Scotland, for instance, is described with exciting energy:

> The wind hurried him along Princes Street. It blew with a bellow and a buffet on his stern and half-lifted his feet from the pavement. It beat his ears with a fistful of snow, and clasped his ribs with icy fingers. It tore the clouds from the sky, and laid bare, as if beyond the darkness, the cold grey envelope of outer space. Heads bent and shoulders thrusting like rugby forwards in a scrum, eastbound pedestrians struggled against it, and westward travellers flew before it with prodigious strides. To the left, towering blackly, like iron upon indomitable rock, was the Castle. To it also the storm seemed to have given movement, for as the clouds fled behind its walls the bulk of its ancient towers and battlements appeared to ride slowly in the wind's eye, as though meditating a journey down the cavernous channel of the High Street to Holyroodhouse, its deserted sister.[19]

In the Orkney-based part of the novel too he naturally and necessarily deals with the wind and not infrequent stormy conditions, and he does so with a matching delight in the violence of the elements. But he also loves the islands when in their more peaceful aspect they inculcate in Magnus a growing beatitude; his arrival home follows a rough voyage from Leith to Kirkwall up the east coast of Scotland:

> It was early June, and there was no darkness on that northern land. The sun had set, but the north-west sky was stained with a rich afterglow. A twilit veil hung over the still fields. The wind had gone, and there was no sound but the lazy booming, muted by distance, of waves on the Atlantic shore.[20]

It was earlier noted how Eric used to say that his failure to be recognised as a serious novelist might have derived in part from his not having imposed on his books his own character, 'his own way of thought and fashion of writing'.[21] Even if it is true of *The Men of Ness* that Eric had so fully adopted the style of the saga-makers that the modern Linklater was invisible (a contentious proposition at best), no such comment could possibly be made about *Magnus Merriman*. No one else could have written it. Its tone and voice are as individual and recognisable as that of, say, D. H. Lawrence, and, it might be argued, as wise and valuable in thought, though richer in entertainment. If Eric failed to win the recognition he wanted and merited, it was not because he failed to develop a style of complete individuality and integrity; and *Magnus Merriman* exemplifies it at its best.

Eric, working in Italy on his biography of the Bruce and practising being a good husband to his heavily pregnant wife, knew that he had written a very good novel in *Magnus Merriman*, but did not then have time to be distressed if its critical reception lacked insight. The public liked it well enough to buy copies in large numbers, and his immediate financial worries were relieved; he was able to contemplate setting up a permanent home, and his thoughts continually inclined to Orkney where, like Magnus, he felt his proper place was.

Life in Italy, especially in the rather circumscribed Villino San Carlo, was mostly work and waiting for the baby to complete its term of gestation. They got to know some people; there were:

> A delightful woman with an enormous villa, who has lived here for thirty years; a retired Admiral (Sir R. Bacon, who wrote a good book about Jutland) and his family; a couple of German refugees; and two or three female artists, nice and elderly—all very respectable, you see.[22]

The delightful woman with the enormous villa was Lady Sybil Lubbock, wife of Percy Lubbock, and the Linklaters' friendship with her led to a change of location as the time for the birth of the child grew closer. In the grounds of the great house called Villa Medici at Fiesole, in which Lady Sybil held court, there was a cottage in which the Marchesa Iris Origo, Lady Sybil's daughter by a previous marriage, was supposed to live. But she preferred to live elsewhere and the Linklaters were persuaded to come to the Villino Medici for a while, on the grounds that 'the nursing-homes of Florence are all quite dreadful—staffed by nuns, who rejoice in suffering—and hardly anyone comes out alive.'[23] Towards the end of March they moved to Fiesole and awaited what Eric referred to as 'zāo', the confinement expected about 21 April.

Eric thought Lady Sybil a most individual woman:

> Irish by birth—her father was an impoverished earl, of great learning and recurrent work—she had an impediment of speech which decorated her conversation with a multiple lisp, and the staple of her conversation was so far removed from ordinary topics, or ordinary values, that rarely, since knowing her, have I had much difficulty in believing fairy-tales.[24]

He did not, however, find it so easy to warm to Percy Lubbock, whom he found rather dry:

> In his garden at Gli Scafari [the Lubbocks' other house, at Lerici] ... I found elements of boredom which seemed to me—in the coarseness of my judgment, the brutality of my taste—comparable to similar elements in his books. But Lady Sybil was pure enchantment of a sort I had never known before, nor have encountered since ... Percy was a scholar and an influential writer, and it may be that Sybil was no more to hold or bind than a will o' the wisp; but as a companion I much preferred her.[25]

To Lady Sybil Eric was further indebted for an Italian phrase, the *'dono di coraggio'* (the gift of courage) in the context of a story she told him about an Italian peasant in the Great War whose conduct was rather like that of Bluntschli in *Arms and the Man*. A dozen years later that phrase and that story, which had been gestating in his mind ever since he first heard it, finally produced the concept of Private Angelo.

Among those whom Eric met at the time were Norman Douglas and his publisher-bookseller friend, Pino Orioli. Orioli, full of comical stories and expansive as the day, won Eric's affection, and his respect, too, when the Italian charmed Eric's mother-in-law 'as clowns and elephants and piebald horses charm children at a circus'.[26] With Norman Douglas he felt rather shy, though they found common ground in their interest in Scotland; Eric recalled:

> I had read most of his books, and I knew the Scottish countryside in which he had been born. His red face beneath a silver coverlet of hair was inscrutable yet seemed benign; but I was over-awed by his scholarship and greater breadth of experience. I had met, at that time, few authors, and I was properly respectful of the author of *South Wind* and *Old Calabria* and *Siren Land*. I was, I think, too respectful for his liking, who preferred enjoyment to honour.[27]

He was well pleased with an armful of books given him by Orioli and

Norman Douglas, and twenty years later, when he was working on *A Year of Space*, he recalled the gift with gratitude.

But the visiting and sight-seeing in which Eric and Marjorie spent much time did not prevent him from working hard: harder indeed than he had intended for, as he told Douglas Walker:

> The omnipresent *Robert the Bruce*, not nearly finished yet, has been much more difficult than I expected: endless disentangling of events and balancing of theories and endeavouring to get dates to fit in: the result is a somewhat bald narrative that shows no sign of the underlying toil and will win nothing in the way of criticism except: 'A perfunctory and slipshod piece of work'.

The anticipation of a cool reception from the reviewers had already become ingrained in him; he grumbled that 'most of the reviews of *Magnus* have been abysmally stupid ... the majority are of such a nature as to convince me that a novelist should add footnotes (for reviewers only), carefully explaining the meaning of simple sentences and telling them, in words of one syllable (with illustrations where possible) just what one is doing.'

He described how he had 'simply sweated' over a preface that Cape had asked him to do for the forthcoming *The Devil's in the News*, and 'only succeeded in getting something reasonable after long agony and multiple re-writing'. Among the pieces he had been writing there was one which showed his political awareness and his outspokenness in a notable way. In Florence he had met some early victims of German oppression, and the premature death of one of these men, a poet and artist, prompted him to write an article combining his pet subject, the advantages of littleness, with an attack on the new monolithic Nazi state.

Nazism was, he wrote, 'a loathsome regime', and he reflected on 'the meanness of the Nazis' brutality' which led them 'to practise on their interned enemies the slow torture of a rancid Prussianism'.[28] He later wrote that it was nonsense to claim that in the 1930s 'we in Britain knew little or nothing of the repression and torment of German concentration camps until they became, during the course of the war, so notorious that they could not be ignored'.[29] He himself was already keenly aware, in 1934, of what he saw as the evils of Communism and of Fascism and its vile companion, National Socialism. He was already beginning to be torn between two notions of what ought to be done about them. That they should be resisted was patently obvious, but whether there might be some other means than the use of force to correct their errant ways exercised him intellectually and emotionally for some years.

To his references to Hitlerism in the magazine *Life and Letters* there was an immediate response. In Germany his publishers, Langen & Müller, were instructed that as Linklater was on record as a hostile critic of

Germany their forthcoming translation of *The Men of Ness* must be abandoned. According to Eric's pleased recollection, 'the translation was publicly burnt'.[30] A year or so later another German publisher approached him about a German edition of *Magnus Merriman*, but started making conditions he did not like. When a local gauleiter warned the press that they must not use the services of a Jewish translator, Eric wrote angrily to Rupert Hart-Davis, who was negotiating the matter:

I don't know whether Goldschmidt is any good as a translator or not, the odds are always on the negative—but if Goverts Verlag refuse to employ him simply because he is a Jew, you can tell them to stuff a large bag of tin swastikas up their fundamental orifices and ride a tandem bicycle to hell. I'm not going to play ring-a-ring-o'-roses with Julius Streicher round a Nazi maypole for anyone or for any money.

When it was further stipulated that Eric must revoke his criticism of the Nazi ethic and the Hitler regime, and promise not to attack it further, he abandoned hope of sales in German markets and replied briskly: 'No! A year ago Germany banned me. Now I ban Germany.' Finally a letter from the President of the Reichsschriftumskammer, dated 9 December 1935, confirmed that Eric was *persona non grata* with the German Government. It delighted him to remember that 'in parting company with Germany I anticipated Neville Chamberlain by almost four years'.[31]

There was a curious sequel to all this some seven years later, when Goebbels issued copies of *Juan in America* to large numbers of his circle, and the *Berliner Illustrierte Zeitung*, in August 1943, printed extracts from it as anti-American propaganda, despite the official taboo on Eric's work. When it came to his notice Eric raged, but the best he could do by way of reply was an angry article featured in the *Daily Mirror* with the headline: 'I'll sue Mr Hitler, says Linklater'.[32]

Hitlerism was not Eric's only target in the mid-thirties. Some readers criticised his comments on Communism, especially when he compared it with Nazism and called it 'an Oriental perversion aggravated by torments and techniques filched from Germanic practice'.[33] There was no doubt in his mind about where the enemies of civilisation were to be found, and financial setback was no obstacle to his saying so. Again his solution to the problems of the day, as developed in 'Growing Like a Tree' and later detailed more fully in *The Lion and the Unicorn*, was for small states (such as a free Scotland as argued for in his by-election manifesto), small businesses, small organisations of every kind, glorying in their individual differences and specialties, ready to join together on occasion to repel monsters.

With splendid timing he completed by the beginning of April the various writing tasks he had undertaken. It had required all his powers of application to do so, considering the temptations to visit and go sightseeing when 'an hour away stood all the rich creation of the Renaissance'. His delight in Marjorie and his concern about and interest in her pregnancy also made it difficult to concentrate. He complained comically in a letter to Phoebe:

> I have just spoken *most* harshly to my poor Marjorie, and told her, in thunderous tones, not to stand dithering at my shoulder: and she simply laughed as heartily as if Eddie Cantor had made a good joke and Peter Arno had drawn it. I try to break her spirit, and all that happens is that I break my own. Marriage is no joke.

Ten days later he wrote to Mackenzie, worried about the possibility that he might have to return to Scotland because of the Wendy Wood libel claim: 'I can't leave Marjorie, and it's too late for her to travel. She's amazingly fit and full of spirits, and I grow more ridiculously in love with her all the time!'

In the strange way that so often seems to happen, their happiness as they entered the last weeks of waiting for the birth was muted by news of a death. Douglas Walker's father, who had in some ways become a father-figure to Eric since Robert Linklater's death in 1916, suddenly became ill. After an apparent recovery he relapsed and died. Eric's letter of sympathy to Mrs Walker shows a rare glimpse of his deeper self:

> I'm terribly sorry ... few people, outside his immediate family, can have had a greater affection for Mr Walker than I had, or a greater admiration of all his fine qualities. He was a type of the best that his generation and his country produced. Not many men have combined such sterling virtue with so charming and endearing a manner: his kindness, his geniality, his abundant vitality—he had so many lovable characteristics, and his inner self was so fine and strong. I have often envied him—not grudgingly, but honestly and admiringly—for the success he made of his life: I don't mean making money, or anything like that, but the wholeness, the completeness, the *satisfactory* happiness of his life. Only a good man can be deservedly happy, as he was—and only a very lovable man can make other people happy, as he did.

But, like the rustics in *The Winter's Tale*, having met with things dying they had to turn to things new born. Alison Sarah, destined to be known as Sally, was born on 28 April 1934. The proud father described his new life to Douglas Walker:

> The Lord has added unto my store a daughter: truly a marvellous child, weighing the quite unusual weight of 3,330 grams. During the early stages of the battle, while Marjorie was really the most important person in the house, and doing her work very nobly, her mother and I behaved with admirable composure; but now, when the infant has taken first place, we—its grand-mother and I—have become a little unhinged, and run about with books by a

man named Truby King—a great liar, I should think—and tell the nurse (a charming girl) that she is doing everything wrong; and whenever the baby goes to sleep we wake it up to see if it's still alive.

For a while his paternal enthusiasm was almost unsupportable; Marjorie told Peg Walker how her husband had got the whole of Truby King's book off by heart and was furious if the young nurse and the mother of the babe didn't get every detail right:

> He throws open windows and assists Alison to bring up wind and questions me sternly about the length of time allowed for feeding.

But the baby was strong and healthy, 'muscular and barrel-chested', Marjorie said, and when he saw that all would be well, Eric's energies were re-directed to his work. A baby, he perceived, was best defined as 'a collection of uncontrolled apertures', and Marjorie's methods of dealing with them, though haphazard, seemed effective.

He was looking forward, now that the child had arrived and the winter was over, to returning home; there were projects waiting to be begun. Besides, life in Italy, especially in Fiesole, was not inexpensive; Eric almost began a thank-you letter to Lady Sybil with the words: 'Dear Lady Sybil, Owing to your very great kindness, we are now almost entirely destitute.'[34] To Douglas, who had to warn him that Mrs Cuthbert was reopening her libel case against him, he wrote: 'This is a charming place indeed, but it's costing us a mint of money—there won't be much left over for Wendy.' He was not, in fact, in danger of insolvency, but was anxious, now that he was father as well as husband, to find a roof of his own under which to establish his family; and although he was still negotiating at long distance for the two islands called The Holms, it was clearly a matter that required his personal attendance in Orkney. Arrangements were made for the family to leave Italy at the end of May. Just before leaving he wrote to Mrs Walker about their plans:

> Now we're on the point of leaving; packing almost finished—it's going to cost thousands of pounds to transport us, and more particularly our baggage—and we leave on Tuesday. I shudder to think of the journey. Alison Sarah is *not* a modest child, in any way. She has a robust and assertive nature, a thoroughly modern regard for her own comfort, and a hell of a voice. In fact, she's rather a pest; and she'll be lucky if she escapes being thrown out of the window.

They were sorry to leave such a lovely place, but idylls must come to an end and life must be got on with. By the last day of May they had arrived in Edinburgh, and a new phase had begun.

12   Orkney Householder

Marjorie had enjoyed holidays in Orkney with her family before she ever met Eric, and had already, as he remembered, 'acquired an affection for the islands which was ready to go hand in hand with my own addiction to their harsh and brilliant, inscrutable and friendly charm'.[1] She was perfectly happy to contemplate living in Orkney, but may not have been altogether heartbroken when Eric's prolonged negotiations for the tiny pair of islands called The Holms finally fell through. They lost no time in returning to Orkney for the summer of 1934, and, while staying with their friends the Scarths at Binscarth, looked for some more permanent answer to their accommodation problem.

In the end it was solved through the generosity of Elizabeth Linklater, Eric's mother. She had been living for some years in Ingleneuk, the house by the Loch of Harray built by her husband in 1910. Standing near it was another little house, The Cottage, which Eric now bought and presented to his mother, and he set about turning Ingleneuk into a much larger house, to which he gave the invented but authentically Norse-sounding name of Merkister. Not particularly practical by nature, he found the process of designing and projecting exciting enough, but the business of persuading builders and craftsmen to work as and when he wanted proved rather more complicated and frustrating. Wishing also to extend the amount of land attached to the house, he found even purchasing a half-acre of field took more energy than he had expected. He explained to Rupert Hart-Davis:

> The current novel is in its third quarter—a ticklish phase—so I couldn't leave it for more than a day or two. The poor thing's had many interruptions already, for intermittently during the summer I was rushing about all over Orkney interviewing builders, contractors, joiners, plumbers and whatnot; and, worst of all, a damned fellow, a cousin of my own, from whom I wanted to buy a bit of land you could put in your pocket—it's taken two months of negotiation and argument, and an extortionate price, to get it—so you perceive that returning to one's native country is not an easy thing to do.

By the end of the summer he had at least set in motion the process of creating his home. He had also done a great deal of work on the new novel despite the distractions of domestic life and business negotiations. The baby continued to make healthy progress; Eric told Douglas Walker in

August: 'Sally has reached the satisfactory weight of fourteen pounds, and her bowels are firing on both cylinders.' But it would be months before the newly extended house would be habitable, and in the meantime they decided to spend the winter in Aberdeen, where Douglas's mother let them rent her house until the following April.

There is a sense, however, in which home-making had not been exactly the first and most prominent matter in Eric's mind since the return from Italy. The month of May had seen the publication of three new Linklater titles that demonstrated incontrovertibly his versatility and continuing experimentation with genre and form, and on arrival back in Britain he was naturally anxious to see how they had been received. *The Revolution*, published in a paperback volume by the White Owl Press and not widely distributed, did not receive much attention and was a relatively minor matter, though the form, that of the short story, soon began to engage him much more fully. Peter Davies's issue of *Robert the Bruce* was politely received and sold satisfactorily; in the United States it was published by Appleton and sold sufficient copies to make it worth publishing, though it created no stir. It was a solid, readable, elegant book, showing unobtrusive but impressive skill in the organisation of a complex narrative and full of powerful feeling for Scotland. There was no unexpected revelation about the character of the Bruce, and no new perception about the political complexities of the time which made him act more than a little deviously in pursuit of his triumph. Eric relied on the standard works: Barbour's poem, *The Brus*; the Lanercost Chronicle; and Thomas Gray's *Scalacronica*. He had also read with particular interest the work of two modern scholars, W. Mackay Mackenzie and E. M. Barron, who had discovered additional details of the conduct of the battle of Bannockburn and the general sequence of events in the wars of independence. Out of this he had hammered a thoughtful and at times poetic narrative combining chivalric romance and hard political in-fighting, and made a book still delightful to read for the polished power of its storytelling. A brief quotation gives something of the particular flavour of the tone of the book:

> Edward mustered a great army and marched to Scotland. He besieged Berwick. His fleet suffered a serious repulse, and his army was infuriated by the barbed invective of the garrison. The walls of Berwick, however, were hardly so robust as Scottish wit, and the English army soon entered the town. By Edward's orders no quarter was given, and eight thousand were massacred in three days of busy discipline.[2]

The book was later reprinted, and then in 1939 bought and reissued by Nelson. In the absence of critical approval, Eric took comfort in the fact that somebody must still be reading it.

But the publication for which he had the greatest hopes was *The Devil's in the News*. He had been tinkering with the play for more than a decade, on and off, re-shaping, adding new elements from more recent experience, and his enthusiasm for it was still enormous. It was, perhaps partly in consequence of its compositional history, rather a curious play, and it is a notable testimony to Eric's persuasiveness that a hard-headed businessman such as Jonathan Cape could be induced to publish it. It mixes together some highly disparate elements: the Faustus story with high-sounding blank verse dialogue; characters and relationships from *The Beggar's Opera* with dialogue in rhyming couplets; lyrics from Eric's student plays; and a satirical tale of modern press barons in a world of lost values with dialogue in a formal, complex, often ponderous prose. In the Preface over which Eric had agonised in Italy, and which became eventually an interestingly personal and humorously self-deprecating essay, he spoke of the frailties of the contemporary theatre and the need for experiment, the problems of finding a recipe for good writing, and questions of morality and propriety in writing. He confessed 'with grudging honesty' that he was not wholly convinced that his play was a good one; he *thought* it was, but only when acted could it really be tested and assessed; and he hoped his Preface would help call attention to the play's need to be produced.

One of the excitements of the summer for him then was an experimental production of the play in London on 17 and 18 June at the Grafton Theatre, Tottenham Court Road. The production was mounted by the Incorporated Stage Society, under the direction of Warren Jenkins. Alastair Sim played the Dominican Friar who is discovered to be none other than Satan himself, come to trade for men's souls; Norman Shelley played Harlequin and Eileen Beldon played Lady Drum, who metamorphoses into Polly Peachum during the action. But their performance, though it gave some pleasure, was not well received. *The Times* commented:

> It is irrelevant but charitable to hope that Mr Linklater's comedy reads amusingly. On the stage it slithers disconcertingly from plane to plane and can scarcely be said to have any life at all.[3]

Mr Linklater sheathed too soon, the reviewer complained, the sword of satire at the expense of the newspaper proprietors and allowed his play to slip into dull slapstick comedy and cloudy symbolism.

Despite its London reception, the play was also staged for a week in November at the Maddermarket Theatre, Norwich, where it enjoyed some success, though insufficient to allow it any further life in the theatre. Eric was disappointed, but perhaps it was necessary for him to get these materials out of his system to clear the way for future work in dramatic writing, for his ambitions were no more than temporarily delayed by the setback.

By December 1934 he had almost completed his new novel. He was grateful when Rupert Hart-Davis wrote with handsome appreciation of what he had read so far, because he had suffered a sudden crisis of confidence about it: 'What if everyone else, bar me alone, decides that *Ripeness is All* is not ripe but rotten? From these ugsome musings you timely rescued me. Thankyou.' He finally brought it to a conclusion early in January 1935 and sent Compton Mackenzie a copy of the dedicatory letter with which he proposed to preface the book. The dedication proudly proclaimed his admiration for Mackenzie's writing and his friendship for so exceptional a man:

> It is a large and delighted friendship; but if I do not protest it now, in public, it may go unspoken for long enough. For as soon as we meet again there will be talk on noisier subjects, more inflammatory subjects, on a multitude of very arguable subjects, and a host of inordinately comical subjects; we shall certainly not bother about a topic as quiet as friendship. Indeed, had a stranger listened to our last debating with Norman Sturrock, and Willy Mackay Mackenzie, and Moray McLaren, he might well have thought we were each and all devoted enemies: for you have the gift of contagious passion on subjects so remote and disparate as, if I remember rightly, Turkish mathematics and the identity of Jack the Ripper.

The novel he had begun to write immediately upon his return to Scotland may seem something of a curiosity, for although its theme is clearly not unconnected with his personal life, and although much later in autobiography he described vividly the agreeable and typical Orcadian life-style he was now able to adopt, his chosen setting for his new book was southern England; indeed, he never wrote about Orkney in his fiction again (except in a short story or two and in a children's book, *The Pirates in the Deep Green Sea*). Not one to repeat himself, he felt he had said what he had to say about Orkney in the novels already published. With a major novel about Scottish life still being widely discussed and his other contributions to the Scottish scene all demonstrating his sympathy for the cause of the Scottish renaissance, he personally was interested in a change of literary scene. Besides, he had already begun marinating in his mind the central idea for his new story long before realising that destiny was going to take him to live in the north. His marriage and accession to fatherhood certainly affected the way he handled his material. *Ripeness is All* was, he later mused, 'a light-hearted, most genial novel ... in the mainspring of which was my exuberant delight in becoming a father.'[4]

The book, like *Poet's Pub*, presents a rich but subtly observed feeling of English life, not without a satirical tinge but generally appreciative and celebratory. It has a carefully plotted story in which all the action is hung on the well-proven device of a peculiar will which provides a powerful motivation for the antagonists. In this case the prize is to go to that descendant of the eccentric Major Gander who has by a given date achieved the largest family. Although the events, when considered from a strictly realistic viewpoint, are ludicrous and unlikely, they are narrated with convincing detail, and the picture of mid-thirties English village life is witty but also authentic. If the characters are no more fully realised than is necessary for them to play their roles in the comic proceedings, some of them linger strangely long in the mind after a reading of the novel. The returning 'black sheep', George Gander, attempting incorrigibly to take the inheritance by cheating, is conventionally amoral and engaging, but there is an unexpected dimension in his Anglo-Indian background and the force of his comments on Hinduism and British governmental relations with India. Similarly there is an oblique comment on the rise of Fascism not immeasurably far away from the traditional peace and quietness of the English village, seen specifically, for instance, in an 'isomorphic' poem devised by Stephen Sorley:

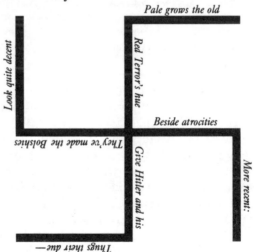

And there is a good deal of comment on the state of poetry, twentieth-century morality, and other questions; Lord Quentin Whicher, for instance, contributes funds to pay for the education of the Vicar's children, and then regrets parting with capital which might more productively have been invested in 'a new process for the mass-production of gas-masks (civilian pattern) for daily use in the next war'.[5]

There is also a typically Linklaterian shadow across the comic action, when the darkness in the human psyche is allowed to dominate unexpectedly for a short cruel while. The potential for the comic to turn horrific is always present in any action; Eric sometimes comes close to exploring what happens when the rules are suddenly ignored: what happens when in the middle of the comic chase the hero's judgement fails and he and his car are smashed under the train. When *Ripeness is All* was published Eric was simply rapped over the knuckles for his lack of decorum; John Brophy, for instance, wrote:

> And his taste has appalling lapses, witness the garden-party in this book (dragged in, for it is not essential to the plot) where an attempt is made to slaughter two pigs, from which they escape alive but not unhurt. Until Mr Linklater learns that grown-up people are not amused by such things, he cannot complain if he is considered, in some respects, still an adolescent.[6]

For Francis Russell Hart, a much more recent commentator, the occasional threat of the bleaker alternative route which Eric indicates as a possibility in his comedy is a highly significant element in his writing. It foreshadows the black humour and the 'sick' joke which became more common to the postwar generations with their greater experience of the unlimited depths to which human depravity can sink. For Hart the pig-slaughtering incident is 'one of the most splendid examples' of Eric's characteristic use of the macabre to shock the reader into reconsidering the material he is perusing: 'The episode is fitting: in an effete postwar pastorality, the gross will to survive tramples less fruitful orders into muddy chaos.'[7] After the garden-party so thoroughly gone wrong, one of the characters who has been presented with a certain sympathy, Lady Caroline, takes cold; pleurisy and then pneumonia set in; and soon she dies. Eric allows the tragic to happen with a kind of ruthless detachment similar to that with which Waugh condemns the innocent little Lord Tangent to death in *Decline and Fall*; but in *Ripeness is All* it is more shocking, because the people are more real than Waugh's, and we have been induced to care about them.

The pursuit of the pigs is both farcically comical and disconcerting; it is described in a passage which has all the energy of Chaucer's account of the chase after the fox in *The Nonne Preestes Tale*, but it is also disturbing, like the episode in *Lord of the Flies* where the boys go to kill their first pig and find mixed emotions attendant upon their success.

Such elements in the writing are, like the more direct references to the horrid in the world of 1935, a kind of substratum of warning in a novel which overtly celebrates 'life, fertility, ripeness'; by the contrasts it throws into relief between the idyllic and the forces which threatened to overwhelm it, it demonstrates, despite its apparent levity, a serious concern with the future of mankind.

It received, on the whole, commendatory reviews and was soon selling with gratifying briskness; according to the *News Chronicle* of 5 April it was the novel most in demand over the past four weeks. For its time it seemed rather daring and there was some fuss about the sexuality of its theme, causing moral problems for reviewers; this was more commonly the response in strait-laced America than in Britain. The *New York Herald Tribune* allowed two of its writers to discuss the novel. Lewis Gannett suggested that Eric might yet 'successfully fuse Wodehouse with Shaw', and that this would be a great triumph. Florence Haxton Britten pointed out that there was more in the book's 'delicious nonsense' than at first met the eye:

> Peeping coyly out from behind the ample skirts of Mr Linklater's humor, there's enough shrewd and able observation of the contemporary scene to fit out several straight-ahead, serious-minded novels with an adequate cargo of sound sense.[8]

No subsequent critic, however, found the novel worthy of comment.

In his *Modern Scottish Literature* (1983), Alan Bold included *Ripeness is All* in a group of 'wildly funny books in which [Linklater's] sense of fun was controlled by a strictly functional and absolutely precise prose style'. He had no more to say specifically about *Ripeness is All*, but commented that the experience of close contact with death when Eric was wounded in 1918 had not unnerved him but given him an extreme distaste for the pretensions of humanity. Consequently:

> His is a black comedy, dedicated to the proposition that the human race is hardly worth running. What makes life worthwhile is the spectacle of the astonishing individual ... Destructive laughter is what Linklater's black comedy suggests.
>
> He is capable of a Swiftian disgust for the brazen mask mankind draws over its imperfections. Linklater pulls back the mask to reveal the individual who— at his or her most vulnerable—deserves perhaps a little sympathy. Linklater's work can be cruel and the end of the cruelty is to encourage the reader to distrust pomposity and posturing. Linklater actually refined, to a literary art, the Scottish supposition that dignity is deceit in disguise.[9]

This is an interesting but overstated and somewhat blinkered view which in pursuit of a particular thesis ('Linklater: Mocking the Heroic') overlooks many balancing and compensating elements in Eric's work. He certainly appreciated the ludicrous, and was a collector of the ridiculous. He paraded them in his novels. But his attitude was not, except on rare occasions, 'Swiftian disgust', but rather an affectionate fellow-feeling which delighted in those comic or bizarre elements that render human personality and society so richly rewarding a study. There is no destructive laughter in *Ripeness is All* for instance at George Gander, who enjoys life in his own way, attempts a mild fraud but does nobody any harm, and accepts defeat with a cheerful grace; there is only pleasure in the projection of the somewhat henpecked Arthur Gander, who finds consolation in the astonishing fertility of his imagination and who provides the reader as well as himself with many delightful moments as he spins his compensatory yarns of heroic experiences in his fancied past. The book offers a whole gallery of comic but sympathetically drawn characters: the splendid English sporting girls, Bolivia Ramboise and Jane Sutton, of the type celebrated similarly in many of the poems of John Betjeman; and the poet Stephen Sorley, with his fear of those same girls and his affectionate relationship with the 'extremely sympathetic young man', Wilfrid, who, it is evident from an early stage of the book, would make Stephen a good wife. The portrayal of Stephen Sorley's problematical love-relationships is light-hearted and touching; he turns, after an excruciatingly funny attempt at courting the rather awe-inspiring Miss Ramboise, to a relationship with the fluttery, domesticated, effeminate Wilfrid and in it finds a sufficient happiness. It might be argued that so tolerant and affectionate a treatment of the theme of sexual inversion is as valid as and more convincing than any number of angst-filled and repetitive pages by some of Eric's more serious-minded and seriously taken contemporaries.

Ripeness is All celebrates enduring values, is funny and moving, and pleases the aesthetic sense with the quality of its writing. Eric's only comment on it in retrospect was that it was 'an exuberant little novel about the joys of parenthood', but he took pleasure in one particular observation:

> In the temper of the time I could not avoid some comment on the politics of those years, and with a curious anticipation of what has now, I believe, become a recognised extension of traditional art forms, I invented concrete poetry.[10]

While waiting for *Ripeness is All* to make its appearance in March, Eric spent some of his winter in Aberdeen again considering the Scottish question and writing a book about the relationship between England and Scotland. This was at the invitation of Lewis Grassic Gibbon, who was editing a series of volumes under the heading 'The Voice of Scotland'. Gibbon had first approached him the previous October, and Eric had immediately indicated his interest, provided that Routledge & Kegan Paul would be a little more specific about the terms they proposed; it would be 'something to come between novels', a pattern of writing he was beginning to settle into happily. Something of a contretemps occurred a couple of weeks later when Gibbon revealed that the publishers were prepared to offer only £50 for the book. Eric, in a document headed 'The Money-Grubbing Business Letter', replied:

> I'm sorry, but £50 is not nearly enough to start the game. I discussed the idea with a Very Distinguished Man of Letters (who has also been asked to contribute a volume) and we agreed that the proper sort of sum was £50 multiplied by 6. This may seem outrageous to Kegan Paul—but £50 seems appalling to me.[11]

The financial arrangements underwent a satisfactory revision and Eric set to work. The volume he produced was eventually published in September 1935, and took its place beside others in the series written by Neil M. Gunn (on whisky), Hugh MacDiarmid (on Scottish eccentrics), Compton Mackenzie (on Catholicism and Scotland), and the Muirs (Willa on Mrs Grundy in Scotland, and Edwin on Scott). *The Lion and the Unicorn*, subtitled 'What England has Meant to Scotland', was a pleasant, sensible, highly individual monograph, full of good things. Its thinking was again generally in favour of autonomy for Scotland, on the grounds that 'people degenerate when they lose control of their own affairs',[12] provided that the benefits of proper partnership and interdependence with England continued to be recognised.

The book is less interesting now as political argument than as a personal rumination, very stylish and rather idiosyncratic, witty and humorous and wise, with speculation of all sorts on interests historical, psychological, literary and social as well as political and economic. The reader may see, in Eric's chapters on Scotland's dark ages and on the influence of the Kirk, more evidence of the fascination with historical topics and the skill in historical narrative which later in life led him to write extensive historical surveys; and in his use of reflective dialogues to carry forward the argument at certain points the germs of a technique of dramatised conversation which he later used to great effect during the Second World War. He did not hesitate either to refer to the larger context in which Scotland's future needed to be considered, and his worries about the darkening clouds in European politics as well as a more general self-image come through in such passages as:

> I am free, as I have said, from racial prejudice. But I have a score of violent intellectual prejudices. I hate Fascism, Communism and all other political or economic systems that cripple and reduce the stature of individual men for the mythical benefit of an imaginary totality. I hate puritanism, teetotalism, and the mental deformity that produces them. I hate stupidity in high places, and only of necessity condone it in myself. I cannot believe that rationalisation of industry, television, and the power to fly to Australia in three days are irrefutable proof of human progress.[13]

For Eric all the arguments could be reduced to a single point:

> The individual is all-important, and the function of the State is to safeguard his security, to provide humus for his growth, and to penalise abuse of the liberty it has established. For yesterday and today men have discovered theory and practice that insistently depreciate the individual. Fascism and its unpleasant brother Hitlerism on the one hand; that well-intentioned Frankenstein, Communism, on the other.[14]

The impression the book gives is partially Shavian in the precise and brilliant use of language and anecdote and ingenious argument, in the urbanity of tone and in the honest and pungent expression of common sense. It is an essay from which one gets a powerful feeling of the individual person behind the print. There are many clues to the personality of the author for those who are interested in such matters, not least, for example, in the chapter called 'Bibulous Interlude', which is a meditation upon whisky. Here Eric took to task those of that 'unhappy multitude that asks, without specification, for "whisky-and-soda": as if, at a railway station, they said "Give me a ticket" or, in a bookshop, tendering their seven-and-sixpence, murmured, "I want a novel".'[15] He tentatively suggested that readers might consider a whisky he had become acquainted with in Orkney, of miraculous qualities, for:

> We have, in Orkney, a distiller of genius. Of the man himself, I need say only this: if indeed it be true that by their fruits we may know men, this is a good man. And of his whisky I cannot say enough. Had I the luminous wings of Shelley I might find an aerial style to praise the felicity with which it comes soaring into the ventricles of the brain. Had I the copious wordage of the Knight of Cromarty I might say something of its bodily virtue and the great galleons of wisdom that sail upon its amber tide. Had I the point and angular precision of Euclid I might prove to a dull world the happiness within its reach.[16]

Sadly and shockingly, Lewis Grassic Gibbon died at the beginning of 1935 before the book he had commissioned was in manuscript. Eric, who had been hoping to make the better acquaintance of a man whose work he much admired, wrote to the bereaved Mrs Mitchell:

> Your husband's death was a calamity, not only to you, but to all of us who are interested in Scots letters ... The quality of his work was so individual that its author must have become a reality to all that read him. Yet a very puzzling reality, for the best of his writing—that magical part which dealt with farm and village gossip—had something like the perfect anonymity of the ballads. He had the faculty—which I take to be genius—of becoming the mouthpiece and translator of a whole people and a whole countryside ... The art of *A Scots Quair* is unique: it is something of its own kind, and only he could have contrived it. I shall always remember the intense excitement and ever-increasing delight with which I first read *Sunset Song.*

Later in the year he wrote with equal enthusiasm of Gibbon's work in the *Fortnightly Library*, saying:

> He was an audacious person. To invent a new prose rhythm and write three full-length novels in it was plumed and high-horsed audacity; and to come so near success as he did was to demonstrate the genius that justified it ... Gibbon's death was a great loss to Scotland.[17]

The Lion and the Unicorn was never reprinted, but makes a pleasing and illuminating volume to set alongside the three autobiographies. It was later in this year, as Eric contemplated his return to Orkney, that he wrote the charming and typically Linklaterian essay on Orkney's scenery to which reference was made in Chapter 2. It was written as a contribution to a book about Scotland's scenery edited by George Scott-Moncrieff and published in the summer of 1935. The love of that windswept archipelago which is conveyed through the vivid descriptions and affectionate anecdotes is most marked, and Eric's favourite theme, of the Viking inheritance of the islands, provides its core; again he referred to the story of Sweyn Asleifson, and one can again trace the long slow process of maturation through which that material went before finding its fullest expression twenty years later. He also proudly mentioned some contemporary Orcadians of renown:

> Edwin Muir—poet and novelist as well as critic—was born in the little island of Wyre, and went to school in Kirkwall; where a schoolfellow, a backward boy, was that admirable artist and custodian of Scotland's art, Stanley Cursiter. Living at Smoogro in Orphir is Storer Clouston, who, having made a reputation as a humorist—his Lunatic was once as famous as Jeeves—neglected it for pious labours in history and archaeology.[18]

There was, he added, throughout the Mainland of Orkney 'a furious addiction to drama'; their efforts were so far not very good, but they were learning their dramatic alphabet. It was such delights as the company of men like Muir and Clouston and especially Cursiter, who had painted portraits of Marjorie and Eric as wedding presents and whose talk about painting and paintings was an education in a subject of ever-increasing fascination to Eric, that convinced Eric he was right to be building his home in the parish of Harray.

The essay was further typical of his attitudes at the time in the way that he was unable to resist comparing the relationship between Orkney and Scotland with that between Scotland and England, and it ended:

> And when I see the decency of the world progressively menaced by such things as the corporate state, and other such heresies of the ant-hill, I remember with comfort the Icelandic proverb that says: 'Little things are the last to be found.'[19]

The essay began with a description of a visit he made to Orkney in March 1935, when he went up to see how the renovations and extensions to his house were coming on. The winter in Aberdeen had been pleasant and fruitful, but he was now anxious to move into his new abode and settle as a resident Orcadian proper. Early in April he was making arrangements for Rupert Hart-Davis and other friends to come up for a house-warming the first week in July; he impressed on Rupert the necessity to make sure too that Sean O'Faolain, notoriously vague, had received his invitation, that he 'reads it, and understands it, and apprehends that he is to come in July, not June, as he thinks, and knows roughly where Orkney is.'

Despite a current financial precariousness—he had, he told Douglas Walker in early April, an overdraft of £400 odd, and his next cheque from Cape was not due till 1 May—the move to Merkister was effected in the first week in May, and the little family began to enjoy a happy sense of having found their rightful place to live at last. There were still problems over building work and uncompleted details but, as pages 151–3 of *Fanfare for a Tin Hat* show, they felt as if they had escaped to an idyllic backwater and they were very pleased with themselves. In *The Man on My Back* Eric wrote that his existence for a couple of years was uneventful: 'It consisted of hard work and contented domesticity, in which there is no tale.' But in *Fanfare* he expanded a little on this, telling of amateur theatricals, and dangerous games of 'mixed hockey on steeply sloping fields obscured by a thickening twilight',[20] and weddings and funerals and haytime and harvest. He recalled the happiness of having maids who were likeable and cheerful, and who appeared to like them:

> Within my expanded house there was a lavatory that opened off the hall, and in summer, when the kitchen windows were usually wide open, one could sit in the lavatory, with its upper window down, and listen to the exuberant conversation of the three maids who served us with genial efficiency. There was a cook, a housemaid and a nursemaid: they were uncommonly pretty girls, and they lived lives of adventure and emotional extravagance—in theory or wishful thinking rather than reality—that reduced our existence to humdrum insignificance. What tales, what jokes, what wild, pretended confessions, and above all, what squalls of soprano laughter came out from the kitchen window to be captured through the window of the lavatory where I sat in admiration and envy of those lovely girls![21]

If one is reminded of John Synge in Aran, listening to the conversations of his hosts in the room below through a hole in his floor and polishing his understanding of the rhythms and inflections of their speech for use in writing such plays as *The Playboy of the Western World*, one might wish that Eric had made greater use of his privileged position than merely to have enjoyed what he heard.

After Rupert and Comfort Hart-Davis had visited Merkister in July, Eric wrote to thank them: 'When we are as good hosts as you are guests, it will be worth your while to return.' With humour and enthusiasm he described the Stromness Regatta and the mistake he had made which cost his crew the chance of winning their race:

> In the All-Comers' Race we got over the line in magnificent style, second, and only a length behind the leader, whom we passed before getting to the mouth of

the harbour; rounded the Black Buoy, hoisted our spinnaker, and sailed away with the whole fleet behind us. We were half a minute ahead of the next one at the Clestron buoy, gibed over and hauled our sheet like professionals, lay down to a fine fresh breeze and headed straight for the next mark, close-hauled but able to make it. We kept our lead and were the first round. Then, close-hauled on the other tack, we pointed for the mouth of the harbour. And presently we made a grievous mistake. For the ebb-tide seemed to be taking us too far over towards Graemsay, and back a bit from the harbour. So I stood in for the back of The Holms ... and found that two other boats, which had kept on for Graemsay, had been helped, not hindered, by the tide ...

I got an awful telling-off from the Towersers for my mistake in the matter of the tide, and Tommy, with pain rather than anger, has been saying ever since, 'But why did you no stand on for Graemsay, Eric?' Why, oh why? It will take me years to live it down.

When he wrote to Rupert again in August he was in the highest spirits, and Rupert's inquiry about who had been handling Eric's translation rights was put aside several times while more important matters were dealt with—more sailing, and shooting of snipe and plover, and an anecdote about an experience at sea:

Sailing one night in the midst of the Flow, being perhaps some five miles south-west of Scapa Pier and three or four miles east-south-east of Houton Head, the air being dusk and a light wind, I heard such a long-drawn cry, melancholy indeed but not untuneful, like fluting in a hollow room, that I turned with every one of my seven remaining hairs standing like lone trees in a desert, and asked with a tremulous and foreboding voice what it might be—for so might the ghost of a drowned chantyman sing in the twilight—and was told it was a Great Northern Diver; and those three words filled me with a feeling semblable to that state of Grace which is one of the three cardinal doctrines of the Christian Church; for in nature—but not in politics or financial circles—that which is called Great is often great indeed, while the North is the region of green ice and solitude unending, and that which Dives by essence, vocation, predestination and nomenclature must be familiar with the dark unknowable depths of the sea wherein we, whom Providence has not created to be Great Northern Divers, would assuredly drown. And I am still encircled by thoughts of that Bird, its singing and its diving and its boreal home, so split me from forehead to fundament if I can remember anything about translation rights.

In the end he confessed that Curtis Brown, who had acted for him previously, owned 'no monopoly in alien transliterations of my ephemeral works' and assured Rupert that he would be grateful for any ducats, dollars or gold moidores he might be able to send his way, for 'the sands of my fortune constantly run out, and since a strange disinclination for work, and incapacity for literary creation—which also was a plague to Samuel Johnson—afflict me in chronic guise or fashion, why, none comes in to replace that which is spent.'

Throughout the summer he had been working on another project, gathering together all his short stories for a volume to be published by Cape in November. He had gradually been drawn more and more to the special demands made by the short story, and had published stories at intervals in a casual way. In July the *Modern Scot* published 'Kind Kitty', destined to be regarded as one of the best of all Linklater short stories, but for the title of his collection he preferred to use the title of another of the stories contained in it. *God Likes Them Plain* appeared on time in a very attractively bound edition, and Eric had presented himself to the public in yet another guise.

As a writer of short stories Eric was given an appreciative welcome by most of the reviewers, who used phrases like 'sardonic and Rabelaisian; Linklater at the top of his form' (*Spectator*); 'a beautiful readableness which comes of a fine style, good subject matter, and humour' (*Book Society News*); and 'a writer of immense gusto and ingenuity' (*Morning Post*). The *Sunday Times* commended him for his 'shrewd gift of allusive comment, quicksilver wit, and a most effective power of building a new situation with the happy verve of a lightning modeller'.

There were sixteen stories in the collection, or eighteen if the three parts of 'The Revolution' be taken separately, as they can be. They ranged in style from realistic, contemporary stories to fanciful fairy-tales, encompassing a variety of tones from the ironic and satirical to the romantic and atmospheric. The language varied from plain, simple and muscular to rich, decorated and aphoristic. There were different degrees of structural complexity, from anecdote to near-novella.

Some of the earlier stories had grown, as suggested in Chapter 7, from his observations of the Indian scene and were a form of reportage. 'Country-born' offered a sympathetic, inquiring little portrait of an Anglo-Indian living and working in Bombay who had successfully concealed his socially unacceptable origins until just before dying of pneumonia. Eric's treatment of the matter, though sympathetic, is not without ambivalence. The onlooker character is faced with O'Driscoll's mother and small brother:

> It was a cruel system, this social philosophy of Englishmen in the East, but looking at the woman and the disgusting small boy, Manderson could not honestly condemn it. It was this racial fastidiousness which had saved England from the fate of Portugal.[22]

Manderson's views may not be those of the writer, and it is arguable that the reader's sense of shock and pity for O'Driscoll and hence for anyone trapped in a similar social position is increased by Eric's realistic attribution to a sympathetic character of a rather cynical attitude.

'Pathans' similarly arose from Eric's Indian observations, and might be seen as an act of homage to the admired Kipling. The story is notable more for its detailed examination of some aspects of the Indian way of life and of the Indian character than for its structural shape, and for the unforced atmospheric vividness of its telling.

'Thieves', again, fictionalises a real event; it is a sort of unsolved who-done-it about the theft of an ancient *Who's Who* from the library of a passenger-ship voyaging from Bombay to Karachi. It offers a skilful study of a group of people against a well-rendered exotic background; it carries a memorable though unspoken comment on human behaviour.

'The Wrong Story' has a neat shape and a surprising ending. The first-person narrator, so closely identifiable as Eric himself that there is no need to pretend otherwise, writes a story based on the love-hate relation-ship of a woman tourist whom he has observed in New Orleans and the tour guide who picks her up. It is rich in atmosphere and the dialogue shows an accurate ear for the rhythms of American speech, but its interest is mostly in the conclusion, where the narrator confesses his ignorance of feminine psychology. The constructional validity of the story is, however, suspect; the revelation of what 'really' happened seems too unlikely a coincidence and is too neatly opposed to what happens in the imagined internal story.

'Wineland', a story in three parts about the discovery of America by Greenland-based Vikings in the tenth century, was evidently a by-product of Eric's reading for *The Men of Ness*. Using a similar kind of bare, stripped language it retells from *Eric's Saga* and *The Greenland Saga* a unified version of how Leif Ericsson, seeking a new land to the west sighted by Bearne, discovers Newfoundland and starts a settlement in a gentle vine-growing country. The story captures in the same vivid and convincing way as *The Men of Ness* the humanity and manners of the Norsemen, and the grim determination of their women. The reader is moved at the end by the pity of things, and the sorry waste of opportunity that makes them turn their backs on such a world of promise. As in the original sagas and in *The Men of Ness*, the wilful and irresistible power of women causes the tragic action; but to the materials of the sagas Eric added a flavour uniquely his own, exemplified in his management of the confused details of the originals. In *The Greenland Saga* the Eskimos (the Scraelings) are at one point frightened by the roaring of the Norsemen's single bull. In *Eric's Saga* Freydis, Leif's sister, frightens off some Scraelings by baring her breasts and slapping a sword on them. Eric pulls the incidents together to give Freydis's rival, Gudrid, a lapidary last word:

> Thorfinn and the other men came up to Freydis and praised her greatly for her courage and gallant behaviour. But Gudrid said, and many heard her, that the Scraelings had previously been frightened by Thorfinn's bull. 'It is clear', she said, 'that they are not used to cattle of any kind.'[23]

Another serious story is 'The Duke', which amplifies an incident in Highland history into a powerful anecdote. The Duke, unnamed but presumably of Sutherland, is the son of the duke who had effected the clearance of the Highlands in his domain to make way for sheep. He now comes to raise a force of his clansmen to send to the Crimea, but to his astonishment they refuse to sign on or to accept the six sovereigns per man which he offers. Their humiliating failure to flock to his cause is their revenge for the way they were robbed and cheated by his father. The story is unfolded with a lofty gravitas rare in Eric's fiction; the bitterness of the people who have been betrayed is shown in such reflections as that the Duke is accompanied by 'a minister of the Church of Scotland who had served his patron well by telling the crofters that eviction from their holdings was an act ordained by God, as a just punishment for their sins.'[24] The story builds up to the moment of crisis with perfect timing, and its climax, when the people baa like sheep at the retreating and discomfited would-be recruiter of soldiery, is extended and developed like a musical coda over two concluding paragraphs. It is as effective and moving a protest at the clearances as has ever been written.

In its way a political story, it is complemented in *God Likes Them Plain* by two others with a more-or-less political basis, though they are different in tone and style. 'The Revolution' consists of three related stories. In the first the Russian actress, Olenina, left in England at the beginning of the Great War, is infected by a wild enthusiasm for the war in which her native country and her adoptive land are allies. She meets an émigré Russian waiter, Glinka, and decides to give him the treat of his life before sending him home to Moscow to join the fighting. When it comes to the point, however, she quails at his grubby coarseness, and inspired with a sudden thought instructs her maid Dunyasha to do the deed for her:

> 'To live is to love and to love is to live,' she said, 'and when living is an unpleasant thing, why, *nos valets le feront pour nous—et pour la Russie, en effet*!'[25]

In the second story, 'The Revolution', Olenina after the war takes up with an actor called John Paris in the kingdom of Baltland, which, though its confused politics are typically European, is in many ways like the England of the first postwar decade. Jean Paris becomes the leader of a revolution which, in the cause of rejecting dullness in all its forms, deposes the King and substitutes a socialist Committee of Five. But when the King is entrained for deportation he discovers in the next compartment his former opponent. Jean Paris and Olenina are also being deported on the grounds that

> They were dangerous to the new Republic by reason of their ability to excite the populace, their unruly and impolitic view of life, their *penchant* for criticism, and their tendency to revolution.[26]

In exile with King Oscar, Jean Paris learns of the misery of Baltland under the Committee of Five, and in the third story, 'Jean Paris', he returns to lead another revolution.

'The Revolution' is a comic trilogy with a polished urbanity of tone and a great display of wit; though not solemn it is a serious and contentious story. Its suave narrative clothes a perceptive inquiry into political motivations and the mechanics of revolution, and its incidental ruminations include a memorable repudiation of the Marxist viewpoint:

> He had always disliked the teaching of Karl Marx, partly because he could not understand it, and partly because he maintained that *Das Kapital*, and Marx's other works, were too badly written to contain anything worth understanding . . . 'The language of Marx is poor and muddy, so I think it probable . . . that his thoughts also are poor and muddy. And what shall it profit a man if he owns the whole world, but doesn't know the difference between a good and a bad book?'[27]

'His Majesty the Dentist', the longest story in the book, also deals with political happenings in Baltland, where Mr Beeston, a dentist, rises to power by virtue of his professional skills. Baltland has been taken over by an infamous dictator, Kempenfeldt, who fortunately suffers fearfully from toothache. Summoned to his aid, Mr Beeston refuses to help until Kempenfeldt begins to ameliorate the lot of the people. Under Kempenfeldt Baltland is a nightmarish reflection of Hitler's Germany, and is still quite horrible despite its Ruritanian excesses and the genial comic tone which Eric maintains as far as is possible. On his way to the Dictator's Palace, Mr Beeston sees a ragged procession of people being herded to the Baltish Marsh, and is told that these are the enemies of the State, for:

> 'A nation is always at war,' said Schweik. 'One must contend with the forces of disorder. With Intellectuals, for instance, who are a reactionary force. With Jews, who are an international force; with Socialists and Pacifists, who are illegal and immoral forces.'[28]

Despite pointing up the absurdities of the Baltish government with its uniforms, its ridiculous ubiquitous salute with a clenched fist which represents totalitarianism, its pride in its little achievements (clean, neat streets and well-disciplined queues) and the ludicrous pains suffered by its leader with his desperately rotten teeth, Eric's attack on such a governmental system is effective; the details, though absurd, are convincing. And at moments the narrative abandons geniality and becomes very unpleasant, as when Kempenfeldt's soldiers are confronted by demonstrators:

> The rebellion was soon suppressed. Some two or three hundred of the rioters were shot dead by the Machine Gun Corps, a large number were clubbed into insensibility by the police, and more than two thousand were arrested and deposited in gaol.[29]

The dispassionate tone, which challengingly suggests that such hideous brutality is a natural part and parcel of a totalitarian system, helps focus a considerable attack on Fascism within the story, and is evidence of Eric's powerful feelings about the ugly things he could see going on in the world. Though he never reprinted it, it was a brave and perceptive story to have published in 1935.

Another story rising from Eric's Indian experience is 'The Prison of Cooch Parwanee'; it tells of an incident in the life of Thomas Motley, an ancestor of Juan, sent out as an agent of the East India Company in the middle of the nineteenth century. It is an unlikely tale, pleasingly ironic, and shows Eric at his best in the business of creating a sense of a particular time and place.

Fantasy is a keynote of all the rest of the stories in *God Likes Them Plain*, even the least successful, 'Mr Timrod's Adventure'. This is a story within a story, Conrad-style; given his opportunity to relate a tale to a group of fellow-passengers on a ship, Mr Timrod tells the story of the one night in his life when something interesting happened to him. Although the inner story is set in the mysterious prehistoric village of Skara Brae, on the West Mainland of Orkney, and Eric allows Mr Timrod plenty of scope to set the Orkney scene and make the most of its atmospheric potential, it is strangely tedious.

Also set in Orkney, and much more successfully, is a story which was destined to become very well known. 'The Dancers' tells of a group of earthy, ordinary people who go for a picnic on the island of Eynhallow on Midsummer Day. They are never seen again. The mystery is never explained to the satisfaction of the public, but one young man discovers the amazing truth: the party have fallen into the power of the Peerie Men, and are happily doomed to spend the rest of their lives dancing in the interior of Eynhallow to the thin, tinkly, tuneful music playing 'the Merry Men of May and the slow, sad Dance of Lofoden ... and the Herring Dance'. It is a local folk tale realised in full circumstantial detail, and the presentation of the fairy element, the evocation of their magical, haunting music and their merry chatter, is done so unsentimentally and convincingly that the reader feels it to be no wonder that the humans never want to return to the seedy unromantic real world.

'Kind Kitty' is a Scottish story, inspired by a poem by Dunbar, one of the makars in whose tradition Eric considered himself to be working. In Dunbar's ballad, Kitty, an old girl with a taste for beer, slips past Saint Peter into Heaven, only to find that heavenly ale is thin and sour, so that she takes her first opportunity to escape back to an earthly ale-house where at least her thirst is satisfied. Eric's Kitty is an old woman in the slums of 1930s Edinburgh, but there is a timeless quality in the writing which could make it any time in the past five hundred years. Edinburgh is a felt and real presence, and indomitable Kitty, smelling of her hens and smoke and unwashed clothes, peering from rheumy eyes and muttering through thin blue lips, might be bumped into round any corner. In Heaven she overhears God chatting with Shakespeare in a brief interlude that foreshadows the 'Conversations in Elysium' which Eric wrote in the 1940s, but returns to the pub outside the Gate where she can enjoy decent ale and the company of her erstwhile employers, Sir Hector and Lady Lavinia McOstrich.

The remaining four stories in the 1935 collection demonstrate more notably still the kinds of imaginative flight Eric loved to make. As in many of the narrative poems considered earlier, the worlds of chivalric and pastoral romance and of fairy-tale fascinated him both as distorting mirrors of the real world and for their own sake as worlds with rules and manners of their own. 'The Crusader's Key', reprinted from the White Owl Press's book version of 1933, was already quite well known. Set in the medieval world of knights and minstrels, the love of which had partly been inspired in Eric by his voracious reading of Scott, it is far from the semi-pornographic tale that Marjorie's mother supposed when hearing its title and seeing its cover-picture; indeed, it is hardly about sexual matters at all.

Jehane is, like Eric's notion of Mary Stewart, rather sexless and somewhat prudish; she never thinks of betraying Bertran until the device fastened about her loins proves a constant reminder of her husband's cynical lack of faith: ' "You are a woman," said Bertran, "and I shall be gone three years." ' More in fury than desire she allows a visiting troubadour to persuade her of a way to lose the belt, but no sooner is it off than she seizes the first excuse to be rid of her persistent would-be lover. It is a funny and disturbing story; the sympathy lies with Jehane and the indignity visited upon her, but there is some ambivalence. She prefers eating to making love, is devious and self-deluding in character, and in the clever ending the story turns against her.

'The Abominable Imprecation' is a comic exercise in the pastoral convention with a hero named Perigot, a princess called Amoret and a wood-nymph called Cleophantis. When Perigot neglects Cleophantis, and she dies, her sister puts on him the curse of Shepherd Alken ('If you are a man, become a woman; if woman, become man'). This rather throws a shadow over his marriage to fair Amoret after he has won her by slaying a dragon, but, on an adventure in Gargaphie, Perigot is again, by fortunate coincidence, cursed with the same imprecation. The language of the story urbanely catches the courtly convention, but there is an extra dimension of occasional contemporary topicality, and the sexuality of the love-affair is more marked than in a traditional pastoral.

In 'The Redundant Miracle' there is similarly an unambiguous sexuality which renders the story modern despite its indefinite folk-tale setting. Two girls, Dowsabell and Beta, whose father is wasting all the family's meagre income on his alchemical search for the philosopher's stone, are looking forward with increasing excitement to the day when they can personally supplement their income by selling their bodies to the fine young soldiers and wealthy merchants who pass their door; frustratingly they are saved from their fate worse than death by the arrival of a passing pilgrim who miraculously causes money to appear out of thin air. But Eric does not deny them their satisfaction; they catch Saint Polydore planting the pennies from a bag he carries and indignantly send him packing as a fraud, leaving them free to make the sacrifice of themselves after all. The main delight lies in the portrayal of the would-be alchemist father, totally unconcerned about how his daughters find money to pay their bills provided they will fetch him the ingredients he needs for his experiments.

The title-story of the collection depends, like 'The Abominable Imprecation', upon a magical exchange; beautiful queen and ugly storyteller pass each into the other's body during a passionate kiss, and their lives are never the same again. In using a storyteller as his protagonist Eric afforded himself an opportunity to make some interesting comments on the art of narrative. Malis is exceedingly ugly but is able to win Queen Perdis's love through the irresistible magic of his art. There may have been some ironic self-projection in the portrayal of Malis, for Eric still regarded himself as being sadly unattractive even after having won the love of the desirable Marjorie; in the story even the children are rude to Malis, so unimpressive a figure is he—until he begins to tell one of his tales:

> [The children] did not trouble to be polite to him as would older people in similar circumstances. On the contrary they assured him that his last story had been shockingly dull, and that his bald head looked more and more like a brown hen's egg every day. At this the man tried to smooth his untidy black hair over the bare dome from which it had receded, but the wind caught it and blew it out like little black wings, and the children laughed louder than ever.[30]

When Queen Perdis is first attracted to Malis, she is troubled because of his reputation for telling bawdy tales about a Balzacian—or Chaucerian—monk, Brother Bonamy, who is famous for his exploits among lovely women. It is Bonamy who in one of Malis's stories coins the phrase 'God likes them plain'. God's ladies, the nuns, are often ugly; this being God's preference, men should by implication confine their attentions to beautiful women. When, after the kiss, Malis has become beautiful (but has lost his linguistic arts) and Perdis has become ugly (but gained in understanding), this saying is Malis's excuse for not kissing her again to restore the status quo. Perdis must learn to live with her ugliness, though she knows 'I am a woman, and cleverness is not everything ... For a woman, beauty is best; strength of arm and intellect is man's good.'[31] A modern feminist reader will not be happy with such a reflection, but it adds a poignancy to Perdis's brave resignation when Malis is unable to bring himself to restore her beauty. 'God Likes Them Plain' is a witty, provocative fairy-tale that makes the reader think about some quite profound matters; and in its genial bawdiness and, in the description of the all-important kiss, its passionate eroticism, it is an intriguing development of the fairy-tale form.

The book provided evidence of a considerable mastery of the short-story form; its humour, variety and sophisticated linguistic skills made it a notable publishing event. Short story collections, however, do not sell in such numbers as successful novels and, extensive though his output in 1935 had been, Eric was by the autumn, before *God Likes Them Plain* had even appeared, anxious to make progress on another novel. He was happy enough with what had been happening: *Ripeness is All* was still selling; *Poet's Pub* was earning a little more money, having been issued as the third of the first ten paperbacks to be published under the Penguin imprint by Allen Lane; *Juan in America* was selling in translation in Hungary and Czechoslovakia. His new books were creating interest and his old ones continued to show vitality. But his feet were itching for travel and an escape from the cosy domesticity into which the past year had brought him. He wrote in October to Rupert Hart-Davis:

> Since sending off the various oddments that will eventually—I hope—take comely shape in *God Likes Them Plain*, I have been living almost wholly in very murky clouds—in tenebrous imagination, lit by fitful gleams that slowly, after long wrestling with darkness, acquired a certain shape and illumination. In plainer words, planning the course of events—shaping the design—constructing and articulating the skeleton of the next *Juan* book in preparation for the first instalment—in China—that must, to some extent, prepare for what follows.

The mysterious East was beckoning, and Eric had found a means of answering its call.

13 Traveller in the Orient

When precisely it occurred to Eric that he might journey to China to do research for a new Juan novel would be hard to say, but some time during the summer of 1935, as he dutifully applied himself to his house renovations and paternal offices and literary obligations, he remembered the intriguingly open ending of *Juan in America*, and a new resolution began to form in his mind. Although he had greatly enjoyed much of his new domesticated life, it was very wearing, as he explained to Phoebe Gilkyson:

> I have also become a householder. I told you I was going to become one. That was in the halcyon past, before I realised the iniquity of builders, masons, plumbers and paper-hangers. We planned to enter into occupation of our house—in Orkney, of course—at the beginning of June. I went up in May to superintend the laying of carpets and the distribution of furniture; and found a mere shell of a house, without a window in it, or a fireplace, and the staircase still in the joiner's shed. After a few weeks we took up residence: but shared our home, for the next three months, with five masons, three or four carpenters, two linoleum and carpet experts, three painters, two plumbers and their passionate assistants, and several odd people whose purpose we never could discover. The maids loved it. So did Sally. Marjorie and I were hardly so well pleased. I got very little work done—except upon the house, for I had to sergeant-major the mercenaries—and Marjorie was often in tears about such things as curtains.

The shoguns at Cape's had urged him to capitalise on Juan; why should he not now do precisely that? He set plans tentatively in motion, with Marjorie's not altogether enthusiastic agreement to his absenting himself for the best part of the winter. An apparent stumbling block was encountered when in September Marjorie realised she was pregnant again, but preparations had gone so far ahead that it was decided he should go nonetheless, making sure he would be home for the accouchement in April. As Eric pointed out, a successful new Juan book would be the basis of next year's bread and butter, and with an extra mouth to feed ... About his decision to go East at this time he later wrote:

> I shall not blame my mother for all that is unstable in my character, but I think she was partly responsible for my reluctance to settle down, sensibly and securely, in the comfort I had created. Our life in Orkney gave me pleasure—as much pleasure as I wanted—but not nearly enough satisfaction. It was absurd,

I thought, to live in a globular world without going round it. I had, moreover, an idea for a novel which needed a Chinese background, and between Orkney and China lay the warm, brown, humming mass of India, of which I had seen so little when I worked there. Perhaps it was my duty to see India again?[1]

He even at that time of writing claimed that 'one of the major reasons for the long continuance of our marriage is that it has often been relieved by my absence abroad. That absence makes the heart grow fonder is not necessarily true, but that recurrent absence relieves the inevitable stress and strain of marriage can hardly be doubted!'

As the winter gales began to come in, rather ahead of their usual time, they discovered 'thirty-seven different leaks' in their brand-new house. 'A purple cloud rose over the land—as I began to swear again—and back came the masons, the joiners, the plasterers and the odd incomprehensible men.'[2] The Linklater family packed up and moved south for the winter near Edinburgh, where Eric established Marjorie, Sally and his mother in a small house called Waverley, at West Calder. There they were close to Marjorie's parents, too, and Eric could feel reasonably happy about going off to the other side of the world.

After lunching with Rupert Hart-Davis in London, he caught the boat-train and was in Marseilles by 9 November. From there he wrote to Rupert that the SS *Strathand*, upon which he was now embarked, was 'a truly superb and magnificent vessel' well adapted to his 'quiet and modest views of entertainment', and with ironic delight described one of his fellow passengers. This was a young man rather in the mould of a Linklaterian hero:

A very masculine-looking young man with red hair and a long, lean jaw . . . who (a) feared the train would go off the rails and our coach was perilously near the front of it; (b) when we went for a short walk, from the Gare de Lyon (where we waited an hour), suspected we would be knifed before we returned, and (c) now thinks there are not enough lifeboats on the ship.

Throughout the voyage to Bombay Eric took pleasure in seeing again the places that he had first seen on his journey out a decade earlier, but as ever with him the greatest delight was in the people he met, such as three soldiers who had served on the North-Western frontier. Listening to their tales by the ship's swimming-pool, he wrote, 'I touched a dangerous low level in moral dissolution when I became slightly intoxicated in a bathing-suit.'[3] He did not allow the occasion to develop, by the ordering of more pink gins, into a disgraceful orgy, however, for he was aware that he wore 'too grave a look to idle gracefully'. And in case his readers should be interested in his appearance, he noted that James Joyce had written in *Finnegans Wake* what could pass for an exact description of him:

He was sair sair sullemn and chairmanlooking when he was not making spaces in his psyche, but, laus! when he wore making spaces on his ikey, he ware mouche mothst secred and muravyingly wisechairmanlooking.⁴

While in the company of the soldiers he observed something that, later, he felt he could not print in the less tolerant days of 1941, but which he was happy to include as an anecdote in *Fanfare for a Tin Hat*:

> Somewhere in the Canal we tied up to allow the northward passage of one of our troopships, homeward bound from India. Also tied up was an Italian trooper, outward bound for the Ethiopian adventure, and as the two ships approached—each crowded with soldiers—there was a hurricane of catcalls and counter-cheers, of Britannic mockery and Roman or romantic patriotism. Then, in the Italian ship, a tall, vociferous, indignant man mounted to the broad top of a railing, unfastened his trousers, unlimbered a penis of impressive size, and directed towards the British trooper an arc of glittering, contemptuous urine. For a moment there was total silence. Our well-disciplined, innately respectable soldiers were deeply shocked by the indecency of such Mediterranean exhibitionism. But one of them quickly recovered his wits, and remembering a common belief of those days, that the Abyssinians mutilated the dead bodies of their enemies in a very offensive way, shouted across the narrow water in a voice as excessive as the Italian's virile member, 'That's all right, mate! Make the most of it while you 'ave it! You won't 'ave it long!'⁵

He discussed with an Australian politician of astonishing hyperbole the wealth of his antipodean continent, which Eric had thought to be, like Giotto's O, 'a circumference of patently sincere endeavour that enclosed enormous emptiness'. He enjoyed the increasing warmth of friendliness as the ship's company got to know each other, and agreed with a girl who said, as the Indian Ocean lay like 'a ruffled plate of lapis lazuli upon a smooth round shoulder of the sunlit world', that she could marry and be happy with almost any man she knew. An exaggeration, he thought, but with a good core of truth in it, 'for with the majority of people, when you have come to know them, you can live on amiable terms'.

Not that he was a free agent to take advantage of the female warmth he discerned about him on board. To Douglas Walker he confided: 'Nor has anything in the way of womanhood tempted me from the strictest canons of marital fidelity. I grow old, old.' Although he concentrated to his utmost on enjoying and deriving the maximum professional benefit from his adventure, his conscience constantly troubled him about his abandoned family, as he confessed to Rupert Hart-Davis:

> Marjorie's news is good and she seems cheerful. But this marriage business isn't good for travellers. I'll be glad to get home again, for though I'm tremendously enjoying myself, there's a bit of my brain that obstinately occupies itself with her and the one-and-a-half infants.

On arrival in Bombay Eric was met surprisingly but gratifyingly by his old servant Laloo Bhika, who announced his attention of accompanying him on his proposed journeys about the Indian subcontinent. He planned to travel by a northerly route to Calcutta, and from there to visit for a while his sister Elspeth and her engineer husband, Freddy Cormack, in Assam. Their first stop was in Jaipur, where Eric savoured the evidence of the excessive, almost theatrical magnificence in which the Rajput princes had lived, and felt tempted to deplore the duller, more bourgeois gentility into which their descendants had incongruously fallen. A few days later he and Laloo were examining the fabulous folly of Fatehpur Sikri at Agra, built by the Great Mogul, Akbar, to celebrate the birth of a son but unfortunately sited in an uninhabitable place. They went, too, to Delhi, built by Akbar's grandson, Shah Jahan, with silver-plated roofs and a solid gold throne. They inspected the Taj Mahal, Shah Jahan's monument for his queen, and Eric mused on how its over-wrought marble wearied the eye; but

> from a couple of hundred yards away, in the early morning, the Taj is un-affected by its wealth and hardly dimmed by all the guidebooks. Look at its reflexion in cool water, between the cypress-trees, and you may still see in it the epicedium of all women who were beautiful, were loved, and died.[6]

Eric's satisfaction with his travels was temporarily dissipated when he fell ill after, as he suspected, catching cold from 'a lean and filthy Mahommedan, sniffling and snuffling, bubbling vilely at the nose', who persuaded him to watch his trained birds for a moment. As his fever grew he began to wonder if it was a punishment from the goddess Kali for misinterpreting her essential character; for he had suddenly seen her as 'Rebel Woman jumping on the corpus of the Ever-Conservative Husband' and made an obeisance to her image in an Amber temple. But he got better, and went for a most instructive fortnight to Shillong, where there was much to see that was wild, exotic and exciting.

Freddy Cormack was, Eric said, one of the creators of modern Assam, for he had supervised the building of the strategic road linking the valleys of the Surma and the Brahmaputra. Visiting it Eric was almost as impressed with it as a work of art as a feat of engineering, and he wrote a sort of prose-poem paean of praise for it in *The Man on My Back*.[7] In company with his brother-in-law he saw some fascinating slices of savage life, visiting a Naga village at Kohima, the Native State of Manipur, a planters' club at Christmas that might have been anywhere in the Empire, and a couple of villages on the border with Tibet peopled by Daflas—'a very jungly and evil-smelling people'. He gave Rupert Hart-Davis a brief account of his stay in Assam:

My brother-in-law did me proud, though a bit of departmental bother prevented him from getting leave when we wanted to go and shoot at a tiger. So that was off. But I'd probably have fallen out of the tree, and the bloody thing would have eaten me. So all may have been for the best. But I saw the noble and comic savages—the Dufflers, Mufflers, Pullovers, Dhotis, Nagas and so forth—and listened to tales of Sex from planters' wives, and insulted the Governor's wife, and sang 'Reilly's Farm' in a Gurkha mess, and read Mr Spender on the Brahmaputra, and slept in dark bungalows, and went to the Wettest Place on Earth, and drove hundreds of miles over tremendous and magnificent and hideous roads, and felt two small earthquakes, and took photographs of a local Joan of Arc—murderess, priestess and rebel—and altogether had a Good Time.

He reported that he had on ship again, making for Singapore, written several thousand words of a kind that would make a reasonable travel-book. 'Lightish, you understand. That peculiar Linklater humour, you know—God save our souls. And some bits not so light. I have touched on some aspects of Indian life—or Anglo-Indian—but, you will be glad to hear, I have *not* attempted to solve the Indian Problem.' For one reason and another the book was never completed and the words saw print only in so far as some of them were incorporated into his autobiography six years later.

All the way from the Hooghly to the Yangtze Kiang Eric enjoyed the company of an Irish padre who challenged him to shuffleboard twice a day and a 'twenty-stone bright red Calcutta businessman—hearty and friendly but limited by Calcutta offices to interests as narrow as his bottom is broad'.[8] The fat man made a considerable impression, and with some modifications as to background and intellect made his way into *Juan in China* (1937) and at intervals almost took it over. Eric, the padre and the corpulent one had dinner at Raffles' as they stopped over at Singapore, and afterwards they went to the pictures, Eric delighting in his fat friend's responses to such sophistications:

> When the faces of the hero and heroine were magnified so that we could more closely study the passion of their kiss, the fat man made a schoolboy noise of derisive appreciation. He was sixty-three years old, a bachelor, and had reduced enjoyment to a manageable size.[9]

Arriving at last in China towards the end of January 1936, Eric went ashore in Shanghai, 'where I had work to do: I had to find material that would fill the background of a novel and energise a story, so like a collector of virtu I amassed views and gossip, the grimace of a passer-by, the smell of a cookshop, the squalor of the town.'[10] His response to Shanghai was highly unfavourable: 'More loudly than any other town I know, it howls to the unfriendly sky the cunning, the cupidity, the helplessness and fearful injustice of mankind.'[11] A good deal of this dislike, even hatred, of the town arose from his immediate recognition and observation of the Japanese presence, of the Japanese commercial influence ('How hideous aniline paintings from Japan are ousting the exquisitely drawn and delicately tinted scrolls of China'[12]) and even more of the nakedly aggressive Japanese imperialist ambitions: 'Taut bullies in their tight blue uniform, I saw the Japanese police and hated them.'[13] In a letter to Compton Mackenzie he called Shanghai: 'A clenched fist of tragedy and comedy'.

The Japanese presence, which erupted into a full-scale war within a few months of Eric's visit, was something he, who had spoken out so firmly against the similar brutishness of European totalitarianism, could not conceivably tolerate. He evidently felt it wiser, however, to steer clear of politics in a jokey interview he gave to a Shanghai newspaper at the time. The inconsequentiality of his replies to the interviewer may also have arisen from his somewhat ironic acceptance of the reporter's idea that Eric and Juan were to be identified as one and the same:

> Asked what he thought of modern women, the author replied, 'I like them.' As for the silver question, he dismissed that with an airy, 'I like silver, too.'
> Religion doesn't bother him a bit. 'I'm all for that,' he said.
> Liquor?—'I'm all for that, too.'[14]

He either did not mind indulging or was deliberately offhand to a reporter who was avid only for gossip; the instance is instructive, for Eric quite often contributed a fair proportion of the trivia which helped develop a public image of him as a superficial entertainer rather than the deeply serious artist he was. The autobiographies and the novel which grew from the Chinese experience, although they inevitably had their hilarious moments, more accurately reflected the grimness and horror of what he had seen. In *The Man on My Back* he admitted that he had rather liked the Japanese people too, who, when encountered on their own territory, displayed great courtesy, humour and charm; but he added:

> There is little wrong with the people of Japan, I suppose, but ignorance, stupidity and want of strength; but their rulers are evil, like the rulers of all the world, who thwart and mislead the many that luxury and profit may drug the vestigial souls of their scanty friends.[15]

Despite his disappointment with Shanghai itself, China as a whole took a powerful hold on his imagination, and his sympathetic understanding of the plight of the people, together with his enthusiastic appreciation of their art, their poetry and their history, are manifest in the work which resulted from his travels.

He had planned to make a visit to Siberia and maybe return across the Soviet Union, but his time began to run out as Marjorie's pregnancy neared its fulfilment. He had done as much as he could expect to, and was anxious to settle to serious work on his novel, so he 'booked a passage for

10 Marjorie and Eric outside her parents' house, The Tower, Murrayfield, in May 1933, a few
weeks before their marriage in Edinburgh

11 Portrait of Eric, 1933, by fellow
Orcadian Stanley Cursiter, RSA—o
a pair of wedding gift portraits, now
hanging in the Linklater Rooms,
Elphinstone Hall, Aberdeen Univer

12 Marjorie and Eric step from the first
aeroplane ever to land on Barra, Ou
Isles, June 1933, to be greeted by
Compton Mackenzie, Chrissie
MacSween (later Lady Mackenzie)
Marie Dauthieu (*l*), a French friend
Chrissie

Japan and Vancouver, and set to work on ship's notepaper'.[16] The voyage home was hardly as comfortable as he might have hoped, for there was a storm in the North Pacific caused by a hurricane blowing under the Kurile Islands. The train from Vancouver was held up by extensive flooding in the eastern states of America, and he somehow lost most of his luggage before embarking for the final transatlantic section of his circumnavigation of the globe. But he arrived home in good time to be with Marjorie for the birth of their second daughter, Kristin, on 22 April 1936. He intimated the successful outcome of this event to Rupert Hart-Davis with a telegram:

FACULTIES PARALYSED IN ANTENATAL SUSPENSE PARTIALLY RESTORED BY BIRTH OF DOLICHOCEPHALIC GERANIUM COLOURED DAUGHTER BUT NOW SUSPENDED IN LIBATORY POSTNATAL ALCOHOLIC PARESIS—ERIC.

When Rupert congratulated him and said how amused he had been by the telegram, Eric indignantly replied:

My telegram was *not* funny. It was a succinct and accurate statement of fact. For three weeks, after landing in Scotland, I was in a curious state of inertia: intellectual non-existence: emotional suspense. I could do nothing ... It was partly weariness after the journey—I wasn't feeling well—and partly a strange incompetence forced on me by Marjorie's condition of merely waiting.

Once Kristin was safely delivered into the world, however, he was able to put the excitement of the five months of globetrotting behind him and settle to a relatively quiet life, at first in Edinburgh and then in Orkney. Among the baggage which he had not lost in the United States there were two or three chapters of the new Juan book already written; there was a great deal more work to be done on it, and to this he set himself in earnest. Life with his growing family and slowly expanding house was sufficient for him between bouts of labour on the novel, though he also found time to earn a fee from his experiences in the Orient with a series of radio talks broadcast between April and June and given the accolade of being printed in the *Listener*.[17] He also took time to write a charming and funny letter to his new daughter, congratulating her on deciding to be a girl, for she would enjoy something new in the history of women—legal equality with men; but she would also, if she was clever (and he was sure she would be), enjoy the traditional privileges of femininity:

You will eat exquisite dinners that fond young men will pay for; you will be disrespectful to peppery old gentlemen who will fill your male contemporaries with fear; and if you are ever shipwrecked, you will be in the front of the queue for lifeboats.

She would learn to be glad that she had been born in Britain, for though it was not without faults and frailties of its own, it was clearly preferable to certain countries that she could easily name for herself ... She would be educated in the classics, and grow to love the sapient laughter of Aristophanes, after which she would no longer be astonished by the behaviour of contemporary peoples and politicians.

> You must also learn to sail a boat, for that is a very great joy. And to swim, for that is useful if the boat capsizes. And to catch fish, for that is invaluable if you swim ashore to a desert island. In fact you are going to learn an enormous number of things—French, and how to cook an omelette, and enjoy Mozart, and lead young men by the ear, which is a very good thing for young men to have done to them—and especially you are going to learn how to be serious without being solemn. This, however, for people born on the island of Britain, is a very difficult thing to learn.

The summer in Orkney, despite Eric's devotion to work on the new book, brought plenty of good times as visitors came to spend a week or two. After leaving Edinburgh at the end of May ('with all the enormous circumstance of a migrating tribe—Grierson might film it, as a Scottish folk movement', he told Mackenzie), the days went by 'swifter than a weaver's shuttle—darkless June, and I trod on my conscience (which was shouting "Work!")', and then Moray McLaren came to stay, and Ursula Balfour a while later, and they were 'beachcombers without memory or duty'. At this time Eric was delighted to receive from Compton Mackenzie an intimation that *The East Wind of Love* was going to be dedicated to him, especially as it was to be the opening volume of what both Eric and McLaren were convinced was going to be Mackenzie's *magnum opus*.

He was working, as usual, harder than he admitted, but modifications to his original conception of the new Juan book called for considerable reorganisation of his material. He explained to Mackenzie how the Chinese part was to have been only an introduction, but after 10,000 words it took charge and became a story all by itself, so *Juan in China* would be its title. Though it still had a long way to go, he was already at intervals turning over in his mind the issues to be treated in his next novel, which was going to be about war and peace. In the summer of 1936 it was clear to him that there was going to be another war, unless something extremely effective were done quickly to prevent it, and with memories of 1918 in mind he was inclined at this point to seek such ways of avoiding another confrontation with the Germans as might be found, despite the incontrovertible unpleasantness of their government. In fact he made some seriously pacifist gestures during the next eighteen months, but in his heart he knew that war was inevitable. His words to Mackenzie in July 1936 don't admit much doubt:

> No, I don't think there's going to be a war just yet. Not till Germany's ready. In New York they said that would be September 1937. But their reasoning was

economic, and economy's the last heresy. 1938 is my bet. I hope it isn't till then; my winter novel is going to be about it, and I'd hate to have it spoiled by reality coming too soon.

When Rupert Hart-Davis complained that his new son, Duff, spent a good proportion of the time crying, it drew forth a word of condolence from Eric who sometimes, when working hard, found his family somewhat too demanding:

> As to howling children, I can thoroughly sympathise: we gave house-room (a week or two ago) to my Indian-memsahib-sister's brat, a boy with the appearance of an infant Bill Sikes, a perpetual voice like an angry guinea-hen, and a nursemaid with a carthorse tread. All this, added to our own ululating fruit, a barking dog and a large bleating sheep and two lambs (which I bought) have made me rather touchy on the subject of noise.

A nasty snag impeded the progress of *Juan in China* when in October Rupert read the first 45,000 words and realised that one of Eric's characters, 'Two-Gun Cohen', could be taken as a libellous portrait of someone of the same sobriquet (and disposition) who had recently been in the news. Eric had never heard of him, but, remembering the Wendy Wood affair, applied himself to the large task of rewriting all the Cohen sections and substituting another character. By a sudden thought which seemed to him quite brilliant he saw how he could resurrect Rocco, Red-Eye Rod Gehenna's bodyguard, from *Juan in America*; he unfolded his reasoning to Rupert:

> Well, times were bad in America, and Red-Eye was going in for kidnapping, which Rocco didn't approve of. So Rocco went to China and got a job with General Tu-Fu. How's that? Cast-iron, isn't it? Rocco's an already established character, he won't be called 'Two-Gun'—though on occasion he uses two, which is a good American habit—and his rank will be no higher than a Colonel.

By the first week in November he had finally brought it to a conclusion. In a letter to Douglas Walker he confessed it had been one of the most difficult things he had tackled; unlike *Juan in America*, which had written itself—'anyone could write a novel about America'—this one had had to be dug from the unwilling clay of its author's 'claudicant and costive brain'; it was not so exuberant as *Juan in America*, but he thought it wasn't bad.

When it appeared, in February 1937, it rapidly found a great many readers; after a month it was, according to a survey published in the *News Chronicle*, Number One in the list of 'What Britain is Reading'.[18] Considering that novels named in the list below it included Margaret Mitchell's *Gone with the Wind* and Compton Mackenzie's *The East Wind of Love*, Eric had no expectation of being disappointed financially. Critical reaction, however, was on the whole merely amused and unable to perceive any special merit in the book. Eric himself made little comment on it at first, contenting himself with the observation that he had 'conceived a high comedy that was set in the misery of war; which offended many, but was inoffensive to the spirit of the Middle Kingdom'.[19] Thirty years later he defended the novel more vigorously:

> When my novel was published, it excited adverse criticism. It was written, some said, in heartless ill taste: it mocked the tribulations of an ancient people who were passionately seeking a *modus vivendi* that would release them from immemorable tyrannies and a static culture that prohibited their advance towards, their enlargement in, the modern world which was the goal of their most enlightened leaders. So far from being heartless, however, the novel disclosed my immediate response to the beauty, grace, gaiety and dignity of the people in China; it harshly denounced the vulgarity of Japanese oppression; and when it mocked the futility of Chinese leadership—the faction that was more destructive than invasion—its mockery was justified by the witless dissension that had crippled the most populous of empires.[20]

Curiously it does not seem to matter that the reader should know much about China or its complicated history or its specific quandary at the time in which the novel is set. As with *Juan in America*, one might argue that it is a historical novel about a world that has gone, but that fails to explain fully its timeless and universal quality. It is rather that Eric's China (or rather, Shanghai) offers not so much a documentary reflection of the real China of 1936 as a distorting mirror's reflection of it; his China, like his America, is sufficiently based in authentic observation to be fascinating and convincing, but has also an extra dimension which makes it part of Wonderland, which is unaffected by time or political change.

Set in Shanghai at the traumatic period just before the outbreak of the Sino-Japanese War of 1937, the novel is held together by a plot involving a secret plan that keeps disappearing, and the account of the sale of some worthless tanks to the Chinese by a loosely concerted group of not unamiable rogues. Juan is involved in the events through his affection for the Chinese woman Kuo Kuo, whom he was last seen pursuing at the end of *Juan in America*, and whom he finds to be a more dedicated guerrilla fighter for Chinese liberty than he had expected.

Juan does little enough to help; he is thrown into the sea of events and bobs along from crisis to crisis, observing, laughing, occasionally precipitating action and reluctantly taking part; but he is often bewildered, sometimes frightened, and ultimately depressed by what he sees. The world is mad, but his answer, which is to laugh at it, does not seem wholly satisfactory. Through the medium of what the reader comes to recognise as a typically Linklaterian *melange* of hilarity, wit, romance, realism, cruelty, grotesquerie, farce and verbal dexterity, a provocative and moving look is taken at life, its satisfactions and pleasures, its disgusting and horrific contradictions, and its mysterious purposes. It is a coolly brilliant exemplification of Eric's ability to do what he proposed that his baby daughter, Kristin, should learn to do: to be serious without being solemn.

Eric always enjoyed greatly what he saw, even in a sense when it repelled him, and his faculty for representing places, individual appearances, spoken exchanges, lovers' emotions and social institutions was rarely better displayed than in *Juan in China*. The same is true of his ability to formulate a laconic aside or a lapidary sentence. The fat man with whom he sailed from Calcutta becomes the basis in the novel for a character called Major Flanders; here is his first appearance in the novel:

> He stood proudly behind his enormous paunch. It was no mere pudding-basin of a paunch, no petty tumescence or adventitious hummock of fat; it was a rolling down, a Border hill that marched from his broad chest to a broader top, and from there declined steeply, but not without dignity, to the spacious anchorage of an heroic pelvis. It was a truly noble paunch. It was far more than the simple consequence of a hearty appetite. It was a monument to his spirit, and a testimonial to the strength of his back. It was a paunch that made one think not of greed but of grandeur, not of gluttony but of the profusion of earth and the magnanimity of mankind.[21]

This is unironic appreciation of the Gargantuan Flanders, who in many ways is like a modern descendant of Falstaff in behaviour, even to his attitude to the notion of honour: 'I was honourable myself once—no, by God, some three or four times—but that's long ago now. Life wears it out, and you lose the knack of it.'[22] In Flanders's delight in exaggeratedly colourful language, and his appetite for food and drink, Eric's own enthusiasms are celebrated, and there is a moral justice in the conclusion when Flanders sails home to a new appointment as Warden of a Home for Fallen Women in Gloucestershire.

Eric's inventiveness showed itself at its most individual in the characters of Varya and Masha Karamazov, 'the only genuine Russo-Siamese twins'. In attempting the delineation of two women so intimately connected he was uniquely bold. It may be that some people would find unacceptable the very idea of using Siamese twins as characters in a novel; their predicament, it might be argued, is so unfortunate, their enforced total intimacy of such an embarrassing nature, their relationship under such unimaginable pressure, that fiction had best make do without them. To add insult to injury, Eric is not concerned to study the problem of their jointure at all seriously; he presents them as two beautiful girls locked in a relationship as much psychic as physical, and moreover as comic characters to be laughed at. A serious novel about Siamese twins, that really tried to explore the nature of their experience sympathetically, might, it was thought, be possible; but to take advantage of the bizarre aspects of such a plight, and to derive some titillation from consideration of the girls' sexuality, was heartless, cruel and too disturbing for words. But this kind of reaction failed to note that comedy often treats its characters with some detachment, and that Varya and Masha are actually drawn with a good deal of affection.

This was one of the aspects of Eric's writing which helped win him a reputation for impropriety, and it is true that in 1930s terms he skated on thin ice. The girls tell, for instance, of a scientist in love with one of them who attaches a sphygmomanometer to the wrist of the other to see if she were, through her inter-connection with her sister, as excited as her sister by his love-making. As 'love-making' could, in the language of those days, mean no more than kissing and cuddling, and as the context was comedy rather than realist fiction, no protest followed (except for the banning of the book in Eire); but it may be perceived that Eric sailed very close to the wind at such times.

The story affords various occasions for mild satire at individual human foibles and at social institutions: Eric's picture of the Europeans at the Shanghai Club is very funny but at the same time convincing. Criticism, great or small, is almost always by implication, but is hardly ever harsh because it is founded upon a delight in eccentricity for its own sake. It leads, moreover, more often than not into some set-piece of more physical farce, such as when Fannay-Brown of the Shanghai Club takes Juan on a mounted paper-chase, and puts him up on a wicked pony named Chang. The account of the chase which follows, reminiscent now of the hunt scene in *Tom Jones*, now of Mr Pickwick and Mr Winkle on their memorable attempt to drive to Manor Farm, is a small masterpiece of comedy.

But beneath the fun and pleasure so often appreciable at the surface of the narrative, there is the under-burden of war, just as in *Juan in America* there is an undertone of violence and occasional horror which contrasts and highlights the comedy. As Juan, newly in New York, is shocked by a suicide, so, newly in Shanghai, is his attention drawn to the darker possibilities of life by an explosion in the Whangpoo River:

> Tugboats sped swiftly under plumes of furious smoke, ferries crossed, and narrow destroyers were anchored in mid-stream. It was, though hardly a peaceful scene, a scene that made no suggestion of war. But suddenly a procession of boats—a tug and two lighters—enormously erupted. A funnel of grey and yellow fumes shot upwards from them, expanded, and spread into cumulus. In the very moment of expansion it was split by a lurid flame, and the city shook to the roar of the explosion. Out of the smoke descended a shower of dismembered arms and legs and other human fragments.[23]

In the novel which follows there is a good deal of violence and unpleasant action, culminating in a battle between Chinese and Japanese forces in which Juan, Flanders and Rocco are unwillingly involved, having been forced to drive the jerrybuilt plywood tanks sold by Rocco to General Wu. The action leaves a field littered with bodies, 'some of them motionless, and others still horribly alive'. It is recorded realistically, with Eric's memories of fighting in Voormezeele providing vivid images—though less is made of them here than in the novel he wrote next, *The Impregnable Women* (1938). The horrors of battle are turned to farce when Juan finds a way to gain a victory. Flanders, who has in his turn been double-crossed, is in possession of quantities of counterfeit money; this Juan shows to the Chinese troops. They crowd about excitedly 'stretching eager and dirty hands towards it', and he tosses the fistful of notes to the wind, which accommodatingly blows them towards the Japanese lines. In pursuing the money the Chinese create a sufficient charge to make their opponents beat a temporary retreat. A little later, when Flanders discovers that Juan has accidentally included five genuine £100 notes in his gift to the winds, and goes lumbering mountainously in the wake of the attack to try to recover them, Juan's response is laughter, and so the book modulates back to the strain of comedy.

The phenomenon of laughter has earlier in the novel been considered very closely, when Juan finds himself in a monastery looking at statues of the gods. One, 'a glaucous deity whose face was twisted in wild and diabolical laughter', is very disturbing; Eric makes Juan turn from it in agitation as 'this dreadful apotheosis of humour'. Juan is more delighted to discover the god Mi-lei-fo, 'the rollicking likeness of a divine toper' (a sort of Oriental Silenus, who would have appealed to Eric), but his experience in the Hall of the Five Hundred Lohan essentially convinces him that the Chinese have no conscience, no sense of sin; and this is alarming because 'innocence is capable of the most appalling misconduct'.

These complex issues are not resolved in the novel though they are so provocatively raised, and perhaps there can be no satisfactory answers. Juan at the end of the battle is shot accidentally, and the book ends with him sailing back to England and comparative sanity in the company of Flanders, contemplating the nature of England and the character of the English, and seeking some understanding of the greatness they have known as builders, conquerors and colonisers.

The topicality of *Juan in China* is no bar to its being read and found rewarding almost fifty years after its first publication because it addresses itself, in a highly intriguing vehicle, to perennial problems in man's personal, social and political life. The storyteller here is no mere entertainer, but a thoughtful and sensitive analyst of life; and he is still a determined celebrant of the good things of life even as he acknowledges and incorporates the bad.

Though the book was not a critical success, one curious feature of its composition was pleasing to Eric in retrospect. Much of the action of the story depends upon a search for a secret plan evolved by Lo-Yu, a guru-chieftain to whom the young revolutionaries look for inspiration. When found at last the 'master-plan' turns out to be a series of quasi-Confucian aphorisms, of little practical use; in this way the ineffective leadership of the day is gently castigated. Eric was greatly amused by the way in which Lo-Yu's 'Precepts for the Individual and Good Counsel for Government' anticipated by many years the Little Red Book of Chairman Mao Zedong and the Chairman's method: 'the control of thought, the instigation of opinion, exercised by the aphorisms and precepts in Mao's little red phylactery'. With some satisfaction Eric concluded his reminiscence:

> I am, of course, prejudiced in favour of Lo-Yu, and I do not expect everyone to share my prejudice. But I am not, I think, unduly arrogant or improperly self-satisfied when I say that his apothegms are more interesting than those of Chairman Mao.[24]

14 Uncertain Pacifist

By the time he was ready to hand over the manuscript of *Juan in China* to Cape in November 1936, Eric was beginning to feel the strain of a long period of application to his writing and of devoted attention to his family. He told Douglas Walker:

> The corpus vile is uncommon weary, and the eager childlike brain is nothing but drooling senility ... I've had a poor summer—five months' hard ... *Juan in China* turned out to be the most difficult thing I've ever tackled ... The casualties of the campaign were a $\frac{\text{nervous breakdown}}{2}$ and a reawakening of my old friend the duodenal ulcer; which, however, responded to treatment and a fortnight on the wagon.

He felt that he owed himself something of a treat, and an invitation via Rupert Hart-Davis to speak at a *Sunday Times* exhibition being held in London in mid-November afforded him an opportunity to get away. Earlier in the year he had been introduced to the Savile Club, and he looked forward to being able to take advantage of his membership, which in the years to come, especially during the war, was a great comfort to him. He also wanted to pay a visit to Blackpool, 'for ulterior motives', as he put it darkly to Douglas, whom he invited to come with him to see the lights:

> In those engaging surroundings, designed for popular folly, we can with loud laughter discuss the more unpopular follies of our time, and congratulate ourselves upon a sound perception and Voltairean eyes for the gimcrack, the sham and the horse's arse.

His purpose in visiting Blackpool was to get background material for the novel which was already occupying much of his thought: *The Impregnable Women*. On 6 November Eric and Marjorie set off for London for their autumn break and Eric gave his talk on 'The Happy Author' at the *Sunday Times* exhibition. When first asked what his topic would be, he told Rupert to expect a learned dissertation upon 'The Chronology of the Samaritan Pentateuch', but, with Christmas coming on, relented; instead, he said, his theme would be 'The Dismal Scrivener'.

After a fortnight Marjorie returned home and Eric, after staying a little longer, went northwards again by a longer route. He made his reconnaissance of Blackpool, remembering no doubt the occasion three years previously when, having engaged himself to be married to Marjorie, he collected her sister Alison Bonfield from the Liverpool hotel where she was working as a housekeeper and took her to Blackpool to see the lights. Having done his bit of research, Eric went north to Edinburgh for a couple of days, and then to Glasgow, where Alison, who had been glad to leave her rather tough and uncongenial job at the Liverpool Adelphi, was now in post as Warden of the Queen Margaret Hostel for University Women. With an Edinburgh architect friend, Robert Hurd, she had helped establish the Saltire Society and was making a name for herself in Scottish cultural life. Eric was very fond of his wife's spirited and intelligent elder sister, and enjoyed a chance of some cheerful flirtation with her even while approving of the young French teacher, Harvey Sheppard, ten years her junior, who had begun to court her with some assiduity and flair.

But Eric's main reason for coming to Glasgow was in fulfilment of a long-standing intention to visit Compton Mackenzie. He flew to Barra from Renfrew, intending to stay no more than three or four days, but then 'from Glasgow to the south of England there was a brown impenetrable fog, and all the aeroplanes sat still as hooded falcons'.[1] His week in Mackenzie's company was enormously rewarding, and he came to admire more and more the energy, wit and conversational brilliance of the older man who, earlier in the year, had dedicated to him his latest novel with the words:

> In dedicating to you the first volume of *The Four Winds of Love*, I have chosen a junior contemporary for whose existing work I have a secure admiration and in whose future work I have an equally secure confidence, but let that pass; a truer and better reason is that I hope to please thereby a friend to whose friendship I owe more than can be paid with words.[2]

A particularly delightful fruit of his days on Barra was the portrait of Mackenzie which Eric wrote in *The Man on My Back*, painting his hero as 'the very top and flourish of good company'. With great vividness the pages project a vision of a many-sided and memorable man, of disconcertingly nocturnal habits, working 'with the persistence of a fanatic' throughout the night, while one of his secretaries kept the air full of music from a pair of enormous gramophones. Eric wrote of Mackenzie's gifted mimicry, of his entertaining recitations from Dickens or Wordsworth, of his astonishingly capacious memory and hugely diverse interests. It is no wonder that Eric was captivated, for in Mackenzie he saw a man after his own heart, a full-blooded romantic, loved by almost everyone who met him.

When the weather moderated a little, Eric returned to the mainland by ferry and went by train to Glasgow, where again he stayed for a few days on hearing that communications with Orkney were interrupted by new gales. Glasgow, where he walked about, as he said to Mackenzie, 'slum-inspecting in the Gallowgate and neighbourhood', was a horrifying revelation. His discovery that the butchers' shops sold mostly offal epitomised a poverty more hideous than he had known to exist in Britain. It seemed to him that it would be best for the Gallowgate if it were burned to the ground: 'There would be a Great Fire of Glasgow, and a good thing too.'[3]

It was December 1936, and the newsboys in Glasgow were shouting of Edward VIII's desire to marry Mrs Simpson. Eric's journey home was further delayed when he was 'held up for a long and weary weekend in Thurso by monstrous great fogs, tempests and bewilderments of snow'[4] in the tedious company of 'two spinsters, one of either sex, who chattered interminably and more platitudinously than you could believe'. He arrived at last, Marjorie very anxious because of the long lack of news, after a merry crossing of the Firth on the mailboat:

> Hoy in front all vast and white in snow—and with a stiff breeze behind us and the tide beneath us we made the fastest passage I've ever done; and happening to have with me a small bottle of brandy, and being on the bridge, the Captain, the Mate and the man at the wheel were all very friendly, talkative and glad to see me.[5]

Once home he began to work more intensively on the new book, but suffered from a number of interruptions and something of a crisis of confidence. He was in London again early in February 1937 for the Foyle's celebratory banquet, where he was interestingly teamed up with Sir Harry Lauder. ('Is this true?' he asked Rupert. 'What a joke. Are we expected to sing a duet? Miss Foyle must have heard about my voice.') Before he returned there was a memorable evening in Rupert's company during the course of which they found themselves, anxious to get to Euston in time for Eric's train, 'in a round-the-houses motor-race which we won at 92 mph' after surging on 'a great tide of vin rosé with undercurrents of Chambéry's Armagnac'.[6] His northward train journey was complicated by a Siamese kitten that he had acquired:

> I spent much of the time on the floors of railway carriages, trying to extract it from a nest of hot pipes; in Inverness, in the Station Hotel, it vanished completely between 12 and 1 a.m. and the Boots and I were to be seen crawling along endless corridors and hissing 'Puss, puss!' in every dark corner. Now it is creating endless turmoil, for it and the dog became enemies at sight and are mortally jealous, and the dog has got a definite neurosis about it.[7]

A week or so later Eric and Marjorie went for an aerial picnic: 'It was a lovely day, and we were invited to fly round the North Isles, landing at Eday and Sanday, where we picnicked—in the bar of the local pub, to be quite truthful about it—and so home by Westray and over the West Mainland.'[8] Such excitements were rare however in a rather stormy winter and Eric spent most of his time at his desk, when he was not called upon to deal with some domestic crisis or with the kitten, which acknowledged no master:

> It bullies my poor dog, is incredibly egotistical, very lovely, totally insensitive to criticism, inclined to be constipated, rather destructive, very much admired, furiously active, and called Kuo Kuo.[9]

He was still spending a lot of money on the house—for 'extension of kitchen premises, Esse stove, dykes, garage, etc'[10]—and didn't quite know whether he was earning as much as he needed; they had decided, he told his sister-in-law Alison, that they must more-or-less economise by living in Orkney through the winters as well as the summers, and calling it local patriotism. When *Juan in China* began to sell quite well and then very strongly indeed in March, at least that kind of worry slipped into the background again, only to be replaced by a kind of frenzy as 'sundry impositions, taxations, assessments, tithes and general suckings of blood'[11] reminded him of the government's interest in his earnings.

The political situation in Europe was preoccupying another part of his mind. His imagination and fears were continually caught by new information about the growth of Fascism in Italy and Germany: Italy's invasion of Abyssinia in October 1935; Germany's reoccupation of the Rhineland in March 1936; and as if they were not enough, the outbreak of the Spanish Civil War in July 1936. When it became evident that the Germans were supporting the rightist rebels in Spain, Eric could no longer resist his awareness that a great crisis was approaching. Before he had finished the Juan book he was working out a literary riposte to the forces of darkness that seemed to be gathering to plunge the whole of Europe into new agonies of war, and for a while, his memories of the useless carnage of the Somme in the forefront of his mind, he set his shoulder to the wheel of the pacifist cart.

It troubled him in later years that he had not, along with other members of the artistic and literary community, gone to join the struggle in Spain, though there were good enough reasons preventing such Quixotic behaviour. 'The meaning of the guns was plain,' he wrote. 'They meant that evil was not only positive in the world, but that evil had mobilised and become aggressive. The world was again at war, and sooner or later we should have to choose our side.'[12] Though his 'sense of decency, and a civilised palate for justice' suggested that he should go to Spain, he realised that he was no longer as young as he had been during his fighting days in the Great War, and he doubted whether the trade of writing had had the effect of encouraging fortitude or developing soldierly muscle; he had reason to doubt his quality as a rifleman after sixteen years of civilian life. More seriously, he 'could not quite stomach the thought of fighting for Communism, even though Communism in Spain was in the right'.[13] At the heart of the matter was a logical problem causing the utmost perplexity, for 'as Franco's cause was sullied by his German and Italian allies, so was the apparently constitutional cause stained and confused by Russian aid.'[14]

Nowhere has Eric referred to what his young wife, pointing no doubt at the two little girls, might have had to say about any idealistic proposal to go and join the Spanish conflict, though her attitude may have had something to do with his decision not to go. He surely realised that the experience would have been invaluable to him as an author; a year or so later, discussing *To Have and Have Not* with Rupert Hart-Davis, he observed prophetically that Hemingway had 'milked the old cow dry ... I'd take a bet that Hemingway's next book will, in a way, be a first novel—the first in a new style and temper ... Spain ought to give him what he wants: he ought to write an absolute winner out of Spain.' But, with the political dilemma insoluble and his domestic circumstances not permitting anyway, he remained at home, and in 1940 wrote: 'The decision weakened me and left a scar.'[15] In 1970 he recalled: 'My conscience was lacerated.'[16]

His work during the spring of 1937, then, was concentrated mainly on devising a novel that would show the folly of war and laugh out of court any notion that it was a viable means of solving great political and economic problems. He had had a considerable predecessor in the field in the person of Aristophanes, whose play *Lysistrata*—not so well remembered in the 1930s as it became later with an important revival in the 1950s—was the last word in mockery of bellicose behaviour. Revering the comic method of Aristophanes as he did, Eric perceived how he could take the classical play as his model and up-date it to underline its sense and the force of its message for the disaster-inviting world of 1937.

The work went slowly, however, for he encountered profound difficulties in the adaptation of the original material to contemporary circumstances, and in solving the problem of tone. It was similar to the problem which *Juan in China* had presented: how, when your vehicle is comedy, to incorporate reference to the worst kind of excesses possible in modern warfare? Eric was the ideal man to attempt such a task, for his comedy had always included the possibility of its antithesis, but for a long time he was dissatisfied with his progress.

Meanwhile there was no avoiding politics in real life and at home as well as abroad. Early in the year Eric, after consultation with Compton Mackenzie who resolved to follow the same course, resigned his membership of PEN, the writers' society, on the grounds that their involvement in politics was too acute and taking them too far to the Left. By a comical irony his sister-in-law Alison, ever busy and active on the fringes of the literary field, became Secretary of Scottish PEN in March, and immediately put it to Eric that he would make an excellent President. He admitted that with her as Secretary the position would be somewhat different, but declined on domestic grounds to allow his name to go forward. He was tempted, but he simply hadn't time. But he wrote Alison a long letter explaining his position about propaganda in literature, the matter which had caused his resignation from P E N and which was one of his own chief difficulties in writing an anti-war novel. He wrote:

> Propaganda is different from criticism. Criticism, of social values, standards, etc is implicit in most kinds of prose writing. But propaganda demands the sacrifice of nearly all the characteristics of literature—individual judgment, aesthetic, a *whole* creation of character, and all the rest of them. Is the sacrifice worth while? Read on.

He argued that Left propaganda was not worth making such sacrifices for, because the programme of the Left was insufficiently humanist, by which he meant it did not combine selected elements of our Christian and classical heritage. Most notably this came down to a recognition of the individual and of the jealous maintenance of Western traditional culture. Under Socialism, as he read the signs, there could be no hope of such desirable policies. He gave examples of the difference between legitimate criticism and unacceptable propaganda:

> The propagandist writes: 'The capitalist system is a monstrous injustice. Workers of the world, unite and destroy it!' The critic says: 'What shall it profit a man if he gain the whole world and lose his soul?' The first is not consonant with literature; the second is. Literature may question, debunk or satirise wealth and power; it cannot—while remaining literature—demand a transference of wealth and power to the proletariat.
> For these, and probably other reasons, I am not to be drawn to the Left. I would say to the proletariat—and I might well be lynched if they heard me—'What shall it profit the proletariat if it gain the whole world, and lose its capitalist and bourgeois literature?'

Perhaps this kind of feeling was part of the reason why, during the late spring, growing impatient for a while with a critical novel that kept wanting to be pacifist propaganda, he put it aside and wrote instead a short and cheerful novel which allowed him to spin stories and indulge in the sort of mild and affectionate satire which he most enjoyed. This was *The Sailor's Holiday* (1937), and once he had introduced his character, Henry Tippus, a simple, fun-loving young man with an extraordinary charm and a gift of storytelling to rival that of Arthur Gander in *Ripeness is All*, the book flowed forward almost effortlessly. If it takes a happy man to write a happy book, this novel suggests that, despite everything, Eric was very pleased with life in his own small corner at that time.

The Sailor's Holiday is set in southern England, and again reveals Eric's versatility and stylistic elegance in a picaresque story that has its farcical elements but which is also full of poetry and interesting reflections on life. In structure it could hardly be simpler. Henry comes ashore after a long hard voyage and resolves never to go to sea again. His travels through England bring him some comical adventures in which he meets a number of odd and interesting people. He is ready to turn his hand to anything in the way of a job, and tries chauffeuring and washing-machine salesmanship among other jobs; he rescues an airman whose plane crashes nearby, and later helps his new friend to kidnap his fiancée so that they can marry; he meets a girl himself and decides to settle down in married life with her. But fate parts them, and in order to avoid the temptations of land-life and remain faithful to his Molly, Henry goes back to sea for another voyage after all.

Wherever he goes, Henry tells stories about himself and his ancestors; they come pouring out upon the slightest stimulus, and are both delightfully imaginative and strangely convincing. He seems to make them up as he goes along, yet they seem to have some possibility of truth in them; those that he does not invent on the spot seem to have descended to him from narrative-spinning forebears who, it is suggested, were also drawing on memories orally passed down through many generations. Thus Henry tells, with fine circumstantial detail, of events at the Battle of Santa Cruz, when his great grandfather witnessed Nelson's behaviour when his right arm was shot off; in another story one of his ancestors appears to have sailed with Raleigh's men up the Orinoco; and to cap it all, in another he tells of an ancestor who sailed long ago in a ship called the *Cargo*. This, it transpires, is a corruption of *Argo*; in Jason's crew there was a man called Tiphys ("'Tippus we always called him in my family," said Henry dreamily"[17]), helmsman on the voyage to Colchis in search of the Golden Fleece. Henry's storytelling facility, and the dimension it adds to the book, are Linklaterian features of great interest; a number of his characters possess it, from Nelly Bly to Edward Gratiano Vanbrugh who, in *Position at Noon*, creates the whole novel out of his stories of his own and earlier generations of his family.

In some ways *The Sailor's Holiday* is not unlike a kind of unusually cultured Wodehouse novel with Dickensian echoes. There is a scene where, to help out a benevolent old gentleman, Henry agrees to exhibit himself as a reformed alcoholic at a girls' school, and somehow finds himself talking about how true Socialism would mean the nationalisation of wives, who would be redistributed to meet the needs of the community. In another scene, Henry helps Tod to kidnap Isobel, who cannot leave her bed because of a sprained ankle; everything goes sensationally and chaotically wrong when they rig up block and tackle to get her out of the house, bed and all, and raise the entire household; the consequences are painfully funny for the reader. Some of the characters are no rounder than they need to be to play their part in the farcical events, but others have a dimension similar to that created by the historical and mythical elements in Henry's stories; they are part of the wider culture of English literature. Eric's England in this novel is like the field full of folk that Piers the Plowman saw, and Henry's encounter with Mr Hacking, a walking personification of the deadly sin of Anger, exemplifies an aspect of the book that relates it to a large and ancient tradition.

At one point Eric had high hopes that it might become the basis for a Hollywood film when his American agents, Curtis Brown, reported that MGM had asked for copies, but nothing came of it. He made no great claims himself for his book, calling it 'a short and idle novelette' when telling Mackenzie about his summer's work; but to Rupert Hart-Davis he wrote of 'that agreeable fairy-tale' and it is plain that he had some affection for it.

One thing that annoyed him was a reference in the *Sunday Times'* review to the sailor's 'Gargantuan vocabulary'. Not for the first time (nor the last) he protested to Rupert that such comments about the extent and strangeness of his word-hoard were nonsensical:

> Is there a word of truth in the suggestion that the sailor has a vocabulary more copious and rich than the generality? Not a word. His speech is deliberately and beautifully simple, and the temper of the whole story is quiet.
>
> Even in my other *opuscula*, where certain characters are admittedly given to wordiness, there's nothing truly remarkable in my vocabulary. It is a good working vocabulary, that's all. True, it is fuller than the two hundred useful words that some of the starveling moderns are contented with. But it is *not* a conjuror's equipment; and I do object to this vulgar attitude of 'look at the big words he uses!' I do not use big words: I use the words which seem—in my limited judgment—to suit the sentences and the situation.

But he may, for all the force of his protest, have had his tongue a little in his cheek; he was no searcher of dictionaries for unusual or unexpected words, but his mind retained words, once encountered, in a way which most people's minds regrettably do not. His implication, that people ought to know more language than they do, is hardly disputable. Whether *The Sailor's Holiday* sold because of or despite the range of its protagonist's vocabulary, it paid Eric's bills and gave him the break he needed from the difficulties he was encountering with the Lysistrata novel.

Before he could resume his work on his major novel there were other demands upon his time. The summer of 1937 was much occupied for the Linklater family by their involvement in a great celebration in Orkney of the 800th anniversary of the building by Earl Rognvald of the Cathedral at Kirkwall in honour of his uncle, Saint Magnus. Together with Storer Clouston, Eric wrote the words for eight scenes of Orkney history, in

13 One of Nancy Kirkham's drawings for
   The Crusader's Key, published by
   White Owl Press, 1933

14 Joan Hassall's wood-engraving for
   the title story in *Sealskin Trousers*,
   published by Rupert Hart-Davis, 1947

Leapt from the rock   Joan Hassall

15 Major Linklater, Royal Engineers, and a Lovat Scout officer en route to Thorshavn Faroe Islands, in May 1941, researching for *The Northern Garrisons*

16 Lt-Col Linklater in apprehensive mood before being catapulted from the carrier HMS *Glory* to visit the British Commonwealth Division near the front line in Korea, August 1951

which they 'showed the coming of the Faith to Orkney, the establishment of Norse power, the triumph of Earl Rognvald, and the inception of the Gay Crusade'.[18] It was a tremendous undertaking, involving innumerable preparations, rehearsals and costume-making, and organising a cast of, if not thousands, several hundred eager actors. Eric and Marjorie took the responsibility for the production of one of the Viking scenes, and Eric held the whole thing together with pieces of interim narrative.

Eric described events in a letter to Compton Mackenzie:

It was, after weeks of utter chaos, a great triumph ... We didn't bother to proclaim our independence, we just realised it. I wish you had been here. It was extraordinary, the way Orkney suddenly perceived the reality of its history. We had, in our scene, a force of sixty Vikings, fine fellows, old and young, and half of them over six feet. They—our lot—were all farmers, and a bit contemptuous of the urban players. During the dress rehearsal, to everyone's consternation, they disappeared; and then we found their leaders, two ex-sergeants, were marching them through Kirkwall, just to show them off. With three words, they'd have sacked the place.

Among the visitors with which the islands were bursting were distinguished guests from Norway, Iceland and the Faeroes—'the President of the Iceland Althing was there, and the Bishop of Nidaros, and a Norwegian training ship'—and at Merkister the Linklaters played host to a singer and an actor both representing the Norwegian government. They were 'both gigantic, perennially thirsty, loud as earthquakes and dogmatically in love', and Eric's enjoyment of their uproarious but exhausting personalities is evident in several hilarious pages devoted to them in *The Man on My Back*. It was a stage in his growing ever more fond of Scandinavia and its people even as they grew more interested in and appreciative of his work. In some ways the pageant was one of the high points of his life; almost forty years later Lord Birsay recalled: 'In 1937 Eric won all Island hearts by his ever-memorable pageant and narration for the octocentenary of St Magnus' Cathedral.'[19]

Eric's work in preparation for the pageant also provided him with a further opportunity to broadcast, and the text of his talk on 'Two Saints of Orkney'[20] shows his delight in a story to which he returned again and again in different work after the war, until it finally formed the basis for the entire book, *The Ultimate Viking* (1955).

Another broadcast, of quite a different kind, followed later in the year when he contributed to a series of 'Imaginary Portraits' for the BBC Scottish Home Service an ironic defence of William Fisher, the 'Holy Willie' of Burns's poem. Affecting to take 'the poet Burns' to task for his denigration of Fisher in the poem, Eric reviewed 'the facts' with humorous solemnity, finding means of excusing the behaviour of the sadly misrepresented Elder of Mauchline in such a way that every sentence became an accusation as potent as those of Burns.

In defence of Fisher's alleged light-fingeredness, for instance, Eric pleaded:

> As an Elder it was sometimes his duty to take charge of the plate or bag into which the congregation put their weekly offering. That he was widely suspected of converting some part of the offering to his own use is very generally known, and those who take but a superficial view of his character may think it a fault in him that he did so. But anyone who has taken the trouble to enter into the very mind and nature of the man will readily perceive that this innocent pilfering was merely an expression of his abounding charity. Charity, as he was well aware, begins at home, and by taking the offering to his own home, where the struggle for life was hard enough, he had the satisfaction of knowing that it was well spent.[21]

If the jokes are a little predictable, the tone is deliciously maintained, and any of Fisher's reputation that may have remained after Burns's onslaught could hardly have survived Eric's defence.

Another of Eric's tasks during the summer was to be editor of a book written by his mother. Elizabeth, whose marvellous tales of the sea and exotic shores had enriched her children's childhood, had been scribbling in exercise books at intervals for several years, and when Eric read her memoirs of youthful months at sea he was sure they were worth publishing. He asked his friend George Blake, the Glasgow novelist, to read the manuscript, and was glad to have his judgement confirmed by someone less emotionally involved. All Eric had to do, said his mother, was to punctuate the manuscript and divide it into chapters. At first he tackled his job without much pleasure, for his mother's typing was, he said, 'impressionistic, and at first glance the manuscript was shapeless'.[22] But he soon realised that Elizabeth had told a fascinating story effectively through native wit and a beginner's good fortune to hit upon an appropriate design. Having 'scattered commas and cemented it with semi-colons' he sent it with some confidence to Cape, who immediately agreed to publish it.

When *A Child Under Sail* appeared in February 1938, with an interesting personal essay by Eric by way of introduction, it was very warmly received. George Blake, whose own novel, *The Shipbuilders*, had been published three years previously, reaffirmed in a letter to Eric the pleasure the book had given him. 'This is really to the address of your mother,' he wrote, 'a woman I revere this side of idolatry. Her little book is a real corker of charm and unusual interest.' He admitted how Elizabeth Linklater's book had stirred his own carefully concealed feeling for his native city of Glasgow, so that 'for what sort of novelist I am, I am settling down for the rest of my life to screw the essence out of that so-typical Scottish community.' His advice to Eric as a fellow novelist was that he, too, should look again to his roots:

Some day, my son, you are going to write the essential Scottish novel, in which all the perdurable elements of *White-Maa, Men of Ness* and *Magnus Merriman* will be beautifully fused. Do you care to know that—admiration for technical qualities apart—one humble critic still likes *White-Maa* best of all and believes that the root of the Link matter was there? That Orkney night haunts us still; likewise the end of *Magnus*.

But by then Eric was already back in the toils of his pacifist novel, and whatever he may have thought of the validity of Blake's words, things generally were moving too quickly for him to give them much consideration. Since he had put the novel aside the world had rolled on, and the confrontation his story was designed to forestall was coming inevitably closer. Nevertheless, it was still possible to enjoy much of life quite normally, and so he did in his November holiday of 1937, as he told Rupert Hart-Davis:

The latter part of my holiday—though discoloured by several bouts of public speaking—was also good, and frequently amusing. I could, indeed, make an agreeable story of my three weeks jaunting if it weren't for the law of libel—Dublin and Edinburgh and Glasgow are full of good material: the RLS Annual Banquet (and Exercises) at which I delivered the oration was, with a flick of the pen, pure farce ... Yes, it was a good holiday, with much in it to show that Linklater novels are rather sad and sober little experiments in understatement.

The holiday was perhaps better than it should have been, for soon after his return to Merkister Eric 'fell sick, and lay in such miserable lethargy that all thought of Christmas was drowned in stagnancy'.[23] He kept to his bed for two or three weeks and recovery was slow and partial, but by the end of January 1938 he was working again with enthusiasm. The Lysistrata book was still causing trouble. He told Rupert in February: 'I have just had the strength of mind to reject my long penultimate chapter, and start it again. It went out of tune, blast it.' At last, however, it was finished. Eric resolved that, to give himself a chance to recover fully from the abdominal miseries that had dogged him for months, he would take the cure at Champneys in Tring, Hertfordshire: 'one of those places where they starve, slap and swab one out'.[24]

Rupert Hart-Davis made the journey out to Tring to visit the invalid once or twice; how could he resist a pleading invitation which offered 'a meal of sorts and, if you cared, you might have a colonic irrigation as well'? With his usual generosity he went loaded with armfuls of books, including Douglas Reed's *Insanity Fair*, an investigation of the state of the world that Eric thought first-rate. Eric admitted that there was not really much wrong with him 'but a little self-pity, a spot of bile, and some masochism' but the treatment did him a great deal of good. 'This morning I was mauled by a wild osteopath—my head nods loosely on my shoulders, like a sun-drunk overblown poppy', he informed Rupert, not without some delight.

It may have been his fears and doubts about *The Impregnable Women* that helped drain his energy, for once it was completed and he had taken his nature cure he was on top of the world again. He was even hopeful that the book would be seen to have turned out rather well; he told Phoebe Gilkyson:

> Till the beginning of March I was doing ten hours a day, being utterly under the spell and compulsion of a novel which now, thank heaven, is finished. And I think it's good. I'm more excited about it than I have been about anything for a long time.

His high spirits shine through the rest of the letter too; he was looking forward to rejoining his 'desolated wife and hapless young' in Orkney; they were all in splendid form: 'Sally very big, and already showing a regrettably literary turn of mind—full of fanciful invention and fond of rhyming—but Kristin, the little one, is just a clown.' Marjorie wanted to increase the family, but 'the cautious male parent is somewhat reluctant to increase his style, responsibilities and expenditure'. He confessed to sharing a general feeling in Britain of guilt over the failure to do anything to help Spain, and confirmed:

> Europe isn't as healthy a playground as it might be. I'm not unduly pessimistic about the future, and certainly not about the war, if it comes: we'd muddle through once again, though sorely hampered by a dry rot in our ruling classes.[25]

He stayed a week in Edinburgh on his way back from Champneys— 'hard going,' he confessed to Compton Mackenzie, for it 'almost put me back where I'd started, but was worth the subsequent discomfort.' But his anxieties about *The Impregnable Women* were growing again; the good news was that the Book Society wanted to adopt it, but this entailed holding back publication until August, and 'every time anybody in Czechoslovakia speaks above a whisper, I get the wind up in case a war starts before then and dishes it completely.'[26]

Writing in June to Neil Gunn, to congratulate him on his having been awarded the James Tait Black Memorial Prize for *Highland River*, Eric mentioned his own hopes for *The Impregnable Women*: he was, he said 'fairly well pleased with it'. His praise of Gunn's novel shows his appreciation of a precise and tactile rendering of experience:

> I had enjoyed *Highland River* more than any of yours since *Morning Tide*: it was more purely Keatsian than any intervening ones: Keatsian in the 'O for a life of sensation' way. You do sensation so well that really you oughtn't to be allowed to think ... Stick to sensation—and narrative.

He praised also Gunn's more recent *Off in a Boat* for its sheer readability and its delicious matter. From the sympathetic way Eric wrote of Gunn's experiences with his boat, it is plain he was remembering his own troubles with *Joy* in 1933:

> I was agonised, utterly agonised by your difficulties in getting the *Thistle* launched ... by the reticence (more dreadful than a scream) with which you treated your discovery of the engine's age and then the previous price of the boat. But you've turned the tables on them all: it's a blessed thing, a pen, that can make use of any mishappening.

In March Hitler had annexed Austria, and few could doubt but that it would be the turn of Czechoslovakia's Sudetenland next. Eric was in an ironic quandary. He wanted the book to succeed, because he needed the money, but he was already unconvinced about the message he had been trying to convey in writing it. A year or two later he put it down to his 'weakness' that his project had 'subscribed to a heresy popular at the time ... that war could prove nothing and that no good ever emerged from it. History demonstrated a hundred times the untruth of this, but the belief was current, and because writing had become my form of action, I sat down to write a novel against war.'[27]

In the darkening days of 1938 the theme of Eric's novel was found very attractive. Following the Aristophanic original, his story of *The Impregnable Women* tells of a Second World War which is brought to a halt through the good sense and powerful effect of the actions of Britain's women, who withdraw their favours from their menfolk until they see reason. The book has much to offer, from convincingly horrible and realistic scenes of modern warfare as recalled by Eric from his 1918 experiences, to magnificent comic set-pieces and forceful satirical attack on government mismanagement, war-profiteering and so on. It has a witty and decisive heroine in Lady Lysistrata Scrymgeour, and a varied team of other women to support her in her revolt. Its powerful, uproarious story is told with all the precision and richness of language, the wealth of comical, startling and symbolic incident, and the brilliant realisation of place and atmosphere which distinguished its predecessors. The tone varies from the coolly detached to the purely romantic, the narrative from the exciting to the grotesque and the farcical; the comedy is offset by harrowing description of the kinds of horrors the First World War had inflicted on its participants and by unsparing sacrifice to those horrors of some of the characters. The second half of the book offers a much sunnier account of the revolt of the women and their occupation of Edinburgh Castle until they win their way; it is joyous and exciting, and the use made of the Edinburgh setting looks forward to *The Merry Muse*, where Eric returns with éclat to celebrate a world that both amused and delighted him.

A detailed commentary could be offered to demonstrate that this book as much as any of his output proves Eric to have been stylistically more rewarding than almost any other writer of his generation; its texture is impeccable. But in conception and structure there are flaws, upon which no one has commented more severely than Eric himself. Francis Russell Hart suggests that it is one of Eric's least successful novels because of its lack of unity: 'Trench realism gives over to mythopoeia, Dionysiac ritual, and farce ... The mixture of fantasy and grotesque farce with serious and plausible adult character is quite typical [of Eric's work]. It is a difficult mixture to manage.'[28] Hart's implication is that though, for instance, in *Juan in America* and, later, in *Position at Noon* and *A Man Over Forty*, Eric succeeded in such a problematical melding of differences, in *The Impregnable Women* something went wrong.

This view may be disputed, though the novel presents one problem that makes the suspension of disbelief in its action almost impossible. This was the logical step which led Eric to postulate a war against France rather than Germany, so that a basically emotional appeal could be made against war in general. This very decision, which came not from his head but from his heart, made something of a nonsense of his thesis, for the enemy was obviously Germany; but Eric 'could not persuade himself into drawing a heroine who would want to make peace with the Nazis'.[29] At which point he might as well have given up his project, for his perception of the true position obviated the possibility of setting his novel in the real world of 1938. Many readers may be glad that he nevertheless soldiered on, for the novel has many facilities which outweigh even so central a flaw.

Among those who liked it very much was Neil Gunn, who in a letter to Eric hit on a compelling symbol for Eric's method. Thanking him for his handsome appreciation of *The Impregnable Women*, Eric replied:

> I don't think it's going to be very popular. A bit near the knuckle at times, perhaps. I was solemnly reproved for it by *The Times* and the *Spectator* ...
>
> You in your letter referred to 'the forgotten congruity of the gargoyle and angelic masonry'—and convicted yourself of second sight. From boyhood (when I was allowed to ring the bells of St Magnus' and perilously admire the gargoyles on its tower) I've been fascinated by them ... And now you've discovered my secret passion! And my belief. One cannot—or at least, if one has any sense, one dare not—build a cathedral without a gargoyle.

Readers of Thomas Hardy may recall the gargoyle which plays its part in *Far From the Madding Crowd* and be interested by the echo. The propinquity of the grotesque and the lovely has a force in a secular novel no less than in a sacred edifice, and in *The Impregnable Women* this characteristic Linklaterian admixture of the two is startling and compulsive.

Eric did not suppose that his novel could affect the future. Indeed, by the time that it was published he no longer wished for it to do so. It was a gesture he had had to make, but in making it he had realised:

> Its theme was the waste and futility of war, but to end one war the rebel women declared another. Against all inclination I had created a situation in which war became rightly purposive and serviceable to humanity.[30]

Embarrassing though he found his position, it was through the writing of *The Impregnable Women*, and being forced to the daft expedient of making France the enemy, that he found his way and exorcised the weakness he felt after failing to go to Spain, for now he recognised what he had known all along, that Germany would have to be fought.

Despite the faults of which the author was so conscious, the book met a need of the time and was received with press comments verging on the rapturous. Sean O'Faolain said that it was even better than Eric's earlier novels, at least three of which were in his opinion 'nonpareil':

> It has a more serious core than any of the other Linklater satires ... We have a tragi-comic satire in which the rage of the satirist constantly rumbles, occasionally erupts, may be muted but never dies out.[31]

Within a few weeks of the publication of *The Impregnable Women*, Germany demanded that the Czechs evacuate the Sudetenland. Eric looked out his soldier's uniform. His pacifist days, such as they were, were over.

15   Soldier to the Wars Returning

Since his university days Eric had maintained occasional contact with the Territorial Army. Now, as Germany moved towards its violation of Czechoslovakian territory, he revived his dormant commission and began to help stir things up in Orkney. The events of September 1938, culminating in the Munich agreement, filled him with horror. Though war had been temporarily averted by Mr Chamberlain's piece of paper, Eric was certain that it was now inevitable, and he declared himself in the fighting camp. He wrote to Alison:

> My mother and sister, whom I went to see last night, are both on your side: peace-at-any-pricers; so the affectionate family visit turned into a nasty family quarrel. In all honesty I can't see the advantage—save for the insect world—of peace with ignominy. For years past I have said—and believed—that Hitlerism is an evil thing, and for years past I have wished that this country would make a stand against it.

Now, he insisted, was a time for a fortification of the British spirit; there must be a general realisation that there was such a thing as evil, an ability to recognise it, and a determination to oppose it. In similar terms he wrote to Phoebe Gilkyson. In August he had spent a holiday with Marjorie in Sweden; he had been given a marvellous reception wherever he went, largely stage-managed by his friend and admirer Karl Ragnar Gierow and his Swedish publishers; he told Phoebe:

> Sweden was grand: a sane, wholesome and lovely country. A great place for hospitality, good eating and fine drinking. A charming people and a delicious landscape ...
> And then we returned to this malodorous country, and life since then has been hell. Rage, humiliation, and thought of what Chamberlain was doing to the poor bloody Czechs has almost driven me crazy. And now, after sacrificing honour, decency and Czechoslovakia, we're in greater danger than we have been since 1917.

Two years later he wrote of his thinking at this time:

> In my youth, when anger and grief had been partners with a certain exuberance, I had taken a romantic view of the world, but when my life ran into broader waters, much of the traffic that I saw was stuff for comedy. I shall not claim that the comic view of life is either whole or ultimately satisfying, but it has no less validity than the tragic or romantic view, or what is known as realism.

And in the years between the two German wars the matter for comedy lay upon the ground as thickly as forest leaves after a storm. But now, against my habit and inclination, my younger and less comfortable perception was beginning to return.

There was good in the world, though worldly goodness was much blemished; there was evil in the world, though evil could whisper excuses for its birth; and when evil menaced the very existence of good, a man must put away the richness of comedy, the luxury of doubt, and stand with the angels. If victory were won, he could wear his conscience among the battle-ribbons on his coat; and if good were to be defeated, let him go down with virtue. In the mythology of the Norsemen, in the heroic age, there was prophesied a last battle, called Ragnarök, and in that fighting the gods would be defeated. But a good man would have his reward. He would be summoned to fight and fall with his gods.[1]

Despite his resolution to put away comedy and concentrate on grim reality as the world grew darker, Eric could not quite abjure laughter either in life or art. Even as he complained to Phoebe Gilkyson, he included this sketch of the progress of his children:

Sally, though ridiculously fat, shows a little sign of mild intelligence, I think, but Kristin is just an amiable nitwit, with an odd taint (there's none in my family) of the lemur—she loves being swung upside down. They're both mercenary, either teary or cheery, and inclined to constipation. Oh, just children, I suppose. Sally is religious, in a patronising way; Kristin agnostic. Sally knows 5 of the 6 facts of life; Kristin will never realise that there are any. They don't think much of me except as a bit of gymnasium apparatus; they're very fond of Marjorie, and either bully or blackmail her. Just children.

Similarly, though he claimed that anger, blowing like a strong wind, cleared his mind and inspired him to write his next novel, and though the theme of the novel was betrayal, and though it is comparatively stark and bare in style, yet as true realism requires it has within it a good deal of a grim humour of character and dialogue similar to that in *The Men of Ness*. The motivation for his move into historical fiction for the first time since his Viking saga was as much linked with propaganda as that of *The Impregnable Women*, as he explained to Douglas Walker: 'In one way it's the other side of the medal to *The Impregnable Women*: there I showed the argument against war; here I show the consequences of peace-at-any-price.' He gave an account of the conception of the novel:

Some months ago I read Conrad Noel's *Life of Jesus*, where he stresses the socio-political side of the state-of-affairs, and was enormously interested. Then I read the Moffatt translation of the *New Testament*, and the gospels in modern English took on quite a shattering reality. So in September, when the world was again presented with an outstanding bit of treachery, my thoughts turned naturally to Judas.

Judas was written, according to Marjorie Linklater, 'in a frenzy of fury over Neville Chamberlain's betrayal of Czechoslovakia', and according to Eric 'in a state of controlled excitement'.[2] He was convinced that what he was doing mattered: 'If this isn't good—well, I may as well shut up shop.' Writing deliberately in a quite different mode, Eric told a story of what seemed to him immense symbolic significance with a subdued artistry with which he was very pleased. To his astonishment it made, on publication in March 1939, practically no impact in Britain.

Among those who did find the novel effective was the reviewer in *Punch*, who gave Eric some pleasure not only by an expression of approval of the book but also by his comment on the author's surprising variety: 'It is a far cry from *Juan in America* to *Judas* in Jerusalem, but Mr Eric Linklater is one of those rare and refreshing authors who are not content to write the same book over and over again.'[3] At least there was someone who appreciated the kind of craftsmanship which Eric had adopted and which he later defended in his autobiographical writings. But a review in the *Spectator* was so cruel as to call an angry reply from Eric, who in one of his very few letters to the press on the subject of his own work pointed out:

> The novel was written with passion that I most sedulously controlled, in a bitterness of spirit that by discipline I translated into a treatment as nearly objective as I might contrive ... It is the story of a man in whom there was much good, but also the elements of disintegration. Judas, in my mind's discovery, was poisoned by that loving regard for security, for property, which in recent years has again unmanned so many.[4]

In this way he related the meaning of his book to the prevailing political situation, which few if any of his reviewers had mentioned, and took to task the *Spectator*'s critic who had inexplicably dismissed *Judas* as 'this vulgar little novel'. As Eric saw it, 'that love of what is good, and perception of the truth, should by human fears and weakness be defeated, is by any standard of criticism a tragic theme; neither vulgar, nor little'.

The only subsequent commentary on *Judas* has been that of Francis Russell Hart, who called it 'a book of stunning economy and tact',[5] and noted Eric's avoidance of simple answers and mere dialogue or parable. Dramatic reality and ideology were carefully balanced, he pointed out.

Very short, the novel is an ingenious and convincing attempt to understand the psychological make-up of one of the most notorious traitors in history. Its narrative examines Judas' behaviour during the seven days of Holy Week, when his breakdown and treachery are seen against the dramatic events culminating in the Crucifixion. The focus is wholly upon Judas; Jesus remains off-stage and we hear of the great sayings and happenings only through the reports of witnesses. Eric used a modern colloquial idiom for the speech of the characters, avoiding any temptation to go for a sort of grand, remote, historical-biblical dialogue; he concentrated on presenting a socio-political background understandable in contemporary terms. New perceptions about the real politics of the Romano-Judaean period made it possible for him to write about the day-to-day life of remote times with a vivid recognition of their similarity to the present. His characters are earthy and real, their concerns about property, political change, secular versus church authority, and nationalism are the concerns of the 1930s—and of today. It is this bringing to earth in realistic and compassionate terms of the airy mysteries of biblical narrative which lends the book its distinction and startling persuasiveness.

As Eric told Douglas Walker, it contained historical figures but was a modern novel. 'Not a trace of historical detail in it, nor anything but the barest minimum of local colour. Nothing but people ... Character and action, nothing else.'

Eric conceives of Judas as a young man earnest in nature and from a good family background. Judas' spirit is broken on the collision of interests between idealism, whose political expression is inevitably Socialism, and respect for property, traditionally ordered society and comfort. He is a pacifist who wants to retain the status quo and have the ills of society solved by some miraculous means which will mean no loss to him and his. When he begins to perceive that Jesus' radicalism extends to political solutions such as the redistribution of wealth and the throwing off of the Roman yoke, and that the mild, visionary preacher can be transformed (as in the Cleansing of the Temple) into a wrathful, soldierly, violent man of action, he is appalled. To save his own conception of Christianity, he sacrifices Christ.

Eric traces the course of these thoughts in Judas with cool and accurate compassion, and renders it the more convincing by his perception of the people in Judas' life. He is a political innocent, no match for the intriguers within the Sanhedrim; his uncle Phanuel with his pragmatic reasonableness, Annas with his ruthless determination and Caiaphas, superficially weak and irresponsible but formidable in his position of authority, are able to manipulate Judas for their purposes. Eric's humour is inevitably subdued, but, with a distinctly Jewish tinge, it plays an important part in the delineation of these characters. All the characters are human and believable, most of all the muddled, sometimes unpleasant, vain, weak but ultimately sympathetic Judas. The book has no grand pretensions; it works on a level of understatement and allusion, but its effect is that of large-scale tragedy.

It did not sell well in 1939, and at the time that was a matter of greater immediate import for Eric than the failure of the critics to appreciate his art; in May he wrote to Rupert Hart-Davis with a certain bitter cheerfulness:

From your letters it appears that nobody except two children and a governess have bought *Judas*. Good. I should also tell you that a couple of months ago, having a little spare money, I was persuaded to make a certain speculative investment. (Ha-ha.) The stock, I believe, is now no longer quoted. Good again. Also, in the early part of the year, being for no reason optimistic, I instituted some interior decoration and landscape gardening: the bills are now coming in. Loud laughter. Furthermore, my Territorial exercises are taking up an ever-increasing proportion of my time, owing to the disappearance of my Commanding Officer, and the consequent devolvement upon me of letter-writing to D.A.D.O.S., O. i/c Records, O.C.S.E.L., O.C.F.D. (Scotland), C.R.E., and other mysterious giants in the military hierarchy. This is ruining my literary style, and, in any case, leaves me little time for practising it. As, however, nobody buys books any longer, it would seem to be a waste of time to go on writing them. So that's all right.

According to my income–expenditure graph, we shall be slowly beginning to starve about midnight 8th/9th October.

Whether because of a real sense of disappointment about the reception of *Judas* or because he became too busy doing other things when war intervened, six years passed before Eric wrote another novel. He devoted his energies to preparing for the coming struggle and, when he had time to write, tried his hand at various genres, including outright propaganda. In an article in the *News Chronicle* in June 1939, boldly headlined WE MUST FIGHT FOR IT, he considered the nature of freedom and the way in which 'the fighters for freedom, from Wat Tyler to Kościuszko, from Galileo to Freud, have had as their intention far more than the freeing of themselves: they have sought freedom for their fellow-men.' In conclusion he invoked that favourite image of the battle of Ragnarök, convinced that 'in a modern Ragnarök, many would prefer the losing side rather than to share in the barren triumph of a tyranny that writes its commandments on the grave-stone of freedom.'

When he did have time to practise his art of writing more seriously he was working at an autobiography, kept at it by repeated encouragement from Rupert Hart-Davis on behalf of Cape. By June he reported quite good progress:

I go slowly with the autobiography. I've written something more than 80,000 words, most of it twice, and I know what happens in the rest of it ... Great strength and a deal of luck might get the opusculum off my meagre chest by the end of August; notes exist for the unwritten part, and I have established the temper. (Uncertainty about the temper was the reason for the early delay.)

Any possibility of its being finished by August was spoiled by events during the summer. After the German invasion of Czechoslovakia in March—ironically just as *Judas* was published—Eric began working very hard in the Coastal Defence unit of the Territorial Army to which he had been attached in Orkney, and increasingly during the summer thought of himself more as a soldier than as an author. A full-scale training camp kept him occupied throughout much of July and early August, and when the inevitable happened on 3 September, he at any rate was ready for it.

On 5 September 1939, Captain E. R. Linklater, Royal Engineers, wrote to Rupert Hart-Davis:

> Our war station—which I must not name, of course—is at the moment in the very midst of a roaring gale such as is characteristic of this locality—which I may not specify. We are surrounded by water (which I cannot otherwise describe than to say that it is in a state of singular commotion) and beaten upon by wind (whose velocity I can only hint at and whose direction I dare not whisper) ... Presently I shall go out and battle for an hour or two with the excessive storm while I inspect the duties and discomforts of my devoted Sappers; who will be on their nightly task of working unmentionable apparatus for an indescribable purpose in circumstances quite unprintable on the edge of a bloody awful cliff.
>
> And—believe it or not—it's rather fun.

Eric was—in a way—in his element. It made him happy to think he was doing something, and commanding Orkney (Fortress), R.E. was obviously something that needed to be done, but already he itched for something more demanding. He wanted to go to France but knew there was no chance of anything like that 'till the Regular gentlemen are provided with decent occupations'.[6] He was taking bets that the war wouldn't last long: one of the few details in which his prescience let him down.

There was plenty to do in Orkney. The Royal Navy was at anchor in Scapa Flow, and the defence of the archipelago was of supreme importance. The excitement of real action came early with the sinking on 14 October of *Royal Oak* by the submarine, U47, and the loss in an air attack on 17 October of *Iron Duke*. Eric described part of the action to Phoebe Gilkyson:

> It was very agreeable to watch a German plane come down in flames. Our people—our good sober Orkney soldiers—very decorously *clapped their hands* when they saw it. To cheer would have been vulgar and emotional ... It is twenty-one years since I was last under fire, but the visceral sensation, when a shell comes anywhere near, remains curiously the same.

His energetic work was rewarded by promotion to Major in November, but he was conscious of a fearful triviality about his mundane administrative duties. He sustained an injury, breaking a rib when aboard a visiting destroyer ('There happened to be an air-raid while I was there, and going up to the bridge in what I thought was a very nimble, jaunty and romantic fashion, I slipped ... and fell with all the heaviness of forty years,' he confessed to Phoebe) but it was not the sort of war-wound he would have preferred. To Rupert he outlined a typical day:

> In pursuit of war aims I have today purchased four stones of stucco; ordered two Sappers to tear down the ceiling of a house; signed my name 143 times; obtained five different estimates of the height of a passing German aeroplane; written three reports which nobody will read; encountered an old friend so disguised by a tin hat that I couldn't recognise him; and eaten a large tea with raspberry jam while trying to persuade a Person with Some Authority to adopt a Certain Policy.
>
> This is war.

As his detailed and witty account of the period in *Fanfare for a Tin Hat* shows, there was throughout the winter of 1939/40 evidence in plenty of 'our ponderous and grave intention' in the form of much work in fortification and training, but after the initial excitement it was felt as a phoney war nonetheless. In quiet moments between official duties he returned to work on the autobiography, but found it difficult to settle to. Gradually reorganisation and an influx of senior officers created a situation in which Eric's authority was superseded and he had himself to face redundancy. For a while he wondered what was to become of him, and he canvassed various avenues of useful employment; 'at one time,' he wrote, 'an offer seemed imminent from MI5, but I laughed at the wrong time—I made an inappropriate joke—and the prospect faded.'[7] The year wore on with little to make his life seem very important or useful. 'I do not like this kind of war,' he confided to Rupert Hart-Davis: 'I have a simple nature: I merely want to shoot a few Germans and go home again.'

In April 1940 there was a great deal of activity as the Royal Navy prepared to launch its not very successful attack on Andalsnes in an attempt to relieve Norway. Eric was surprised to receive a peremptory summons to go aboard a ship newly arrived in the Flow, but was delighted to discover it came from O. H. Mavor, 'the Glasgow doctor who in the theatre made himself improbably famous as the dramatist, James Bridie'.[8] Bridie, aged over fifty, had managed to secure a commission in the Royal Army Medical Corps and was on his way to see active service. Eric had known and admired him since the early 1930s, and this brief reunion with so vital a man gave him great pleasure.

Eric was, by April, almost threequarters of the way through his autobiography, and he sent to Compton Mackenzie the chapter in which he had written a portrait of his friend. He complained of being up and down with 'a misbehaving heart, into which apparently got a streptococcus or two during an attack of 'flu'. He did not like the war, he said, but he thoroughly approved of it, and longed to see 'those beasts whining for mercy'. A week or so later he again wrote to Mackenzie to tell him that *The West Wind of Love*, newly published, 'put the seal of absolute assurance on the whole novel. It is going to be a great and memorable work ... *The West Wind* is ripe and whole, and I love every page of it.'

The autobiography was at last finished in May. At about the same time Marjorie and the children and Eric's mother were evacuated to the mainland for their safety. They settled in St Boswell's, in Roxburghshire, together with Marjorie's sister Ida Hume and her children, and remained there, at first fairly discontented with their lot, for about a year. Eric went down to London briefly in June to discuss publication details of the autobiography with Macmillan. He had not left Cape for good and all, he told Mackenzie, but felt a need to establish his independence—'Cape was beginning to feel he had proprietary rights in me'—and besides, there had been a little difference of financial opinion.

Back in Orkney he was, he wrote to Marjorie in St Boswell's, 'bored—bored—bored'. Looking for something other than petty administrative jobs to do, he made some efforts to remind people of his occasional broadcasting experience during the 1930s, and an approach to James Fergusson at the BBC in October promised to bear fruit. After a tentative beginning Eric was given an opportunity to make a broadcast in the 'Britain Speaks' series, in which people such as Leslie Howard, J. B. Priestley, Hugh Walpole and others tried to tell listeners in Canada and the United States what it felt like to be in Britain at war. Eric thought it would be interesting to describe something of how the Orkney community had been involved in the northern defences; he wrote to Fergusson:

> I consulted the General about the propriety of such a talk and, with the proviso that I should not mention the number of troops in the Islands or their disposition, he concurred.[9]

Eric was diffident about his quality as a broadcaster; after a postponement of the broadcast because of pressure of work, he wrote to Fergusson: 'I hope devoutly that I read it decently.' He may have been justified in his fears, for the day after the first transmission of the talk ('We Guard Scapa Flow', 21 November 1940) Fergusson was obliged to report: 'You do not seem to have been quite successful in "putting it over".' The Americans had apparently found something unsympathetic in Eric's delivery, and Fergusson had to say, 'Until we have found the right channel for your talents we cannot pursue the plan I outlined to you of applying for your release for regular work of that sort.' Fergusson tried to find some other niche for Eric in the BBC's work and in mid-December brought him to London for two days to talk to people and discuss some script ideas. Eric was reasonably hopeful that he would find employment in broadcasting until another adverse report on his reception landed on Fergusson's desk on 31 December; its comment was that 'from the overseas point of view his voice was not suitable', and that seemed to be that. 'I am more than sorry', wrote Fergusson, conveying the bad news, 'that we could not fix up anything between you and my own department.'

This somewhat abortive beginning was far from the end of the story of Eric's association with broadcasting, though there was an interval of a year before he got another chance. Anyone who has heard the warm, deep, humorous voice with which he made innumerable broadcasts later in the war and afterwards may wonder in what way it seemed unsuitable to the anonymous judges of 1940; the explanation on record is that he spoke too regularly or 'monotonously'. Fortunately, he was later allowed to learn a more satisfactory technique and to try again.

Before the judgement that there was to be no career in broadcasting for him, Eric was quite cheerful in the autumn of 1940. In late September, looking forward to a brief leave to be spent in St Boswell's with his 'widowed family' he wrote to Rupert Hart-Davis: 'It's odd how this ridiculous life returns one to the emotions of boyhood: end-of-term feeling is in my blood. And also, perennially, the feeling that one is going to be found out.' After his few days in Roxburghshire he described how things were to Phoebe Gilkyson:

> I've just come back from leave, a pleasant lazy week and all the family well. A house full of children ... So breeding goes on, like the production of aeroplanes, and our children are sempiternal raspberries to Adolf and his crazy gang.

And to show the spirit awake in Britain, he included 'a pleasant story for you':

> A man was telling me of a bomb that had fallen behind a neighbour's house. 'It blew everything forward. Blew all the furniture through the front windows. Blew old So-and-so and his wife out through the front door. By God, it was the first time they'd gone out together for twenty years!'

Ironically, Eric was invited to spend Christmas Day 1940 in his own house which was, in the absence of Marjorie and the children, temporarily being occupied by one of Eric's fellow Sapper officers and his wife, who by some anomaly had been allowed to come to Orkney just as everyone else's family was being evacuated elsewhere. Their dinner was interrupted when a German Ju 88 bomber crash-landed in the next parish, and Eric and his host rushed out in time to arrest the German crew and prevent them from blowing up their abandoned aeroplane. Accepting a cigarette, the German flight-lieutenant said that there was no need to give cigarettes to all of his crew, one of whom was not an officer. Eric's reaction was typical:

> To the wounded man who was not an officer I gave my packet of Gold Flake, and with a rebuke that seemed called-for, but in my gentlest voice, said to the flight-lieutenant, 'I think, when you are talking to me, you should stand at attention.' To my great surprise he, and the two others who held commissioned

rank, responded with a disciplined alacrity that I had seldom seen in my own Territorial Company.[10]

It was not the only encounter Eric had during the war with the crew of a downed aeroplane, for on leave in 1943 he went to the rescue of two young naval officers whose Walrus aircraft was stuck on a shoal in the Loch of Harray just by a little island called the Holm of Kirkness, one of Eric's favourite fishing places. After a couple of hours of hard rowing about in his little boat he helped them get off again, but not before one of the men had fallen into the loch. In *A Year of Space* Eric described with great amusement his thoughts when he heard no word of thanks later for his assistance to the young officers; he concluded:

> I have not told the story, after nearly a decade, to complain of their neglect; but as a fisherman I cannot omit from the game-book one sub-lieutenant of the Royal Navy. In his waterlogged flying-suit, as I netted him, he must have weighed at least two hundred and fifty pounds; which raises my average appreciably.[11]

Although Eric knew during the later months of 1940 that his Orkney job was dwindling and that some alternative would have to be found, he took great pleasure in one last task for the Orkney garrison. This came about when General Kemp, in command of the now numerous and widely scattered troops on the islands, decided that they needed a newspaper, not so much to provide news for its own sake as to combat the old enemy of boredom as the war in the north quietened and excitement turned to routine. Eric was recruited to the foundation of such an organ, and for several busy weeks bustled around to find editorial assistance and a supply of newsprint, and to secure the use of the local newspapers' printing machinery. Named appropriately for the decidedly stiff breezes so frequently experienced in the islands, the *Orkney Blast* made its first appearance on 17 January 1941. Eric had been warned that he could not be kept on as editor once he had got the enterprise going, and after the first edition he officially handed over the reins to Private G. M. Meyer, a cockney trooper with some peacetime experience of newspaper work.

The first number was an instant sell-out, and not surprisingly for it was attractively and professionally done. There was a pleasant title-piece depicting 'a mermaid in partial uniform—she wore a cap'[12]; a strip-cartoon about an ATS girl called Audrey Allbust (Orkney's answer to the *Daily Mirror*'s 'Jane'); a comical thriller by General Kemp; an article on St Magnus' Cathedral by Storer Clouston; and an imitation Beachcomber column supplied by Eric; and quite a lot more. In his editorial Eric pointed out that 'our readers must also be our writers', and commented on an astonishing phenomenon of the first batch of contributions received from the troops:

These were nearly all written in verse. There must be something in the Orkney air that drives a man to poetry, as duller places will drive him to drink. Verses, at any rate, were constantly arriving from privates and sergeants, from gunners and sappers and quartermasters and rugged sentimentalists in the R A O C. Our office, at the moment, is so full of lyrics and limericks that we can hardly move without treading on a sonnet or tripping over a few heroic couplets.[13]

Soldiers who got articles printed, he suggested, could send a marked copy of the *Orkney Blast* to their young women, which would help them a lot; because a young woman was instantly attracted to any author, thinking fondly that his next lucubration would be about her. He ended by offering a prize: the best of the biographical articles that they received would be printed right alongside an article by Mr Winston Churchill—'If Mr Winston Churchill sends us an article, that is.'

The *Orkney Blast* flourished throughout the war; when the war was over, 'Geremy' Meyer decided to remain in the place he had come to love, and until 1983 he edited the *Orcadian*. With some satisfaction Eric, looking back in 1970, reflected: 'I had more success in establishing a newspaper than in demolishing railway bridges.' But after the launch of the *Orkney Blast* there was no more wartime employment for him in Orkney.

No sooner had he got the first number of *Blast* to the press than he was sent, in January 1941, to the School of Military Engineering at Ripon on courses designed, he said, to make him absorb sufficient instruction to make him eligible, with reduction in rank, for a field company. He was not the least bit practically minded, however, and his brain was of the wrong kind for arithmetical calculation; on his own admission he had by the end of the course revealed, as a Sapper, total ineptitude.

From his depression when he returned to Orkney, where he expected to be condemned to go off to perform some pedestrian office as, say, a Railway Transport Officer, he was rescued at last by an invitation from the War Office to do a job for the Directorate of Public Relations. This office had just been taken over by the former Secretary of State for Scotland and Minister of Health, Walter Elliot, who as a Chamberlain supporter lost his Cabinet post when Churchill took over the government. Elliot knew Eric through their mutual friend James Bridie, and thought of him now when he needed some first-rate writers to explain and report on the military effort of the time.

Eric's first, very congenial, task during the spring of 1941 was to 'compose, for publication by the Stationery Office, a pamphlet in which [he] would describe—with unfailing accuracy but in a manner designed for popular reading—the peculiar conditions of garrison service in our northernmost outposts: Iceland, the Faeroes, Shetland and Orkney.'[14] Something of the pleasure which the undertaking gave him is evident from the twenty pages of *Fanfare for a Tin Hat* and two or three pages in *A Year of Space* which he devoted to memories of his jaunts about the northern archipelagos.

The booklet, in the Ministry of Information/War Office series 'The Army at War', which he wrote in the summer after his journeyings in the North Atlantic, shows equally his pride and his pleasure in the job he had been asked to do. *The Northern Garrisons* (1941) is the sort of excellent writing which gives propaganda a good name. Full of Eric's warmth of personality, humour and perception, of vivid and economical description, and of devotion to the cause, it celebrates a convinced and convincing notion of the British soldier as essentially decent and efficient, doing a difficult job with patience and application. Beside the strong sense of admiration of the soldiers, sailors and airmen which is manifest there is also a warm appreciation of the local inhabitants of the various islands and of their history and culture; and there is above all a clear and unshaken feeling that the war, which in an introduction he called 'the war between the Sensibles and the Stupids', was right and necessary. And he wrote as if the possibility of not eventually winning it had never entered his head.

While he was gathering material for his pamphlet his autobiography was published in March 1941 and attracted a great deal of attention. He had planned at one time to call his book *Position at Noon*, but in the event this pleasing title was reserved and eventually used for a novel in 1958. Later he had considered calling it *Gazebo*, but by the beginning of 1941 had settled for *The Man on My Back*. Even this was not completely satisfactory, for it led to a basic misapprehension of his purpose. He had hit on it, he said, after reading an essay by Montaigne about a man whose travels had 'neither improved his temper nor enlarged his understanding, for wherever he went he carried himself on his back, and the burden was too much'.[15] Modestly accepting this as having some application to himself, he asked Macmillan to print it as an epigraph on the title-page, but the quotation and/or the instruction went astray.

Ironically, Eric had within the book quoted in part of his narrative an old Norse proverb: 'Bare is his back who has no brother.'[16] Readers linked the phrase to the title and supposed, embarrassingly, that Eric was 'posing and posturing as his brother's keeper' as he unhappily recalled in 1970: 'In 1941, when the book was published, the acceptance of unwelcome responsibilities had been common form; but I was not trying to win favour by a show of timely virtue.'[17] On the contrary, his decision to write an autobiography at the early age of forty had been made as a means of coming to terms with himself, for:

I did not like myself. I was ashamed of the vast and dreary spaces of my ignorance, I deplored my diffidence, I despised my timidity, I abominated my

false disguise in these indecencies. I deprecated the impacted layers of repression that prevented me from being frank and free and emotional; and when
repression loosened a little and out I came, frank and free and too emotional, I
was covered with confusion to hear the horrid noise I made.[18]

Having found that he lost all interest in the people and circumstances of a
novel as soon as he had written it, he thought he would similarly be able to
banish from his mind all thoughts of himself by writing an autobiography,
by writing himself out of his system, by composing some sort of record of
his life that should reduce his ego to 'a little i with whom I could live and
never notice him'.[19]

Whatever his motive for writing *The Man on My Back*, it was recognised
as a fine achievement in both Great Britain and, later, the United States,
and was in gratifying demand in the bookshops. L. P. Hartley said 'his
book is of altogether unusual value, both as a personal record and as a
commentary on life'.[20] The *Manchester Guardian* commented:

> It is a very good autobiography, avoiding the Scylla of ultimate personal
> revelation and the Charybdis of the gossip column. It reflects rather than
> describes the contemporary scene and the varying moods, social and political,
> between Britain's two wars ... Mr Linklater as his own hero is as entertaining
> as, and more interesting than, any of his predecessors.[21]

Most reviewers expressed similar views and several agreed that the
central jewel was Eric's portrait of Compton Mackenzie. About a year after
it was published C. W. Taylor summed up: 'This is the very pearl of
autobiographies ... It reads not like an autobiography but like a novel, a
perfect one.'[22]

As must be plain from the many citations of *The Man on My Back* in this
book, it is unusually well written. In its maintenance of a recognisably
Linklaterian tone it creates a voice which delights not only with what is
being said but also the very satisfying way in which it is said. All Eric's
skills as narrator, observer, wit, poet and philosopher went into it, and
many would agree that it is among the best books he wrote. As autobiography, however, it is not altogether satisfactory. It omits much; it
distorts things for various reasons, for example to make better jokes, or to
secure better artistic effects, or to protect identities, or to present a
self-justification that avoids self-revelation. Eric admitted as much when
writing a third volume of autobiography at the age of sixty-nine, explaining that he now intended to fill in some gaps and straighten some impressions he had formerly given, for while *A Year of Space* had 'violent
deviations' in time and place it was 'an accurate and trustworthy chronicle;
and that cannot be said of its predecessor.'[23]

When he had completed *The Northern Garrisons* and was waiting for some
new commission from Walter Elliot, he spent his spare time at his conge-

nial London club; later it seemed to him that he had been able to pass so much time within its comfortable portals that he used to tell people that he had fought the Second World War in the Savile Club. In fact, he also spent a fair proportion of it in Orkney, where, he persuaded his mentors, he could best do his writing once his researches were complete. Writing *The Northern Garrisons* in Orkney in May, after Marjorie and the children were allowed to return from their enforced evacuation, he found time to attend to his domestic duties so satisfactorily that in October he was able to tell Mackenzie:

> My family, all in Orkney, are well at the last hearing. Marjorie in high spirits, and dropping another small Linklater into the world next February. To stop breeding now, merely because of Hitler, would be sheer defeatism, she said. Look at France, and to hell with safety first. I think she is right.
>
> Sally, aged 7½, is already committed to literature; but Kristin shows no signs of perversion as yet.

By the time *The Northern Garrisons* was published in August 1941, Eric had been given another assignment, this time to put together an interim account of the British Expeditionary Force's four-day struggle to defend Calais in May 1940. It was a more difficult job, but the resulting pamphlet, *The Defence of Calais* (1941), was extremely successful when published in December. The entire edition was rapidly sold out at fourpence a copy; as collectors' items, twenty years later, they were changing hands at more than seventy-five times that price, and Eric could not help regretting that none of his other books appreciated quite so much in value.[24] The merits of the account were its apparently straightforward and simple style with strong narrative drive which diverted attention from the constructional skill and selection of detail which made it so effective. It was, furthermore, without being partisan, so appreciative of the heroism and duty shown by the trapped forces, while so British in its cool and even humorous portrayal of desperate and doomed action, that the booklet, despite its admitted incompleteness, remains memorable.

Equally popular was his next undertaking for the series 'The Army at War', which was 'to sew a patchwork quilt: the story of the Highland Division, the 51st, of which the greater part went into involuntary retirement after being surrounded—its ammunition spent—at the little port of St Valéry-en-Caux.'[25]

The news of the surrender of the 51st (Highland) Division on 12 June 1940 had come to Scotland 'like another Flodden', and part of Eric's function was to repair the damage done to the Division's reputation and morale by its failure and the apparent shame of its capitulation. He wanted to insist that 'the black morning at St Valéry does not tell the whole story. Before the Division walked into that disastrous trap it had fought well, endured with hardihood.'[26] He succeeded in putting together, in considerable detail and with the utmost conviction, an exciting and persuasive account of the Division's actions up to the surrender, and in doing so won the eternal gratitude of all Highland soldiers. His mastery of detail, perception of the main issues and force of narrative impressed and moved those who only read of as well as those who had participated in the débâcle.

Pursuit of the details necessary for the task involved Eric in a long and problematical chase. Anthony Walker, who, in 1941, was a young subaltern in the 154th Brigade of the re-forming Highland Division, remembers Eric arriving in the autumn of the year to seek information. As Mess Secretary, Walker was detailed to look after the visitor:

> He was polite but extremely distant. I was not to know, but he felt his position acutely and was deeply embarrassed at the assignment. He remained in the Mess for weeks, making occasional forays to our battalions and ancillary units in the area from Tain southwards ... He drifted in and out, always politely distant.[27]

However, when the disaster occurred which was the subject of Compton Mackenzie's *Whisky Galore*, urgent business on Skye suddenly called Mr Walker to the island, and he returned with two gallons of whisky in his utility truck. While the officers were wondering how to make best use of their windfall, Eric offered to show them how to make 'heather honey whisky', indistinguishable from Drambuie—and did so, with great success.

It is a glimpse of Eric at work that shows the less ebullient side of his character, for at times a very substantial reserve and decorum kept well hidden the exuberance which at other times seemed his foremost characteristic. Such glimpses reinforce his own words in *The Man on My Back* about his lack of self-liking, and the personal hurdles he had to surmount before being able to play in public the confident, witty, sometimes autocratic and overbearing man that many took him for—a role which, after all, he often played even within his own family, sometimes frightening the children when his volatile temper led to a shouting-match. His moods were rooted in lack of self-confidence and occasional self-disgust which he had to work hard to overcome. When his humour was tickled, when things went right, then he could become the life and soul of the party; but when things were otherwise, when he was upset, or embarrassed, or intellectually bored, then he could be formidable in quite another way. Fortunately one person was never overawed by him, and to her he was married.

Even Marjorie had her moments of worry, however, especially when for some reason his shortness of temper impinged upon his tendency to be jealous of his wife. She was ten years younger than he, extremely attractive, affectionately disposed and rather demonstrative, and as flirtatious when she wanted to be as was her husband in his best moods. When they were separated by the war in 1940, Marjorie participated in a scheme to 'adopt' a Polish or Czech airman who had escaped from Europe and joined the RAF. She corresponded with one Čenek Chaloupka; the matter seemed so trivial that she didn't mention it to Eric. But then Čenek—or 'Čenda', as he called himself—announced early in 1941 that he would like to spend ten days' leave with Marjorie and her sister at Monksford, St Boswell's. Marjorie's story continues:

> The very next day Eric rang up to say he had a few days' leave before embarking in a trawler for Iceland. I thought it would be better *not* to have Čenda at the same time and wrote accordingly.
>
> So, at the end of his visit I took Eric to the station and parted with a long and lingering farewell. The train drew out from the station, north to Edinburgh, and there on the platform was the tall, dark and handsome Czechoslovakian sergeant-pilot, Čenek Chaloupka ...
>
> [The next day] Eric rang up to say his departure had been postponed and he would return for a few days. From this distance in time [1976] it seems ridiculous that this announcement should have caused the consternation which it undoubtedly did.—'I am *so* glad. How wonderful to have you back. By the way, we have a Czech airman staying.'

As it happened, Eric liked Čenda very much; a year later, when Čenda was a prisoner in Colditz Castle, he told Pat Reid (author of *The Colditz Story*) that he was Eric Linklater's adopted son. After initial explanations, therefore, there was no difficulty, but it is instructive that for a while Marjorie feared an explosion. For his part Eric was not unamused by her trepidation, and confessed that his temper was immoderately volcanic. After a bout of fury on another occasion he wrote to Marjorie to apologise:

> I am the last person in the world to defend my naturally bad temper, which is quite abominable and which I heartily deplore. It isn't as bad as it used to be, however, and if I spend the remainder of it on you, the children will be spared.

While gathering information for the Highland Division pamphlet towards the end of 1941 Eric was given new opportunities to broadcast as the first two little books became talking points. He had evidently improved his technique and rapport with his listeners, for after a series of news talks recorded in the field during an invasion exercise in November and some guest appearances on Home Service programmes, he was invited to deliver one of the prestigious 'Postscript' broadcasts on St Andrew's Day and acquitted himself well. The script of his talk, 'Nemo Me Impune Lacessit', all about the Scottish regiments, was published in the *Listener*.

His return to broadcasting coincided with an interesting aerial by-product of his work while attached to the Directorate of Public Relations.

Discussing with Walter Elliot one day the difference between information, which they both thought they were disseminating, and propaganda, Eric mentioned that he would like to write something more obviously carrying a message than the pieces he had already done, which essentially did no more than scrupulously report facts.[28] What Eric had in mind when preparing his first draft of *The Cornerstones* (1941) was something inspirational in the form of a 'conversation-piece'; although conceived as a philosophical dialogue among several voices on the meaning and purposes of the war, there is no evidence that he intended it for broadcasting. When Elliot saw the MS he approved it for publication, and it was offered to Macmillan, who unhesitatingly accepted it. The first edition appeared in December 1941.

Though he was not the first writer to use the idea of placing great men from the past and present together in some isolated location to compare viewpoints, nobody had thought of reviving the notion to provide a forum for the discussion of the war, and Eric's use of the form struck deep into a vein of current feeling. He wrote 'a conversation-piece, pleasantly sited in the Elysian Fields, in which Abraham Lincoln, Lenin, Confucius and a fighter pilot of the Royal Air Force argued about humanity, their own countries, and the possibility of building peace on a fourfold alliance'.[29] But despite his experience as a broadcaster and scriptwriter towards the end of 1941, he did not think of offering it to the BBC.

After the tremendous success of the piece as a radio play, followed in time by four similar dramatic essays, it became commonplace to look upon them as having been composed specifically for radio; such an intention became obvious in retrospect, so that a reviewer could write authoritatively: 'These imaginary conversations ... were intended and used for broadcasting, and have the spaciousness and wide application this medium calls for and so seldom gets.'[30] But there were precedents for the conversation as a written form, most obviously in Landor's *Imaginary Conversations*. Eric had briefly experimented with it in 'Kind Kitty' and in *The Lion and the Unicorn*. Some commentators invoked not only Landor but also Shaw as influences on Eric's development of the form of dialogue for didactic and reflective purposes.

It was not until late January 1942 that interest in the little book began to build up in the BBC, when Robert Speaight, receiving a copy from Lovat Dickson at Macmillan, passed it on to Moray McLaren with the observation: 'You have probably already come to the fairly obvious conclusion that this is heavensent broadcasting material.' McLaren, to whom no such thought had occurred, set wheels turning rapidly. Val Gielgud accepted the book as a drama script, at a fee of thirty guineas, and the first broadcast was heard on Sunday 15 March 1942.

Reaction, both in the press and from the listening public, was highly favourable, and the play was quickly repeated. Within weeks Val Gielgud wrote to Eric requesting more of the same:

> The Corporation was particularly pleased with the effect of the broadcast of *The Cornerstones*, and we are all most anxious that the effect should be repeated ... I don't think I am overstating the case to say that this is precisely the sort of contribution that it is desirable that my department should make regularly to the national morale.

The success offered new hopes of a firmer attachment to the Directorate of Public Relations for Eric, who had felt rather insecure during the latter part of 1941. At one stage in September he had been excited by a prospect of going to the Middle East on attachment to the Indian Army. He seemed the ideal man for the job, and had the enthusiastic backing of Walter Elliot. He packed his bags, received his inoculations and vaccinations, and was ready to go. But, frustratingly, the approval of the Indian Government was withdrawn at the last minute, and he had to settle down to his more-or-less freelance existence in London again.

At least this meant that he was home for the new Linklater arrival in February 1942. He wrote to Compton Mackenzie:

> Will you so much honour us as to become godfather to a male child born in this parish about two o'clock in the morning of February 21st, the infant being sound in wind and limb, with rather—for the moment—a Neolithic appearance, and the given names of Magnus Duncan?
>
> Marjorie, I am glad to report, is very well, and extremely cock-a-hoop about this bit of war-production. I wanted to call the child Snaebjorn Stalin, but she just wouldn't listen; women are so tiresomely conventional.

And, asking Phoebe Gilkyson to be godmother to the new infant, he promised that her responsibilities would be limited to introducing Magnus to some attractive girls when he first visited the United States.

At the end of 1941 Walter Elliot left the Directorate of Public Relations, more than a little frustrated by the low status accorded his position and the consequent difficulty of getting things done exactly as he wanted them. He was succeeded by a Territorial Army soldier, General Lawson, who later as Lord Burnham became the owner of the *Daily Telegraph*. At about the same time, Eric's position in the War Office was called in question by administrators who could not find that appropriate paperwork existed to confirm his transfer from regimental duties. Though he was working, with Lawson's approval, on a successor to *The Cornerstones*, he was instructed to report to Yorkshire where a suitable job awaited him. He described his position to Rupert Hart-Davis, who was now Adjutant of a Guards regiment:

> I've walked all unwittingly into the noxious web of that bloated spider, A.G.T. Reason? Establishment, my dear fellow. That deadly word. A.G.T. discovered

(after a year or more) that the D.P.R. had no establishment for me, and insisted on posting me here. To a depot battalion (the lowest form of life) where I command a huge motley company ... I correspond chattily with Magistrates' courts about Bastardy summonses, and send for half-witted sappers to explain that, until a debt of £19 19s 4d has been paid off, their cash-issues will be limited to 1d a day. With intense zeal I preside over Handing-Over-Boards— counting blankets, teaspoons ... As a reward for long service (and for making hundreds of pounds for the Stationery Office), I have, of course, been allowed to revert to the rank of Captain.

He appealed to Val Gielgud to pull such strings as he could grasp to secure him a permanent transfer to the War Office, saying:

I'm so sorry to put you to all this trouble, but I've got caught in a regular spider's web of departmental nitwittery, and I can only get out by making a thunderous nuisance of myself, and by persuading other people to attack from the outside. I have here one of the dullest jobs in the army ... And as, when I left London, I was as full as a tanker (Eastbound) with good ideas and irking to get to work on them, the sense of frustration is fairly bloodily acute. Because good ideas (like Fortune) need to be taken on the tide.

Gielgud's efforts were successful, and in May Eric was officially inducted into the Public Relations Department with duties related to 'Propaganda and Publicity Literature'; he was 'to co-operate with the BBC in so far as the time at his disposal will allow him for the preparation of features calculated to put across the army in the right light.'[31]

His first official task was to complete his new radio piece; to his delight he was able to persuade his seniors that this could best be done in the bosom of his family and went to Orkney for six weeks. Half-way through June he sent a script to Gielgud with the message:

I hope it may do. But—at this stage—I am not one of your confident blokes. Gloom assails me and doubt constricts my inner parts ... The second one, a sequel to *The Cornerstones*, is into the last lap and should be finished within a few days. It has been a wrestling-match, but I may bring it off.

He had no need to doubt whether the new plays would be acceptable. Gielgud wrote:

Many thanks for *The Raft*. I am enormously excited by it, and think it first-rate ... I can't tell you what an oasis in the desert the arrival of a piece of this quality is like.

Socrates Asks Why was also received with delight, and the two new plays were broadcast to similar accolades in August and early October, and were published together in a volume by Macmillan shortly afterwards. Ivor Brown commented:

Eric Linklater is rapidly qualifying as the Plato of the people. He puts in dialogue form the problems of eternity and the hour, speaking either through such major foghorns of historic sapience as Dr Johnson and Abe Lincoln or even Socrates himself, or by the mouths of modern combatants ... He has the knack of turning sense into good listening and righteousness into lively reading.[32]

There was another product of that summer of 1942, of lowlier aim but perhaps of more lasting consequence; Eric described its genesis very amusingly in *Fanfare for a Tin Hat*. Having taken his rather reluctant daughters for a walk on Sunday morning, in order to allow Marjorie an interval of comparative peace with the baby boy, and finding the girls even more difficult when they were surprised by rain, Eric in desperation began to tell them a story of something that happened to two extremely naughty little girls, who fell under the influence of the wind on the moon. On his return home he immediately began to write down the story which had so unexpectedly come into his mind, and at intervals during the next eighteen months added to it, until it was at last completed in 1944, with illustrations by Nicolas Bentley, and published by Macmillan. Nominated as the best children's book of the year by the Library Association, *The Wind on the Moon* was awarded the Carnegie Medal. Eric commented: 'It was successful far beyond my expectation, and still brings me a little comfort. Those dear children, bellowing their anger ... How grateful I was!'[33]

Eric's base in the second half of 1942 was effectively the Savile Club, and in London there were many pleasant occasions when he dined with friends such as Peter Fleming and his wife, Celia Johnson; Moray McLaren; Arthur Koestler; Lovat Dickson; Ralph Richardson and his wife, Mu; and others.

From his London base Eric did a good deal of travelling about the country to unravel stories told by soldiers, sailors and airmen. Among these he met and enjoyed a brief friendship with Richard Hillary, and exchanged letters with him two or three times. Hillary, author of a single but famous book, *The Last Enemy*, was a young pilot who had been shot down during the Battle of Britain and sustained terrible burns to face and hands. He had been restored to life by the miraculous plastic surgery of Sir Archibald MacIndoe and the devoted care of his nurses, and, still somehow full of gaiety and courage after all that, was walking testimony of all that was finest in English youth. Much moved, Eric watched his fight back to health and his determination to fly again, and heard with horror of his fatal crash at the controls of a Blenheim bomber on 8 January 1943. Later in the year he contributed a preface to a special reissue of *The Last Enemy*, and a long and moving essay about his friend was included in *The Art of Adventure* (1947).

The information he gleaned from his interviews with men who had experienced military action in various theatres of war became material for further broadcasts and pamphlets on military themes, and a series of accounts of notable actions from the first two years of the war was published in *Illustrated*, with paintings by Eric Kennington, between March and August 1943. His commission for these had been 'to disinter not forgotten tales but tales that had never been told, and now had lost much of their savour'[34] and his stories, as of 'The Hampshire Bayonets', 'Worcestershires at Keren' and 'Their Motto was "Sans Peur"' (about the 2nd Battalion of the Argyll & Sutherland Highlanders' rearguard action against the Japanese at the Muda River), were meticulously told and stirring in a pleasingly understated way.

Eric's travels took him to Scotland, Wales and Cornwall, and some of them are recalled in *Fanfare for a Tin Hat*. He even found himself summoned to Liverpool to open an exhibition of Chinese art and gave a talk on China's destiny as a great force for peace and sanity in the postwar world to which they were all looking forward. He told Marjorie that he was sure that nobody in his audience had understood a word he was saying, and that Lord Leverhulme, replying to his speech, had fumbled for some time before coming up with the word 'informative' to describe it.

During one of his assignments, to observe and report on a Scottish Command 'experiment in the selection of officers by psychological divination',[35] he met Evelyn Waugh, who was being vetted for promotion by this system and who had some typically lapidary observations to make about it. But Eric thought the system seemed sound and reasonable and less revolutionary than he had been led to expect.

Really he still felt that he was rather adrift; 'surplus to requirement' was the way he put it. The Public Relations Office had accepted him, but wasn't sure what to do with him. For many months he was set to working on a planned Grand Book of the Army, designed to explain to the British public the structure, ethos and functions of the new British Army, but just as he was beginning to make some headway in what he considered an almost impossible task the project was called off. The only fruit of his attempt to find a way through the immense complications of his task was a radio talk, 'The March Past of the British Army', broadcast ultimately in December 1943. Long before that he had accepted defeat and turned to other things.

One aspect of the war as it continued he found very encouraging. He commented to Phoebe Gilkyson upon the good feeling created by the Americans in Britain:

It's extremely difficult for soldiers to behave properly in a foreign country, but yours have been excellently taught and the result is a diplomatic victory . . . It was charming to see them playing baseball in Green Park—a perfect symbol—while Grosvenor Square was rapidly becoming Eisenhowerplatz ... We had a regular London fog the other night, as dense as it could be, and your soldiers appeared to think it the greatest joke imaginable; in these parts they played Blind Man's Buff with the ATS and liked it: both parties.

His observation of the Americans brought him no new friendships, but there was at least one new acquaintance that became very important to him indeed. This was with John Moore, eight years younger than Eric, a pilot in the Fleet Air Arm and attached to the Admiralty. Moore had some reputation as a writer of novels and short stories celebrating his native Gloucestershire; he was scholarly and fun-loving, and a fanatical enthusiast for the countryside and country life. In common with Eric he, too, loved to fish. From their first meeting they felt like close friends. In January 1943 Eric described to Marjorie a walk he and John Moore had taken through war-ravaged London after dining at the Gargoyle: 'We strolled thereafter through moonlit London to admire the Venetian effect, in that light, of the many lagoons that have been filled in readiness for the next fire-blitz. And while we stood by one we were accosted by a French tart in trousers.' Declining her wicked delights on the grounds that they were weary after a heavy day of war-work, they went on to the Savile and there sat talking until very late.

After the war, when Moore's new book about the life and people of a Gloucestershire country town was published, it was dedicated 'To Eric Linklater, with love'. The book, *Portrait of Elmbury*, was the first of the very highly regarded 'Brensham Trilogy', and for Eric no more pleasing declaration of friendship could have been possible.

Conscious that his absence from home was not altogether pleasing to Marjorie, especially when his war-work seemed of less than national importance, Eric wrote to her fully and frequently about his London acquaintances; one letter provided glimpses of the home-life of the somewhat self-destructive Moray McLaren and his wife Aline that made Eric write: 'I returned to the Club feeling that I had emerged from an unpublished chapter in one of Evelyn Waugh's earlier novels'; in another he told of dining with Koestler 'and his lovely girl at their tiny little house in Chelsea'. Life had its divertissements.

At the same time he was working, having conceived ideas for two further dialogues to complete what Macmillan's called his 'pentastyle edifice' when they ultimately published them the following January. The first of these was received again with considerable excitement at the BBC, and was given special treatment in May 1943 when, with John Gielgud and James McKechnie in the cast, it was broadcast three times in one week. Those used to the apparently unlimited quantities of repetition offered on contemporary radio and television may find it difficult to credit that the repeated broadcasts of *The Great Ship* were seen as a welcome novelty in 1943. Observing that it was 'immeasurably better than most radio plays', Herbert Farjeon praised Eric's 'blend of realism, mystery and allegory, well and boldly conceived', in a script 'by a radio-writer with a feeling for writing *and* radio', and went on:

> Much virtue in repetition ... A good radio play should be good enough to be broadcast three or four times a year for two or three years in succession. If this were a customary practice, it would be an encouragement to writers far above pearls and rubies.[36]

Eric's conversation-plays were among the first to be so treated. Another measure of their effect was the great volume of correspondence they evoked from listeners, some of it extremely moving. Asking Val Gielgud to send a spare script to one such listener, Eric wrote:

> She is the mother of a Wing-Commander who disappeared after a marvellous fighting record. I got from her one of those bloody heart-rending letters that make you feel, every time they say 'thank you', the veriest shit for sitting safely at home and writing about the people who go out and die.

Rabelais Replies, the fifth and last of the dialogues, broadcast in July 1943, rounded off the series by pulling together the philosophical threads explored in the first two 'conversations in Elysium' and insisting that the most important concept now was the future; what would the victorious Allies do to recreate the world in a better image after the tragedy of war? For Eric the answer clearly lay in Education and, taking up a theme hinted at in *Socrates Asks Why*, when Voltaire urges: 'It would be useful to begin your campaign in a few selected schools',[37] he went on to argue in his final dialogue that the future belonged to the children, and could be secured only by educating them for life. They should be taught 'language as an instrument of pleasure ... history ... that will convince them that they are growing things and part of a greater thing that is also growing', and should be given 'their rights: right of shelter and food, of health and joy, of growth and teaching.' So he called ringingly for a Charter of Rights for all children, a 'guarantee that soldiers' children shall be the beneficiaries of their fathers' valour.'—'I say with you,' are Rabelais' final words, 'let them be given what you in England were given at Runnymede, a charter of rights and justice: a Great Charter of the Children!'[38]

The words and feelings caught with accuracy and felicity the sentiments of the time, and helped fire the mood of reconstruction which, well before the end of the war, began to set up the new welfare state, and to put its faith so signally into the possibilities of a revitalised education system.

Eric personally took pleasure in the evidence afforded by his work in these radio pieces that 'our rulers in Britain—no matter what faults they had—believed in freedom of speech, and gave remarkable latitude to the BBC'.[39] Certainly his characters freely expressed scepticism and doubts about the purpose of the war. Socrates is able to ask questions like:

> The Allied nations, being in agreement about whom they are fighting against, will probably win the war. But unless they are in equal agreement about the cause they are fighting for, they will not be able to make a good and fruitful peace. And I ask you yet again: does a positive cause exist?[40]

Eric wrote:

> That was the question which the BBC, Val Gielgud and I dared to ask when, from Alamein, the Eighth Army, after much tribulation, was at last advancing with a prospect of victory before it; and I am still astonished that we were allowed to ask it.[41]

He wrote no more such plays for radio, however, though his interest in the further possibilities of the genre was not exhausted. He first applied himself to a new commission from Val Gielgud, which was to script a version of Cervantes' *Don Quixote* as a radio serial. This he worked at in Orkney, for in May 1943 he was released from the Army for six months' leave of absence without pay, or 'relegation to unemployment' as he put it in a letter to Ralph Richardson. The *Don Quixote* scripts—an enterprise which he described to Rupert Hart-Davis as 'turning Don Quixote into The Exploits of Elaine in six parts'—proved more difficult to do than he had expected, but his first draft met with approval when delivered to the BBC in August. With that out of the way he applied himself to investigating another outlet for his skill in setting the most highly revered of the Ancients talking together in the Elysian Fields, this time for the stage rather than for radio. It had occurred to him to expand the whole notion into a full-length play, and when John Gielgud expressed interest during rehearsals for the broadcast of *The Great Ship*, he resolved to put it to the test. He began to write *Crisis in Heaven*.

These concerns were interrupted on his return to Army employment at the end of October by a pleasant though in the end abortive visit to Gibraltar. He flew out with Lt-Cdr Ralph Richardson RNVR and Vincent Korda to look into the possibilities of making a film about the Rock. After a couple of weeks soaking up the atmosphere, talking to soldiers and sailors who had served in the Mediterranean, travelling also across to Tangier to investigate 'that evil fairyland', and strengthening his greatly valued friendship with Richardson, he returned to England to concoct a suitable story for the proposed film. Sadly nothing came of it, for, he wrote, 'my film-script on Gibraltar was heartily disliked by the brigadier to whom it had been submitted for criticism'.[42] The only published product of the excursion was his brilliantly evocative recollection of it in Chapter 22 of his last autobiography, and a vivid story illustrating Ralph Richardson's astonishing dramatic art. Eric wrote:

> I had, I thought, invented a story that was full of brooding excitement—too wildly plotted, perhaps—and deeply sympathetic with the sturdy patience of the soldiers on the Rock. But it failed to find approval, and I had to swallow my disappointment.

His scenario can no longer be found, but later Eric attempted to turn it into a novel, the typescript of which was among his papers at his death. With the working title of *The Rock* it reads well enough to suggest that the Army's rejection of Eric's film-script may have been lacking in judgement. Eric, however, was never sufficiently satisfied with it to offer it to his publishers. Whether that would have been Cape in 1943 is problematical, for Eric was still having his differences with them. In July he had written to Cape:

> I think I really do realise something of a publisher's difficulties in war-time: and I fancy I am aware of some of his advantages ... I still maintain the opinion that I expressed in my last letter: to wit, it would be profitless, and therefore inequitable, for me to send you any new book in the present circumstances. For if you haven't enough paper to keep in print books that would sell, you can't have very much to speculate on books that might sell.

For that reason he took *The Wind on the Moon* to Macmillan, who had pleased him with their handling of his autobiography and the conversation-pieces, and told Jonathan Cape that he intended to continue to go hawking until Cape's returned to supplying him in the lavish way they had formerly done.

He returned from Gibraltar late in 1943 to exciting preparations in connection with the *Don Quixote* scripts and the play about life in Elysium that he had begun in the summer. Both had found favour and work on them was proceeding. *Crisis in Heaven* was produced at the King's Theatre, Edinburgh, late in February 1944, directed by John Gielgud. In May 1944 it came to London to the Lyric Theatre. Despite having a good cast, including Ernest Thesiger, Barry Morse, Herbert Lomas, Dorothy Dickson and Esmond Knight, and a luxurious production with costumes designed by Cecil Beaton, the play received a rather disappointed and lukewarm welcome.

Macmillan published the play a few weeks later, giving people an opportunity to test Ivor Brown's judgement that as a script the play promised more than the production delivered: 'I had the pleasure of reading it a few months ago,' he wrote. 'What seemed to me spirited then came over somewhat limply last Wednesday.'[43] Reviewers generally felt that the play might have worked better in the same medium as the dialogues; on the stage, the attempt to make it visually pleasing notwithstanding, its relative prolixity and lack of action became marked.

Crisis in Heaven was never revived, and for that its topicality and patriotism may be sufficient explanation. The play is rather wordy and could have done with some pruning, but that kind of thing might have been seen and dealt with at the rehearsal stage if it was obvious to the distinguished director and his cast. It may have been unfortunate in some aspects of its production. On the page it still looks promising; the conception is neat, the development ingenious, the dialogue witty, and it makes a firm, even passionate statement about man's need for peace. The work, whatever its theatrical history, relates interestingly to the conversations for radio, and most notably enshrines Eric's admiration of and faith in the soldier and the essential decency of the common man.

Ivor Brown's observation that Eric should study the theatre more closely was probably justified, though it may have rung an ironic note for Eric at a time when he had been visiting the London theatre more consistently and frequently than for years. He had been taking full advantage of his residence in London, where he often met and talked theatre with actors and directors at the Savile Club, to see all the new plays, and felt that his old attraction for the theatre was at last leading to a significant place in it for him. He shrugged off disappointment however with his usual resilience; there were other things to do; there would be other chances.

A letter from Marjorie to Phoebe Gilkyson ended with the observation that, in spite of her shortcomings, she and Eric remained devoted to each other. A new consequence of their devotion was already in evidence as Eric rushed to complete the final episodes of his *Don Quixote* adaptation before taking to his travels again in April; and in a letter to Marjorie from London his pride and joy are manifest:

> How delightful to hear your voice, an hour or two ago. Such charming music it made—and how gratifying to find that I can still, after eleven years of marriage, elicit from you the liquid laughter of courtship. And that before lunch! What a man I am! What a woman, you!
>
> I am, I think, quite truly delighted to hear that you may be breeding again . . . The deed was done, moreover, not idly but in love. And that is the ultimate justification.

The Adventures of Don Quixote in Eric's radio adaptation met with much greater acclaim than his Elysian play. In mid-April he broadcast a talk to introduce the serialisation, and on seven Sunday evenings between 30 April and 11 June 1944 the episodes were listened to by a large audience. With Ralph Richardson as the Don and George Robey as Sancho Panza, the series was 'an outstanding success' according to D. Shaw-Taylor in the *Sunday Times* and Eric was hailed for his craftsmanship and for his sensitivity to the material he was adapting. Despite the success of the enterprise, Eric never again attempted to adapt classical material for radio, nor was he approached by the BBC to do so. It seems a curious oversight. In fact he never heard any of the *Don Quixote* broadcasts, for before they went on the air he was out of the country, and in those days such programmes often went out unrecorded. As he left also before *Crisis in Heaven* was brought to the Lyric Theatre, he never saw the end-result of much of his work during the previous four or five months. Given the choice, he would willingly have sacrificed such satisfactions in return for the adventure on which he now embarked.

Eric's new assignment was to follow the Allied attack on Italy and to gather together materials for a preliminary history of the campaign. He went aboard HMS *Flint Castle*, a corvette, at Liverpool on 19 April 1944, and had so interesting and exciting a voyage to Algiers that he devoted thirteen pages of *Fanfare for a Tin Hat* to describing it.

In Algiers he remained for a fortnight or so, talking to people who had witnessed parts of the struggle in Sicily and the Toe of Italy. The world being a small place, one of the first people he met was Walter Lucas, with whom he had travelled overland home from India in 1928. The materials he had been promised turned out not to have been neatly gathered together after all, and he began to get an inkling of how huge a job he had taken on. There were compensations; one evening he dined with Harold Macmillan and Lady Dorothy; on another he attended a French music-hall which he found hilariously bad.

In late May he joined forces with Christopher Stone, the BBC war correspondent, who had just arrived, and they flew together to Naples on 29 May. Eric found it a moving experience to arrive in Italy again after so long an absence and in such circumstances. 'To return to Europe by sliding round the corner of Vesuvius was delightful,' he wrote to Marjorie; and his mind was full of the fact that it was eleven years almost to the day since their wedding; and that the letters he had hoped to find awaiting him from her had not arrived.

For almost six months he followed the fighting in various parts of Italy. It was a powerfully enriching experience, providing material for essays, broadcasts and for one of his finest novels, as well as for the voluminous official preliminary history of the campaign. Starting from the Garigliano and the Liri Valley, he was later present at the entry into Rome, and followed the action northwards to Florence, encountering some old friends and new heroes on the way. In Rome he met Philip Jordan, the journalist, and kept company with him for several days; they made a journey to Pontecorvo and Cassino which, Eric told Marjorie, they found 'though extremely interesting, very horrible: the destruction, I mean. Cassino is pure horror: it must have required incredibly heroic fighting to take it, but the shapeless ruin of the place is appalling.' Almost a year later he returned to Cassino and drove up to the Monastery to see the unbelievably difficult terrain over which the Gurkhas had somehow fought their way; his imagination was overwhelmed with the evidence of horror:

> The town itself is white and crumbled, like a dead leper with his bones sticking through. There are dead, and fragments of dead, still in the ruins and among the scree on the mountains, and all the trees for miles around are shredded and charred, like burnt matches.[44]

On 5 July 1944 Eric saw the Pope in the Vatican; as he did so he noticed the Pope's 'red embroidered carpet slippers (only the carpet was velvet)'[45] and later, he said, came to the conclusion that they must have been magic slippers, because the Pope seemed rather to float, or to be wafted about, than to walk. Two or three weeks later, after being summoned by the Army Commander, General Oliver Leese, he was delighted to be among some war-correspondents who were introduced to King Umberto; he reported to Marjorie:

> He talked for quite a while—eight sentences, I should say—well, seven at any rate—about what I was doing, and then said, 'I've read your books, of course.' *Of course.* So there!

In Rome he was much moved when he saw Churchill, who 'walked, as it seemed, in his own climate',[46] unaffected by the August heat as he gave a press conference. To Marjorie he wrote: 'I fell quite in love with him. I had no idea he was so sweet. A dear little plump pink man, smoking a cheap American cigar, talking very genially the most sonorous good sense, interspersing it with charming little gaieties and moments of real emotion.'

He met Evelyn Waugh and Philip Jordan again, convalescing after their miraculous escape from a blazing aircraft in Yugoslavia. And he met Wynford Vaughan Thomas, blazing a trail as one of the BBC's most individualistic and daring war correspondents, carrying with him the primitive and weighty apparatus on which he recorded such reports as his account of the landings at the Anzio beachhead. In Vaughan Thomas's company Eric enjoyed the great adventure to which he gave the best part of Chapter 25 of *Fanfare for a Tin Hat*.

They were travelling towards Florence when they stopped to visit the 8th Indian Division and in particular Captain Unni Nayar, of the Mahratta Light Infantry, whose acquaintance Eric had made in Rome. His battalion headquarters were being established in a large house above a valley; Eric was astonished to discover that it was the Castello di Montegufoni, the property of Sir Osbert Sitwell. It was in this house, only 2,000 yards from the German forward positions, that Eric and Vaughan Thomas discovered an incredible treasury of great paintings, including the *Primavera* of

Botticelli, which had been moved there from Florence for safety and were now somewhat vulnerable to the depredations of ignorant Allied troops. It was a wonderful discovery, and though it fell to Vaughan Thomas, the accredited war correspondent, to announce it to the world through a broadcast, Eric told the story again and again during the next few years and felt it as a major incident in his life. Though he made no reference to it in his first account, in *Town and Country*, May 1945, in a letter to Marjorie he confessed that he had been so moved as to seize his moment and kiss one of the ladies in *Primavera*. In later re-tellings this became the climax of his story; it helps confirm the sense of the eternal romantic which constantly underlay the more hard-boiled pose he favoured.

After taking steps to ensure the safety of the paintings, Eric continued his travels in search of facts and impressions of the Allies' advance. In July and August, in response to a request from General Leese that he should 'broadcast, over some far extension of the BBC's wartime network, occasional reports of his army's progress and successes',[47] he gave talks on some aspects of the campaign, and later in September contributed items to the BBC's *Radio Newsreel*. Becoming very concerned about the way in which the image of the British Army was being overshadowed by a sense that the American effort was immensely more significant in the prosecution of the war, he 'composed a long memorandum pointing out the folly or imprudence of letting the Americans assert, over the Mediterranean, a monopoly of its history'.[48] He had noted that the Americans had a competently manned and lavishly supported Historical Section that was hard at work collecting, assessing and indexing documents of every sort, and it perturbed him that the British counterpart was so small as to be barely visible. With the assistance of Lt-Col Raymond Kittoe, Eric's memorandum came to the attention of General Alexander, and after Eric had been called to dine with the great man to discuss the problem, Alexander told Eric to go back to England and argue his case with the authorities.

He arrived back in England in October 1944 and for about six months was left with a fair amount of free time. With Marjorie now in an advanced state of pregnancy, he could hardly have planned things better. After a short period in London, discussing the position with his chiefs at the War Office, he was able to tell Rupert Hart-Davis:

> Now it is fixed that I am to write a history of the whole campaign, and I have persuaded my masters that I can best employ myself at home for the next month or so. This period—by pure coincidence!—will cover old fruitful Marge's fourth lying-in, which is scheduled for early December.

Marjorie was in a house she had taken in Edinburgh for the winter. There Eric joined them, and was able to welcome the arrival on 10 December 1944 of his fourth child, Andro. He wrote to John Moore:

I live in a pullulation of infants. My second son—making two pairs in all—arrived in good order nearly three weeks ago, and now wears a curious resemblance to a nestling fallen from a tree. So much so that I have been wondering whether Marjorie, during my absence, was attacked by a large white bird. Has Jove been at it again, do you think? What a responsibility, if he has.

The idea, hatched in his brain by observing the temporary presence of an avian strain in his son's features, did not go away, but gradually grew into the long short-story written two years later: 'The Goose-Girl', included in *Sealskin Trousers* (1947). It is not often that it is possible so precisely to observe the conception of a story. In the same letter Eric confessed to making slow progress on the Italian history; 'my conscience would burn hotly were I not pretty sure that the War Office, the Ministry of Information and the Stationery Office will, in any case, sit on it with such infinite sloth that my worst turn of speed will presently look, in comparison with them, like a V2 coming down.' Here again he showed some prescience, for *The Campaign in Italy*, though finished in 1948, was not published until 1951. But another reason for his slowness was that his energies had been diverted onto a new novel arising from his experiences in Italy. He had started writing it in August, and by Christmas had done 40,000 words which he thought highly promising.

His official task at home was to canvas various authorities for support for his idea that 'history as well as the Eighth Army required a more balanced view'[49] of the war in Italy, from the Director of the Office of Public Relations at the War Office through various Members of Parliament to Sir Edward Bridges, Secretary to the Cabinet. He was later convinced that he had not presented the case as well as he might have if he had not been personally involved; he did not wish to seem to be arguing for his own advancement, and the shy man behind the ebullient exterior was embarrassed to be in such a position. His mission was not without some success, however, and Kittoe was later established with much better provision in a Historical Unit which Eric, though warmly invited, did not join.

As well as his military jobs during the winter he was able to do various things besides make progress on the new novel. The publication of *The Wind on the Moon* in October 1944 brought him a fair amount of attention, and he made a broadcast on 'New Judgements on Robert Louis Stevenson' in December. By March 1945 he had reached, he told Rupert Hart-Davis, 'the third battle of Cassino, which I am fighting with the New Zealanders and the Indians; and a pretty heart-breaking job it is even to write about it.' Then Marjorie went back to Orkney with the four children, and Eric returned to Italy.

He continued to gather impressions of the now rapidly advancing war, gaining material as valuable for his novel as for his history, but working doubly hard to appease his conscience on the matter. When he came later to settle down in earnest to his history of the Italian campaign, he found his notes gathered in the field added little to the final account, which was firmly and necessarily based on a huge load of official documents sent to him from Kittoe's Historical Section, though 'they were of real value in that they gave me a remembered background for the events I then had to plot and measure.'[50] The vividness of the background, the strong sense of lived experience, and the powerful pictures of the novel, *Private Angelo* (1946), however, manifestly could not have been derived from any other source than his year in Italy.

Other fruits of the time were his visits to the honeymoon villa at Fiesole, to Ferrara and Venice, and particularly to Settignano where he met Bernard Berenson who, as an essay later included in *The Art of Adventure* suggests, made a deep impression on him. Berenson told him, 'I refuse to be heroised', but typically Eric could not do other than respond with warm admiration to the splendid old man, demanding: 'Should one refrain from lauding so lively and greedy and generous a pursuer of beauty, and the truth of its creation, and art's life everlasting?'[51]

As he worked in Italy, Eric was forced by Marjorie's letters to consider his domestic future. He acknowledged in April:

> I am filled with melancholy and deep sympathy for you in your many difficulties, toils and troubles. Your first letter was all about east wind, smoking chimneys and fratricidal strife between Magnus and Andro; and your second (written in great sadness) about money.

She was lonely; she, more than he, was affected by financial worries; she had had enough of the remoteness of Orkney and the wildness of its winters; she was worried about the education of the children. Thinking it over, he realised that changes would have to be made. They had better consider a city with good day-schools if they were to keep the children at home as long as possible, he wrote in May. Would Marjorie like to live in Edinburgh?

So he allowed the possibility of leaving Orkney to become a topic for discussion, though perhaps at that stage he still thought his return to full-time residence at home after the war might make such a move less necessary. When the war ended, however, he did not hurry home, for there was much still to be done in gathering and organising material. The Historical Unit with which Eric was working received instructions to transfer to new headquarters at Klagenfurt in Austria, and for a while he contemplated going with them. But in mid-June homesickness, thoughts of the fishing in the Loch of Harray, and a sense that he had done as much as he could, combined to convince him it was time to go home. The war was over, and it was time to rediscover the secret of living a civilian, peaceful, domestic life.

III

HIGHLAND GENTLEMAN

16 Leaving Orkney

When Eric arrived home in Orkney in time for the summer fishing, his heart sank at the prospect of uprooting himself and his family and seeking new pastures. There was much to do in the way of writing, with *Private Angelo* to complete and the Italian campaign to be recorded; these duties, together with those of rediscovering his family and attending to neglected household repairs, provided a reason for not too quickly settling down to serious discussion of the future. Furthermore there was summer and newly achieved peacetime life to enjoy, and at that stage of the year nothing was more important, he said to Compton Mackenzie, than 'exercising my remnant intellect on the problem of extracting trout from a large sheet of water, aided by Doyne Bell, who makes a charming guest and fortifies me in idleness'.

Doyne Bell was an eminent doctor at St Thomas's Hospital in London; Eric had met him with Stephen Potter at the Savile Club, and had admired the energy and efficiency with which he had organised the underground shelter medical services during the bombing raids. He was one of several cronies with whom Eric regularly took fishing holidays in Orkney for several years after the war. Another was Nick Roughead, co-founder with A. D. Peters of the literary agency which represented Eric. Also friendly with Bell, 'Roughie' was venerated as the erstwhile Captain of the Scottish Rugby XV. But he had served below decks in the Navy throughout the war; when it was over at last the toll it had taken was too great, and he gave up his partnership with Peters. Only now did he meet Eric, when Bell introduced them and persuaded Eric to invite 'Roughie' to Orkney for the fishing to help him through his depression. It became a regular appointment. Marjorie recalled:

> Eric and Nick were absurdly alike in appearance; both sturdily built, 5′ 8″, bald, and wearing old-fashioned spectacles—Eric's rimless and Nick's National Health steel-rimmed. When the summer sun caught their heads and faces they went an identical shade of salmon-pink.

Though fishing took pride of place, Eric went often to his writing-table, and by September he was able to report to Rupert Hart-Davis that he had completed *Private Angelo*: 'I think—I am pretty sure—that the novel is a good one.' He had done little of the military history, and was resolved to do no more until he could persuade someone in authority to give him an

official commission to complete the work and to make clear the terms
offered to him to do so. For he was, as he explained to Phoebe Gilkyson, a
soldier no more:

> I was demobilised in mid-July; or rather, because I have a permanent commis-
> sion, I was what they sinisterly call 'disembodied'. The word has a ghostly ring,
> and I have a notion that, being in such a state, I may disclaim all responsibility
> for my actions. Now, I thought, I shall return to my proper business of being an
> author, and how pleasant it will be—after the rude noises of war—to live in my
> Ivory Tower. I found, however, that the Ivory Tower was somewhat over-
> crowded. Marjorie and our own quartet of young; Marjorie's sister Ida (her
> husband still being in the Far East) with another couple; and my sister Elspeth
> in the offing with a brace who talk quite respectable English but prefer to swear
> in Hindustani—a sanitary inspector would have been *appalled* by my Ivory
> Tower ... For the last few weeks I have relapsed into such delicious unshaven
> idleness as would make me the ideal companion for Huckleberry Finn's papa.
> He, I think, will be my model henceforth. A *foutre* for the world and ground-
> lings base ... This is boasting, of course. What I am, in fact, on the point of
> becoming is a docile, broken-spirited household serf. Marjorie continues ro-
> bust in spirit, my daughters (now at school in St Andrews) are going to be young
> women of deplorably individual character, and the two little boys have appe-
> tites that require continual stoking. What hope for me but domestic peonage?

In October Eric went to Edinburgh for a couple of weeks, staying at the
University Club, membership of which he cherished as highly as that of
the Savile in London. Although his summer had been so 'idle', he had
turned his hand 'to one or two things'. One was a radio script written at the
behest of Stephen Potter, who had asked him to contribute to a new series
in which well-known people took a trip back to their places of origin and
explored them verbally on the air. To be called generically 'Return
Journey', it was the series to which Dylan Thomas later gave a famous
poetic evocation of the Swansea of his youth. Eric's inaugurating script,
broadcast on 31 October 1945, has never been published, though it might
have been deemed to merit a place in one of the volumes of stories and
scripts he issued later. Consisting of an idiosyncratic mixture of poetic
description, humorous self-disparagement, historical reflection, natural
history observation and interludes of talk among members of his family
and local people, it reads well and must have made a delightful broadcast.
The management of viewpoint is very impressive, so that the listener
always has a precise notion of where he is and what can be seen, swooping
from the cliffs above Hoy in an aeroplane to a bird's-eye view, or entering
into domestic establishments or prehistoric burial chambers. It never
occurred to Eric that, since the first twelve years of his life had been spent
there, a 'Return to Cardiff' might have been an appropriate theme.
Though he was in fact considering leaving Orkney, and had not been born

there, he wrote for the announcer the introductory words: 'In the first of the series, Eric Linklater describes the birthplace which is still his home—the Islands of the Orkneys.'[1]

After thirty years of telling the story, he thought it was true.

Meanwhile November brought two particular pleasures. First there was the announcement that the Library Association had chosen *The Wind on the Moon* to win the Carnegie Medal as the best children's book of the previous year; then, a few days later, he was to his own amazement elected Rector of his old University of Aberdeen in succession to Sir Stafford Cripps. Explaining the office of Rector in his autobiography over twenty years later, Eric modestly suggested that he had merely been fortunate enough to be the youngest and least establishment-identified figure among the candidates just at the time when the students were beginning to resent the traditional order. Instead of choosing one of the pillars of the establishment who had offered their candidature, they elected Eric, and he recalled:

> My election was basically an act of insurrection, a murmur of dissent. I was put forward as a figure of revolt—at the mature age of 46 I was the protagonist of youth and its impatience with the old regime—and sadly I betrayed my supporters. I behaved with the utmost decorum, and my Rectorial address was a model of what should be said from the platform to which I had been elevated. But my election opened a breach in the ancient walls of custom.[2]

Whatever he may have said later, he was enormously pleased with his election and remained a popular Rector with the students and friends of the University for the next three years. He was also delighted with the honorary degree with which he was invested when installed as Rector; he wrote to Rupert Hart-Davis:

> I have—as a piece of history—already taken the chair at a meeting of the University Court, wearing a tasteful robe of scarlet trimmed with a broad lace of gold. They will also give me an LL.D. with which, if the worst comes, I can set up practice in the hinterland of Southern Rhodesia. 'Old Doc Linklater's black draught, it certainly kills or cures.'

One of his earliest undertakings as Rector of Aberdeen was to exercise the kind of talent he had shown as a student when he had written dialogue and lyrics for the Rag Week musicals. He now adapted Scott's *Rob Roy*, making a light-hearted parody of the central story and writing lyrics for a handful of songs to be set to traditional Scottish tunes. The Aberdeen students produced *To Meet the MacGregors* in April 1946. Although rehearsals and disagreements with the director drained Eric almost completely of patience, the production was sufficiently successful to attract the attention of James Bridie, who staged it at the Glasgow Citizens' Theatre in the autumn. The play is pleasant to read; inconsequential perhaps, but witty, charming and full of fun, and showing ingenuity and skill in the use of the theatrical situation. It has genial satire on such topics as Scottish and English character; the historical background of the two countries; the current postwar situation; bureaucracy in general; the relationships between men and women, soldiers and civilians, servants and masters; and accents and dialects. The lyrics of the songs are neat and funny, and Eric thought highly of the tunes which he had found in a collection of Scottish airs published between 1787 and 1803 by James Johnson, who had collaborated with Burns.

The production of *To Meet the MacGregors* in the Citizens' Theatre marked the beginning of a considerable association between them and Eric, while his friendship with their founder, James Bridie, became ever more important to him.

But all this was in the future when Christmas 1945 brought Eric less joy than it might have; he told Compton Mackenzie:

> I hope you had a merry Christmas. I hadn't. I was shooting four weeks ago—hit nothing and got soaked to the skin—cold encircled my bowels and I suffered fever, sweating and earthquake-sickness—the distemper then settled down as jaundice and I'm still in bed, though getting better now.

It should have been some compensation that, thanks partly to Mackenzie's influence, the Book Society had just before Christmas told Eric that *Private Angelo* was to be their March selection. From that moment it mattered much less what the reviewers might say about his book, but he was beginning to be greatly annoyed by the way in which casual and imperceptive reviews affected not only his reputation but also his income. Though he need not have worried about responses to the new novel, he was not satisfied with its warm reception, and many years later he still thought that it had probably been published too soon after the war to be generally appreciated. He wrote:

> I had written of war without apparent bitterness, without manifest anger and open denunciation of its folly; and in the aftermath of war it was obligatory to make one's disapproval of it obvious ... War, in Italy, was a drunken, destructive and impertinent clown; to deal justly and truthfully with it, one had to keep one's temper cool, one's judgment clear, and write a comedy.[3]

It is not clear why he felt the need to write defensively about *Private Angelo*. Several commentators in 1946 thought it his best novel, even including *Juan in America* (the book most frequently invoked when the name of Eric Linklater was under discussion). The reviews in the United States were also complimentary. Eric was pleased to receive a great many letters from former members of the Eighth Army 'who recognised its accuracy'; and its reception in Italy was gratifying; he received a telegram of congratulation from King Umberto. But though it sold well enough, the novel attracted no permanent attention. This was what most hurt Eric in his secret heart, for he thought, and with good reason, that he had written as fine a novel as was likely to come out of the experience of the war.

Private Angelo embodies the best of all Eric's skills as a writer and all his best qualities as a human being. Unexpectedly, for a war novel by a Briton, it has as a central character a highly sympathetic Italian soldier. In the novel all Eric's qualities of concrete evocation of scene and mood are harnessed to the expression of a mature philosophical attitude, so that his own experiences in following and observing the campaign are distilled into a moving and hilarious story full of wisdom and poetry. Angelo is first cousin to Juan and shares with him an ancestor in Candide. There is something in him, too, of Jaroslav Hasek's *The Good Soldier Schweik*, which Eric had enjoyed in 1940 and had mentioned in a *Time and Tide* article.[4] He is essentially an innocent whose hapless adventures in war-torn Italy offer the reader a viewpoint immensely attractive for its simple perceptions and honest love for the greater part of humanity.

Angelo is presented as lacking somehow in moral fibre; he does not have, complains his amoral father Count Piccologrando, the *'dono di coraggio'*— the gift of courage. Unwilling though he may be to face the enemy soldiers in battle if such confrontation may be avoided, Angelo proves to be the possessor of enviable moral courage; he may not have much appetite for war, but he copes admirably with life and love, even when sorely buffeted by fate.

Starting very specifically on 8 September 1943, the day the Italians capitulated to the Allies and tried to withdraw from the contest, the action follows the rest of the war in Italy and concludes some time after the coming of peace. As the manuscript was completed in the autumn of 1945, Eric was in the final chapter projecting the life of his characters a couple of years into a period of postwar reconstruction that had not yet happened. In so doing he underscored the optimistic belief in the ultimate triumph of the human spirit that informs the whole book, and that characterises all his novels.

Angelo, himself illegitimate but good-looking and attractive and un-troubled by guilt, sees the war through innocent and wondering eyes, occupying a significant middle position from which to observe the libera-tion of Italy. He thinks a great deal about what he sees, and his reflections on the problems of being liberated (a recurring theme) demonstrate something of the witty and ironic tone of much of the book:

'Then let us go at once!' cried Lucrezia. 'I cannot bear to stay here any longer. I want to be in Pontefiore.'

'It would be wiser', Angelo said, 'to wait and see whether Pontefiore is going to be liberated, or lucky enough to be ignored.'

'Are you not eager for it to be liberated?' asked Lucia.

'It is sometimes necessary to go to the dentist,' said Angelo, 'but I have never seen anyone eager to go ... Before a village can be liberated it must be occupied by the Germans, and the Germans will rob it of everything they can find; but that is of no importance, that is merely the Overture. Liberation really begins when the Allied Air Forces bomb the town; that is the First Movement, the *Allegro* so to speak. The Second Movement is often quite leisurely but full of caprice: it occurs when the Allied artillery opens fire to knock down what the bombs have missed, and may be called *Andante Capriccioso*. After that has gone on for some time the liberating infantry will rush in: that is the Third Movement, the *Scherzo*, and though the Allied soldiers do not loot, of course, they will find a number of things such as geese and hens and wine, that apparently belong to no one—for the local inhabitants have taken to the hills or are hiding in their cellars—and to prevent the wine and the geese from being wasted, the soldiers will naturally take care of them. Then comes the Last Movement, when the officials of the Allied Military Government arrive and say to the inhabitants, 'No, you cannot do that, you must not go there, you are not allowed to sell this, and you are forbidden to buy that.'[5]

It is typical of Eric that the writing continually sparkles with wit and humour while not far away the immanent threat of death and destruction which war entails is manifested in the black comedy and cruel grotesqueries of some of the incidents. The horrors are not skimped. But through incidents sometimes violent and unpleasant the reader is brought with understanding, sympathy and joy to Angelo's declaration of faith at the end of the novel. The way has been prepared by the extraordinary vitality and pleasure in life which comes through the whole narration. Much of this is brought about by the contrast between the Germans on the one hand, seen always as gratuitously unpleasant, and the British who, although they muddle through with at times alarming inefficiency, yet represent decency and determination to restore civilised values. Most of all there is Angelo with his ingenuous perceptiveness, his innocent philosophical animadversions, his love of life and Italy and his comical but touching relationships with women. In Angelo, Eric was able to project his own enthusiasms and around him he built a narrative that forcefully imparts a huge delight in being alive, a particular feeling for Italy, its scenery, its culture and its people, and a well-documented impatience with war and its adjuncts.

While the reviewers were still reading their copies of *Private Angelo*, Eric was being fêted, wined and dined in Scandinavia where he had gone to give some lectures for the British Council and to attend some parties thrown for him by Norstedt's, his Swedish publishers. He took great pleasure in meeting again Karl Ragnar Gierow, his poet-dramatist friend whom he had not seen since a brief encounter in London in 1943. He enjoyed himself so well that, inevitably, he later suffered duodenal eruptions; he wrote to Phoebe Gilkyson:

I had an excellent time in Norway, Sweden and Finland in February and March, lecturing on some odd topics and nearly dying of hospitality. The richness of the food was something one had quite forgotten.

And to John Moore he confessed:

I've been a bit unwell—guts—duodenal gone bad, merely the result of over-indulgence in Scandinavia, and since then of trying to mitigate a feeling of gloom-in-general and distaste-for-work in particular by drinking rather too much.

But he had been working, especially on a new project which became increasingly associated with Rupert Hart-Davis. Rupert, who had expected after the war to rejoin Cape's in a senior position, had been disappointed by Jonathan's reception of him, and was looking into the possibility of setting himself up in a new publishing firm of his own, perhaps in partnership with David Garnett. Eric encouraged him:

The tone of Jonathan's last letter is very curious. It suggests, more than a little, that he feels his feet cold, and his effort to be ingratiating is obvious—but equally obvious is his determination *not* to give you another cut off the joint ... He would have made an excellent character for Balzac—but, regarded less impersonally, his dogged greed is infuriating.

In April 1946 Rupert's plans had advanced to a secure decision to set up entirely on his own, and Eric found two ways to help him. After discussion with his old friend and financial adviser, Douglas Walker, he put £1,000 into Rupert's new firm. And he offered Rupert the opportunity to publish some new short stories he had been writing, sending him one as an example. This was 'The Goose Girl', under its working title of 'Mr Tindall'. Eric said that he was disposed to think well of it. Rupert's reply was rapturous:

The story, my dear Eric, is a smasher ... Am I wrong in spotting a new Eric Linklater? An even surer touch, a different, simpler prose style, perfectly suited to its subject ... I consider it an astonishing success ... I can scarcely wait to see the other stories—If they're anything like as good as this one, the book will be colossal, and the firm's fortune is made!

Encouraged by such warm words, Eric continued to work at his short pieces for several months, as well as at a book of essays for Macmillan's. For this he used as a title-piece and declaration of theme his Rectorial address, 'The Art of Adventure', which was also published separately as a pamphlet by the Aberdeen University Press in October 1946.

As usual he insisted to his friends that he was hardly working at all, but spending most of his time thigh-deep in water; he told Phoebe Gilkyson:

A new boat, a new rod and tackle, on to the loch, and death to the trout: that was my programme as soon as I came out of the army last summer, and this spring I wilfully and wickedly put off work until I had glutted my desire for fish.
Literature? An ephemeral joy.
But *fishing*—now that is something.

At the end of June Eric had to go to Edinburgh to attend the funeral of his father-in-law, Ian MacIntyre—'my naughty old father-in-law', as Eric described him to Phoebe, 'who, after a long and combative and cheerful life, died at 77 in two seconds of an apoplexy'. He told Rupert:

The old boy's death was a great shock to us, and Edinburgh now seems rather like a familiar bit of coast without the remembered lighthouse on it. But he had the luckiest death a man could wish for ... I went down to help bury him— or cremate him, rather—and the ceremony was greatly enlivened by Ida (Marjorie's sister), who, showing a great sense of occasion—but, alas, of the wrong occasion—turned up dressed as for a fashionable wedding.

In September, after attending Bridie's improved version of *To Meet the MacGregors* in Glasgow, he went to London for a few days, and then to Dublin—'just for the hell of it—so it may seem to the casual observer', he told Rupert, 'but really (in a mystical apprehension of the truth) in your service. For the little book of short stories needs a very little one to go in the middle, and I have a *feeling* that I shall find it in Dublin.' He did indeed find inspiration in Ireland, and 'Joy as it Flies', one of his more popular short stories, was in Rupert's hands by early December.

But the work of a publisher, especially one newly established in a difficult period immediately following a war, is complicated and lengthy, and the collection of stories did not see the light under Rupert's imprint until October 1947. By then the Linklater family had lived through one more winter in Orkney and they were agreed that enough was enough. The fearful winter of 1947 was the last straw, though in comparison with the flooding after snow suffered by John Moore in Tewkesbury their troubles had not, Eric wrote, been too bad:

Here we endured only the ordinary discomforts of a sub-arctic winter. For several weeks I spent my mornings in breaking a hole in the frozen loch from which to carry water for *all* domestic purposes; and the afternoons dragging a sledge to the village shop for some paraffin and a loaf of bread and a sausage or two. Just like an old Lapp.

Eric himself had, even before the war, begun to find that Orkney, 'deeply though I loved its fluent hills and shining waters, was not a sufficient environment for the sort of life which I had chosen'.[6] At one stage he had even discussed with Marjorie the possibility of going to live in the Caribbean, where he would find nourishment for his writing in a complete change of scene, people and circumstances. The war had brought changes to the islands of Orkney, where the 'soldiers' ungainly colonisation' had left 'brutal scars ... woefully apparent'.[7] Partly for the sake of the children's education, partly to find 'a larger beauty than the Loch of Harray could reflect', and partly to have a larger estate than Merkister where there was no possibility of expansion, the Linklaters decided the time had come to leave Orkney for the mainland.

After considerable searching they found, in the spring of 1947, a small estate in Easter Ross, a lovely old house with a superb view across Nigg Bay to Ben Wyvis. According to Marjorie, they had 'made a study of the climate all over Scotland and discovered that Easter Ross had as much sunshine as the Isle of Wight'.[8] Eric's daughter Sally recalled:

> One of the reasons for choosing Easter Ross ... was its nearness to Cromarty, the birthplace of Sir Thomas Urquhart, whose translations of Rabelais in the seventeenth century almost equalled its original in the robustious bawdiness of its vocabulary. Next to Aristophanes I'd say that Rabelais was my father's greatest literary hero.[9]

Eric put it differently:

> With the house, moreover, I acquired a circumference of land, a little wood, a small croft, and a long narrow strip of foreshore: enough to satisfy my peasant appetite.[10]

Merkister was sold—it is a hotel today—and Eric moved his family to Pitcalzean (pronounced Pitcalyan) House, Nigg, Ross-shire in May 1947. The move heralded something of a metamorphosis. Eric began to become a Highland gentleman.

17   Lure of the Theatre

Settling into their new home at Pitcalzean proved only one of a thousand things that pressed to be done as Eric moved into the two most busy and demanding decades of his life. Between bouts of home-making (engagingly described in one of the parenthetical flashbacks of *A Year of Space*)[1], he worked on various writing projects while slowly being drawn into playing a more and more notable role as an important and influential citizen. Though he shared his energy around with prodigal generosity, one thread of interest became more markedly central for a while, as his desire to write for performance found some encouragement. Late in 1946 he collaborated with Val Gielgud again, this time on a radio version of *Crisis in Heaven*, Gielgud having written: 'I say this with diffidence, but I think you know that in my view the stage version suffered from inadequate casting and a certain lack of grip from the production angle.' Gielgud was sure that his Drama Department would do better, but in the event advisers within the BBC cared little for the idea, and it was not until August 1948 that, after much revision, a shortened version of the play finally achieved production on the Home Service. But what with this and the presentation of his 'trifling playlet for the students' at the Citizens' Theatre he had the old dream in his mind again, and he looked for the opportunity to write another play.

At the beginning of May 1947 he flew with Naomi Mitchison to Switzerland for the International PEN Conference in Zurich. One evening he fell in with Alec Waugh, who recalled:

> What attracted me about these conferences was the finding myself unexpectedly without premeditation having a long confidential talk with a fellow-writer whom I had long respected but never really got to know ... Of Zurich I cherish particularly the memory of a long talk after an evening *conversazione* in the garden of the Bar du Lac with Eric Linklater ... We had lunched together a couple of times, but we had never had a real talk together, and we were never to have another, but after that evening in Zurich I knew we spoke with the same idiom. What a wicked wit he had, what a terrible twinkle in his eye, what a good writer.[2]

Such rewarding moments also pleased Eric, as did the opportunity to meet again old friends such as Storm Jameson, who worked so hard and generously within the PEN movement, and whose perceptive and appreciative criticism of his books had always meant a great deal to him.

He had flown to Switzerland to save time, for he should have been working. Just before leaving Merkister he had received a present from the Army's Historical Section, as he told John Moore:

> I myself feel very like a miner at present—a miner buried under a sudden fall—for after waiting eighteen months for them, the documents from Italy did arrive, and some weeks ago I plucked up courage to go to work again on the history—and when I shall dig my way through to daylight, God alone knows. It's a hideous task. Military history—as literature—became impossible when red coats were discarded and battles couldn't be finished between dawn and dark.

Daunting though the task was, he chipped away at the mountain of information—'four packages that weighed, in all, two and a half hundredweight'—to such effect that six months later, sympathising with the labours of Moore who was himself almost overwhelmed with work on a long new novel, he was able to tell him: 'I hammer also—now at the last chapters—on my Italian history, that has lain upon me like the upper mill-stone for a year and a half—but when we break through, how glorious it will be!' By December it was done; but much water flowed beneath the bridge before it was at last set up in print. Not that Eric much minded, once his part in the Herculean labour had been honourably completed.

From time to time during the summer he was involved in helping Rupert Hart-Davis to complete the production work on the book of short stories he had given him. Joan Hassall was engaged to produce some wood-engravings, and Eric was wholly delighted with them, especially since, when Rupert had been temporarily embarrassed for cash to pay her for her work, Eric had written: 'As to the £100: lop it off my whack and give it me back some time if circumstances warrant it, and you can afford it. That's all the agreement we need.' The book was printed, elegantly, in The Netherlands, but one last upsetting mistake could not be rectified: the intended dedication to John Moore was missing. Seeing Rupert's distress, Eric wrote:

> Say no more. I have written to John Moore. I told him you were only a young publisher. That harsh reproof now would bruise your tender spirit . . . I have promised to write another book, and dedicate it to him. It will be a nuisance to write another book. But it is my trade. Oh dear.

He had also been working during the spring and summer at the book of essays for Macmillan, so there was an exciting time in October when both *The Art of Adventure* and *Sealskin Trousers* were published.

The Art of Adventure received a good press, showing as it did Eric's writing skills in yet another guise. Dedicated to one of Eric's heroes, Lord Wavell, the book is made up of half a dozen portraits of people he knew well and admired: General Alex, James Bridie, Evelyn Waugh, Richard Hillary and Bernard Berenson, and the more obscure but equally heroic figure of Trevie Napier, a naval officer whom Eric had first met at Fiesole in 1934, whose destroyer he had visited in Scapa Flow in 1940, and who, not unlike Eric's father in 1916, died virtually of strain and exhaustion in the autumn of 1940. Then there is a trio of pieces about Burns and Jean Armour, and an entertaining account of the life and work of the Duke of Wellington's Scottish Inspector-General of Hospitals, one Doctor James McGrigor. A clutch of 'episodes' from Eric's own adventures follows; being autobiographical they were later incorporated into *Fanfare for a Tin Hat*. The address to the students of Aberdeen, made on his inauguration into the office of Rector of the University, suitably ends an idiosyncratic and characterful book. In its advocacy of the need for adventurous spirits—for 'it is a world in which, if we want to enjoy peace, we must wage peace'—and in the beautifully turned phrases of a satisfyingly urbane, civilised and comfortable style, it offers much pleasure, not only to the reader whose desire is to know more about the man behind the words.

Rupert Hart-Davis was so sure of the quality of Eric's new stories and of the drawing power of his name that he printed a first edition of 20,000 copies of *Sealskin Trousers*. Considering that it appeared in a period of postwar austerity, it was a handsome if slim volume—bound in a good blue cloth of prewar quality and with twenty-four wood engravings by Joan Hassall, three of them full-page and extremely fine. Except in *Time and Tide*, however, to which during the year Eric had begun to contribute regular articles in a series destined to continue almost ten years, the little book was not seriously noticed.

Perhaps one reason for the critical neglect of Eric's new stories was their failure to be rooted in the grim miseries of the time. It was only a year or so before the publication of Orwell's *Nineteen Eighty-Four*, which in grim realism more accurately mirrored the anxieties of the period. But Eric's stories, though given modern settings, have as Robert Lockyer observed 'roots which strike down into myth and ballad and poetry'[3] and their force is of a kind which may not have seemed important just then. Although one of the stories is a tribute to the people of Finland who had so stoically borne their suffering through their wars, it may have seemed that the collection generally lacked relevance in a world which, having survived the horrors of death and destruction, had now to shoulder the sober responsibility of rebuilding its towns and recreating its societies.

Two of the stories in *Sealskin Trousers* are strange, half-way between the real and the fanciful; in one a soldier is cuckolded by a giant gander and his wife gives birth to a second Helen; in another a girl is courted by a seal-man and goes to live with him in the depths of the sea. The settings, however, are solid contemporary, and it is the grafting onto the modern of elements of faery or folk-tale which makes the stories so effective, rather as in 'The Dancers' from his 1935 collection. When the seal-man takes Elizabeth to live in the sea, it is a direct condemnation of modern civilisation that she goes willingly; when Robert Lacey Tyndall considers his marriage to Lydia Manson and acknowledges the strange provenance of his beautiful daughter, he is forced to contemplate his own destiny—which arises from the paradox that soldiers, whose aim is to defend the peace, must inevitably foster war. 'The Goose Girl', as Eric argued to Rupert, combines the Leda theme, which provides a 'heroine', with a theme of destiny or fate, and this renders Tyndall not a mere narrator but 'a haunted figure who must dree his weird as inevitably as Lydia herself'. The story is impressively written, with moments of compulsive and visionary strangeness; such as when Tyndall finds his little daughter in a kind of colloquy with the gander, which has unexpectedly returned:

> She stood with her back to me, in her favourite position, her hands clasped behind her, and not until I had come within a few yards of her did I see the gander. He was afloat in a little smooth backwater of the burn, but as soon as he caught sight of me he came ashore, his broad feet ungainly on the snow but moving fast, and I thought he was going to attack me. The child turned and I called to her: 'Come here, Nell! Come here at once!'
>
> But she stayed where she was and the gander came up behind her and opened his wings so that she stood by his breast within a screen of feathers as hard as iron and as white as the snow beyond them. It must have been the whiteness of the fields, with the bright haze of the sun upon them, that dazzled me and deluded me into thinking that the gander had grown three or four times his proper size. His neck seemed a column of marble against the sky, his beak was bronze, and his black eyes reflected the sun like shafts from a burning-glass. A low rumbling noise, like the far-off surge of the sea on a pebble-beach, came from his swollen throat.[4]

The other three pieces in the collection are quite different. 'The Dreaming Bears' and 'The Three Poets' are almost more essay than story, though both have a narrative framework; one celebrates aspects of the Finnish, the other of the Swedish, national character and ethos. Both are poetic, humorous and admiring; both were greatly appreciated in Scandinavia. 'Joy as it Flies', set in Edinburgh and Dublin, is a pleasing, teasing love-story, completely contemporary, a little nostalgic, about two brief but delightful moments of real contact between a man and a woman for whom life otherwise holds separate destinies. A charming story, typically celebrating life and its possibilities, it has been anthologised more than once.

Despite the lack of attention from the reviewers, the little book sold more than 16,000 copies over the next four years. Though it was not the huge success Rupert had hoped for, Eric had no time to be rueful, for he was far too full of energy and plans for other things.

Before the publication of his two new books in October, the first Edinburgh International Festival of Music and Drama had been held, and Eric had begun his long association with it. In those gloomy days of austerity his infectious enthusiasm and lively personality did much to publicise and support the efforts of the organisers of the Festival. He had taken a strong dislike to the tighten-your-belts, put-up-with-the-second-rate, generally drab and colourless policies of the postwar Government, as may be gathered from some of his occasional journalism of the period. In one article he compared Britain of 1947 with a remote and ailing Eskimo community which had discovered a grave injustice in their social system:

> A family more industrious than its neighbours could live better, and when spring came would be visibly fatter. Nothing was done to prevent self-seeking individuals from fishing as long as they chose, or to hinder alert and energetic men from going to far-off and therefore dangerous—but often better holes.[5]

Clearly something will have to be done; the community duly nationalises its fishing industry and builds a top-heavy system of observers, inspectors and administrators to look after it, until for one actual fisherman there are forty-four members of parliament, civil service officers, educators and other non-producers; and the poor Eskimos are on the verge of starvation.

In a handful of poems published a little later in the year he included an Audenesque ballad attacking the inaction and ineptitude of the Government in which bureaucracy had run wild:

> In Durham mines black solitude,
>   And Lothian fields all bare—
> The waving fields men ploughed for food—
>   Nothing grew there!
>
> But London's loud with game and glee!
>   And, wreathed in civil smiles
> The Civil Servants take their tea
>   And pass their files.[6]

It was therefore with real hope and sense of involvement that he saw the Edinburgh organisers setting up their Festival. He found it a joyful and fulfilling occasion, and said so in a report heralding the new spirit it symbolised, emerging like a small patch of blue in a dense grey sky. A difference, he wrote, had come over Edinburgh, comparable to the difference between Shakespeare's and Verdi's versions of the Macbeth story, the one grim and black, the other full of ceremony and splendour: 'The stern Caledonian, isolated under his northern sky, has melted in a genial throng ... since the air of festival, the harlotry players, and the breeding sun have come to town.'[7] Here was a sign, he felt, for Britain; addressing the Scottish PEN Centre he said: 'Here in Edinburgh is the sort of air that should have clothed all Britain after its historical triumph in

1945. Here it seems—despite our alleged poverty—is a realisation of our victory.'[8] With a like hope and determination he returned to the Festival year after year, several times writing plays for production as part of the official programme, and always taking a great interest in the organisation and promotion of the event. Through the encouragement of the arts lay the way to a better Britain, and it was in this belief that in 1948 he accepted appointment to the Arts Council.

The winter of 1947–8 was occupied with various tentative undertakings after he had, 'in black exhaustion',[9] finished his Italian history at the New Year. In the spring he began a second children's novel, this time intended for his two boys; and conducted what he described to John Moore as 'a hot flirtation with the film boys'. After the pleasing news that *Private Angelo* would be the May selection for the World Books book club, bringing in a reasonable financial reward, came the equally palatable information that Peter Ustinov wanted to make a film of it. In September Eric went to Italy and had an excellent fortnight watching some of the filming for *Private Angelo* in the Tuscan village of Trequanda. 'Sunshine and buckets of red wine and lots of people and familiar scenes,' he told Compton Mackenzie. He said nothing about the filming itself, but was a little uneasy about some aspects of what he saw, and his doubts were sadly confirmed when the film was released the following year. The talented but very young Ustinov had, as the credits rather insisted, taken over the story so completely that little Linklater remained; it was 'written, produced and directed by Peter Ustinov', and he also acted the main role. Reviewers regretted the way in which the director had somehow missed the point that Angelo should be, before anything else, an *Italian*, and that the film would have done better to capitalise on Eric's use in the novel of strongly national types to point an international message.

But there were good things in Ustinov's film, and it has given a good deal of pleasure in its gentle way over the years to audiences both in the cinema and on television. Eric's disappointment was that it was not *his* Angelo; it would probably have been a better film if it had been. Eric did not fall out with Ustinov but continued to admire his undeniable gifts, and it was not long before they were working happily and fruitfully together again.

The film of Eric's second novel, *Poet's Pub*, directed by Frederick Wilson for Aquila Films and with a screenplay by Diana Morgan, was released at about the same time in 1949. Although inhabited by some well-known comic players, including James Robertson-Justice, Joyce Grenfell, Derek Bond and Barbara Murray, the film was another disappointment. Neither the critics nor the public liked it, and little was heard of it. Eric, remembering the rejection of his screenplay for a film about Gibraltar a few years earlier, began to wonder whether he had been mistaken in his wooing of the spirits of the flickering screen.

He was also wooing the spirit of drama without notable success. While tinkering with the proposed radio version of *Crisis in Heaven* he became acquainted with Basil Ashmore and, interested in Ashmore's enthusiastic notions about revitalising Marlowe for the modern age, agreed to furnish a foreword for his edited version of *Tamburlaine the Great*. Eric seized the opportunity to urge the need for 'some infusion of Elizabethan speech into our shrivelled vocabulary, as well as some infection of our minds with the Elizabethans' robust spirit'. He extolled Marlowe as:

> The most Elizabethan of the Elizabethans ... To an age of strenuous inspiration he gave commensurate speech, and for the reckless grandeur of his thought created a prosody that set free a music, new to experience, that could equally enthral a crowd and haunt a lonely mind.[10]

Eric was naturally interested in Ashmore's excited insistence that he had what was necessary to be a significant writer for the theatre and, with some sense of indulging the young man, dug out *The Devil's in the News* to consider whether, with Ashmore as his mentor, something might yet become of it. According to Ashmore:

> Eric Linklater was really meant to be a dramatist with even more wit and variety than the charming James Bridie. Unfortunately he had little initial feeling for dramatic form. I thought the start of *The Devil's in the News* was splendid, but it went to pieces ... We worked on it, and he finally came up with a magnificent text, written as a ballad-opera. It was a smash-hit.

Whether it might in fact in its new version have fared better than the old did in 1934 will never be known, for sadly the famous London producer to whom Ashmore triumphantly sent the manuscript lost it[11]; Eric had kept no copy; and that was that. Given a new lease of energy by Ashmore's encouragement, however, Eric began work in the summer of 1948 on a new comedy asked for by James Bridie for his Citizens' Theatre.

The result was *Love in Albania*, which turned out to be Eric's most successful play in production. First staged in Glasgow in February 1949, it was sufficiently well noticed for Peter Ustinov, attracted by Eric's work in general, to mount a production for the Bath Festival in May. The play provided a rich and toothsome role for Ustinov himself, and the production delighted its audiences. Eric recognised and generously acknowledged Ustinov's remarkable work in the interpretation of the role of Sergeant Dohda which particularly contributed to the play's success:

> The difference between the two productions, the first in Mr Bridie's Citizens' Theatre and the second under the prodigious hand of Mr Ustinov, has induced in me a modesty, a humility indeed, that may be most salutary. As a novelist I exercise a masterly control over my characters; as a tentative and incipient dramatist I am bound to realise, in consequence of Glasgow and Mr Ustinov,

that my control is no more than that of any parent whose offspring, in our modern times, have survived their infancy. In Glasgow Mr Douglas Campbell as Sergeant Dohda, the most conspicuous character in the play, surprised and delighted me by a genial representation of the part that I had never envisaged, but which, when I saw it, convinced me of its truth; while in Bath, and later in London, Mr Ustinov daunted my parental mind with so masterly and huge a realisation of the mere germ I had conceived, that I was divided between pride in my share of him and wonderment at his conquest of me.[12]

Ustinov recalled the play as 'an affectionate kind of literary comedy' in which he played 'one of the more simple-minded purveyors of America's cosmic message, a military policeman of Albanian origin searching Europe for his long-lost partisan daughter'; Peter Jones was 'a stuttering, exasperated individual'; and Robin Bailey 'a suburban husband faced with these lunatic intruders'.[13] The play was far-fetched and preposterous but full of situations that kept the audience intrigued and amused, and the players, sometimes themselves overcome by hilarity, enjoyed it as much as the audiences.

From Bath the play was taken first to the Lyric Theatre, Hammersmith, and eventually in mid-July to the St James's Theatre, where it enjoyed a respectable run. Reviewers were divided about whether it was really a rather literary play or a genuinely theatrical experience, but they said encouraging things about its wit, originality and style, and Eric was persuaded that he had made something of a breakthrough.

Heady though the experience was, and determined though he might be to follow his success as a playwright, Eric was not one to be content with only one iron in the fire at a time, and he was busy with several enterprises. An adaptation for radio of *Sealskin Trousers*, however, brought him considerable distress in August; he had not been consulted about the production, and afterwards he told Rupert Hart-Davis:

> I hope you didn't hear it. It was horrible, and Mr T—— [the actor who played the seal-man], I think, must have been chosen because he is, in fact, an Airedale. He has never been a seal, of course, but—yes, I'm almost sure that he used to be an Airedale.
>
> As for the girl: who would *not* have thrown her off the cliff? Oh dear, it made me so unhappy.

Much work fell to him when he undertook to edit an anthology of prose and poetry by living Scottish authors, designed to raise some money for the Scottish Centre of PEN, which was to host in Edinburgh in 1950 the International Congress of the PEN Club. Letter-writing and acknowledgements and arrangements occupied a great deal of his time for well over a year before the project could safely, and just in time, be left in the hands of the printers. He started making his requests of people whom he cornered while they were visiting Edinburgh for the Festival in August 1948. The occasion also afforded him a memorable meeting with Dylan Thomas, which he described gleefully in a letter to Marjorie:

> And there, looking very drunk, was one of my poets from the luncheon party—Dylan Thomas.
>
> He is Welsh, and his poetry is usually described as 'apocalyptic'. He is small, plump, and has rather an embryonic look: goggle-eyes and curly hair, but otherwise the appearance of a well-fed foetus. He was hiccuping badly, so I took him out for a little walk, and suggested that if he could belch instead of hiccup, it might be good for him. Belching turned out to be an accomplishment of which he is very proud, and he belched a great deal to show me how good at it he was...
>
> 'There!' he exclaimed proudly—but a moment later he became gloomy and cried: 'It's no good! It's got me, it's got me!'
>
> 'Drink?' I asked.
>
> 'No, sex!' he shouted...
>
> Then most violently he exclaimed, 'If you've had the pox in Hull, you know how to avoid the pox in Hull!' And we went back to the party.

The autumn was sadly marred by the news that his brother-in-law, Freddy Cormack, had died suddenly and unexpectedly, leaving Elspeth not too well provided for. There was some distraction from this sadness for their mother when Rupert Hart-Davis proposed to bring out a new edition of her book *A Child Under Sail*. Once again Cape showed a certain meanness of spirit, demanding half the royalty if he was to release the title to Rupert. Eric wrote:

> If one did a lithotomy on Jonathan, one would discover, I believe, a calcareous mass extending from his Adam's apple—itself a pebble from Southend perpetually agitated in an old tin can—down to his perinaeum, which I take to be constructed, rather cheaply, of indifferent concrete. A man of crumbling but persistent stone.

Although there were many distractions, he began in the autumn of 1948 a new novel; it was, he told Rupert, 'a highly improbable tale by which I am worried for most of the week and occasionally elated'. But he had to spend all his time writing letters to say he couldn't open bazaars in Auchtermuchty or addressing Debating Societies in Droitwich: 'I *must* write a book, and everyone is trying to prevent me,' he complained. The new novel he declared to be 'a *very* serious tale, the seriousness of which is concealed by a debonair and sometimes hilarious manner ... I doubt if Mr Cape or Mr Howard will like it—but I think I shall.' He had completed during the summer his second fantasy for children, *The Pirates in the Deep Green Sea*, and the vein of fantasy continued into his adult novel. *The Pirates in the Deep Green Sea* had two small boys as central characters; they were somewhat older than the six-year-old Magnus and four-year-old Andro to whom the book was dedicated, but they might have recognised themselves.

The boys in the book live on an Orkney island called Popinsay, where cannon-balls and gold coins from a sunken Spanish galleon are occasionally washed up. (Eric used to keep on his desk such a cannonball, found on a beach on the west Mainland of Orkney.) The boys' father 'was a very good man, but he had a very bad temper. He had fought in two wars, and in one he had lost his left eye, and his left hand, and in the other his left leg had been shot off just below the knee . . . When he lost his limbs, he lost his temper too.'[14] Several of Eric's protagonists in the novels he wrote after the war are in some way crippled or otherwise saddled with physical deficiencies. In this book for children this mocking but distinct reference to himself and his bad temper aligns him with those of his characters who suffer as a result of physical damage or inferiority, and reminds the reader anew of the consequences for Eric of the traumatic head-wound and emotional experiences which took their toll of him in 1918.

In *The Pirates in the Deep Green Sea* the boys' father's war-wounds merely render him one of a gallery of eccentric comic characters, to be placed alongside Sam Sturgeon and Gunner Boles, or the piratical Inky Poops and Dan Scumbril, or the magical animals, especially the octopus Culliferdontofoscofolio Polydesteropouf, or Cully for short. When published in April 1949 the book immediately found favour, and won the British Annual of Literature Medal for the best children's book of the year. Like all the best children's books, it has a level at which it can delight adult readers as greatly as the children to whom it is addressed. Eric makes no evident concessions to the presumed childishness of his readers, either in tone or language, so that there is no irritation for an adult reader but rather a constant pleasure in the wit, invention and characterisation. One reviewer at the time compared it with T. H. White's *The Sword in the Stone* and commended also the 'much history and natural history which will be painlessly absorbed by the young reader.'[15] The adult reader will savour its affectionate pastiche of elements from *Treasure Island* but also its specific and unmistakable Linklaterianism. It is exciting, funny and stylish. Whatever the fate of Eric's other novels, it seems likely that his two children's books will continue to live as minor classics.

The world of fantasy and fairy-tale always delighted and intrigued Eric. Although his short stories had drawn upon it, however, he had not, up to now, allowed it into his adult novels. In *A Spell for Old Bones* the strain comes into its own. In his final assessment of his work, on the last page of his last autobiography, he referred rather wonderingly to the way in which during the last twenty years of his life some of his novels had failed to make any impression: 'I am very fond, for example, of a fable called *A Spell for Old Bones*, which fell as unnoticed as a snowflake in Lapland.'[16] It was not exactly unnoticed, for it received enthusiastic reviews from, among others, Peter Quennell, C. P. Snow and Richard Church. But it did not sell, and fairly soon disappeared as if it had never existed. Its neglect is not easy to explain. Anyone who has read George Orwell's *Animal Farm* and who has noted the power that 'A Fairy Tale' can engender will find a similar charge generated by Eric's *Spell*. Inspired by an inscription at Kirkseton ('When the giants fell, old bones revived'), Eric wrote a kind of cross between a historical novel and a fairy tale in which to explore the basic human themes of love and war. Set in south-west Scotland in the first century of the Christian era, the novel has as its central figure a poet, Albyn. He becomes involved with the two giants, Od MacGammon and Furbister, who between them dominate the whole country, and whose rivalry eventually leads to an epic confrontation in the Battle of the Blind Glen.

Fantastic though it is, the story is told with utter conviction and the universal issues with which it deals are given a new lease of life in their curious vehicle. Eric imagines the giants with wonderful concreteness and their characteristics and conflicts are enormously entertaining, full of black and wicked humour. In his treatment of the giants, Eric inevitably remembers Rabelais and his Gargantua, and the writing has a pictorial richness. At Furbister's wedding to the mighty Bala, the giant leans his weight on the table end and tips it up:

> The long board inclined towards the giant at an increasing angle, and down its slope slid the remnants and the debris of the feast. Beef bones and ribs of mutton, the little splintered bones of hares, the glutinous vertebrae of cod and haddock, oyster-shells and the sharp hooves of pigs' trotters—down they all came, and hastening their descent was the flood of ale and mead from horns upset and mugs turned over. One half of this rushing spate cascaded against the skirt of Furbister's wedding-robe, but the other half tumbled, as if over a waterfall, into the open gulf of Bala's gown, and down the deep valley of her prodigious bosom fell the shins of cows, the skulls of sheep, crusts of oatbread, drumsticks, and fishbones, pigs' feet and oyster-shells—all carried on a mingled flood of ale and mead that drenched her to the knees and roused her, by its chill, to loud complaint.[17]

Albyn's story is straight from fairy-tale in incident but of the stuff of human life in atmosphere and dialogue, and the particular focus on the way in which he is torn between the desire to settle down with his wife and children on the one hand and to go out and drink deep of the wine of life, even in war and soldiering, gives the novel a special validity. Full of reflections on the pleasures and satisfactions of life: food, poetry, the love of women, and of those problematical human urges to power and domination of others which makes political behaviour so fascinating, the book may be read at different levels, each satisfying in a different way. One of the levels is that of profound parable about the human condition. It is a beautiful, tender, hilarious and provocative novel which haunts the imagination.

Before the children's book and *A Spell for Old Bones* were published Eric, after a flying visit to Sweden, Finland and Denmark in April 1949, where he 'talked a great deal of hot air for the British Council',[18] had begun a new story which this time he offered to Rupert Hart-Davis, feeling justified in taking it to him rather than to Cape's because it would be only a short novel of 40,000 words or so. Besides, not only had he completed his contract with Cape's, but also he was very disappointed with Jonathan's response to the typescript of *A Spell for Old Bones*; he had still not heard a word over a fortnight after delivering it. 'Jonathan, dear old man, has no idea what it's all about,' Eric told Rupert. The new book was to be a 'sort of superior thriller-diller', he explained:

> Out of my original, rather scampering notion have come, I think, some real (and very unpleasant) characters, and a story that is quite horrible in parts. Not *merely* horrible, of course: there isn't a drop of blood from beginning to end. It may, after a modern fashion, amount to something in the Jekyll and Hyde category.

Rupert was only too delighted to accept what he immediately recognised as a winner, and he scheduled publication of *Mr Byculla* for early 1950.

The cool reception of *A Spell for Old Bones*, his first new novel for three years, did not affect Eric's work rate; after completing his new thriller he was more fully occupied than ever. Now fifty years old, he was still in some ways an *enfant terrible*, full of surprises; in others, visibly becoming part of the literary establishment, moving among the senior men with a certain crusty authority. In a very important year for the Scottish Centre of PEN he became its President, and had much to do in preparing to host the Twenty-Second International Congress of the PEN Club held in August 1950. The anthology of Scottish writing which he had put together to publicise the Conference was duly published as *The Thistle and the Pen* early in the year, and he found time for many articles, broadcasts and interviews. He also undertook, with fresh confidence after the success of *Love in Albania*, to provide another new play for the Glasgow Citizens' Theatre.

Recalling the origins of his new play, he wrote of how he had 'a long time ago' conceived an exuberant admiration for Ben Jonson and written a book about him.

> His play called *The Alchemist* was built upon a situation, familiar to Elizabethan audiences, that again became common in our own times. Plague in the 17th Century drove the well-to-do from London as bombs did in the 20th Century, and in both ages knavery found sustenance in folly. I wrote a light-hearted play of which the scene was a mansion in Belgravia, whose owner had fled from the menace of the Luftwaffe and whose empty rooms were exploited by a batch of contemporary coney-catchers.[19]

He sent his draft to James Bridie, and, after much revision, first at the instance of Bridie and later in consultation with Tyrone Guthrie who agreed to direct it, *The Atom Doctor* was produced as part of the official programme of the 1950 Edinburgh International Festival on 24 August. It raised roars of approbation from its audience, and Eric was chuffed by a report in the *Daily Record* of 6 September that The Queen and Princess Margaret had thoroughly enjoyed it. The play's success in Edinburgh was not so great as to attract the immediate attention of the West End, but a year or so later it was revived by George Devine. A promising provincial tryout led to its transfer on 30 April 1952 to London. The production had an excellent cast, with Pamela Browne, Roger Livesey, George Ralph and Mona Washbourne, and was expensively mounted, but somehow the Edinburgh triumph was not repeated. Eric wrote later:

> In a false confidence I waited for the opening night, at Brighton, and I thought the performance went very well. But a few weeks later, at the Duke of York's Theatre, a chilly air descended on the third act, in which I thought was the prettiest comedy, and I shivered slightly in the falling temperature. The play lingered for a while, and gently expired.[20]

The text of the play, under its new title, *The Mortimer Touch*, was nevertheless issued by Samuel French later in the year and for some years proved popular with amateur dramatic societies. But though he was far from the end of his efforts to master the arts of theatre, Eric's experience of seeing his work on the West End stage finished with this failure.

If ultimately let down by his play, however, Eric was far from failure in other undertakings in 1950. Rupert Hart-Davis had in May published *Mr Byculla*, the book which Eric had described to him as a thriller rather than a novel; he was thinking of the way Graham Greene used to distinguish his 'novels' from his 'entertainments'. The book, declared by the reviewers to be exceedingly effective, proved to be Eric's most lasting and financially rewarding publication for several years.

The idea on which *Mr Byculla* is based is gruesomely simple, and derives from Eric's interest in things Indian founded in his working days there in the 1920s. Taking yet another new path, he wrote with superb confidence something quite unlike anything he had yet attempted. It is a crime story impeccably structured and with a smoothly horrific tone of utter urbanity. The eponymous protagonist is of complicated Anglo-Indian descent; his real name is McKillop, but he calls himself Byculla: 'To remind myself, every day, of the vanity of human wishes,' he says.[21] He has studied the art of Thuggee in deeply scholarly fashion, and has turned to practising its skills in what he conceives to be the interest of humanity in general and certain selected individuals in particular. As the reader realises the situation he is gradually drawn into a powerful and frightening drama which raises some difficult questions about life and its sanctity. The conception and presentation of the plausible and insidiously persuasive villain, and the bleak picture of the society through which he moves on his deadly way, combine to make the story much more than the mere entertainment implied by categorising it as a crime novel. The writing, plainer and more subdued than in many of Eric's novels, relies on subtle tonal values and on the perfect construction of the narrative for its effect.

Eric's interest in criminality had been developing since the days of his study of Mary Queen of Scots and the murder of Darnley. *Mr Byculla* also gave advance notice of his fascination with dreams and dream psychology, an element which featured most potently in his last published novel. Several readers at the BBC thought that it would be ideal for broadcasting, but it was rejected with some asperity by Harman Grisewood, then Head of the Drama Department, with the words: 'Very exceptionally we might try a dramatised version of a book, but it would have to possess outstanding qualities, which I don't see in this novel by Linklater.'[22] The rejection and the reason for it seem to imply an astonishingly blind critical attitude in a man in such a position. It is further difficult to read the book without thinking what a good film it would make, but though an option was bought on the title in the United States, nothing came of it. Fourteen years after its publication a television adaptation by Leon Griffiths was shown in the BBC 'Story Parade' series.

Towards the end of 1950, Jonathan Cape began issuing a special uniform edition of all Eric's books, starting with *Magnus Merriman* and *Juan in China*. The launch of 'The Orkney Edition' of his books capped a crowded and successful year for Eric. It had been one of the most highly charged and busy periods of his life, and there was a good deal of satisfactory acknowledgement of his work. Praising an open-air tribute paid by him to the poet Robert Fergusson at his bicentenary ceremonies on 2 September, the *Scotsman* called it 'one of the highlights of the Festival period' and commented:

> Most men of normal constitution would have been incapable of making a speech of even modest merit after being subjected, as Mr Linklater has been, to weeks of severe strain. It was no little accomplishment on his part to steer a difficult PEN Conference so successfully through its tough sessions ... More than anyone else Mr Linklater has had to personify, in public, our Scottish culture during the past weeks, and for undertaking these duties so willingly, so seriously, and with such good nature and modesty, Edinburgh owes him a special vote of confidence.[23]

James Bridie in the Festival number of *Music and Drama*, after demonstrating that Eric was a man of distinct literary achievement, sketched him thus:

He is an adventurer and a gentleman. He is a middle-aged man of middle height. On his homely face are a pair of strong spectacles, a moustache, and a poker-player's unchanging and innocent regard. His carriage is erect, his gestures few, and in his gait there is something of the military automaton. In his costume he affects a neat compromise between the Bohemian and the country laird. His manners are austere and gracious, and his conversation is witty and well-informed ... His laugh is a cavernous 'Haw, Haw' often observed in essentially *good* men. He has many friends, and his friendship is deeply valued by those who enjoy it.

The PEN Conference was a great success, though just before it happened Eric told Compton Mackenzie: 'The whole thing is now becoming a nightmare, but I hope to survive it,' and afterwards he told Rupert Hart-Davis it had been 'all very wearing, extremely expensive, and largely, I think, a waste of time'. He had enjoyed his work in close proximity with Rebecca West, Edwin Muir, T. S. Eliot, Compton Mackenzie and others, not to mention the Lords Provost of Edinburgh and Glasgow and the Secretary of State for Scotland, but a reaction against so much literary and establishment-based company quickly and inevitably set in, so that he could not wait to return to his relatively practical open-air-minded friends away from the scene. He wrote to Rupert:

Now I am trying to gather the scattered threads of a more normal life again, and plait them into something useful. But my fingers are not very willing.

And to John Moore, promising to come down to the Cheltenham Festival of which Moore was Director, he said that he was coming only to see Moore, and Lucile his wife, and Emma Smith:

Without any sense of responsibility ... It is a great mistake to be public-spirited, and in future I shall not make even the smallest effort to be dutiful and to do good.

His mood was real enough. But it soon passed.

18　Old Warrior Goes Walkabout

Three years of life at Pitcalzean had shown that, though it had its inconveniences, it was a good place to live. The girls had to go away to school, but Nigg Bay was a fine place to come home to at holiday time, and the little boys, until they in turn went off to school, found they were being raised in a natural paradise. The house was big and old and really too expensive; Sally, the elder daughter, recalled:

> The long corridor from kitchen to dining-room which meant that all meals arrived well-chilled; the extra bedrooms and sitting-rooms tacked on at the back that no one could use; the bees making honey in the attic. For Eric these things were not important ... Every day he would walk out of his front door, contemplate the view across the Cromarty Firth to Ben Wyvis, and then turn and walk back slowly to his writing-desk.

Rupert Hart-Davis remembered:

> It was a lovely house in a desolate place, right on the edge of a wood, and the sea outside, and nothing in sight. He had three Highland cattle—little hairy things with long horns—just for fun in a bit of the garden, fenced off.

Eric told Phoebe Gilkyson in March 1950:

> We are slowly getting the house into reasonable condition, though there is still a great deal to do. It was very run-down and ramshackle, both inside and out, when I bought it, but the situation is so good it was worth taking some trouble to put in order. We have a large and very good garden, and with the romantic idea of market-gardening—truck-farming, in your language—I employ two gardeners, and lose a lot of money for the very good reason that we haven't got a market, and neither Marjorie nor I can keep accounts.
>
> We look out over a large shallow bay with high hills beyond it, and the place is so rich in bird-life—mainly waders, geese and ducks—that the whole area is likely to be made a sort of game-reserve.

Easter Ross was, compared with Orkney where everyone knew each other and each other's business, positively feudal, Sally said. All around there were clan chiefs and scions of ancient houses living in crumbling mansions or castles among portraits of their ancestors and stags' heads, growing steadily poorer and more eccentric. Eric was fascinated by them and their setting, and made friends with a range of them, from farmers to retired Admirals and from clan chieftains to the occasional writer or artist who lived in the neighbourhood of the Black Isle. Among these were, at one time or another, Gavin Maxwell, whom Marjorie and Eric found one of the strangest, most difficult and most interesting men they had ever met; Jane Duncan, 'such a nice woman', who came home to Poyntzfield from the West Indies in 1958, just as her 'My Friend' novels were about to win her a wide readership; and James Robertson-Justice, who became particularly close and in whose company Eric spent many a convivial evening. In Sally's words:

> If you can imagine two men with rapier-sharp points to their toes doing a sword-dance, with one of them occasionally letting off a revolver, then you'll have a fair idea of those conversations. Either Eric or James would introduce a topic and then they'd pursue it hotly, up comic hill and down erudite dale, until the whole party was so exhausted with laughter and surprise that nothing would revive us—except perhaps another glass of Glenmorangie whisky, or another helping of whatever delicious dish had been prepared by Irina von Myerndorff, the charming German actress who lived with James.

Not far away lived Neil Gunn, to whom Eric with typical generosity offered hospitality at Pitcalzean when Gunn was given notice to quit his tenancy of Braefarm House in the spring of 1949:

> If you are turned out before you have found something really suitable, don't forget that I have a cottage which—though no proper dwelling for a noble fellow like yourself and another noble fellow like Daisy—could, perhaps, shelter you for a few months while you continued your search.

But Gunn settled at Kincraig on the edge of the Cromarty Firth, and Eric's offer was not taken up.

Eric's energy was partly devoted to his notions for preparing his two boys to face the world. They didn't quite know what to make of him. His moods were changeable and his temper when roused formidable. Being bald he looked older than he was, and Magnus felt that he had always seemed remote and old from their earliest memories of him. But he had such physical enthusiasms that made him at times quite boyish himself. He taught the boys to box and fish, and with what Magnus recalls as a quite devastating lack of normal adult concern for matters of safety encouraged them to ride their ponies, or to go rock-climbing, or to sail their dinghy or canoes without insisting on formal training or wearing hard hats or life-jackets; he even let Magnus take his old twelve-bore shotgun and pot at targets by the shore when he was still quite young.

At other times, as he had always been, he could be tyrannical. If his work was going well, or the company was good, meal-times, for instance, could be very jolly; but if the boys' manners were forgotten, or they ate without gentlemanly concern for the feelings of others at the table, he might suddenly become extremely angry. He did not like to be contradicted at all, by Marjorie any more than by the children. Sally remembered:

> Reprimand was at times unstinted. My father never raised a finger to punish us physically, but his tongue was formidable. His favourite threat was 'I'll beat you to within an inch of your life!' and when he was really angry this became 'I'll beat you to within an inch of your life with rusty barbed wire!' I truly believed he would. He seemed to come out of the fairy tales by Andersen or Grimm. Sometimes he was very funny, but often he was as frightening as the giant in the legendary castle.

Magnus once went into the room where his mother and father had 'had one of their shouting-matches'. Eric had gone, and Marjorie was standing there surrounded by fruit—Eric had been so infuriated about something that he had evidently picked up the fruit-bowl and emptied it over her— there were apples and oranges all over the room.

There were times, when Eric was working, when they hardly saw him for weeks at a time. What he was working at in the autumn of 1950 was a consequence of his 'hot flirtation with the film boys'. He had sketched out for Charles Crichton at Ealing Studios a scenario for a film about salmon-poaching in Scotland. It was not what they wanted. Eric requested the return of his story-line, saying that he wanted to make it into a novel, and promising that the film rights in the novel would belong to Ealing. This was the origin of *Laxdale Hall*, at which he laboured through the winter and into the spring of 1951, when he told Rupert Hart-Davis:

> I am in the last third of a novel, half blind and wholly hag-ridden. It would be nice to be a genius, and sure that one's work was going to be worth the trouble. But it would be horrible to think one was a genius, and then discover that no one else thought so. In between these extremes there is a grim pleasure in cutting a piece of wood to shape, and even occasional excitement when it seems possible that the shape will be true. But a workman's life, not a gentleman's!

He told John Moore: 'I still battle with the current novel, which gets longer and longer without any sign of coming to an end. It may, indeed, be concluded on page 484 with a broken sentence and the honest declaration, "I can do no more".'

Finish it he did, however, on Easter Sunday, and then drew breath before plunging into the last great adventure of his life. Some time earlier he had arranged with the British Council to go on an antipodean lecture tour in the autumn of 1951; to recharge his batteries ready for this after his winter's toil he went at the beginning of April to Sweden, partly to enjoy what proved to be a rather strenuous holiday in the enthusiastically hospitable Scandinavian surroundings he found so congenial, partly to see his play *Love in Albania* in a Swedish translation being mounted by the Gothenburg State Theatre and, a few days later, at a Malmö theatre.

While in Sweden he received from Sir Robert Fraser at the Central Office of Information a challenge to take on a commission that would render his 'year of space' even more momentous. The invitation was to go to Korea and act as an official observer of the conduct and achievement of the British and Commonwealth troops involved in the new war there. He demurred, for remembering the war in Italy he felt afraid of the pain he knew he would suffer at the sight of new ruins, new refugees:

> I did not want to breathe again the smell of shattered houses, the stink of humanity on the run, and see its tear-stained children. What, I wondered, was the Korean for 'Niente mangiare'?[1]

But he saw that it could be fitted in neatly at the beginning of his projected schedule of travels in Australasia, and admitted with wry humour:

> My sense of duty is nothing like so large or robust as once it was, but a vestige remains; and no one had a better claim to it than the soldiers who had twice saved our century. If they wanted a clerk to record their latest bravery, it would indeed be shabby to refuse them.

Marjorie was less than overjoyed at the prospect of managing without Eric for perhaps six months rather than the planned two or three, but at the end of June 1951 he returned to uniform with the temporary rank of Lieutenant-Colonel and flew via Cairo and Karachi to Singapore. His service began with a series of dinner-parties with officers stationed there, and of conversations with wounded men brought out of the Korean battlefields. On 11 July he flew to Hong Kong, writing to Marjorie while aboard a Sunderland flying-boat:

> And you, my love, my poor deserted one—how are you? Cheerful, I hope, but not *unduly* cheerful, and in rude health—but not *too* rude. I am truly grateful to you for letting me go off on this trip without raising emotional storms and difficulties.

He thought, after his time with the wounded, that he was right to have accepted the additional job; the soldiers were so decent, they had had a hell of a rough time, they didn't really know what it was all about—his heart had gone out to them, and he felt that he ought to do something (or try to) to let them see that what they had been doing was important, and to make other people see that what they had been doing had been done damned well.

His period in Korea and its environs (fully recounted in *A Year of Space* which began as a diary of an unusually exotic taste of life) took him from Hong Kong to Okinawa and Japan initially. From Sasebo, near Nagasaki, he was taken aboard the NZ frigate *Rotoiti*, and thence to the RN frigate

Cardigan Bay into Korean waters and eventually to Inchon. The rest of July was spent examining the territories of the Imjin River confrontations and talking to men of the 29th Brigade about their experiences in that battle. Early in August he was flown from Seoul in a little Firefly to land on board the aircraft carrier *Glory*; after several days observing the work of the Fleet Air Arm he was much moved in more ways than one when catapulted off the carrier for his return to the capital in Seoul. He explained how reading *Pride and Prejudice* helped control his excitement and apprehension during the violent take-off:

It worked almost at once. The sublime confidence of Miss Austen was infectious, and in her company it was ill-mannered to suffer from nerves.[2]

In Seoul he saw something of what the war had meant to the Korean populace and later vividly evoked the shattered landscape and despairing circumstances of their life. To Marjorie he wrote:

All around are the depressing ruins of Seoul—such ruins!—and a thin scattering of Koreans ... Between here and Inchon the country is a kind of suburban wreckage, rice-fields between broken villages and small, wrecked factories, under a drab and clouded sky.

In *A Year of Space* he quotes someone who said: 'I don't know who's going to win this war, but it's God-damned certain who's lost it: and that's the poor bloody Koreans.' In his survey of the degradation and tragedy brought by war he tried to understand the larger politics which had caused it:

The tragedy of Korea was made more shocking by its general ugliness; and to endure the sight of it one required the absolute conviction that what had happened there might have prevented a larger war, for the third and last time, in Western Europe ... War is an evil thing, a persistent thing. We have not yet found the cure for it, but to localise it is empirically a useful beginning to preventive treatment. And I am selfish enough to prefer a war localised in an Asiatic peninsula to a war let loose on my own heritage.[3]

This honest declaration notwithstanding, he was sore at heart at what he had seen, and found unusual difficulty in writing the report he had been commissioned to produce. Modern war was technically difficult to describe because the operations were on too vast a scale to be adequately represented in a few words, and morally difficult because a civilised person could no longer write of war with relish and a hearty assurance that victory would be commensurate with the soldiers' efforts. Nor did he feel that he had seen enough to appreciate fully 'the unique and savage truth of a Korean battle'. Nevertheless his account, when published six months later, justified his hope that 'bare facts by proper arrangement would find in themselves a little eloquence'.

In *Our Men in Korea* (1952), Eric's simple narrative gains life from occasional images, as in 'The south-going stream [of traffic] was flowing again. Trucks, tanks and tank-transporters, like ice-floes in a melting river, growled and screamed in their narrow bed'; and vivid pictures:

> The dark sky was lighted by the flames of ruin, and huddled in their casual warmth lay a wretched few of the many thousands of panic-struck, frost-bitten, wailing refugees who, to shame humanity, came like a doomed migration of lemmings from the terror of the north.

His praise of the soldiers' deportment and actions rings true, as do his comments on their essential decency and compassion:

> No hardship of their own so troubled the spirit of the Commonwealth soldiers as the dreadful spectacle of Korea's misery on those frozen wastes. It stayed in their minds, an aching memory, long after their own sores and danger had been turned, by time and the genial temper of the Army, to indulgent jokes and mockery.[4]

The narrative is both exciting and involving, and nowhere is its habitual understatement more effective than in two passages where it has to present the frightful effects of American attacks accidentally directed onto hapless Commonwealth troops instead of the enemy. The particular matters which Eric selected for fuller treatment, such as the Gloucesters' glorious stand at the Imjin River and the contribution of the 60th Indian Field Ambulance, help to give the reader a strong feeling of scene and ambience, and the pamphlet serves as a notable example of Eric's competence as a professional writer.

After a further period with units of the Commonwealth soldiers—Australians, Canadians and Indians—involved in the fighting and a visit to the site of the Battle of the Kapyong River Eric had, by mid-August, exhausted the time available for the Korean project. He made his way to Japan, and after some delay caused by a typhoon which, as he solemnly informed his wife, was codenamed MARGIE, but which afforded him an excuse for some pleasant bathing and sightseeing in Tokyo and Iwakuni, he was flown in a Sunderland to Darwin. One further hop brought him to New Zealand just in time for the first of his British Council lectures.

His eight weeks in New Zealand and subsequent six weeks in eastern Australia proved to be a rewarding and stimulating period, and he found plenty of material for his proposed diary-cum-travel-book. Though he was somewhat hampered as a sightseer in New Zealand by the necessity of writing his Korean booklet and by the need to devise and polish up suitable lectures for his scheduled audiences, his enthusiasm for and judicious appreciation of the country were unaffected. From the sunlit northern end to the extreme southerly community of Stewart Island, a territory which despite its wild beauty he found curiously sinister, he journeyed, talked and wrote. By the end of his two months' stay he had not only seen a great deal with a keen vision that missed nothing, but had also successfully delivered his series of lectures and readings and gratefully completed his account of the British and Commonwealth contribution in Korea.

Free at last to do nothing but enjoy himself for a while, he crossed the Tasman Sea back to Australia, where he planned a northerly journey from Sydney towards the Great Barrier Reef, northern Queensland, and ultimately New Guinea, to make as much as he could of an Australian vacation before returning to his lectures in India and Africa on the long way home. Two chapters of *A Year of Space* treat of his impressions of Australia, from a perception of essential contradictions between realistic thought and romantic practice in Australian behaviour to a moment of pure pleasure as he realises the special qualities of youth and sea-washed beauty possessed by the Saturday morning shopping-crowd in Sydney; and from accounts of spear-fishing in the Great Barrier Reef to a vividly evoked circular flight round cattle-stations and ghost towns of the outback, taken on the recommendation of Nevil Shute whom he had met in Sydney. It is travel writing of the finest quality, full of atmosphere and unforgettable sensuous effect as well as life, humour and anecdote.

He had a good time, though much harassed as in New Zealand by reporters with whom, sometimes, he was a little short, as he confessed in a letter to John Moore written aboard SS *Monowai* 'on the stormy Tasman Sea which is in fact merely showing a tantrum between the blue water astern and clear sky ahead; it being the anniversary of Trafalgar, 1951':

> A young man has just interrupted me, confound him, to say that he was looking for me in Christchurch, hunting me in Wellington, seeking me out in Auckland. 'Who are you?' I ask. 'I'm in broadcasting.' 'Then I'm glad you didn't find me,' I bark; and return to my letter.

Everywhere he went, both in New Zealand and Australia, he met exiled Scots and Orcadians, and far-flung Linklater cousins, and men who remembered him from some previous meeting. He told Moore: 'I behaved very well, on the whole, till I got to Sydney; but in Sydney there was a certain liveliness. I wasn't on duty there.' What the liveliness amounted to must remain a matter for conjecture. While in flight from Sydney to Brisbane he wrote to Marjorie:

> Sydney was social and amusing. Several parties, including one very good one at which (if my memory serves) I sang 'Reilly's Daughter'. I tell you everything, you see—and you will observe, I trust, that this was the first party of that sort I have had since leaving home. The Australian air is more exuberant than New Zealand's comfortable domestic atmosphere.

In one of his efforts to remind Marjorie both of his opportunities for roguery and Juanism and of his essential fidelity, he mentioned a meeting with writers and journalists in the long bar of the Australia Hotel, adding: 'There was a delightful barmaid at the Australia: I felt I could have been better employed.' When in the mood, and in the company of a woman prepared to hold her own with him at his own level of intellect and wit, then he could and would put aside the element of chauvinism in his nature and respond with a most engaging flirtatiousness. Georgina O'Sullivan, a reporter on the *Australian Woman's Weekly*, was utterly charmed:

> He is an exhilarating fellow.
>
> He is not obviously attractive. Nature was generous with the amused brown eyes and the mouth which quirks easily. But she detracted by handing him a longish face and the sort of hair which did not stand a chance of lasting on top beyond his thirties. He is now 52.
>
> But in her endowment of mind and personality, Nature was lavish . . .
>
> After half an hour with him I decided he is one of the most attractive men I have interviewed—and that includes Lord Louis Mountbatten and Anthony Eden.[5]

Eric liked what she said sufficiently to cut the article out and send it to Marjorie.

After some idyllic days in north-eastern Australia, based at Daydream Island and later at Cairns, he visited Papua New Guinea, and there, on a flight from Port Moresby to a place called Tapini in the remote interior, he found a dramatic setting that demanded to be used in a story. There was no road from the coast, and on foot an eight days' journey of great difficulty would have been necessary, but in an aeroplane an hour or so was sufficient. He was enormously impressed by the site of Tapini in 'a particular valley in a countryside that consisted entirely of deep and shadow-laden valleys between truculent, high-rearing, narrow-crested ridges',[6] and more than a little excited by the skill of the pilot as they landed safely on what seemed a hideously dangerous and almost inaccessible shelf of cleared ground above a precipitous three thousand foot drop. Two years later he lovingly recreated this extraordinary valley as the scene of the central action of *The Faithful Ally* (1954). His explorations in New Guinea were curtailed by illness which he later discovered to have been caused by salt loss through sweating, but which was a worry and a nuisance at the time.

He had now been away from home for five months, and he was getting tired. With a great desire to see his wife and children again, and to come to grips with the paper mountain of work he wanted to do, and to see for himself how his 1951 publications were faring, he cut short the rest of the Australian jaunt, cancelled the lecture tours in India and Africa, and embarked on the P & O liner *Stratheden* for the first stage of his homeward journey.

Eric arrived home with perfect timing on Christmas Eve; after six months of almost perfect health in exotic climes he had caught a roaring cold, 'the bequest of British Railways, every one of whose filthy carriages is deeply infected in every cushion',[7] on the last lap, and he entered the New Year with some feeling of lethargy.

During his absence his novel *Laxdale Hall* had appeared from Cape's in October, and *The Campaign in Italy* had at last been published by HMSO in November. *Laxdale Hall* is a comedy set in the limited and specific location of a coastal village in western Scotland. It was not much noticed by reviewers, who generally seemed to read it as a kind of imitation or exploitation of Compton Mackenzie's type of light-hearted romp as in *Whisky Galore* or *Hunting the Fairies*, but Richard Church was enthusiastic about its powerful satirical undercurrents and its poetic, idiosyncratic flavour. The novel brings the little community richly to life, and the concerns of the people of Laxdale are brought out through a multiplicity of threads in the plot. Love affairs, the capture of a gang of salmon-poachers, the production by the villagers of a classical Greek play and an identity-mystery all contribute colour and complexity to an account of a visit from a Member of Parliament to try and resolve the villagers' quarrel with the Government over the provision of a good road to the outside world. The assembly of characters at the Hall talk about aspects of modern life with wit and asperity, as if the old house were full of guests from one of Thomas Love Peacock's gatherings.

Eric's vision in the novel of the Hall and village and their interaction may be a little idealised and unreal from a 'serious' point of view, and the machinery may seem no more than well-oiled conventions smoothly whirring into professional entertainment. In fact through them Eric presents a model of life where its possibilities are more fully developed than in most of this television-watching civilisation, and the memory of his vision lingers and inspires after the laughter fades.

Though only moderately successful in terms of sales, the story brought Eric a pleasant reward two years later, for after being rejected by Ealing Studios it was filmed instead by Group 3, a production company set up by the National Finance Corporation to use as a testing-ground for new talent. There was a tenuous connection with Ealing still, since Michael Balcon, John Grierson and John Baxter were in charge of the enterprise, but the film was made by Alfred Shaughnessy and John Eldridge. Released in April 1953 with Ronald Squire, Raymond Huntley, Kathleen Ryan, Prunella Scales and Roddy MacMillan in the cast, it became by far the most popular of the three films made from Eric's books.

The Campaign in Italy made a handsome book, very well bound and produced, of 480 pages with fifty-one maps and twelve pages of photographs, an astonishing half-guinea's worth. In humorous retrospect Eric wrote:

In the history there are more than a quarter of a million words. It is painstakingly accurate, and illuminating in parts; but much of it, when I look at it again, reminds me of Kipling's poem about infantry columns in the South African war:

> We're foot-slog-slog-slog-sloggin' over Africa—
> Foot-foot-foot-foot-sloggin' over Africa—
> (Boots-boots-boots-boots—movin' up an' down again!)
> There's no discharge in the war![8]

In truth the punctilious attention to detail may defeat the casual reader, but the writing has a particular flavour of dry wit which, with the fine craftsmanship of the sentence structures and the individual tone attributable to Eric's choice of words, renders the book more attractive as art than might be expected. A sentence taken at random illustrates something of this quality: 'An attack on the town from the north was the logical next step; but logic was defeated by topography, for the northern approach was dominated by Castle Hill which rose, unassailable, on a sheer cliff.'[9] On the same page he writes of the 'marvellous' speed of the sappers in bridging certain streams; such commitment adds significantly to the tone. It exemplifies Eric's practice, which was to write history almost as he wrote novels, seizing the narrative centre and exploiting the human aspects of the story and writing with humour, wit and an individual elegance of style.

The Campaign in Italy opens with an introductory essay of great interest. Divided into three sections, it raises difficult questions about the nature and purpose of war, about the possibility of satisfactorily recording a war as military history, and about the conduct of the specific part of the Second World War with which the book has to deal. Recalling first the observation of Clausewitz that war is the continuation of policy, Eric suggests that the modern experience is very different: 'A major war, it is clear, can no longer be regarded, with Sadowa for an example, as the continuation of policy; but, with the ruins of Western Europe before us, as the collapse of policy.'[10] In answer to the question of what use or purpose was the disinterring and reconstructing from complicated records the story of a campaign which was, in fact, no more than a consequence of humanity's failure to be sensible and an example of the slenderness of its claim to be civilised, Eric proposed the value of considering the soldiers' role as

Scapegoats of a flock incapable of securing its peace by sagacity; as the scapegoat who suffers, and by his suffering redeems the people from the failure of their policy; as the scapegoat who, in extremity, reveals unsuspected virtues that might perhaps have saved his country—and the enemy's—from the calamity of war if means had been found, before its outbreak, to enlist and deploy them in the cause of peace.[11]

Thus he had found in his burdensome task a congenial function to set alongside his delight in storytelling, and had grasped the opportunity to continue his championship of the soldier which he had begun in the wartime pamphlets and radio conversations. The dedication of the work, to 'Field Marshal the Viscount Alexander and the Soldiers of Five Continents who in a Brotherhood of Arms and Obedient to their Vision of the Truth Served in Italy the Troubled Causes of Freedom, Justice and Peace', is revealing both of Eric's motivation and of his personality.

Besides occasional broadcasting and journalism, and the excitement associated with the abortive attempt to make a success of *The Mortimer Touch* on the London stage, Eric's first objective in 1952 was to write an account of his recent travels. Meeting some difficulty in deciding how to shape it, he made several false starts and the spring passed without much progress having been made. How he finally solved the problem is described in the last pages of the book he made:

> Somewhere I have confessed the uneconomic habit of my work—the laborious waste of time, the patient fishing of a sluggish hook till the fish begin to rise—and because the rise often comes late in the day I seldom go to bed before the next morning, and to keep the balance I do not get up very early. I breakfast alone, and for company I take almost at random a book from the shelves . . . And one morning, after some dispiriting days when I could not make my story seem fresh and sound true, and as many pages were thrown away as were written, I came down and took by chance the picaresque *Adventures of a Bookseller*, by Pino Orioli.[12]

His perusal of this book at breakfast led to memories of Orioli from the days in Fiesole in 1934, and of Norman Douglas whom he had met in Orioli's company and who had recently died. Finding on his shelves a copy of *Paneros*, written by Douglas and published by Orioli in a limited edition, and given to Eric by Douglas, he suddenly realised, 'Of all the minor gifts, books are the most agreeable.' With this idea in mind he set out to write his new book as a present for thirty people or so to whom, for one reason or another, he felt inclined to give a present, and this at least partially solved his problems of selection and tone by providing a specific, known audience. He wrote:

> I went back to my table. I tore up a few more pages, rewrote what I had written, and started another chapter. Beyond my window the summer painted new colours on the hills and like a *pointilliste* enlivened the dancing sea; but I stayed indoors. I turned my back upon the growing summer—oh, the perversions of mankind!—and sat at work. That was the end of my walkabout year.

It still took him longer than he expected to get it done. In June he stopped for a break and went for a week with Marjorie to Paris, though he could not really justify it, he said to John Moore, for: 'My current play has flopped, my book-in-hand is but half-done, and my next play can be described only as work-in-progress.'

The next play on which he was tentatively working was *The Faithful Ally*. He was not encouraged, however, by A. D. Peters' relative lack of enthusiasm for his attempts at writing for the theatre, and after a while he put his draft aside and began planning a new novel instead. In August he declared to Rupert Hart-Davis:

> I have been living underground for a long time. Not in the romantic style of a political refugee, but as a miner at the coal-face, cramped but enduring, patiently hacking away at a dark subterranean rock which may, when brought to the surface, give a little warmth; but, of course, may prove only to be rubble such as the Coal Board sells. I have, in fact, been writing a book. Yes, another bloody book. A sort of extension of *The Man on My Back*, based on my travels of last year, but ranging also a little in time.

A Year of Space, when finished at last and published in January 1953, was very well received and indeed very highly praised in some quarters; Lord Birkenhead was especially pleased by it:

> He unfolds his rich experience swiftly, in sparse and sinewy prose, but he has always been a master of words and again and again amid the hurrying narrative an arresting phrase glistens like a jewel in an Ethiop's ear.[13]

Eric had reason to be gratified by the sale of the book, for there were many who, although not included in the list of thirty or so to whom Eric wanted to give a present, found the book a veritable gift. The following year it was adopted by World Books and reissued in a Reprint Society edition. The income was a godsend, for as usual he was not far ahead of the tax-hounds on the one hand and the bank manager on the other. For a while he was even convinced that they would have to move from their Highland home; he explained to Rupert Hart-Davis:

> Pitcalzean is now advertised for sale. It's too expensive for me, partly because maintenance costs a lot, and partly because railway fares get higher and higher, and with all my brood getting their miseducation—or none at all—in the south, and my own journeys to the Smoke, the proportion of my income that goes to British Railways is clearly excessive.

He would look for somewhere, preferably to rent, closer to Edinburgh and near enough to Berwick to shorten the voyage to London, he said. In the event his income improved again and no buyer emerged anyway, so the house was retained and they continued to manage somehow.

After his walkabout year, Eric had begun to settle into the routine of hard work, occasional holidays, and excursions to talk, broadcast or lecture which became so much a pattern that in *Fanfare for a Tin Hat* he gave the entire period no more than a page of review. It was more interesting, however, than this implies.

19 Honoured by The Queen

Eric spent some time in the winter of 1952–3 playing with the notion that he and John Moore would together write a musical comedy:

> It might usefully start in a select and superior bar of the very sort you took me to in Tewkesbury, where we heard tales of fiddling and diddling ... There could be a bored and decorative barmaid who is the repository of all secrets and yet is perfectly innocent, because she believes that the world of fiddling and diddling is the only one and the natural one.

The idea turned into a sort of half-serious running joke that crept into all their correspondence on and off for the next ten years, but in the end both men were too busy with their own projects to find the time to get together; it was probably little more than an excuse to spend more time in each other's company anyway.

More immediately Eric worked on an article for *Collier's* magazine about 'the violence of boreal weather' which involved him in a flight to Orkney in the company of Karl Gullers, the Swedish photographer, to find some suitable pictures. 'The things we do!' he exclaimed to Moore; but the money offered made it irresistible. He found Gullers to be a very pleasant companion, and the commission brought about the beginning of a long friendship with some interesting co-productions.

But his main concern was with a new novel; not yet the one in which he could make use of the fantastic jungle setting he had observed in New Guinea, but one set partly in an area of Scotland very important to him though previously untouched in his novels. This was the wild and remote north-west, more familiar to him since he had come to live in Easter Ross and had begun to strike westwards to investigate the fishing or to take the boys for manly excursions on the raw hills. The novel, he told Moore, had required all the dwindling store of his senile energy, and with single-minded application he had made some progress—but not very much, and all other occupation had fallen into desuetude and decay. As usual his protestations of idleness and incapacity had little foundation, though he was a little ill at the end of the year: 'I celebrated the New Year on milk,' he told Compton Mackenzie, 'because of my familiar duodenal collapse in the face of hard work—and, in honesty, I must confess, of a *leetle* too much drinking about Christmastide.' Among other undertakings, he had to prepare an address to the Edinburgh Sir Walter Scott Club, of which he had been elected President.

He presided at their 45th Annual Dinner on 20 January 1953, and took advantage of the occasion to combine a forthright declaration of Scott's greatness with some animadversions on the current literary scene and on the curious fluctuations of literary reputation. Noting that 'Sir Walter no longer lives in the warm centre of general admiration, where once he was at home', he considered others whose reputations had suffered only to be reinstated later, and predicted that 'within the generation of the next three years the light of benign interest will fall again upon the Waverley novels'.[1] Scott was, he said, a great storyteller, comparable both in stature and untidiness with Cervantes, Balzac, Dickens, the giants of literature, with whom Scott shared 'a creative faculty that enables them to give their readers a sensation that approximates to a real experience of life'. He was surely thinking of himself too when he went on to discuss modern criticism and its singular lack of interest in the art of storytelling: 'The modern critic ... has been much inclined to see virtue only in those writers who self-consciously make writing a rarefied art, an esoteric enterprise.'

Throughout February Eric sat writing *The House of Gair*, and outside the elements raged, contributing conceivably by their excess something to the unusually melodramatic scenes in the resolution of his story. He described to John Moore the scene from his window:

> We have been barricaded against a tank-attack of fallen trees. We lost about 300 in the gale—all big ones—and the house is almost unapproachable. Now, with snow on the ground, and brilliant sun, and the earth standing up in vast dollops, and the trees lying down in utter confusion, our view is apocalyptic.

By mid-March his work on the novel was almost done, and his attention was turning again to the possibilities of the film industry. There was some anxiety when Marjorie hurt her back in an accident; finding with relief that no permanent harm had been done, Eric described it to Compton Mackenzie:

> Seized by a romantic impulse, on a fine spring morning, Marjorie resolved to clean a window; and stood outside, on a window-ledge, to do it. Then she let go, and fell some fifteen feet to the cellar-entrance. We took her to hospital, and now she's home again, still in bed and won't be out of it for some weeks, but in very good health and spirits. She squashed two of her vertebrae a bit, and her left knee suffered the same sort of damage. But she will be all right, and that's a miracle of good luck; for she might easily have crippled herself for life. The neighbours come in droves to look with awe at the scene of defenestration.

When the film of *Laxdale Hall* was released in April, Eric went to London at the invitation of the British Lion Film Studios to try a stint as a screenwriter. The conditions of work were really not to his taste, but a payment of £250 a week seemed a sound reason for giving it a trial. To Marjorie he wrote:

> The truth of it is—the strange, unnatural truth—that I have been working hard and living sober. Ever since I arrived, till this weekend, I have been up and out of the house by *8a.m.*, and at it all day until 6 or 7 ... The work is interesting because Carol Reed is so clever at making something out of nothing; and that is what I have to do, too. Because the story of the film is utter nonsense ... and although I have written quite a lot, I'm still not quite sure what the film is *about.*

He returned home briefly after Easter, bearing triumphantly the news that the Commissioners of Inland Revenue had, after an appeal, finally agreed that the market garden at Pitcalzean was a legitimate commercial proposition and that its losses might therefore be set against his income. 'We ought to get some refund of tax. Most satisfactory,' he told Marjorie. Two weeks later he went back to Shepperton, but found that the charm of novelty had worn off the film business. He was much taken with the newly arrived German actress, Hildegarde Neff—'a perfect fizzer,' he told Marjorie, 'pale, pale yellow hair, and black eyebrows, black lashes, and pale, sea-green, transparent eyes. Oh my!' The occasional company of Miss Neff on the one hand and Claire Bloom on the other was for a while almost sufficient compensation for the fact that the film was in his estimation getting sillier and sillier. There was also a pleasant weekend in Gloucestershire with his new friend, Robert Henriques, the soldier and novelist, whom he had met in the company of John Moore. He fished, without result, a narrow dry-fly stream that he found very difficult, and John and Lucile Moore came over to Robert's comfortable Cotswold house in the evening.

He finished his film work in mid-May and, determining to give no more time to such uncongenial labour, drew up and got his employer to sign a reference for him:

BRITISH LION FILM STUDIOS

FROM: Sir Carol Reed

TO: Whom it may concern

Linklater has been employed by me for five weeks, and leaves only at my request. His job was to create dialogue, for which my minimum requirements were that it should be, at one and the same time
   a) Simple
   b) dramatic
   c) exciting
   d) funny but not vulgar
   e) fraught with tears
   f) immortal

His failure to reach this standard has been admirably consistent and shows real integrity. He is clean, diligent, respectful, and frequently sober; and I can recommend him for employment elsewhere.

DATED: 13–5–1953   SIGNED: Carol Reed

His comic memento of the occasion notwithstanding, the experiment had not been very happy. It was the last he had to do with the cinema. However, he took home one trophy from London which was most satisfying. Hanging at the Savile Club was a Peploe painting which Eric craved for his walls at home; feeling at last sufficiently well off, and with the combined excuse of the imminence of the Coronation of Queen Elizabeth and of the twentieth anniversary of his wedding to justify the extravagance, he bought the painting and took it home as his present to Marjorie to mark the great occasion. On the way back to Edinburgh he called in to see Sally at Cambridge. He told John Moore: 'Sally brought several of her young friends from Girton to dine with me, and I sat purring like a contented old cat in the midst of them—and told some catty tales to amuse them.'

In the summer he contemplated anew his play about life in a village just like Tapini and decided he could, as Peters suggested, make better use of the material. Writing to Cape to thank him for his kind words about *The House of Gair*, which was now being made ready for publication, he said:

> The theme of my next novel has been clear to me for some time—but a lot of the detail needed clarifying. I began to think of it, and light descended. A contemporary story set in the western Pacific. A social comedy hyperimposed on a tale of unrest.

He had decided to turn his play into a novel; though his words to John Moore show that he did not expect the task to be easy: 'You must have been alarmingly industrious to have brought your novel to within sight of the finish already. I stand reluctant before the frightful effort of starting another, shivering like a little boy on the river-bank and whimpering "It's cold!"' There was a moment when he thought he might, after machinations on his behalf by Compton Mackenzie, be given a lucrative and irresistible contract to write a biography of the Aga Khan and thus delay having to work on the novel; but, as he told Mackenzie's secretary, Chrissie MacSween:

> A later communication said it was off, because apparently the *Daily Mail* holds a lien on the life, and the *D.M.* insists that a tame, anonymous ghost should do it. Alas—I should have been well pleased to spend a few months at Antibes as His Highness' guest and interpreter.

So he began the novel *The Faithful Ally*, and at the same time started work on another idea that he had long intended to develop: an account of the Orkney Vikings and their connection with the whole Norse adventure.

Eric (*l*), John Gielgud, Barry Morse (*r*) at rehearsal for *Crisis in Heaven*, February 1944

Eric and Peter Ustinov confer during the filming of *Private Angelo* (1949) in Italy

19 Pitcalzean House, looking out over Nigg Bay, Easter Ross, where the Linklaters lived from 1946 to 1971

20 Eric and Marjorie enjoying a crack at Pitcalzean, 1955, under the gaze of their sons Andro (*l*) and Magnus, painted by Mary Potter; on top of the bookshelves is a photograph of Norman Douglas

In a letter to Rupert Hart-Davis in August he explained why he had for weeks abstained from any correspondence:

> Having been in that miserable, broody state that authors and villatic fowl too well do know. I have a novel in the early chapters, a lightly critical and dubiously historical work in an earlier phase—and I crouch above them both, trying to lend them the failing warmth of my enfeebled body, and uttering to all who come near me a croaking, hostile noise.

On its publication in October, *The House of Gair* received little attention outside Scotland. *The Times* declared itself positively disappointed with 'an average, cultivated, undistinguished book',[2] saying that it was a mystery why a novelist of Mr Linklater's talent was ever impelled to write it. *The House of Gair* follows up Eric's interest in criminality as first fully explored in *Mr Byculla*. It is a finely plotted mystery story, the very ending of which leaves a question hanging still in the reader's mind. Eric told Cape before it was published:

> I am glad indeed that you like *The House of Gair*. Much of it grew, almost unbidden, from a simple idea that came to me when I was driving one day in the gaunt north-west—and I think it moves with a natural development of excitement.

Eric's sixteenth novel was his first to use a first-person narrative, and he evidently found pleasure in the discipline both in plotting and style required by this method. Its most interesting feature is the character of Hazeldon Crome, the complex and curiously attractive old man whose amorality and criminal activities involve the narrator, a somewhat humorless novelist called Stephen Coryat, in the action. Crome, who operates from his hideous old house on the rocky Atlantic shore of Sutherland, has been a writer from the days of the Yellow Book, talks with familiarity of Beardsley, Max Beerbohm, 'Bosie' Douglas and others, and has dealt for many years in blackmail and forgery. Yet in his way he is a devoted writer of integrity, and Eric puts so much of his own philosophy about literature and criticism into his mouth that at times it has the feeling of an ironic and destructive kind of self-portrait. Marjorie thought that Hazeldon Crome was the most complete and satisfying character Eric had yet devised—'I am rather alarmed by this preference,' said Eric to Cape—and many will agree with her. Crome's reflections on art and literature and his elegant and insidiously logical brand of evil lend the novel a curious tone, while Eric's use of a gothic-romantic machinery to tell the story is dextrous and effective. Vividly descriptive and evocative of the different settings in the Highlands, in the south of England, and in the Mediterranean, the writing however has a sparer and tenser texture than the luxurious and uproarious language somewhat thoughtlessly associated with the name of Eric Linklater, and Eric's chief satisfaction was in the discipline by which a means of expression appropriate to the content and the apparent narrator has been secured.

His work during the summer on *The Faithful Ally* and on the preliminary soundings for *The Ultimate Viking* which were involving him in much reading and thinking about history had been productive but exhausting, and by the end of October he was ready for his autumn holiday. Asking Rupert Hart-Davis if he would like to be taken out to a play and some supper ('I know you poor Londoners never go to the theatre unless you're dragged there by us provincials. I leave the choice to you; I've seen nothing, I know nothing'), he confessed he was feeling 'passé, cassé et lassé'. His historical researches had led to two scholarly essays, 'The Scottish Monarchy in the Fourteenth Century' in *History Today*, and 'The Battle of Largs' in the *Orkney Miscellany*, and the return to matters of history and especially Viking history was proving very satisfying. With a shrug for the reviewers who had failed to appreciate *The House of Gair*, he left for the south in late October and enjoyed a break which took in, among other things, a visit to Cambridge on 3 November to speak against Stephen Potter in a Union debate on the motion that 'This House admires its Victorian ancestors'. Although already in some moods beginning to adopt his pose as the last of the Victorians, he roundly attacked the motion and, with 'a really good debating speech' in which 'wit was often bubbling to the surface but never permitted to obscure the issues',[3] secured its total rejection.

Early in 1954 Eric accepted from John Moore an invitation to come and play a part in the Cheltenham Festival:

> I don't feel that Cyril Connolly will be quite such hilarious company as Dylan [Thomas], but I'm willing—I am almost eager—to debate the thesis you put forward . . . that 'The essence of a novel is the story' . . . I have marked 6 October in my diary; but as I always lose my diary that may not be so much help as you think.

Moore comically replied a little later that Cyril Connolly, on hearing that Eric was to be his opponent, had hurriedly said that he was going to be abroad, and that he didn't like public speaking anyway, and had clearly been frightened to death at the prospect. Now he was hoping to get V. S. Pritchett instead.

The spring passed quietly as Eric completed *The Faithful Ally*. Michael Howard, who had now joined his father Wren Howard at Cape's, was very hopeful for the new novel. Wren Howard, knowing of Eric's predilection for writing alternately fiction and non-fiction, had suggested in January that he might consider doing a biography of Winston Churchill, but after some excited thought Eric realised he was alarmed by the magnitude of the task:

I've been thinking a good deal about your Winstonian idea—Too much for comfort. I'm attracted to it strongly, but am shaken by the difficulties ... Isn't it possible that someone with the advantage of personal association and political inner knowledge is already at work on a biography that would claim more authority than mine?

In the end he preferred to 'scrap the Winstonian idea—the odds against are too long' and keep on with his Viking book, though he promised to keep an open mind about doing a biography of Wavell when the papers eventually became available. In fact he became very keen on writing the life of Wavell, and it was one of his bitterest disappointments when his hero's widow, who had apparently approved of the choice of Eric as official biographer, afterwards appointed John Connell instead.

One fine early summer day in 1954 the post brought a most pleasant surprise as a representative of Her Majesty wondered diplomatically whether Mr Linklater would, in the event of its being offered, be disposed to accept nomination for appointment to the rank of Commander of the Order of the British Empire. Eric accepted the CBE, both pleased and exhilarated by the honour.

In June he went as usual to Orkney with Nick Roughead for a fortnight's fishing, and then in July flew to Iceland for further researches in Viking history. The expenses of Icelandic life appalled him, as he told Rupert Hart-Davis:

I have now discovered it costs £8 a day to hire a car, so I shall have to go round by bus, and spend some nights, I fear, in rather dubious comfort. Also— believe this or not—this hotel, and such others as exist, are DRY! Who says I do not suffer for my art?

After his return he described his trip to John Moore:

I enjoyed myself very much under the Arctic Circle, after I had got acclimatised, and I managed to visit all the places I wanted to see on the south-west and north coasts, and catch a few fish as well. I had in all about 3 days' fishing, in three different rivers, and took 8 salmon up to 12½ lbs—and the best day was in the wildest river.

There had been much correspondence between Eric and John Moore since February specifically about arrangements for the Cheltenham Festival. Alan Pryce-Jones was going to oppose Eric in the debate about story as the heart of the novel, and Eric had undertaken also to chair a poetry-reading and to address an audience of schoolchildren on 'Reading for Fun'. But all their plans came to nothing when in late September Eric suddenly became ill—struck down by leprosy, he told Michael Howard—with an irritating and unpleasant dermatitis. Feeling like 'Maclean and Fuchs both rolled into one' he cancelled his engagement: 'I shall be in an Edinburgh nursing-home covered in tar.' Very equably in the circumstances Moore sent sympathetic words hoping for a speedy recovery and recommending for reading the Book of Job.

Marghanita Laski good-naturedly spoke to the schoolchildren in Eric's stead, but using her own words; Eric's talk on the pleasures of reading was too personal to him for someone to use successfully. In it he would have begun with his personal delight in travel books, such as Patrick Leigh Fermor's *The Traveller's Tree* or Arthur Grimble's *A Pattern of Islands*, not to mention *The Travels of Baron Munchausen*. He wrote:

> The study of literature can be lightened if you approach it not, as it were, from the west end, but from the east. When you feel it an intolerable burden to be called upon to show your appreciation of really good poetry, you can sometimes escape, for a little while, by enjoying what is clearly bad poetry.

The proposition was proven by a lengthy quotation from McGonagall's 'The New Railway Bridge over the Silvery Tay', and from there he proposed to range through samples from Harry Graham, Hilaire Belloc and John Skelton, the ballad of 'The Strange Visitor' and a passage from *Nicholas Nickleby* in a demonstration of 'reading for pleasure, which is the only proper way of reading'. The whole highly entertaining tour through some 'oddities and curiosities of English literature' was intended to reach a high point with a suggestion that one should scrape an acquaintance with the giants of literature through biography, and as an illustration he offered the account of Wordsworth and his friends at a literary party which became a disaster as recorded in his *Autobiography* by Benjamin Haydon. The story was a personal favourite of Eric's, and he returned to it two or three years later when it was clearly the inspiration for a wonderful chapter in *Position at Noon* (1958). To finish his Cheltenham talk, Eric played the game of designing a suitable library for a desert island:

> You would of course be sure to take a complete Shakespeare, *War and Peace*, Boswell's *Life of Johnson*, *Candide*, and perhaps *Don Quixote* ... and that perennial entertainment, Mark Twain's *Huckleberry Finn*.

It is a pity the speech was never delivered; it gives a good idea of the catholicity of Eric's taste and of his sensible and down-to-earth approach to literature. The children would have enjoyed it and benefited from it.

The autumn saw the publication of *The Faithful Ally* which, as Eric explained in the World Books broadsheet when his novel was later selected by the Reprint Society, had had a very long period of gestation indeed:

> A novel has to grow before it's written, and sometimes it grows as slowly as a tree on a timber-line ... In the winter of 1935 I was in India ... and spent a pleasant weekend in a club where I felt curiously at home. I say 'curiously' because the other members of the club were all Indians. They were charming

people ... and they were amusing, impressive, dashing, boring, in a very English way. They had acquired English habits, mannerisms, turns of speech, and only in appearance did they seem different from my clubs in London and Edinburgh: the Indians seemed much more handsome. It occurred to me then that long after England had shed the last rag of its imperial mantle there would probably be other races who, taught by the English, would still go about their business with a fine, untroubled air and such a proud, happy confidence as no one had seen in England since 1912 ... That was the beginning of *The Faithful Ally*, and it stayed comfortably in my mind until 1951 when, by a most improbable turn of fortune, I found myself in New Guinea; and in New Guinea I found a highland setting that demanded a dramatic action for its high-pitched solitude ... I began to write, but ... the first effort got into a contrary current and went adrift ... All I can say, with any assurance of truth, is that the first seed fell into my mind in 1935.[4]

The novel met with a reception that went some way to restoring Eric's confidence, with reviewers finding it not only witty and entertaining but also decently serious in theme. J. W. Lambert in the *Sunday Times* remarked that it was somewhat too professionally skilled and easy, an observation which has a certain irony in the light of Eric's account of the long period over which the book had sought its shape, and the discussion of the problems of writing a novel which he had included in *A Year of Space*:

> It is one of the hazards of the trade, and one of the writer's penalties, that hard work can be put into failure as inconspicuously as into success. A good novel or play conceals the labour of its making.[5]

The Faithful Ally had evidently concealed its labour only too well. But it sold steadily, and brought him a most acceptable lump sum from the Reprint Society in 1956, and this, as he said more than once, was the professional writer's proper criterion of success. In the United States, under the title of *The Sultan and the Lady* (which Eric hated), it was noted approvingly.

At the heart of the novel is a vivid account of an uprising among the stone-age savages of 'Namua' against the British authorities. Involved in dealing with the insurrection are half a dozen characters whose interaction both before and after the central conflict is the main source of interest, especially the charming, able, amoral, anglicised Sultan, a descendant of the 'Faithful Ally' of the title, and his most recent companion, the mysterious and beautiful Mrs Nottingham. A very subtle portrait is that of the British Commissioner, the unfortunate James Morland, whose death in a later rebellion is a spring of the action of *The Merry Muse*. In observing this cast of characters in their social, personal and political dance, Eric comments lucidly on the modern world and its relationship with the past through witty and urbane dialogue, while offering a story that, despite its laughter and excitement, has elegiac tones, a sense of past greatness and of talents now tragically wasted.

Eric's winter work was mainly spent on Viking lore, but he took time out to write another play at the instigation of James Bridie for the Citizens' Theatre. When duly produced in late February 1955 with Fulton Mackay and William Franklyn in the cast, *The Isle of Women* seemed to have some promising life in it, but nothing came of it and it was never published. Eric reported to John Moore:

> I've had a dullish winter—grinding slowly like the mills of God—a play that had a two weeks' run in Glasgow and quietly died—my interminable Norse book, that now bashfully approaches its last quarter—some preparation for the next novel . . . Oh, yes, and I've been planting trees. That's virtuous, anyway.

At one stage Barbara Bray of the BBC, hearing of the new Linklater play, wrote asking for a copy of the script to assess its potential for broadcasting, but readers in the Drama Department decided it was not up to scratch. Little that Eric could do as a scriptwriter was good enough for readers at the BBC at this time, though oddly enough he was just entering on a period where his personality as an impromptu broadcaster on panel programmes became much in demand, at least in Scotland.

He was deeply touched in March when, through Robert Henriques who had agreed to help run it, John Moore asked him again to come to the Cheltenham Festival. Concerned about the way he had, as he felt, let them down so badly the previous year he promised: 'I shall be very glad if I can do anything to make up for that failure.' He suggested the organisers should ask the schoolboys and girls to nominate a topic for debate; or, if they didn't care for that, what about 'That fiction is truer than history'? It was arranged eventually that he would oppose Marghanita Laski on 'That reading is a dangerous drug', and he looked forward greatly to the encounter.

Meanwhile, once he had finished *The Ultimate Viking*, he was enjoying a summer of 'beachcombing'; he told John Moore:

> I have been scandalously and almost shamelessly idle. I can scarcely get into my study for unopened correspondence, among which there may be the most frightful intimations of disaster. But meanwhile the sun is shining and there's still a bottle or two in the cupboard.

He went to fish in Skye with Doyne Bell, but had a disappointingly unrewarding time with his rod. On his return, Marjorie kept him busy socially, as he told Compton Mackenzie:

> I live, for the moment, in the midst of monstrous frivolity: we entertain (and are entertained by) the most glittering Admirals, and all the telephone wires are occupied by high-spirited arrangements and re-arrangements of parties. A

bazaar for Lord Roberts' Workshops and a Harvest Festival (for God, presumably) further complete the atmosphere. Marjorie is indignant with the Rector for arranging his Harvest Festival on the same day as she is having a luncheon-party.

But after his 'dissolute, irresponsible, vagrant and most agreeable' summer, he buckled on his harness again and this time got to Cheltenham and made a characteristically breezy and enjoyable contribution to its success. Then he settled to a new novel, the basis of which had been knocking at the back of his mind since 1941.

At this time Rupert Hart-Davis, whose business was in financial difficulties and who was being made rather ill with worrying about what to do, wanted to know what Eric, as an original stockholder, suggested. Eric advised him not to sell out to Heinemann, as Rupert was tempted, for a rather poor return:

> I want to keep my money on you. I know as much about publishing and bookselling as anyone not in the trade, and there's no doubt you are still the best animal over the literary jumps since 1945 ... Go *on*—take in new stable-boys, new jockeys, new corn-merchants, but run under the same colours, and to hell with the notion of 'pulling' at this stage.

A few weeks later he was offering Rupert further encouragement as a prospect of a possible arrangement with Eyre & Spottiswoode offered a solution:

> I am desperately sorry that all your worry and hard work and disappointment have made you ill ... I do hope the E. & S. proposal materialises, and fatly. But if it doesn't, well, it's not worth hanging on if you're going to make a wreck of your health ...
>
> I'm in the middle of a horribly difficult book. Wading breast-high against a strong current, on a rocky and treacherous bottom, and although there are fish in the water, they're damned sullen and slow to move. What a ridiculous life one leads. Shall we give it up and do a Gauguin? Sell your business for what it will fetch, and we'll go to Tahiti or some such place. Tell your secretary to get a shipping-list.

The novel causing such technical difficulties was *The Dark of Summer*. While he was in the early stages of it, *The Ultimate Viking* was published in early November, and received reasonably appreciative reviews, about as good as he had learned to hope for, though hardly as enthusiastic as he would have liked after all the work that had gone into it. He had devoted himself to doing something very close to his heart in his survey of the Sagas and his attempt to understand the realities and the motivations of the people who figure in those stories. 'Admittedly,' he said to Rupert,

> I wrote the *Viking* with some notion of duty in mind, and when I finished it I said, 'Well, I've paid my debt to Orkney.' But I only do agreeable duties, and I

took great pleasure—though it was damned hard work—in trying to find what underlay all the blood and axe-work in the north.

His book proudly disclaimed professional historical validity, but showed evidence of wide reading, individual thinking and enormous delight in its subject. More a personal document than a historical treatise, *The Ultimate Viking* advances theories—about the aesthetic motivation of the Norsemen and the importance in British history of the Norse strain in the blood—which are not universally acceptable but which are the product of dedicated studies by a most perceptive and thoughtful investigator. It is also highly entertaining; the versions of selected tales are written with all the laconic immediacy of *The Men of Ness*, and the arguments are marshalled and related to the evidence with great narrative skill.

A handsomely produced edition issued by Harcourt, Brace in the United States also attracted a fair amount of attention, and some eulogistic reviews; likely though it be that a fair number of new readers were brought by the book to interest in the Vikings, their history and their literature, however, it was not sufficiently successful in either country to achieve a second edition. However, he had not yet done with the Norsemen, and as his impulse to fiction during the next decade was increasingly defeated by unappreciative reviews and falling sales figures, so he turned back to the Vikings, and to historical and topographical writing in general.

20 Eclipse at Noon

In October 1955 Eric gave the inaugural address for the new academic year at the Leeds School of Medicine. With his own distant studies as a medical student vividly present in his mind, he reflected on the current state of the medical profession after ten years of the National Health Service, and spoke wittily and inspiringly on the lessons of the past and the challenge of the future.

He invoked the Prometheus legend to consider how the advance of science had brought its problems, for, amid all the new knowledge, a great deal of the old knowledge had been lost. Prometheus stole fire, which became the precursor of all human arts and crafts; but fire was difficult to control, and had brought bane as well as blessing:

> So we, who are about to enjoy the increasing power and comfort of our Promethean age, enter our inheritance with a feeling of guilt, a sensation of fear ... because fire in untaught hands can easily consume those hands, and all their neighbours.[1]

We had need of the hope which is given humankind in another chapter of the Promethean myth, he said; and our best hope lay in the certainty that human nature would not change. Although a witness in a slaughter-house might be impressed by the anatomical similarities between animals and human beings, a moment's reflection would recall the human advantages of laughter and the compulsion to work. These were important faculties for a potential doctor, for in dealing with humankind,

> You will have the permanent satisfaction of reading, simultaneously, a detective story that abounds in clues and has no end, and a poem, occasionally sublime, whose strength and tenderness, pathos and beauty, do not exclude some rough humour.

This sentence summarises well what had been his own attitude to life throughout his books, and his romantic enthusiasm was further revealed in the rest of his speech. Comparing 'the convoluted tubules of the kidney, the rhythmical capsule of the spleen, or the infinite benignity of the gall-bladder' with a steam-engine such as Kipling celebrated in 'M'Andrew's Hymn', he said:

> Here are mechanisms far more delicate, exact and perdurable than any steam-engine, and equally designed to work 'at ony tilt an' every rate o' speed'. But the

greatest, the wildest poetry is seen, not in the post-mortem room, but in the labour ward; for that emerging head may contain murder or genius.

Eric's address, ranging from high-spoken enthusiasm to earthy and dry-witted medical jokes, ended with the cheerful prediction that 'though you may die of overwork, it is quite unlikely that you will perish of boredom'.

Despite his frequent protestations that his life had been benighted by his own incurable idleness, Eric himself was in more danger of the penalties of overwork than boredom. The winter was occupied principally with overcoming the technical difficulties of the new novel, *The Dark of Summer*. His reading of the Norse sagas and the visits to Orkney, Shetland and Iceland to brush up his topographical knowledge had stirred memories of his wartime service in the northern archipelagos. From that basis in experience had evolved a complex story concerning the adventures during and after the war of a man called Chisholm, whose life becomes enmeshed in an ancient family quarrel in Shetland. Getting the structure right required much jiggling of elements and rewriting, but Eric was fascinated by the problems. Much later he confessed to Rupert Hart-Davis:

Since re-reading it I have felt, with horrid discomfiture, that I made a mess of the construction. Chisholm's development—his coming to life— ... should have led strongly to the end of the Wishart story ... and this doesn't happen as it should because the major excitement is all in the first half ... It was the lure of the rounded shape that misled me. How difficult it all is!

Not all readers of *The Dark of Summer* would agree that its construction is unsatisfactory. It certainly did not seem so to Eric when in the spring of 1956 he delivered the novel to Cape's and, with a sigh of relief, took a holiday. Marjorie had for a long time been persuading him to take her to Africa and this he now did, though unenthusiastic about quite so dramatic a change of scene.

The holiday was intended as an opportunity for them to escape decisively from a domestic background and routine in which Marjorie especially was aware of some loosening of the bonds that held them together. They hoped in the greatness and novelty of Africa to rediscover their former totality of commitment to each other. They had been married for twenty-three years, their eldest children had grown up, and Eric, because of the nature of his work and of his temperament, had failed to see the danger signs of Marjorie's lack of real contentment. The ten-year age gap between them for a while became significant for Marjorie; now in her forties, she subconsciously knew that if any change in her life was going to be made, it would have to be soon. Her election to the Ross and Cromarty County Council in 1954 had given her a lot more to do, but it did not fulfil her sufficiently to dispel an ache for a more romantic life while she was still young and pretty enough to take it if a chance should come.

Eric wrote to Rupert from Entebbe describing the African adventure:

Having a wonderful time—wish you were here—if only to take a spell at the wheel; we've already done 1400 miles in a small hired-car, most of it on horrid roads through splendid country (mountain and forest) and Marjorie is still untired and clamouring for more—but the Old Man is a little jaded. High spot was the Q.E. National Park on the border of the Belgian Congo, with elephant, buffalo, hippo, flamingo and all the rest of it; and this place, on the edge of Lake Victoria, is wonderfully trim, well-gardened, and peaceful though hot. At the end of the week we fly to Southern Rhodesia.

Instead of bringing them closer together, the trip was almost fatal to their marriage, for Marjorie found the opportunity she half wished for, half dreaded, and fell into a liaison with the dashing figure of a naval officer whom they met—not exactly by chance.

When Eric discovered what had happened, he was at first appalled at having been, as he felt, betrayed, and divorce suddenly and sadly became a possibility. But, faced with all that that would entail, Marjorie realised the folly of her behaviour, and Eric, perhaps understanding though not openly acknowledging his own contribution to their breakdown, sought for ways by which to subdue his hurt pride and to avert the disaster that seemed imminent. Sensibly, though not altogether quietly, they talked their problems through, and to the relief of both came to the realisation that they both still needed each other.

Some time after the main crisis Marjorie told her sister Alison what had happened, and Alison, who had always resented aspects of Eric's treatment of his wife, nearly upset matters again by declaring her sympathy for Marjorie. Eric wrote to Alison:

When the truth emerged, I forgave her. I did this at very great cost to myself and after a period of extreme agony of mind. And I was rewarded by seeing in Marjorie such apparent happiness, such peace of mind, as she hadn't enjoyed for quite a long time. I was rewarded, I say, because I love her, and it gave me great easement to see her happy again.

In her reply Alison grasped the opportunity to tell Eric a few home truths about his attitude to Marjorie, calling his reaction to her little peccadillo 'Victorian melodrama' and urging:

Marjorie loves you; I know that from her letters. Her worst punishment has been the knowledge that she has hurt the person she loves best. But what she needs from you is a little tenderness; some appreciation of herself as a person; more love and gentleness—she has always needed more of these than you have been able to give. If you can now give her what she needs, then the future holds happiness for you both. But if you are harsh to her; if you are suspicious and jealous and possessive; if you try to separate her from her friends, then the prospects are not rosy. I do not mean that she would ever deceive you again; but she might cease to love you.

I always feel that Marjorie has never quite grown up. *You* are to blame for that, Eric. You have treated her as a child; talked down to her; snubbed her in public (I've heard you); not treated her as an intellectual equal—in spite of this, Marjorie has always loved you and never allowed any criticism of you.

Eric took Alison's words to heart, and answered with some humour a week or so later, confessing that he had been something of a 'resentful clown', but insisting that adultery could never be insignificant, and that sexual jealousy was inevitable where there was strong physical love—as in him for Marjorie, the fact that he was not far off sixty notwithstanding. He had, he said, always offered Marjorie tenderness, but she had seemed to regard it as a tiresome Victorian remnant. It was very difficult to please. And he acknowledged:

> That I have behaved to Marjorie, from time to time, with a sad imperfection, I have already admitted to her. That her behaviour has sometimes deserved less than an Alpha Plus has also (I think) been admitted . . . Now, out of our double unhappiness, we have 'made it up'; and look to the future with bold intention and timorous hope.

The exchange of letters with Alison cleared the air and set the seal on their intention never again to break faith with each other. Eric tried to reduce the force of his overbearing manner, and succeeded to an extent, partly by turning it into more of a joke than it had been, partly by achieving with age a greater equanimity. If there were moments when he was moody and depressed, or when he still spoke more harshly than was desirable— and there were—both knew a little better how to deal with it. Few people ever knew how close they had come to parting.

Before the matter came to light Eric went in July to Scandinavia for a fortnight. He wanted to write a programme about Norway for the BBC, and he wanted to get together with Karl Gullers again and discuss some possibilities of work with him. He behaved, he told Marjorie, like a regular tourist, going up to the Arctic Circle to see the midnight sun, voyaging round the tiny offshore islands at Bergen with the Postmaster in attendance, and taking advantage of a chance to catch three salmon in the river skirting the country-house of a shipowner who was his temporary host.

On his return he dined in London with Rupert Hart-Davis at the Garrick Club; in a thank-you letter to Rupert he recalled it, and the behaviour of Doyne Bell in particular:

> I thought Doyne looked a trifle embarrassed when I saw him a day or so later. Given a few drinks he recaptures, I think, the youthful emotion of 'Let's all go round to Tony's place.' Only to find that youth is gone and Tony's is deserted.

The Dark of Summer was published by Cape's in September. A striking, original and compelling novel, it was read by the reviewers without notice-able perception. *The Times* said, for instance, 'Mr Linklater is a most persuasive storyteller, and although he breaks the rules in *The Dark of Summer*, the spell cast by his twilight story holds.'[2] Eric could not under-stand why an experimental structure in his book should be characterised as 'rule-breaking' and reluctantly condoned, while in the books of certain other writers such experiment would be seen as the vital element which rendered possible high-level critical discussion. The novel received quite good selling reviews, and was a Recommendation of the Book Society, though not its Choice. A year or so later it was the selection of the Popular Book Club run by Odham's Press and was quite widely circulated, so at least it made him a little money. It ought to have earned him increased respect as a novelist.

In *The Dark of Summer* Eric examines minutely the theme of treachery, a theme as deep, serious and important as any he ever attempted. As in *The House of Gair* he uses a first-person narrative, and controls the tone and language to project a superficially rather humourless, pedestrian narrator. The story is again complex, as in *The House of Gair*, but with a much wider and deeper canvas, both in time and space. Two plot threads are inter-woven to throw light upon each other, so that Tony Chisholm's journey through wartime and peacetime experience towards understanding and acceptance of himself is recounted in the context of an ancient mystery with which he becomes involved in Shetland, where he has settled. Despite the fears he confided to Rupert Hart-Davis, in his technical mastery of the narrative Eric is quite dazzling. The writing is economical and intelligent, without the Linklaterian rumbustiousness that would be inappropriate to its narrator, but with most effective communication of the peculiar lonely beauty of the Faeroes and Shetland, and with an evocation of wintry conditions and storm at sea reminiscent of the power of *The Men of Ness*. Eric was remembering his own journey of 1941 when he wrote:

> Now the gale was at its height, but the movement of the sea was still increasing. It was no longer merely very rough. It became a huge and vehement, an abysmal violence, on which roughness supervened. Now the movement came from great depths that had been slow to answer the gale's demand, but now, as it seemed, were rolling in a cosmic tide from whose gigantic billows, rising dark and high above the bridge, the storm tore a continuous spray: and in whose sickening troughs an undertow, or contrary swell, often laid us low upon our side. Into these deep valleys of the sea the trawler sank and shuddered; then, with its bow pointing to the sky and the gun on its forward deck aiming at high clouds, it climbed to mountainous and tattered crests that filled its main deck with white water, and with a roll and a twist rushed down again, out of the wind, but into the roaring menace of the next great wave.

Time lost its ordinary measure. Time was measured only by the black hills we must climb, the monstrous valleys into which we swooped.[3]

The Dark of Summer has as part of its mechanism a book within the book, reputedly written by the strange, rather magnificent but tragically deluded Mungo Wishart, whose activities in wartime Shetland Chisholm has to investigate. Inspired by a Scottish *cause célèbre* of the nineteenth century, in it Eric/Wishart tells a complicated and riveting tale of a quarrel over an inheritance, following the fortunes of a family from generation to generation. As in the Prologue to *Juan in America*, and the explanation of the Gander inheritance in *Ripeness is All*, these genealogical concerns become valid almost for their own sake in 'The Wishart Inheritance' within *The Dark of Summer*, and mark a step towards the similar concerns of Eric's next novel, *Position at Noon*. Eric's interest in history, its importance and its uses, was growing palpably stronger.

About this time he stepped up his work as a broadcaster, taking part frequently, for instance, in BBC Scotland's *Arts Review* programme. George Bruce, responsible for directing the programmes during the years 1957 to 1965, found him to be a curious and sometimes unpredictable colleague. At first he was impressed by Eric's veneer of unshakeable confidence ('the commanding officer type'), and was surprised and rather touched to find that the brusque military exterior was a manufactured cover for a sensitive and rather insecure man. This role led Eric sometimes into making rather cruel, even coarse observations on personal matters, especially on one occasion recalled by Bruce when he had 'taken more liquor than desirable'. Yet at other times he could be 'wholly human, generous in remark, witty, discreet in his entries into the discussion'. In his prepared material he was never disappointing, full of brilliant and pointed comment and showing what Bruce thought an unusually wide range of sympathies; he recalled:

> As might be expected, his review of *The Playboy of the Western World* at the Pitlochry Festival Theatre on 6 July 1957 was rich in imaginative comment, as were his reviews of eighteenth-century plays, Congreve and the like. But I also asked him to review *The Making of Classical Edinburgh* by A. J. Youngson, and also *The Cherry Orchard*. The singular appropriateness of his response seemed to me to transform the man who enjoyed letting off verbal fireworks with the enjoyment of showmanship into a quite different persona. First there was the careful scholar responding to the architectural excellence of the neo-classical building of Georgian Edinburgh, and then ... his unexpected understanding of the inwardness of Chekhov.[4]

Revivals of Eric's earlier pieces, *Socrates Asks Why* and *Sealskin Trousers*, were broadcast on the BBC's Home Service in May and July 1956, and his Norway revisited piece, 'Sunburnt Girls on the Rocks' in October. But a suggestion by Finlay Macdonald that he should produce a radio version of *The Dark of Summer* was rejected firmly by a BBC reader who pronounced the writing 'mawkish and sentimental'; an idea that Eric should go to Israel and make a programme was received lethargically and later shelved; and a new conversation-piece that he had written and sent to Val Gielgud was rejected with an even more scathing report by a BBC reader. As this piece, 'Invention for Four Voices', was later published in *A Sociable Plover* (1957), anyone interested can try to assess why it was found lacking. For whatever reason, his work as a scriptwriter seemed less than welcome at the BBC in London even as his work as a performer in Scottish programmes brought in regular supplements to his income.

During the year 1956–7 Eric enjoyed the highest honour his old school could bestow upon him when he was installed as President of the Former Pupils' Club. He appeared, said his eulogist in the Aberdeen Grammar School Magazine, to be superseding as Most Venerable (but not, of course, Most Ancient) Former Pupil one, George Gordon, Lord Byron, whose sojourn at the school was commemorated through the piety of an older generation in imperishable bronze. Was there no guidance to be found in their example, he demanded. Eric who, as the writer anticipated, would certainly not have wanted his statue next to that of Byron outside the school gates, was nevertheless delighted to be President of the FPC, and he fulfilled his duties in that capacity during the year with gravely humorous decorum.

He spent the winter polishing a long short story that he had promised some time earlier to offer to Rupert Hart-Davis, and in February sent it, together with two other short stories and two radio pieces, to him for his consideration. He wrote:

> Frankly, unambiguously, but perhaps ego-swayed to a higher rating than they deserve, I think well of these tales. But if you don't, you will say so with the brutality inculcated under Slough and fortified by Geo. Monk's Regt of the Second Guards. It will please me very greatly if you decide to publish. And if you don't, I'll drop a tear in secret and never tell you where it fell.

In March he went for a fortnight to stay with Robert Henriques at Théoule Supérieure on the French riviera. Marjorie joined him for the second week. 'Wonderful weather here, lots to eat and drink, otherwise idle,' Eric reported to Rupert. And he told Douglas Young:

> The riviera is very fine for a few days of idleness, and Robert's house, on a red peninsula falling precipitous to the sea, is handsome and comfortable and kindly attended. But God keep me from living there: OK for the rich, the pansy and the sedentary snob, but not for us young men of high endeavour.

His spirits were as high as the endeavour he claimed. Rupert had written approvingly of his stories and, with the effect of making his financial situation quite comfortable for at least two or three years, he was about to begin work on a commission from Rio Tinto Zinc to write a history of their organisation. As this would involve him in more extensive travelling, to Spain, Canada, the United States and Australia at least, he was well satisfied with life, specially as the unhappy marital troubles now seemed well behind them.

His first trip for the RTZ project was to Spain in April; he told John Moore about it:

> I had a nice little jaunt in Spain, and went down a mine and saw some gipsies in Seville and that sort of thing: in fact, I did a bit of work and had a bit of fun—and saw (and was properly surprised at) the Prado for the first time in my mis-spent life. Also—what was very interesting—ran into curtains of reticence about the part played by the Rio Tinto miners in the Civil War. I'll have to do some tactful but penetrating exercises there.

In mid-May, feeling 'as empty as an old tin bucket in the desert' after working on a play which, he told Rupert, had been hell to do, he went to London to see the galley-proofs of *A Sociable Plover* which was already in production. He and Rupert went to the theatre, an occasion which Rupert recalled:

> I told him that what he (as a bucolic barbarian) needed was a spot of culture but he said he'd prefer 'a leg show'. By the time I picked him up at his club he had failed to get seats for *Grab Me a Gondola* or anything else, so I reverted to culture and dragged him unwillingly off to the Arts Theatre to see Genet's play *The Balcony* ... The actors were all appallingly bad, the play pretentious and windy—rather like the reverse of the Maeterlinck model—instead of 'Moonshine' they repeatedly said 'Shit' and 'Bugger'. We stuck it to half-time and then repaired to the Ivy for an excellent meal.[5]

In July Ralph Richardson and his wife, Mu, came to Pitcalzean, and after their departure Eric wrote to thank them for being the most generous of guests, who reversed the natural order of things; for normally it was the host who gave and the guest who received:

> But you, ignoring all precedent and convention, shower rich gifts upon your trumpery host—I still await the two dancing girls you promised—and leave them lapt in the luxury of Havana's enchanted perfumes. What a lovely box to get! I dote on cigars—but Havanas only—and with my Scotch background am always too mean to buy them.

Everything seemed to be going well. He had that day been fishing on a Highland river, forty miles away, and after terrible exertion had caught the noblest fish of his experience:

21 William Hewison's cartoon
of Eric in *Punch*, 1958

ERIC LINKLATER

*In Juan's day we knew a roistering
Linklater;
He only started seriously to think later.*

22 Emilio Coia's caricature in pastel of Eric from a
sitting arranged in James Robertson-Justice's
house at Spinningdale, Sutherland, where Coia
was the weekend guest. Eric was a near neighbour
and drove over specially for the sitting; all three
were well known to each other. Easter 1967

23 Distant roots: Eric enjoying the sunshine in the old university town of Uppsala, 1964. His maternal grandfather was a Swedish sailor

Such a terrible and splendid fighter, my spirit died and triumphed three times over—and then I brought him in, his silver skin laced with his golden blood when the gillie gaffed him—$11\frac{1}{2}$lbs of pure beauty and virtue.

And then, in September, just as he and Marjorie were about to set off for New York on the *Queen Mary* for a visit to Canada and the United States in the RTZ interest, the worst thing happened that they could have imagined. Their eldest daughter, who had graduated from Cambridge and was teaching in Malvern, was badly hurt in an accident. Eric described it to John Moore:

Poor Sally took a toss from one of those horrid little Italian scooters … She fractured both jaws, and got a deep contusion on the right temple that has gravely injured the optic nerve. What deeper brain injury there *may* be we don't yet know, for she's still unconscious after 24 days.

It was a terrible time. For weeks as Sally lay in a coma, Eric and Marjorie were full of anxiety. The American journey was cancelled; 'the Rio Tinto people were immensely kind,' Eric told Rupert, and all arrangements had been indefinitely postponed. After seven weeks, when Sally began to emerge from the coma, Eric had to go to London on business; his relief was so great that there was an evening in which, as Rupert told George Lyttelton, tension was released in alcohol:

After leaving the Garrick he collected some friends from the Savile and spent most of the night in some frightful nightclub. Next morning he awoke when the bar opened, spent three hours over lunch, and arrived at Soho Square [where the Hart-Davis headquarters were established] very merry indeed. Somehow I propelled him to some nearby binders, where by means of astonishing will-power he managed to make a creditable shot at signing sixty copies of a limited edition of his new book.[6]

'When troubles come,' Claudius said to Gertrude, 'they come not single spies, but in battalions.' Just as it was becoming evident that Sally, though physically scarred, had not suffered serious brain damage, Eric's mother died. She was ninety years old, and had had a good deal of pleasure and success in her long life. In an obituary notice, *The Times* recalled with approval her book of recollections of life at sea. But her parting came inevitably as a blow. 'I expect', said George Lyttelton, commenting to Rupert on the bad time Eric was going through, 'that like most Scots he is used to the bludgeonings of fate.'[7]

By the Christmas of 1957 they had received encouraging reports of Sally's progress at Bangour Hospital near Edinburgh; Marjorie and Eric both felt that they had been drawn even closer together during the period of worry and strain over their daughter; and life was looking more hopeful again. His new book of short stories, however, despite some favourable and some highly enthusiastic reviews, and despite having been produced attractively with wood-engravings by Reynolds Stone, was selling only slowly; in January Eric acknowledged Rupert's rueful sales report:

> I'm so sorry for both of us. It really is sickening to think that nowadays, to get any attention, you have to behave like an Oriental beggar—sit on the pavement outside the Fitzroy and display your sores and pitch into a lazar's whine when you explain how you came by them.

The highest praise of the stories in *A Sociable Plover* had come from Douglas Young, who drew attention to the funny and revealing dedication of the book to 'Robert Henriques, a good soldier, a successful farmer, who for fear of too much happiness has committed himself also to literature'. Eric's commitment to literature and his mastery of his chosen forms are manifest in all five pieces in the book. Besides the two 'conceits'—conversation-pieces written for radio but entertaining and provocative on the page—there are three short stories. 'Escape Forever' is a rollicking and exciting tale about a convict who escapes and travels the breadth of Scotland to exact his revenge on his faithless fiancée and her new husband. He finds his trip abortive and it ends in gales of laughter and the moral that 'there's no one goes unpunished who takes a woman to his house'.[8] 'The Masks of Purpose' reconstructs the massacre at Glencoe and imaginatively inquires into the political reasons why it happened; it is a moving and convincing account of a horrifying episode. At the time of publication, most commentators gave it pride of place among the five components of the book.

But the title story, a novella of supernatural revenge set in the Outer Isles, is the most satisfying and intriguing achievement in the book. It has two narrators, the interweaving of whose contributions is brilliantly controlled and rich in implications. One of them is a novelist whose circumstances and life-views are so similar to Eric's own that it would be tempting—though quite wrong—to believe that his narrative is an exercise in autobiographical fiction. The working out of the plot, when the novelist is tormented for former misdeeds by a 'fetch' in the shape of a bird that rarely visits Scotland, is done with a suggestive and compulsive skill that may remind the reader of the Henry James of *The Turn of the Screw*. A section where Malone prophetically dreams that he follows the Hound of Cuchullin into the loch to drown is very potent, and adumbrates the dream-ridden life of Evan Gaffikin in Eric's last novel. 'A Sociable Plover' demonstrates the substance of Moray McLaren's declaration:

> Linklater can write well indeed about the sun and the south and hard practical matters. Seldom, however, are his power and imagination more potent than when he is dealing with the North and the supernatural of the North.[9]

A product of Eric's visit to Sweden in July 1956, when he stayed with the photographer Karl Gullers and his family at their summer house on the west coast in Bohuslän, *Karina with Love* was published by Macmillan in January 1958. Gullers, a very tall man, had a troop of beautiful blonde daughters whom Eric's elder son Magnus remembered as 'these devastating girls'; Karl used to send out Christmas cards with photographs of the girls in descending order of height, each with an arm outstretched to rest on the slightly lower shoulder of a younger sister. Eric too was captivated by the daughters, and with Karl he collaborated on a children's book, about three girls living in a remote Swedish forest and what happens when the youngest of them goes off to follow the course of the felled trees when they are floated down the river to the distant sea. Karl supplied a portfolio of monochrome photographs and Eric provided the words. The book was given a tentative welcome, and one reviewer said:

> A lovely book, both to look at and to read ... Strictly speaking, this is not a children's book, but a book for the young at heart. Those who buy it to give to some young relation will on second thoughts find it impossible to part with.[10]

But the Linklater of the high-spirited and fantastic *The Wind on the Moon* and *The Pirates in the Deep Green Sea* was not in evidence; instead the story proceeded by a plain, rather subdued narrative which was intended to take second place to Gullers' beautiful and evocative pictures but which lacked sufficient variety and verbal dash in the event to attract a following. Magnus was gravely disappointed in his father's new story, and thought it rather wet. As children at sixteen are inclined to, he thought his old man was going soft. But the book is oddly haunting and atmospheric, and it is a pity it was never reprinted.

At intervals throughout the winter Eric had also been working on a new play for which he began to have the highest hopes. Provisionally called 'A Man of Business' it was set in France in the Middle Ages, and Eric was greatly enjoying the opportunity it gave him to explore with all his wit and panache but also with genuine philosophical concern a number of themes very relevant to modern life: power and authority; love; religion; soldiers and their value to society; the best way to live. The play's construction and use of theatre suggest that he had learned a great deal about dramatic writing from his earlier experiences; it offers some splendid roles and situations, a strong human story as well as wide-ranging debate, dialogue that is witty and stylish, and a single set against which the whole could be played without scene changes. It follows the traditional dramatic unities without strain or artifice, and seems on the page to have tremendous promise.

Among those who read the typescript and thought its potential to be high was Eric's old admirer, Basil Ashmore, who wrote:

I had dedicated two books to him 'as a bribe to get more plays written by a potentially great dramatist'. Finally he sent me *Breakspear in Gascony*. It was all I ever hoped for.[11]

Arrangements were set in hand for it to be produced, under its new title, at the 1958 Edinburgh International Festival, and Macmillan's, in anticipation of the event, published a finely produced edition in May. By the time the book appeared, however, something had gone wrong, and the plans for a Festival production that year had fallen through. Ronald Mavor, James Bridie's son, commenting on this disappointment, suggested that there was some mystery that needed to be cleared up:

> Either the author has since withdrawn the play, as O'Casey did in Dublin, or the Plays Committee at the Festival have decided not to perform it. Although the play has some rumbustious bawdry in it, I do not think that the Lord Chamberlain has put down his stockinged foot ... Could it be that the Plays Committee simply did not like the play? The said committee having shown less than genius in their choice of play in previous years, such a conclusion would not imply any rebuke to Mr Linklater.[12]

In the spring of 1958, as encouraging reports from hospital promised an eventual very good recovery for Sally, and positive responses to his new play came his way, Eric was writing what he became increasingly convinced was his best novel for years. The words of his doomed character Torquil Malone in 'A Sociable Plover' might have been his own: 'I have been working with my old, forgotten zest and with full confidence in the worth of what I write. This is the best of my novels, no doubt of that.'[13] Later, looking back at that year of 1958 when first *Karina with Love*, then *Breakspear in Gascony*, and finally his new novel were all born to enjoy only a brief and unappreciated life, Eric wondered what he had done to suffer such continuous eclipse. He was never able to understand why *Position at Noon*, published by Cape's in October, did not do better; on the last page of *Fanfare for a Tin Hat* he could not resist a sad little reference to the novel which he himself cherished beyond anything else that he had written, at least since 1950:

> I was more deeply disappointed by the indifference which attended the publication of *Position at Noon*: in conception, as well as in execution, it is the wittiest novel I have written, and wit is a quality that I value and expect to be valued.[14]

It was not that the book failed to achieve any notice. Issued in an excellently bound and produced edition, with comical line drawings by Hans Tisdall as decorations to the text, it received enthusiastic reviews from several quarters, and was published soon afterwards in the United States under a different title (*My Fathers and I*) but to a similar welcome.

Pamela Frankau in England said: 'I was taken with some of the helpless giggles that shook me long ago when I first read *Juan in America*. I found acids, fantasies, Rabelaisian interludes and history diabolically re-told.'[15] And P. G. Wodehouse wrote:

> One of the great moments in my life was when I read Chapter One of *Juan in America* ... and now Mr Linklater has obliged with a long book in the same vein. Reading this book is like being escorted through the portrait gallery of some stately home of England by a kindly guide of immense charm and erudition ... He holds you, not with a glittering eye, but by some subtle magic which is difficult to analyse.[16]

In manner *Position at Noon* is a return to the wonderfully polished, sophisticated writing of the earlier Linklater after the deliberately more workmanlike surfaces of *The House of Gair* and *The Dark of Summer*. The stylistic excellence of the book is a feast in itself. Edward Gratiano Vanbrugh tells his personal story in the opening chapters, and explains it by tracing his ancestry backwards through seven previous generations and noting ironically how each Vanbrugh in turn blames some aspect of failure in his life on a fault in his father before him. The middle chapters are effectively a brilliant series of related short stories, given coherence by the theme of the interaction of generations. Eric's friend James Fergusson wrote to him to say that though this was one of the most captivating books he had ever written, there was a problem of overall unity inherent in the form Eric had chosen. But the centrality of the idea that the sins of the fathers may be visited on the sons even unto the second and third generations, and of Eric's implicit rejection of the notion, is sufficient to create a palpable unity. This manifests itself most clearly when Edward, having shown himself to be the product of all that has gone before, finds the vitality necessary to show that the whole thesis may be rejected, or its effects cancelled by action. He severs his links with England, wife, children, lover, all, and goes off to start a new life in the United States. His very rehearsal of his excuses leads him to the realisation that a man may always choose for himself what he will be.

The sense of period and place which distinguishes the various narratives, together with their cultured, sometimes bizarre humour, and their ingenious critical episodes, makes the book a high point in Eric's career. His disappointment when it failed to engage critical attention was very great.

At the time of its publication he was in Canada, for it was a year since Sally's accident had prevented the journey of exploration of Rio Tinto's American empire, and now it was time to take up again the work for which he had contracted. He sailed on R MS *Carinthia* in late September; it was a rough crossing, but there was a hugely comic compensation:

The Atlantic really is a brute: such a vast and wild desolation of black water torn to shreds ... How different from the film I saw this afternoon: it was called *The Vikings*, and I haven't laughed so much since grandpa died. All the seas the Vikings sailed were bright blue and flat as a dish of curds—they ate and drank and shared elementary jokes with prodigious laughter—they all talked like characters in Li'l Abner—the heroine wore a white afternoon-frock and was called Morgana (pronounced 'Murganner')—and the concluding line, after the hero had been killed, was 'Prepare a Viking's funeral'. I waited breathlessly for the addition 'And don't spare the expense'—but alas, it didn't come. That however was my only disappointment.[17]

From Montreal he went to Toronto and thence to Elliot Lake and Blind River to see the uranium miners. He went down a mine, and was given masses of technical information that he didn't really know what to do with, and kept cheerful despite a persistent and heavy rain that obliterated the fabled beauty of the country. After a visit to an exploring party in the wilds of northern Quebec he was flown to Vancouver where, he told Marjorie:

I was immediately met by two kind and enthusiastic people who, indifferent to the fact that I had been 11 hours in the air, began to entertain me with a rolling spate of information about mining, geology, geophysics, finance, the economy of British Columbia, and so forth—but this I quickly interrupted with a demand for drink, and then, after a little delay, I was taken to the Vancouver Club where indeed I was handsomely received.

More explorations in the north and in the canyons of the Fraser River followed ('Very magnificent, but far too much of it') and then he returned to Toronto, where he was taken for 'a little trip' on Thanksgiving Day by one of the people in his Canadian publisher's office who wanted to try out his new Buick. They covered 345 miles and Eric thought it would never end. The next day he signed copies of *My Fathers and I* in innumerable bookshops, did a television interview, and went to a dinner in his honour which was rather spoiled for him by a lamentable Canadian practice of eschewing alcohol at such functions in favour of iced water. At first he thought it was some kind of joke. He came home on the *Queen Mary* on 29 October after spending a few days with his old friends, the Gilkysons, and a day or two in New York.

By December he was already working on a new novel; 'Nothing to report from here but unhealthy stuffing,' he wrote to Rupert Hart-Davis a day or two after Christmas, 'though despite it the old lag gets another rousing chapter out of his Parker 51.' But his energy was unabated, and in March, just after his sixtieth birthday, he was off on his travels again. He told Compton Mackenzie in eager anticipation of his journey:

I go to London on Tuesday night and take off for Melbourne on Thursday morning. The rain-drenched forests of western Tasmania, down in the Roaring Forties, and the sun-whitened deserts of northern Queensland will be my principal ports of call, and I ship myself for home again on 9 May. What fun we have!

Fun he had indeed, as well as work. He wrote to Marjorie from Melbourne:

The Tasmanian trip was strenuous and full of interest, and not without an occasional laugh. It went without accident except when I lost my grip on a greasy rope and went arse-over-tip down a mountainside—but I landed, like a little koala bear, in a soft pile of eucalyptus leaves, quite unhurt, but looking silly.

The rest of the trip kept him fully occupied, trying to record and master facts about mining and prospecting and to relate them to their social and economic consequences. Again he found the northern parts of Australia 'strangely exciting—a savage, untamed land', and enjoyed some parties, one of which, he told Marjorie,

was given by a delightful man called John Rodd, a lawyer of power and influence here, whose wife paid me the compliment of laughing so much at my simple little jokes that her eyelashes swam off in a flood of tears.

His observations of the mining industry done, he sailed for home from Perth aboard SS *Strathmore*, spending his time working on a play he had conceived about Samson and Delilah and, as he assured his wife, behaving alarmingly well. His fellow passengers were mostly 'hearty extravert Australians who play games with tireless enthusiasm from morning till night, and often the swimming-pool is full of chunky girls—but just as often full of ridiculous bald heads, so that it looks as if some gigantic sea-fowl had laid a clutch of eggs there.'

After a quiet summer, in which fishing in Orkney with Nick Roughead was the part that mattered, he prepared himself for a new attack on the theatre. Since the Plays Committee still, after the discussion and complaints of the previous year, did not want to make *Breakspear in Gascony* its official choice, and since no London management had shown any interest since its publication, Eric decided to allow a provincial company to stage it at Edinburgh during the Festival. Basil Ashmore recalled:

I knew that this would be a disaster, and begged him to wait for an all-star production so that his *style* would be allowed to make itself known. Unfortunately, he was too kind-hearted. He felt it would 'help a struggling little rep'. I had not the heart to see it staged, but I foresaw the results.[18]

Ashmore's forebodings proved only too accurate. *The Times* was gravely disappointed when the Perth Repertory Company's production appeared at Edinburgh's Gateway Theatre in August. W. A. Darlington later wrote regretting the missed opportunity, insisting that in its initial production a play, no matter how good, would fail unless a great actor were given the chance to *create*, not merely *play*, the main role.[19] As Darlington and Ashmore expected, and as Eric ruefully learned to accept, the play's essential life had been extinguished by its inadequate production, and *Breakspear in Gascony* was never heard of again. Ashmore later regretted once more its banishment to the back shelves of obscure libraries, saying:

> No one seems even aware of the existence of a play which should be one of the peak attractions of the National Theatre. *Breakspear in Gascony* rivals Congreve in its verbal pyrotechnics, Rabelais in its salty wit, and John Whiting for its powerful depth of thought, yet remaining as Linklaterian as anything he had written at his peak.[20]

At the BBC producer Gordon Gildard and reader Helena Wood enthusiastically proposed a broadcast version, but the idea was overthrown by a sudden burst of savagery from Eric's old friend Val Gielgud, who said:

> I am not in favour of our handling this play. Linklater's particular style does not lend itself to dramatic compression, and the play itself is, I am convinced, a thoroughly inferior example of his work.

The play could not survive such a torpedo-strike, and that was the end of that.

With some trepidation Eric awaited the publication in early September of the novel he had finished just before going to Australia. To his relief the reception of *The Merry Muse* was warm enough, especially in Scotland where its evident love and simultaneous drily satirical view of Edinburgh was greatly appreciated. And Evelyn Waugh wrote enthusiastically in a personal letter:

> What a treat it has been! I think it your best novel, ingenious, admirably constructed and written, strong and funny. What boobies most of the reviewers are! I think they positively dislike correct syntax and a rich vocabulary and I am sure they resent your being Scotch. But I'm sure you won't repine. You have the confidence of a good workman.

The novel portrays a vivid impression of the city of Edinburgh while handling with consummate ease a story of the discovery of a group of sixteen hitherto unknown erotic poems by Robert Burns and the effect this find has on the lives of a closely observed cross-section of Edinburgh citizens—and indeed on a much wider community before the tale is done. Dominated by the characters of the splendidly vital Max Arbuthnot, who finds life very satisfactory, and Hector MacRae, the poet known as Eachain Dubh (or Yacky Doo), who is intent on committing suicide to quit an unsatisfactory world, the story has a controlling machinery in the adventures of a book which keeps getting lost or stolen and returning only to disappear again; and there are many high points in the accounts of dinner parties, confrontations, the mysterious Dionysiac fever which for a while has the whole of Edinburgh in its grip and, above all, two gloriously imagined funerals where the arrangements of men gang agley. In his black-comic treatment of death Eric anticipates by some ten years the tone of Joe Orton's *Loot*. Partly a celebration of Eric's father-in-law's indomitable *élan vital*, it is also a steady and unshaken contemplation of his own state of life, and the optimistic statement that is confided through Max's exuberance is one of the most affecting aspects of the book. For the first time but not the last Eric, as he begins to confront the inevitability of his own old age and death, embodies in his fiction his thoughts and feelings about it; the product is a novel that is both uproariously funny and strangely moving.

While on the subject of Edinburgh, as it were, Eric happily accepted an invitation to write a celebration of the city, and his researches for this project occupied much of his working time-table in the winter of 1959–60. In November he went to Jonathan Cape's eightieth birthday party in London; in February he was writing to Wren Howard about Jonathan's death:

> He seemed to have survived so much that the presumption was that he would run on for ever. But what a good run for his money he had! And what wonderful satisfaction he must have had—and you still have—in looking back to the great Doughty and T. E. Lawrence adventures, and contemplating the vast literary colony you and he established in consequence of that very daring and rather curious pioneer effort . . . And so, although one deplored the old man's going, one couldn't feel that it was a sad and sorry occasion—but the end (as far as he was concerned) of a really great achievement.

The winter had taken its toll of Eric, and in March he went back to the establishment at Tring which had by its unpleasant regimen greatly helped him in the 1930s. He wrote to John Moore:

> A winter of indifferent well-being collapsed into a damned nasty dermatitis, so I resolved on medical attack and came down here to do a three-week cure. A kill-or-cure—and at the moment, so cold it is, so little I've eaten (I've lost a stone and a half), I'm feeling more dead than alive. But I'm looking forward to tomorrow week and a glorious resurrection—and I can almost see great mugs of drink leaping to my hand, and huge collops of beef soaring to my lips.

Much recovered after his session at Champneys he set about enjoying the summer. In June he went with Nick Roughead to Ireland for some fishing, taking Marjorie 'to keep on call as chauffeuse', he told Rupert Hart-Davis. 'We spent a few comical weeks in Ireland,' he reported to John Moore in July—'lots of fun and good food, but very few fish—and I'm just off to Denmark tomorrow to talk some nonsense to someone or other.'

Adjusting to being in his sixties was not easy, and determined enjoyment of the good things of life kept giving way to more contemplative moods. The death of friends became a feature of the day's news, a constant reminder. In July Compton Mackenzie's wife Faith died, and Eric wrote to Mackenzie:

> Though it must have been a merciful release for her—and the termination of long, long anxiety for you—there's no escaping sadness when someone dies who has been part of one's life ... Oh dear, what a lot of remembering a death incurs.

And to John Moore he observed:

> I find myself in the sad position of spending more money than I earn but strangely, perhaps suicidally not bothering. Oh the fearful irresponsibility of old age! And ah! the vanished high-seriousness of youth.

In such a mood, between the sadness and the laughter which this awareness of old age occasioned in him, he reported to Michael Howard at Cape's that he had had an unpleasant year, except for a couple of good patches, and that it hadn't been a good working year because of 'a recurring dermatitis of a mysterious sort—under sedatives much of the time'. He was writing intermittently, but there wouldn't be a 'regular down-to-earth novel—and the children needing boots again. Oh dear, dear.' What he did not mention to Howard was that among the bits and pieces he had been working on was an experimental novel about old age and memories which he was going to offer to Rupert Hart-Davis. This was *Roll of Honour*, for which he had high hopes indeed.

21 A Man Over Sixty

In September 1960 the fruit of Eric's labours during the previous winter was published by George Newnes: not so much a conventional guide-book, the blurb of *Edinburgh* claimed, but more an 'appraisal, full of love, pride, discomfort and shame; a characteristically frank and witty view of a not altogether blameless city'. Decorated with comical line drawings and endpaper maps of the Old and New Towns drawn by Don Pottinger (Unicorn Pursuivant of Arms), and with many photographs from various sources, the book was a very individual piece of work. As stylishly written as anything Eric had ever done, the book celebrates the city from several points of view—personal, historical and social—with a warm and lively appreciation of its people, its architecture, its cultural and even its criminal associations. There are chapters devoted to walking about the city, on eating in the city, on the ghosts that haunt the city. Even those who have no intention of going to Edinburgh, for its Festival or for any other reason, will enjoy its Linklaterian panache and its hodgepodge of anecdote, impression and information.

Eric's devotion of time during this year to the kind of reading needed to produce such a book really marks his entry into a new phase of life. He had always liked to have writing of different kinds under way together, as from the beginning when he had found it possible to alternate novels and biographies. Now the emphasis began to fall more on non-fiction. Rupert Hart-Davis in retrospect thought: 'Towards the end his creative gift petered out and he was obliged to turn to historical hack-work to make ends meet.'[1] While Eric certainly wondered whether he had lost his touch, this was more because of the cruel critical neglect of his novels and something of a slackening-off in the devotion of his paying public than any true inner conviction that his gift had gone. His confidence had been shaken, but ultimately it was not a feeling that he could no longer do it that led to his abandonment of fiction. Rather it was simply no longer worth the candle to write fiction, when his non-fiction was in greater demand.

Not that money was everything, even if his children did need boots. The Rio Tinto project, on which he had spent so much time and energy, was not completed though it was a lucrative commission; Marjorie explained:

Eric visited Canada and Australia and then the West Indies, gathering information. At first the early history of the company entranced him. It went back to the ancient days of copper in Spain, the original Rio Tinto . . . But gradually he became aware of the ruthless political intrigue governing the company's affairs . . . He decided he could not go on, and sacrificed the £2000 or more due to him. He abandoned the manuscripts. They lay in our attic at Pitcalzean and when we left Eric destroyed the lot.[2]

He had always loved history; it had always had some part in his writing; now it became the staple of his output. But not before he had, through the experience of writing four more novels, become convinced that his fiction was no longer wanted and that he had best retire from the fray.

Roll of Honour, which he first mentioned to Rupert Hart-Davis as a novel-in-progress in early 1961, was different in yet another way from anything he had written before, and he awaited Rupert's opinion with some anxiety:

> I have been writing a sort of irregular or 'off-beat' novel, on which I should be grateful to have the opinion of someone whose judgment I can respect: and since the death of Edward Garnett, there's no one in this phylum except you.

The response from his old friend after receiving the typescript in April was all he could have hoped for, and arrangements were made for it to appear under the Hart-Davis imprint the following October. Meanwhile Eric set about the year's other tasks with renewed vigour. He told Rupert of another little commission he had much enjoyed:

> I've just finished an amusing trifle in the *son et lumière* line to be done at Stirling Castle; everything in it but the kitchen sink: Bannockburn, Mary Queen of Scots, the Thin Red Line and Kenneth Muir's VC in Korea—the Castle has been, till this year, the Argylls' depot. Bagpipes and ballads and soldiers' boots: lots of fun.

His real interest was set on plans to go to Greece for a few weeks—'I feel I *need* Greece at this moment'—with the possibility of starting another travel-autobiography book. He had hoped that John Moore or A. D. Peters might be able to accompany him, but when their plans were frustrated he determined to go alone. Just before leaving for the Mediterranean he went with Andro, who was now sixteen, to Tarbert on Loch Fyne to take over a little boat he had bought there, and together they managed to bring it back to Inverness. It was quite an adventure, he told John Moore:

> We had a couple of days of jolly rough weather—for a small open boat (a Shetland skiff with a small motor)—but in spite of a bit of accident here and there, got her up in 5 days . . . Very amusing, and I'm still stiff and tired.

His Greek trip, too, was great fun, he reported to Rupert. 'Oh, much more than that. Deeply impressive and most moving. Such things as Delphi, Delos, Patmos, Mycenae—however familiar as ideas—are tremendous in visible reality.' And to John Moore:

Greece was a winner: absolute and unqualified winner, except for the last jaunt to Hydra, which disappointed. But all the mainland stuff—Delphi, Mycenae and so forth—was supernacular, the island-voyage enchanting—Crete, Rhodes, Cos, Patmos, Delos, Mykonos—and I had a week on Paros which I enjoyed immensely, save for a sad visit from Michael Ayrton, who wasn't well, and who later in Athens fell dangerously ill. But he's home again now.

Although the projected travel-book did not materialise, the Greek background was later incorporated in a novel to very good effect. The summer was occupied mostly with work on *Roll of Honour*, and there was much discussion when Rupert tried to persuade Eric to modify the end of the book; to him it seemed that the farcical conclusion was out of tune and temper with the rest of the novel, but Eric insisted that his central figure's collapse among the books was symbolically rich and necessary:

> That's due to my feeling that we don't want a dying fall for the conclusion, but a little tune of modest triumph . . . Birnie, you see, has at last triumphed over Old Gilmour, of whom he's been afraid all his life. He's discovered that Old Gilmour is not invulnerable; and in his reading of the Roll his spirit has been raised in spite of the sorrow he feels.

He contributed some reviews to the *Sunday Times*, notably of Wynford Vaughan Thomas's *Anzio* and Bernard Fergusson's *Wavell: Portrait of a Soldier*; he broadcast on Hemingway; he wrote letters to *The Times* on such subjects as the Loch Ness monster. New visitors to Pitcalzean included the young historian Ian Grimble, to whose *The Trial of Patrick Sellar* Eric generously contributed an Introduction, and whom he undertook to educate regarding the character of Mary Queen of Scots. As the publication date for *Roll of Honour* approached he was gratified by a letter from Ruth Simon, Rupert's much-valued colleague and later his wife, saying 'the nicest possible things about the novel in the most intelligently nice way',[3] and by the commendations of David Garnett. He was really pleased with the pre-publication copy of the book: 'You've made an excellent job of it, and very nice it looks,' he wrote to Rupert. 'What a nice piece to have! I hope many will think so.'

To his intense disappointment, many did not think so. *The Times* wrote that Mr Linklater deserved louder cheers than he had been getting of late and showed approval of 'a mosaic which vividly depicts life in a small, academically slanted town', but as it in the same review suggested that 'Miss Sparks' new novel, *The Prime of Miss Jean Brodie*', afforded little motive or cue for enthusiasm, its judgement might be considered less than perceptive. Cuthbert Graham praised the novel as 'Dr Linklater's most serious and perhaps his best', and Moray McLaren compared it advantageously with Evelyn Waugh's *Unconditional Surrender* which had just appeared. But no one else had much to say about it. That Eric was angry is apparent from his letter to Rupert soon after:

They were shitty little reviews, weren't they? But for a good long time the cockney reviewers—all but a very few—have been distinguished either by professional ineptitude or personal silliness; and in some instances by both.

Roll of Honour never sold many copies, at least not compared with the thousands his name would have been good for in his prime, no matter what the reviewers said. A couple of years later Rupert reluctantly remaindered it. These facts are quite extraordinary for the novel is, despite its lack of recognition, beautiful and fully achieved. Anthony Burgess acknowledged something of its quality:

> Eric Linklater, one of the finest craftsman of the century, shamefully under-valued, achieved a very successful verse-prose compromise in *Roll of Honour*. This is a gentle, minor work in which a retired schoolmaster reminisces about some of his pupils, dead in the war, and it reserves a loose verse-form for his elegiac musings; for the rest, we have Linklater's fine narrative prose.[4]

More might usefully be said. The change of tone between this novel and its predecessor is startling. As in *The Merry Muse* Eric's subject is death and age, but the ebullient writer whose delight in life and its drolleries produced the vibrant prose of *Position at Noon* and *The Merry Muse* has given way to a more subdued and contemplative observer. The novel is an elegy for the boys of the Cathedral School of 'Inverdoon' whose lives were lost in the Second World War, and it proves to be a vivid and moving document. The reflections of Andrew Birnie about the dead men are presented in an unusual way, using lines of irregular length designed to represent the uneven flow of thoughts in an old man's mind. Because this makes the lines on the page look rather like modern free verse, this narrative form was taken to be intended as poetry, but Eric denied having any such intention. (He had always been scornful of contemporary forms of verse which eschewed traditional rhythms or any kind of rhyme.) Poetry or no, it is a very effective device for summarising the brief lives and sudden deaths of a large number of young men, and for setting off Birnie's inner narrative against the outer story concerning the present. At one stage Eric contemplated incorporating one or two factual mistakes or contradictions into the thoughts thus presented, to show the unreliability of memory alone, but decided that that might be going too far and that it might prove confusing.

Linking Birnie's memories there is a narrative of his own life in the past and up to the present, through which a convincing and affectionate portrayal of a small town very like Aberdeen emerges. Though subdued in tone and elegiac in mood, the novel contains some beautiful comedy, and at the end it is Birnie's affirmation of his own continuing appetite for life which makes the point of the novel manifest. Taken together with *Private Angelo*, *Roll of Honour* makes an almost incomparable contribution to the literature of the Second World War.

Though shaken by the failure of another of his favourites, Eric did not throw in the towel. Looking forward to a spring visit to the Caribbean in 1962, he spent the winter repeating the exercise of turning a play into a novel, this time as a result of A. D. Peters' doubts about 'A Husband of Delilah' which Eric had started on the way home from Australia a couple of years earlier. Discovering that it went well as a novel, he had it completed before setting off with Marjorie for Jamaica in March.

He enjoyed the West Indies enormously; almost too much, he told Ian Grimble: 'We had a splendid jaunt to Jamaica, but it has demoralised me. I cannot find any impulse to work, or to think seriously about life and letters.' In May they were off again; Eric described to John Moore their visit to Ireland:

> We made an almost complete circuit of that beautiful and bewildering island. We went for fishing and sight-seeing: the sight-seeing was good, and productive of a lot of fun, but the fishing was ludicrous: one 10 lb salmon and one 1 lb trout, and that's all ... So we intermitted fishing by driving over some splendid hills to see Bridges Adams; where we spent a delightful day, and had a great deal of hilarious conversation.

Writing to Rupert Hart-Davis to congratulate him on his excellent edition of Oscar Wilde's letters ('You needn't bother to do anything else. This is your sufficient monument'), Eric said he felt sure his holiday had helped him appreciate Rupert's work:

> I think an Irish tour—Dublin, Wexford, Kerry, Mayo—was a good preliminary to reading [the letters], for there's a fecklessness in the whole tale of Ireland which narrows to a glittering point in Oscar. The genius that he put into his life was dislocated long before his birth ... Well, as you see, your scrupulous labour has brought out—out from obscurity—a tale of terrible impact; which means that you, who call yourself an editor, have really done with infinite skill a job of genuine creation. And I congratulate you with all my heart.

After his fortnight's fishing in Orkney in June, he began tinkering at home with a new novel which would make use of some of the exotic locations he had recently been enjoying. In August he spent a few days with John Moore at his new home at Lower Mill Farm near Tewkesbury, not at all perturbed by Moore's warning: 'There are quite a lot of small trout in the stream immediately outside the sitting-room window, but Lucile won't let me catch them, and I don't expect she'll let you catch them either.' Thanking Lucile for her hospitality, Eric described his own family life:

> We have one of our young at home, but the others have made Europe their common market; one in Sweden, one in Austria, and one on the way to Poland—while the old rustics remain grumpily at home, fiddling with their television machine.

It was becoming his not-altogether-ironic habit to see himself as retired and countrified, sitting at home and wielding a pen; later he fed the phrase 'an old peasant with a pen' to various reporters, and congratulated them on their perspicacity when they used it. His interest, however, as October approached was decidedly literary. For his new novel, retrieved from the ashes of a play his agent had not cared for, Eric had told the story of Samson and Delilah from the Book of Judges in the Old Testament, his purpose being, he said, to 'refurbish the core of reality in a heroic myth'. His treatment of biblical material was similar to his approach to the Judas story in 1938, though why in 1960 the story of Samson should have begun to interest him is less clear. It may be that Eric, like his admired friend James Thurber, really did still believe in 'the war between men and women', and that he could not consequently overlook so notable a defeat for the male as that of the great Israelite, any more than he could ignore Lysistrata's victory.

Commercially *Husband of Delilah* was considerably more successful than some other of his more recent novels, but it was treated by the reviewers as no more than a pleasant piece of storytelling. *The Times* found it 'remarkably faithful and, as is to be expected from a master of narrative description, a colourful and rousing piece of fiction'. But, the reviewer objected, 'celluloid vulgarisation has spoiled its chances—one looks for, and finds not an awesome Miltonic giant in torment, but a muscular amiable superman'.[5] Eric's point was that Milton had already done the 'giant in torment' bit; he wanted to understand the roots of the myth in what might have really happened to start it, and his aim, brilliantly realised, was through an imaginative recreation of the relationship between Samson and Delilah to bring the Old Testament world to convincing and comprehensible life. His firm grasp of the political and economic realities of the day, and his projection onto the protagonists of manners understandable in twentieth-century terms, renders Samson's world with the utmost credibility. The balanced point of view does not detract from but rather creates tremendous sympathy for Samson, who is not Superman but someone rather resembling, say, Willie-John McBride, except in his propensity to lose his temper rather sweepingly.

The story is related with great relish and evocative detail. Despite the humour which constantly enlivens the presentation of Samson himself and the interrelationships of the characters, and despite the down-to-earth ordinary realism with which incidents and motivations are analysed, the events seem to take on their original epic stature as a great and terrible meaning emerges from the pages of the book. It is storytelling of peculiar power, and its mythic force is not diminished but intensified by Eric's highly individual vision of it.

At least it did better in the bookshops than some of his postwar novels, and for that the professional writer in Eric was grateful. And as a professional novelist, his back was still not broken. In the autumn he worked with confident application at the new novel which, firmly set in the television age, challenged him also to catch the flavour of a range of new backgrounds explored in his recent travels. A week in Sweden in mid-November reinvigorated him, and by Christmas the novel was almost finished.

In November Rupert Hart-Davis and Wren Howard were perturbed when Lovat Dickson showed them the typescript of his autobiography, *The House of Words*. In it he told of how Eric had come to him at Macmillan's with *The Man on My Back* in 1941 because he was disgusted with Cape's *défaitisme*. Rupert and Wren Howard felt they were unfairly tarred with this brush, and wanted to know what Eric had to say. He told them:

> I do remember being hopping-mad with old Jonathan. He was *défaitiste* from the start—I think you can confirm this—and in 1940 or 1941 I almost broke with Cape altogether. What prevented me from doing so (and I admit this without shame, for I was sorely in need of the money) was a handsome bonus Jonathan sent me in compensation for his neglect of my interests as an author.

He suggested a re-wording of Dickson's paragraph that proved acceptable, and the crisis passed. In case further declaration of his old affection for Rupert were needed, he told him he had dedicated his new novel to him:

> I hope you won't object. It would be pretty humiliating if you did. Macmillan will publish it in September or October, unless they go all dreamy, which sometimes they do. It's called *A Man Over Forty*, and I think it's pretty funny in parts.

All was quiet in Pitcalzean, he reported, with the children scattered about Europe:

> So we're all practically European except me—the old peasant just sits here grunting and hoeing his row with labour intermitted only by an occasional bottle. Marjorie continues to interfere with local constitutional arrangements, and spends most of her time on the roads—which, of course, is a different thing from on the streets.

The labour included a contribution to a book 'to be called *My Favourite Crime*, or some such thing', he told Ian Grimble, and he was going again all over the Mary Stewart ground as he tried to solve 'The Murder of Darnley'. He had also undertaken to write a book on Orkney and Shetland for Robert Hale. These tasks did not prevent him from writing to the *Observer* and *Spectator* in defence of the reputation of Field Marshal Haig which had been attacked by Kenneth Tynan and by Joan Littlewood's production of *Oh What a Lovely War!* He wrote:

> Of friends of my own age, all but a handful were either killed or died in the years after the war of their gas-infected wounds, and that was the common experi-

ence. But we did not associate our traumata with Haig: that was left to a later generation, when the traumata of folk-memory coalesced into one vast impersonal trauma, and the search began for someone to blame. Then Haig, as the victor, became also the victim.[6]

His thoughts were forcibly returned to the unhappy far-off days of the First World War a few weeks later when he was desolated to hear that Douglas Walker had died. He had seen rather less of Douglas of late but they had been best friends for fifty years; Douglas was one of the very few of Eric's friends to survive the First World War; his death reminded Eric of all the good things they had known together and filled him with sorrow at the thought of their loss. He wrote to Peg:

> Don't think me selfish when I say that Douglas's death reminds me, overwhelmingly, of the death of my own youth. We were so much together—not only he and I but you and he and I: that house in Hamilton Place was a focus of so much that we did and enjoyed—and my God, how we enjoyed it!—in the days of our youth that now, inevitably, seem like the sunset of a golden age. I think of all the splendid parts of Scotland where Douglas and I walked together, from Mount Keene to the Moor of Rannoch, from Speyside to Orkney, and all the great fun we had, with Isobel and Charles and Jean and Archie Hyslop when we were concocting those absurd little Gala Week plays . . .
>
> I remember when Douglas came back, in uniform from OTC camp in Edinburgh, to take his Dux's medal at the Grammar School; and how jealous I was because he'd got into uniform before me . . . I remember him, standing beautifully straight and speaking with brilliant clarity, in one of old Harrower's Greek plays. I remember coming back to Aberdeen, after some great walk about Tarfside, with him and Dickie Garden and James Sutherland, every one of us tight as a tick . . . I remember.

Eric was sixty-four, and had more than a decade to live, but such a *memento mori* inevitably coloured his views, and thoughts about life approaching its close increasingly found their way into his work.

A Man Over Forty was greeted on its appearance in September 1963 with expressions of pleasure and approval in the popular press, though not taken very seriously by the influential reviewers in the quality papers. Inspired by a famous television incident in which Gilbert Harding, the well-known television 'personality' of the time, suffered something of a public breakdown when being hard pressed by the interviewer John Freeman, Eric made such an event the starting-point for his book, and a considerable sale was achieved to a public that was interested for this topical reason. Some of his readers may have wondered what to make of the novel, and might have preferred a straight telling of the Gilbert Harding story, but Eric's concern was quite different.

Eric's 'television personality extraordinary', Edward Balintore, is nothing like Gilbert Harding, and his story after his public collapse is not remotely like Harding's; the plot in fact invoked echoes of the *Oresteia* and *The Family Reunion*. The novel is devoted to searching out the causes and consequences of Balintore's unexpected and dramatic breakdown. In the course of it Eric is able to explore many aspects of contemporary life with a keenly satirical eye and to develop a challenging philosophy of life. Balintore's flight from his personal Furies allows Eric to exploit locations in Jamaica, Ireland and Greece with all his old verve and skill, and the gradual revelation of the mystery in Balintore's background provides an unfolding theme that holds the elements strongly together. *A Man Over Forty* is full of funny dialogue, sharply etched characters, and comic incidents in which an element of the macabre has its place, and Eric's control of an ironic tone through an unmistakably Linklaterian use of language is total.

In 1963, with an encouraging sale for *A Man Over Forty*, Eric was not displeased with life. At the same time *New Saltire*, under the editorship of Magnus Magnusson, published his updated versions of Dunbar's poems, and as ever the Linklater versatility was publicly demonstrated. There followed a period in which he was quietly reading his history books, writing occasional letters to the press, appearing from time to time on television and radio, and taking part in the social life of Easter Ross. Late in 1963 he joined in vociferous opposition to the proposed rail cuts which would badly affect the Scottish Highlands. *The Times* reported him as saying that 'intense indignation' was the reaction locally to the 'stark injustice' of Dr Beeching's proposals:

> Because we have fewer votes, that is, a smaller political power, it seems to certain people that it is safe to neglect us ... There are faceless ones, the cockney leatherbottoms by whom increasingly we are ruled. The arguments they employ are not arguments which recommend themselves by their honesty.[7]

Behind the scenes Eric devoted a good deal of time and energy to this cause and undertook to compose the Memorandum on behalf of the North of Scotland Transport Conference which was submitted to the Prime Minister in 1964. It was a considerable labour, and inevitably fared little better than any of the other nationwide protests against the destruction which economics and Dr Beeching demanded of huge proportions of the national railway system. But he had tried his best, and had coolly and persuasively voiced the indignation of the Scottish people; as always when he had completed a writing task, successfully or otherwise, he cleared his desk and turned to the next interest.

In 1964 his main concern was with the Orkney and Shetland guide and various bits and pieces, as he called them: the text for a book of photographs of Sweden by his friend Karl Gullers[8]; an introduction to a book of translations of Norse literature by Jacqueline Simpson[9]; and a commission from a whisky firm to write an account of the flight of Bonnie Prince Charlie after Culloden. He paid visits to Italy in March, lecturing for the British Council, and Denmark in April. 'I should be working hard,' he told John Moore, 'but in fact I've been scandalously idle for a long time.' He compared himself detrimentally with Compton Mackenzie who, they had heard, was seriously ill; but when Eric rang him up,

> His voice came strong and resonant, and he spoke cheerfully of soon completing the Fourth Octave of his Auto B, and then going to France to write Volume Five and simultaneously a novel that would do for World War One what Tolstoy did for that little job with Napoleon—I began to realise, as I listened, that while I am growing old and feeble and frail, Monty was enjoying another episode in his sempiternal resurrection.[10]

He had in Italy met people who remembered him from the war, including a little man who had been at Montegufoni when Eric and Wynford Vaughan Thomas discovered the Uffizi paintings, and who now disarmingly said: 'Oh, I was just another Private Angelo.' But he no longer felt impelled to write about such encounters, as he would once; or indeed about anything. 'This business of writing bores me,' he said, revealing just how disillusioned he temporarily was. Moore had been working for a long time on a novel, and Eric advised him:

> It's high time you gaffed that novel of yours. You've been playing it far too long. Is it depraved in temper? Sullen or despairing in mood? Sadistic in action? Wilfully obscure in diction? And filthy in dialogue? If you score 3 out of 5 you can be assured of modest success. 4 out of 5 will make it a bestseller on both sides of the Atlantic. And 5 out of 5 will assure your presence at Miss Foyle's next literary luncheon.

These sardonic words about the state of the contemporary novel explain why Eric could not, though it was his business, get down to writing another novel just then; he felt that all the old values, for which he stood, had somehow faded away. A month or two later, when Rupert Hart-Davis told him he would have to destroy or remainder his unsold copies of *Roll of Honour*, Eric's pain was acute:

> That bloody book—well, I needn't tell you—was written in the light that comes through a blur of tears, for I'm old enough to have known and felt the impact of death-on-youth in two generations ... I thought it so good, and I still think it good, that I didn't anticipate failure; so the taste of failure is rather sour. Not bitter, but just sour. For I don't blame myself, I blame our god-awful critics and an overstuffed populace. From individuals in that populace—quite a large number—I've had the warmest commendation for that little book ... Well, you can't shape public taste, even if you're a dictator, and if public taste wants something between the Beetles [sic] and Henry Miller, I'm not in the field, and don't want to be.

Even so, the bits and pieces kept him so hard at work that he complained about it to John Moore, whom he had not managed to visit as intended:

> One of the worst disabilities of work is that it is profoundly anti-social. To maintain a really warm and lively social life, one should be completely idle; except for such social work as shooting, fishing, love-making and so forth … How wretched a thing is work, that inhibits so much pleasure!

The published evidence of his continuing application to this disagreeable self-immolation in 1964 was his contribution 'The Murder of Darnley' to *Fatal Fascination: A Choice of Crime* (in which, alongside Eric, Nigel Balchin, Christopher Sykes and C. S. Forester each wrote about a historical crime that intrigued them), and the account of *Gullers' Sweden.* For the time being his desire to write fiction was in abeyance, though not quite extinguished.

During the winter he began to work on a commissioned history of the Norman Conquest, the first of a series of large-scale popular histories which paid his bills quite satisfactorily during the next few years. John Moore, on hearing of Eric's attack on the '1066 and all that' theme, suggested they should go together to Bayeux to pay their respects to the Tapestry and any decent French wine they could find. At the suggested time, however, Eric was at sea with the Royal Navy, writing a couple of articles for *The Times* about the partnership of modern technology and traditional values in the Senior Service. When, in April, he took a holiday from work he wrote to invite the Moores to Pitcalzean in the summer:

> It's a long, long time since you were there, and you should see it again before the roof collapses. The lawn being what it is, we play a sort of *field*-croquet; but, on the other hand, we no longer expect guests to assist at tree-felling and scrub clearance.

He had, he said, been fishing in Argyll while Marjorie was smartly gallivanting in the south; and he was moved to wonder *why* he was so spending his time:

> I have been stubbornly angling under permanent rain and skies of aching, sodden grey for the reward of two rather long and lanky trout and a wet arse. There is more masochism in our nature than we are commonly prepared to admit.

He deserved a holiday for he had worked so hard through the spring that the 'William the Conk book' (as Moore rudely referred to it) was finished; and now, while he stood thigh-deep in a trout stream at Portsonachan, he found, resist it though he might, a new novel building in his mind. He returned to Pitcalzean and began to write again, though 'in a leisurely, amateurish sort of way', he told Moore. But then in August, just as *The Prince in the Heather* appeared, he was offered another commission for a survey, this time of the history of Scotland from Roman times to the present. He applied himself perforce to finishing the novel before burying himself once more in history.

The Prince in the Heather was splendidly produced in an edition illustrated with many atmospheric and beautiful photographs by Don Kelly and sponsored by the Drambuie Liqueur Company, to whom Eric shortsightedly sold the copyright outright, not realising how successful such a book might be. It was a pleasing and memorable version of a story that might run the risk of over-exposure in a less polished telling.

Three months later his guide to Orkney and Shetland was also published to enthusiastic reviews. It is for a guidebook surprisingly and pleasingly personal, with Eric's characteristic voice and tone coming through a large amount of information about the islands' geography, history and society devotedly researched. True to several prognostications that it would be a long time before this book on the islands could be superseded, *Orkney and Shetland* has remained in print, having been updated in 1971 by the addition of two new chapters on recent developments in the archipelagos. As a guidebook to a region it is vivid and reliable; as an indicator of aspects of the character and personality of the author, it is revealing.

Before it appeared, Eric had completed what was to be his last novel and begun the new 'monstrous historical work'[11] that had been commissioned by Doubleday. He had, he told Rupert Hart-Davis, 'rather a shrinking feeling' as he began to tackle the enormous amount of work it entailed, observing that for a basically indolent person he seemed to have spent a great deal of time on the treadmill. But 'the good Macmillan's appear to like the novel I sent to them in September', and with hope that 1966 would be a more rewarding year he settled to his absorbing task.

Though occasionally during the winter he emerged from his study to make a radio broadcast on *Arts Review*, or something of the kind, most of the time he was bent over his book of Scottish history to such good effect that by April considerable progress had been made. He broke off for a fortnight's cruise with the National Trust in the ship *Meteor* in May—after which, as Compton Mackenzie told John Moore, Eric never wished to look a rhododendron in the face again.[12]

In September both *The Conquest of England* and *A Terrible Freedom* came out within a few days of each other. If the warm recognition afforded the history and the cool, even hostile response given to the novel had only been the other way around, Eric might have offered the world a good deal more in the way of fiction, and it is quite conceivable that the rest of his life would have been both different and happier. As it was, the reviewers of the novel, with few exceptions, were either disappointed or positively sneering in their observations. Zulfikar Ghose in the *Western Mail* said that the novel was very good indeed: 'The writing is polished and consistent in style; there is humour as well as thought and the evocation of the Scottish landscape is quite brilliant. Mr Linklater is at his best.'[13] And Eric was so delighted with praise in a review by Jocelyn Brooke, the author of *The Military Orchid*, that he wrote to thank him for it. But most of the others either got their hatchets out or ignored the book altogether. Considering it briefly at the tail-end of his list, *The Times*' reviewer selected elements from the book in such a way as to suggest that it was almost complete nonsense, and concluded: 'It is tempting generously to believe that Mr Linklater has his tongue in his cheek in this silly, self-indulgent novel. But has he?'[14] One of the Scottish reviewers saw Eric's undertaking in the novel as 'an ambitious project' somehow not carried through, as if 'once embarked, he doesn't set store enough by his own ambition'.[15]

Eric's idea in the novel was to explore the relationship between life and dream. One may conclude, from the internal evidence in this and some of his other writings (notably 'A Sociable Plover' and *The Dark of Summer*), that he himself dreamt with astonishing and puzzling vibrancy, and that in writing the book he made use of personal experience which was in its way as shattering as that which led Evelyn Waugh to write *The Ordeal of Gilbert Pinfold*. In a proposed blurb for the novel Eric declared that though it was not intended as a solemn book, it was serious: 'Nothing truly written about the human condition could be solemn. Serious, yes, for most of us are condemned to play on a tragic string, and farce is inescapable; and that keeps solemnity at bay.'[16] When the interlocutor in this blurb-dialogue asks: 'Is there a conclusion to your tale?' Eric replies: 'Death. There's quite a lot about death in the story. But as my principal character is as old as I am, there's no mourning.'

The novel is powerful, experimental in method, and profound in its effect. Evan Gaffikin finds his dream life becoming more interesting and important to him than his real life, where he is trapped in an unrewarding round of business and family affairs with little opportunity to escape except into the world of the imagination. The book consists of an inter-leaved recounting of the two lives. The dreams are wonderfully compelling, being comic, bawdy, bizarre and lurid, and bear a complicated symbolic relationship with the realities out of which they spring and with which they significantly contrast.

After recounting the events of Gaffikin's past life up to the present through a well-organised narrative full of vividly recalled flashbacks, Eric brings the story to a weird climax when his protagonist takes a sailing holiday on a chartered boat along the west coast of Scotland and then to the Outer Isles, to culminate in a dramatic and mysterious merging of the two worlds of reality and dream. Evan Gaffikin is a wonderfully worldly character, deeply confused by a romantic streak in his basically practical make-up, and other characters in the book are among Eric's most memorable people: especially the brothers Roderick and Andrew McPhee, on whose boat Evan sails to his strange destiny, and Lindy, the unusual but vital American girl in love with Evan's son William. *A Terrible Freedom* renders life with assured conviction; it is most provocative in its attitudes and ideas, and satisfying in its narrative.

As with earlier books, where he sternly forbade his readers to assume that his fictions were disguised autobiography, this book should be weighed purely as a novel, and as such it can stand very well on its own feet. But no reader who knows something of Eric's life can fail to be moved by certain correspondences between his experiences and those he gives Evan Gaffikin. Evan's experience in two wars, his family life, his likes and dislikes, his awareness of his own advancing age and the death that must come, all parallel in some ways those of his creator. Here are snatches from what William Gaffikin says about his father in the final chapter:

> [My mother] was not a clever woman ... but she was by no means as stupid as my father showed her ... My father was unduly impatient, and frequently so rude to her as to be embarrassing...
>
> I cannot excuse my father's behaviour to my mother, but I do realise and acknowledge the unhappiness that darkened much of his life. It was the unhappiness of extreme and conscious loneliness. More than once, in this narrative, he speaks of the desolating effect, on his mind and body, of the war in which most of his contemporaries and all his friends were killed, and it is perfectly clear that he never recovered from the psychological wounds of that war.[17]

Eric was not writing a self-portrait; but at times he gave his own experience very much as it had been to certain of his characters. Here he had a son considering his father very much as, in certain moods, his own sons might have considered him; it is this kind of thing he meant when, pressed to make statements about himself, Eric said: 'Anyone who really wants to know me may find me in my books.'

He had put everything he could into *A Terrible Freedom*, and nobody wanted to know. His haunting, dark, wildly funny, deeply touching, philosophically invigorating and stylistically pleasing story had failed. What could be going on? He railed comically against the critics in letters to his friends, and essayed a shrug; but the rejection of this novel finally made him doubt himself. Almost persuaded that the spring of his fictive talent had run dry, he resolved to put up the shutters. There were other ways by which he could earn money by his pen.

22 An Old Peasant with a Pen

The Conquest of England received on its appearance in September 1966 a good deal of approval among reviewers and a public who very much liked the energy and individuality which radiated from Eric's writing of history. The book had been commissioned by Orville Prescott, the American editor of Doubleday's 'Crossroads in World History' series, who wanted a new popular account of England up to the Conquest ready for publication on the nine hundredth anniversary of the event. Eric's reading and natural Norse sympathies led to a rather different version of the story than might have been expected, for he developed a thesis that the Conquest was in fact the culmination of the great outburst of Viking ability that had been in evidence over two preceding centuries.

He placed the Conquest firmly in the context of the Norse achievement: their voyages of plunder, battle and settlement; their impact on France and Ireland and England; their colonisation of Iceland and Sicily; their legal system and forms of government; their literature; and the Norse characteristics which emerged in the countries they invaded. He wrote:

> It was in England that the Norse propulsion, which found its ultimate and formative strength in the Norman Conquest, had its greatest and most lasting success.[1]

Eric made no mention of the historians who tended to doubt whether the Norman knights who crossed the Channel with William in 1066 really were descendants of the Viking raiders to whom Charles the Simple ceded Normandy in 911. For him there was no doubt, and his positive approach gave to his story a powerful and exciting unifying theme; one commentator said that the thesis had made it possible for Eric to write 'a saga edged with crimson splendour'.[2] The book was an extension of work continued in *The Ultimate Viking* from groundwork done for *The Men of Ness* thirty years before, and dealt with material very close to his heart. As usual he managed the action and characters much as if he were writing a novel. The language, urbane in tone, polished in structure, sometimes unobtrusively dry and humorous, but also direct and economical, is unmistakably that of a man who found a good deal of pleasure in his work.

It is a most readable book and it is not surprising that it was a success on both sides of the Atlantic. While it may be a matter for regret that he published no more novels, it is some compensation that his ability to organise narrative, substantiate a theme, set character in action against strongly realised backgrounds, and control the whole through an individual, serene and highly civilised diction, was able to find other sources of employment.

With the disappointment over *A Terrible Freedom* partly reduced by the positive acclaim for *The Conquest of England*, Eric continued to display a great deal of energy in his activities. In November he and Marjorie, the differences between them precipitated by an earlier visit to Africa now long forgotten, took another holiday there; on their return Eric told John Moore:

> Our expedition to East Africa was successful far beyond expectation, and I seriously suggest that you and Lucile look into the possibility of doing likewise. The only disadvantage is that returning from the snows of Kilimanjaro to the harsh and dissolute snow of northern Scotland is a shattering experience, and one realises that no reasonable creature would voluntarily spend the winter in these islands of Britain.

Immediately on returning from Africa Eric was on duty at St Andrews University where he delivered the Dow Lecture. With all his characteristic wit and enthusiasm he spoke about Scotland, its great men, its history and its influence in the world, taking great pleasure in speaking where Walter Elliot, W. S. Morrison and Lord Cameron had preceded him. Scotland, he said, had if anything gained by its submission to England:

> It did not disappear. It was not destroyed. In some ways, indeed, it became more manifestly Scottish than it had been before ... When their ship sank beneath them—the old ship called *Independence*—the people of Scotland showed a remarkable buoyancy ... They were individuals, and it was individualism that gave them the buoyancy to float and swim. Scotland has always been deficient in coagulant or agglutinative elements.
>
> Let us ... without any concern for modesty remember that David Hume, most amiable of philosophers, once wrote: 'Really it is admirable how many Men of Genius this Country produces'; and this country, I repeat, cannot be measured on the map. This country lives in the deeds and creations of its sons and grandsons—Scots of the diaspora as well as the native-born.[3]

Eric's own buoyancy was a little deflated when, in January 1967, Robert Henriques died after a long illness, and sadness at the loss of a friend again affected life. Shockingly at the same time Rupert—now Sir Rupert— Hart-Davis's new and dearly loved wife Ruth died, and Eric hardly knew how to comfort his friend. Writing to John Moore about these losses, he said: 'What a bloody world we do live in, to be sure. You must come up here this autumn, or we'll be gone too.' Although Moore had suffered a good deal from diverticulitis, neither of them had any reason to guess how truly Eric spoke.

Eric wrote an obituary notice on Robert Henriques for *The Times*, and commented to Moore:

> Poor old Robert! I was, for a good many years, alternately bloody fond of him and bloody exasperated by him. When we stayed with him and Vi in Jamaica he was, for a little while, at his very worst—and in his agony and nonsense he could still remember to be sweet and generous. And at his best I've never known anybody more brilliantly alive, more vividly intelligent.

Eric's winter task had been to write a companion book to *The Conquest of England*. He was much encouraged by a wildly enthusiastic response to his first draft by a reader at Doubleday's called Maggie Cousins, who reported:

> This is a marvellous book ... It is superb because it communicates to the reader the absolute reliability of the author's information; the author's blazing interest in his subject; and because his style, which is easy, graceful, literary without being stuffy, is such a delight ... It is filled with delicious asides ... I think this may be Linklater's *magnum opus*.[4]

Certainly Eric's longest book at 160,000 words, *The Survival of Scotland* was one he was glad to have finished by April 1967; after which laborious work, he told John Moore, he had relapsed into total idleness. Strangely, he used this idle period to write to Moore the longest letter that he had had time for in all their acquaintance, in reply to the longest he had received. Moore wrote about his new novel, about the world crisis over Egypt and the Israelis, about the uselessness as he saw it of the United Nations Organisation and of the British Government under Harold Wilson, about a meeting of the Royal Society of Literature at which he had taken the chair for Compton Mackenzie, about a Foyle's luncheon where he had met John O'Hara. Eric went to town on an answer, blowing off his frustrations about 'the bloody world we live in'; the wickedness of Colonel Nasser; the imminent destruction of the world by over-population; the 'futile whimperings of Mr Wilson—who, more and more, strikes me as being a left-over comic character from an unknown work by Charles Dickens'; about his sympathy for Israel; his hatred for the new order in China; the horrors of football hooliganism; about John's horses at Kemerton; about John O'Hara and the disappointment attendant on his writings after the brilliance of *Appointment in Samarra*; and about the deep and sad divisions he had observed in Philadelphia between those who existed on opposite sides of the railway tracks.

They had hardly drawn breath from their exchanges, which they were looking forward to continuing orally in the autumn, when Moore in mid-July entered hospital suffering from an oesophagal stricture. A fortnight later, after an operation which appeared to have been successful, he died. He was not yet sixty years old.

It was almost a month after the funeral before Eric could pull himself together sufficiently to write to Moore's widow. Then he said:

I was uncommonly fond of John, and because we were nice, normal creatures we never made much of it, but just went on quietly liking each other from a distance—now and then exchanging letters—now and then meeting at the Savile and getting loudly and genially plastered ... I told John, once in a while, that he was the best writer about country topics in England since old Gilbert of Selborne died—and that was true. It was truly scandalous that his splendid last novel [*The Waters under the Earth*] was never given the appreciation it deserved. I think John—the most genial, the most engaging, the most cheerful, the most delightful companion I have had in my latter years—was really and truly a man saddened by the destruction of the England he had known so well ... He was a man who loved England ...

Except for two occasions, the renewal of grief (in my life) has never approached the misery (of the loss of friends in the First World War). The first exception was Richard Hillary's death, for he and I—though he was young enough to be my son—had become close friends. And since Richard's death I have never known real, down to the soil of the soul grief, till John died.

Life went on regardless; Eric's moods were sometimes charged with sadness, but at other times he was as full of fun and vitality as ever. Late in the summer he was visited by Francis Russell Hart, an American scholar who was in Scotland collecting material on Neil Gunn and Jane Duncan, with a book on Scottish literature in mind. Hart recalled:

He sat me down in his ample book-lined study and paraded up and down— what a solid, SQUARE, short man he was!—and asked me if I knew what was WRONG with modern fiction ... He assured me that Dostoevsky had ruined it by making it all PSYCHOLOGY. Across from my chair was one floor-to-ceiling book-case and on a protruding front border at waist height stood a framed portrait photo of Compton Mackenzie, very handsome and theatrical. He referred to him as Monty and asked me somewhat aggressively if I had read *The Four Winds of Love* ... He opined that he thought of himself as one of only three or four people who had read *all* of it, and assured me it was worth the trouble ... My impression then and there was of a learned man, a lover of books and history ... and later in the day, of a playful man who loved children ... Finally, he spoke warmly of his friend Jane Duncan and asked with some tender regret about Neil Gunn, whom he had not seen for some time and who, he seemed to feel, had withdrawn and given up on him as a friend.[5]

In October Eric was again honoured in Scandinavia when a special Dinner was given for him in Stockholm by the Royal Ministry for Foreign Affairs; a note from Karl Gullers told him that this was the first time such a party for an author had ever been held. Here he met again with great pleasure his friend Frans G. Bengtsson, the novelist whose *The Long Ships* had been inspired by *The Men of Ness* and who was known, he was proud to say, as 'the Eric Linklater of Sweden'. Sometimes it seemed odd to Eric that his work was taken so much more seriously in a country where he could speak so little of the language than it was in his home country, but he enjoyed his respectful treatment there none the less.

In 1968 Eric became a Deputy Lieutenant for Ross and Cromarty, and enjoyed, though not so much as his wife did, the occasional duties incurred in the role. But he was still more concerned with his literary than with his social reputation, and in April he awaited with some concern the response to his *The Survival of Scotland*. He need not have worried, for even very scholarly reviewers showed appreciation of the qualities in his writing and did not make too much play with what they considered inaccuracies of detail or eccentricities of emphasis. In *The Times Literary Supplement* its felicities were listed: lucid accounts of battles, perceptive characterisation, sketches of old ways of life, digressions on the achievements of Scots ex-patriates, agreeable comments, commonsense views, and the whole clearly and beautifully written.[6]

Jo Grimond exclaimed:

> I never knew that Linklater knew so much! ... It is an essay in the grand classical manner ... It is weak, by modern standards, in the same way as Gibbon and Macaulay are weak. But how splendid to be borne along by Mr Linklater's splendid wave, rather than pick a tedious path through the usual suet of modern social and economic research.[7]

Richard Church, too, wrote with generous enthusiasm of Eric's poetic vision and the 'humour and challenging recklessness of mood and idea' in his writing of history.[8] The public liked it too, and though it was not the blockbuster which Maggie Cousins had forecast it sold steadily over the years and Eric's hard labour in the winter of 1966–7 was rewarded.

Later in the year there was a very gratifying reaction when Macmillan's brought out a collected edition of *The Stories of Eric Linklater*. There were no new stories in it—'unfortunately', as Robert Nye observed[9]—but a considerable welcome was extended to the reappearance in such a handsome volume of the old stories, many of which had long been out of print. There were good reviews in Australia, too, and in Scotland, where Eric's stature was still immense, the publication of the short stories met with special approval. Alexander Scott pointed out that such a body of stories represented a major achievement.[10] The omission of several stories from *God Likes Them Plain*, most notably 'Wineland' and the second and third parts of 'The Revolution', and from the later books passed without comment; even without them, the range and variety of Eric's writing is dramatically exemplified in the 1968 volume. In his introduction Eric refused to apologise for having failed to let discretion rule invention and his pen, so that his territory might be properly marked out, like that of a well-behaved cock robin or a three-spined stickleback; he preferred to think that readers 'may believe, with Dr Johnson, that "the great source of pleasure is variety" '. His book is a fair demonstration of the tenability of that position.

Pleased with the satisfactory reception of his review of Scottish history, Eric took a deep breath and during the winter of 1968–9 plunged into a third massive historical undertaking. This was an account of the Stewart family from their origins in the eleventh-century Breton Steward, Flaald fitzAlan, through the great days when his descendants ruled in Scotland and England, on past their decline and loss of rule, and to their tenuous survival in the blood of Queen Victoria. He finished his work just before his seventieth birthday—'another bloody great tome', he called it when writing to Bernard Fergusson with whom, newly returned to Scotland after five years as Governor-General of New Zealand, he now renewed and developed a warm friendship.

The seventieth anniversary of Eric's birth was duly celebrated in the Scottish press and marked by the BBC with a new radio production of his play based on *Magnus Merriman*. Marjorie in her element planned a party attended by seventy or more guests, including Ronald Mavor, Jane Duncan, Lord Kilbrandon and Professor Grieve of the Highlands and Islands Development Board, and told a reporter from Aberdeen that her husband was 'in top form and so full of life that it's impossible to believe that he's seventy'.[11] Eric enjoyed the party so much, he told Bernard Fergusson, that 'the following morning I thought I'd spread-eagled my own wicket'. Weakly surviving, he gathered himself together, and he and Marjorie went to Malta for a fortnight to recover.

The *Scotsman*, on his birthday, featured an article which the journalist, Raeburn Mackie, ended with a quotation from Eric: 'No, I am just an old peasant with a pen.' The joke he had made so often in private became public. The role of peasant was one which he played quite seriously at times; the croft which he had bought with Pitcalzean had about fifteen acres of land, and had been the scene of an attempt at commercial market gardening involving the employment of a full-time gardener. As such it had been, he told another journalist, 'a fearful failure: I can turn a sentence with tolerable felicity, but I cannot always expect the right answer when I do sums.'[12] But it had, after a famous battle, been accepted by the Inland Revenue as a legitimate loss to set against his earnings from writing, so its failure had not been altogether disastrous. What was more significant about the peasant role was its symbolisation of the way in which he felt out of touch with the accelerating pace of modern life and contemporary adjustments in moral attitudes. The more he found himself disapproving of new developments in writing, the more he retreated towards the past and the idea of himself as a rural reactionary. He told Graham Lord of the

Sunday Express: 'I'm just an old hayseed. A rustic. I always have been. My wife is on all sorts of committees, but I'm just a selfish old man.'[13] But it was just another of the roles he played, to make sure that the real inner man never showed through.

A few weeks after his seventieth birthday his first grandchild was born to Magnus and his wife Veronica; Magnus had become a journalist and was working in London on the *Evening Standard*. Their son was called Alexander Ragnar. The four Linklater offspring had all grown up and more or less left home: Sally was painting in Edinburgh; Kristin was in the United States working as actor, teacher and director in theatre; and Andro was teaching in England. Eric and Marjorie were beginning to see more of friends whose own children had also grown up and left the nest, leaving the parents free to meet and spend holidays together. Especially they now saw more of Ursula Balfour, Marjorie's friend from before marriage, and her husband Jimmy Dallmeyer whom she had married in 1939. Ursula recalled a typical evening spent at Pitcalzean when James Robertson-Justice and his wife were also present:

> I remember a game of croquet played at Pitcalzean which continued until it was too dark to see the next hoop. Eric, who was my partner, kept altering the rules, but Jimmy and James Robertson Justice were formidable opponents. Marjorie kept pleading with us to go and eat the excellent dinner which was getting cold.
>
> Eric and J R J were old friends and sparring partners. Both were intensely well-informed and that evening they reminded us of two small boys trying to get the better of each other. I don't need to tell you how much Eric enjoyed a convivial evening.[14]

Apart from a few reviews Eric published nothing in the year of his seventieth birthday except a rather odd little booklet about salmon-fishing. In *The Secret Larder* he put forward a revolutionary and, among salmon fishers, rather sensational theory about the perennial mystery of why and how salmon return to the rivers of their origin to spawn at the end of their life-cycle. According to Eric, or rather to two fishing friends of his, salmon recognise their own river by the smell in it of the rotting corpses of the previous year's kelts (salmon that died after spawning) and, contrary to received opinion, feed on the very dilute broth created in the stream by infinitesimal bits of old salmon mixed with the water. As an example of the variety and intensity of Eric's interests the pamphlet is a fascinating document. He later told a correspondent, General Holden:

> I wrote it of course as one flies a kite: to see what will happen. None of the vested authorities agrees with me, but I've had some very interesting—and interested—letters, and I still hope that what Campbell and Vass did on the Shin will be repeated elsewhere.

Early in 1968 Eric had been asked by the editors of *Twentieth Century* to contribute some personal reminiscences to a special edition of the magazine to be called 'Turning Points', the aim of which was to establish something of 'What determines the shape and pattern of our lives? Parents, genes, class, luck, events or consciously willed decisions?' Eric provided an account of some turning points in his own life, determined, he said, 'by ancestry, honesty and the thickness of one's skull',[15] and the exercise of writing it was a contributing factor to his decision to write the third volume of autobiography which he began in the autumn of 1969. For some months he was not very well; he told Bernard Fergusson:

> I have been on and off sick parade in the most tiresome way. It started with an allergy, which is a convenient modern word for anything the doctors can't diagnose, and settled into a sort of dermatitis. Well, as we all know, dermatologists are clever chaps who specialise in that sort of thing because their patients never die, never call them out at night, and never get better.

A particular nuisance of this was that it had affected his eyelids and he tended to cry rather a lot:

> I used to cry only at noble spectacles, such as Trooping the Colour, but nowadays the most trifling things—300 orphans trampled to death by mounted police in Bolivia; 48 elderly widows drenched in petrol and set on fire in Vietnam; 3800 villagers drowned in a tidal wave at Cox's Bazaar—even that sort of thing starts a flood of tears.

Nevertheless he had made good progress on his new volume of autobiography, and by the spring it was in the hands of Macmillan's. He told W. R. Aitken, a bibliographer who had been in touch with him about an article he had written about Eric, that in the book 'I have tried to make some assessment of myself as a writer. It is, I think, a pretty cool and balanced assessment.' And he commented:

> I haven't—as you say—had much critical appreciation, but long ago I realised that my dreadful mistake was threefold: to write comedies; to write with evident enjoyment of what I was writing; and to live so far from London that I have never been able to buy, for critics, the strong drink they need. For about forty years, however, I have been able to live in tolerable comfort by writing what I choose to write, and having enjoyed such good fortune it would be absurd to grumble.

To recuperate after his winter's work he went with Marjorie to India on a package tour that lasted an exhausting but rewarding three weeks; *Blackwood's Magazine* published in June and July 1970 his full and detailed account of the holiday. In June he went to Finland for a week, and then almost immediately upon returning he and Marjorie met Ursula and Jimmy Dallmeyer for the first of several holidays they all took together. They had hired a fifty-foot converted motor fishing vessel called *Old 797,* and planned a voyage to the Outer Isles. In a lively description of the holiday, also published in *Blackwood's*, he wrote:

> We were not going to be adventurous; we were intent on pleasure rather than sea-faring, and we had decided that a circumnavigation of Skye, a little dodging about between Rum and Loch Torridon, would give us what we wanted, and that was a seaward view of the Inner Hebrides, and the sense of freedom which only the sea and a boat of one's own can give.[16]

Ursula remembered Eric sitting up late to talk to the skipper:

> We heard him make his way to the Linklater cabin, and a commanding voice said: 'Marjorie.' No answer. Again, even louder: 'Marjorie, get up and take my boots off!' At this there were muffled but explosive sounds from Marjorie's bunk. We knew quite well that she would do no such thing.
>
> Eric liked to see himself as a dominating husband, and in the early days of their marriage I was often distressed by his tone. Very soon, however, Marjorie learned to cope. I am afraid that as often as not his sneering comments on her opinions or his impeccably phrased criticisms would reduce onlookers to helpless laughter. Nothing could subdue Marjorie, and we have seen her at their dinner table launch forth with immense courage into some passionately held opinion, her voice trailing into silence as she caught Eric's eye at the head of the table. He had bright chestnut-coloured eyes which seemed to protrude on stalks when he was roused; his looks would have withered a lesser woman.[17]

If he published little in 1969, he made up for it in 1970. In May came his selection from John Moore's writings together with linking comments, published as a tribute to his dead friend. The following month saw the publication of *The Royal House of Scotland*. Once again press opinions were warm and great appreciation was expressed of Eric's style, knowledge, individuality in judgement, and fluent narrative skill. It is a delightfully readable and entertaining history, with Eric's ability to depict eccentric characters and his witty asides providing palpable evidence of his authorship. Antonia Fraser, who later covered much of the same ground as Eric, especially in her book on Mary Queen of Scots, praised his combination of warmth and knowledge and his liberal use of quotations from Scottish poetry.[18] A feature of the book is its infectious enthusiasm, not so commonly found in septuagenarians. In his discussion of the version of the Bible authorised by James VI, Eric's feeling for language and joy in the particular beauty of Elizabethan English finds new expression, and his statement of the debt owed to James by succeeding generations is unequivocal:

> In the greatest age of English writing King James's Bible—regarded as literature, not as revelation—cannot be bettered by *Hamlet* or *Lear*, by Bacon or Donne; and in the oldest sense of 'author'—of him who gives existence—the King must be accepted as its prime and motivating author ... The non-

professing critic can hardly deny the impact, on believer or unbeliever, of an imagery presented in a style that might substantiate divinity though no other proof of it could be found.[19]

And in a couple of sentences, taken at random from the chapter on James IV, may be detected the tonal quality which makes Eric's writing of history a particular pleasure:

English reprisals followed, and in 1491 Henry VII, the Welshman who had acquired the English throne, was involved in a very curious transaction. To the Earl of Buchan, James's great-uncle, and Sir Thomas Tod, the Master of the Mint, he offered the cheese-paring sum of £266 13s 4d to kidnap the King and his younger brother. It is not known whether Buchan or Tod took the offer seriously or regarded it as a Tudor aberration about which it was better to say nothing; but the plot, if it was a plot, was still-born.[20]

A courtesy copy of *The Royal House of Scotland* was sent to The Duke of Edinburgh, who liked it so much that the Linklaters were invited to stay at Balmoral. They spent a memorable weekend there in September. Eric joked about hobnobbing with royalty, but it was an occasion that he treasured.

With the approach of winter Eric settled to a new task, having accepted a commission from George Rainbird and John Murray to write, for publication in 1972 to mark the centenary of its departure from Portsmouth, an account of the great scientific voyage of HMS *Challenger*. He began to examine some introductory material, telling Bernard Fergusson:

I've been sent some hefty volumes, and I have a feeling that by merely looking at them—and perhaps laying down my head and sleeping on them for an hour or so a day—I can absorb some useful information without actually reading them.

In November the final volume of his autobiography appeared from Macmillan's, to receive some of the best notices he had had for years. *The Times Literary Supplement* seemed anxious to compensate for its recent coolness towards him, saying:

It has been his literary virtue that he has tried his hand at many different types of book, instead of creating his own terrain, Linklaterland ... and yet Mr Linklater's character has been very consistent ... Wit is the quality which gives his recollections an astringency rare in those practising the usually self-indulgent art of autobiography.[21]

Fanfare for a Tin Hat, like its predecessors in autobiography, is no longer available, but does both on its own and as part of a trilogy constitute an impressive achievement. At the end of 1970 Eric had no complaints about its reception and his readers could have no doubt of his continuing energy, sense of fun and faculty of eloquent and elegant narrative.

The year was crowned with a coveted honour when he was proposed by Lord Balerno, Stanley Cursiter and others for election as a Fellow of the Royal Society of Edinburgh. Duly elected a Fellow in early 1971, he found the boy in him delighted by the new letters he could place after his name to add to a considerable string; he was now, for the record, E.R. Linklater, Esq., CBE, MA, LLD, DL, TD, FRSE, and in certain moods the accumulation of alphabetic distinctions pleased him almost as much as in other moods he found the accretions comic.

Although part of the winter was taken up with preliminary reading for the *Challenger* book, his main project was again historical but this time concerned more with recent history than was his wont. As in his essay 'The Murder of Darnley' he was really working less in the field of history than that of criminology; the old interest which had surfaced before in *The House of Gair* and *Mr Byculla* was now fully extended in a non-fictional context.

Eric had first been excited by the trial of Steinie Morrison for the murder of Leon Beron when, almost twelve years old, he had avidly followed the sensational accounts in the newspapers. As he explained in the Preamble to the book which he now wrote, he had suspected as a schoolboy that justice had not been done. Various later accounts of the case, notably those of Fletcher Moulton and Edgar Lustgarten, had at intervals reminded him of this feeling and confirmed his sense of its rightness; he wrote:

> It was almost by chance, a few years ago, that I pulled Fletcher Moulton's narrative from a book-case to read over a solitary breakfast: a working writer's day rarely corresponds with the nicely time-tabled habits of his house; and as my custom then was to work late into the night, and get up late, I breakfasted alone and for half an hour or more read casually, for entertainment only, in the book I had happened to choose. But on that day the book held me much longer than usual. I went on reading it for most of the morning, and again and again I found my thoughts interjecting rank disbelief into what I read.[22]

An idea took him to the National Library of Scotland in Edinburgh where, reading contemporary accounts of the case, he noticed some associated phenomena which finally persuaded him that:

> It was worth my while, and possibly of advantage to the truth, to re-tell Steinie's lamentable tale and set it in a context that would, to some extent, illustrate the temper and material environment of that age and so, perhaps, prompt reassessment of his supposed guilt.

He saw how he could use, as part of his argument, Conrad's novel *The Secret Agent*, which had appeared some four years before the Beron murder but which, in dealing with a public outrage deliberately arranged by a foreign (Russian) conspiracy, offered an alternative view of the motivation of the murderer to that attributed to the hapless Morrison. According to Eric, the murder of Beron was committed by Russian *agents provocateurs* who were also active in the contemporaneous Houndsditch Murders and the Siege of Sydney Street; and their aim was to inflame the British Government to repressive action against all anarchists and to give the British bourgeoisie a memorable fright—all in the cause of Russian nationalism which, certain Russian patriots felt, would benefit from the discomfiture of other countries.

When it appeared in November 1971, *The Corpse on Clapham Common* attracted some attention. Dennis Johnson found the evocation of the period 'engrossing from our new perspective ... now that anarchism is fashionable again'.[23] H. R. F. Keating said Eric's book wrung 'much savoursome juice concerning the intellectual climate of the day' and was 'a fair *coup d'intellect*'; but however stimulating it might be, 'the corpse on the common lacks the final juiciness'.[24] So apparently the public found, for the book sold only in relatively small numbers and was remaindered after three years. It had however been a labour of love and in its reconstruction of the period was vivid and atmospheric, while its organisation and linguistic flavour were rewardingly Linklaterian. Eric did not regret the time spent on it.

In the summer before it was published Eric and Marjorie made up a foursome again with the Dallmeyers to go on another boating expedition. Eric told Bernard Fergusson: 'We are venturing into Irish waters—the Shannon, Lough Derg, perhaps others—in a chartered 30-footer, and sailing directions make Lough Derg appear to be much more dangerous than the broad Atlantic.' Ursula recalled:

> We had an idyllic time ... This time there was no Captain, or rather Eric was Captain and Jimmy First Mate ... It was only on the last day we discovered the chart was marked in feet, not fathoms ... One of the pleasantest aspects of the cruise was that one met the birds on the water 'eyeball to eyeball' as Marjorie put it. Eric remarked that it was like going for a walk in beautiful countryside without the trouble of using one's legs.

In one of the bars they visited a friendly local inhabitant tried to guess what profession Eric and Jimmy followed; Jimmy said he would always remember with pleasure the look on Eric's face when he was unhesitatingly cast as a bank manager.

He returned home to further work on the *Challenger* story, writing about a voyage of rather more epic proportions, and was sufficiently advanced with it to be overjoyed when, in November, Bernard Fergusson asked him to consider a commission to write the history of their old regiment, The Black Watch. Eric had been a lance-corporal in it; Bernard Fergusson had been Commanding Officer of its First Battalion and was now Colonel of the Regiment; but their friendship was based on equal pride in it and in one another. Fergusson wrote to Eric:

I am thrilled, and so will all me cobbers be when they know ... that there is a good chance of your taking on the book. There is *nobody* who could do it anywhere near so well, and there is no subject I could think of more apt to your own gifts.

It was some time before the matter was settled, but from the time the idea was broached it filled Eric with anticipatory pleasure and excitement. As soon as *The Voyage of the Challenger* had been delivered to George Rainbird for publication by John Murray, he began his researches into the history of The Royal Highland Regiment, ransacking the National Library in December and visiting The Black Watch Museum at Riemore in January. An exciting prospect opened up of flying out to the Mediterranean in April to visit some wartime scenes of battle, but the trip had to be cancelled when Fergusson found himself not well enough to travel.

As it happened, there was a good reason why Eric did not mind deferring the jaunt to Crete and Tunisia quite as much as he might otherwise have done. During the last few years he had been distressed by the way his retreat in Easter Ross had become increasingly less remote. The modern world and its developments threatened the Bay of Nigg, like so many other pleasant backwaters, and in 1971 he felt he could stand it no more. *The Times'* diarist recorded the Linklaters' capitulation in March:

Progress (if that is the correct word) is forcing Eric Linklater, the author, to leave his home, Pitcalzean House, at Nigg overlooking the Cromarty Firth where he has lived for the past twenty-five years ... The progress which has caused their departure began a couple of years ago when a giant aluminium smelter was erected at Invergordon across the water from his house. When he moved there, Linklater said, he could claim 'one of the best views in Scotland. The smelter has not improved it.' More recently, peace and quiet have been destroyed by a firm making giant oil rigs on the beach at the bottom of his garden. 'Everyone around here wanted it except me,' he said. 'Unemployment is very serious in these parts. If I had stood out against it I should have been the most unpopular man in Ross-shire!'[25]

Perhaps in fact he would not have left even then, but for a combination of circumstances. The coming of the very industry which was despoiling their comfortable life brought in people with sufficient money to make a much better offer for the house than they could have expected; and a timely suggestion came from their friend the Earl of Haddo, who had on his estate near Aberdeen 'a decentish, 1820-ish house',[26] the lease of which he offered to the Linklaters.

Before he succeeded to the Earldom of Haddo, Major David Gordon and his wife June had set up a choral society with Haddo House as its centre. For several years Eric and Marjorie had been keen supporters of this enterprise, which had gradually turned Haddo into a sort of northern Glyndebourne. In 1970 Eric had written a pamphlet about their work; this was the idea of June Gordon, Lady Haddo, who, as Eric told General Holden, 'in the nicest possible way—of course—commanded me to do it.' In *The Music of the North* Eric wrote:

> I cannot sing in tune, I have no aptitude for woodwind or strings, but I can recognise virtue in others, and when Lady Haddo asked me to write a short and simple account of the Haddo experiment—the experiment that grew to accomplishment—I said immediately, 'Yes, of course'; because that process from experiment to accomplishment deserves and demands celebration, and it is an honour to be associated with it, however tenuously.[27]

Out of the association with the Haddos, soon to become Marquess and Marchioness of Aberdeen, came Eric's chance to escape from the encroaching modernity of Nigg to the rural quiet of the elegant former farmhouse called The Mains of Haddo. The move was scheduled for April 1972, just when he would have been gallivanting in the Mediterranean if Bernard Fergusson's plans had worked out. He was glad—or quite glad—not to have had to leave Marjorie to look after everything on her own; he told Fergusson:

> To pack up for Tunisia on the 12th would have meant leaving Marjorie with the burden of settling in, for which, of course, I would again have felt *faintly* guilty, while now, instead of guilt, I shall merely have to endure fearful discomfort. How I shall hate it—but how bright and clean will be my conscience.

Not without some pain and heartache, when it came to the day, the Linklaters took up residence in The Mains of Haddo. Eric had come almost full circle, back to Aberdeen, and to his last home.

EPILOGUE

23 Sentinel Stone

The change of scene was not greatly conducive to work on The Black Watch book, but the flurry of things that needed to be done helped for a while to stave off feelings of uprootedness and regret for Pitcalzean. Eric told Bernard Fergusson:

> I have done shamefully little of my task, because we have been living in ever-increasing chaos and work has been impossible ... Marjorie really enjoys choosing wallpapers and carpets and deciding that blue curtains will go very nicely with a yellow wall; all that sort of *garrulous* activity. But oh, how bored I get.

But as they settled in and he got back to work, he began to enjoy his task, not least the travelling about Scotland and the meetings with soldiers that it involved. Other undertakings included an essay on contemporary Scottish politics for a book being put together by A. M. Dunnett.

This interesting document demonstrates the essential and perennial Linklater, for while it draws together so much of the thinking that Eric had expressed about Scotland in various places over forty years, it also retained a youthful vigour and cutting edge of wit which suggested powerful feeling.

In a brief survey of the political relationship between Scotland and England since the Act of Union, Eric suggested that though there had been mistakes in the past, the union was still mutually desirable. Some anger towards England might be justified by memories of its early treatment of Scotland, for 'Scotland was a nation, not a company bought on the Stock Exchange by a richer company',[1] but since then things had much improved. Considering any claim that Scotland might have to govern itself, he pointed out that it was difficult to perceive any evidence of far-sighted and trustworthy leaders in Scottish domestic politics. In a devastating look-round at the recent achievements—or lack of them—of the city fathers of four important Scottish cities, he implied that grave consequences would follow should the Scottish people trust such men with rule of the whole country. As examples he castigated Edinburgh's lack of imagination in all except that which might yield 'a quick and easy profit'; Glasgow's indiscreet and ineffective substitution of high-rise ghettos for communal tenements; and Aberdeen's absurd betrayal of its educational superiority by submission to government edict about comprehensive schools. The chief hope for Scotland lay in its rediscovery of the old phenomenon that Scots flourish best abroad, away from their fellow Scots. Let them travel and work in the newly available territories of the EEC, and let Scotland be content to prosper in its symbiotic mutually advantageous relationship with England.

A month or two after the move to the Haddo estate, Eric was the subject of a talk by Ian Grimble in one of a BBC radio series about 'Highland Novelists'. In a sympathetic and enthusiastic review of Eric's career, Grimble compared him with Rabelais and with Sir Thomas Urquhart as examples of great satirists who show 'the true hallmark of compassion, smiling at the frailty of our species in all their infinite diversity'.[2] Grimble had much to say about Eric's Viking blood and sympathies, and the work which had arisen from them, from *The Men of Ness*—'In fact there's nothing in modern literature quite like *The Men of Ness*, and only the greatest of the classical sagas can stand beside it'—to his retelling of 'The Battle of Largs'. Similarly, Grimble emphasised his 'deep understanding of human nature' and 'his splendid gift for bringing the past to life' in his historical works as well as in his novels. It was an appreciative and perceptive tribute, and Eric was touched. He wrote to Grimble:

> I have just been listening, with the greatest pleasure, to all the charming things you say about me. A *real* surprise—and thank you very much ...
>
> I still regret the abandonment of Pitcalzean and Easter Ross—though we are very comfortable here, in the middle of a large and handsome estate—but we couldn't possibly have stayed on to see the devastation of the bay of Nigg, where dreadful things are being done.

Eric's account of the voyage of the survey ship *Challenger*, jointly sponsored in 1872–5 by the Admiralty and Edinburgh University, was published in September 1972 and found an appreciative market. It was the most expensive book he had had to do with; selling at £5 in a large-format edition produced by George Rainbird for John Murray, it contained numerous illustrations in colour and monochrome and was a pleasing example of the bookmaker's art. Unlike most 'coffee-table' books, however, the heart of the book lay not in its pictures but in its text, in which Eric economically, vividly and stylishly as ever unfolded his narrative. The *Challenger*'s was a pioneer expedition of great importance, with the ambitious aim of charting the depths, movements and contents of the seas, surveying the marine life and seeking mineral wealth as well as clues to climatic phenomena. If its consequences were not so dramatic as those of the voyage of the *Beagle*, its story was nevertheless full of human as well as scientific interest. In Eric's treatment the people involved acquire depth like characters in a novel, and the descriptive writing is masterly.

The reviews were good and the book received a new lease of life three years later in paperback. It was the last book Eric completed. Though he did a fair amount of work on some ideas for novels, after the disastrous failure of *A Terrible Freedom* he could not believe his fictions were good enough, and none was finished. Instead he plugged away at his history of The Black Watch, which was at least a topic in which he was emotionally involved and a commission which, in the absence of the confidence to complete a new novel, gave him a good deal of pleasure.

In September he took a very special holiday, flying off with Marjorie on what he described to Bernard Fergusson as 'a high-spirited jaunt—a jaunt exceptional, a jaunt of superior dimensions'. Their immediate destination was Fiji, their purpose there, a little Pacific island-hopping. 'The good Thos. Cook—and, of course, his invaluable Son' had, he said, included in their plan not only visits to various places in Fiji, but also two voyages ('quite short, of course') and a chance to see Apia, Pago Pago and Tonga as well. The jaunt was supremely enjoyable, and included an introduction to the King and Queen of Tonga. As a tribute to their Majesties, Eric took a copy of *The Voyage of the Challenger* which had, he was relieved to recall, some complimentary things to say about their kingdom.

Settling down after their return from the South Pacific to his winter's work on The Black Watch story, Eric found the way difficult and the going slow. The tale was really too vast to be fitted into the relatively short book which the publishers required. Eric told Fergusson:

> I started very cheerfully, but too lavishly, and presently discovered that if I continued in that style the book would run to 150,000 words. So I had to re-think and re-shape all that I had written ... I decided to omit—for the time being—everything from Waterloo to Magersfontein, and tackle what was clearly going to be the most difficult part: World War One.

The difficulties, work at them though he might, would not go away, and he still had much to do as the spring of 1973 brought on thoughts again of holiday. In May, together again with the Dallmeyers, Eric and Marjorie visited Crete, Rhodes and Athens. It was a good trip. Ursula remembered how they persuaded Eric to buy a nautical hat, 'as his poor naked dome was peeling. Wherever he went he carried a shepherd's crook, and Marjorie said he looked like a cross between St Christopher and the Ancient Mariner.' Marjorie's throat was still rather uncomfortable after a winter cold, and Eric said she would be all right if she'd only hold her tongue for three or four months. Couldn't she get a job as a housekeeper in a Trappist monastery? Eric christened himself 'the old hippo' when the Dallmeyers commented with amusement on the curious noises they could hear coming from his room as he woke up in the morning. And Ursula remembered:

> Eric had a booming voice ... Marjorie, thinking we might be snoozing on an adjacent balcony, evidently made some sort of grimace in an attempt to keep

him quiet. 'Marjorie, don't bare your teeth at me,' he thundered. 'Go down and buy some gin.'

In a letter to the Dallmeyers, thanking them for being 'perfect *compagnons de voyage*' on 'a cracking good jaunt', Eric wrote:

I enjoyed every hour of it, despite Marjorie's insistence that I must keep going for yet another 100 up-hill steps, and her absurd belief that 'exercise', which produces only exhaustion, is good for Old Age Pensioners ... Do you miss ouzo? I do, for gin and tonic now seems thinly flavoured. And our outlook, on gay green fields, is less exciting than the deep-hearted blue of the farthest Mediterranean. But we *had* a good time, and bless you for enhancing the charm and beauty of immortal Hellas. *Xairete*!

He never really enjoyed anything so much again. His work went well for a while, and then was increasingly interrupted by minor illness and a degree of lassitude. Bernard Fergusson, who had by then become Chairman of the British Council as well as Lord Ballantrae of Auchairne and the Islands, felt that he detected a waning in Eric's spirit, and so did Marjorie. It showed only from time to time, but the joy of their summer holiday could not be recaptured on a Christmas visit to Malta, and as he began to approach his seventy-fifth birthday he worried Marjorie with frequent references to death.

Early in 1974 he took her back to Orkney and showed her the place in the Harray churchyard where, he said, he wanted to be buried. He discussed with her the type of stone to be set at the head of the grave, and insisted that there should be no words on the stone but his name and the dates that indicated his life-span. 'He did not seem in the least morbid about it,' said Marjorie; 'it was just that arrangements had to be made, and he couldn't trust them to me, a mere woman. He seemed to be taking great pleasure from a last look round the places he had loved since he was a boy. It was simply as if he knew his life was over and now, having greatly enjoyed it, he was preparing himself with equanimity for death.'

In early March a *Guardian* writer, Diane Morgan, visited Eric at Haddo and reported: 'As far as work is concerned, he has something on the stocks as ever, but admits that his output is slowing down a little and suspects that he might be getting a little lazy.'[3] He seemed lively enough, however, for her to suggest that 'he might do another novel, perhaps about North Sea oil?' Despite his inner assurance, which he did not keep from Marjorie, that the party was over, he kept a bright and interested face turned towards the world, and took part spiritedly in the various celebrations of his seventy-fifth birthday.

These included a dinner given in his honour at Edinburgh's New Club on 15 March. Mentioning the occasion in the *Orcadian*, George Mackay Brown added:

Eric Linklater is one of Scotland's best storytellers ever ... Besides being a novelist, he is a masterly short-story writer ... I often wish that he had spent more time on the short story—he is such a consummate artist ... He has a marvellous lyricism, a delight in the land and shifting seas and skies of the north.[4]

No tribute could have pleased Eric more, though he was also deeply moved by a BBC broadcast in his honour on his birthday. Contributions from Stanley Cursiter, Magnus Magnusson, Harald Leslie (Lord Birsay), Jack House and Sir Ralph Richardson praised his work with readings from typical extracts, and he could not but glow as he realised how fully some had appreciated him both as an artist and a man.

But his health in the summer was not good, and his work made little progress. Ian Grimble came with a film crew and recorded a long interview in which for a while Eric seemed almost his old self again, full of droll comments and firmly and fluently expressed opinions. Parts of the interview were used in a film about Eric's life and work, written by Jeremy Bruce-Watt and directed by Laurence Henson; entitled *A Stone in the Heather*, it gives an affecting and perceptive glimpse of Eric in the last months of his life.[5]

He took considerable interest, too, in a celebratory exhibition of Linklateriana set up by Stanley Simpson at the National Library of Scotland and open to the public from July till September. Eric lent a number of items, including the famous helmet with two holes in it, and there were letters, pictures and books from various sources; but the Library was able to supply most of the exhibits from its own extensive collection, which had by good fortune been greatly improved by the acquisition of a large pile of old papers that Eric had sold a few years previously to K. D. Duval, a dealer in books and manuscripts, and forgotten. There were original manuscripts, copies of special editions, copies of Linklater books in German, Dutch, Swedish, Norwegian, Italian, Romanian, French and other languages, drawings, photographs, medals and paintings: an impressive suggestion of a full and successful and vastly entertaining life.

At the end of the summer, almost without warning as it seemed, Eric suffered a thrombosis attack and was taken to St John's Nursing Home in Aberdeen. After a period of illness he seemed to rally a little, but did not seem very pleased with his doctor's observation that alcohol was forbidden for the foreseeable future. He joked with Andro about leaving him 'only the paperbacks and the cheap red wine' and reminded Marjorie not to go cluttering up his tombstone with verbiage.

The next day, 7 November 1974, he died. There was little doubt in Marjorie's mind that he simply did not wish to live any longer.

He was buried in Orkney after a service at St Olaf's Church on 11

November. His grave in the high and windy Harray churchyard commands a view over the Loch of Harray and the house called Merkister and all the surrounding countryside that meant so much to him as he forged his youthful image of himself as Orcadian, Viking, Scot. At the head of the grave is a magnificent stone over six feet high that Marjorie found in Caithness, like a stone from one of Orkney's mysterious standing circles, and on its polished surface are the words, carved quite small:

ERIC LINKLATER

1899–1974

PRAISE BE TO GOD

Eric's last undertaking, the history of The Black Watch, was completed by Andro, whom Eric named as his literary executor, and published in 1977. Lord Ballantrae was eminently satisfied with the result, saying that Andro had done the work superbly, in the fine tradition of the Regiment about which they had written, where sons had traditionally followed fathers throughout two centuries.

Marjorie returned to Orkney, a year or so later, to live in Kirkwall. She gave to Aberdeen University, in Eric's name, a dozen of the forty or so paintings which he had bought and given to her during their lifetime together. Hung together as a group in Elphinstone Hall, they are known as 'the Linklater Bequest', and include paintings by Michael Ayrton, James Cowie, Stanley Cursiter, David Donaldson, Joan Eardley, J. D. Fergusson, William Gillies, George Leslie Hunter, S. J. Peploe, Robin Philipson and Anne Redpath. The collection of paintings is an interesting memorial, throwing a little more light on the romantic, beauty-loving character and generous nature of an extraordinary man. But the gift he gave to the world, of twenty-three novels, two children's novels, three autobiographies and three collections of short stories, is his finest memorial.

Notes on Sources

The principal sources for this biography are Eric Linklater's more than seventy books; several boxes of papers (manuscripts, notes, cuttings, letters and memorabilia) in the possession of Marjorie Linklater; eleven boxes of papers (manuscripts, typescripts, notes and some correspondence) held by the National Library of Scotland; six boxes of papers (typescripts and letters, mostly to A. D. Peters) held in the Humanities Research Center, University of Texas; extensive files of correspondence and a collection of radio scripts held at BBC Written Archives Centre, Caversham, Reading; letters between Eric and numerous correspondents (some in the possession of Marjorie Linklater, some in the possession of their original recipients or their families and made available to me by their kindness); and the personal reminiscences of those who knew him, mostly received in the form of letters to me, but some from oral interviews, of which some were tape-recorded. Assuming that readers would want as little interruption to the narrative as possible, I have kept documentation to a minimum. In copying manuscripts I have sometimes spelled out abbreviations for the sake of clarity.

The Selected Bibliography offers detailed listings. In the following notes, letters are cited only where it is not plain from the text who was writing to whom. All letters quoted are, unless otherwise indicated, in the possession of their recipients. Books cited in these notes are the particular editions in my possession, and page numbers may vary in other editions.

Letters not in the possession of their recipients are held as follows:

EL to Phoebe Gilkyson, General Holden, Douglas Walker, Mrs Walker, Lesley Storm, David Wise, Bernard Fergusson, Alison Linklater, Elspeth Cormack—all in the possession of Marjorie Linklater.

EL to Isobel Walker—National Library of Scotland, Dep 220.

EL to John Moore—in possession of Mrs Lucile Bell.

EL to Compton Mackenzie, Evelyn Waugh, Richard Church, Clifford Bax, Jocelyn Brooke, A. D. Peters, Herman Ould—Humanities Research Center, University of Texas at Austin.

EL to Jonathan Cape, Wren Howard, Michael Howard—Cape Archive, Reading University Library.

EL to Douglas Young, Neil M. Gunn, Lewis Grassic Gibbon (J. L. Mitchell)—National Library of Scotland.

EL to James Fergusson, Val Gielgud—BBC Written Archives Centre, Caversham.

1 CHILD IN EXILE

1 EL in a letter to W. R. Aitken, 17.3.1970.
2 *The Man on My Back* (London: Macmillan, 1944) p. 9. The many quotations from this book are indicated below by the abbreviation: *M B* and page no.
3 *Fanfare for a Tin Hat* (London: Macmillan, 1970) pp. 27–8. This book is indicated below by the abbreviation: *F T H* and page no.
4 ibid, p. 29.

5 ibid, p. 28.
6 Elspeth Cormack in a letter to MP, 17.6.1976.
7 R. H. Edwards in a letter to MP, 30.10.1975.
8 *A Child Under Sail* by Elizabeth Linklater (London: Rupert Hart-Davis, 1949). From EL's 'Foreword', p. 9.
9 *F TH*, p. 27.
10 ibid, p. 31.
11 ibid, p. 36.

2 ORKNEY YOUTH

1 *FTH*, p. 40.
2 ibid, p. 41.
3 *M B*, p. 3.
4 ibid, p. 8.
5 *Scottish Country* ed. George Scott-Moncrieff (London: Wishart, 1935). From an essay by EL: 'Orkney', p. 82.
6 *F TH*, p. 39.
7 'The Great Gales of Orkney'; article by EL, ts in possession of Marjorie Linklater, p. 2. Commissioned by *Collier's Magazine*, publication date not known, but *c.* April 1953.

8 ibid, p. 1.
9 *M B*, p. 11.
10 Marjorie Linklater in a letter to MP, 28.10.1982.
11 *Scotland – 1938: Twenty-Five Impressions* ed. John R. Allan (Edinburgh: Oliver & Boyd, 1938). From an article by EL, 'The Orkney Farmers', p. 6.
12 'Return Journey: Eric Linklater on the Orkneys'; script by EL for a radio programme, produced by Stephen Potter, broadcast 31.10.1945. Ts in possession of Marjorie Linklater, pp. 11.–12.

3 SCHOOLBOY IN ABERDEEN

1 *FTH*, p. 41.
2 ibid, p. 42.
3 *M B*, p. 19.
4 ibid, p. 9.
5 ibid, p. 10.
6 *F TH*, p. 43.
7 *M B*, p. 9.

8 *F TH*, p. 45.
9 *M B*, p. 9.
10 Letter to MP from Marjorie Linklater, 5.9.1982.
11 *F TH*, p. 51.
12 *M B*, p. 24.
13 ibid, p. 25.

4 A SNIPER IN FRANCE

1 *FTH*, p. 52.
2 *M B*, p. 29.
3 ibid.
4 ibid, p. 30.
5 ibid, p. 31.
6 ibid, p. 19.
7 *F TH*, p. 57.
8 ibid, p. 54.
9 ibid, p. 56.
10 ibid, p. 65.

11 *M B*, p. 45.
12 ibid, p. 39. What the Annamese workers were doing in France in 1918, I do not know.
13 'Joy as it Flies', *Sealskin Trousers and other stories* (London: Rupert Hart-Davis, 1947). Rupert Hart-Davis questioned the use of 'inenarrable' and EL replied: 'An illiterate age! A generation insulse from birth and uncultivated by

art. A Boeotian spawning, undisciplined in youth, analphabetic in its dull caducity.—One of it, squinting from time to time through its bleary lippitude, perceives in a printed book—which it handles gingerly, being unused to letters—a word somewhat longer and more mellifluous than the gross monosyllables with which it is familiar—for all its own literary exercise is writing them on the wall of a jakes—and, querulous and rathe, exclaims: "Why, that's not English! There's no such word in English. I'm English myself, and I ought to know, oughtn't I?" His own deficiency he construes as wholeness; his general cachexy he assumes to be perfect health; and any normal man who enjoys a sound knowledge of his mother-tongue, sufficient for quotidian needs, he will accuse of an apolaustic sesquipedalianism. (6.1.1948).'

14 *MB*, p. 39.
15 *FTH*, p. 67.
16 *MB*, p. 19.

17 EL to John Moore, 5.4.1959.
18 *FTH*, p. 67.
19 *MB*, p. 19.
20 Marjorie Linklater in a letter to MP, 10.4.1983.
21 *MB*, p. 46.
22 *FTH*, p. 71.
23 ibid, p. 11.
24 The Linklater Exhibition was held in the National Library of Scotland, July–September 1974. A catalogue of the items shown is held at the office of the Assistant Keeper of Manuscripts. Sir Rupert Hart-Davis says that he saw the helmet hanging on a wall at Merkister in 1935; underneath was a notice: NONE IN FRONT.
25 *MB*, p. 55.
26 ibid, p. 56.
27 *Edinburgh* (London: Newnes, 1960), p. 10.
28 *MB*, p. 58.
29 ibid, p. 59.
30 *FTH*, p. 57.

5 STUDENT

1 *MB*, p. 62.
2 *FTH*, p. 80.
3 ibid, p. 77.
4 *MB*, p. 74.
5 James Sutherland in a letter to MP, 24.8.1982.
6 *FTH*, p. 82.
7 *White-Maa's Saga* (London: Penguin, 1963) pp. 12–13.
8 *MB*, p. 67.
9 *The Scottish Tradition in Literature* by Kurt Wittig (Edinburgh: Oliver & Boyd, 1958), p. 329.
10 *White-Maa's Saga*, pp. 165–75.
11 *A Year of Space* (London: Reprint Society, 1954), p. 216. Hereafter abbreviated to *YS*.
12 ibid, p. 215.
13 Gordon L. McCullough in a letter to MP, 1.11.1975.
14 *MB*, pp. 71–2.
15 ibid, p. 74.
16 Alan J. Grant in a letter to MP,

10.7.1976.
17 McCullough letter op. cit.
18 *Aberdeen Evening Express*, 3.4.1923.
19 *White-Maa's Saga*, p. 43.
20 *MB*, pp. 115–18.
21 ibid, p. 297.
22 Isobel Walker in a letter to MP, 1.10.1975.
23 *MB*, p. 66.
24 McCullough letter op. cit.
25 *Alma Mater*, 21.10.1925.
26 *FTH*, p. 79.
27 *Stella the Bajanella*, performed in 1922. EL gave the manuscript to Jean Mackay (now Mrs Jean Cruickshank) who played the role of Stella, and she sent MP a photocopy, 28.10.1977.
28 EL to David Wise, 4.6.1965.
29 *FTH*, p. 82.
30 ibid, p. 89.
31 ibid.
32 ibid, p. 85.

6 JOURNALIST IN BOMBAY

1 *MB*, p. 79.
2 *FTH*, p. 90.
3 *After These Many Quests* by Marsland Gander (London: Macdonald, 1949), p. 81.
4 L. A. Stronach in a letter to MP, 30.10.1975.
5 *FTH*, p. 92.
6 *MB*, p. 83.
7 *FTH*, p. 91.
8 ibid.
9 'The Unknown Pathan' by E. R. R. Linklater. Source unknown; cutting in possession of Marjorie Linklater, prob- ably *c.* 1926.
10 *MB*, p. 111.
11 ibid, p. 105.
12 *FTH*, p. 98.
13 EL to Douglas Walker, 11.3.1926.
14 *MB*, p. 119.
15 *After These Many Quests*, op. cit., p. 209.
16 *MB*, p. 120.
17 ibid, p. 122.
18 EL to General Holden, 15.12.1968.
19 *MB*, p. 123.
20 ibid, p. 139
21 ibid, p. 153.

7 POET MANQUÉ

1 *Alma Mater*, 21.1.1920.
2 James Sutherland letter to MP, op. cit.
3 *MB*, p. 71.
4 EL to Isobel Walker (NLS, Dep 220).
5 *Alma Mater*, 23.11.1921.
6 ibid, 30.1.1924.
7 ibid, 6.2.1924.
8 ibid, 12.5.1923.
9 ibid, 25.10.1922.
10 *Scottish Student Verse 1919–23* (Edinburgh: 1923).
11 *Alma Mater*, 26.10.1921.
12 ibid, 19.1.1921.
13 ibid, 21.11.1923. Repr. in *Poobie* (Edinburgh: Porpoise Press, 1925).
14 *MB*, pp. 70–1.
15 *FTH*, p. 86.
16 *Poet's Pub* (London: Penguin, 1935), p. 13.
17 *Magnus Merriman* (London: Mayflower Dell, 1966), p. 51.
18 ibid, p. 55.
19 *A Dragon Laughed* (London: Cape, 1930), p. 13.
20 *Alma Mater*, 18.5.1921.
21 *A Dragon Laughed*, p. 15.
22 ibid, p. 51.
23 ibid, pp. 105 ff.
24 *MB*, p. 120.
25 ibid, p. 121.
26 *Scots Review*, June 1947, pp. 40–1.
27 *New Saltire*, no. 9, 1963, pp. 18 ff.

8 COMMONWEALTH FELLOW

1 'As Luck Would Have It', *Twentieth Century*, vol. 176, no. 1036, 1968, p. 15.
2 *MB*, p. 174.
3 *As I Walked Down New Grub Street* by Walter Allen (London: Heinemann, 1981), p. 36.
4 *MB*, p. 125.
5 EL in interview with Mary Marquis, BBC Television (Scotland): 'Writers in Britain: Eric Linklater', transmitted 1971.
6 George C. Morrison in a letter to MP, 26.7.1982.
7 Charles T. Rioch in a letter to MP, 14.8.1982.
8 *MB*, p. 175.
9 ibid, p. 176.
10 ibid, p. 120.
11 ibid, p. 178.
12 ibid.
13 ibid, p. 179.
14 ibid.
15 'As Luck Would Have It', op. cit.
16 ibid.
17 *MB*, p. 180.
18 ibid, p. 181.
19 *FTH*, p. 100.
20 ibid, p. 101.
21 EL to Mary Marquis, op. cit.
22 *MB*, p. 187.
23 *FTH*, 104.
24 ibid.

25 *MB*, pp. 108–9.
26 ibid, p. 189.
27 *Juan in America* (London: Cape, 1931), p. 291.
28 *MB*, p. 185.
29 *FTH*, p. 102.
30 ibid, p. 103.
31 *MB*, p. 182. The name of Eric's companion was not Smith, but it has not been possible to establish his identity.
32 ibid, p. 193.

33 *FTH*, p. 109.
34 EL to Douglas Walker, 16.7.1929.
35 ibid.
36 EL to Phoebe Gilkyson, July 1929.
37 EL to Douglas Walker, 16.7.1929.
38 *Listener*, 9.9.1931, p. 418.
39 *MB*, p. 191.
40 EL to Douglas Walker, 16.7.1929.
41 EL to Phoebe Gilkyson, 17.12.1929.
42 EL to Mary Marquis, op. cit.
43 EL to Mrs Walker, 29.3.1930.

9 PROFESSIONAL WRITER

1 *FTH*, p. 125.
2 ibid, p. 124.
3 *Edward Garnett: A Life in Literature* by George Jefferson (London: Cape, 1982), pp. 251–2.
4 *Daily Mail*, 17.3.1931.
5 *Now and Then*, no. 38, Spring 1931.
6 *Daily Express*, 17.3.1931.
7 *FTH*, p. 134.
8 'Looking Around' by Ernest Marwick, *Orcadian*, 8.4.1972.
9 *Beyond Culture* by Lionel Trilling (London: Penguin, 1967), paraphrased in *The Critical Enterprise* by Raymond Cowell (London: Allen & Unwin, 1975), p. 58.
10 *Now and Then*, op. cit, p. 17.
11 *MB*, p. 199.
12 *FTH*, p. 103.
13 *White-Maa's Saga*, p. 228
14 ibid, p. 12.
15 'Looking Around' by Ernest Marwick, op. cit.
16 *Sunday Times*, 22.10.1929.
17 *Poet's Pub*, p. 130.
18 W. D. Taylor, *Aberdeen University Review*, vol. xviii, 1933, p. 22.
19 Eric Linklater as Comic Novelist' by Andrew Rutherford, *Literature of the North* ed. D. Hewitt & M. Spiller (Aberdeen: The University Press, 1983), p. 153.
20 *FTH*, pp. 122–3.
21 *MB*, p. 198.
22 EL quoted by Ian Grimble in 'Highland

Novelists: Eric Linklater', BBC Radio 4, transmitted 23.6.1972; the script is held at the BBC Written Archives Centre, Caversham, Reading. This source is abbreviated to 'BBC' in further references.
23 'Eric Linklater: Novels and Short Stories' by John MacRitchie, unpublished BA dissertation, University of Strathclyde, 1979.
24 *FTH*, p. 114.
25 *MB*, p. 198.
26 *Juan in America*, p. 74.
27 ibid, pp. 25–6.
28 ibid, pp. 88–9.
29 *The Modern Age From 1920* by David Daiches (London: Cresset Press, 1958), p. 304.
30 EL to Mary Marquis, op. cit.
31 Thomas Mann, quoted by T. R. Whitaker, *Twentieth Century Interpretations of The Playboy of the Western World* (New York: Prentice Hall, 1974), p. 4.
32 *Juan in America*, p. 315.
33 ibid, p. 326.
34 *The Scottish Novel: A Critical Survey* by Francis Russell Hart (London: John Murray, 1978), p. 250.
35 'Eric Linklater as Comic Novelist' op. cit.
36 *MB*, p. 222.
37 *FTH*, p. 114.
38 *MB*, p. 223.
39 ibid.

10 SCOTTISH NATIONALIST

1 *FTH*, p. 129.
2 ibid, p. 126.

3 *MB*, p. 225.
4 ibid, pp. 225–6.

5 *The Ultimate Viking* (London: Macmillan, 1955), p. 295.
6 *MB*, p. 228.
7 *FTH*, p. 132.
8 *Lyttelton-Hart-Davis Letters*, vol. V, ed. Rupert Hart-Davis (London: John Murray, 1983), p. 26.
9 Peg Walker in a letter to MP, 24.8.1983.
10 *MB*, p. 228.
11 ibid.
12 *FTH*, p. 134.
13 ibid, p. 135.
14 ibid, p. 134.
15 *Then and Now*, Winter 1932, pp. 32–4.
16 *The Scottish Tradition in Literature*, op. cit., p. 326.
17 *The Ultimate Viking*, p. 8.
18 *The Men of Ness* (London: Panther, 1959), p. 32.
19 ibid, p. 24.
20 ibid, p. 7.
21 *The Scottish Novel*, op. cit., p. 252.
22 *My Life and Times*, Octave VII, by Compton Mackenzie (London: Chatto & Windus, 1968), p. 77.
23 *MB*, p. 230.
24 *FTH*, p. 135.
25 EL to General Holden, 15.12.1968.
26 *Manifesto*, East Fife By-Election, 1933 (Edinburgh: National Party of Scotland, 1933).
27 *MB*, p. 230.
28 *Memoirs* by Jo Grimond (London: Heinemann, 1981), p. 103.
29 *MB*, p. 231.
30 *FTH*, p. 138.
31 ibid, p. 139.
32 *FTH*, p. 137.
33 *MB*, p. 232.
34 ibid.
35 *The Times*, 25.6.1933; 26.6.1933; 21.2.1967; 23.2.1967.
36 *MB*, p. 232.
37 *My Life and Times*, op. cit., p. 141.
38 *Mary, Queen of Scots* (London: Peter Davies, 1933), pp. 144–5.
39 *Record and Mail* (Glasgow), 21.2.1933.
40 *FTH*, p. 140.

11 FAMILY MAN IN ITALY

1 Marjorie Linklater in a letter to MP, 7.2.1978.
2 *FTH*, p. 240.
3 Marjorie Linklater letter op. cit.
4 *My Life and Times*, op. cit., p. 106.
5 *FTH*, p. 141.
6 *Orcadian*, 6.4.1933. Repr. *Orcadian*, 7.4.1983.
7 *Orcadian*, 11.4.1983.
8 *My Life and Times*, op. cit., p. 121.
9 EL to Compton Mackenzie, 9.8.1933.
10 Marjorie Linklater in a letter to MP, 8.9.1983.
11 Alison Sheppard in a letter to MP, 27.10.1982.
12 *Lyttelton-Hart-Davis Letters*, op. cit., vol. V, p. 77.
13 EL to Compton Mackenzie, 21.11.1933.
14 EL to Lesley Storm, 14.1.1934.
15 EL to Douglas Walker, 26.12.1933.
16 EL to Jonathan Cape, 17.7.1933.
17 *The Scottish Novel*, op. cit., p. 252.
18 *The Scottish Tradition in Literature*, op. cit., p. 328.
19 *Magnus Merriman* (London: Mayflower Dell, 1966), p. 28.
20 ibid, p. 162.
21 *FTH*, p. 133.
22 EL to Lesley Storm, op. cit.
23 *FTH*, p. 143.
24 ibid.
25 ibid, p. 146.
26 ibid, p. 147.
27 *YS*, p. 316.
28 'Growing Like a Tree', *Life & Letters*, April 1934, pp. 72–8.
29 *FTH*, p. 147.
30 ibid, p. 148.
31 ibid.
32 *Daily Mirror*, 3.9.1943.
33 *FTH*, p. 149.
34 *MB*, p. 238.

12 ORKNEY HOUSEHOLDER

1 *FTH*, p. 152.
2 *Robert the Bruce* (London: Daily Express Books, 1936), p. 23.
3 *The Times*, 19.6.1934.
4 *FTH*, p. 149.
5 *Ripeness is All* (London: Cape, 1943), p. 192.
6 *Daily Herald*, 28.3.1935.
7 *The Scottish Novel*, op. cit., p. 253.
8 *New York Herald Tribune*, 12.5.1935.
9 *Modern Scottish Literature* by Alan Bold (London: Longman, 1983), pp. 185–6.
10 *FTH*, p. 149.
11 EL to Lewis Grassic Gibbon, 15.11.1934 (NLS Acc 6253).
12 *The Lion and the Unicorn* (London: Routledge & Kegan Paul, 1935), p. 26.
13 ibid, p. 20.
14 ibid, p. 148.

15 ibid, p. 140.
16 ibid, p. 142.
17 *Fortnightly Library*, no. 144, p. 621.
18 *Scottish Country*, op. cit., p. 93.
19 *The Lion and the Unicorn*, op. cit., p. 97.
20 *FTH*, p. 153.
21 ibid.
22 *God Likes Them Plain* (London: Cape, 1935), p. 93.
23 ibid, p. 71.
24 ibid, p. 79.
25 ibid, p. 253.
26 ibid, p. 261.
27 ibid, p. 268.
28 ibid, p. 287.
29 ibid, p. 308.
30 ibid, p. 44.
31 ibid, p. 58.

13 TRAVELLER IN THE ORIENT

1 *FTH*, p. 155.
2 ibid.
3 *MB*, p. 241.
4 ibid, p. 245.
5 *FTH*, p. 156.
6 *MB*, p. 254.
7 ibid, pp. 269–71.
8 EL to Rupert Hart-Davis, 27.1.1936.
9 *MB*, p. 289.
10 ibid, p. 293.
11 ibid.
12 ibid, p. 294.
13 ibid.

14 *North China Daily News*, 12.2.1936.
15 *MB*, p. 294.
16 ibid, p. 296.
17 *Listener*, 22.4 / 20.5 / 27.5 / 10.6 / 17.6.1936.
18 *News Chronicle*, 12.3.1937.
19 *MB*, p. 295.
20 *FTH*, p. 157.
21 *Juan in China* (London: Cape, 1937), p. 53.
22 ibid, p. 71.
23 ibid, p. 31.
24 *FTH*, p. 158.

14 UNCERTAIN PACIFIST

1 *MB*, p. 303.
2 *The East Wind of Love* by Compton Mackenzie (London: Rich & Cowan, 1936).
3 *MB*, p. 310.
4 EL to Douglas Walker, 14.12.1936.
5 EL to Compton Mackenzie, 14.12.1936.
6 EL to Rupert Hart-Davis, 12.2.1937.
7 ibid.
8 ibid.
9 EL to Compton Mackenzie, 4.3.1937.
10 EL to Alison Bonfield, 14.3.1937.
11 EL to Douglas Walker, 14.12.1936.

12 *MB*, p. 332.
13 ibid.
14 *FTH*, p. 159.
15 MB, p. 333.
16 *FTH*, p. 159.
17 *The Sailor's Holiday* (London: Panther, 1958), p. 101.
18 *MB*, p. 323.
19 *Year Book of the Royal Society of Edinburgh*, 1976, p. 56.
20 *Listener*, 11.8.1937.
21 Unpublished radio script, BBC Scotland, transmitted 9.11.1937, quoted

from copy in possession of Marjorie Linklater.
22 *FTH*, p. 153.
23 EL to Alison Bonfield, 27.12.1937.
24 EL to Rupert Hart-Davis, 16.3.1938.
25 EL to Phoebe Gilkyson, 4.4.1938.

26 EL to Compton Mackenzie, 28.5.1938.
27 *MB*, p. 332.
28 *The Scottish Novel*, op. cit., p. 256.
29 *MB*, p. 333.
30 ibid.
31 *John O'London's Weekly*, 8.7.1938.

15 SOLDIER TO THE WARS RETURNING

1 *MB*, p. 334.
2 EL to Douglas Walker, 20.12.1938.
3 *Punch*, 19.4.1939.
4 EL to Editor of *Spectator*, 14.4.1939.
5 *The Scottish Novel*, op. cit., p. 256.
6 EL to Rupert Hart-Davis, 5.9.1939.
7 *FTH*, p. 181.
8 ibid.
9 EL to James Fergusson, 11.11.1940 (BBC).
10 *FTH*, p. 180.
11 *YS*, p. 48.
12 *FTH*, p. 183.
13 *Orkney Blast*, vol. 1, no. 1, 17.1.1941.
14 *FTH*, p. 185.
15 ibid, p. 9.
16 *MB*, p. 334.
17 *FTH*, p. 9.
18 *MB*, p. 331.
19 ibid, p. 332.
20 *Sketch*, 19.3.1941.
21 *Manchester Guardian*, 6.6.1941.
22 *Catholic World*, 27.2.1942.
23 *FTH*, p. 9.
24 ibid, p. 209.
25 ibid.
26 *The Highland Division* (London: HMSO, 1942).
27 Anthony Walker in a letter to MP, 21.5.1976.

28 *FTH*, p. 214.
29 ibid, p. 215.
30 *Punch*, 18.11.1942.
31 Brigadier Turner (War Office) to Val Gielgud, 12.5.1942 (BBC).
32 *Observer*, 22.11.1942.
33 *FTH*, p. 199.
34 ibid, p. 221.
35 ibid, p. 227.
36 *Listener*, 20.5.1943.
37 *The Raft & Socrates Asks Why* (London: Macmillan, 1942), p. 115.
38 *The Great Ship & Rabelais Replies* (London: Macmillan, 1944), p. 64.
39 *FTH*, p. 231.
40 *The Raft & Socrates Asks Why*, op. cit., p. 105.
41 *FTH*, p. 232.
42 ibid, p. 243.
43 *Observer*, 19.5.1944.
44 EL to Marjorie Linklater, 15.4.1945.
45 EL to Marjorie Linklater, 7.7.1944.
46 *FTH*, p. 293.
47 ibid, p. 273.
48 ibid, p. 291.
49 ibid, p. 304.
50 ibid, p. 272.
51 *The Art of Adventure* (London: Macmillan, 1947), p. 107.

16 LEAVING ORKNEY

1 *Return Journey*, op. cit., p. 1.
2 *FTH*, p. 321.
3 ibid, p. 316.
4 'Soldiers and Books', *Time and Tide*, 11.10.1940.
5 *Private Angelo* (London: Penguin, 1958), p. 155.
6 *FTH*, p. 323.

7 ibid, p. 332.
8 'Marjorie Linklater' by Ann Tweedy, *Leopard* (Aberdeen), May 1976, p. 15.
9 'The Cave in Father's Head', a talk about EL given by Alison Linklater, who sent MP a copy of her script, 1982.
10 *FTH*, p. 325.

17 LURE OF THE THEATRE

1 *YS*, pp. 27–9.
2 *The Best Wine Last* by Alec Waugh (London: W. H. Allen, 1978), p. 240.
3 *Time and Tide*, 28.2.1948.
4 *Sealskin Trousers*, op. cit., p. 42.
5 'Crisis in Baffin Bay', *Observer*, 11.5.1947.
6 'New Poems', *Scots Review*, June 1947.
7 *Time and Tide*, 6.9.1947.
8 *Public Opinion*, 19.9.1947, p. 163.
9 E L to John Moore, 3.2.1948.
10 *Christopher Marlowe's Tamburlaine the Great*, in a special version by Basil Ashmore (London: Blandford Press, 1948). From E L's 'Foreword', p. 7.
11 'The Fourth Musketeer' by Basil Ashmore, *Punch*, 29.11.1974.
12 *Two Comedies* (London: Macmillan, 1950), p. vii.
13 *Dear Me* by Peter Ustinov (London: Heinemann, 1977), p. 170.
14 *The Pirates in the Deep Green Sea* (London: Macmillan, 1949), p. 7.
15 *Illustrated London News*, 10.12.1949.
16 *FTH*, p. 326.
17 *A Spell for Old Bones* (London: Cape, 1949), p. 93.
18 E L to Rupert Hart-Davis, 3.5.1949.
19 *YS*, p. 309.
20 ibid, p. 314.
21 *Mr Byculla* (London: Chatto & Windus, Landmark Library, 1970), p. 41,
22 Harman Grisewood to Barbara Bray, 23.4.1951 (BBC).
23 *Scotsman*, 2.9.1950.

18 OLD WARRIOR GOES WALKABOUT

1 *YS*, p. 23.
2 ibid, p. 112.
3 ibid, p. 117.
4 *Our Men in Korea* (London: HMSO, 1952), pp. 30–1.
5 *Australian Women's Weekly*, 5.9.1951.
6 *YS*, p. 267.
7 E L to John Moore, 8.2.1952.
8 *FTH*, p. 325.
9 *The Campaign in Italy* (London: HMSO, 1953), p. 177.
10 ibid, p. 1.
11 ibid.
12 *YS*, p. 315.
13 *Daily Telegraph*, 23.1.1953.

19 HONOURED BY THE QUEEN

1 *Annals of the Sir Walter Scott Society*, vol. 45, 1953.
2 *The Times*, 7.10.1953.
3 *Varsity*, 7.11.1953.
4 *World Books Broadsheet*, July 1956.
5 *YS*, p. 308.

20 ECLIPSE AT NOON

1 'Prometheus and Tomorrow', *British Medical Journal*, 24.12.1955, p. 4955.
2 *The Times*, 6.9.1956.
3 *The Dark of Summer* (London: Cape, 1956), pp. 118–19.
4 George Bruce in a letter to MP, 18.8.1982.
5 *Lyttelton Hart-Davis Letters*, vol. II, p. 107.
6 ibid, p. 190.
7 ibid, p. 192.
8 *A Sociable Plover and other stories and conceits* (London: Rupert Hart-Davis, 1957), p. 222.
9 *Scotsman*, 14.4.1957.
10 *Weekly Scotsman*, 1.3.1958.
11 Basil Ashmore in a letter to MP, 1.10.1977.
12 *Scotsman*, 6.6.1958.
13 *A Sociable Plover*, op. cit., p. 51.
14 *FTH*, p. 326.
15 *Bookman*, Winter 1958.
16 *New York Times*, 12.3.1959.
17 E L to Marjorie Linklater, 29.9.1958.
18 Basil Ashmore in a letter to MP, 1.10.1977.
19 *Daily Telegraph*, 23.11.1959.
20 'The Fourth Musketeer', op. cit.

21 A MAN OVER SIXTY

1 Sir Rupert Hart-Davis in a letter to MP, 18.1.1978.
2 Marjorie Linklater in a letter to MP, 10.4.1983.
3 EL to Rupert Hart-Davis, 27.9.1961.
4 *The Novel Today* by Anthony Burgess (London: Longman for British Council, 1965), p. 31.
5 *The Times*, 5.10.1962.
6 *Spectator*, 17.5.1963.
7 *The Times*, 24.12.1963.
8 *Gullers' Sweden* (Stockholm: Almqvist, 1964).
9 *The Northmen Talk* by Jacqueline Simpson (London: Dent, 1965).
10 EL to John Moore, 1.5.1964.
11 EL to John Moore, 15.8.1965.
12 John Moore to EL, 28.6.1966.
13 *Western Mail*, 3.9.1966.
14 *The Times*, 1.9.1966.
15 *Glasgow Herald*, 3.9.1966.
16 NLS Acc 5665.
17 *A Terrible Freedom* (London: Macmillan, 1966), p. 222.

22 AN OLD PEASANT WITH A PEN

1 *The Conquest of England* (London: Hodder & Stoughton, 1966), p. 297.
2 Cuthbert Graham, *Press and Journal* (Aberdeen), 17.12.1966.
3 *Notes for a Scottish Pantheon* (Edinburgh: Oliver & Boyd, 1967), pp. 5–6.
4 Note in possession of Marjorie Linklater.
5 In a letter to MP, 4.8.1982.
6 *Times Literary Supplement*, 2.5.1968.
7 *Guardian*, 5.4.1968.
8 *Country Life*, 16.5.1968.
9 *Scotsman*, 20.7.1968.
10 *Glasgow Herald*, 18.7.1968.
11 *Press and Journal* (Aberdeen), 28.2.1969.
12 *Scotsman*, 23.3.1968.
13 *Sunday Express*, 26.3.1970.
14 'Turning Points', *Twentieth Century*, op. cit.
15 EL to W. R. Aitken, 17.3.1970.
16 *Blackwood's*, vol. 308, no. 1862, p. 481.
17 Hon Mrs C. J. Y. Dallmeyer in a letter to MP, 22.10.1983.
18 *Financial Times*, 25.6.1970.
19 *The Royal House of Scotland* (London: Sphere Paladin Books, 1972), p. 151.
20 ibid, p. 48.
21 *Times Literary Supplement*, 27.11.1970.
22 *The Corpse on Clapham Common* (London: Macmillan, 1971), p. 2.
23 *Guardian*, 9.12.1971.
24 *The Times*, 25.11.1971.
25 ibid, 1.3.1972.
26 EL to Sir Bernard Fergusson, 20.2.1972.
27 *The Music of the North* (Aberdeen: Haddo House Choral Society, 1970).

23 SENTINEL STONE

1 'The Political Scene', *Alistair Maclean Introduces Scotland* ed. A. M. Dunnett (London: André Deutsch, 1972), p. 116.
2 'Highland Novelists: Eric Linklater', BBC talk by Ian Grimble, op. cit.
3 *Guardian*, 6.3.1974.
4 *Orcadian*, 12.3.1974.
5 *A Stone in the Heather*, film directed by Laurence Henson, written by Jeremy Bruce-Watt, produced by International Films (Scotland) Ltd, for Films of Scotland and the Scottish Arts Council, 1974.

Selected Bibliography

There is no complete bibliography of Eric Linklater's published work. The following is a list of Eric's books (based on W. R. Aitken's checklist in *The Bibliothek*, vol. 5 (1967–70, pp. 194–7), with additions by myself with help from Allan Colquhoun), of the locations of principal manuscripts used in this study, and of other works cited. Detailed references are included in the Notes on Sources.

I BOOKS BY ERIC LINKLATER

(a) *Novels*

White-Maa's Saga (London: Cape, 1929; repr. London: Cape, 'The Orkney Edition', 1952; London: Penguin, 1963).

Poet's Pub (London: Cape, 1929; New York: Cape & Smith, 1929; repr. London: Penguin, 1935; London: Cape, 'The Orkney Edition', 1952; London: Consul Books, 1964).

Juan in America (London: Cape, 1931; New York: Cape & Smith; repr. London: Cape, 'The Orkney Edition', 1953; London: Penguin, 1956; London: Panther, 1965; Edinburgh: Macdonald Publishers, 1983).

The Men of Ness (London: Cape, 1932; New York: Farrar & Rinehart, 1933; London: Daily Express Books, 1935; London: Cape, 'The Orkney Edition', 1952; London: Panther Books, 1959; Kirkwall: The Orkney Press (with Introduction by Marjorie Linklater), 1983).

Magnus Merriman (London: Cape, 1934; New York: Farrar & Rinehart, 1934; repr. New York: Armed Services Editions, 1934; London: Cape, 'The Orkney Edition', 1950; London: Penguin, 1959; London: Mayflower Dell, 1966; Edinburgh: Macdonald Publishers, 1983).

Ripeness is All (London: Cape, 1935; New York: Farrar & Rinehart, 1935; repr. London: Cape, 'The Orkney Edition', 1954; London: Pan Books, 1952; London: Penguin, 1962).

Juan in China (London: Cape, 1937; New York: Farrar & Rinehart, 1937; repr. London: Cape, 'The Orkney Edition', 1950; London: Penguin, 1958; London: Panther, 1965).

The Sailor's Holiday (London: Cape, 1937; New York: Farrar & Rinehart, 1938; repr. London: Cape, 'The Orkney Edition', 1954; London: Panther, 1958).

The Impregnable Women (London: Cape, 1938; New York: Farrar & Rinehart, 1938; repr. London: Cape, 'The Orkney Edition', 1952; London: Penguin, 1959).

Judas (London: Cape, 1939; New York: Farrar & Rinehart, 1939; repr. London: Cape, 'The Orkney Edition', 1956; London: Panther, 1959).

Private Angelo (London: Cape, 1946; New York: Macmillan, 1946; repr. London: The Reprint Society, 1948; London: Cape, 'The Orkney Edition', 1953; London: Privately printed for Sir Allen Lane, the first book in Britain to be wholly set without metal type by photocomposition, 1957; London: Penguin, 1958; London: Panther, 1965).

A Spell for Old Bones (London: Cape, 1949; New York: Macmillan, 1950; repr. New York: Arno Books, 1978).

Mr Byculla (London: Rupert Hart-Davis, 1950; New York: Harcourt, Brace, 1951; repr. London: Chatto & Windus, 'Landmark Library', 1970).

Laxdale Hall (London: Cape, 1951; New York: Harcourt, Brace, 1952; repr. London: Cape, 'The Orkney Edition', 1956; Edinburgh: Macdonald, 1982).

The House of Gair (London: Cape, 1953; New York: Harcourt Brace, 1954; repr. London: Cape, 'The Orkney Edition', 1960).

The Faithful Ally (London: Cape, 1954; New York: under new title *The Sultan and the Lady*, Harcourt, Brace, 1954; repr. London: Reprint Society, 1956).

The Dark of Summer (London: Cape, 1956; New York: Harcourt, Brace, 1957; repr. London: Popular Book Club, 1958).

Position at Noon (London: Cape, 1958; New York: under new title *My Fathers and I*, Harcourt Brace, 1958; repr. London: Penguin, 1964; Edinburgh: Macdonald, 1980).

The Merry Muse (London: Cape, 1959; New York: Harcourt, Brace, 1960; repr. London: Consul Books, 1962).

Roll of Honour (London: Rupert Hart-Davis, 1961).

Husband of Delilah (London: Macmillan, 1962; New York: Harcourt, Brace, 1962; repr. London: Pan Books, 1966).

A Man Over Forty (London: Macmillan, 1963; repr. London: Pan Books, 1966).

A Terrible Freedom (London: Macmillan, 1966).

(b) *Short Stories*

The Crusader's Key (London: White Owl Press, 1933; New York: Knopf, 1933; repr. in *God Likes Them Plain*, q.v.).

The Revolution (London: White Owl Press, 1934; repr. in *God Likes Them Plain*, q.v.).

'Sinbad the Sailor' in *The Fairies Return* (London: Peter Davies, 1934).

God Likes Them Plain (London: Cape, 1935).

Sealskin Trousers and other stories (London: Rupert Hart-Davis, 1947).

A Sociable Plover and other stories and conceits (London: Rupert Hart-Davis, 1957).

The Stories of Eric Linklater (London: Macmillan, 1968; New York: *The Horizon Press*, 1969) (Stories selected from *God Likes Them Plain*, *Sealskin Trousers* and *A Sociable Plover*.)

(c) *Children's Books*

The Wind on the Moon (London: Macmillan, 1944; New York: Macmillan, 1944; repr. London: Puffin Books, 1972).

The Pirates in the Deep Green Sea (London: Macmillan, 1949; repr. London: Puffin Books, 1973).

Karina with Love (London: Macmillan, 1958).

(d) *Verse*

Poobie (Aberdeen: Porpoise Press Broadsheets, 1925).
A Dragon Laughed and other poems (London: Cape, 1930; repr. London: Cape, 1943).

(e) *Plays*

Rosemount Nights (Aberdeen: W. W. Lindsay, 1923).
The Prince Appears (Aberdeen: W. W. Lindsay, 1924).
The Devil's in the News (London: Cape, 1934).
The Cornerstones (a conversation-piece) (London: Macmillan, 1941).
The Raft & Socrates Asks Why (two further conversation-pieces) (London: Macmillan, 1942).
The Great Ship & Rabelais Replies (two further conversation-pieces) (London: Macmillan, 1944).
Crisis in Heaven (London: Macmillan, 1944).
Two Comedies (*Love in Albania*—repr. London: English Theatre Guild, 1951; and *To Meet the MacGregors*) (London: Macmillan, 1950).
The Mortimer Touch (originally performed as *The Atom Doctor*) (London: Samuel French, 1952).
Breakspear in Gascony (London: Macmillan, 1958; New York: St Martin's Press, 1958).

(f) *Autobiographies*

The Man on My Back (London: Macmillan, 1941; New York: Macmillan, 1941).
A Year of Space (London: Macmillan, 1953; repr. London: Reprint Society, 1954).
Fanfare for a Tin Hat (London: Macmillan, 1970).

(g) *Biographies*

Ben Jonson and King James (London: Cape, 1931; New York: Cape & Smith, 1931; repr. London: Academy Books, 1938).
Mary, Queen of Scots (London: Peter Davies, 1933; repr. London: Nelson, 1939; London: Dobson, 1952).
Robert the Bruce (London: Peter Davies, 1934; New York: D. Appleton-Century, 1934; repr. London: Nelson, 1939).

(h) *Essays and Histories*

The Lion and the Unicorn (London: Routledge & Kegan Paul, 1935).
The Northern Garrisons (London: HMSO, 1941).
The Defence of Calais (London: HMSO, 1941).
The Highland Division (London: HMSO, 1942).
The Art of Adventure (Aberdeen: The University Press, 1946).
The Art of Adventure (London: Macmillan, 1947).
The Campaign in Italy (London: HMSO, 1951; repr. London: HMSO, 1976).
Our Men in Korea (London: HMSO, 1952).
'The Memory of Sir Walter Scott' in *The Forty-Fifth Annual Dinner* (Edinburgh: Sir Walter Scott Club, 1953).

The Ultimate Viking (London: Macmillan, 1955).

Edinburgh (London: Newnes, 1960).

Gullers' Sweden (Stockholm: Almqvist, 1964).

Memorandum on the Conditions in the North of Scotland which Necessitate Revision of those Parts of the Beeching Report which Recommend the Closing of Railways North and West of Inverness (Inverness: North of Scotland Transport Conference, 1964).

'The Murder of Darnley' in *Fatal Fascination: A Choice of Crimes* (London: Hutchinson, 1964; Boston: Little, Brown, 1964; repr. London: Arrow Books, 1968).

The Prince in the Heather (London: Hodder & Stoughton, 1965; repr. Panther Books, 1976).

Orkney and Shetland (London: Robert Hale, 1965; repr. with two additional chapters, London: Robert Hale, 1971; repr. with revisions by J. R. Nicolson, London: Robert Hale, 1980).

The Conquest of England (London: Hodder & Stoughton, 1966; New York: Doubleday, 1966).

Notes for a Scottish Pantheon (Edinburgh: Oliver & Boyd, 1967).

The Survival of Scotland (London: Heinemann, 1968; New York: Doubleday, 1968).

Scotland (with Edwin Smith) (London: Thames & Hudson, 1968).

The Secret Larder or How the Salmon Lives and Why it Dies (London: Macmillan, 1969).

The Royal House of Scotland (London: Macmillan, 1970; repr. London: Sphere Cardinal Books, 1972).

The Music of the North (Aberdeen: Haddo House Choral Society, 1970; repr. with Postscript by Marjorie Linklater, Aberdeen: Haddo House Choral Society, 1978).

The Corpse on Clapham Common (London: Macmillan, 1971).

The Voyage of the Challenger (London: John Murray, 1972; New York: Doubleday, 1972).

The Black Watch (with Andro Linklater) (London: Barrie & Jenkins, 1977).

(i)   *Anthologies*

The Thistle and the Pen: An Anthology of Modern Scottish Writers (London: Nelson, 1950).

John Moore's England (London: Collins, 1970; repr. London: Country Book Club, 1971).

(j)   *Contributions to Books*

'Letters' in *Scotland in Quest of her Youth* ed. D. G. Thompson (Edinburgh: Oliver & Boyd, 1932).

'Introduction' to *The Heart of Scotland* by George Blake (London: Batsford, 1934).

'Preamble to a Satire' (Verse satire) in *Towards a New Scotland: A Selection from 'The Modern Scot'* ed. J. H. Whyte (London: Maclehose, 1935).

'Orkney' in *Scottish Country* ed. George Scott-Moncrieff (London: Wishart, 1935).

'The Orkney Farmers' in *Scotland – 1938* ed. J. R. Allan (Edinburgh: Oliver & Boyd, 1938).
'Introduction' to *A Child Under Sail* by Elizabeth Linklater (London: Cape, 1938; repr. London: Cape, 'Florin Books', 1942; repr. London: Rupert Hart-Davis, 1949; repr. New York: Brown & Ferguson, 1978).
'Introduction' to *Kabloona* by G. de Poncins (London: Cape in association with Readers' Union, 1942).
'Preface' to *The Last Enemy* by Richard Hillary (London: Macmillan special memorial edition, 1943).
'Foreword' to *Sheet-Anchor* by Eve Stuart (London: Sidgwick & Jackson, 1944).
'Introduction' to *Poetry Scotland No 3* ed. M. Lindsay (Glasgow: McLellan, 1946).
'Christopher Marlowe and Basil Ashmore' in *Christopher Marlowe's Tamburlaine the Great*, a special version by Basil Ashmore (London: Blandford Press, 1948).
'Foreword' to *The Atlantic Islands* by Kenneth Williamson (London: Collins, 1948).
'Introduction' to *Scottish Student Verse* (Glasgow: Ettrick Press, 1949).
'PEN and UN' in *Scottish Arts & Letters, 5th Miscellany* (Glasgow: McLellan, 1950).
'Introduction' to *England: photographed by Karl Gullers* (London: Odhams, 1951).
'Foreword' to *James Bridie and his Theatre* by Winifred Bannister (London: Macmillan, 1955).
'Introduction' to *The Life of Charles XII* by F. G. Bengtsson (London: Macmillan, 1960).
'Introduction' to *Scots in Sweden* by Berg and Lagercrantz (Stockholm: Nordiska Museet & Swedish Institute, 1962).
'Introduction' to *The Trial of Patrick Sellar* by Ian Grimble (London: Routledge & Kegan Paul, 1962).
'Foreword' to *The Korean War* by Robert Leckie (London: Barrie & Rockliff, 1963).
'Foreword' to *The Northmen Talk* by Jacqueline Simpson (London: Dent, 1965).
'Introduction' to *The Social Life of Scotland* by H. G. Graham (London: A. & C. Black, 1969).
'The Political Scene' in *Alistair Maclean Introduces Scotland* ed. A. M. Dunnett (London: André Deutsch, 1972).

II PRINCIPAL MANUSCRIPTS

A National Library of Scotland, Edinburgh. Letters of EL to Isobel Walker (Dep 220); Letters of EL to various correspondents (ACC 5799; ACC 5709; Dep 209); tape copy of radio programme for EL's 70th birthday (Acc 6102).

B National Library of Scotland, Acc 5665. Eleven boxes of manuscripts and typescripts of novels, histories, radio scripts; a few cuttings, sketches, draft letters.

C Reading University Library. Holds on deposit correspondences of house of Jonathan Cape, including approximately 100 letters between EL and J. Cape and Wren Howard.

D Humanities Research Center, University of Texas. Holdings include letters of EL to Compton Mackenzie, Edward Garnett, Herman Ould, Clifford Bax,

Richard Church, J. B. Priestley; notes on proceedings of Scottish P E N Club; six boxes of correspondence between E L and the A. D. Peters Literary Agency 1943–63; the typescripts of three plays: *A Man of Business* (afterwards published as *Breakspear in Gascony*); *A Husband of Delilah*; and *The Faithful Ally.*

E Marjorie Linklater's private collection. Contains letters of E L to Marjorie Linklater, Elspeth Cormack, Douglas Walker, Peg Walker, Mrs Walker, Phoebe Gilkyson, and others; the collection is uncatalogued. Contains also manuscripts of two unpublished novels, poems, talks, newspaper cuttings, review clippings and memorabilia. Mrs Linklater is also in possession of a correspondence between E L and General Holden on the subject of Eric's writings, especially certain ephemera.

F Rupert Hart-Davis's private collection. Includes approx. 170 letters of E L to Rupert Hart-Davis.

G Mrs Lucile Bell's private collection. Includes approx 250 letters of E L to John Moore with carbon copies of some of Moore's letters to E L.

H Ronald Mavor's private collection. Includes approx 10 letters of E L to O. H. Mavor ('James Bridie').

I Ian Grimble's private collection. Includes approx 20 letters of E L to Ian Grimble.

J 'The Cave in Father's Head'—ts of talk given by Alison Linklater about her father. In possession of Mrs Alison Betley.

K Transcripts of tape-recorded interviews between Michael Parnell and Sir Rupert Hart-Davis; Magnus Linklater; Mrs Alison Sheppard. In M. Parnell's possession.

L 'Eric Linklater: Novels and Short Stories'—ts of unpublished B A dissertation by John MacRitchie, University of Strathclyde, 1979; on loan to M. Parnell from J. MacRitchie.

M B BC Written Archives Centre, Caversham Park, Reading. Holds correspondence of E L with Val Gielgud, James Fergusson, and others, and large collection of internal correspondence on the subject of EL writings.

N Letters to MP from the following correspondents: W. R. Aitken; Basil Ashmore; A. W. Badenoch; Mrs Lucile Bell; Sir John Betjeman; John L. Broom; George Mackay Brown; George Bruce; Mrs Margaret Chapman (Storm Jameson); Mrs Margaret Clarke; Allan Colquhoun; Mrs Elspeth Cormack; Mrs Jean Cruickshank; Hon Mrs C. J. Y. Dallmeyer; Monja Danischewsky; Lt-Col R. J. Edwards; L. Marsland Gander; Dr Karl Ragnar Gierow; Alan J. Grant; Dr Ian Grimble; Rt Hon Jo Grimond, MP; Karl W. Gullers; H. Forsyth Hardy; Francis Russell Hart; Sir Rupert Hart-Davis; Jack House; Mrs Margaret Cursiter Hunter; Lt-Col Jack Lambert; Mrs Marjorie Linklater; Mrs Alison Betley (Sally Linklater); Andro Linklater; Magnus Linklater; David Machin; Gordon L. McCullough; Finlay J. Macdonald; Colin Mackenzie; Alan Maclean; John MacRitchie; J. Montgomery MacRoberts; Magnus Magnusson; Ronald Mavor; Bruce Marshall; Lady (Naomi) Mitchison; J. E. Morpurgo; George C. Morrison; Sean O'Faolain; J. B. Priestley; Sir Ralph Richardson; Charles T. Rioch; Andrew Rutherford; Stewart F. Sanderson; Mrs Alison Sheppard; Mrs

Annabelle Skarda; Margaret Stephens; L. A. Stronach; James Sutherland; Dr Ragnar Svanstrom; Anthony Walker; D. P. Walker; Mrs Isobel Walker; Mrs Peg Walker; Dame Rebecca West.

III OTHER PUBLISHED SOURCES

Abbott, Donald, 'Eric Linklater 1899–1974', *University of Edinburgh Journal*, 1976, xxvii.

Aitken, W. R., 'Eric Linklater', *The Bibliothek*, vol. 5, (1967–70).

Allen, Walter, *As I Walked Down New Grub Street* (London: Heinemann, 1981).

Blake, George, *Annals of Scotland* (London: BBC, 1955).

Bold, Alan, *Modern Scottish Literature* (London: Longman, 1983).

Bold, Alan, 'Introduction' to *Magnus Merriman* by Eric Linklater (Edinburgh: Macdonald Publishers, 1982).

Bridie, James, 'A Profile of Eric Linklater', *Music and Drama* (London: Edinburgh Festival No., August 1950).

Brown, Ivor, *Old and Young* (London: The Bodley Head, 1971).

Bruce, George, *Festival in the North* (London: Robert Hale, 1975).

Burgess, Anthony, *The Novel Today* (London: Longman for British Council, 1963).

Chandos, John, 'The Story-Teller from Orkney', *Picture Post* (London: 2 April 1955).

Coote, Colin, *A Companion of Honour: The Story of Walter Elliot* (London: Collins, 1965).

Daiches, David, *The Present Age from 1920* (London: Cresset Press, 1958).

Dickson, Lovat, *The House of Words* (London: Macmillan, 1963).

Gander, L. Marsland, *After These Many Quests* (London: Macdonald, 1949).

Gibbon, Lewis Grassic (J. L. Mitchell) & Hugh MacDiarmid (C. M. Grieve), *Scottish Scene* (London: Jarrolds, 1934).

Gielgud, Val, *Years of the Locust* (London: Nicolson & Watson, 1947).

Gielgud, Val, *Years in a Mirror* (London: The Bodley Head, 1965).

Gifford, Douglas, 'Scottish Fiction Since 1945', *Scottish Writing and Writers* (Edinburgh: Ramsay Head, 1977).

Gifford, Douglas, 'In Search of the Scottish Renaissance', *Cencrastus*, no. 9, Summer 1982.

Grimond, Jo, *Memoirs* (London: Heinemann, 1980).

Hart, Francis Russell, *The Scottish Novel: A Critical Survey* (London: John Murray, 1978).

Hart, Francis Russell & J. B. Pick, *Neil M. Gunn: A Highland Life* (London: John Murray, 1981).

Hart-Davis, Rupert, *The Lyttelton Hart-Davis Letters* (London: John Murray, vol. I, 1978, vol. II, 1979, vol. III, 1980).

Hayman, Ronald, *Gielgud* (London: Heinemann, 1971).

House, Jack, *Pavement in the Sun* (London: Hutchinson, 1967).

Howard, Michael, *Jonathan Cape: Publisher* (London: Cape, 1971).

Jefferson, George, *Edward Garnett: A Life in Literature* (London: Cape, 1982).

Jenkins, Alan, *Stephen Potter: Inventor of Gamesmanship* (London: Weidenfeld & Nicolson, 1981).

Lindsay, Maurice, *History of Scottish Literature* (London: Robert Hale, 1977).

Mackenzie, Compton, *My Life and Times* (London: Chatto & Windus, Octave VII, 1968, Octave VIII, 1969, Octave IX, 1970, Octave X, 1971).

McLaren, Moray, 'Eric Linklater', *The Sketch* (London: 16 August 1950).

Marwick, Hugh, *Orkney* (London: Robert Hale, 1951).

Massie, Allan, 'Ludic Linklater', *New Edinburgh Review*, no. 59, Autumn 1982.

Meikle, Henry, *Scotland: A Description of Scotland and Scottish Life* (London: Nelson, 1947).

Moore, John, 'Eric Linklater', *Cheltenham Festival Handbook* (Cheltenham: Festival Committee, 1954).

Morpurgo, J. E., 'Eric Linklater', *Contemporary Novelists* ed. J. Vinson (London: 1972).

M., R. J., 'Eric Linklater: President of the Former Pupils' Club', *Aberdeen Grammar School Magazine* (Aberdeen: June 1956).

Parker, Stanley, 'Eric Linklater', *John O'London's* (London: 17 December 1959).

Pitman, Robert, 'The Mystery of Eric Linklater', *Sunday Express* (London: 12 January 1958).

Pound, Reginald, *APH* (London: Michael Joseph, 1976).

Reid, J. M., *Modern Scottish Literature* (Edinburgh: Oliver & Boyd, 1945).

Rodger, Ian, *Radio Drama* (London: Macmillan, 1982).

Royle, Trevor, *The Macmillan Companion to Scottish Literature* (London: Macmillan, 1983).

Rutherford, Andrew, 'Eric Linklater as Comic Novelist', *The Literature of the North* ed. David Hewitt & Michael Spiller (Aberdeen: The University Press, 1983).

Sanderson, Stewart F., 'Eric Linklater', *Twentieth Century Fiction* ed. George Woodcock (London: Macmillan, 1983).

Shaughnessy, Alfred, *Both Ends of the Candle* (London: Peter Owen, 1978).

Thomas, Wynford Vaughan, *Trust to Talk* (London: Hutchinson, 1980).

'The University', 'Open Letter to Eric Linklater, President of the Union', *Alma Mater* (Aberdeen: The University Press, 27 May 1925).

Ustinov, Peter, *Dear Me* (London: Heinemann, 1977).

Tweedy, Ann, 'Marjorie Linklater', *Leopard Magazine* (Aberdeen: vol. 2, no. 7, May 1976).

Waugh, Alec, *The Best Wine Last* (London: W. H. Allen, 1978).

Wittig, Kurt, *The Scottish Tradition in Literature* (Edinburgh: Oliver & Boyd, 1958).

NB also:

A Stone in the Heather: Eric Linklater 1899–1974, a film directed by Laurence Henson, written by Jeremy Bruce-Watt, produced by International Films (Scotland) Ltd, for Films of Scotland and the Scottish Arts Council, 1974.

Highland Novelists: Eric Linklater, a radio talk by Ian Grimble, broadcast on BBC Radio 4, 1972.

Writers in Britain: Eric Linklater, a television film of an interview with Eric Linklater by Mary Marquis, for BBC Scotland, 1971.

Index

Abbott, Claud Colleer, 41, 69
Aberdeen, 3, 5, 11, 14, 15, 46, 77, 95, 98, 102, 103, 126, 127, 167, 173, 176, 318, 334, 341, 342, 345, 349
Aberdeen Evening Express, 35
Aberdeen Grammar School, 15, 16, 303, 322
Aberdeen University, 19, 28, 30, 38–9, 41, 43, 74, 116, 251, 260, 350
Aberdeen University Review, 41
Adams, Bridges, 319
Adams, Prof. Quincy, 82
Aelingaklaet, Cristi, 11
Africa, 149, 239, 279, 280, 298, 299, 300, 330, 341–2
Aga Khan, 288
Agate, James, 157
Aitken, W. R., 336
Alexander, Field Marshal Viscount, 244, 260, 283
Alice's Adventures in Wonderland (Carroll), 108
Allen, Walter, 77
Alma Mater, 35, 38, 45, 61, 62, 65, 66, 67
Amis, Kingsley, 104
Animal Farm (Orwell), 268
Anthony Adverse (Allen), 257
Aquila Films, 263
Argyll & Sutherland Highlanders, 236
Aristophanes, 194, 205, 213, 257
Armour, Jean, 260
Arno, Peter, 164
Arts Council, 263
Arts Review (BBC Scotland), 302, 326
Ashmore, Basil, 128, 264, 307, 311, 312
Atkinson, Miss, 116, 135
Auden, W. H., 262
Australia, 174, 189, 278–80, 304, 310–12, 315, 319, 333
Australian Women's Weekly, 280
Austria, 213, 246, 319
Ayrton, Michael, 317, 350

Bacon, Sir Francis, 337
Badenoch, Alex, 43
Bailey, Robin, 265
Balch, Emily, 119
Balchin, Nigel, 325
Balcon, Sir Michael, 281
Balcony, The (Genet), 304
Baldwin, Stanley, 86, 123
Balerno, Lord, 339
Balfour, The Hon Ursula (Mrs C. J. Y. Dallmeyer), 146, 194, 335, 336, 337, 340, 347, 348
Balmoral, 338
Balzac, Honoré de, 185, 255, 286
Bannockburn, 167, 316
Barra, 147, 148, 149, 150, 156, 202
Barrie, J. M., 154
Barron, E. M., 167
Bath Festival, 264–5
Baxter, John, 281
BBC, 127, 223, 232, 234, 237, 239, 242, 244, 258, 271, 294, 300, 302, 303, 312, 334, 346, 349
Beachcomber, 225
Beaton, Sir Cecil, 240
Beaverbrook, Lord, 120, 139
Beerbohm, Sir Max, 289
Beggar's Opera, The (Gay), 57, 61, 65, 66, 168
Beldon, Eileen, 168
Bell, Doyne, 249, 294, 300
Belloc, Hilaire, 63, 64, 67, 292
Bengtsson, Frans G., 332
Bennett, Arnold, 101
Bentley, Nicolas, 235
Berenson, Bernard, 246, 260
Berkeley, University of California at, 90–1
Betjeman, Sir John, 173
Bhika, Laloo, 48, 191
Bible (Authorised Version), 337
Binscarth, 152, 153, 166
Birkenhead, Lord, 284
Birmingham, 26, 77
Black Watch, The, 21–3, 26, 27, 340, 341, 345, 347
Blackpool, 201

Blackwood's Magazine, 60, 77, 336, 337
Blake, George, 123, 152, 210, 211
Bloom, Claire, 287
Bold, Alan, 172
Bombay, 36, 47, 49, 51, 54, 179, 180, 188, 190
Bond, Derek, 263
Bonfield, Mrs Alison (Mrs Harvey Sheppard), 145, 146, 153, 202, 204, 205, 206, 216, 299, 300
Book Society, 97–8, 179, 212, 252, 301
Boulogne, 21, 22, 26
Brahmaputra, 190, 191
Bray, Barbara, 294
Brecht, Bertholt, 66
Bridges, Sir Edward, 245
Bridie, James (Dr O. H. Mavor), 123, 222, 226, 251, 252, 256, 260, 264, 270, 271, 294, 308
Britain, 193, 194, 203, 212, 223, 224, 228, 235, 262, 330, 340
British Annual of Literature Medal, 267
British Army, 236, 276, 277
British Council, 254, 269, 275, 279, 324
British Lion Film Studios, 286
Britten, Florence Haxton, 172
Brooke, Jocelyn, 327
Brophy, John, 71
Brown, George Mackay, 348
Brown, Ivor, 234, 240, 241
Browne, Pamela, 270
Bruce, George, 302
Bruce-Watt, Jeremy, 349
Buchan, John, 140
Buchanan-Ridell, Sir Walter, 81
Burgess, Anthony, 318
Burns, Robert, 128, 209, 210, 252, 260, 312
Byron, George Gordon, Lord, 16, 62, 108, 110

Cabell, James Branch, 88
Cairns, 280
Caithness, 350

Calcutta, 190
California, 90–2, 94, 114
Cambridge, 288, 290, 305
Cameron, Lord, 330
Campbell, Douglas, 265
Canada, 91, 193, 223, 304, 305, 309, 310, 315, 319
Candide (Voltaire), 109, 112, 253, 254, 292
Cantor, Eddie, 164
Cape, Jonathan, 72, 83, 91, 95, 96, 97, 98, 99, 107, 110, 116, 121, 125, 126, 135, 139, 155, 156, 157, 162, 168, 210, 223, 240, 255, 266, 269, 271, 288, 289, 313, 321
Cape, Jonathan, & Co, 98, 116, 120, 127, 130, 135, 177, 179, 187, 201, 240, 255, 269, 281, 290, 298, 301, 308, 314, 321
Cardiff, 3–6, 8, 11, 14, 15, 250
Caribbean, 256, 319
Carlyle, Thomas and Jane, 154
Carnegie Medal, 235, 251
Carolina, South, 88, 114
Caspian Sea, 58, 59
Cassino, 242–3, 245
Castlerosse, Lord, 139, 151
Cervantes, 239–41, 286, 292
Chaloupka, Čenek (Čenda), 231
Chamberlain, Neville, 163, 216, 218, 226
Champneys, 211, 212, 213, 313
Chaucer, Geoffrey, 171, 185
Cheerful Weather for the Wedding (Strachey), 120
Chelmsford, Lord, 81
Cheltenham Festival, 272, 290, 291, 294
Cherry Orchard, The (Chekhov), 302
Chesterton, G. K., 64
Cheyne, A. I., 37, 40
Child Under Sail, A (Elizabeth Linklater), 6, 210, 266, 305
China, 56, 188, 191–2, 196, 199, 236, 331
Church, Richard, 268, 281, 333
Churchill, Randolph, 121
Churchill, Sir Winston, 16, 226, 243, 290, 291
Citizen of the World, The (Goldsmith), 108
Citizens' Theatre, Glasgow, 251, 258, 264, 269, 294
Clausewitz, 282
Clouston, J. Storer, 13, 124, 153, 176, 208, 225

Cold Comfort Farm (Gibbons), 120
Colditz Story, The (Reid), 231
Coleridge, S. T., 63, 134
Collier's Magazine, 285
Commonwealth Fund, 77, 81, 85, 91, 94
Communism, 162, 163, 174, 204
Confucius, 200, 232
Congreve, William, 302, 312
Connell, John, 291
Connolly, Cyril, 290
Conrad, Joseph, 23, 96, 183, 339
Constantinople, 53, 58, 59
Coolidge, Calvin, 85, 108
Cormack, Freddy, 190, 266
Cornell University, 82, 85, 87
Cornwall, 129, 236
Cousins, Maggie, 331, 333
Cowie, James, 350
Crichton, Charles, 275
Cripps, Sir Stafford, 251
Cromarty, 108, 257, 273, 274
Culloden, 324
Cursiter, Stanley, 176, 339, 349, 350
Curtis Brown, 126, 128, 178, 208
Czechoslovakia, 186, 212, 213, 215, 216, 218, 220

Daiches, David, 113
Daily Express, 119
Daily Mail, 55, 60, 130, 140, 288
Daily Mirror, 163, 225
Daily Record, 270
Daily Telegraph, 233
Dane, Clemence, 97
Darlington, W. A., 311–12
Davies, Peter, & Co, 126, 140, 155, 156, 167
Denmark, 269, 313, 324
Devine, George, 270
Dickens, Charles, 101, 105, 109, 139, 198, 202, 207, 286, 292
Dickson, Dorothy, 240
Dickson, Lovat, 232, 235, 321
Dodd, Sarah, 6
Don Juan (Byron), 16, 108, 109, 115
Donaldson, David, 350
Donne, John, 116, 337
Dostoevsky, Fyodor, 332
Doubleday & Co, 326, 329, 331
Doughty, Charles, 313
Douglas, Lord Alfred, 289
Douglas, Norman, 161, 162, 283
Drambuie Liqueur Co, 236
Drayton, Michael, 71

Drummond of Hawthornden, William, 4
Dublin, 103, 111, 211, 256, 261, 308, 319
Duke of York's Theatre, London, 270
Dunbar, William, 70, 76, 115, 130, 183, 323
Duncan, Garry, 32, 38
Duncan, Jane, 274, 332, 334
Dunnett, A. M., 345
du Pont, Frank, 117, 118, 119
Duval, K. D., 349

Ealing Studios, 275, 281
Eardley, Joan, 350
East Fife By-Election (1933), 136–8, 147, 163
Easter Ross, 108, 257, 273, 323, 333, 341, 346
Eden, Sir Anthony, 280
Edinburgh, 26, 27, 95–6, 123, 127, 139, 140, 145–7, 151, 159, 165, 183, 188, 193, 194, 202, 211, 212–13, 231, 244, 246, 250, 256, 261, 265, 270, 284, 286, 305, 312, 313, 322, 345, 346, 348
Edinburgh, The Duke of, 338
Edinburgh International Festival, 117, 262, 266, 270, 271, 308, 311, 315
Edward VIII, 203
Edwards, Roy, 5
Eldridge, John, 281
Eliot, T. S., 42, 68, 69, 70, 272
Elizabeth II, H M The Queen, 270, 288, 291
Elliot, Sir Walter, 226, 228, 232, 233, 330
England, 174, 176, 179, 181, 199, 206, 207, 208, 244, 254, 289, 293, 309, 329, 330, 332, 345
Esslemont, Dr Mary, 43
Evans, Todger, 5
Everyman, 140

Faerie Queene, The (Spenser), 110
Faeroes, 226, 301
Fairbairns, Denis, 128
Falstaff, Sir John, 65, 71, 134, 197
Family Reunion, The (Eliot), 323
Farjeon, Herbert, 238
Farrar & Rinehart, 126, 130
Fascism, 162, 170, 174, 183, 204
Fauré, Gabriel, 112
Faustus, Dr John, 168
Fergusson, Sir Bernard (Lord

Ballantrae), 20, 54, 75, 317, 334, 336, 338, 340–2, 345, 347, 348, 350
Fergusson, James, 223, 224, 309
Fergusson, J. D., 350
Fergusson, Robert, 128, 271
Fiji, 347
Finland, 255, 260, 261, 269, 336
Firbank, Ronald, 105
fitzAlan, Flaald, 334
Flaubert, Gustave, 80
Flecker, James Elroy, 67
Fleming, Peter, 235
Forester, C. S., 325
Forster, E. M., 157
Fort George, 27
Fort William, 135
Fortnightly Library, 175
Foyle, Christina, 203, 324
France, 123, 214, 215, 221, 229, 307, 329
Franco, General, 205
Frankau, Pamela, 309
Franklyn, William, 294
Fraser, Lady Antonia, 337
Fraser, Sir Robert, 276
Freeman, John, 322
French, Samuel, & Co, 270
Freud, Sigmund, 220

Gala Week (Aberdeen University Rag), 39, 56, 251, 322
Galsworthy, John, 101
Gander, Leonard Marsland, 47, 57
Gannett, Lewis, 157, 172
Garden, Dickie, 322
Gargantua, 197, 208, 268
Garnett, David, 255, 317
Garnett, Edward, 95, 96, 99, 110, 121, 130, 132, 316
Garrick Club, London, 300, 305
Gascoyne, David, 68
Gateway Theatre, Edinburgh, 311
Gauguin, Paul, 295
George V, 37
George VI, 37
Georgia, 59
Germany, 17, 24, 163, 182, 204, 205, 214, 215, 216, 220, 254
Ghose, Zulfikar, 326
Gibbon, Lewis Grassic (J. L. Mitchell), 4, 120, 122, 135, 140, 173, 175
Gielgud, Sir John, 237, 239, 240
Gielgud, Val, 232, 233, 234, 238, 239, 258, 303, 312
Gierow, Karl Ragnar, 216, 254

Gilkyson, Hamilton, 87, *passim*
Gilkyson, Phoebe, 91, 92, 93, 99, 119, 137, 148, 155, 164, 187, 212, 216, 217, 221, 224, 233, 236, 241, 250, 254, 255, 256, 273, 310
Gillies, William, 350
Gibraltar, 239, 240, 263
Gildard, Gordon, 312
Glasgow, 126, 127, 202, 203, 210, 211, 256, 258, 264, 265, 294, 345
Glasgow, Ellen, 93
Gloucestershire, 237, 287
Goebbels, Josef, 163
Gone with the Wind (Mitchell), 195
Good Soldier Schweik, The (Hasek), 253
Goodbye to All That (Graves), 96
Gordon Highlanders, The (4th Company), 41
Gothenburg State Theatre, 275
Gould, Gerald, 101
Goverts Verlag, 163
Grafton Theatre, London, 168
Graham, Cuthbert, 317
Graham, Harry, 292
Grant, Alan J., 34, 38, 43, 44
Greece, 316, 317, 323
Greene, Graham, 120, 270
Grenfell, Joyce, 263
Grierson, John, 194, 281
Griffiths, Leon, 271
Grimble, Ian, 317, 319, 321, 346, 349
Grimond, Jo, 138, 333
Grisewood, Harman, 271
Guardian (Manchester), 228, 348
Gullers, Karl, 285, 300, 307, 323, 332
Gunn, Neil M., 123, 130, 131, 132, 135, 212, 213, 214, 274, 332
Guthrie, Tyrone, 270

Haddo, Earl of, 341–2
Haddo, Mains of, 342, 348
Haig, Field Marshal Earl, 21, 321, 322
Hale, Robert, 321
Harcourt, Brace & Co, 296
Harding, Gilbert, 322–3
Hardy, Thomas, 104, 214
Harper's Bazaar, 128
Harray, Loch of, 3, 8, 36, 225, 246, 257, 350
Harrower, Prof. John, 40, 322
Hart, Francis Russell, 115, 132, 134, 157, 171, 214, 218, 332

Hart-Davis, Duff, 195
Hart-Davis, Sir Rupert, 75, 96, 125, 145, 154, 163, 166, 169, 176, 177, 178, 186, 188, 189, 190, 193, 195, 201, 203, 205, 208, 211, 219, 220, 221, 222, 224, 233, 239, 244, 245, 249, 251, 255, 256, 259, 260, 261, 265, 266, 269, 270, 272, 273, 275, 284, 289, 290, 291, 295, 298, 299, 300, 301, 303, 305, 310, 313, 314, 315, 316, 317, 319, 321, 324, 326, 330
Hartley, L. P., 228
Hassall, Joan, 259
Haydon, Benjamin, 292
Heinemann, William, & Co, 295
Hemingway, Ernest, 157, 205, 317
Henriques, Robert, 287, 294, 303, 306, 330, 331
Henry VII, 338
Henryson, Robert, 70, 130
Henson, Laurence, 349
Herder, Gottfried, 123–4
Hergesheimer, Joseph, 88
Highland Division, The 51st, 229, 230, 231
Hillary, Richard, 235, 260, 332
History Today, 290
Hitler, Adolf, 163, 182, 213, 224, 229
HMSO, 226, 234, 245, 281
Holden, General, 335, 342
Hoover, Herbert, 83, 85–6
Houghton Mifflin Co, 121, 126
House, Jack, 349
Howard, Leslie, 223
Howard, Michael, 290, 291, 314
Howard, Wren, 97, 99, 100, 117, 118, 119, 120, 121, 124, 125, 127, 128, 130, 139, 266, 290, 313, 321
Hume, David, 330
Hume, Ida and Julian, 153, 223, 250
Hunter, G. L. 350
Huntley, Raymond, 281
Hurd, Robert, 202
Huxley, Aldous, 105, 107, 120, 157

Iceland, 209, 226, 231, 291, 298, 329
Icelandic Sagas, The (Craigie), 124
Illustrated, 236
Imaginary Conversations (Landor), 232

India, 46–58, 82, 86, 122, 170, 179, 183, 188, 190, 191, 233, 245, 276, 279, 280, 292, 293, 336
Ingleneuk, 8, 12, 126, 166
Insanity Fair (Reed), 211
Inverness, 15, 127, 203, 316
Ireland, 198, 256, 313, 319, 323, 329, 340
Irvine, Sir James, 81
Israel, 303, 331
Italy, 154, 155–65, 204, 205, 242–6, 252, 254, 259, 260, 263, 283, 324

Jack, Prof. A. A., 34, 41, 69, 77, 80, 135
Jamaica, 319, 323, 331
James IV, 123, 338
James VI and I, 116, 117, 337
James, Henry, 306
Jameson, Storm, 130, 258
Japan, 192, 193, 196, 276, 278
Jenkins, Warren, 168
Jessop, Gilbert, 5
Johnson, Celia, 235
Johnson, Dennis, 340
Johnson, James, 252
Johnson, Samuel, 178, 235, 334
Jones, Peter, 265
Jonson, Ben, 4, 81, 82, 84, 85, 97, 99, 116–18, 269
Jordan, Philip, 243
Joseph, Michael, 126, 128
Joy (boat), 148–52, 213
Joyce, James, 101, 103, 104, 111, 188

Keating, H. R. F., 340
Keats, John, 75, 212
Keir, David, 139
Kelly, Don, 326
Kemp, General, 225
Kennington, Eric, 236
Kilbrandon, Lord, 334
King, Truby, 165
King's Theatre, Edinburgh, 240
Kinross, Lord, 146
Kipling, Rudyard, 44, 57, 63, 96, 180, 282, 297
Kirkham, Nancy, 128
Kirkwall, 11, 12, 104, 152, 160, 176, 208, 209, 350
Kittoe, Lt- Col Raymond, 244–6
Knight, Esmond, 240
Knopf, Alfred, 121
Koestler, Arthur, 235, 237
Korda, Vincent, 239

Korea, 276–9
Kricorissian, Edward, 128

Lambert, Jack, 145
Lambert, J. W., 293
Lane, Sir Allen, 107, 186
Lanercost Chronicle, The, 167
Laski, Marghanita, 292, 294
Lawrence, D. H., 101, 103, 104, 160
Lawrence, T. E., 313
Lawson, General (Lord Burnham), 233
Leeds School of Medicine, 297
Leese, General Oliver, 243–4
Leith, 148, 150, 160
Lerici, 155–61
Leslie, Harald (Lord Birsay), 349
Lettres Persanes (Montesquieu), 108
Leverhulme, Lord, 236
Lewis, Sinclair, 119, 157
Life and Letters, 162
Life of Jesus, The (Noel), 217
Life of Johnson (Boswell), 292
Lincoln, Abraham, 232, 235
Linklater, Alexander Ragnar, 335
Linklater, Alison (Sally), 154, 164–7, 187–8, 212, 217, 229, 235, 257, 273–5, 288, 305, 308
Linklater, Andro, 244, 246, 273, 274, 275, 316, 335, 349, 350
Linklater, Mrs Elizabeth (Elizabeth Young), 6, 31, 36, 116, 149, 166, 187–8, 210, 223, 305
Linklater, Elspeth (Mrs Freddy Cormack), 4–6, 149, 190, 223, 250, 266

LINKLATER, ERIC
NOVELS
The Dark of Summer (1956), 295, 298, 301–3, 309, 327
The Faithful Ally (1954), 280, 284, 288, 290, 292–4
The House of Gair (1953), 286–9, 301, 309, 339
Husband of Delilah (1962), 311, 319
The Impregnable Women (1938), 28, 199–201, 208, 211–15, 217
Juan in America (1931), 72, 82, 86–8, 94–100, 107–15, 121–6, 131, 157, 163, 186, 187, 195–8, 214, 218, 252, 302, 309
Juan in China (1937), 71, 186–7, 191, 193–200, 204, 205, 271
Judas (1939), 217–20, 320

Laxdale Hall, 106, 275, 281; Film, 286
Magnus Merriman (1934), 3, 69, 70, 75, 102, 104, 107, 135, 138–9, 152, 154–60, 162–3, 211, 271, 334
A Man Over Forty (1963), 214, 321, 322
The Men of Ness (1932), 3, 100, 125–6, 128–32, 135–40, 160, 163, 180, 211, 217, 296, 301, 329, 332, 346
The Merry Muse (1959), 75, 213, 293, 312–13, 318
Mr Byculla (1950), 269, 270, 289, 339
My Fathers and I (see *Position at Noon*)
Poet's Pub (1929), 69, 75, 83–4, 91, 93, 105–7, 112, 121, 169, 186; Film, 263
Position at Noon (1958), 207, 214, 227, 292, 302, 308–10, 318
Private Angelo (1946), 161, 245–6, 249, 252–4, 263, 318, 324; Film, 263
Ripeness is All (1935), 75, 169–73, 186, 206, 302
The Rock (unpublished), 240
Roll of Honour (1961), 15, 314, 316–18, 324
The Sailor's Holiday (1937), 107, 206–8
A Spell for Old Bones (1949), 75, 266–8, 269
The Sultan and the Lady (see *The Faithful Ally*)
A Terrible Freedom (1966), 306, 326–8, 330, 347
White-Maa's Saga (1929), 3, 14–15, 30, 32, 36, 67, 80, 83–4, 91, 93–4, 99, 101–3, 112, 221

SHORT STORIES (referred to in the text)
'The Abominable Imprecation of Shepherd Alken', 128, 184–5
'The Actress Olenina', 181
'Country-born', 56, 179
'The Crusader's Key', 128, 146, 184
The Crusader's Key (1933), 128
'The Dancers', 183, 261
'The Dreaming Bears', 260–1
'The Duke', 181
'Escape Forever', 306

'God Likes Them Plain', 185–6
God Likes Them Plain (1935), 179–86, 333–4
'The Goose Girl', 245, 255, 261
'His Majesty the Dentist', 182
'Invention for Four Voices', 303
'Jean Paris', 182
'Joy as it Flies', 256, 261
'Kind Kitty', 27, 76, 179, 183, 232
'The Masks of Purpose', 306
'Mr Timrod's Adventure', 183
'Mr Tyndall' (see 'The Goose Girl')
'Pathans', 56, 180
'The Prison of Cooch Parwanee', 56, 183
'The Redundant Miracle', 184–5
'The Revolution', 182
The Revolution (1933), 156, 167, 333
'Sealskin Trousers', 261, 265
Sealskin Trousers and other stories (1947), 150, 245, 259
'A Sociable Plover', 306, 308, 327
A Sociable Plover and other stories and conceits (1957), 303–6
The Stories of Eric Linklater (1968), 333
'Sunburnt Girls on the Rocks', 302
'Thieves', 180
'The Three Poets', 261
'Wineland', 180, 333
'The Wrong Story', 180

CHILDREN'S BOOKS
Karina With Love (1958), 307–8
The Pirates in the Deep Green Sea (1949), 169, 266–7, 307
The Wind on the Moon (1944), 235, 240, 245, 251, 307

PLAYS
The Adventures of Don Quixote (unpublished radio script, 1944), 239, 241–2
The Atom Doctor (see *The Mortimer Touch*)
Breakspear in Gascony (1958), 307–8, 311–12
The Cornerstones (1941), 232–3
Crisis in Heaven (1944), 109, 239–42, 258, 264
The Devil's in the News (1934), 57, 61, 66, 156, 162, 167–8, 264
The Great Ship (in *The Great Ship*

& Rabelais Replies, 1944), 238–9
The Isle of Women (unpublished, performed 1955), 294
Love in Albania (in *Two Comedies*, 1950), 264–6, 269, 275
A Man of Business (see *Breakspear in Gascony*)
The Mortimer Touch (1952), 270, 283
The Prince Appears (1924), 40
Rabelais Replies (in *The Great Ship & Rabelais Replies*, 1944), 239
The Raft (in *The Raft & Socrates Asks Why*, 1942), 234
Rosemount Nights (1923), 40, 53
Socrates Asks Why (in *The Raft & Socrates Asks Why*, 1942), 234, 238, 302
Stella the Bajanella (unpublished, performed 1923), 40
To Meet the MacGregors (in *Two Comedies*, 1950), 251, 256, 258

VERSE
'The Adversary', 72
'Baghdad', 73
'Behind the Sea', 73
'Carousal', 63, 71
'The Christmas Mumps', 63
'De Amicitia', 64
'Death from Croup', 67
'Don Juan—Lamb', 38, 62
A Dragon Laughed and other poems (1930), 72–5, 95
'The Faithless Shepherd', 70, 72
'Iraq Railway', 73
'Miss Poobie', 67
'Mr Benn', 63
'The Narrow Bed', 73
'The Naughty Broomstick', 73
'Navajo Sand-Painting', 89
'New Lamps for Old', 67
'Pan', 67
'The Persian Gulf', 73
Poobie (1925), 67, 127
'A Province for Adam', 72
'The Queen of Scots', 42, 74
'Rosemount Nights; in Memoriam', 65
'Rubáiyát of Omar K. Lamb', 63
'Rumbelow', 73
'Silenus', 71–2
'Song for an Able Bastard', 73
'Sophonisba', 67
'Spilt Wine', 63, 66

'To My Good Friend, J. R. Sutherland', 65
'Wedding Morning', 73

AUTOBIOGRAPHIES & BIOGRAPHIES
Ben Jonson and King James (1931), 100, 118, 130
Fanfare for a Tin Hat (1970), 3, 25, 30, 46, 82, 90, 120, 139, 177, 189, 222, 227, 235, 236, 240, 242, 243, 260, 284, 308, 336, 338
The Man on My Back (1941), 3, 12, 19, 23, 26, 27, 28, 30, 32, 46, 47, 57, 75, 82, 88, 123, 138, 146, 177, 190, 192, 202, 209, 220, 222, 223, 227, 228, 230, 284, 321
Mary Queen of Scots (1933), 140–1
Robert the Bruce (1934), 4, 155, 156, 160–2, 167
A Year of Space (1953), 36, 162, 225, 227, 228, 258, 276, 277, 279, 284, 293

ESSAYS, HISTORIES, ARTICLES, FOREWORDS, ETC
'The Art of Adventure', 255
The Art of Adventure (1947), 255, 259, 260
'The Battle of Largs', 290, 346
The Black Watch (1977), 350
The Campaigns in Italy (1951), 245–6, 249, 259, 263, 281–3
'The Cash Value of a Scottish Accent', 140
The Conquest of England (1966), 325–6, 329–31
The Corpse on Clapham Common (1971), 339–40
The Defence of Calais (1941), 229
Edinburgh (1960), 27, 315
'The Eleventh Hour of Christopher Marlowe', 128
'Foreword' to *The Northmen Talk* (1965), 323
'Growing Like a Tree', 163
Gullers' Sweden (1964), 325
'The Hampshire Bayonets', 236
The Highland Division (1942), 229–31
'Introduction' to *The Trial of Patrick Sellar* (1962), 317
Jaipur (1926), 57
John Moore's England (1970), 337
The Lion and the Unicorn (1935), 4, 127, 163, 173–6

'The March Past of the British Army' (Radio), 236
Memorandum . . . on the Beeching Report (1964), 323
'The Memory of Sir Walter Scott', 286
Mount Abu (1926), 57
'The Murder of Darnley' in *Fatal Fascination: A Choice of Crimes* (1964), 325, 339
The Music of the North (1970), 342
'Nemo Me Impune Lacessit', 231
'New Judgements on Robert Louis Stevenson' (Radio), 245
The Northern Garrisons (1941), 227–9
Notes for a Scottish Pantheon (1967), 330
'Orkney' in *Scottish Country* (1935), 9
Orkney and Shetland (1965), 323, 326
Our Men in Korea (1952), 278
'The Political Scene' in *Alistair Maclean Introduces Scotland* (1972), 345
'Preface to *The Last Enemy* (1943), 235
The Prince in the Heather (1965), 324–6
'The Prodigal Country', 140
'Reading for Fun', 291
'Return to Orkney' (Radio), 250
The Royal House of Scotland (1970), 334, 337–8
'The Scottish Monarchy in the 14th Century', 290
'Scottish Nationalism', 140
The Secret Larder; or How the Salmon Lives and Why it Dies (1969), 335
The Survival of Scotland (1968), 326, 331, 333
'Their Motto was *Sans Peur*', 236
The Thistle and the Pen (1950), 269
'Two Saints of Orkney', 209
The Ultimate Viking (1955), 132, 209, 290, 294–6, 329
The Voyage of the Challenger (1972), 338–41, 346–7
'We Guard Scapa Flow' (Radio), 223
'Why Scots Succeed', 140
'Worcestershires at Keren', 236

Linklater, Kristin, 193, 197, 212, 217, 229, 235, 335

Linklater, Magnus, 8
Linklater, Magnus Duncan, 229, 233, 235, 273–5, 307, 335
Linklater, Marjorie (see MacIntyre, Marjorie)
Linklater, Robert Baikie, 4, 8, 15, 17–18, 164, 260
Listener, 119, 128, 193, 231
Littlewood, Joan, 321
Livesey, Roger, 270
Lockyer, Robert, 260
Lomas, Herbert, 240
London, 26, 95, 119, 122, 127, 145, 154, 159, 223, 235, 249, 256, 262, 270, 284, 286, 303, 310, 336
London *Evening News*, 101, 140
London *Evening Standard*, 156, 335
London Mercury, 46, 70
Loot (Orton), 313
Lord, Graham, 334–5
Lord of the Flies (Golding), 171
Loti, Pierre, 57
'Love in the Valley' (Meredith), 63
Low, Sir Francis, 55
Lubbock, Percy, 160–1
Lubbock, Lady Sybil, 160–1, 165
Lucas, Walter, 57, 59, 242
Lustgarten, Edgar, 339
Lynd, Sylvia, 97–8
Lyric Theatre, London, 57, 240, 265
Lyttelton, George, 125, 154, 305

McBride, Willie-John, 320
MacCormick, John M., 136
MacDiarmid, Hugh, 69–70, 115, 122, 135
Macdonald, Finlay J., 303
Macdonald, W. B., 35
McFee, William, 157
McGrigor, Dr James, 260
McIndoe, Sir Archibald, 235
MacIntyre, Ian, 146, 256
MacIntyre, Marjorie (Mrs Marjorie Linklater), 153–5, 160–2, 164–6, 185, 187–8, 192–3, 201, 203, 209, 212, 216–18, 223, 229–31, 235–7, 241–3, 244–6, 249–50, 257, 273–4, 276, 279–80, 283, 287–8, 294–5, 298–9, 303, 305, 310–13, 315, 319, 321, 325, 330, 333–6, 340–2, 347–50
Mackay, Fulton, 294
McKechnie, James, 237
Mackenzie, Colin, 146
Mackenzie, Sir Compton, 121, 123, 135, 138–40, 147–8, 152, 155–7,

164, 169, 192, 194–5, 202, 205, 208–9, 212, 222–3, 228–9, 233, 249, 252, 263, 272, 281, 285–6, 288, 294, 310, 314, 324, 326, 331–2
Mackenzie, W. Mackay, 167, 169
MacRitchie, John, 109
McLaren, Moray, 120–3, 127, 145–6, 169, 194, 232, 235, 237, 306, 317
Macmillan & Co, 223, 227, 232, 234, 240, 255, 259, 307–8, 321, 326, 333, 336, 338
Macmillan, Harold, 242
MacMillan, Roddy, 281
McNeil, Roderick (The Crookle), 148
MacOwan, Michael, 145
MacSween, Chrissie, 152, 288
Maddermarket Theatre, Norwich, 168
Magnusson, Magnus, 323, 349
makars, the, 114, 130, 183
Mann, Thomas, 114
Margaret, H RH Princess, 270
Marlowe, Christopher, 264
Marwick, Ernest, 100–1, 103
Marxism, 182
Mary, Queen of Scots (Mary Stewart), 4, 74, 126, 135, 145, 147, 184, 271, 316–17, 321, 337
Masefield, John, 63
Mavor, Ronald, 308, 334
Maxwell, Gavin, 274
Mediterranean, 119, 239, 289, 317, 341–2, 347–8
Merkister, 8, 166, 177, 209, 211, 257, 259, 350
Meyer, G. M., 225–6
Miller, Henry, 324
Mitchison, Lady (Naomi), 123, 258
Modern Scot, 179
Montaigne, 227
Montegufoni, Castello di, 243, 324
Moore, John, 75, 237, 240, 255–6, 259, 263, 272, 275, 279, 283, 285–8, 290–2, 294, 304–5, 313–14, 316, 319, 324–6, 330–2
Moore, Lucile, 272, 287, 331
Morgan, Diana, 263
Morgan, Diane, 348
Morning Post, 179
Morrison, George, 78
Morrison, Steinie, 339–40
Morrison, W. S., 330
Morse, Barry, 240
Moulton, Fletcher, 339

Mountbatten, Lord Louis, 280
Muir, Edwin, 120, 123, 176, 272
Muir, Kenneth, 316
Murdoch, Iris, 104
Murray, Barbara, 263
Murray, Basil, 139
Murray, Gilbert, 139
Murray, John, Ltd, 338, 341, 346
Murray, Marris, 44, 118, 128, 129
Music and Drama, 271

Napier, Trevie, 260
National Library of Scotland, 25, 339, 341, 349
National Party of Scotland, 139
Nayar, Captain Unni, 243
Nazism, 162–3, 174, 214, 216
Neff, Hildegarde, 287
New Saltire, 76, 323
New Testament (Moffat translation), 217
New York, 82, 88, 94, 118, 310
New York Herald Tribune, 172
New Zealand, 245, 278–80, 334
Newnes, George, 315
News Chronicle, 171, 195, 220
Nicolson, Sir Harold, 99, 120, 157
Nigg Bay, 257, 273, 341–2, 346
Nineteen Eighty-Four (Orwell), 260
Norris, Rev. J. Frank, 83
Norse sagas, 13, 123–4, 130, 180, 217, 295–6, 323
Norstedt's, 121, 254
Norway, 117, 209, 222, 255, 300, 302
Now and Then, 130
Nye, Robert, 333

Observer, 101, 321
O'Casey, Sean, 308
O'Connor, Philip, 68
Odhams Press, 301
O'Faolain, Sean, 91, 121, 123, 177, 215
O'Hara, John, 331
Old 797 (boat), 336
Orcadian, 151, 226, 348
Origo, The Marchesa Iris, 160
Orioli, Pino, 161, 283
Orkney, 3, 6, 8–9, 11–14, 36, 66, 95, 99, 100–4, 116–18, 123–4, 126–7, 132–3, 146, 152–3, 156–69 *passim*, 175–6, 183, 187, 193–4, 202–4, 208–9, 216, 221, 223, 225–6, 229, 234, 239, 246, 249, 256–7, 267, 273, 285, 288, 291, 295, 298, 311, 319, 321, 348, 349, 350

Orkney Blast, 225–6
Orkney Miscellany, 290
Orr, John Boyd, 41
Orton, Joe, 313
O'Sullivan, Georgina, 280
Owen, Hamilton, 93

Papua New Guinea, 279–80, 285, 288, 293
Pattern of Islands, A (Grimble), 292
Peacock, Thomas Love, 101, 105–6, 281
PEN Club, 24, 206–8, 258, 262, 265, 269, 271–2
Penguin Books, 107
Peploe, S. J., 288, 350
Perth Repertory Company, 311
Peters, A. D., 97, 249, 284, 288, 316, 319
Philipson, Robin, 350
Piers the Plowman (Langland), 208
Pinckney, Josephine, 88–9, 93
Pitcalzean House, 257–9, 272, 274, 284, 287, 304, 316–17, 321, 325, 334–5, 341, 345–6
Pitlochry Festival Theatre, 302
Playfair, Nigel, 57
Plomer, William, 157
Popular Book Club, 301
Porpoise Press, 67, 127
Potter, Stephen, 249, 290
Pottinger, Don, 315
Prescott, Orville, 329
Pride and Prejudice (Austen), 277
Priestley, J. B., 97–101 *passim*, 120, 157, 223
Primavera (Botticelli), 243–4
Prime of Miss Jean Brodie, The (Spark), 317
Pritchett, V. S., 290
Pryce-Jones, Alan, 291
Punch, 218

Quennell, Peter, 268

Rabelais, 64, 103, 108, 115, 157, 238, 257, 268, 309, 312, 346
Radio Newsreel, 244
Ragnarök, 217, 220
Rainbird, George, 338, 341, 346
Raleigh, Sir Walter, 116, 207
Ralph, George, 270
Redpath, Anne, 350
Reed, Sir Carol, 287
Reid, P. R., 231
Reith, Sir John, 127
Reprint Society, 284, 292–3

Richard Coeur de Lion (Wilkinson), 140
Richards, Grant, 79
Richardson, Sir Ralph, 235, 239–41, 304, 349
Rio Tinto Zinc Corporation, 304–5, 309, 315
Rioch, Charles, 78
Robertson, Billy, 12
Robertson-Justice, James, 263, 274, 335
Robey, George, 241
Rodd, John, 311
Roth, Philip, 104
Roughead, Nick, 249, 291, 311, 313
Routledge & Kegan Paul, 173
Royal Society of Edinburgh, 339
Royal Society of Literature, 331
Rutherford, Prof. Andrew, 107, 281
Ryan, Kathleen, 281

St Andrews, 123, 124, 126–7, 139, 250, 330
St Boswells, 223–4, 231
St James' Theatre, 265
St Magnus' Cathedral, 208–9, 214, 225
Saltire Society, 202
Savile Club, London, 201, 235, 237, 249–50, 288, 305, 332
Scalacronica (Gray), 167
Scandinavia, 209, 254–5, 261, 300, 332
Scapa Flow, 30, 178, 221, 260
Scarth, Hester and Robert, 152, 166
Schumacher, Eugene, 123
Scotland, 117, 122–3, 139–41, 157, 159, 161, 163, 167, 173–6, 236, 257, 268, 285, 289, 294, 306, 312, 322–3, 330, 333, 345–6
Scots Review, 75
Scotsman, 271, 334
Scott, Alexander, 333
Scott, Tom, 12
Scott, Sir Walter, 128, 157, 184, 251, 286
Scott-Moncrieff, George, 176
Scottish Nationalism, 4, 122–8 *passim*
Secker, Martin, 79
Service, Robert W., 63
Shakespeare, William, 114, 116, 164, 183, 262, 292, 337
Shaughnessy, Alfred, 281
Shaw, George Bernard, 31, 118, 161, 172, 175, 232

Shaw-Taylor, D., 241
Shelley, Norman, 168
Shetland, 226, 298, 301, 321
Shute, Nevil, 279
Silenus, 38, 44, 64, 71, 199
Sim, Alastair, 168
Simon, Ruth (later Lady
  Hart-Davis), 317, 330
Simpson, Jacqueline, 323
Simpson, Stanley, 349
Sinclair, Johnny, 13
Sitwell, Sir Osbert, 243
Smith, Bill, 87–93
Smith, Emma, 272
Smith, Sir George Adam, 42
Smith, Harrison, 93, 95, 126
Smith, Sydney Goodsir, 115
Snow, C. P., 268
Socialism, 122, 206
Socrates, 235, 239
Spain, 204–5, 212, 215, 304, 316
Spark, J. A., 35
Speaight, Robert, 232
Spectator, 179, 214, 218, 321
Spender, Sir Stephen, 191
Spring, Howard, 157
Squire, Sir John, 70–1
Squire, Ronald, 281
Stephen, Dan, 13
Stevenson, R. L., 89, 128, 211, 245,
  267
Stewart, Captain Jimmy, 20
Stirling Castle, 316
Stone, Christopher, 242
Stone in the Heather, A (film), 349
Stone, Reynolds, 306
Storm, Lesley (Mrs Mabel Clark),
  34, 42, 80, 155
'Strange Visitor, The', 292
Strauss, Ralph, 105
Streicher, Julius, 163
Stronach, L. A., 47–8
Sturrock, Norman, 169
Sunday Express, 151, 335
Sunday Times, 105, 179, 201, 208,
  241, 293
Sutherland, James, 31, 36, 38, 61,
  63–5, 322
Swan, Annie S., 118
Sweden, 121, 216, 255, 261, 269,
  275–6, 307, 319–23, 332–3
Sweyn the Viking, 63, 66, 176
Swift, Jonathan, 108, 172
Sword in the Stone, The (White),
  267
Sykes, Christopher, 325
Synge, J. M., 123, 177

Tauchnitz Press, 121
Taylor, C. W., 228
Taylor, John Stevenson, 41, 43
Territorial Army, 216, 220, 233
Thesiger, Ernest, 240
Thistle (boat), 213
Thomas, Dylan, 250, 266, 290
Thompson, Dorothy, 119
Thomson, David Cleghorn, 127,
  129
Thomson, George Malcolm, 97,
  127
Thurber, James, 108, 320
Time and Tide, 253, 260
Times, The, 140, 168, 214, 289, 301,
  305, 311, 317, 320, 323, 325,
  327, 331, 341
Times Literary Supplement, The, 95,
  118, 333, 338
Times of India, The, 46–7, 55, 57
Tisdall, Hans, 308
Tom Jones (Fielding), 198
Touch and Go (Starke), 120
Towers, Tommy, 178
Town and Country, 244
Travels of Baron Munchausen, The,
  292
Travellers' Tree, The (Fermor), 292
Trilling, Lionel, 101
Trollope, Anthony, 101
Twain, Mark, 108, 250, 292
Twentieth Century, 336
Tynan, Kenneth, 321

Umberto, King, 243, 252
UNO, 331
Updike, John, 104
Urquhart, Sir Thomas, 108, 175,
  257, 346
USA, 81–99, 107–10, 121–2, 130,
  172, 193, 223, 228, 233, 236,
  252, 271, 293, 296, 304, 308,
  309, 310, 330
USSR, 192, 205, 340
Ustinov, Peter, 263–5

Vaughan Thomas, Wynford,
  243–4, 324
Venusberg (Powell), 120
Vikings, 11, 104, 117, 124, 126–7,
  132–3, 176, 180, 209, 288–96
  passim, 310, 329, 346
Vikings, The (Mawer), 124
Voltaire, 109, 157, 210, 238

Wain, John, 104
Walker, Anthony J., 230

Walker, Dr Charles, 41, 117, 129,
  322
Walker, Douglas, 41, 43, 45,
  49–52, 54, 56, 61, 65, 78–9, 83,
  85–6, 90, 93–5, 97, 118, 121,
  128, 150, 153, 155–6, 162,
  164–6, 177, 189, 195, 201, 217,
  219, 255, 322
Walker, Isobel, 38, 41, 42, 50–6,
  63, 67, 117–18, 121, 129, 150,
  322
Walpole, Sir Hugh, 97, 99, 120,
  157, 223
War and Peace (Tolstoy), 292
War Office, The, 226, 233–4, 245
Washbourne, Mona, 270
Waugh, Alec, 258
Waugh, Evelyn, 105, 107, 120, 139,
  171, 236–7, 243, 260, 312, 317,
  327
Wavell, Field Marshal Earl, 259,
  291
Wells, H. G., 101
West, Dame Rebecca, 272
West Indies, 274, 315, 319
Western Mail, 326
Whisky, 175, 230, 274, 324
White, Sir Dick, 91, 94
White, Gilbert, 332
White Owl Press, 128, 156, 167,
  184
Whiting, John, 312
Wilde, Oscar, 319
Williams, Evan, 55
Wilson, Frederick, 263
Wilson, Sir Harold, 331
Wister, Owen, 119
Wittig, Kurt, 32, 130
Wodehouse, P. G., 105, 157, 172,
  207, 309
Wood, Helena, 312
Wood, Wendy, 158, 164–5, 195
Woolf, Virginia, 101
Wordsworth, William, 63, 105, 202,
  292
World Books, 263, 284, 292
World War, First, 18, 20–8, 161,
  204, 213, 324, 328, 332, 347
World War, Second, 24, 109,
  194–5, 213, 221–46, 252, 318

Yeats, W. B., 72, 123, 124
York, Duke of, 37
Yorkshire, 21–2, 233–4
Young, Douglas, 303, 306
Young, James (James Ljung), 6ff

Zedong, Chairman Mao, 200